BECOMING A TEACHER

10th EDITION

FORREST W. PARKAY
Washington State University

PEARSON

Boston Columbus Indianapolis New York San Francisco Upper Saddle River
Amsterdam Cape Town Dubai London Madrid Milan Munich Paris Montreal Toronto
Delhi Mexico City São Paulo Sydney Hong Kong Seoul Singapore Taipei Tokyo

Vice President and Editorial Director: Jeffery W. Johnston
Senior Editor: Julie Peters
Editorial Assistant: Andrea Hall
Development Editor: Bryce Bell
Marketing Manager: Chris Barry, Krista Clark
Executive Managing Editor: JoEllen Gohr
Production Editor: Mary Beth Finch
Senior Operations Supervisor: Deidra Skahill
Senior Art Director: Diane C. Lorenzo

Cover and Text Designer: Candace Rowley
Cover Image: Shutterstock
Media Producer: Autumn Benson
Media Project Manager: Allison Longley
Full-Service Project Management: Kelli K. Jauron
Printer/Binder: Courier Kendallville
Cover Printer: Courier Kendallville
Text Font: ITC Garamond Std Light, 10/12

Credits and acknowledgments for material borrowed from other sources and reproduced, with permission, in this textbook appear on the appropriate pages within the text.

Every effort has been made to provide accurate and current Internet information in this book. However, the Internet and information posted on it are constantly changing, so it is inevitable that some of the Internet addresses listed in this textbook will change.

Alexander Trinitatov. Shutterstock, p. 307; Annie Pickert Fuller. Pearson Education, Inc., p. 60; Armadillo Stock, p. 394; David Kostelnik/ Pearson Education, Inc., p. 366; Baronb, p. 383; Bettman, p. 163; Bikeriderlondon. Shutterstock, p. 42, 226; Bill Aron, p. 404; Blend Images, pp. 224, 318, 320; M. Scott Brauer, p. 377; Comstock Stock Photography, p. 344; Corbis, p. 158; David Smith, p. 287; Dennis MacDonald, p. 170; Design Pics, p. 465; Fotolia, p. 260; fstockfoto. Shutterstock, p. 213; © Gina Sanders, p. 23; Golden Pixels/Alamy, p. 125; H. Mark Weidman, p. 338; Iakov Filimonov / Shutterstock, p. 57; Jeff Greenberg, p. 180; Jim, p. 283; Library of Congress, pp. 164, 167; Lisa F. Young / Shutterstock, pp. 84, 372; © matka_Wariatka, pp. 121, 353; Michaeljung. Shutterstock, p. 307; Michael Karlsson, p. 250; © Monkey Business, p. 47; Monkey Business Images / Shutterstock, pp. 4, 74; Monkey Business Images, pp. 266, 269, 304, 361, 415, 420, 442, 457; moodboard, p. 390; MShieldsPhotos, p. 446; Northwind Picture Archive, p. 150; Olesya Feketa. Shutterstock, p. 307; Peteer Byron/PhotoEdit, p. 81; Philidor, p. 335; Photographer: Ron Sachs/REX, p. 201; racorn. Shutterstock, pp. 112, 313; ©Rido, p. 367; Robin Nelson / PhotoEdit, p. 51; Shawn Pecor. Shutterstock, p. 297; Spencer Grant, p. 364; Studio 8. Pearson Education Ltd, p. 189; Susan Montgomery/ Shutterstock, p. 144; © Syda Productions, p. 419; Terrie L. Zeller. Shutterstock, p. 191; Tim McCabe/USDA, p. 134; Tracy Whiteside / Shutterstock, p. 106; UPI, p. 209; Vanessa Davies (c) Dorling Kindersley, p. 307; VIPDesign, p. 407; William Perugini / Shutterstock, p. 17.

Library of Congress Cataloging-in-Publication Data

Parkay, Forrest W.
   Becoming a teacher / Forrest W. Parkay. — Tenth edition.
       pages cm
   Includes bibliographical references and index.
   ISBN-13: 978-0-13-386841-8
   ISBN-10: 0-13-386841-9
   1. Teaching—Vocational guidance.   2. Education—Study and teaching—United States.   I. Title.
   LB1775.P28 2014
   371.10023'71--dc23

                                                                                              2014037971

10 9 8 7 6 5 4 3 2 1

PEARSON

ISBN-10:   0-13-386841-9
ISBN-13: 978-0-13-386841-8

PREFACE

I hope you share my belief that teaching is the world's most important profession. Teaching is exciting, rewarding, and uplifting; teachers receive great satisfaction from making a difference in their students' lives. In today's climate of accountability, high-stakes testing, and new federal programs such as Race to the Top, however, becoming a successful teacher requires high levels of professionalism and commitment.

The 10th edition of *Becoming a Teacher* continues to listen to the voices of those who care deeply about teaching—professionals and expert teachers, novices just learning the ropes, students in America's classrooms, and preservice learners deciding if teaching is their best career path—to help readers discover the answer to the question, "Is teaching for me?"

With the help of these stakeholders, the 10th edition focuses on teacher quality and provides in-depth coverage of:

- teacher leadership, political activism, and change facilitation
- diversity and culturally competent teaching
- social justice and democracy

Becoming a Teacher embraces and articulates the changing field of education, outlining ways to be an agent of change in the profession, pinpointing meaningful uses of technology in education, clarifying realities of diversity in the classroom, and clearly outlining past, present, and future thoughts on curriculum, instruction, management, philosophy, and issues in education. This down-to-earth and straightforward approach provides students with the tools and information necessary to answer the questions, "What does it take to become a high-quality teacher?" and "Do I want to teach?"

A THOROUGHLY REVISED NEW EDITION

The 10th edition is thoroughly revised and draws attention to the rapidly changing climate in education. I approached this revision of *Becoming a Teacher* with an eye toward providing readers with cutting-edge information impacting the teaching profession. In response to reviewers' feedback, new research, and emerging trends, the 10th edition reflects the following changes and additions.

NEW INTERACTIVE ETEXT

The medium in which you are reading this content might be an eText or a print loose-leaf version. To be more portable and accessible as well as affordable, we produced this text with the digital version in mind first. You'll notice the following characteristics and features in the 10th edition's Pearson eText:

- **Dear Mentor/Dear Student** pieces on Part Openers feature audio clips of exchanges between new teachers and their mentors.

- Embedded **videos** help to illustrate key chapter content.

Watch this video to observe various characteristics needed to be an effective teacher.

- **Professional Reflection** interactive features include videos followed by reflective questions, helping students begin to develop their thinking as professionals.

PROFESSIONAL REFLECTION
Listen as this teacher gives you advice for succeeding in your first year of teaching.

- **Teaching on Your Feet** features, which describe classroom scenarios, include pop-up windows where students can analyze the scenarios and respond to reflective questions.

TEACHING ON YOUR FEET
Half of Teaching Is Learning

"You have a screen name?" they query in disbelief. Screen name, IM, blogging, DVD, iPod, podcasts, YouTube, MySpace, HDTV, text messaging, iMac . . . this is the jargon of the *millennials*—my seventh-grade students. Their world is filled with technology; they accept it—and expect it. They use it to communicate, connect, and create. And they use it constantly and confidently.

Yes, I tell them. I have a screen name . . . It's mrsheebz. I blog, instant message (IM), Google, make podcasts, publish online books, and text message. I visit MySpace, Facebook, and YouTube. I use Garageband, Comic Life, iPhoto, iTunes, Frontpage, iMovie, Keynote, and Noteshare. I love the world of technology. Of course, my students think I'm kidding when I tell them I grew up with a rotary phone . . . and a black-and-white TV with three stations of snow. No microwave, no World Wide Web, no cell phones . . . and certainly no computers. But my family did own a typewriter and a complete set of World Book Encyclopedias. I had all the tools necessary to give me an edge in school—then.

Fast-forward 40 years. The 12-year-olds I teach still have the encyclopedia as a wonderful window to the world. But the typewriter is long gone. Instead they possess iMac G4 laptops with the World Book just one of the many promising programs at their fingertips. It's a powerful tool that gives my kids—and me—an edge on learning.

There is no tool that has changed my teaching practice as much as the laptop. All seventh and eighth graders in the state of Maine have 24/7 access to their own wireless laptops. In 2001, the Maine Learning and Teaching Initiative (MLTI) was voted and approved; as a result, 1 percent of Maine's educational funds was spent on one-to-one computing—a laptop for every seventh grader in the state. The following year, the eighth grade was added, for a total of 35,000 laptops. This was a lofty goal aimed at evening the digital divide by providing the World Wide Web to all students in our largely rural state. This was a true democratic ideal: equal opportunity regardless of economic status. At this time, this initiative was the only program of its kind in the world. . . . Teachers spouted clichés like a potato sprouts eyes: a mixed blessing, throwing money in the wind, a two-edged sword, Christmas in July, can't teach an old dog new tricks. The program was embraced by some teachers, scorned by others. I chose to embrace. To learn. Or at least try to learn. For to teach "is to learn twice" (Joseph Joubert). And that has made all the difference in who I am as a teacher.

Using technology has transformed my curriculum and my teaching style. In particular, one-on-one computing has made the single biggest impact on my 27 years of teaching. My entire belief system has been tested and strengthened not only by the advent, but also by the intrusion of the laptop into my classroom. I'm no longer the expert, the disseminator of all-that-needs-to-be-known. I'm a learner, growing along with my students and along with my colleagues. We are a true community of explorers compelled by the MLTI motto: "If you know how to do it, teach someone else. If you don't know how, ask someone else." It's an energizing environment in which to learn: it's the environment of the connected generation.

Today's students are often more technologically savvy than their teachers. At many schools, students play an important role in integrating technology into teaching. What are the benefits of this approach to technology integration?

I teach seventh-grade language arts in a coastal town in southern Maine. The majority of my students come from professional families who have the ability to travel, vacation often, own lovely homes, and pay for higher education. It's a homogeneous community, with poor and minority students few and far between. Ninety-two percent of the families in my district had access to the Internet at home when the MLTI program began, so the digital divide was never a huge issue for my students. Yet access to computers at school for word processing and research had always been minimal. Prior to the laptop program, I'd been lucky to obtain an hour a week in the computer lab for my students. Laptops have given us a portable writing lab, instant access to research, and assistive technology.

My teaching philosophy is simple. I strive to create a democratic classroom—an energetic community of caring people engaged in learning. The laptop is a tool, a powerful communication device that has increased my ability to enact democratic ideals on a daily basis. Engagement, energy, and caring: these are more important to me than the content I teach.

ANALYZE & REFLECT

Click here to analyze and reflect on this scenario you have just read.

Merry Herbert teaches seventh-grade language arts at a middle school in MAINE.

The preceding is excerpted from her contribution to the National Network for Educational Renewal's Teacher Case Story Collection. The Collection is "dedicated to providing a public forum for teachers to share their stories." National Center for Educational Renewal. © 2006. Retrieved and adapted from http://nnerpartnerships.org/stories/herbert.html.

- Audio clips in **Teacher's Voices: Walk in My Shoes** features allow teachers to share their classroom experiences, describe their perspectives on a career in teaching, and even offer advice and tips. In the first chapter, this feature includes a video of the author himself sharing about his own teaching experiences.

TEACHERS' VOICES
Walk in My Shoes
"I hold the potential to change a child's life."
Cheryl Beene
Center Hill High School,
Olive Branch, Mississippi

- **Chapter Quizzes** at the end of each chapter help students gauge their understanding of the material covered.

STOP

CHAPTER QUIZ

Take this quiz to check your understanding of the content covered in this chapter.

- **Glossary** terms can be clicked on to read definitions.

AN EMPHASIS ON STANDARDS TO PREPARE PROSPECTIVE TEACHERS TO MEET KEY PERFORMANCE STANDARDS

- The 10th edition of *Becoming a Teacher* provides prospective teachers with guidelines for acquiring the knowledge and skills necessary to meet the performance standards developed by InTASC, NCATE, TEAC, PRAXIS, NBPTS, and the newly created Council for the Accreditation of Educator Preparation (CAEP). The book also prepares readers to meet the accountability criteria contained in the No Child Left Behind (NCLB) Act and the current administration's *A Blueprint for Reform: The Reauthorization of the Elementary and Secondary Education Act*.

- The text's appendix, **Preparing for Certification: Your Guide to Licensure**, provides students with a brief tutorial of FAQs, test-taking tips, and sample test questions intended to remove some of the intimidation of this important professional step. Correlations to content in the book demonstrate why *Becoming a Teacher*, 10th edition, is the ideal preparation guide for becoming a licensed teacher.

AN EMPHASIS ON THE DIVERSITY OF STUDENTS AND THEIR TEACHERS

- **Focus on Diversity** These sections in each chapter address cultural and ethnic diversity, student ability, the impact of socioeconomic status, as well as linguistic diversity in today's classrooms. The sections introduce readers to culturally competent teaching and help them learn how to meet students' diverse needs in every classroom.

- **Comprehensive State Coverage** To ensure that students and teachers from all over the country see themselves mirrored in the content, the 10th edition specifically highlights master teachers, instructional issues, and curriculum initiatives from across the United States. An index of highlighted states is presented at the end of the Preface.

NEW CHAPTERS

- CHAPTER 11, School Curricula and Standards
- CHAPTER 12, Assessing Student Learning

NEW PEDAGOGY AND UP-TO-DATE CONTENT

- Learning Outcomes at beginning of each chapter
- New Readers' Voices open each chapter
- More than 250 new references to reflect the most recent information about the teaching profession in the United States

LATEST TRENDS IN TECHNOLOGY AND TEACHING

A thoroughly revised technology chapter explains how teachers can integrate technology into teaching in order to engage today's tech-savvy students fully and to adjust to the reality that technology has transformed how, when, and where students can learn. From blogs and wikis, to podcasting and 3-D virtual worlds, the 10th edition is filled with case examples of how teachers are integrating technology and transforming their teaching to foster collaboration, discovery, and understanding of the "big ideas" in the curriculum.

NEW AND EXPANDED COVERAGE TO ADDRESS THE MOST CURRENT TRENDS AND ISSUES

Chapter 1, Teaching: Your Chosen Profession

- Revised chapter now covers classroom observations, induction into the profession, gaining practical experience for becoming a teacher, and benefits of having a mentor.
- Characteristics principals look for when hiring teachers (NEW)
- Timeline for efforts to reauthorize the Elementary and Secondary Education Act (ESEA) and change the No Child Left Behind (NCLB) Act (NEW)
- Revised section on "Teaching and the National Economy"
- Latest data on school enrollments, school staffing, and teacher salaries

Chapter 2, Today's Teachers

- Revised chapter now covers the role of teacher leaders in transforming the profession, the U.S. Department of Education's "Respect Project," and seven "critical components" for transforming teaching.
- Influence of different groups on hiring process in schools (NEW)
- Model for teacher's thought processes while teaching (NEW)
- Model for multi-stage career ladder for teachers (NEW)
- Updated demographic information on U.S. public school teachers

Chapter 3, Today's Schools

- Revised chapter now covers educational opportunities for children of lower-income families, and provides analysis of America's continuing dropout problem, homeless children and youth, and extent of child maltreatment in the United States.
- Updated data on child well-being in the United States, drug use among students, crime in public schools, discipline problems, and dropout rates

Chapter 4, Philosophical Foundations of U.S. Education

- Eight guidelines for facilitating a Socratic discussion (NEW)
- Matrix for comparing five philosophical orientations to teaching (NEW)
- Matrix for comparing three psychological orientations to teaching (NEW)
- Model for an eclectic philosophy of education and teaching (NEW)
- Teaching on Your Feet, "Reluctant Readers" (NEW)
- Being an Agent of Change, "Every Day Is Filled with Deep Thinking and Contemplation" (NEW)

Chapter 5, Historical Foundations of U.S. Education

- Revised chapter now covers Common Core State Standards Initiative (CCSSI), continuing efforts to reauthorize the Elementary and Secondary Education Act (ESEA), and "EASA flexibility."

- Section that describes the European antecedents of American education (NEW)
- Timeline for European influences on American education (NEW)
- Illustration of the seven liberal arts (NEW)
- Updated historical timeline for U.S. education
- Walk in My Shoes, "Understanding the Past Is the Best Compass for the Future" (NEW)

Chapter 6, Governance and Finance of U.S. Schools

- Revised chapter includes updated, expanded coverage of: Chicago School Reform and 2014 school closings; state takeover of the School District of Philadelphia; summary of Obama administration's education reform efforts through 2014; up-to-date analysis of research on charter schools by Stanford University and the National Education Policy Center; and critical analysis of the performance of for-profit schools.
- Sections that describe innovative approaches to school governance in New York City; Washington, D.C.; Memphis, Tennessee; and New Orleans, Louisiana (NEW)
- Section that discusses role of teacher leaders in school governance, including teacher involvement in teacher education, certification, and staff development (NEW)
- Section that discusses the District of Columbia School Choice Incentive Act (NEW)
- Discussions of education–business partnerships: GE Foundation and Bill and Melinda Gates Foundation (NEW)
- Updated figures and tables for data on 10 largest U.S. school districts, school expenditures, distribution of expenditures, sources of school revenues, state education revenues, and funding priorities for education philanthropy

Chapter 7, Ethical and Legal Issues in U.S. Education

- Revised chapter includes updated, expanded coverage of court cases involving teachers and online social networking, student expression on social networking sites, dress codes, cyberbullying, and homeschooling.
- Updated references throughout chapter reflect the most recent court rulings on legal issues in U.S. education
- Legal advice for your student teaching experience (NEW)
- Section on Employment Non-Discrimination Act (NEW)

Chapter 8, Today's Students

- Revised chapter includes updated, expanded coverage of minority groups and academic achievement and Afrocentric schools.
- Updated figures and tables for data on children of immigrant families, English language learners (ELLs), and poor children and low-income families in the United States
- Nation's Report Card: 2013 Mathematics and Reading (NEW)
- Technology in Action: "High School Teacher Earns Online Master's Degree in Multicultural Education" (NEW)

Chapter 9, Addressing Learners' Individual Needs

- Revised chapter includes updated, expanded coverage of multiple intelligences, and Individual Education Plans (IEPs).
- Graphic to illustrate Piaget's stages of cognitive growth (NEW)
- Strategies for teaching children at Piaget's stages of cognitive growth (NEW)
- Updated figures and tables for data on children with disabilities
- Walk in My Shoes, Anthony Mullen (NEW)
- Being an Agent of Change, "Creating an inclusive environment . . . has always been my mission" (NEW)

Chapter 10, Creating a Community of Learners

- Revised chapter includes updated, expanded coverage of cooperative learning and cross-cultural interaction, successful classroom management, and assertive discipline.

- Graphic of authentic learning activity (NEW)
- Updated figures and tables for data on discipline problems at school and assertive discipline policy
- Data on importance of what teachers can do for parents (NEW)
- Professional learning environment for teachers (NEW)
- Teaching on Your Feet, "I see a story in every learner" (NEW)
- Sections on how teachers build learning communities and participate in teacher collaboration (NEW)

Chapter 11, School Curricula and Standards (NEW)

- Model for four kinds of curricula students experience (NEW)
- Model for three noncognitive factors that contribute to academic achievement (NEW)
- Coverage of global awareness; grit, tenacity, and perseverance; academic mindset; mindfulness/meditation skills; curricula to enhance noncognitive strengths; and Common Core State Standards Initiative (CCSSI) (NEW)
- Walk in My Shoes, "I Learned That I Love Learning" (NEW)
- Being an Agent of Change, "A 'Techno-Librarian' Shares New Ideas Across the Globe" (NEW)

Chapter 12, Assessing Student Learning (NEW)

- Latest data on students' mathematics, reading, and science performance on the Program for International Student Assessment (PISA) (NEW)
- Map of state high school exit exam policies (NEW)
- Sections on the role of assessment in teaching, standardized assessments, international assessments, "high-stakes" tests and accountability, and portfolio assessment (NEW)
- Being an Agent of Change, "Good Teachers Don't Shy Away from Assessment Data" (NEW)

Chapter 13, Integrating Technology into Teaching

- Revised chapter includes updated, expanded coverage of how technology is transforming teaching, virtual schools, availability and use of technology in schools, and the latest research studies on the use of educational technology.
- Figure to illustrate how teachers "embrace" digital technology (NEW)
- Sections on the traditional educational model and the digital "learning farm" model, how students use cell phones in learning, teachers' use of digital tools, and online activities teachers assign to students (NEW)
- Sections on the performance of cyberschools, flipped classrooms and flipped teaching, and "wired" students and their ability to focus (NEW)
- Three vignettes of how teachers use technology (NEW)
- Map of states with multi-district fully online schools (NEW)
- Data on percent of teachers reporting the availability of various technology devices (NEW)
- Data on students' use of educational technology during their classes (NEW)
- Being an Agent of Change, "Is Blended Learning Worth the Hype?" (NEW)

POPULAR FEATURES TO ENGAGE READERS

VOICES FROM THE FIELD

Throughout the 10th edition, the voices of preservice, new, and master teachers are heard.

- **"Dear Mentor" Feature** Success during the first years of teaching is a challenge for new teachers. Ask any experienced teacher to identify the key to success and most, if not all, will stress the importance of mentors. To facilitate your students' journey to becoming high-quality teachers, the popular Dear Mentor feature that opens each part of the book continues, enlisting the help of four novice teachers who pose important questions to four highly accomplished mentor teachers.

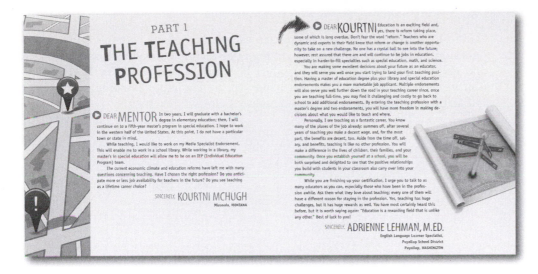

- **Readers' Voices** This feature at the beginning of each chapter provides comments by undergraduate teacher education majors about the importance of chapter content and helps readers feel confident about joining the wider community of those preparing to teach.

- **Teachers' Voices: Being an Agent of Change** This feature brings in the voices of experienced teachers—many of them National Teachers of the Year award winners—to focus on how teachers can effect change in the classroom and the community for the benefit of their students.

TEACHERS' VOICES ➡ BEING AN AGENT OF CHANGE

GEORGE WATSON

**Preparing "Citizens of the World"
Who Respect Cultural Differences**

Buenos dias. I teach Spanish at Walpole High School in Walpole, **MASSACHUSETTS.** I am also the department head of foreign languages for grades 6 through 12. When I was a student many years ago, I really looked up to my teachers. I saw them as people who had devoted themselves to a very noble profession, and that belief has not changed. Teaching, along with parenting, is probably the most important job that any one individual can do in any society, in any culture, on any continent.

I teach because I believe that every child wants to learn, is able to learn, and must learn. Furthermore, I teach because I believe that every child should have access to foreign language education. And every child should have access no matter what their reading level, no matter what their learning style and, really, no matter what grade they are in.

Over the course of my career, I have had the privilege to give my students the skills to communicate effectively in a second language and to give them confidence to navigate in a foreign culture. And I've seen students who have had very difficult middle school years come to my ninth-grade freshman Spanish class and achieve success. I've seen students from both Walpole, Massachusetts, and Palmares, Costa Rica, participate in our exchange program and establish friendships and bonds that last for years and years. I've seen

students who over the course of their 4 years in high school achieve incredible linguistic success and progress, so by the time that they are seniors in my AP class I know that they're going to be successful in college; I know that they are going to eventually participate in a global economy, which is more than just rewarding for me personally, it's nationally critical.

And last, it's wonderful for me as a teacher and a department head to celebrate the achievement of students—this is so very important; we just don't do this enough, I think, in public education. In Walpole, we have a very special foreign language awards night where we do just that, and we highlight not just what students have learned, but what students can do with the skills that we've provided them.

Yes, I am a teacher. I want to do my part to prepare my students to be citizens of the world, to be lifelong, self-confident learners, to be students who appreciate and respect cultural differences—those cultural differences that make our society and our world so fascinating and so very, very rich.

QUESTIONS

1. With respect to the subject area and grade level for which you are preparing to teach, how can you help students become "citizens of the world"?

2. After you become a teacher, what are some ways that you can demonstrate to students your own love of learning?

George Watson was Massachusetts Teacher of the Year for 2009.

- **Teaching on Your Feet** This feature has been revised to present examples of how successful teachers have turned potential problem situations in the classroom into "teachable moments." Written by real teachers, this feature illustrates how professional reflection and inquiry enable teachers to meet the numerous, unpredictable challenges that are part of teaching in today's schools.

- **Teachers' Voices: Walk in My Shoes** This margin feature of audio-recordings profiles teachers whose philosophy and professional contributions reflect commitment to touching others' lives through teaching. These teacher leaders share their insights, challenges, and accomplishments and encourage future teachers to "walk in their shoes."

AN EMPHASIS ON TODAY'S TECHNOLOGIES

- **Technology in Action** These features in each chapter have been revised to highlight how teachers are integrating cutting-edge technologies—such as virtual labs and text-to-speech programs—into their teaching. A practical **"Try It Out"** section in each feature gives readers hands-on directions for learning more about integrating the highlighted technology into their own teaching.

INSTRUCTOR'S RESOURCE CENTER

The Instructor Resource Center at www.pearsonhighered.com has a variety of print and media resources available in downloadable, digital format—all in one location. As a registered faculty member, you can access and download pass code–protected resource files, course-management content, and other premium online content directly to your computer.

Digital resources available for *Becoming a Teacher,* 10th edition, include the following:

- *Instructor's Resource Manual and Test Bank,* which includes:
  - Chapter-by-chapter materials, including a Chapter-at-a-Glance organizer for each chapter of the text, which correlates chapter outlines, learning objectives, and teaching supplements; an Annotated Lecture Outline, which provides examples, discussion questions, and student activities; suggestions for additional readings and media extend chapter learning; and handout masters, which provide additional lecture support materials.
  - A Test Bank of multiple choice and essay tests
- TestGen
- PowerPoint presentations specifically designed for each chapter.

To access these items online, go to www.pearsonhighered.com and click on the Instructor option. There you will be able to log in or complete a one-time registration for a user name and password. If you have any questions regarding this process or the materials available online, please contact your Pearson representative.

ACKNOWLEDGMENTS

I would like to thank the many members of the Pearson Education team who provided expert guidance and support during the preparation of the tenth edition of *Becoming a Teacher.* Clearly, Julie Peters, Senior Editor, and Mary Beth Finch, Production Editor, head the list. From skillful coordination of the revision process, from beginning to end, to addressing the challenges of preparing a new interactive eText and a print loose-leaf version, their hard work is deeply appreciated. Additionally, I am forever grateful to Meredith D. Fossel for her skill and professionalism in making critical arrangements for the tenth edition revision of this book.

I extend a very special thanks to Jeffery W. Johnston, Vice President and Editorial Director; Bryce Bell, Development Editor; and Kelli K. Jauron, Full-Service Project Manager, all of whom were steadfast in their support of the tenth edition.

I also extend a special thanks to Donald Finn for writing the Test Bank and preparing the Instructor's Resource Manual and PowerPoints for this edition.

For their patience, encouragement, and understanding while their dad has worked on revisions of this book since its first edition in 1990, I give warm thanks and a hug to each of my wonderful daughters: Anna, Catherine, Rebecca, and Anchitta. And, for her friendship, spiritual support, and encouragement during the revision process, I thank my wife, Phensri. Her ability to maintain a positive outlook while meeting life's inevitable challenges is remarkable; each day, she brings sunshine and joy into my life.

In addition, Michael Trevisan, Dean of the College of Education at Washington State University; Kelly Ward, Chair of the Department of Educational Leadership, Sports Studies, and Educational/Counseling Psychology; and the faculty, teaching assistants, and research assistants in the department gave me much-appreciated encouragement and support. Gail Furman, Professor of Educational Leadership, and Paul Pitre, Associate Professor of Educational Leadership, provided invaluable ideas for this edition of the book, as did Eric J. Anctil, Associate Professor of Education and Director for Innovation at the University of Portland. I give a sincere thanks to students (many of them now teachers and school administrators) in the classes I have taught at Washington State University. Conversations with them over the years have been thought provoking and professionally rewarding. I extend warm thanks to Ingrid Spence and her colleagues and students at the University of Idaho for their excellent suggestions for this edition. And, for demonstrating the power of professional inquiry, I owe a profound debt to a great teacher, mentor, and friend, the late Herbert A. Thelen, Professor of Education at the University of Chicago.

I am also grateful to the many people throughout the United States who have used the previous edition and provided suggestions and materials for this edition, including my students at Washington State University. I also wish to thank the following reviewers, who provided concise, helpful suggestions during the developmental stages of this book: Tina Allen, University of Louisiana at Monroe; Robert A. Schultz, University of Toledo; and Curtis Visca, Saddleback College; as well as the following reviewers of earlier editions: Tami Baker, East Tennessee State University; Kara Dawson, University of Florida; Larry Froehlich, Kent State University; Lynne Hamer, University of Toledo; Judy Jackson May, Bowling Green State University; Sandi McCann, Columbus State University; Lois Paretti, University of Nevada, Las Vegas; Sarah Swicegood, Sam Houston State University; and Barbara Taylor, Western New Mexico University.

STATE COVERAGE

The 10th edition of *Becoming a Teacher* considers educational issues and contributions as they apply to teaching across the country. You'll see specific state coverage throughout the chapters.

CHAPTER 1: TEACHING: YOUR CHOSEN PROFESSION

California
Colorado
Delaware
Florida
Georgia
Hawaii
Illinois
Kansas
Maryland
Massachusetts

New York
North Carolina
Ohio
Pennsylvania
Rhode Island
Tennessee
Texas
Washington
Washington, DC

CHAPTER 2: TODAY'S TEACHERS

California	Maryland
Connecticut	Massachusetts
Idaho	Pennsylvania
Louisiana	Texas

CHAPTER 3: TODAY'S SCHOOLS

Alabama	New Jersey
California	New York
Florida	Ohio
Hawaii	Oklahoma
Illinois	Pennsylvania
Massachusetts	Texas
Minnesota	Washington
Mississippi	Washington, DC

CHAPTER 4: PHILOSOPHICAL FOUNDATIONS OF U.S. EDUCATION

Arkansas	Ohio
California	Texas
Indiana	Washington

CHAPTER 5: HISTORICAL FOUNDATIONS OF U.S. EDUCATION

California	Virginia
New Hampshire	West Virginia

CHAPTER 6: GOVERNANCE AND FINANCE OF U.S. SCHOOLS

Arkansas	New Mexico
California	New York
Colorado	North Carolina
Florida	Ohio
Illinois	Pennsylvania
Kentucky	South Carolina
Michigan	Texas
Minnesota	Virginia
Missouri	Washington
Nebraska	West Virginia

CHAPTER 7: ETHICAL AND LEGAL ISSUES IN U.S. EDUCATION

California	New Hampshire
Florida	Pennsylvania
Louisiana	Virginia
Missouri	

CHAPTER 8: TODAY'S STUDENTS

Alaska	Minnesota
Arizona	New Mexico
California	New York
Colorado	Oklahoma
Florida	Texas
Illinois	Utah
Indiana	Washington

CHAPTER 9: ADDRESSING LEARNERS' INDIVIDUAL NEEDS

California	Maine
Connecticut	Nevada
Florida	Oregon
Illinois	Texas
Indiana	

CHAPTER 10: CREATING A COMMUNITY OF LEARNERS

Kansas	Virginia
Texas	Washington

CHAPTER 11: SCHOOL CURRICULA AND STANDARDS

Alabama	New York
Alaska	North Dakota
Arizona	Ohio
California	Oklahoma
Colorado	Oregon
Connecticut	Rhode Island
Florida	South Carolina
Hawaii	South Dakota
Maine	Texas
Massachusetts	Virginia
Nevada	Washington
New Jersey	Wyoming

CHAPTER 12: ASSESSING STUDENT LEARNING

Alabama	Maine
California	Michigan
Connecticut	North Carolina
Florida	Vermont
Georgia	Washington
Hawaii	West Virginia
Idaho	Wisconsin
Illinois	

CHAPTER 13: INTEGRATING TECHNOLOGY INTO TEACHING

Alabama	North Carolina
California	Ohio
Colorado	Oregon
Connecticut	South Dakota
Delaware	Tennessee
Florida	Texas
Georgia	Vermont
Indiana	Virginia
Kansas	Washington
Nebraska	West Virginia
New Mexico	Wisconsin
New York	

BRIEF CONTENTS

CONTENTS

CHAPTER SIX

Governance and Finance of U.S. Schools 180

CHAPTER SEVEN

Ethical and Legal Issues in U.S. Education 224

PART 3
THE ART OF TEACHING 264

CHAPTER EIGHT
Today's Students 266

CHAPTER NINE
Addressing Learners' Individual Needs 304

CHAPTER TEN
Creating a Community of Learners 338

SPECIAL FEATURES

ABOUT THE AUTHOR

Forrest W. Parkay is Professor of Educational Leadership and Higher Education at Washington State University. He was Professor of Educational Leadership at the University of Florida for eight years and at Texas State University for five years. Forrest received his B.A. and M.A. degrees in English education from the University of Illinois–Urbana. He earned his Ph.D. in education at the University of Chicago, and he is a graduate of Harvard University's Management Development Program (MDP). For eight years, Forrest taught at DuSable High School on Chicago's South Side, and he served as Chairman of DuSable's English Department for four years.

Forrest is the author or co-author of more than 60 refereed journal articles and several books, including *Curriculum Leadership: Readings for Developing Quality Educational Programs* (Pearson, 2014). His research has appeared in the field's leading peer-reviewed journals, including *Phi Delta Kappan, American Journal of Education,* and *Educational Administration Quarterly.*

A former Fulbright Scholar at Kasetsart University's Center for Research on Teaching and Teacher Education, in Thailand, Forrest has facilitated educational reform programs and conducted cross-national research in China, Thailand, Korea, Japan, Pakistan, India, and Singapore. He has been a Visiting Professor at Beijing Normal University and at Assumption University in Thailand.

His hobbies include classic cars, camping, kayaking, and photography. Forrest is the proud father of four daughters: Anna, Catherine, Rebecca, and Anchitta.

PART 1
THE TEACHING PROFESSION

▶ DEAR MENTOR In two years, I will graduate with a bachelor's degree in elementary education; then, I will continue on to a fifth-year master's program in special education. I hope to work in the western half of the United States. At this point, I do not have a particular town or state in mind.

While teaching, I would like to work on my Media Specialist Endorsement. This will enable me to work in a school library. While working in a library, my master's in special education will allow me to be on an IEP (Individual Education Program) team.

The current economic climate and education reforms have left me with many questions concerning teaching. Have I chosen the right profession? Do you anticipate more or less job availability for teachers in the future? Do you see teaching as a lifetime career choice?

SINCERELY, KOURTNI MCHUGH

Missoula, MONTANA

▶ DEAR **KOURTNI** Education is an exciting field and, yes, there is reform taking place, some of which is long overdue. Don't fear the word "reform." Teachers who are dynamic and experts in their field know that reform or change is another opportunity to take on a new challenge. No one has a crystal ball to see into the future; however, rest assured that there are and will continue to be jobs in education, especially in harder-to-fill specialties such as special education, math, and science.

You are making some excellent decisions about your future as an educator, and they will serve you well once you start trying to land your first teaching position. Having a master of education degree plus your library and special education endorsements makes you a more marketable job applicant. Multiple endorsements will also serve you well further down the road in your teaching career since, once you are teaching full-time, you may find it challenging and costly to go back to school to add additional endorsements. By entering the teaching profession with a master's degree and two endorsements, you will have more freedom in making decisions about what you would like to teach and where.

Personally, I see teaching as a fantastic career. You know many of the pluses of the job already: summers off, after several years of teaching you make a decent wage, and, for the most part, the benefits are decent, too. Aside from the time off, salary, and benefits, teaching is like no other profession. You will make a difference in the lives of children, their families, and your community. Once you establish yourself at a school, you will be both surprised and delighted to see that the positive relationships you build with students in your classroom also carry over into your community.

While you are finishing up your certification, I urge you to talk to as many educators as you can, especially those who have been in the profession awhile. Ask them what they love about teaching; every one of them will have a different reason for staying in the profession. Yes, teaching has huge challenges, but it has huge rewards as well. You have most certainly heard this before, but it is worth saying again: "Education is a rewarding field that is unlike any other." Best of luck to you!

SINCERELY, **ADRIENNE LEHMAN, M.ED.**
English Language Learner Specialist,
Puyallup School District
Puyallup, WASHINGTON

CHAPTER ONE
Teaching: Your Chosen Profession

learning outcomes

After reading this chapter, you will be able to do the following:

1. Explain why you want to teach.
2. Identify the benefits of teaching.
3. Identify and explain the challenges of teaching.
4. Explain what society will expect of you as a teacher.
5. Describe the job outlook for teachers.
6. Explain what you can learn from observing in classrooms.
7. Explain why your induction into teaching is important.
8. Explain how you can gain practical experience for becoming a teacher.
9. Explain how you will become a highly qualified teacher.
10. Explain how you can benefit from having a mentor.

READERS' VOICES

Why do I want to teach?

Teachers have been a profound influence in my life. They have inspired me in so many ways. Now I am becoming a teacher because I want to help my students grow, just as my teachers helped me.

—MARCUS, Teacher Education program, first year

Congratulations on deciding to become a teacher! Teaching is exciting, rewarding, and uplifting. Teachers receive great satisfaction from knowing that they really make a difference in their students' lives. I hope you share my belief that teaching is the world's most important profession and is vitally important to our nation's future. As President Obama said in his 2011 State of the Union Address, "To every young person who's contemplating their career choice: If you want to make a difference in the life of our nation; if you want to make a difference in the life of a child—become a teacher. Your country needs you" (January 25, 2011).

I also hope your commitment to teaching will become deeper and stronger as you move through your teacher education program. And I hope your experiences will be similar to those a student teacher recently shared with me: "When I came to the university I had various majors—electrical engineering, architecture, journalism—but I wasn't really happy until I went into teaching. Now it's really becoming a passion."

Teaching is a challenging but rewarding profession—one that is not for everyone, however. This book will orient you to the world of teaching and help you answer your own questions about the career you have chosen. What is teaching really like? What rewards do teachers experience? What are the trends and issues in the profession? What problems can you expect to encounter in the classroom? What will you need to know and be able to do to become a highly qualified teacher?

I believe that successful teachers know why they want to teach. They examine their motives carefully, and they understand why, at first, they might have been uncertain about choosing to become a teacher. The first chapter of this book, then, addresses the 10 learning outcomes listed on the previous page, which will help you decide if teaching is the right profession for you.

The learning outcomes in each chapter of this book address *your future* as a teacher. Achieving these learning outcomes will provide you with a reality-based look at the world of teachers, students, classrooms, and schools and their surrounding communities. After reading this book, you will have a broad understanding of one of the world's most exciting, satisfying, and honorable professions. And you will know if teaching is the right profession for you.

WHY DO I WANT TO TEACH?

You may want to teach for many reasons. Your desire to teach may be the result of positive experiences with teachers when you were a child. You may be attracted to teaching because the life of a teacher is exciting, varied, and stimulating. Or you may see teaching as a way of making a significant contribution

TABLE 1.1 Teacher characteristics that principals look for when hiring (percentage)

Teacher Characteristic	In Top Three Reasons	Most Important Reason
Superior Teaching Skills	64.8	36.4
Content Knowledge	65.9	26.1
A Passion for Teaching	27.3	11.4
Cares About Children	42.0	8.0
Willingness to Work as Part of a Team	30.7	6.8
Classroom Management Skills	45.5	6.8
Willingness to Do Something Extra Beyond Classroom Teaching	12.5	0.0
Other	8.0	4.5

Note: The survey item was worded as follows: "What characteristics do you look for when hiring a classroom teacher?"

Adapted from Glazerman, S. A., Protik, B., Teh, J., Bruch, N., & Seftor, N. (2012). *Moving High-Performing Teachers: Implementation of Transfer Incentives in Seven Districts* (NCEE 2012-4051). Washington, DC: National Center for Education Evaluation and Regional Assistance, Institute of Education Sciences, U.S. Department of Education, p. 38.

to the world and experiencing the joy of helping children grow and develop. Table 1.1 shows that caring about children is among the most important characteristics elementary and middle-level principals have in mind when they hire new teachers.

Desire to Make a Difference in Students' Lives

Although teaching may be challenging and teachers' salaries modest, most teach simply because they care about students. Teachers derive great satisfaction when their students learn—when they make a difference in students' lives. In fact, 59 percent of teachers in a national survey reported that they are "very satisfied" with teaching as a career, and 75 percent said they planned to continue working in education after retirement (Harris Interactive, 2010, p. 45).

As a teacher, your day-to-day interactions with students will build strong bonds between you and them. Daily contact will enable you to become familiar with your students' personal and academic needs. Concern for their welfare will help you cope with the difficulties and frustrations of teaching. The teacher's potential to make a difference in students' lives can be profound; for example, the National Education Association (NEA) has posted at its website comments by the following highly accomplished individuals that pay tribute to the teachers who have touched their lives:

- Oprah Winfrey, entrepreneur
- Dan Rather, national news commentator
- Charles Platt, science fiction novelist
- Carl Jung, world-renowned psychoanalyst

Like most teachers, you appreciate the unique qualities of youth. You enjoy the liveliness, curiosity, freshness, openness, and trust of young children or the abilities, wit, spirit, independence, and idealism of adolescents. As one teacher told me, "I know I make a difference in my students' lives, especially those who may not see themselves as 'good' students. It is so rewarding when they tell me that they *can learn*, that they can 'change the world.'"

As a teacher, you will also derive significant rewards from meeting the needs of diverse learners. Students from our nation's more than 100 racial and ethnic groups and students with special needs are increasing in number, so your classroom will be

PROFESSIONAL REFLECTION

Listen as this teacher gives you advice for succeeding in your first year of teaching.

enriched by the varied backgrounds of your students. To ensure that you can experience the satisfaction of helping all students learn, significant portions of this book are devoted to **student variability** (differences among students in regard to their developmental needs, interests, abilities, and disabilities) and **student diversity** (differences among students in regard to gender, race, ethnicity, culture, religion, sexual orientation, and socioeconomic status). Your appreciation for diversity will help you to experience the rewards that come from enabling each student to make his or her unique contribution to classroom life. In addition, you can be proud of your role in promoting social justice and helping our nation realize its democratic ideals.

Like the following two teachers, a likely reason you have been drawn to teaching is the privilege of working with children and youth, regardless of their stages of development or their life circumstances:

> I don't know another job where you laugh every day; where you get hugs consistently; where thinking is a requirement; where you can have snack time; where you are loved by 30 people; where you can get lost in a good story; where you play and create; and where you meet heroes and where you get to be one, too. (Harris Interactive, 2006, p. 66)

> The rewards are great, when you see a child suddenly grasp a concept or write that poem that he/she thought [he/she] couldn't, these are the moments that let me know that I am in the right profession! (Harris Interactive, 2001, p. 118)

A Passion for Teaching

Table 1.1 also shows that a "passion for teaching" is among the most important characteristics principals look for when hiring teachers. What does it mean to be *passionate* about teaching?

A PASSION FOR THE SUBJECT

You may be passionate about teaching because you are passionate about teaching in your discipline. Teaching can give you an opportunity to share with students your passion for science, computers, sports, or the outdoors, for example. When students see that you *really do love* a subject, they will respond—their interest will be aroused, and they will appreciate that you have shared an important part of your life with them. As evidence of this, recall how your own interest has been piqued whenever your teachers shared their passion for the subject. What you experienced during those moments was a special "invitation" to share a teacher's excitement about an important part of his or her life.

A PASSION FOR THE TEACHING LIFE

Perhaps you are eager to experience the "joy of teaching" that motivated a teacher who taught Arnie Duncan, now U.S. Secretary of Education: "A reason to go into teaching is that it's a total joy. And, yes, it's hard work, but it's a gift" (U.S. Department of Education, May 7, 2010). The life of a teacher appeals to you—to be in an environment that encourages a high regard for education and the life of the mind, and to have daily opportunities to see students become excited about learning. Albert Einstein, for example, regretted that he did not devote his career to the teaching life, commenting on children's openness to knowledge and how much he enjoyed being with them.

Teachers can play a critical role in shaping the future of young people. What positive effects might this teacher have on these students?

A PASSION FOR THE TEACHING–LEARNING PROCESS

You may be passionate about teaching because you are excited about helping students learn. The prospect of thinking on your feet and capitalizing on teachable moments is appealing. Perhaps you had expert teachers who made you appreciate the "artistic" dimensions of teaching, and you marveled at their ability to maintain students' interest in learning from moment to moment and to improvise on the spot.

The great educator and philosopher John Dewey explains how skilled teachers improvise. Teachers, he said, are sensitive to the inner lives of children and therefore aware of what students are learning (or not learning) as a result their teaching. He explains:

> As every teacher knows, children have an inner and an outer attention. The inner attention is the giving of the mind without reserve or qualification to the subject at hand. . . .
>
> To be able to keep track of this mental play, to recognize the signs of its presence or absence, to know how it is initiated and maintained, how to test it by results attained, and to test apparent results by it, is the supreme mark and criterion of a teacher. (Dewey, 1904, pp. 13–14)

Philip Jackson describes the unpredictability of teaching in his well-known book *Life in Classrooms*: "[As] typically conducted, teaching is an opportunistic process. . . . Neither teacher nor students can predict with any certainty exactly what will happen next. Plans are forever going awry and unexpected opportunities for the attainment of educational goals are constantly emerging" (Jackson, 1990, p. 166).

Research tells us that teachers may make up to 3,000 low-level decisions in a single school day (Jackson, 1990). Most decisions are easy and natural, but some require critical thinking. Stepping into the minds of teachers to see how they turned a negative situation into a positive learning experience for students is the purpose of the Teaching on Your Feet feature in each chapter of this book. For example, students at risk need teachers who can recognize opportunities in the classroom to build up their confidence as learners, as Jennifer Michele Diaz illustrates in the Teaching on Your Feet feature for this chapter.

Influence of Teachers

The journey toward becoming a teacher often begins early in life. Although few people are born teachers, their early life experiences often encourage them to become teachers. With the exception of parents or guardians, the adults who have the greatest influence on children are often their teachers. A positive relationship with a teacher may have been the catalyst for your decision to become a teacher. Perhaps you had teachers similar to those described by several young people in the following:

> *She was a good teacher because she was able to make learning fun, and she related to our lives. She was able to find fun ways to learn, instead of the boring "textbook approach."*
>
> —15 year-old

> *She listened to what I had to say.*
>
> —10 year-old

> *He was able to talk to us like a person and not a teacher. Treated us with respect but joked around but kept the line of teacher and student.*
>
> —14 year-old

> *Mr. C. always told me I was smart when I didn't feel like it.*
>
> —10 year-old

I learned more from this one teacher because she didn't just have us do stuff from a book, she did creative things to help us learn about stuff.

—12 year-old (Harris Interactive, 2008, p. 86)

Similar to most people who become teachers, you may have been more influenced by your teachers as people than as subject-matter experts. Often, the process of becoming a teacher begins early in life. For example, a teacher's influence during your formative years may have been the catalyst that started you thinking about the possibility of, one day, becoming like that teacher. Over time, the inspirational memory of that teacher led you to the teaching profession.

Desire to Serve

You may have chosen teaching because you want to serve others. You want your life's work to have meaning, to be more than just a job. As Arnie Duncan, U.S. Secretary of Education, put it, "No other profession carries a greater burden for securing our economic future. No other profession holds out more promise of opportunity to children and young people from disadvantaged backgrounds. And no other profession deserves more respect" (U.S. Department of Education, February 15, 2012).

Your decision to serve through teaching may have been influenced by your experiences as a volunteer. One such teacher is Noah Zeichner, a former volunteer teacher

Watch this video to observe various characteristics needed to be an effective teacher.

TEACHING ON YOUR FEET
The Abolishment of "I Can't"

Thirty-two little hands burst into the air as I reached into a jar of student numbers to randomly select a student to read aloud. It was the second week of school for my fourth graders, and the second week of my first year of teaching. The students were excited and enthusiastic about the possibility of being selected to read aloud from the new brightly colored social studies textbook.

"Congratulations, student number three! Let's follow along as we listen to Anthony read aloud," I said, when I pulled Anthony's number from the jar. Several students dropped their hands back down to their desks in disappointment. (My students seemed to think that if they raised their hands while rising slightly out of their seats their number would magically be selected. Their sense of naïveté melted my heart.)

Silence fell over the classroom, and Anthony gazed at the book. He squirmed in his chair and began to rock back and forth gently. He began to stumble through the words "The state of California is . . . ." Then he blurted out, "I can't read, Miss Diaz," and began to giggle, perhaps hoping to give the impression that a fit of laughter was the cause of his inability to read aloud.

Anthony's laughter sparked giggles among his classmates but caused me to feel panic. I knew that Anthony had been retained a year. The fact that he was a year older than his classmates yet several years behind them in terms of reading ability alarmed me. How should I, as a first-year teacher, respond to his near-illiteracy?

Quickly bringing myself back to the immediacy of a classroom of 32 students, I praised Anthony for being courageous enough to read aloud and helped him read the rest of the short paragraph. Setting

the social studies lesson aside, I took the opportunity provided by Anthony's comment to insert a mini-lesson on the need to eliminate the phrase "I can't" from my students' vocabulary. I noted that even though Anthony may have felt that he could not read aloud, he did in fact read (albeit, with my guidance).

During my mini-lesson, one student suggested that we ban the phrase "I can't" from our classroom. As a class, we then collectively created a list of phrases that could be used instead of "I can't" when we become frustrated with a challenging task. These phrases included "I do not understand . . ."; "I am confused about . . ."; and "I need some extra help/extra time with. . . ." Our time quickly ran out, and it was time to go to lunch. As my long line of fourth graders made its way to the cafeteria, I could hear the voices of several students echoing in the halls as they chanted, "There's no such thing as 'I can't'!" Although our social studies lesson was delayed, it was well worth the boost in confidence and understanding that filled our classroom because Anthony was now encouraged rather than embarrassed.

ANALYZE & REFLECT

Click here to analyze and reflect on this scenario you have just read.

JENNIFER MICHELE DIAZ
**Fourth-Grade Teacher,
Westmont Elementary School
Anaheim, CALIFORNIA**

in Ecuador who now teaches at Chief Sealth High School in Seattle, **WASHINGTON**. His Ecuadorian students, he says, "had the desire to learn, in spite of overwhelming economic hardships. I figured if I could be successful there—with 12 students ages 12 to 18—I could do it in the United States" (Berry et al. 2011).

After the terrorist attacks of 9/11, many people reported that the uncertainty caused by the attacks led them to consider teaching as a career. According to school officials, the national wave of soul-searching after the attacks swelled the number of people seeking jobs as teachers. Clearly, they saw teaching as a way to serve.

The desire to serve others and give something back to society is a key attraction of **Teach for America**, a national corps launched in 1990 by Wendy Kopp as an outgrowth of her senior thesis at Princeton University. Teach for America corps members, recent graduates from some of the best colleges and universities in the United States, are assigned to teach for a minimum of 2 years in urban and rural school districts with severe shortages of science, math, and language arts teachers. Corps members complete 5 weeks of intensive training during a summer institute in Atlanta, Houston, Los Angeles, New York City, Philadelphia, Phoenix, Detroit, or San Antonio. After two years of teaching, being monitored by state and school authorities, and taking professional development courses, Teach for America teachers can earn regular certification. Upon completion of their 2-year assignment, corps members return to their chosen careers in other fields, although more than half remain in education as teachers, principals, and educational administrators. During 2013, Teach for America had 6,000 first-year corps members, 39 percent of whom were people of color and 39 percent from low-income backgrounds (Teach for America, 2014). At the start of the 2013–2014 school year, 11,000 corps members taught in 48 regions of the country (Teach for America, 2013).

Explore more deeply your reasons for becoming a teacher by completing the activity presented in Figure 1.1. The figure presents several characteristics that may indicate your probable satisfaction with teaching as a career.

TEACHERS' VOICES
Walk in My Shoes
"Welcome to the exciting, dynamic profession of teaching!"
Forrest W. Parkay

FIGURE 1.1   Why do I want to teach?

Explore your reasons for becoming a teacher. Rate each of the following characteristics and experiences in relation to how each describes your motivation for choosing teaching as a career. Rate each item on a scale from 1–5 (1 = "very applicable"; 5 = "not at all applicable"). Which factors are most applicable to you? What is your strongest reason for becoming a teacher?

	Very applicable				Not at all applicable			Very applicable				Not at all applicable
1. A passion for learning	1	2	3	4	5	**7.** Good verbal and writing skills	1	2	3	4	5
2. Success as a student	1	2	3	4	5	**8.** Appreciation for the arts	1	2	3	4	5
3. Good sense of humor	1	2	3	4	5	**9.** Experiences working with children (camp, church, tutoring, etc.)	1	2	3	4	5
4. Positive attitude toward students	1	2	3	4	5	**10.** Other teachers in family	1	2	3	4	5
5. Tolerance toward others	1	2	3	4	5	**11.** Encouragement from family to enter teaching	1	2	3	4	5
6. Patience	1	2	3	4	5	**12.** Desire to serve	1	2	3	4	5

WHAT ARE THE BENEFITS OF TEACHING?

Perhaps you are drawn to teaching by its practical advantages. Teachers' hours and vacations are well-known advantages. Although the hours most teachers devote to their jobs go far beyond the number of hours they actually spend at school, their schedules are more flexible than those of other professionals. Teachers who have young children can often be at home when their children are not in school, and nearly all teachers, regardless of years of experience, have numerous holidays and a long summer vacation. On the other hand, teachers at the nation's nearly 3,000 public year-round schools in 46 states have three or four mini-vacations throughout the year (National Association for Year-Round Education, 2008). Teachers at year-round schools welcome the flexibility of being able to take vacations during off-peak seasons.

Salaries and Benefits

Although intangible rewards are a significant attraction to teaching, teachers want the public to acknowledge the value and status of teaching by supporting higher salaries. According to a poll of 2,500 adults, 69 percent of the public supports increasing teacher salaries (Howell & West, 2009). As a result of the public's support for higher teacher salaries, teachers' salaries have increased steadily since the new century began. The average salary of all teachers in 1999–2000 was $41,807; as Table 1.2 shows, for 2013–2014, the average salary was $56,689 (National Education Association, 2014).

Although the general consensus is still that teachers are underpaid, teacher salaries are becoming more competitive with those of other occupations. In fact, salaries could become an attraction of the profession if schools like The Equity Project (TEP) Charter School in New York City become more common. All TEP teachers earn $125,000 per year and are eligible for a $25,000 annual bonus based on schoolwide performance (Galante, 2012). The school, which opened in 2009, was designed on the basis of research showing that teacher quality is the most important school-based factor in the academic success of students, particularly those from low-income families (Goldhaber & Anthony, 2003). The school uses what it calls the "3 Rs" to recruit master teachers: Rigorous Qualifications, Redefined Expectations, and Revolutionary Compensation. The school does not fundraise to support its investment in teachers' salaries; instead, "TEP's mission is to demonstrate that schools can make a radical investment in teacher equity by reallocating existing public funding" (TEP, 2014).

A teaching career at TEP involves weekly peer observations and co-teaching, an annual 6-week Summer Development Institute, and a mandatory sabbatical once every 5 or 6 years. These Redefined Expectations are based on the realization that student achievement is increased when teachers have the time and support to improve their craft.

When comparing teachers' salaries state by state, remember that higher salaries are frequently linked to a higher cost of living, a more experienced teaching force, and a more desirable location. In addition, many districts have salary policies that attract the best graduates of teacher education programs, encourage quality teachers to remain in the classroom, or draw teachers into subjects and geographic areas in which there are shortages. These policies can increase a teacher's salary by thousands of dollars. For example, from 2007 through 2010, the United Federation of Teachers (UFT) and the New York City Department of Education implemented a teacher incentive program and distributed almost $75 million to teachers in over 200 high-need schools (Fryer, 2011, p. 4).

Teachers' salaries are typically determined by years of experience and advanced training, as evidenced by graduate credit hours or advanced degrees. When you become a teacher, you may be able to increase your salary by taking on additional duties,

TABLE 1.2

Estimated average instructional staff and teacher salaries, 2013–2014

| | Average Salaries | |
Region and State	Instructional Staff	Elementary and Secondary Teachers
U.S. AND D.C.	**58,873**	**56,689**
ALABAMA	50,604*	48,413*
ALASKA	68,063*	66,739*
ARIZONA	51,109*	51,109*
ARKANSAS	50,398*	46,950*
CALIFORNIA	71,285*	70,126*
COLORADO	53,039*	50,651*
CONNECTICUT	70,584*	70,584*
DELAWARE	64,338*	60,571*
D.C.	73,162*	73,162*
FLORIDA	48,050	46,691
GEORGIA	55,420	52,924
HAWAII	58,524	56,291
IDAHO	53,088*	50,945*
ILLINOIS	60,098*	60,124*
INDIANA	50,942*	50,644*
IOWA	54,196	51,662
KANSAS	49,571*	48,221*
KENTUCKY	53,022	50,705
LOUISIANA	55,342*	52,259*
MAINE	50,762	49,232
MARYLAND	69,249*	64,868*
MASSACHUSETTS	73,736	73,736
MICHIGAN	62,141*	61,866*
MINNESOTA	62,891*	57,230*
MISSISSIPPI	43,918*	42,187*
MISSOURI	52,498*	48,329*
MONTANA	51,494*	49,893*
NEBRASKA	49,545	49,545
NEVADA	57,879*	57,391*
NEW HAMPSHIRE	57,026*	57,057*
NEW JERSEY	74,625*	70,060*

(continued)

TABLE
1.2 (continued)

Region and State	Average Salaries	
	Instructional Staff	**Elementary and Secondary Teachers**
NEW MEXICO	48,209*	45,727
NEW YORK	78,835*	76,566*
NORTH CAROLINA	45,355	45,355
NORTH DAKOTA	50,622*	48,666*
OHIO	62,473*	57,270*
OKLAHOMA	46,198	44,277
OREGON	61,492*	58,597*
PENNSYLVANIA	65,956*	64,072*
RHODE ISLAND	70,411*	64,696*
SOUTH CAROLINA	51,441	48,425
SOUTH DAKOTA	41,649	40,023
TENNESSEE	50,355*	48,049*
TEXAS	52,191	49,270
UTAH	52,806*	50,659*
VERMONT	55,265*	53,656*
VIRGINIA	51,490*	49,233*
WASHINGTON	56,182*	52,236*
WEST VIRGINIA	48,298*	45,583*
WISCONSIN	58,847*	54,717*
WYOMING	60,023	57,910

*Data reflect NEA estimates rather than estimates by state departments of education.

Note: "Instructional staff" includes teachers, principals, consultants or supervisors of instruction, guidance personnel, librarians, psychological personnel, and other instructional staff.

Adapted from Rankings & Estimates: Rankings of the States 2013 and Estimates of School Statistics 2014. Washington, DC: National Education Association, March 2014, p. 92. Data used with permission of the National Education Association © 2014. All rights reserved.

such as coaching an athletic team, producing the yearbook and school newspaper, or sponsoring clubs. In addition, your district may offer limited summer employment for teachers who wish to teach summer school or develop curriculum materials. Additionally, about one-fourth of the nation's approximately 3.2 million public school teachers moonlight (i.e., hold a second job) to increase their earnings.

Teachers also receive various **fringe benefits**, such as medical insurance and retirement plans, which are usually given in addition to base salary. These benefits vary from district to district and are determined during collective bargaining sessions. When considering a school district for your first position, carefully examine the fringe benefits package as well as the salary schedule and opportunities for extra pay.

WHAT ARE THE CHALLENGES OF TEACHING?

Like all professions, teaching has undesirable or difficult aspects. Frank McCourt, a teacher at four New York City high schools over a 30-year period and a noted author after his retirement from teaching, said a teacher needs to be "a drill sergeant, a rabbi, a disciplinarian, a low-level scholar, a clerk, a referee, a clown, a counselor, and therapist" (McCourt, 2005).

As a prospective teacher, you should consider the challenges as well as the satisfactions you are likely to encounter. You can make the most of your teacher education program if you are informed. Awareness of the realities of teaching will enable you to develop your personal philosophy of education, build a repertoire of teaching strategies, strengthen your leadership skills, and acquire a knowledge base of research and theory to guide your actions. In this manner, you can become a true professional—free to enjoy the many satisfactions of teaching and confident of your ability to deal with its challenges. Table 1.3, based on a survey of almost 3,000 teachers, shows factors that help and hinder teachers in their efforts to provide students with the best education possible. Later chapters in this book will address the factors that hinder teachers the most. The sections that follow, however, discuss three challenges that are part of teachers' daily lives: long working hours, accountability for student learning in a high-stakes-testing environment, and motivating today's tech-savvy students.

Long Working Hours

The length of a teacher's workday may appear attractive, but teachers' actual working hours are another matter. Teachers' contracts do not include additional hours for lesson planning and evaluating students' work, nor do they include noninstructional

TABLE 1.3 Relative rankings of factors that helped and hindered teachers most in their efforts to provide the best service in their teaching positions, 2001 and 2006

	Helped Teachers Most			Hindered Teachers Most	
Rank	**2001**	**2006**	**Rank**	**2001**	**2006**
1	Cooperative/competent teacher colleagues/mentors	Cooperative/competent teacher colleagues/mentors	1	Heavy workload, extra responsibilities, paperwork, meetings	Heavy workload, extra responsibilities, paperwork, meetings
2	Training, education, and knowledge of subject matter/professional development	Help from administrators/specialists	2	Incompetent/uncooperative administrators	Testing demands/teaching to the test
3	Interest in children/teaching, other personal characteristics	Interest in children/teaching, other personal characteristics	3	Negative attitudes of public, parents, and state legislators	Discipline and negative attitudes of students
4	Help from administrators/specialists	Good materials, resources, facilities	4	Discipline and negative attitudes of students	Incompetent/uncooperative administrators/lack of support from administrators
5	School environment/organizations, freedom to teach	Training, education, and knowledge of subject matter/professional development	5	Lack of materials, resources, and facilities	Lack of preparation/planning time
6	Good materials, resources, facilities	School environment/organization, freedom to teach	6	Lack of funds/decent salary	Lack of materials, resources, and facilities

Source: National Education Association, *Status of the American Public School Teacher, 2005–2006: NEA Research,* March 2010, pp. 92–93. Data used with permission of the National Education Association © 2010. All rights reserved.

assignments found at all levels of teaching—from recess duty to club sponsorship and coaching. Teachers devote an average of 52 hours a week to their jobs, with approximately 37 hours devoted to the required workweek, and 12.7 hours devoted to non-compensated teaching tasks (National Education Association, 2010, pp. 47, 53).

The need to keep accurate, detailed records of students' academic progress, absences, and lateness, as well as other forms of paperwork, is one of the teacher's most time-consuming tasks. Other nonteaching tasks include supervising students on the playground, at extracurricular events, and in the hallways, study halls, and lunchrooms; attending faculty meetings, parent conferences, and open houses; and taking tickets or selling concessions for athletic events. Nonteaching responsibilities often are enjoyable and provide opportunities to interact informally with students; however, they can lessen the amount of time and energy teachers have available for teaching-related tasks.

High-Stakes Testing and Increased Accountability

A significant challenge for today's teachers is the emphasis placed on **high-stakes tests**. Each state has mandated a standardized test to assess students' mastery of academic standards. For example, 4th-, 7th-, and 10th-grade students in WASHINGTON State must take the Washington Assessment of Student Learning (WASL) based on the state's Essential Academic Learning Requirements (EALRs) in reading, writing, listening, and mathematics. In TEXAS, students must take the Texas Assessment of Knowledge and Skills (TAKS), which assesses how well they have mastered the Texas Essential Knowledge and Skills (TEKS) in English language arts, mathematics, science, and social studies. High-stakes tests are also used increasingly to determine whether a student can participate in extracurricular activities or graduate, or whether teachers and administrators are given merit pay increases.

In 2002, President George W. Bush, to fulfill his pledge to "leave no child behind," signed into legislation the **No Child Left Behind (NCLB) Act**, reauthorizing the Elementary and Secondary Education Act (ESEA) launched in 1965 as part of President Johnson's Great Society program. NCLB mandated statewide testing in reading and mathematics each year in grades 3–8. Also, NCLB required that, by the end of the academic year 2013–2014, public schools guarantee that all students are prepared to pass state proficiency tests. An additional key provision of NCLB was for schools to provide evidence each year that students were making **adequate yearly progress (AYP)**. Schools that failed to make AYP could be identified as "in need of improvement." The first year a school did not make AYP, it must provide transportation for pupils who want to enroll in another public school. If the school failed to make AYP again, it must pay for supplemental services, including tutoring.

Since 1965, Congress has reauthorized (revised and renewed) ESEA approximately every 5 years. In 2010, the Obama administration released **A Blueprint for Reform**, calling for the reauthorization of ESEA and significant changes to NCLB. The *Blueprint* emphasized the following "key priorities":

- College and Career–Ready Students
- Great Teachers and Leaders in Every School
- Equity and Opportunity for All Students
- Raise the Bar and Reward Excellence
- Promote Innovation and Continuous Improvement

The proposed reauthorization would also eliminate the 2014 deadline for all students to attain academic proficiency, and schools no longer would be singled out for not making "adequate yearly progress" as evidenced by students' test scores.

However, as Figure 1.2 shows, Congress has yet to act on the Obama administration's call to reauthorize ESEA. While waiting for Congress to reauthorize ESEA, the Obama administration announced in 2011 that states could voluntarily seek "EASA flexibility" that would exempt them from certain requirements of NCLB. To be granted flexibility, a state would have to submit a comprehensive plan to improve educational outcomes for all students, close achievement gaps, increase equity, and improve the quality of instruction. As of 2013, 45 states submitted plans for ESEA flexibility, and 42 of these plans were approved.

FIGURE 1.2   Timeline for reauthorization of the Elementary and Secondary Education Act (ESEA)

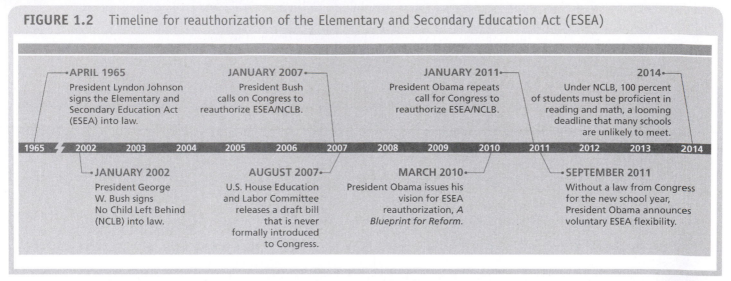

Source: U.S. Department of Education, *Bringing Flexibility & Focus to Education Law: Looking Back and Moving Forward n.d.* Retrieved September 30, 2014, from http://www.ed.gov/sites/default/files/looking-back-moving-forward.pdf.

A key piece of *A Blueprint for Reform* is the **Race to the Top Program**, designed to foster state-level educational reform. According to President Obama,

> Race to the Top says: Instead of Washington imposing standards from the top down, let's challenge states to adopt common standards voluntarily, from the bottom up. That doesn't mean more standards; it means higher standards, better standards, standards that clarify what our teachers are expected to teach and what our children are expected to learn—so high school graduates are actually prepared for college and a career. This is different from No Child Left Behind, because what that did was it gave the states the wrong incentives. [Some] states watered down their standards so that school districts wouldn't be penalized when their students fell short. And what's happened now is, at least two states that lowered standards in response to No Child Left Behind are now raising those standards back up, partly in response to Race to the Top. (The White House, July 29, 2010)

Under Race to the Top guidelines, states submit comprehensive plans to reform schools and compete for federal funding. In the first round of competition held during 2010, 41 states applied, and **DELAWARE** and **TENNESSEE** won grants of $100 million and $500 million, respectively. In the second round, 35 states and the District of Columbia submitted applications, and the winners were the **DISTRICT OF COLUMBIA**, **FLORIDA**, **GEORGIA**, **HAWAII**, **MARYLAND**, **MASSACHUSETTS**, **NEW YORK**, **NORTH CAROLINA**, **OHIO**, and **RHODE ISLAND**. By 2013, more than $4 billion in Race to the Top funding had been awarded to 19 states.

In 2012, the Obama administration expanded Race to the Top to include competition for school districts. That year, 55 districts received awards totaling $400 million. Commenting on the districts that received awards, U.S. Secretary of Education Arne Duncan said, "Districts have been hungry to drive reform at the local level, and now these winners can empower their school leaders to pursue innovative ideas where they have the greatest impact: in the classroom. Race to the Top-District grantees have shown tremendous leadership though developing plans that will transform the learning environment and enable students to receive a personalized, world-class education" (U.S. Department of Education, December 11, 2012).

Today's Tech-Savvy Students

Understanding how technology affects students and schools and integrating technology into teaching come easy for some teachers; for other teachers, however, it can be a challenge. Students in your classroom can be viewed as "digital natives"—that is, they were born *after* digital technologies were introduced on a wide scale. Today, "many students have a mobile device in their pockets with more computing power than the early supercomputers" (U.S. Department of Education, February 2013, p. 1), and much of their time is spent using technology. For example, young people 8–18 years old use cell phones, iPods, and other electronic devices for an average of 7 hours and 38 minutes a day. Because today's students are multitaskers, the figure jumps to 10 hours and 45 minutes of engagement with media and includes 4½ hours watching TV and 1 hour and 10 minutes of video games (Rideout, Foehr, & Roberts, 2010).

Many schools have not kept up with the rapid changes in technology. "Schools have kept new digital technologies on the periphery of their core academic practices. Schools . . . do not try to rethink basic practices of teaching and learning. Computers have not penetrated the core of schools, even though they have come to dominate the way people in the outside world read, write, calculate, and think" (Collins & Halverson, 2009, p. 6). Today's students have iPods, smartphones, video cameras, laptops, and digital cameras. Websites like Facebook, Twitter, and MySpace are changing the way students communicate, socialize, and network. Sites like YouTube and iTunes bring media to students seamlessly, whether at home, school, or on the move. Media content comes into schools through smartphones, the Internet, e-mail, text messages, and general entertainment (music, video, and blogs, for example). " . . . [W]e no longer live in an information push-out world where we passively receive information that is broadcast out to us by large, centralized entities. Instead, we now live within multi-directional conversation spaces in which 15-year-olds can reach audiences at scales that previously were reserved for major media companies, large corporations, and governments" (McLeod, 2011, p. 1).

For these students, using advanced technology is an everyday part of their lives. How can teachers remain up-to-date regarding the role that technology plays in their students' lives?

To keep up with the media and technology environment today's students inhabit outside school, teachers must integrate technology into their teaching. For example, students of Neelam Mishra, who teaches Hindi at Edison High School in **NEW JERSEY**, use Skype to interact with Hindi-speaking students at St. Gregorios High School in Mumbai, India. Her students ask their peers about Hindi words, after-school activities, and Indian history. According to Mishra, "My students enjoy my class, but when they talk to their peers, they feel more comfortable sharing." In addition to online collaboration with native Hindi speakers, Mishra's students use technology to develop projects on topics such as Gandhi's life, school days in India, or Indian tourism. Her students share many of these projects with the Mumbai students, for example, performing a skit during a Skype videoconference (George Lucas Educational Foundation, 2010).

Another teacher who has integrated technology into teaching is Loveland, **COLORADO**, high school French teacher Toni Theisen. Her students use wikis, VoiceThreads, and Voki avatars; they comment on class films in real time using a free chatroom site called TodaysMeet; and they answer questions using their cell phones and the Poll Everywhere site. In addition, they learn French by creating videos with Animoto.com and comic strips with ToonDoo.

Theisen uses technology to connect her classes with people around the world. For instance, when her students were reading *Le Petit Prince*, Theisen came across a Twitter post from a New Zealand teacher who mentioned that her class was reading it, too. Within days, Theisen set up a wiki for the two classes to share, and students began posting audio podcasts describing the character they most identified with and creative videos interpreting the text. Today, Theisen's students manage a wiki with a partner school in La Réole, France, and through videos, podcasts, and VoiceThreads, Loveland students practice French and La Réole students practice English. Theisen's students even created a Flip cam tour of Loveland High for their French peers (George Lucas Educational Foundation, 2010).

TECHNOLOGY in ACTION
Wikis in 10th-Grade Social Studies

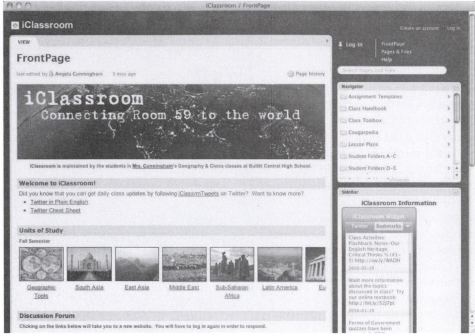

Source: PBwiki, Inc. http://pbworks.com/content/edu+overview?utm_campaign=nav-tracking&utm_source=Home navigation (accessed March 5, 2011). Used by permission of PBworks and Angela Cunningham.

Maria Valquez has asked her 10th-grade social studies students to track and report on 2012 national election activities. She has organized her four social studies classes into 28 groups of 3 students each. Each group is assigned an aspect of the election to cover, such as specific political parties, an individual candidate, hot topic issues, media campaign messages, and so on. Maria wants her students to share the information they find with the rest of the school and the community. In addition to researching election activities, she hopes that students will find common ground and form a consensus on controversial issues. To facilitate this communication and sharing of information, Maria needs a technology tool that is not controlled by a single group or individual. She needs a tool that allows all students in her social studies classes to have an equal say. She decides to create a wiki.

WIKIS: As part of the social networking movement on the Internet, wikis follow the logic that many voices are better than one. A wiki is a website that allows collaborative work by various authors. A wiki website allows anyone or designated members of a group to create, delete, or edit the content on the website. Several free wiki services are available to educators. A simple Google search yields promising results.

POSSIBLE USES: By using a wiki, students can explore a book, an events calendar, a field trip, and so on. A wiki can be a long-term exploration, such as the results of a newly formed conservation club, or a short-term event, like your high school basketball team going to the state tournament. In addition, many school districts use wikis for staff professional development. For example, the Avon Grove School District in **PENNSYLVANIA** uses a wiki for curriculum development, new teacher induction, and peer coaching.

Effective teachers recognize that technology can be a powerful tool for enhancing students' inquiry, reflection, and problem solving. They also realize that technology cannot be grafted onto existing teaching strategies; it must be integrated into those strategies. Chapter 13 of this book is designed to help you become a tech-savvy teacher. In addition, the Technology in Action feature in each chapter demonstrates practical applications of technology in real classrooms, by real teachers. These features also include technology-based learning activities designed to give you hands-on experience at integrating technology into teaching. The above Technology in Action **feature** explains how your classmates can create a wiki to use during the term to discuss issues and content presented in *Becoming a Teacher*.

WHAT WILL SOCIETY EXPECT OF ME AS A TEACHER?

The prevailing view within our society is that teachers are public servants accountable to the people. As a result, society has high expectations of teachers—some would say too high. Entrusted with our nation's most precious resource, its children and youth, to-day's teachers are expected to have advanced knowledge and skills and high academic and ethical standards. Although promoting students' academic progress has always been their primary responsibility, teachers are also expected to further students' social, emotional, and moral development and to safeguard students' health and well-being. Increasingly, the public calls on teachers and schools to address the social problems and risk factors that affect student success.

Watch the many roles a teacher exhibits each day in the classroom.

The Public Trust

Teaching is subject to a high degree of public scrutiny and control. Because of its faith in the teaching profession, the public invests teachers with considerable power over its children. For the most part, parents willingly allow their children to be influenced by teachers and expect their children to obey and respect teachers. The public appears to have great confidence in local schools; however, attitudes toward schools elsewhere in the nation is significantly lower. For example, the 2013 annual Gallup Poll of the Public's Attitudes Toward the Public Schools revealed that a majority (53 percent) of citizens gave public schools in their community a grade of "A" or "B," whereas only 19 percent gave the same grades to the nation's schools (Bushaw & Lopez, 2013).

Teacher Competency and Effectiveness

Society believes that competent, effective teachers are important keys to a strong system of education. Moreover, society understands that "We have to give teachers the support they need to ensure that children get the high quality education they deserve" (U.S. Department of Education, September 30, 2011). As a teacher, you will be expected to be proficient in the use of instructional strategies, curriculum materials, advanced educational technologies, and classroom management techniques. You will also be expected to have a thorough understanding of the developmental levels of students and a solid grasp of the content you teach. To maintain and extend this high level of skill, you will be expected to keep informed of exemplary practices and to demonstrate a desire for professional development.

Watch how a **teacher motivates students to learn a unit of study.**

Teacher competency and effectiveness include the responsibility to help all learn-ers succeed. Although today's students come from diverse backgrounds, society will expect you to believe in the potential of *all* children. Regardless of your students' eth-nicity, language, gender, socioeconomic status, sexual orientation, religion, family back-grounds and living conditions, abilities, and disabilities, you will have a responsibility to ensure that all students develop to their fullest potential. To accomplish this, you will be expected to have a repertoire of instructional strategies and resources to cre-ate meaningful learning experiences that promote students' growth and development.

Teacher Accountability

Teachers must also "be mindful of the social ethic—their public duties and obligations embodied in the practice of teaching" (Hansen, 1995, p. 143). Society agrees that teachers are primarily responsible for promoting students' learning, although different members of society are not always in agreement about what students should learn. As a teacher, you will be expected to understand how factors such as student backgrounds, attitudes, and learning styles can affect achievement. You will be expected to create a safe and effective learning environment for your students, and you will be accountable for equalizing educa-tional opportunity, promoting social justice, and maintaining high professional standards.

WHAT IS THE JOB OUTLOOK FOR TEACHERS?

When you think ahead to a career in teaching, a question you are likely to ask yourself is, What is the job outlook for teachers? From time to time, figures reflecting **teacher supply and demand** have painted a rather bleak picture for those entering the teach-ing profession. At other times, finding a position has not been difficult. Even during

FIGURE 1.3   Actual and projected public school enrollment in grades prekindergarten (preK) through 12, by grade level: School years 1970–1971 through 2021–2022

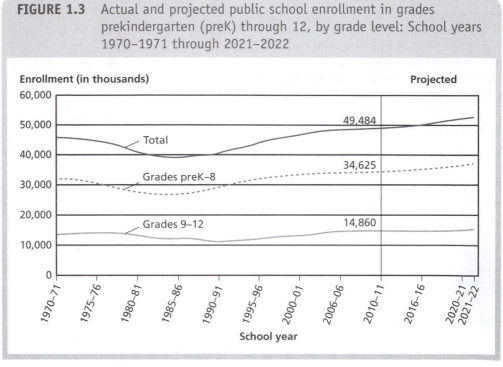

Source: Aud, S., Wilkinson-Flicker, S., Kristapovich, P., Rathbun, A., Wang, X., & Zhang, J. (2013). *The Condition of Education 2013* (NCES 2013-037). Washington, DC: U.S. Department of Education, National Center for Education Statistics. Retrieved from http://nces.ed.gov/pubsearch.

times of teacher surplus, talented, qualified teachers are able to find jobs. Teaching is one of the largest professions in the United States; out of a national population of about 310 million, about 49.5 million attended public elementary and secondary schools during 2010–2011, where they were taught by about 3.2 million teachers (National Center for Education Statistics, 2012). Figure 1.3 shows that public elementary and secondary school enrollment is projected to increase from 49.5 million students in 2010–2011 to 53.1 million by 2021–202, an increase of 7 percent. Within such a large profession, annual openings resulting from retirements and career changes alone are numerous.

Employment of K–12 teachers is expected to increase from almost 3.7 million in 2013 to more than 4.1 million by 2021, an 11 percent increase (Hussar & Bailey, 2013, p. 55). The job outlook is brightest for teachers in high-demand fields such as science, mathematics, and bilingual and special education, and in less desirable urban or rural school districts. In addition, the number of teachers retiring will continue to increase for the foreseeable future, and this will create many job openings (Ingersoll & Merrill, 2010).

Teaching and the National Economy

In 2008, the nation entered what many financial experts saw as the worst financial crisis since the Great Depression of the 1930s. Nationwide, the unemployment rate rose from less than 5 percent at the end of 2007 to about 10 percent by the end of 2009. State funding for education dropped dramatically, and many school districts, facing large budget deficits, were forced to lay off teachers and to close schools. To keep teacher layoffs to a minimum, school districts trimmed their budgets in other areas—eliminating summer school programs, after-school programs, bus routes, and days from the school calendar, for example.

In response to the funding crisis for America's schools, the American Recovery and Reinvestment Act of 2009 included $100 billion for education. That stimulus money enabled school districts to avoid thousands of scheduled teacher layoffs and to rehire teachers previously laid off. At the beginning of the 2010–2011 school year, the federal government provided another $10 billion for school districts to retain or rehire teachers and other educational staff.

The nation showed a few signs in 2011 of emerging from what some called the Great Recession, and many school districts reported fewer layoffs during the 2010–2011 academic year than expected. Nevertheless, the recession had a dramatic impact on every segment of American society, including the teaching profession. During previous recessions, which often resulted in layoffs for workers in other sectors of U.S. society, teachers tended to enjoy a higher level of job security, in part because of the widespread practice of tenure. **Tenure** is job security granted to teachers after satisfactory performance for a specified period, usually 2 to 5 years.

In spite of the nation's lingering economic woes, there will be many job opportunities for teachers in the near future. Currently, many school districts are luring teachers from other states and districts with bonuses and higher pay. In addition, increasing enrollments of students from minority groups and a shortage of teachers from minority groups are leading to increased efforts to recruit minority teachers. Also, the number of non-English-speaking students has grown dramatically, especially in **CALIFORNIA** and **FLORIDA**, creating a demand for bilingual teachers and teachers of English as a second language.

In response to a current shortage of teachers in some locations and anticipated teacher retirements, many states are implementing policies that will encourage more college students to become teachers. Some states give large signing bonuses that are distributed over the teacher's first few years of teaching. Some are increasing state scholarships, issuing loans for moving expenses, and implementing loan-forgiveness programs (U.S. Department of Labor, 2013).

For the foreseeable future, there will be exceptional job opportunities for teachers from diverse racial and ethnic backgrounds and for teachers with disabilities. Students from diverse racial, ethnic, and cultural backgrounds and students with disabilities benefit from having role models with whom they can easily identify. In addition, teachers from diverse groups and teachers with disabilities may have, in some instances, an enhanced understanding of student diversity and student variability that they can share with other teachers.

FOCUS ON DIVERSITY: DEMAND FOR TEACHERS OF COLOR

Nearly 48 percent of public school students were considered part of a minority group during 2011 (Keaton, 2012a). Before the middle of this century, more than half of the nation's students will be minority-group members (U.S. Census Bureau, 2012a). In the nation's 25 largest cities, students of color represent half or more of the student population (National Center for Education Statistics, July 2012).

When contrasted with the diverse mosaic of student enrollments, the backgrounds of today's teachers reveal less diversity. Teachers of color represent about 17 percent of public school teachers in the United States (Boser, 2011). This shortage is due in part to the fact that minority students frequently attend our nation's most impoverished schools. At such schools, students receive little motivation to become teachers; and, if their school experiences are negative, they have little incentive to pursue a career in teaching.

The typical undergraduate candidate preparing to teach is a young, White female who recently graduated from high school and is attending college full-time (National Research Council, 2010). Post-baccalaureate-level individuals preparing to teach tend to be older, to include slightly more people of color and more males, to be transitioning into teaching from an occupation outside the field of education, to have prior teaching-related experience, and to be attending college part-time (Feistritzer, 1999). Figure 1.4 illustrates the differences between the racial and ethnic composition of students enrolled in U.S. public schools and that of teachers at those schools.

FOCUS ON DIVERSITY: DEMAND FOR TEACHERS WITH DISABILITIES

Contrary to what some people may think, research indicates that people with disabilities can be effective teachers (Educators with Disabilities Caucus, Council for Exceptional Children, 2008). In addition, a teacher with a disability may have an "advantage" in working with students who also have the same disability. The teacher may understand more

FIGURE 1.4 (a) Percentage distribution of U.S. public school students enrolled in Prekindergarten through 12th grade, by race/ethnicity: selected years, fall 2000–fall 2021 (b) Total number of public school teachers and percentage distribution of school teachers, by race/ethnicity, school type, and selected school characteristics: 2011–12

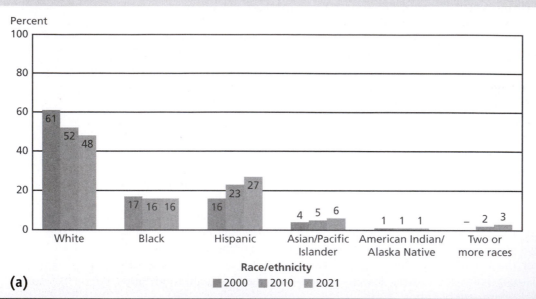

(a)

School type and selected school characteristic	Total number of teachers	Percent of teachers by race/ethnicity						
		Hispanic, regardless of race	White, non-Hispanic	Black, non-Hispanic	Asian, non-Hispanic	Native Hawaiian/ Pacific Islander, non-Hispanic	American Indian/ Alaska Native, non-Hispanic	Two or more races, non-Hispanic
All public schools	3,385,200	7.8	81.9	6.8	1.8	0.1	0.5	1.0
School classification								
Traditional public	3,269,500	7.6	82.3	6.6	1.8	0.1	0.5	1.0
Charter school	115,600	13.1	69.9	11.8!	2.8	‡	0.6!	1.7!
Community type								
City	‡	‡	‡	‡	‡	‡	‡	‡
Suburban	1,096,400	7.6	83.6	5.7	1.5	‡	0.3!	1.2
Town	411,00	5.6	87.7	3.6	1.6!	0.1!	0.6	0.8
Rural	916,600	4.7	88.7	4.2	0.7	‡	0.8	0.8
School level								
Primary	1,626,800	8.7	81.2	7.1	1.7	‡	0.4	0.8
Middle	592,100	7.0	81.6	7.7	1.7	0.2!	0.4	1.3
High	961,300	6.8	83.6	5.6	2.1	0.2!	0.5!	1.2
Combined	206,000	7.4	80.9	7.9!	1.2!	‡	1.1	1.3

(b)

a. *Note:* Detail may not sum to totals because of rounding. Data for 2021 are projected.
Source: U.S. Department of Education, National Center for Education Statistics, *Projections of Education Statistics to 2021;* and Common Core of Data (CCD), "State Nonfiscal Survey of Public Elementary and Secondary Education," selected years, 2000–2001 through 2010–2011. Retrieved August 15, 2014, from http://nces.ed.gov/programs/coe/pdf/Indicator_CGE/COE_CGE_2013_03.pdf.
b. ! Interpret data with caution. The coefficient of variation (CV) for this estimate is between 30 percent and 50 percent (i.e., the standard error is at least 30 percent and less than 50 percent of the estimate).
‡ Reporting standards not met. The coefficient of variation (CV) for this estimate is 50 percent or greater (i.e., the standard error is 50 percent or more of the estimate) or the response rate is below 50 percent.
Note: Black includes African American and Hispanic includes Latino. Teachers include both full-time and part-time teachers. Detail may not sum to totals because of rounding and because some data are not shown.
Note: Table above adapted from Goldring, R., Gray, L., and Bitterman, A. (2013). *Characteristics of Public and Private Elementary and Secondary School Teachers in the United States: Results From the 2011–12 Schools and Staffing Survey* (NCES 2013-314). U.S. Department of Education. Washington, DC: National Center for Education Statistics. Retrieved September 28, 2013, from http://nces.ed.gov/pubsearch.
Source: U.S. Department of Education, National Center for Education Statistics, Schools and Staffing Survey (SASS), "Public School Teacher and Private School Teacher Data Files," 2011–12.

readily how to meet the needs of those students. He or she knows, first-hand, how that disability influences students' learning.

Teachers with disabilities can also be inspirational to students without disabilities. Such teachers model for students how challenges that are part of life can be overcome. Students learn from their teachers that inner resources such as drive, commitment, and perseverance help one achieve goals in life.

The percentage of children with disabilities receiving special education in public pre-K to 12 schools is approximately 10 percent (Hardman, Drew, & Egan, 2013), and the current critical need for special education teachers is expected to continue for the next few decades.

Demand for Teachers by Geographic Region and Specialty Area

Through 2021, elementary and secondary school enrollments are projected to rise more slowly than in the past, as children of the baby boom generation will leave the school system. Enrollments will vary widely across the nation, however. The West and South will experience the largest increases, whereas enrollments in the Midwest will remain about the same, and those in the Northeast will decline (Hussar & Bailey, 2013). The ease with which you will find your first teaching position is also related to your area of specialization. In 2015, for example, job seekers able to teach bilingual education, special education, English as a second language (ESL), mathematics, chemistry, or physics were in an especially favorable position.

Teachers with disabilities can be highly effective at teaching students in "regular" classrooms. In what ways can teachers with disabilities be role models for students without disabilities?

WHAT CAN YOU LEARN FROM OBSERVING IN CLASSROOMS?

Classroom observations are an excellent way to develop knowledge about teaching. Most teacher education programs require that students participate in **field experiences** that include classroom observations. Students report that these experiences help them make a final decision about becoming a teacher. Most become more enthusiastic about teaching and more motivated to acquire the essential knowledge and skills; however, a few decide that teaching is not for them.

Recognizing the value of observations, many teacher education programs are increasing the amount of field experiences and placing such fieldwork earlier in students' programs. For example, at **WASHINGTON** State University (WSU), students preparing to become elementary teachers complete 1 week of classroom observations as part of their first education course. Later in their program, WSU students complete two 45-hour blocks of observations in K–8 classrooms and a 5-week advanced practicum (or field experience) that requires several hours of classroom observation each week.

Technology and Classroom Observations

Distance learning—the use of technology such as video transmissions that allows students to receive instruction at multiple, often remote sites—now enables preservice teachers on campus to observe in school classrooms off campus. For example, at the University of **NEBRASKA**, a two-way audio-video conferencing system called PictureTel allows remote viewing of any classroom with an Ethernet connection to the Internet (Austin & Adcock, 2002). The university instructor has a remote control so the camera at the school can follow the teacher around the room or zoom in on a small-group activity. The small camera makes almost no sound, so it does not disrupt the class. Strategically placed microphones pick up the voices of the teacher and the students.

Focused Observations

Observations are more meaningful when they are focused and conducted with clear purposes. Observers may focus on the students, the teacher, the interactions between the two, the structure of the lesson, or the setting. More specifically, for example, observers may note differences between the ways boys and girls or members of different ethnic groups communicate and behave in the classroom. They may note student interests and ability levels, study student responses to a particular teaching strategy, or analyze the question-and-response patterns in a class discussion.

Observations may also be guided by sets of questions related to specific areas. For instance, because beginning teachers are frequently frustrated by their lack of success in motivating students to learn, asking questions specifically related to motivation can make an observation more meaningful and instructive. Figure 1.5 presents a helpful set of focused questions on motivation. Similar questions can be generated for other focus areas, such as classroom management, student involvement, questioning skills, evaluation, and teacher–student rapport.

FIGURE 1.5 Guiding questions for observing motivation

Directions: As you observe, note the ways that students are motivated intrinsically (from within) and extrinsically (from factors outside themselves).

Intrinsic Motivation	Extrinsic Motivation
What things seem to interest students at this age?	How do teachers show their approval to students?
Which activities and assignments seem to give them a sense of pride?	What phrases do teachers use in their praise?
When do they seem to be confused? Bored? Frustrated?	What types of rewards do teachers give (e.g., grades, points, tangible rewards)?
What topics do they talk about with enthusiasm?	What reward programs do you notice (e.g., points accumulated toward free time)?
In class discussions, when are they most alert and participating most actively?	What warnings do teachers give?
What seems to please, amuse, entertain, or excite them?	What punishments are given to students?
What do they joke about? What do they find humorous?	How do teachers arouse concern in their students?
What do they report as being their favorite subjects? Favorite assignments?	How do students motivate other students?
What do they report as being their least favorite subjects and assignments?	What forms of peer pressure do you observe?
How do they respond to personalized lessons (e.g., using their names in exercises)?	How do teachers promote enthusiasm for an assignment?
How do they respond to activity-oriented lessons (e.g., fieldwork, project periods)?	How do teachers promote class spirit?
How do they respond to assignments calling for presentations to groups outside the classroom (e.g., parents, another class, the chamber of commerce)?	How do teachers catch their students' interest in the first few minutes of a lesson?
How do they respond to being given a choice in assignments?	Which type of question draws more answers—recall or open-ended?
	How do teachers involve quiet students in class discussions?
	How do teachers involve inactive students in their work?
	In what ways do teachers give recognition to students' accomplishments?

Observation Instruments

A wide range of methods can be used to conduct classroom observations, ranging from informal, qualitative descriptions to formal, quantitative checklists. With reform efforts to improve education in the United States has come the development of instruments to facilitate the evaluation of teacher performance, a task now widely required of school administrators. Students preparing to teach can benefit by using these evaluative instruments in their observations. An example is the Florida Performance Measurement System (FPMS) Screening/Summative Observation Instrument, which is presented in Figure 1.6.

The Florida instrument is based on educational research that has identified what effective teachers do. The FPMS was the first research-based performance system to be implemented on a statewide basis. Beginning teachers in **FLORIDA** must now demonstrate behaviors in six domains: planning, management of student conduct, instructional organization and development, presentation of subject matter, verbal and nonverbal communication, and testing (student preparation, administration, and feedback). Figure 1.6 presents the "effective" and "ineffective" behavioral indicators for four of those domains.

WHY IS YOUR INDUCTION INTO TEACHING IMPORTANT?

The retention of public school teachers is a problem in the United States. Each year, scores of beginning teachers enter classrooms with vigor and determination; regrettably, however, many soon leave the profession. The attrition rate among teachers during the first 3 years is 9.1 percent. Attrition is highest among special education teachers (12.3 percent) and English teachers (10.5 percent). Attrition is lowest among arts/music teachers (4.1 percent) and early childhood teachers (5.6 percent). High school teachers are more likely to leave teaching (8.8 percent) than elementary teachers (7.5 percent). Attrition is lower in cities (7.5 percent) than in rural (8.4 percent) or suburban schools (8.3 percent). Surprisingly, attrition is lowest in schools with more than 75 percent of students eligible for free or reduced lunch (5.1 percent), and highest (10.3 percent) in schools with 35–49 percent eligibility (Keigher, 2010). Clearly, beginning teachers need support, guidance, and encouragement to become confident, skilled professionals.

Some beginning teachers eventually give up their chosen profession because their problems and concerns go unattended. Veteran teachers, who recall their own early struggles as beginning teachers, may have a "sink-or-swim" attitude toward the difficulties encountered by those just entering the profession. "Since I learned to cope with the challenges of beginning teaching on my own, today's teachers either have to sink or swim," they reason. In addition, beginning teachers may think they should be as skilled as master teachers with many years of experience.

Feedback from new teachers suggests that they want to talk about the problems they encounter in their work. They want assistance to help them to be successful during the first few years of teaching. Instead, they may experience isolation and have few opportunities to share their experiences with colleagues.

Problems and Concerns of Beginning Teachers

The problems and concerns of beginning teachers can be extensive. The following problems cause some beginning teachers to think about leaving the profession: maintaining classroom discipline, motivating students, responding to individual differences, assessing students' work, maintaining positive relationships with parents, organizing

FIGURE 1.6 Florida performance measurement system: screening/summative observation instrument

FRAME FACTOR INFORMATION (PLEASE PRINT)

Teacher's Name

_____ _____ _____
(Last)   (First)   (Middle)

SS# __ __ __ - __ __ - __ __ __ __

Institution of Graduation _____ Inst. # _____

Graduated from a College of Education ☐ 1. Yes   ☐ 2. No

Number of Complete Years of Teaching Experience _____

District Name _____ Number _____

School Name _____ Number _____

Observer's Name

_____ _____ _____
(Last)   (First)   ☐   (Middle)

SS# __ __ __ - __ __ - __ __ __ __

Position ☐1. Principal ☐2. Ass't Principal ☐3. Teacher ☐4. Other

Class _____ Grade Level (Specify one level only–For Adult Ed. mark level 13
For Kindergarten or Preschool mark Level 00.)

Subject Area Observed

☐ 1. Language Arts   ☐ 9. Home Economics
☐ 2. Foreign Language   ☐ 10. Other Vocational Ed.
☐ 3. Social Sciences   ☐ 11. Arts
☐ 4. Mathematics   ☐ 12. Music
☐ 5. Science   ☐ 13. Exceptional Stud. Ed.
☐ 6. Physical Education, ROTC ☐ 14. Other (Specify)
☐ 7. Business Education, DCT, CBE
☐ 8. Industrial Arts/Education   _____

Type of Classroom/Facility in Which the Observation Occurred

☐ 1. Regular Classroom—Self-contained, Open, Pod
☐ 2. Laboratory or Shop
☐ 3. Field, Court, Gymnasium
☐ 4. Media Room or Library

Total Number of Students in Class _____

Observation Information   Date ___/___/___

Type of Observation   ☐ 1. Prof. Orien.   ☐2. Dis. Assess
                      ☐ 3. Other (Specify) _____
Screening Obs.   ☐1.   ☐2.   ☐3.   ☐4.
Summative Obs.   ☐1.   ☐2.   ☐3.   ☐4.

Time Observation Begins __ __:__ __   Observation Ends __ __:__ __
Test Begins __ __:__ __   Test Ends __ __:__ __

Methods Used in the Observed Lesson
☐ 1. Lecture
☐ 2. Interactive/Discussion
☐ 3. Independent Study/Lab or Shop Work

Teacher's Signature _____

Observer's Signature _____

Number of Students Not Engaged
1☐   2☐   3☐   4☐

DOMAIN	EFFECTIVE INDICATORS		TOT. FREQ.	FREQUENCY	FREQUENCY	TOT. FREQ.	INEFFECTIVE INDICATORS
3.0 Instructional Organization and Development	1. Begins instruction promptly						1. Delays
	2. Handles materials in an orderly manner						2. Does not organize materials systematically
	3. Orients students to classwork/maintains academic focus						3. Allows talk/activity unrelated to subject
	4. Conducts beginning/ending review						4.
	5. Questions: academic comprehension/ lesson development	a. single factual (Domain 5.0)					5a. Allows unison response
		b. requires analysis/reasons					5b. Poses multiple questions asked as one
							5c. Poses nonacademic questions/nonacademic procedural questions
	6. Recognizes response/amplifies/gives correct feedback						6. Ignores student or response/expresses sarcasm, disgust, harshness
	7. Gives specific academic praise						7. Uses general, nonspecific praise
	8. Provides practice						8. Extends discourse, changes topic with no practice
	9. Gives directions/assigns/checks comprehension of homework, seatwork assignments/gives feedback						9. Gives inadequate directions on homework/no feedback
	10. Circulates and assists students						10. Remains at desk/circulates inadequately
4.0 Presentation of Subject Matter	11. Treats concepts—definition/attributes/examples/ nonexamples						11. Gives definition or example only
	12. Discusses cause-effect/uses linking words/applies law or principle						12. Discusses either cause or effect only/uses no linking word(s)
	13. States and applies academic rule						13. Does not state or does not apply academic rule
	14. Develops criteria and evidence for value judgment						14. States value judgment with no criteria or evidence
5.0 Communication: Verbal and Nonverbal	15. Emphasizes important points						15.
	16. Expresses enthusiasm verbally/challenges students						16.
	17.						17. Uses vague/scrambled discourse
	18.						18. Uses loud, grating, high pitched, monotone, or inaudible talk
	19. Uses body behavior that shows interest—smiles, gestures						19. Frowns, deadpan or lethargic
2.0 Management of Student Conduct	20. Stops misconduct						20. Delays desist/doesn't stop misconduct/desists punitively
	21. Maintains instructional momentum						21. Loses momentum—fragments nonacademic directions, over dwells

Observer's Notes: _____
_____
_____

Source: Florida Department of Education, Division of Human Resource Development, Tallahassee, FL. State of Florida, Department of Education, Used with permission. Retrieved May 1, 2011, from http://education.ucf.edu/clinicalexp/docs/FPMSForm.pdf

classroom activities, securing adequate teaching materials and supplies, and dealing with the problems of individual students.

In some cases, teachers experience frustration related to lack of preparation time, conflicts with principals, difficulties with student misconduct, and undesirable teaching assignments (for example, larger class sizes than those of experienced teachers). Lack of dialogue with their peers about teaching, minimal involvement in schoolwide decisions about curriculum and instruction, and the absence of a shared technical culture are additional reasons why teachers leave the profession (Glickman, Gordon, & Ross-Gordon, 2014).

Induction into the Profession

One solution to the problem of teacher attrition is to offer beginning teachers induction programs that provide them with support during their first years in the profession. "Indeed, everyone in the schoolhouse ought to be dedicated to assisting new teachers and accelerating their continuous-improvement journey. . . . Induction programs and well-trained and dedicated mentors can make a difference" (Nash, 2010, p. xxvii).

Approximately half of the states require and fund mentoring programs for new teachers (Olson, 2008), and many local school districts, often in collaboration with colleges and universities, have begun teacher induction programs. Among the programs that have received national attention are the **FLORIDA** Beginning Teacher Program, the **CALIFORNIA** Beginning Teacher Support and Assessment (BTSA) program, the **TEXAS** Beginning Teacher Induction and Mentoring (BTIM) program, the **VIRGINIA** Beginning Teacher Assistance Program, and the **KENTUCKY** Beginning Teacher Internship Program. As noted, about half of the states require and fund induction and mentoring programs for beginning teachers, but only five require an individual growth plan (Olson, 2008).

Induction programs provide beginning teachers with continued assistance at least during the first year. As Figure 1.7 illustrates, the key outcomes of induction

FIGURE 1.7   Conceptual framework for the effects of teacher induction programs on teacher and student outcomes

Source: Isenberg, E., Glazerman, S., Bleeker, M., Johnson, A., Lugo-Gil, J., Grider, M., Dolfin, S., & Britton, E. (2009). *Impacts of Comprehensive Teacher Induction: Results From the Second Year of a Randomized Controlled Study* (NCEE 2009-4072). Washington, DC: National Center for Education Evaluation and Regional Assistance, Institute of Education Sciences, U.S. Department of Education, p. 6.

programs are improved teacher practices, increased student achievement, and increased teacher retention. In addition, induction programs promote the personal and professional well-being of beginning teachers by improving their attitudes toward themselves and the profession. Induction programs also help beginning teachers learn about the culture of the school system within which they work.

To achieve these outcomes, induction program components include those illustrated in Figure 1.7: orientation to the induction program, assessment of performance, professional development workshops based on teacher-identified needs, mentoring and peer coaching, small-group meetings to provide support, and observations by and follow-up conferences with individuals not in a supervisory role.

HOW CAN YOU GAIN PRACTICAL EXPERIENCE FOR BECOMING A TEACHER?

Your teacher education program is designed to give you opportunities to experience, to the extent possible, the real world of the teacher. Through field experiences and carefully structured experiential activities, you will be given limited exposure to various aspects of teaching, from curriculum development to classroom management. Observing, tutoring, instructing small groups, analyzing video cases, operating instructional media, performing student teaching, and completing various noninstructional tasks are among the most common activities.

Classroom Experiences

Opportunities to put theory into practice before student teaching are important. Thus, many teacher education programs enable students to participate in microteaching, teaching simulations, analyses of video cases, field-based practical and clinical experiences, and classroom aide programs.

MICROTEACHING

Introduced in the 1960s, microteaching quickly became popular and is widely used today. When **microteaching**, students teach brief, single-concept lessons to a small group of students (i.e., 5 to 10). Microteaching gives students opportunities to practice specific teaching skills, such as positive reinforcement. Often the microteaching is video-taped for later study.

As originally developed, microteaching includes the following six steps:

1. Identify a specific teaching skill to learn about and practice.
2. Read about the skill in one of several pamphlets.
3. Observe a master teacher demonstrate the skill in a short movie or on videotape.
4. Prepare a 3- to 5-minute lesson to demonstrate the skill.
5. Teach the lesson, which is videotaped, to a small group of peers.
6. Critique, along with the instructor and student peers, the videotaped lesson.

SIMULATIONS

Simulations can provide opportunities for vicarious practice of a wide range of teaching skills. In **teaching simulations**, students analyze teaching situations that are written, filmed, or videotaped. Typically, students are given background information about a hypothetical school or classroom and the pupils they must prepare to teach. After this orientation, students role-play the student teacher or the teacher who is confronted with the problem situation. Next, students discuss the appropriateness of solutions and work to increase their problem-solving skills and their understanding of the teacher's role as a decision maker in a complex setting.

Some teacher education programs are experimenting with computer-based simulations that enable students to hone their classroom planning and decision-making skills.

The **WEST VIRGINIA** Department of Education, in collaboration with West Virginia University, has created a space within the virtual world Second Life for use in teacher training. According to a developer of the virtual space, "The possibilities of this virtual world appear to be endless. If you can think it, you can do it in Second Life. This community allows developers to take a snapshot of any real-life classroom situation or even some imaginary scenarios and put them to practice in a world where users may experience learning without actually being in a traditional classroom" (Ashby, 2010). Visitors to the virtual space will interact with avatars controlled by West Virginia Department of Education officials and visit traditional classrooms and those equipped with the latest state-of-the-art technologies.

Although progress is being made in the development of virtual reality (VR) technology, its application to teacher education is hard to predict. Current simulations are limited to specific skills such as classroom management or tutoring highly motivated individuals. As VR technology improves, however, one day we may see simulations of classrooms that show a variety of students with differing needs as learners.

VIDEO CASES

Teacher education students who view, analyze, and then write about video cases have an additional opportunity to appreciate the ambiguities and complexities of real-life classrooms, to learn that there are no single, simple solutions to complex problems that can arise in the classroom. Viewing authentic video cases enables students to see how "teaching tradeoffs and dilemmas emerge in the video 'text' as do the strategies teachers use, the frustrations they experience, the brilliant and less-brilliant decisions they make" (Grant, Richard, & Parkay, 1996, p. 5).

PRACTICA

A **practicum** is a short-term field-based experience (usually about 2 weeks long) that allows teacher education students to spend time observing and assisting in classrooms. Although practica vary in length and purpose, students are often able to begin instructional work with individuals or small groups. For example, a cooperating teacher may allow a practicum student to tutor a small group of students, read a story to the whole class, conduct a spelling lesson, monitor recess, help students with their homework, or teach students a song or game.

CLASSROOM AIDES

Serving as a teacher aide is another popular means of providing field experience before student teaching. A teacher aide's role depends primarily on the unique needs of the school and its students. Generally, aides work under the supervision of a certified teacher and perform duties that support the teacher's instruction. Assisting teachers in classrooms familiarizes college students with class schedules, record-keeping procedures, and students' performance levels, as well as providing ample opportunity for observations. In exchange, the classroom teacher receives much-needed assistance.

Student Teaching

The most extensive and memorable field experience in teacher preparation programs is student teaching. Student teaching will provide you with an opportunity to assess your strengths as a future teacher, to identify areas for improvement, and to develop skills in classroom management. Student teaching will be a time of responsibility. As one student teacher told the author, "I don't want to mess up [my students'] education!" It will also be an opportunity for growth, a chance to master critical skills.

States require students to have a 5-week to semester-long student teaching experience in the schools before certifying them as teachers. The nature of student teaching varies considerably among teacher education programs. Some programs even pay student teachers during the student teaching experience. Most likely, you will be assigned to a cooperating (or master) teacher in the school, and a university supervisor will make periodic visits to observe you.

During your student teaching assignment, you will probably spend about half of your time teaching, with the remaining time devoted to observing and participating in classroom activities. The amount of time actually spent teaching, however, is not as important as your willingness to reflect carefully on your experiences. Two excellent ways to promote reflection during your student teaching experience are journal writing and maintaining a reflective teaching log.

STUDENT TEACHING JOURNAL

Your supervisors may require you to keep a journal of your classroom experiences so that you can engage in reflective teaching. The following two entries illustrate how journal writing can help student teachers develop strategies for dealing with the realities of teaching. The first entry is by a student teacher at a rural high school. The second is by a student teacher at a middle school in an urban setting.

Entry 1: If there is one thing that really drives me crazy about the kids in my fifth-period class, it's how they don't listen to directions. It's a remedial class, and I know I shouldn't be surprised if they have trouble following directions. Today, we were working on writing paragraphs that are clear and well organized. All they had to do was rewrite a paragraph—not make corrections, just rewrite and make sure their paragraphs had a clear introduction, body, and conclusion. I explained the directions once. Then I even had one of the students read them out loud again. Then I asked for any questions—none. So I thought, "Good, they understand; they know what to do." Then as soon as I said "Begin to rewrite now," the questions started flying. What really got me was that they were questions I had already explained or that were right there on the directions for rewriting paragraphs I gave them. Eventually, I told them they would have to ask their neighbors for answers to any questions they still had. Well, that was a mistake, because the room started to get noisy with all the talking. I had to raise my voice to get them to be quiet and start writing. It was so frustrating. At the end of the day, Mrs. B. [cooperating teacher] suggested that I tell them next time that I would explain the directions once and ask for questions—then, that would be it. They wouldn't have to ask someone else! Mrs. B. assured me that I would become better at giving directions. Somehow, when she gives directions to students, they usually know what to do. Today, for me, it was the opposite—confusion! I notice that she writes directions on the board and then explains them, step-by-step, to students. Next time, that's what I'll do. Tomorrow, my lesson is on using adjectives to describe the nouns in their writing. If I have a chance before fifth period, I will ask Mrs. B. to look at my directions and let me know if they are clear.

Entry 2: Today I taught a lesson on the solar system, and the kids seemed so bored. I called on my strongest readers to read the material out of our science book. One by one, they would read a paragraph or two, and then I would explain it. I was surprised at how much they struggled with the reading. I thought they were strong readers. I guess I was wrong about that. The material was basic—like we have nine planets in our solar system. These planets circle around the sun. Mr. J. [cooperating teacher] told me later that I was spoon-feeding them too much. Tomorrow, I think I will put them into small groups and have each group work on one or two questions rather than give them the answers like I did today. That way, all the students can be involved in talking about the material, not just those who are reading out loud. I hope I don't get those glazed looks on their faces tomorrow. I feel badly if they don't understand and don't seem to be interested. Mr. J. is great—he is understanding and supportive. He says I'm doing just fine. He had similar problems when he was a student teacher. That's hard to imagine; he seems to communicate so well with the kids. They really pay attention when he's teaching, and they all seem to understand. Actually, I find myself trying to act like Mr. J. while I am teaching. I'm even conscious of moving around the room and trying to build up suspense like he does while he's teaching. He tells the kids things like "What I am going to tell you now you will hardly believe it's true, but it is; so pay close attention." The kids love it when he says things like that.

Unstructured, open-ended journals such as these enable student teachers to reflect on the student teaching experience.

REFLECTIVE TEACHING LOGS

To promote more analytical reflections, some supervisors ask student teachers to use a structured form of journal writing, the **reflective teaching log**, in which the student briefly describes the daily classroom activities, selects a single episode to analyze, explains the reason for selecting the episode, and discusses what was learned from the analysis and how that might be applied in the future. To illustrate a reflective teaching log, a partial entry for one episode follows. The entry shows how a college student can disagree with a supervising teacher's response to a classroom situation.

> **Log for December 1—Erin Tompkins**
> *Sequence of Events*
>
> 1. Arrival—end of eighth period
> 2. Ninth period—helped Sharad study science
> 3. After-school program—worked on science with Ricki, P.K., and Tom
> 4. Late bus duty with Ms. Soto
> 5. Departure
>
> *Episode*
> I was helping Ricki and P.K. fill out a table about the location and function of the different cell parts. P.K. asked me a question and two other students laughed at him. I began to answer his question when Ms. Soto came over to the table where we were working and yelled at P.K. She said, "P.K. I don't need you distracting other students who are trying to get their work done." He started to tell her what he asked me and she said, "I don't care. You can leave the room if you don't knock it off. Just do your work and be quiet or you're out!" She then apologized to me and went back to helping another student.
>
> *Analysis*
> I was very frustrated after this episode. This is the first time I've seen Ms. Soto raise her voice with a student and accuse him of causing problems when he was getting his work done and other students were being disruptive. P.K. had asked me a legitimate question; the other students who laughed at him were the problem. I was frustrated because Ricki and P.K. were working hard and asking me good questions. I was annoyed that P.K. was being reprimanded for asking a question that was relevant to the topic we were working on. I also felt helpless because I wanted to tell Ms. Soto that it wasn't P.K. who was the problem. I didn't feel it was my place to correct her in front of her students and kept quiet. I decided that my saying something would only make things worse because it would encourage P.K. to continue arguing with Ms. Soto and he would be in more trouble. (Posner, 2005, p. 122)

Although student teaching will be the capstone experience of your teacher education program, the experience should be regarded as an initial rather than a terminal learning opportunity—your first chance to engage in reflection and self-evaluation for a prolonged period. The benefits of reflection are illustrated in the following comment: "Being a good teacher means . . . thinking about teaching, in a long-term, systemic way. By asking the right questions, by continuously critiquing and improving your practice, and by continuing to examine the work you do in your classroom and how it connects with the larger world, you can achieve your vision and become the teacher you hope to be" (Salas, Tenorio, Walters, & Weiss, 2004, p. 8).

Substitute Teaching

Upon completion of your teacher education program and prior to securing a full-time teaching assignment, you may choose to gain additional practical experience by **substitute teaching**. If you are unable to locate a full-time position, you may decide to substitute, knowing that many districts prefer to hire from their pool of substitutes when full-time positions become available.

Substitute teachers replace regular teachers who are absent due to illness, family responsibilities, personal reasons, or attendance at professional workshops and conferences. Each day, approximately 270,000 substitutes are employed in schools across the United States, and one full year of a student's K–12 education is taught by substitute teachers (Substitute Teaching Institute, 2011).

Qualifications for substitutes vary from state to state and district to district. An area with a critical need for subs will often relax its requirements to provide classroom coverage. In many districts, it is possible to substitute-teach without regular certification. Some districts have less stringent qualifications for short-term, day-to-day substitutes and more stringent ones for long-term, full-time substitutes.

In many districts, the application process for substitutes is the same as that for full-time applicants; in others, the process may be more brief. Often, substitutes are not limited to working in their area of certification; however, schools try to avoid making out-of-field assignments. If you decide to substitute-teach, contact the schools in your area to learn about the qualifications and procedures for hiring substitutes.

Despite the significant role substitutes play in the day-to-day operation of schools, "research tells us that they receive very little support, no specialized training, and are rarely evaluated. . . . In short, the substitute will be expected to show up to each class on time, maintain order, take roll, carry out the lesson, and leave a note for the regular teacher about the classes and events of the day without support, encouragement, or acknowledgment" (St. Michel, 1995, pp. 6–7). Although working conditions such as these are certainly challenging, substitute teaching can be a rewarding, professionally fulfilling experience. Figure 1.8 presents several advantages and disadvantages of substitute teaching.

FIGURE 1.8   Advantages and disadvantages of substitute teaching

Advantages
- Gain experience without all the nightly work and preparation
- Compare and contrast different schools and their environments
- Be better prepared for interviews by meeting administrators and teachers
- Teach and learn a variety of material
- Get to know people—network
- See job postings and hear about possible vacancies
- Gain confidence in your abilities to teach
- Practice classroom management techniques
- Learn about school and district politics—get the "inside scoop"
- Choose which days to work—flexible schedule

Disadvantages
- Pay is not as good as full-time teaching
- No benefits such as medical coverage, retirement plans, or sick days
- Lack of organized representation to improve wages or working conditions
- May receive a cool reception in some schools
- Must adapt quickly to different school philosophies
- Lack of continuity—may be teaching whole language one day, phonetics the next

Source: John F. Snyder, "The Alternative of Substitute Teaching," in *1999 Job Search Handbook for Educators*. Evanston, IL: American Association for Employment in Education, p. 38.

HOW WILL I BECOME A HIGHLY QUALIFIED TEACHER?

"Quality teachers have a greater influence on pupil achievement than any other school-based factor," according to *Teachers for a New Era,* a teacher education reform effort led by the Carnegie Corporation of New York (2008). **Highly qualified teachers (HQTs)** for all students were also a key provision of NCLB. According to NCLB, "highly qualified" teachers would have (1) a bachelor's degree, (2) full state certification, and (3) knowledge of each subject they teach. In his introduction to the 2010 *Blueprint for Reform,* President Barak Obama continued the previous administration's emphasis on quality teachers: "Our goal must be to have a great teacher in every classroom" (U.S. Department of Education, March, 2010, p. 1).

How will you make the transition from being a student to being a "great," highly qualified teacher? At this point in your journey to become a teacher, you can do a great deal to make your entry into teaching professionally rewarding and to ensure that you will become a highly qualified teacher. During your journey toward becoming a highly qualified teacher, you will become immersed in the world of professional standards.

Professional Standards

To ensure that all students are taught by highly qualified teachers, several professional associations and state departments of education have developed standards that reflect what teachers should know and be able to do. Most likely, the teacher education program in which you are enrolled will use one or more of these sets of standards to evaluate your progress toward becoming an effective teacher. During your training, you are sure to hear repeatedly about plans instituted by state departments of education to assess teachers and students alike on an ongoing basis. After you become a teacher, you may learn even more about state standards if you have a mentor like Carla Hudson, author of this chapter's Teachers' Voices: Being an Agent of Change. Hudson represents her school on **WASHINGTON** State's Teacher/Principal Evaluation Pilot (TPEP), a statewide program launched in 2011 to evaluate teachers and principals.

The professional standards that have had the greatest impact on teacher education programs nationally (as well as on teachers' ongoing professional growth and development) are those developed by the **Interstate Teacher Assessment and Support Consortium (InTASC)**, the **National Council for Accreditation of Teacher Education (NCATE)**, the **Teacher Education Accreditation Council (TEAC)**, the **Praxis Series: Professional Assessments for Beginning Teachers**, and the **National Board for Professional Teaching Standards**. Figure 1.9 provides an overview of their standards. How have these standards influenced the teacher education program in which you are enrolled? Does your state have a set of professional standards that also applies to your teacher education program?

CONSOLIDATION OF NCATE AND TEAC

The National Council for Accreditation of Teacher Education (NCATE) and the Teacher Education Accreditation Council (TEAC) consolidated and launched a new accrediting body in July 2013: the **Council for the Accreditation of Educator Preparation (CAEP)**. "CAEP's goals and mission include raising the performance of candidates as practitioners in the nation's P–12 schools, but also raising standards for the evidence which supports claims of quality" (CAEP, 2010).

CAEP set five standards for the accreditation of teacher education programs. Standard 1: Content and Pedagogical Knowledge, specifies "that candidates develop a deep understanding of the critical concepts and principles of their discipline and . . . are able to use discipline-specific practices flexibly to advance the learning of all students toward attainment of college- and career-readiness standards" (CAEP, 2013, p. 2). Standard 1 also requires that candidates demonstrate understanding of the 10 InTASC

InTASC Core Teaching Standards

InTASC is a consortium of states that has developed standards used by 38 states for initial teacher licensure. In 2010, InTASC released a revised set of "professional practice" standards to apply throughout the developmental stages of a teacher's career. Beginning and accomplished teachers differ in the degree of sophistication reflected in their mastery of ten standards in four key areas. Each standard consists of "Performances," "Essential Knowledge," and "Critical Dispositions" (InTASC, July 2010)

The Learner and Learning
1. Learning Development
2. Learning Differences
3. Learning Environments

Content Knowledge
4. Content Knowledge
5. Innovative Application of Content

Instructional Practice
6. Assessment
7. Planning for Instruction
8. Instructional Strategies

Professional Responsibility
9. Reflection and Continuous Growth
10. Collaboration

TEAC Quality Principles and Standards

TEAC, founded in 1997, currently accredits 88 teacher preparation programs (TEAC, May 25, 2010). TEAC-accredited programs must fulfill three quality principles. The overall goal of *Quality Principle I*, presented in the following, is to produce "competent, caring, and qualified teachers."

1.0 QUALITY PRINCIPLE I: Evidence of candidate learning

1.1 Subject matter knowledge

The program candidates must understand the subject matter they will teach.

1.2 Pedagogical knowledge

The program candidates must be able to convert their knowledge of subject matter into compelling lessons that meet the needs of a wide range of pupils and students.

1.3 Caring and effective teaching skill

The program candidates must be able to teach effectively in a caring way and to act as knowledgeable professionals.

1.4 Cross-cutting themes

The program must provide evidence that its candidates have addressed the following three cross-cutting liberal education themes:

1.4.1 Learning how to learn: Candidates must demonstrate that they have learned how to learn information on their own, that they can transfer what they have learned to new situations, and that they have acquired the dispositions and skills of critical reflection that will support life-long learning in their field.

1.4.2 Multicultural perspectives and accuracy: Candidates must demonstrate that they have learned accurate and sound information on matters of race, gender, individual differences, and ethnic and cultural perspectives.

1.4.3 Technology: Candidates must be able to use appropriate technology in carrying out their professional responsibilities.

NCATE Standards

NCATE standards are for the accreditation of colleges and universities with teacher preparation programs. Currently, about half of the 1,300 institutions that prepare teachers are accredited by NCATE. While NCATE standards apply to teacher education programs, not to teacher education students per se, NCATE believes that "the new professional teacher who graduates from a professionally accredited institution should be able to" do the following (NCATE, February 2008):

- help all pre-kindergarten through twelfth grade (P–12) students learn;
- teach to P–12 student standards set by specialized professional associations and the states;
- explain instructional choices based on research-derived knowledge and best practice;
- apply effective methods of teaching students who are at different developmental stages, have different learning styles, and come from diverse backgrounds;
- reflect on practice and act on feedback; and
- be able to integrate technology into instruction effectively.

Praxis Series

Based on knowledge and skills states commonly require of beginning teachers, the Praxis Series assesses individual development as it corresponds to three steps in becoming a teacher. These three areas of assessment are Pre-Professional Skills Tests: entering a teacher education program (Praxis I); Subject Assessments: licensure and certification for entering the profession (Praxis II); and Teacher Performance Assessments; the first year of teaching (Praxis III). Praxis III assessment is conducted in the beginning teacher's classroom and measures knowledge and skills in four interrelated domains (Educational Testing Service, 2010):

1. Organizing content knowledge for student learning (planning to teach)
2. Creating an environment for student learning (the classroom environment)
3. Teaching for student learning (instruction)
4. Teacher professionalism (professional responsibilities)

NBPTS Standards

This board issues professional certificates to teachers who possess extensive professional knowledge and the ability to perform at a high level. Certification candidates submit a portfolio including videotapes of classroom interactions and samples of student work plus the teacher's reflective comments. NBPTS evaluators who teach in the same field as the candidate judge all elements of the assessments. NBPTS has developed five "core propositions" on which voluntary national teacher certification is based (NBPTS, 2010):

1. Teachers are committed to students and their learning.
2. Teachers know the subjects they teach and how to teach those subjects to students.
3. Teachers are responsible for managing and monitoring student learning.
4. Teachers think systematically about their practice and learn from experience.
5. Teachers are members of learning communities.

standards in the following areas: The Learner and Learning; Content Knowledge; Instructional Practice; and Professional Responsibility.

Certification and Licensure

Successful completion of a college or university teacher preparation program will not automatically enable you to teach. State certification or licensure is required for teaching in the public schools and in many private schools as well. The terms *certification* and *licensure* are essentially synonymous in the teaching profession; some states issue teaching certificates, whereas others issue licenses. States also differ in the types of certificates offered; teachers can be granted provisional certificates, professional or permanent certificates, or emergency certificates. In some cases, large cities (e.g., Chicago, New York, Buffalo) have their own certification requirements that must be met. And certain local school districts have additional requirements, such as a written examination, before one can teach in those districts.

A **teaching certificate** is actually a license to teach. The department of education for each of the 50 states and the District of Columbia sets the requirements for certification or licensure. A certificate usually indicates at what level and in what content areas one may teach. One might be certified, for example, for all-level (K–12) physical education or art, secondary English, elementary education, or middle-level education. Currently, about two-thirds of the states offer certification for teaching at the middle school or junior high level—an increase from 1987 when about half of the states offered such certification. In addition, a certificate may list other areas of specialization, such as driver's training, coaching, or journalism. If you plan to go into nonteaching areas such as counseling, librarianship, or administration, special certificates are usually required.

The Praxis Series

Nationwide, 35 of the 43 states that include tests as part of their licensure process require completion of the *Praxis Series: Professional Assessments for Beginning Teachers* developed by Educational Testing Service (ETS) in consultation with teachers, educational researchers, the National Education Association, and the American Federation of Teachers. The Praxis Series (*praxis* means "putting theory into practice") enables states to create a system of tests that meet their specific licensing requirements.

The Praxis Series, which replaced the National Teacher Examination in the mid-1990s, consists of three components:

Praxis I: Pre-Professional Skills Tests—Praxis I covers the enabling skills in reading, writing, and mathematics that all teachers need, regardless of grade or subject taught. Two formats, computer-based and pencil-and-paper versions, are available for the Praxis I assessment, which is given early in a student's teacher education program. To help students pass Praxis I, ETS offers online practice test items. Additionally, for students who need help in improving basic academic skills, LearningPlus is an interactive computer software program that provides instruction and diagnostic placement tests in reading, writing, and mathematics.

Praxis II: Subject Assessments—Praxis II measures teacher education students' knowledge of the subjects they will teach. In most cases, Praxis II tests are taken after completion of an undergraduate program. The tests, available in more than 70 subject areas, have a core content module required by every state, with the remaining modules selected on an individual basis by the states. Each state can base its assessment on multiple-choice items or on candidate-constructed response modules. In addition, Praxis II includes the Principles of Learning and Teaching (PLT) test and the Professional Knowledge test; each is a 2-hour test to assess teachers' professional knowledge. The PLT is available in three versions: K–6, 5–9, and 7–12.

TEACHERS' VOICES ➡ BEING AN AGENT OF CHANGE

CARLA HUDSON

NECESSITY AND THE ART OF DIFFERENTIATION

Some may say that necessity is the mother of invention, but in my classroom, necessity is the mother of *differentiation*.

Three years ago, my school district assigned me to the Beaver Valley School in Plain, WASHINGTON. Beaver Valley is one of only 8 "remote and necessary" schools in Washington, and one of less than 400 in the United States. *Remote and necessary* is the current term for what was formerly known as a *one-room schoolhouse*. I approached my new assignment with trepidation. At various times, I had taught kindergarten, first grade, and third grade. Now I was being asked to teach grades 1–4 all at the same time and in the same classroom.

Differentiation is a word regularly utilized in education circles. In general, it refers to modulating instruction so that all students learn at a pace and on a level suitable for their academic abilities. Most teachers agree with the goal of differentiation, but find it hard to implement in practice. Faced with four grades and 22 beaming faces, I realized very quickly that differentiation was not optional in this classroom.

To set up my classroom for success, I differentiated my classroom in three ways: (1) by establishing flexible groupings across grades; (2) by organizing reading and math into grade-level rotations; and (3) by utilizing paraprofessional, parent, and community support.

FLEXIBLE GROUPINGS

Flexible grouping enables me to place students at certain times of day according to their ability level. The advantage to a multigrade classroom is that I have all of the curricula for each of the grades available at my fingertips. In the early morning, my children enter the class and begin work on a short math and reading review. Children work independently and on their own level. For instance, I have a third grader who works on fourth-grade math during this time, but does his reading review on the second-grade level. The combinations vary widely, but the activity is independent and the shared learning spontaneous. For some children, this is a time of enrichment; for others it is a time of review.

GRADE-LEVEL ROTATIONS

To ensure that each student is exposed to the grade-level expectations, I keep my reading groups in grade-level bands. I've organized the reading and math times into rotation centers.

During the 1½-hour reading block, I meet with each grade level for 30 minutes (grades 3–4 combined). While I am with a reading group, the other grade levels rotate between the computer center and the silent reading/workbook center. Focused instruction on the learning standards is provided during this time. Math is organized similarly so that each grade is taught independently even though the class remains intact. Timed fast-fact drills, however, are naturally differentiated. I have a first grader who is working on multiplication facts, while some older children are still mastering addition and subtraction.

PARAPROFESSIONAL, PARENT, AND COMMUNITY SUPPORT

Successful differentiation requires that a support system is in place. I utilize my paraprofessional teacher with parents and community volunteers. While I am working with one grade level, they are supervising the work of the other children in their various centers. In addition, because we don't have any specialized services available to our students, the support team also helps with progress monitoring and provides extra assistance to those students who need a bit more instruction in order to be successful.

CONCLUSION

My colleagues from other schools often shake their heads in amazement when I tell them that I teach four grades in one classroom. They wonder how it is possible to meet the needs of such a wide range of children at multiple grade levels. A deliberate focus on differentiation has been the key to making my multigrade classroom function efficiently. However, now that I have navigated the differentiation waters successfully, I see no reason why the same system would not work at a single grade level. Success requires developing a well-organized curriculum, putting learning systems into place, and efficiently utilizing school and volunteer personnel. Necessity is truly the mother of differentiation.

QUESTIONS

1. Hudson says her approach to differentiation (i.e., teaching four grades in one classroom) could "work at a single grade level." To what extent do you agree with her? Disagree?

2. According to Hudson, one key to her success is "efficiently utilizing" volunteers. How might volunteers help you be successful during your first year of teaching?

Carla Hudson is a multigrade teacher at Beaver Valley School in Plain, Washington.

Praxis III: Teacher Performance Assessments—Praxis III is a performance-based assessment system, not a test. Developed after extensive job analyses, reviews of research, and input from educators, Praxis III involves the assessment of the actual teaching skills of the beginning teacher. The assessments focus on the four domains of the Praxis Series, which are illustrated in Figure 1.9 (see page 34): planning and preparation, the classroom environment, instruction, and professional responsibilities. In addition, Praxis III assesses the teacher's sensitivity to developmental levels and cultural differences among students. In-class assessments and pre- and post-observation interviews conducted by trained state and local personnel are the main components of Praxis III. The observations are supplemented by work samples—for example, lesson plans. Following Praxis III assessments, which normally are completed by the end of the first year of teaching, the state makes a decision about whether to grant a license to teach.

State Licensure Certification Requirements

For a person to receive a license to teach, all states require successful completion of an approved teacher education program that culminates with at least a bachelor's degree. To be approved, programs must pass a review by the state department of education approximately every 5 years. In addition to approval at the state level, most of the nearly 1,300 programs in the nation have regional accreditation, and about half voluntarily seek accreditation by the National Council for Accreditation of Teacher Education (NCATE), the Teacher Education Accreditation Council (TEAC), or the newly-formed Council for the Accreditation of Educator Preparation (CAEP). Currently, all states require an average of six to eight semester credits of supervised student teaching. Alabama, Colorado, Idaho, Indiana, Nevada, New York, and Virginia require a master's degree for advanced certification; and Arizona, Maryland, Montana, Oregon, and Washington require either a master's degree or a specified number of semester credits after certification (Kaye, 2012). Additional requirements may also include U.S. citizenship, an oath of loyalty, fingerprinting, a background check, or a health examination.

A few states, including Iowa, New Mexico, North Carolina, and Oklahoma, waive state licensing requirements for teachers certified by the National Board for Professional Teaching Standards (NBPTS). About half of the states issue a license to a person from another state who holds a valid NBPTS certificate. For a current listing of state and local action supporting NBPTS certification, visit the website for NBPTS.

Nearly all states now require testing of teachers for initial licensure. States use either a standardized test (usually Praxis) or a test developed by outside consultants. Areas covered by the states' tests usually include basic skills, professional knowledge, and general knowledge. Many states also require an on-the-job performance evaluation for licensure.

Today, most states do not grant a teaching license for life. Some states issue 3- to 5-year licenses, which may be renewed only with proof of coursework completed beyond the bachelor's degree. And, amid considerable controversy, several states, including Connecticut, Maryland, Massachusetts, New Hampshire, Rhode Island, South Carolina, and Wisconsin, have enacted testing for **recertification** of experienced teachers.

Licensure requirements differ from state to state, and they are frequently modified. To remain up to date on the requirements for the state in which you plan to teach, it is important that you keep in touch with your teacher placement office or the certification officer at your college or university. You may also wish to refer to *Requirements for Certification of Teachers, Counselors, Librarians, Administrators for Elementary and Secondary Schools* (The University of Chicago Press), an annual publication that lists state-by-state certification requirements. Or you may contact the teacher certification office in the state where you plan to teach. Currently, 47 states and the District of Columbia are members of the **National Association of State Directors of Teacher Education and Certification's (NASDTEC) Interstate Agreement**, a reciprocity agreement whereby a certificate obtained in one state will be honored in another. If you plan to teach in a state other than the one in which you are currently studying, you should find out whether both states are members of the NASDTEC Interstate Agreement.

More than 464,900 teachers, many of whom are noncertified, teach in the growing system of private, parochial, for-profit, and charter schools in the United States (Goldring, Gray, & Bitterman, 2013, p. 7). Private and parochial schools supported largely by tuition and gifts, and for-profit schools operated by private educational corporations, usually have no certification requirements for teachers. Also, teacher-created and teacher-operated charter schools, although they are public, are often free of state certification requirements. A school's charter (an agreement between the school's founders and its sponsor—usually a local school board) may waive certification requirements if the school guarantees that students will attain a specified level of achievement.

Alternative Certification

Despite the national movement to make certification requirements more stringent, concern about meeting the demand for new public school teachers and attracting minority-group members into the teaching profession has resulted in increasing use of **alternative teacher certification** programs. In 1983, only eight states offered alternatives; by 2009, alternative certification programs existed in each state and produced about 20 percent of the nation's teachers (Feistritzer, 2009).

Alternative certification programs are designed for people who already have at least a bachelor's degree in a field other than education and want to become licensed to teach. In 2006, more than 50,000 people were licensed through alternative certification programs (Feistritzer, 2009). Most alternative certification programs are collaborative efforts among state departments of education, teacher education programs in colleges and universities, and school districts. For example, Washington State University, in collaboration with area school districts, has a federally funded program to prepare paraprofessional educators (teachers' aides, for example) in southwest Washington to become bilingual/ESL teachers. Also, many school districts offer teaching fellows programs that provide provisional certification and tuition for graduate-level study in education (National Research Council, 2010). Compared with recent college graduates who enter teaching directly from a traditional college-based teacher preparation program, those who enter teaching through alternate routes tend to be "older, more diverse, and more willing to teach wherever the jobs are and in high-demand subjects than are traditionally trained teachers" (Feistritzer & Haar, 2008, p. 126).

HOW CAN YOU BENEFIT FROM HAVING A MENTOR?

When asked "[what] steps might be taken to attract good people into teaching and to encourage good teachers to remain in teaching," 82 percent of respondents to the MetLife Survey of the American Teacher said "providing mentoring and ongoing support for new teachers" would "help a lot" (Harris Interactive, 2001, p. 125). The following teacher-mentor explains how she provides help and support for beginning teachers:

> I go into their classrooms frequently to observe them and to give them feedback on what they ask for feedback on, or what they need feedback on. Mostly they will ask, "How am I doing with my questioning strategies?" or something like that. They will give me a focus that they want to look at. I let them know that I am on their side and want to help them. I will do whatever I can to facilitate their professional growth. (Peck, 2008, p. 123)

In reflecting on how my own professional growth was enhanced by my relationship with my mentor, Herbert A. Thelen, I defined **mentoring** as

> an intensive, one-to-one form of teaching in which the wise and experienced mentor inducts the aspiring protégé [one who is mentored] into a particular, usually professional, way of life. . . . [T]he protégé learns from the mentor not only the objective, manifest content of professional knowledge and skills but also a subjective, nondiscursive appreciation for how and when to employ these learnings in the arena of professional practice. In short, the mentor helps the protégé to "learn the ropes," to become socialized into the profession. (Parkay, 1988, p. 196)

An urban middle school intern's description of how his mentor helped him develop effective classroom management techniques exemplifies "learning the ropes": "'You've got to develop your own sense of personal power,' [my mentor] kept saying. 'It's not something I can teach you. I can show you what to do. I can model it. But I don't know, it's just something that's got to come from within you'" (Henry, Huntley, McKamey, & Harper, 1995, p. 114).

Those who have become highly accomplished teachers frequently point out the importance of mentors in their preparation for teaching. A **mentor** can provide moral support, guidance, and feedback to students at various stages of professional preparation. In addition, a mentor can model for the protégé an analytical approach to solving problems in the classroom. For example, an effective mentor might use the following strategies to help a beginning teacher solve classroom-based problems:

- Sharing the mentor's own experiences
- Suggesting strategies for handling situations
- Demonstrating techniques and strategies
- Critiquing lesson plans
- Rehearsing planned classroom activities
- Role-playing various classroom situations with the new teacher
- Reviewing the day's events and exploring alternative approaches

SUMMARY

Why Do I Want to Teach?

- Individual reasons for becoming a teacher may be intrinsic (desire to work with young people, passion for the subject, influence of teachers, a desire to serve others and society) as well as extrinsic (work hours, vacations, job security).

What Are the Benefits of Teaching?

- Practical benefits of teaching include on-the-job hours at school, vacations, increasing salaries and benefits, job security, and a feeling of respect in society.

What Are the Challenges of Teaching?

- The challenges of teaching include long working hours, meeting the accountability demands of high-stakes testing and federal legislation that emphasizes closing the achievement gap and the need for "great" teachers in every classroom, and understanding the pervasive influence of technology on today's children and youth.

What Will Society Expect of Me as a Teacher?

- Society expects teachers to be competent and effective, and it holds teachers accountable for student achievement, for helping all learners succeed, for promoting social justice, and for maintaining high standards of conduct.

What Is the Job Outlook for Teachers?

- The job outlook for teachers is positive, especially for teachers in high-demand fields and in less desirable urban or rural school districts.

- The economic recession that began in 2008 resulted in budget crises for school districts around the country, and many teachers were laid off. Federal stimulus money in 2009 and 2010 enabled school districts to avoid scheduled teacher layoffs and to rehire teachers previously laid off.

- In contrast to the diversity of student enrollments, the backgrounds of today's teachers are less diverse; thus, teachers from diverse racial and ethnic backgrounds and teachers with disabilities will experience exceptional employment opportunities for the foreseeable future.

- Teacher supply and demand in content areas and geographic regions influences finding a teaching position.

What Can You Learn from Observing in Classrooms?

- You can gain practical experience through field experiences, focused classroom observations, and the use of various observation instruments.

- Observation instruments range from informal, qualitative descriptions to formal, quantitative checklists.

Why Is Your Induction into Teaching Important?

- In response to the problem of teacher attrition, many states and school districts provide beginning teachers with induction programs that offer support during their first years in the profession.

- Induction programs offer beginning teachers various types of support, including workshops based on teacher-identified needs, observations and feedback from experienced teachers, mentoring, and support group meetings.

How Can You Gain Practical Experience for Becoming a Teacher?

- Microteaching, teaching simulations, analyses of video cases, field-based practica and clinical experiences, classroom aide programs, student teaching, and substitute teaching are among the ways teacher education students can gain practical experience.

How Will I Become a Highly Qualified Teacher?

- Six sets of professional standards have a great impact on teacher education programs nationally (as well as on teachers' ongoing professional growth and development): standards developed by the Interstate Teacher Assessment and Support Consortium (InTASC), the National Council for Accreditation of Teacher Education (NCATE), the Teacher Education Accreditation Council (TEAC), the Praxis Series: Professional Assessments for Beginning Teachers, the National Board for Professional Teaching Standards (NBPTS), and the newly-formed Council for the Accreditation of Educator Preparation (CAEP).

- State certification is required for teaching in public schools and in many private schools. Some large cities and local school districts have additional criteria for certification. Certification requirements for teachers vary from state to state and are frequently modified. Some states waive licensing requirements for teachers certified by the National Board for Professional Teaching Standards (NBPTS).
- Most states require testing of teachers for initial certification, and some require recertification after a 3- to 5-year period.
- States that are members of the Interstate Certification Agreement Contract honor teaching certificates granted by certain other states.

How Can You Benefit from Having a Mentor?

- Mentoring can be a source of professional growth for experienced teachers and enables the protégé to learn about the profession.
- A mentor can model for the protégé an analytical approach to solving problems in the classroom.

PROFESSIONAL REFLECTIONS AND ACTIVITIES

Teacher's Journal

1. Think about a time when a teacher truly motivated you to learn. What did that teacher do to motivate you? Do you believe other students in the class had the same reaction to this teacher? Why or why not?
2. Consider your reasons for deciding to become a teacher. How do they compare with those described in this chapter?

Teacher's Research

1. Locate information in newspapers, magazines, and on the Internet that is related to one of the following "key priorities" emphasized in *A Blueprint for Reform*: College and Career–Ready Students, Great Teachers and Leaders in Every School, Equity and Opportunity for All Students, Raise the Bar and Reward Excellence, Promote Innovation and Continuous Improvement. Synthesize the information and present your findings to the rest of your class.
2. Formulate a research question concerning demographic aspects of teachers in the United States.

Your question might relate to one or more of the following topics:

- Teachers' attitudes
- Characteristics of the teaching force
- Teacher recruitment
- Teacher supply and demand
- Teaching salaries and benefits

Begin your data search at the website for the U.S. Department of Education's National Center for Education Statistics. Present a brief oral report to the rest of your class that summarizes the results of your data search.

Observations and Interviews

1. In a small group of three or four of your classmates, visit a local school and interview teachers to learn about their perceptions of the rewards and challenges of teaching. Share your findings with other members of your class.
2. Interview one or more teachers at a local elementary, middle, junior, or senior high school. Ask the teacher(s) to identify the characteristics of "great," highly qualified teachers.

Professional Portfolio

To help you in your journey toward becoming a teacher, each chapter in this textbook includes suggestions for developing your professional portfolio, a collection of evidence documenting your growth and development while learning to become a teacher. At the end of this course, you will be well on your way toward a portfolio that documents your knowledge, skills, and attitudes for teaching and contains valuable resources for your first teaching position.

For your first portfolio entry, identify significant experiences in your life that have contributed to your decision to become a teacher. In your entry (or videotaped version), discuss your reasons for becoming a teacher and the rewards teaching will hold for you. Before developing your portfolio entry, you might wish to visit the website for the National Teacher of the Year Program, co-sponsored by the Council of Chief State School Officers (CCSSO) and the Pearson Foundation. Here, you can watch short videos in which Teachers of the Year from 2007 to the present explain "Why I teach."

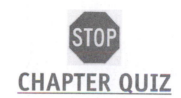

CHAPTER QUIZ

Take this quiz to check your understanding of the content covered in this chapter.

CHAPTER TWO
Today's Teachers

learning outcomes

After reading this chapter, you will be able to do the following:

1. Describe the work of teachers in different types of schools and in different subject areas.
2. Explain how teachers are role models for students, spontaneous problem solvers, and reflective thinkers.
3. Explain the four types of essential knowledge that today's teachers must have.
4. Explain the extent to which teaching meets the commonly agreed-upon characteristics of a full profession.
5. Describe the major professional organizations to which teachers belong.
6. Explain how teacher leaders are transforming the profession of teaching.

WHO ARE TODAY'S TEACHERS?

The answer to this question is not as simple as you might think. Today's teachers teach in schools with different grade configurations, they teach in different subject-matter and specialized areas, and they teach students with different types of learning needs.

Teaching is the largest profession in the United States. Kindergarten, elementary school, middle school, and secondary school teachers, not including special education teachers, total about 3.5 million. Of those teachers, about 179,200 are kindergarten teachers, 1.48 million are elementary school teachers, 641,700 are middle school teachers, and 1.01 million are secondary school teachers (U.S. Department of Labor, 2013).

Table 2.1 shows that today's public school teachers are well educated—almost half have a master's degree, compared to 27 percent who had that degree in 1971 (National Education Association, December 2010); and 40 percent of teachers have 15 or more years of classroom experience. The table also shows that virtually all teachers enhanced their knowledge and skills by participating in professional development during the previous 12 months.

Today's teachers also have higher grade point averages (GPAs) and standardized achievement test (SAT) scores than teachers did several years ago. According to a study by the developers of the Praxis Series, the percentage of teacher candidates who took the Praxis and reported a 3.5 GPA or higher increased from 27 percent during 1994–1997 to 40 percent during 2002–2005. Additionally, candidates' verbal SAT scores rose 13 points and math scores rose 17 points (Educational Testing Service, 2007).

Schools and Grade-Level Designations

Teachers in U.S. schools teach students who are approximately 3 through 17 years of age and attend schools from the pre-kindergarten (pre-K) through high school levels. Figure 2.1 shows that pre-K, elementary, middle, and high school programs in the United States have various grade configurations. A common arrangement is elementary schools that include pre-kindergarten or kindergarten through 5th-grade levels, middle schools that include 6th- through 8th-grade levels, and high schools that include 9th- through 12th-grade levels. A less common arrangement beyond the elementary level is junior high schools that include 6th- through 9th-grade levels, and senior high schools that include 10th- through 12th-grade levels.

TABLE 2.1 · Public school teachers in the United States

Total Number of Teachers	
Traditional public school	3,269,500
Charter school	115,600
Sex	
Male	23.7%
Female	76.3%
Number of Teachers by School Level	
Primary school	1,626,800
Middle school	592,100
High school	961,300
Combined grade school	205,000
Average Age	
Traditional public	42.6
Charter school	37.4
Highest Degree Earned	
No bachelor's degree	3.8%
Bachelor's degree	39.9%
Master's degree	47.7%
Higher than master's degree	8.7%
Years of Teaching Experience	
Less than 4 years	11.3%
4–9 years	28.6%
10–14 years	20.9%
15 or more years	39.3%
Average Hours per Week on Selected Activities	
Delivering instruction to students	30.8
Total hours on teaching and school-related activities	52.2
Salary Supplements (average amount)	
Extracurricular activities, $2,500	41.8%
Additional compensation based on student performance, $1,400	4.4%
Other school system sources (state supplement, etc.), $2,100	7.9%
Job outside school system, $4,800	16.1%
Average Class Size	
Primary schools, self-contained classes	21.6
Primary schools, departmentalized	26.2

(continued)

TABLE 2.1 (continued)

Average Class Size	
Middle schools, self-contained classes	16.7
Middle schools, departmentalized	25.5
High schools, self-contained	17.7
High schools, departmentalized	24.2
Combined grade schools, self-contained	16.6
Combined grade schools, self-contained	19.0
Type of Professional Development Participated in During Previous 12 Months	
Any professional development	99.0%
Content of subject(s) taught	84.8%
Use of computers for instruction	67.2%
Reading instruction	56.7%
Student discipline and classroom management	42.5%
Teaching students with disabilities	37.4%
Teaching limited-English proficient students or English-language learners	26.8%
Other	35.7%

Adapted from Goldring, R., Gray, L., and Bitterman, A. (2013). *Characteristics of Public and Private Elementary and Secondary School Teachers in the United States: Results from the 2011–12 Schools and Staffing Survey* (NCES 2013-314). U.S. Department of Education. Washington, DC: National Center for Education Statistics, pp. 6, 8, 10, 12, 14, 16, and 18–19. Retrieved November 13, 2013, from http://nces.ed.gov/pubsearch.

PRE-K TEACHERS

The ages included in **pre-K education** (also termed **early childhood education** and, less frequently, nursery school education), according to the National Association for the Education of Young Children (NAEYC), range from birth to age 8. Pre-K teachers play a critical role in the development of children. What children learn and experience during their early years shapes their views of themselves and the world and influences their later success in school, work, and their personal lives.

If you had a pre-K educational experience, you probably remember learning through play and interactive activities. Your pre-K teacher(s) most likely used play to further your language and vocabulary development (storytelling, rhyming games, and play acting, for example), improve your social skills (cooperating with other children to build a small town in a sandbox), and introduce scientific and mathematical concepts (learning to balance and count blocks when building a skyscraper or mixing colors for fingerpainting).

Pre-K teachers use a less structured approach than teachers of older students. Children at the pre-K level are involved in small-group lessons; one-on-one instruction; and learning through creative activities such as art, dance, and music. Play and hands-on activities are used also by kindergarten teachers; however, academic learning becomes more important in kindergarten classrooms. Letter recognition, phonics, numbers, and basic understanding of nature and science are introduced at the kindergarten level.

Watch as this teacher uses effective instructional strategies.

ELEMENTARY TEACHERS

Elementary school teachers usually teach one class, from grades 1 through 6, of about 25 children in several subjects. In some elementary schools, two or more teachers work as a team with a group of students in at least one subject. In other elementary

FIGURE 2.1   The structure of education in the United States

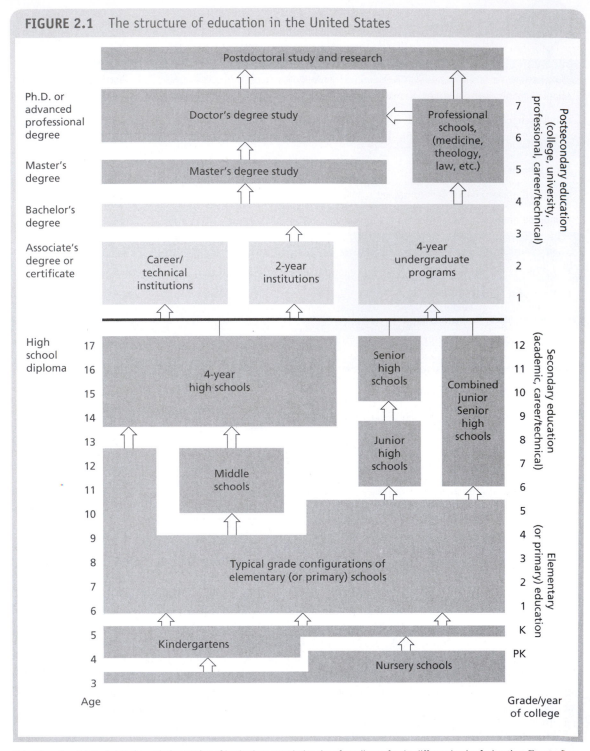

Note: Figure is not intended to show relative number of institutions nor relative size of enrollment for the different levels of education. Figure reflects typical patterns of progression rather than all possible variations. Adult education programs, while not separately delineated above, may provide instruction at the adult basic, adult secondary, or postsecondary education levels.

Source: Snyder, T. D., and Dillow, S. A. (2012). *Digest of Education Statistics 2011* (NCES 2012-001). National Center for Education Statistics, Institute of Education Sciences, U.S. Department of Education. Washington, DC, p. 12.

schools, a teacher may teach one subject—often music, art, reading, science, arithmetic, or physical education—to a number of classes. Increasing numbers of teachers teach in **multiage**, or multigrade, **classrooms**, with students from different grade levels. Elementary school teachers introduce children to mathematics, language, science, and social studies. They use games, music, artwork, films, books, computers, and other tools to teach basic skills.

Elementary school teachers write daily lesson plans based on school or state requirements, and they record student attendance each day. They assign homework, grade papers, and record grades on tests and homework. At regular intervals they evaluate each child's academic progress and write progress reports for parents. On the progress report, they note any behavioral or social problems and disciplinary actions. Elementary teachers also supervise activities on playgrounds, in cafeterias, and in other areas of the school.

Elementary teachers also meet with parents or guardians to discuss student progress or problems. If a child is not adjusting well to school, teachers work with the child; administrators; and parents, guardians, or other family members to find solutions.

Some elementary school teachers teach subjects such as art or music. Art teachers develop art projects, maintain art supplies, and help children develop art skills. Music teachers teach music and lead singing groups, and sometimes they direct the school band. Other teachers teach physical education to help children develop physical coordination. Often, these teachers work at several schools during a week. Some elementary teachers coordinate volunteer groups and/or oversee special projects in addition to their regular duties.

Elementary teachers frequently work with parent volunteers in the classroom. They also attend in-service workshops to learn about new instructional methods and materials. Typically, elementary teachers meet regularly with other staff members to discuss school issues.

MIDDLE SCHOOL TEACHERS

Middle school teachers help students learn more about the subjects studied in elementary school. Most middle school teachers specialize in a specific subject, such as English, mathematics, or science, and they teach several classes a day in that subject area. However, some middle school teachers work in self-contained classrooms and teach all major subjects to one group of students.

During the middle school years, young adolescents are at a unique stage of life. They are dealing with an array of physical, intellectual, emotional, and social challenges. Some mature rapidly, whereas others mature more slowly. Some may be physically mature yet socially immature. Middle school students have very different developmental needs. Middle school teachers understand these needs and are skilled at providing students with

Middle-level students are at a unique stage of life and have different developmental needs. Why is it important that teachers understand their students' developmental needs?

developmentally appropriate learning activities. They also understand that students must believe that teachers really care about their lives. Teachers convey genuine caring when they actively listen to students' concerns, when they show interest in the important events in students' lives. An event that may seem trivial to an adult—a minor disagreement with a friend, for example—can have huge importance to a middle school student.

HIGH SCHOOL TEACHERS

Most high school teachers teach four or five courses within a single content area. For example, a high school math teacher might teach two classes of Algebra I, a trigonometry class, and two geometry classes. An English teacher might teach two classes of sophomore English, one advanced-placement (AP) English literature class for which students receive college credit, one honors English class, and one journalism class.

In addition to teaching, some high school teachers monitor study halls and homerooms or supervise extracurricular activities. On occasion, they may supervise events such as school dances or athletic contests or accompany students on field trips. They may also counsel students regarding classes to take at the high school and/or plans for college, training, or employment after high school.

High school teachers also participate in faculty meetings, professional development workshops, and educational conferences. If they have students with behavioral or academic problems, they may meet with those students, their parents or guardians, and administrators to resolve the problems. They may also identify students with physical or mental difficulties and refer them to the school counselor, special education teacher(s), or other professionals.

Teachers in Nontraditional School Settings

In addition to teachers who work in pre-K, elementary, middle, and high school programs, some teachers teach in nontraditional school settings, such as private schools, charter schools, alternative schools, and magnet schools.

PRIVATE SCHOOL TEACHERS

Teachers in private schools often have smaller class sizes and more control over determining the curriculum and standards for performance and discipline. Their students also tend to be more motivated because private schools can be selective in their admissions processes. Although private school teachers may earn less than public school teachers, they may have other benefits, such as free or subsidized housing.

Religious sects operate a total of 22,731 schools across the country, and an additional 10,635 schools are nonsectarian (Broughman, Swaim, & Hryczaniuk, 2011). There are schools founded on the Christian, Jewish, Muslim, Quaker, and Seventh-Day Adventist faiths, to name a few. The Catholic Church has one of the largest networks of religious schools in the country—5,472 elementary/middle schools and 1,213 secondary schools. Total Catholic school enrollment for the 2013–2014 academic year was more than 1.4 million at the elementary/middle level, and more than 586,000 at the secondary level (National Catholic Education Association, November 14, 2013). Other Christian denominations operate a total of almost 7,500 schools across the country, and the Jewish faith operates more than 800 (Broughman et al., 2011).

CHARTER SCHOOL TEACHERS

Charter schools are independent public schools, often founded by teachers, that are given a charter to operate by a school district, state, or national government. For a charter school to be approved, the school must agree to document students' mastery of predetermined outcomes. To some extent, teachers at charter schools have freedom from many of the regulations that apply to traditional public school teachers. However, charter school teachers must account—usually to a state or local school board—for producing positive academic results and adhering to the charter contract.

The first charter school opened in Minnesota in 1992. From 1999–2000 to 2010–2011, the number of students enrolled in public charter schools increased from 0.3 million to 1.8 million students. During that same period, the number of charter schools increased from 1,500 to 5,300. In 2010–2011, California enrolled the most students in charter schools (364,000), and the District of Columbia enrolled the highest percentage of public school students in charter schools (38 percent or 27,000 students) (Aud et al., 2013).

Charter schools will continue to expand during the coming decade, as the Obama administration's *Blueprint for Reform* announced competitive funding for "the expansion of high-performing public charter schools" (U.S. Department of Education, March 2010, p. 6). However, a debate has emerged about whether charter schools outperform traditional schools in meeting the needs of underachieving students. For example, in New Orleans, **LOUISIANA**, most public schools were turned over to the privately run Recovery School District (RCD) after Hurricane Katrina in 2005. Before Katrina, two-thirds of students attended schools labeled as "failing" by state standards; during the 2010–2011 academic year, fewer than one-third of students attended such schools (Laskow, 2010). On the other hand, critics argue that "difficult-to-teach" students have been "abandoned" by the RCD. "New ideas on how to teach disruptive and unmotivated students have not emerged from charter schools . . . they are an outcast group, thrown into an abyss," according to a former superintendent of public schools in New Orleans (Gabor, 2013).

ALTERNATIVE SCHOOL TEACHERS

To find better ways to educate all students and to reduce problems with violence, weapons, and drugs in schools, many school districts have established alternative schools. There is no single commonly accepted definition for an **alternative school** or program (Lange & Sletten, 2002); however, an alternative school is usually a small, highly individualized school separate from the regular school. Sixty-four percent of public school districts have at least one alternative school or program for at-risk students (Carver & Lewis, 2010).

Alternative schools are designed to meet the needs of students at risk of failure and dropping out. In general, students are referred to alternative schools and programs if they are at risk of educational failure, as indicated by low grades, truancy, disruptive behavior, suspension, pregnancy, or similar factors associated with early withdrawal from school.

Because they often have small class sizes and the freedom to be creative in meeting students' needs, alternative school teachers usually find their work very satisfying. As a teacher at one alternative school said, "Here, you finally have a sense of ownership as a teacher. You have to come in the morning and create something and keep working at it, and it's a tremendous experience" (Firestone, 2008).

MAGNET SCHOOL TEACHERS

A **magnet school** offers a curriculum that focuses on a specific area such as the performing arts, mathematics, science, international studies, or technology. Magnet schools, which often draw students from a larger attendance area than regular schools, are frequently used to promote voluntary desegregation. In 2008, teachers taught at over 2,700 magnet schools in the United States (Keaton, 2012b).

Some evidence suggests that teachers at magnet schools may experience greater levels of autonomy, influence on school policies, and professional development than teachers at traditional schools (Evans, 2002). One example of a professional magnet school teacher is Tere Pujol-Burns, who teaches kindergarten through fifth grade at Sunset Elementary School in Miami, **FLORIDA**. Selected as Magnet Schools of America's 2013 National Teacher of the Year, Pujol-Burns is the Lead Teacher of the International Studies Magnet Program at her school. She developed the *Change for Change* program and brought together teachers, students, and parents to identify areas of need in the local and international community and to provide service-learning opportunities for students. Her students have raised funds for kangaroo adoption, rain-forest preservation, Save the Waves Coalition, and UNICEF (Magnet Schools of America, 2013; Miami-Dade County Public Schools, 2013).

Teachers in Specialized Areas

Some teachers, regardless of level, teach in specialized areas such as art, vocational education, music, or physical education. Others teach in areas differentiated according to the learning needs of students in various groups, for example, special education teachers who specialize in teaching students with disabilities and/or special needs. Other teachers specialize in teaching students whose first language is not English (often called English language learners [ELLs]). The following sections present brief job descriptions for teachers in these specialized areas.

ART TEACHERS

From elementary school through high school, art teachers teach students the visual arts—painting, sketching, designing, and sculpting, for instance. Art teachers may specialize in teaching one or more areas of art, such as illustration, art history, or commercial art, and at times they may organize student art contests or arrange for student artwork to be exhibited. In some cases, art teachers travel from school to school.

More than other areas of the curriculum, art and music (discussed in the following subsection) have had an insecure position. When schools face budget cutbacks or increased pressure to prepare students for high-stakes tests, eliminating art and music is often considered.

MUSIC TEACHERS

Music teachers instruct students in vocal or instrumental music and foster music appreciation. Elementary and secondary school music teachers often direct the school chorus, choir, orchestra, or marching band, as well as give group and private lessons. They instruct students in the technical aspects of music, conduct rehearsals, and evaluate student performances. School music teachers sometimes take students on field trips to musical presentations, or the students may perform off campus under the direction of the teacher.

VOCATIONAL EDUCATION TEACHERS

Vocational education teachers (sometimes called vocational/technical education [votech] teachers) train students to work in fields such as healthcare, business, auto repair, communications, and technology. About 14,400 teachers taught vocational education at the middle school level in 2010, and 88,600 taught at the high school level (U.S. Department of Labor, 2013). They often teach courses that are in high demand by area employers, who may provide input into the curriculum and offer internships to students. Many vocational teachers play an active role in developing and overseeing these internships. To prepare students for the real world of specific vocational or technical careers, vocational education teachers use a hands-on approach to teach academic and vocational skills.

PHYSICAL EDUCATION TEACHERS

Physical education teachers teach students from the elementary through high school levels. The ultimate aim of their teaching is to introduce students to physical activities that develop within them a desire to maintain physical fitness throughout life.

At the high school level, physical education teachers often teach one or two classes of health, coach one or more sports, or teach driver education. Physical education teachers teach individual and team sports that promote the development of students' physical abilities. They organize and referee indoor and outdoor sports, such as volleyball, football, baseball, and basketball. They teach students beginning or advanced calisthenics, gymnastics, or corrective exercises. They teach and demonstrate the use of gymnastic and training equipment such as trampolines and weight-lifting equipment.

At one time, physical education teachers placed greater emphasis on highly competitive team sports. Many students, however, did not do well at such sports and may have experienced a lowered sense of self-esteem as a result. Today's physical education teachers offer activities to meet the needs and abilities of all students, not just the athletically talented. In addition to traditional team sports such as football, basketball, and baseball, and individual sports such as swimming and wrestling, students participate in activities such as aerobics, badminton, gymnastics, volleyball, golf, soccer, and yoga.

SPECIAL EDUCATION TEACHERS

Special education teachers work with children and youth who have a variety of disabilities. Special education teachers held a total of about 459,600 jobs in 2010. About 222,800 worked at the preschool, kindergarten, and elementary level; 98,100 worked at the middle school level; and 138,700 worked at the high school level (U.S. Department of Labor, 2013). Most special education teachers work in public and private educational institutions. A few work for individual and social assistance agencies or residential facilities, or in homebound or hospital environments.

Often, special education teachers specialize in working with students who have specific disabilities—learning disabilities, autism, and brain injuries, for example. Special education teachers must develop an **individualized education program (IEP)** for students and work collaboratively with regular classroom teachers, parents, social workers, school psychologists, and other school staff. Special education teachers are trained to use advanced educational technologies—for example, word-prediction software, voice-recognition computers, and speech synthesizers—to help students with special needs learn.

As schools become more inclusive, special education teachers and general education teachers increasingly work together in general education classrooms. Special education teachers help general educators adapt curriculum materials and teaching techniques to meet the needs of students with disabilities.

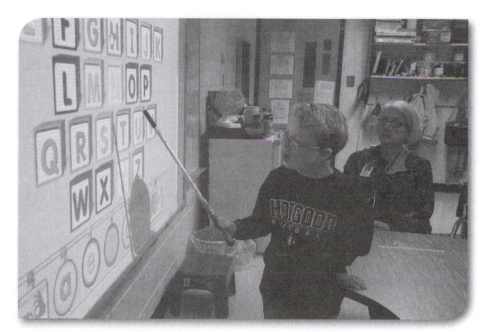

The Individual Education Program (IEP) for this student with multiple disabilities provides for educational technology to help him learn.

They coordinate the work of teachers; teacher assistants; and related personnel, such as therapists and social workers, to meet the individualized needs of the student within inclusive special education programs. A large part of a special education teacher's job involves communicating and coordinating with others involved in the child's well-being, including parents, social workers, school psychologists, occupational and physical therapists, school administrators, and other teachers.

Special education teachers work in a variety of settings. Some have their own classrooms and teach only special education students. Others work as special education resource teachers and offer individualized help to students in general education classrooms. And others teach alongside general education teachers in classes that have both general and special education students. Some teachers work with special education students for several hours a day in a resource room, separate from their general education classroom.

In schools that use the **response to intervention (RTI) model**, special education teachers work with general education teachers on schoolwide screenings and progress monitoring to ensure that students are "responsive" to instruction they receive in the classroom. According to the response to intervention (RTI) model, students who do not make adequate academic progress and who are at risk for reading and other learning disabilities receive increasingly intensive instructional services. The RTI model is designed to determine, as early as possible, if a student's low achievement is due to instructional or behavioral factors or whether the student has a possible learning disability. The goal is to provide the student with appropriate instruction and educational assistance *before* he or she experiences years of low achievement.

FOCUS ON DIVERSITY: TEACHERS OF ENGLISH LANGUAGE LEARNERS (ELLs)

Many teachers, whether they have specialized training or not, teach students whose first language is not English (often called **English language learners [ELLs]**). About 21.8 percent of children ages 5–14 speak a language other than English at home (U.S. Census Bureau, August 2013). Ten percent or more of public school students in the following states are ELLs: Oregon, Hawaii, Alaska, Colorado, Texas, New Mexico, Nevada, and California (Aud et al., 2013). Among the population five years and older who spoke a language other than English at home during 2011, more than 15 percent spoke English "not well, and 7 percent spoke English "not at all" (U.S. Census Bureau, August 2013).

Only 30 percent of teachers who instruct ELL students have received training to teach ELL students, and fewer than 3 percent have earned a degree in English as a second language (ESL) or bilingual education (Aud, Fox, & KewalRamani, 2010). Nevertheless, as comments by the following teacher who has no ELL training illustrate, professional teachers are committed to teaching *all* their students: "They [ELL students] need to be in the classroom. . . . My job is to teach the kids. If they don't know English, that's my job" (Valli & Buese, 2007, p. 532).

Seeing ELL students develop as learners can be very rewarding. Most teachers find their ELL students eager to learn. Once they realize that their teachers want them to succeed, ELL students, in turn, will want to please their teachers by being successful in the classroom. As a result, they are willing to work hard to adjust to an English-language environment. For example, one ELL teacher told the author how much "fun" she now has teaching students from three different language backgrounds—Spanish, Somali, and Russian—in her high school classroom. Now, two months after the start of the school year, her students are participating actively in class activities, and she takes tremendous satisfaction knowing that she is "making a difference in students' lives." According to her, "My ELL students are good kids—I can tell that they really want to learn. They are so cooperative. Also, they really appreciate it when they know that I am interested in learning about their cultures. In a way, I learn as much from my students as they learn from me."

WHAT DO TEACHERS *DO* IN THE CLASSROOM?

At first, this question may appear easy to answer. From your own experiences as a student, you know that teachers assign learning tasks. They ask questions and evaluate students' responses. They lecture and, on occasion, demonstrate what students are to do. They assign chapters to read in the text and then conduct recitations or give quizzes on that material. They praise some students for right answers or good work, and they prod, chastise, and at times embarrass others in the hope that their work will improve. And near the end of the term or semester, they decide who has passed and who has failed. However, the role of today's teachers includes responsibilities that go beyond actual teaching in the classroom. For example, many teachers attend monthly meetings where they might discuss topics such as the following with their colleagues: a budget cut that affects the purchase of grade-level supplies, recruitment strategies for the parent-teacher association (PTA), students' academic performance, and a forthcoming field trip.

Teaching is more than the sum of the behaviors that you have observed in your own teachers. As you move ahead in your journey toward becoming a teacher, you will discover that teaching involves more than performing certain behaviors in front of a group of students. A significant portion of the teacher's work is mental and involves problem solving in response to unforeseen events that emerge in the classroom.

Teaching is a creative act in which teachers continually shape and reshape lessons, events, and the experiences of their students. A former teacher and now head of an organization that creates small, personalized, public high schools in collaboration with their communities describes the creative dimensions of teaching this way: "The act of being a teacher is the act of . . . using your skills and love for kids to figure out how to create the best environment to help your students [learn]" (Littky, 2004, p. 12).

Although your teachers reflected different personalities and methods, your experiences as a student are similar to the experiences of other students. Our recollections about teachers who were good or bad, easy or hard, interesting or dull are drawn from a commonly shared set of experiences. The universality of these experiences leads us to conclude that we know "the way teaching is" and what teachers do. However, in a seminal article aptly titled "The Way Teaching Is," noted educational researcher Philip Jackson points out that teaching is "fleeting and ephemeral" because of the "fragile quality of the psychological condition that is created by the teacher" (Jackson, 1965, p. 62).

The following sections examine three dimensions of teaching that illustrate how, on the one hand, teaching involves "enduring puzzlements, persistent dilemmas, complex conundrums, [and] enigmatic paradoxes" (Eisner, 2006, p. 44) while, on the other, it offers opportunities for "saving lives, rescuing a child from despair, restoring a sense of hope, soothing discomfort" (p. 46). Effective teachers understand that they are role models for students, spontaneous problem solvers, and reflective thinkers.

PROFESSIONAL REFLECTION
Watch as this teacher effectively uses journals to keep students motivated to learn.

Teacher as a Role Model for Students

Clearly, teachers are role models for their students. In the elementary grades, teachers are idolized by their young students. At the high school level, teachers have the potential to inspire students' admiration if they model positive attitudes and behaviors. Teachers teach not only through what they *say* and *do* in the classroom—they teach through who they *are* as people. They have the power to influence their students' lives in the present; and, often, this influence endures into the future and has a profound effect on students' development throughout life. One teacher who is a strong, positive role model for his students is Lincoln Johnson, the mathematics teacher profiled in Teachers' Voices: Walk in My Shoes on page 54.

In *Listening to Urban Kids: School Reform and the Teachers They Want* (Wilson & Corbett, 2001), students express the following expectations about their teachers' attitudes and behaviors:

I heard teachers talking about people, saying "Those kids can't do nothing." Kids want teachers who believe in them. (p. 86)

A good teacher to me is a teacher who is patient, willing to accept the fact that she might be dealing with students who have problems. (p. 87)

Since this is one of his first year's teaching, I give him credit. He relates, but he also teaches. . . . He advises us. He not only tries to teach but gets involved with us. (p. 88)

Developing positive relationships with students is important, particularly in today's culturally diverse classrooms. To develop learning activities that are interesting and relevant to their students, teachers must learn about their backgrounds and experiences. Teachers use this knowledge to make decisions about the curriculum, teaching methods, classroom management, and assessment of students' learning.

Teachers also model attitudes toward the subjects they teach and show students through their example that learning is an ongoing, life-enriching process that does not end with diplomas and graduations. Their example confirms the timeless message of

Sir Rabindranath Tagore that is inscribed above the doorway of a public building in India: "A teacher can never truly teach unless he is still learning himself. A lamp can never light another lamp unless it continues to burn its own flame."

FOCUS ON DIVERSITY: TEACHER AS A MODEL OF CROSS-CULTURAL COMPETENCE

In this chapter's Teachers Voices: Being an Agent of Change, George Watson discusses the role of teachers in a dynamic, global world. Teachers have a responsibility to prepare students to be successful in a global, interdependent economy, according to Watson. Toward that end, he and his colleagues are developing a global issues program at his school that would bring together a variety of high school courses organized around an international theme. In addition, Watson believes that teachers should develop students' appreciation for diverse cultures and the ability to communicate cross-culturally. For more than a decade, he has been "working/fighting" to have more foreign languages offered at the middle and elementary school levels. Watson models to students his own love of learning and the importance of cross-cultural competence—in addition to Spanish, he speaks French and has studied Italian and German. He is also studying Chinese and hopes to start an exchange program with China, in addition to the school's exchange programs with Costa Rica and France.

Teacher as a Spontaneous Problem Solver

In the classroom, teachers must respond to unpredictable events that are rapidly changing, multidimensional, and fragmented. Furthermore, "day in and day out, teachers spend much of their lives 'on stage' before audiences that are not always receptive. . . . Teachers must orchestrate a daunting array of interpersonal interactions and build a cohesive, positive climate for learning" (Gmelch & Parkay, 1995, p. 47).

When teachers are preparing to teach or reflecting on previous teaching, they can afford to be consistently deliberate and rational. Planning for lessons, grading papers, reflecting on the misbehavior of a student—such activities are usually done alone and lack the immediacy and sense of urgency that characterize interactive teaching. While working face-to-face with students, however, you must be able to think on your feet and respond appropriately to complex, ever-changing situations. You must be flexible and ready to deal with the unexpected. During a discussion, for example, you must operate on at least two levels. On one level, you respond appropriately to students' comments, monitor other students for signs of confusion or comprehension, formulate the next comment or question, and remain alert for signs of misbehavior. On another level, you ensure that participation is evenly distributed among students, evaluate the content and quality of students' contributions, keep the discussion focused and moving ahead, and emphasize major content areas. In the Teaching on Your Feet feature for this chapter, you can see how one teacher responded to several unpredictable events in the classroom.

During interactive teaching, the awareness that you are responsible for the forward movement of the group never lets up. Teachers are the only professionals who practice their craft almost exclusively under the direct, continuous gaze of up to 30 or 40 clients. To be watched closely in this manner is a one-of-a-kind experience, according to the author of *Life in Classrooms:* "The immediacy of classroom events is something that anyone who has ever been in charge of a roomful of students can never forget" (Jackson, 1990, p. 119).

Teacher as a Reflective Thinker

Teaching involves a unique mode of being between teacher and student—a mode of being that can be experienced but not fully defined or described. On your journey to become a teacher, you will gradually develop your capacity to listen to students and to convey an authentic sense of concern for their learning. Unfortunately, there is no precise, easy-to-follow formula for demonstrating this to students. You will have to take into account your personality and special gifts to discover your own best way for showing this concern.

TEACHERS' VOICES
Walk in My Shoes
"My students have given me reason, purpose, and triumph . . ."

Lincoln Johnson
Special Education
Mathematics Teacher
Locke Launch to College Academy Los Angeles, California

The above is excerpted from Johnson's article that appeared in *Teaching Tolerance*, Number 37, Spring 2010, p. 9. Used by permission of Teaching Tolerance, www.tolerance.org.

TEACHERS' VOICES ➡ BEING AN AGENT OF CHANGE

GEORGE WATSON

PREPARING "CITIZENS OF THE WORLD" WHO RESPECT CULTURAL DIFFERENCES

Buenos dias. I teach Spanish at Walpole High School in Walpole, **MASSACHUSETTS.** I am also the department head of foreign languages for grades 6 through 12. When I was a student many years ago, I really looked up to my teachers. I saw them as people who had devoted themselves to a very noble profession, and that belief has not changed. Teaching, along with parenting, is probably the most important job that any one individual can do in any society, in any culture, on any continent.

I teach because I believe that every child wants to learn, is able to learn, and must learn. Furthermore, I teach because I believe that every child should have access to foreign language education. And every child should have access no matter what their reading level, no matter what their learning style and, really, no matter what grade they are in.

Over the course of my career, I have had the privilege to give my students the skills to communicate effectively in a second language and to give them confidence to navigate in a foreign culture. And I've seen students who have had very difficult middle school years come to my ninth-grade freshman Spanish class and achieve success. I've seen students from both Walpole, Massachusetts, and Palmares, Costa Rica, participate in our exchange program and establish friendships and bonds that last for years and years. I've seen students who over the course of their 4 years in high school achieve incredible linguistic success and progress, so by the time that they are seniors in my AP class I know that they're going to be successful in college; I know that they are going to eventually participate in a global economy, which is more than just rewarding for me personally, it's nationally critical.

And last, it's wonderful for me as a teacher and a department head to celebrate the achievement of students—this is so very important; we just don't do this enough, I think, in public education. In Walpole, we have a very special foreign language awards night where we do just that, and we highlight not just what students have learned, but what students can do with the skills that we've provided them.

Yes, I am a teacher. I want to do my part to prepare my students to be citizens of the world, to be lifelong, self-confident learners, to be students who appreciate and respect cultural differences—those cultural differences that make our society and our world so fascinating and so very, very rich.

QUESTIONS

1. With respect to the subject area and grade level for which you are preparing to teach, how can you help students become "citizens of the world"?
2. After you become a teacher, what are some ways that you can demonstrate to students your own love of learning?

George Watson was Massachusetts Teacher of the Year for 2009.

One reason it is difficult to describe teaching is that an important domain of teaching, **teachers' thought processes** (including professional reflection and decision making), cannot be observed directly. Figure 2.2 shows how personal characteristics influence a teacher's thought processes while teaching. In addition, the unobservable domain of the teacher's reflection and decision making is influenced by the teacher's classroom experiences and curricular and instructional goals. Teachers' thought processes are influenced by many factors, including their theories and beliefs about students and how they learn. A teacher's thought processes and actions can be constrained by the physical setting of the classroom or external factors such as the curriculum, the principal, or the community. On the other hand, teachers' thought processes and actions may be influenced by unique opportunities, such as the chance to engage in curriculum reform or school governance. The model also suggests a further complexity of teaching—namely, that the relationships among teacher behavior, student behavior, and student achievement are reciprocal. What teachers do is influenced not only by their thought processes before, during, and after teaching but also by student behavior and student achievement. This complexity contributes to the uniqueness of the teaching experience.

In Internet blogs many teachers maintain, they frequently comment on how reflection has helped them become successful in the classroom. For example, Nicholas Provenzano, a high school English teacher and technology curriculum specialist for Grosse Pointe Public Schools in **MICHIGAN**, explained in a blog post how **reflection** helped him become a better teacher (Provenzano, September 26, 2013). In particular, reflection helped him identify changes he needed to make in his classroom practice.

Now a successful teacher and leader for his profession, Provenzano recognized early in his career that the hallmark of professionalism is the ability to reflect upon

TEACHING ON YOUR FEET
Opening the Gates to Empower Students

It is said that mathematics, and especially algebra, is the greatest of gatekeepers. Indeed, it is the subject that prevents most students from aspiring to higher education. I teach mathematics at a school that is mostly comprised of students of color (75 percent Hispanic, 8 percent African American). Here, roughly 50 to 60 percent of the students will manage to graduate within their four years. Furthermore, less than 20 percent of those who do graduate go on to pursue a 4-year college degree. Needless to say, as a teacher of Mexican descent, my teaching and the learning of mathematics is a personal endeavor.

A few years ago, I took my geometry class on an excursion throughout our campus. We were studying shapes and their angles. Students sketched and described the geometrical relationships of the school's buildings and their features. My objective for my students was to allow them to discover not only the usefulness of mathematics but its liberating power to those who can maneuver through it and make it their own. I wanted to empower them to move past academic barriers to a life with more choices. As my students scattered to explore and investigate the architectural geometry that is our school,

two boys asked me if they could simply go back to the classroom. They saw no point in the activity. They were bored.

Rather than have them meander back to our classroom and cause any disruptions, I asked them what is it that they saw besides a cluster of impersonal and inanimate objects such as buildings. They looked dumbfounded at my odd question. "What do you mean?" they asked me. "Look around you. Who is always cleaning the trash and filth that the students carelessly leave behind after lunch? And now think who is in the office making decisions about your education?" I did not have to say much after that. The point of my questions was clear to the boys as they saw men who looked like them cleaning the campus.

ANALYZE & REFLECT

Click here to analyze and reflect on this scenario you have just read.

SERGIO MORA
Montclair High School
Montclair, CALIFORNIA

FIGURE 2.2   Influences on a teacher's thought processes while teaching

one's experiences in the classroom. He learned that teaching is a complex act—one that requires thoughtfulness, insight into the motivations of others, and good judgment. Interviewed several times by the *New York Times* about his innovative use of technology in the classroom, Provenzano is also co-host of a talk show on the BAM! Radio Network that features leading education experts and advocates for quality education. He received the 2013 Technology Using Teacher of the Year Award from his state.

WHAT KNOWLEDGE AND SKILLS DO TODAY'S TEACHERS NEED?

Just as people hold different expectations for schools and teachers, there are different views of the knowledge and skills teachers need to teach well. In addition to being knowledgeable about the subjects they teach, teachers must have the ability to communicate, inspire trust and confidence, and motivate students, as well as understand their students' educational and emotional needs. Teachers must be able to recognize and respond to individual and cultural differences in students and employ different teaching methods that will result in higher student achievement. They should be organized, dependable, patient, and creative. Teachers must also be able to work cooperatively and communicate effectively with other teachers, support staff, parents, and members of the community.

To respond effectively to the complexities of teaching, you must have four kinds of knowledge: knowledge of yourself and your students, knowledge of subject, knowledge of educational theory and research, and knowledge of how to integrate technology into teaching. The following sections examine these four forms of essential knowledge.

Self-Knowledge

Effective teachers understand themselves and are sensitive to students' needs. "They recognize that the child's personality is a fragile work in progress" (Erickson, 2008, p. 225). Naturally, you should understand your students as much as possible. What is the connection, however, between self-knowledge and the ability to promote student learning? If you understand your own needs (and can satisfy those needs), you are in a better position to help students learn. A teacher's self-understanding and self-acceptance help students to know and accept themselves.

Your self-evaluations as a teacher are influenced by the feelings you may experience while teaching—feelings that may range from great joy and satisfaction to anxiety or loneliness. For example, teachers can experience anxiety when starting to use a new, more complex teaching strategy.

As a teacher, you will experience feelings of happiness, excitement, and wonder as a result of the time you spend with students. You may also experience occasional feelings of loneliness or isolation because most of your time will be spent with children and youth, not adults. Although teachers are behind the classroom door most of the day, today's teachers have more opportunities to collaborate with their colleagues, whether it be serving on a school improvement committee, developing new curricula, or mentoring new teachers.

Parents or guardians can be a teacher's greatest partners in determining the success of his or her students. What are some ways you can reach out to know your students' parents or guardians and gain their support?

Knowledge of Students

Without doubt, knowledge of your students is important. Student characteristics such as aptitudes, talents, learning styles, stages of development, and readiness to learn new material are among the essential knowledge you must have. The importance of this knowledge is evident in comments made by an intern at a middle school: "To teach a kid well you have to know a kid well. . . . Teaching middle school takes a special breed of teachers who understand the unique abilities and inabilities . . . [of] those undergoing their own metamorphosis into teenagers" (Henry, Huntley, McKamey, & Harper, 1995, pp. 124–125). An important part of your preparation for teaching involves learning about the diverse groups of students who comprise to-day's school population. In addition, after you become a teacher, you will expand your knowledge of students through additional study, observation, and interactions with students.

Knowledge of Subject

Teachers are assumed to have extensive knowledge. People who are not teachers expect a teacher to have knowledge far beyond their own. Without doubt, teachers who have extensive knowledge of their subjects are better equipped to help students learn.

However, knowledge of subject matter does not translate into an understanding of how to impart that knowledge to students—a point illustrated in a case study conducted by the National Center for Research on Teacher Learning. The case focused on "Mary," an undergraduate literature major enrolled in a teacher education program at a major university. By any standards, Mary was a subject-matter expert—she was valedictorian of a large, urban high school; had straight A's in the literature courses she had taken; and had a sophisticated understanding of literature, especially poetry. The case study revealed that Mary had little understanding of classroom activities that would show her students how to read with sophistication and concluded that "some prospective teachers may come to teacher education unaware of how they have learned the processes they use and that render them expert. Unaided by their disciplines in locating the underpinnings of their expertise, these skilled, talented, and desirable recruits may easily become, ironically, those who can do but who cannot teach" (Holt-Reynolds, 1999, p. 43).

Extensive knowledge of subject matter, as the National Board for Professional Teaching Standards (2002, pp. 10–11) puts it, "entails more than being able to recite lists of dates, multiplication tables, or rules of grammar. [Accomplished] teachers possess what is sometimes called '**pedagogical content knowledge**.' Such understanding is the joint product of wisdom about teaching, learning, students and content. It includes knowledge of the most appropriate ways to present the subject matter to students through analogies, metaphors, experiments, demonstrations and illustrations."

Knowledge of How to Use Educational Theory and Research

Theories about learners and learning will guide your decision making as a teacher. Not only will you know that a certain strategy works, you will also know why it works. Because you realize the importance of theories, you will have a greater range of available options for problem solving than teachers who do not have a repertoire of theories. Your ultimate goal as a professional is to learn how to apply theoretical knowledge to the practical problems of teaching.

Research on students' learning does not set forth, in cookbook fashion, exactly what you should do to increase students' learning. Instead, it may be helpful to think of educational research as providing you with "rules of thumb" to guide your practice, or, to recall a comment by noted educational psychologist Lee

Cronbach (quoted in Eisner, 1998, p. 112), "[educational research] is to help practitioners use their heads."

Educational researchers are still learning *what* good teachers know and *how* they use that knowledge. As a result, many people believe that a knowledge base for teaching should consist of not only what educational researchers have learned about teaching but also what teachers themselves know about teaching—often called teachers' craft knowledge or practitioner knowledge (Burney, 2004; Hiebert, Gallimore, & Stigler, 2002; Kennedy, 1999; Leinhardt, 1990). **Teachers' craft knowledge** is developed by teachers in response to specific problems of practice.

Knowledge of How to Integrate Technology into Teaching

As a teacher, you will be expected to know how to integrate technology into your teaching. And throughout your teaching career, you will be expected to be familiar with newly emerging technologies and how they can be used in the classroom. To increase your skills in using advanced technologies to enhance student learning, this chapter's Technology in Action feature focuses on e-portfolios. E-portfolios not only show the finished product, which could be a paper, artwork, project, musical score, and so on; they also highlight the process that the student engaged in and the stages the work went through to achieve the finished product.

Using technology to enhance students' learning requires more than knowing how to use the latest hardware and software. Conducting classroom demonstrations augmented with multimedia, using presentation graphics to address students' varied learning styles, and designing lessons that require students to use technology as a tool for inquiry should be second nature for teachers.

Reflection and Problem Solving

The preceding discussion of essential knowledge and skills for teaching highlights the fact that teaching is complex and demanding. As you use your knowledge and skills to meet the challenges of teaching, you will be guided by reflection and a **problem-solving orientation**. As Figure 2.3 shows, reflection and problem solving

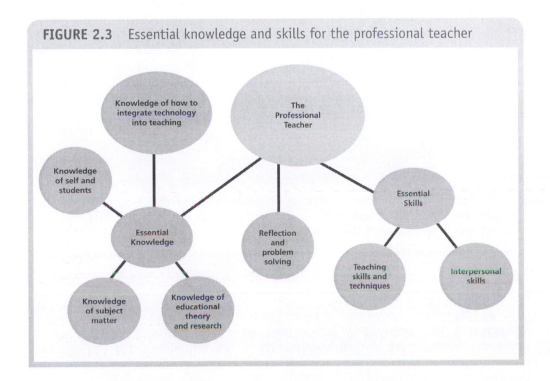

FIGURE 2.3   Essential knowledge and skills for the professional teacher

TECHNOLOGY in ACTION
E-Portfolios in 12th-Grade Industrial Arts

Bill Thompson has taught in the industrial arts automotive technology program for over a year. His students are diverse in terms of interest, gender, and ethnicity. However, they share pride in the work they do in Mr. Thompson's classes. He knows the importance of having his students do more than rebuild engines. They learn to problem solve; work in teams; and think critically about the possible effects of the decisions they make on safety, the environment, and personal finances. However, Mr. Thompson is bothered by the fact that the school and even some of his own students see his classes as for "gearheads" only. Mr. Thompson wants to show the school and his students that the outcomes of his program go beyond just building a neat car.

At lunch one day, he is talking with Mrs. Watson, the technology coordinator for the school, and she suggests that his students might enjoy creating an e-portfolio to share with others. She explains that an e-portfolio is an electronic portfolio of a student's work. Students could upload text, video, audio, and graphics of individual projects they work on and then share that site with other students in their class, the school at large, or even the community.

The next day, Mr. Thompson explains to his students that they will be required to develop an e-portfolio of their work during the school year. Students are to use the e-portfolio to document work, explain processes and decisions, show and discuss stages of work for each project, and provide a personal reflection statement about their group work. Outside his office, he sets up a computer workstation that uses a free e-portfolio website as a home page. He also provides a digital camera, a video camera, and a microphone.

During the school year, students develop their e-portfolios. Mr. Thompson shares some of the e-portfolios with his principal, who shares them with the school board. Some of his students even get summer jobs because they shared e-portfolios with prospective employers.

E-PORTFOLIO: An e-portfolio is an electronic collection of work. The purpose of an e-portfolio is not merely to show the finished product, which could be a paper, artwork, project, musical score, or other creation, but also to highlight the processes the student engaged in and the stages the work went through before becoming a finished product. Students use text, audio, visuals, and web links to describe what they have done. Some e-portfolios allow visitors to ask questions of the e-portfolio owner.

VISIT: To get an idea of how to use an e-portfolio, visit one of the free e-portfolio services available on the Internet. If you need more features and options, you can purchase additional services as well. At most e-portfolio websites, you can view sample e-portfolios.

POSSIBLE USES: The primary use of an e-portfolio is to document student work. This documentation can be used for college admission, for employment, and as a way to update parents on student work. Students can document their growth in writing performance; highlight various research projects they conducted; document their artistic expression with digital stills of their work; and then provide context with narrative text, audio/video, and supporting images and documents.

TRY IT OUT: Visit a website that offers free e-portfolio services for teachers and students. After creating an account, you will usually be directed to a page that asks for your e-mail address and personal information, and to accept the terms of agreement. Once completed, you will be asked for detailed information. Here, you will decide whom you would like to view your work—from private (no one can see it), to open access to everyone, and a few points in between. After you have completed your registration, you will be sent an e-mail that will ask you to verify your registration. Once you click on a link in the e-mail, you will be prompted to create a password, and from there you will be directed to your new e-portfolio page. Good luck!

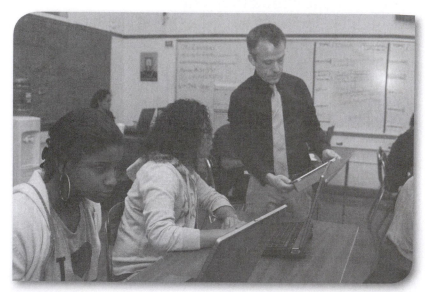

With a teacher's guidance, students can use a free e-portfolio service to upload text, video, audio, and graphics to a Web site that features examples of their work.

---

will enable you to determine how to use knowledge of self and students (including cultural differences), knowledge of subject matter, knowledge of educational theory and research, and knowledge of how to integrate technology into teaching to create optimum conditions for student learning. The figure also shows that you can use reflection and problem solving to decide which essential skills to use and how to use them.

TO WHAT EXTENT IS TEACHING A FULL PROFESSION?

People use the terms *professional* and *profession* quite frequently, usually without thinking about their meanings. Professionals "possess a high degree of specialized theoretical knowledge, along with methods and techniques for applying this knowledge in their day-to-day work. . . . [And they] are united by a high degree of in-group solidarity, stemming from their common training and common adherence to certain doctrines and methods" (Abrahamsson, 1971, pp. 11–12).

From several sociologists and educators who have studied teaching come additional characteristics of occupations that are highly professionalized; these characteristics are summarized in Figure 2.4. Before reading further, reflect on each characteristic and decide whether it applies to teaching. Then continue reading about the extent to which teaching satisfies each of these commonly agreed-upon characteristics of a full **profession**. Do my perceptions agree with yours?

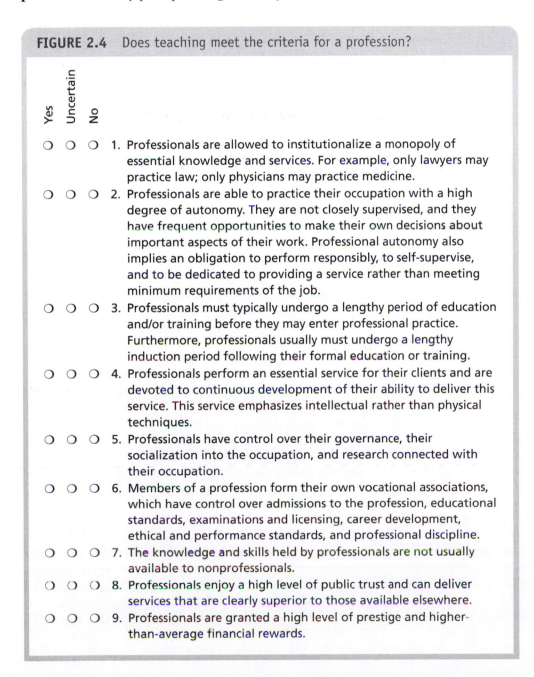

FIGURE 2.4   Does teaching meet the criteria for a profession?

Yes Uncertain No

1. Professionals are allowed to institutionalize a monopoly of essential knowledge and services. For example, only lawyers may practice law; only physicians may practice medicine.

2. Professionals are able to practice their occupation with a high degree of autonomy. They are not closely supervised, and they have frequent opportunities to make their own decisions about important aspects of their work. Professional autonomy also implies an obligation to perform responsibly, to self-supervise, and to be dedicated to providing a service rather than meeting minimum requirements of the job.

3. Professionals must typically undergo a lengthy period of education and/or training before they may enter professional practice. Furthermore, professionals usually must undergo a lengthy induction period following their formal education or training.

4. Professionals perform an essential service for their clients and are devoted to continuous development of their ability to deliver this service. This service emphasizes intellectual rather than physical techniques.

5. Professionals have control over their governance, their socialization into the occupation, and research connected with their occupation.

6. Members of a profession form their own vocational associations, which have control over admissions to the profession, educational standards, examinations and licensing, career development, ethical and performance standards, and professional discipline.

7. The knowledge and skills held by professionals are not usually available to nonprofessionals.

8. Professionals enjoy a high level of public trust and can deliver services that are clearly superior to those available elsewhere.

9. Professionals are granted a high level of prestige and higher-than-average financial rewards.

Institutional Monopoly of Services

On one hand, teachers do have a monopoly of services. As a rule, only those who are certified members of the profession may teach in public schools. On the other hand, varied requirements for certification and for teaching in private schools weaken this monopoly. (Although state certification and teacher education courses are generally not required to teach in private schools, a college degree is a minimum requirement.)

Any claim teachers might have as exclusive providers of a service is further eroded by the practice of many state systems to approve temporary or **emergency certification** measures (or waivers) to deal with teacher shortages. According to the U.S. Department of Education's *Eighth Report on Teacher Quality* (November 2011, p. 48), 1.4 percent of teachers were on waivers in 2008, with more teachers on waivers in high-poverty districts (2.0 percent) than in all other school districts (1.1 percent). Pointing out that "student access to qualified, competent and motivated teachers is critical," the Obama administration continued to support the goal of No Child Left Behind (NCLB) to have a "highly qualified teacher" (a teacher with "full state teacher certification") in every classroom. In addition, emergency certification is strongly resisted by professional teacher organizations and several state departments of education.

The widespread practice of out-of-field teaching also weakens teachers' monopoly of services. For example, the percentage of middle school classes taught by teachers with neither certification or a major in the subject taught is 42 percent. At the high school level, the figure is 17 percent. In high-poverty schools, the rate of out-of-field teachers is 27 percent, compared to about 14 percent in low-poverty schools (Education Trust, 2008). Thus, teaching is the only profession that allows noncertified individuals to practice the profession.

Perhaps the most significant argument against teachers claiming to be the exclusive providers of a service, however, is the fact that a great deal of teaching occurs in informal, nonschool settings and is done by people who are not teachers. Every day, thousands of people teach various kinds of how-to-do-it skills: how to water-ski, how to make dogs more obedient, how to make pasta from scratch, how to tune a car's engine, and how to meditate.

Teacher Autonomy

In one sense, teachers have considerable autonomy. Teachers usually work behind a closed classroom door, and seldom is their work observed by another adult. In fact, one of the norms among teachers is that the classroom is a castle of sorts, and teacher privacy a closely guarded right. Although the performance of new teachers may be observed and evaluated on a regular basis by supervisors, veteran teachers are observed much less frequently, and they usually enjoy a high degree of autonomy.

Teachers also have extensive freedom regarding how they structure the classroom environment. They may emphasize discussions as opposed to lectures. They may set certain requirements for some students and not for others. They may delegate responsibilities to one class and not another. And within the guidelines set by local and state authorities, teachers may determine much of the content they teach.

However, there are constraints placed on teachers and their work. Teachers, unlike doctors and lawyers, must accept all the "clients" who are sent to them. Only infrequently does a teacher actually reject a student assigned to him or her.

Teachers must also agree to teach what state and local officials say they must. And the work of teachers is subject to a higher level of public scrutiny than that found in other professions. Because the public provides "clients" (students) and pays for schools, it has a significant say regarding the work of teachers. Nevertheless, evidence suggests that the following prediction about "leveling" in the professions has become a reality: "More of the work of the traditional high-status professions, particularly medicine, will occur in bureaucratic or large organizational settings under the watchful eye of managers. [While] doctors are accepting more and more regulation, school teachers . . . will slowly break out of long-established bureaucratic hierarchies and share more of the autonomy previously enjoyed by members of the high-status professions" (Grant & Murray, 2002, pp. 231–232).

Years of Education and Training

As sociologist Amitai Etzioni (1969) points out in his classic discussion of the "semi-professions," the training of teachers is less lengthy than that required for other professionals, for example, lawyers and physicians. The professional component of teacher education programs is the shortest of all the professions—only 15 percent of the average bachelor's degree program for a high school teacher is devoted to professional courses. However, several colleges and universities have begun 5-year teacher education programs. Similarly, the National Commission on Teaching and America's Future recommended that teacher education be moved to the graduate level. If the trend toward 5-year and graduate-level teacher education programs continues, the professional status of teaching will definitely be enhanced.

In most professions, new members must undergo a prescribed induction period. Physicians, for example, must serve an internship or a residency before beginning practice, and most lawyers begin as clerks in law firms. In contrast, teachers usually do not go through a formal induction period before assuming full responsibility for their work. Practice teaching comes closest to serving as an induction period, but it is often relatively short, informal, and lacking in uniformity.

Until recently, induction into the profession of teaching has been minimal. Due to the "flat" career paths of teachers (a veteran of 30 years has essentially the same status as a beginner), experienced teachers may have devoted little effort to inducting beginning teachers into a professional culture or way of life. Today, however, increasing numbers of veteran teachers are helping new teachers "learn the ropes." Veteran teachers are helping new teachers identify with the profession, contribute to school-based learning communities, and assume leadership responsibilities.

Drawing from the career structure of other professions, the U.S. Department of Education has suggested a multistage career ladder for teaching (see Figure 2.5). The first stage would be that of a *Resident* teacher. For 1 year, a *Resident* teacher would work under a *Master* teacher's supervision. Unlike a practice teacher, a *Resident* might be paid about $20,000 during his or her residency. After a 1-year residency and demonstrating a minimum level of knowledge and skills for teaching, the *Resident* would be certified as a *Beginning* teacher. The *Beginning* teacher

FIGURE 2.5   A multi-stage career ladder for teachers

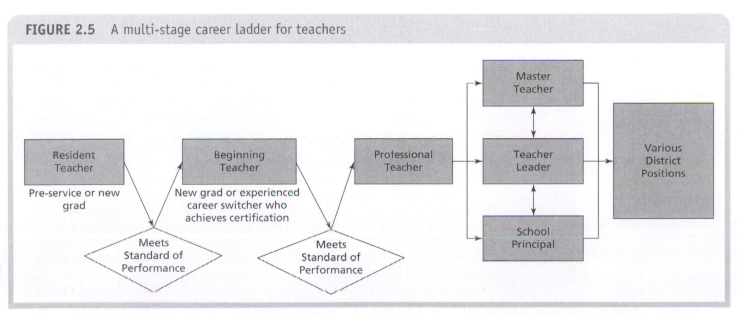

Source: U.S. Department of Education. (April 2013). *Blueprint for Recognizing Educational Success, Professional Excellence and Collaborative Teaching (RESPECT)*. Washington, DC, p. 24.

would have full teaching responsibilities and receive careful mentoring, nurturing, and evaluation by a *Master* teacher. After 2 to 5 years of successful teaching, a *Beginning* teacher might apply for promotion to *Professional* teacher. Promotion to *Professional* teacher would require consistent evidence of teaching effectiveness and might include the granting of tenure. *Beginning* teachers who do not meet the criteria for promotion to *Professional* teacher would not continue in the profession. *Professional* teachers might remain in this role for their entire careers, or they might choose to pursue various leadership roles.

A *Master* teacher is a "teacher of adults" and provides constructive feedback to *Resident* and *Beginning* teachers, while also serving as a key member of a school's leadership team. A *Master* teacher might spend half of each day teaching and the other half supporting his or her colleagues. Similarly, a *Teacher Leader* might teach part time and devote the remaining time to various leadership activities—for example, working with the principal and other members of the leadership team, directing a school-based research project, or developing an evaluation system for *Resident* and *Beginning* teachers.

Provision of Essential Service

Although it is generally acknowledged that teachers provide a service that is vital to the well-being of individuals and groups, the public does need to be reminded of this fact from time to time. This importance was driven home on a large scale during the early 1980s when reports such as *A Nation at Risk* linked the strength of our country to the quality of its schools, or more than 30 years later when NBC News hosted its fourth-annual weeklong "Education Nation Summit" during October 2013. The Summit stressed the connection between education and America's future and the need "to provide information to Americans so they can make decisions about how best to improve our education system both in the near and long terms, and to shine a spotlight on one of the most urgent national issues of our time" (NBC News, Education Nation, June 10, 2013).

The ability to function as the spark that stimulates young people to learn and grow can give teachers a sense of meaning and fulfillment they might not find in other professions. A foreign language teacher who immigrated to this country described for the author what many teachers feel about their profession: "I feel that I get satisfaction . . . that I am a useful member of the society. I feel this is the field in which . . . I can contribute more to society than in any other field. . . . I am doing a job which is good [for] the American society" (Parkay, 1983, pp. 114–115).

Degree of Self-Governance

Without doubt, if members of a profession feel empowered, they have higher morale. If they participate in decisions about job-related policies and if their expertise is acknowledged, they are more invested in their work. The limited freedom of teachers to govern themselves, however, has detracted from the overall status of the profession. In many states, licensing guidelines are set by government officials who may or may not be educators, and at the local level, decision-making power usually resides with local boards of education, largely made up of people who have not taught. As a result, teachers have had little say over what they teach, when they teach, whom they teach, and—in extreme instances—how they teach.

However, efforts to empower teachers and to professionalize teaching are creating new roles for teachers and expanded opportunities to govern important aspects of their work. At schools throughout the country, teachers are developing leadership skills and playing a greater role in decisions related to curriculum development, staffing, budget, and the day-to-day operation of schools. For example, Figure 2.6 shows that teachers play a significant role in selecting and hiring new teachers at their schools.

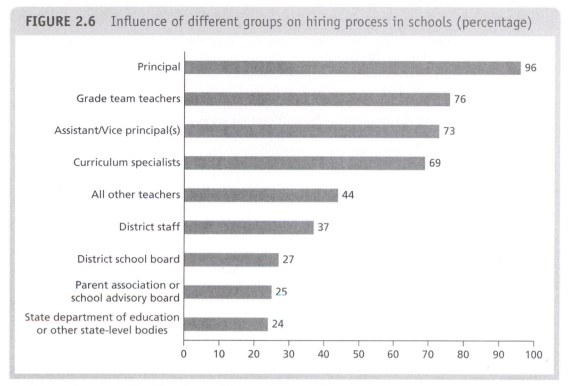

FIGURE 2.6 Influence of different groups on hiring process in schools (percentage)

Note: The survey item was worded as follows: "How much influence does each of the groups or individuals listed below have on the process of selecting and hiring new full-time classroom teachers at your school?" For each group or individual, principals could choose "Major Influence," "Moderate Influence," "Minor Influence," or "No Influence/NA." Groups or individuals were considered to influence the hiring process if the principal indicated that they had moderate or major influence. Responses are from both elementary and middle school principals.

Adapted from Glazerman, S. A. Protik, B. Teh, J. Bruch, N. Seftor, N. (2012). *Moving High-Performing Teachers: Implementation of Transfer Incentives in Seven Districts* (NCEE 2012-4051). Washington, DC: National Center for Education Evaluation and Regional Assistance, Institute of Education Sciences, U.S. Department of Education, p. 39.

Although teachers differ significantly in the amount of influence they believe teachers have, teachers should experience greater self-governance as principals respond to increasing pressure to become more effective at facilitating collaborative, emergent approaches to leadership. Increasingly, principals realize that "leadership in instructional matters should emerge freely from both principals and teachers. After all, teachers deliver the instruction in the classroom; they have expertise in curriculum and teaching, and they have mastered a substantive body of knowledge" (Hoy & Hoy, 2013, p. 2).

Professional Knowledge and Skills

Professionals are granted a certain status because they possess knowledge and skills not normally held by the general public. Within the profession of teaching, however, the requirements for membership are less precise. In spite of the ongoing efforts of educational researchers, there is less-than-unanimous agreement on the knowledge and skills considered necessary to teach. This lack of agreement is reflected in the varied programs at the 1,300 or so colleges and universities that train teachers.

Since it was established in 1987, the National Board for Professional Teaching Standards (NBPTS) has made significant progress toward clarifying the knowledge base for teaching and enhancing the status of the profession. The NBPTS (the majority of whose members are teachers) offers board certification to teachers who possess a high level of NBPTS-identified knowledge and skills. Similar to board-certified physicians and accountants, Board Certified teachers have demonstrated mastery of rigorous standards through intensive study, self-assessment, peer review, and evaluation by

PROFESSIONAL REFLECTION
Watch a teacher reflect on professional development.

panels of experts. To date, the NBPTS has granted national certification to more than 100,000 individuals (NBPTS, January 8, 2013).

According to the president of NBPTS, "Teachers who become National Board Certified are highly effective and strengthen student achievement. They demonstrate the powerful impact that accomplished teachers have daily in their classrooms" (NBPTS, January 8, 2013).

In addition, Board Certified teachers frequently have a positive impact beyond the classroom. For example, a Board Certified science teacher was appointed to the Distinguished Educators Council (DEC) in **OREGON**. He and other teachers on the DEC conducted research on effective educational practices and presented a set of recommendations to legislators at the state capital in Salem. Several of their recommendations were reflected in bills that eventually became law (NBPTS, October 18, 2013).

Trust in the Teaching Profession

Although all professions have some members who might be described as unprofessional and not worthy of the public's trust, teaching is especially vulnerable to such charges. The sheer size of the teaching force makes it difficult to maintain consistently high professional standards. Moreover, teaching is subject to a level of public scrutiny and control that other, more established professions traditionally have not tolerated. However, the era of widespread public trust may be running out for these other professions as well. The mushrooming number of malpractice suits against doctors, for example, may be a sign that here, too, public confidence has significantly eroded. Table 2.2 shows that the public considers teachers to be highly trustworthy.

Prestige, Benefits, and Pay

Although "many teachers and school administrators . . . are thought to be of a more elite social class than the majority of the population in the United States" (Parker & Shapiro, 1993, p. 42), this higher status is based on level of education attained rather than wealth. Thus, teachers have not received salaries in keeping with other professions requiring approximately the same amount of schooling. Nevertheless, there is significant support for reducing the salary gap. For example, the U.S. Department of Education (April 2013) proposed the following salary structure for teachers:

> . . . starting salaries for fully licensed professional teachers should be $60,000–65,000, adjusted as appropriate to the cost of living in different regions. Additionally, salaries would increase faster than they do today, and maximum salaries would be higher, so that Master teachers and other teacher-leaders would have the ability to earn as much as $120,000–150,000 after about 7–10 years. Principals would earn comparable salaries. Whereas today's compensation tends to be linked solely to years of service or professional credentials, under this new vision, salary would reflect the quality of a teacher's work, his or her effectiveness helping students to grow academically, and the scope of the teacher's responsibility. (p. 23)

Professional Associations

Like other professionals, teachers have formed vocational associations that focus on issues such as admission to the profession, educational standards, examinations and licensing, career development, ethical and performance standards, and professional discipline. It is clear, though, that national teacher organizations have not progressed as far as other professions have in gaining control of these areas.

TABLE 2.2 Whom would you generally trust?
"Would you generally trust each of the following types of people to tell the truth, or not?"

	Would Trust (%)	Would Not (%)	Not Sure/Refused (%)
Doctors	85	12	3
Teachers	83	15	2
Scientists	77	19	4
Police officers	76	21	3
Professors	75	19	6
Clergy or priests	74	22	4
Military officers	72	26	3
Judges	70	24	5
Accountants	68	28	3
Ordinary man or woman	66	26	8
Civil servants	62	32	6
Bankers	62	34	3
The president	48	47	4
TV newscasters	44	51	5
Athletes	43	47	10
Journalists	39	58	3
Members of Congress	35	63	3
Pollsters	34	54	12
Trade union leaders	30	60	10
Stockbrokers	29	63	8
Lawyers	27	68	5
Actors	26	69	5

Source: The Harris Poll® #61, August 8, 2006. Based on telephone interviews of 1,002 U.S. adults, July 10–16, 2006.

TO WHAT PROFESSIONAL ORGANIZATIONS DO TEACHERS BELONG?

The expanding leadership role of teachers has been supported through the activities of more than 500 national teacher organizations (*National Trade and Professional Associations of the United States,* 2013). These organizations and the scores of hardworking teachers who run them support a variety of activities to improve teaching and schools. Through lobbying in Washington and at state capitols, for example, teacher associations acquaint legislators, policymakers, and politicians with critical issues and problems in the teaching profession. Many associations have staffs of teachers, researchers, and consultants who produce professional publications, hold conferences, prepare grant proposals, engage in school improvement activities, and promote a positive

Listen to a teacher discuss effective collaboration.

image of teaching to the public. Two national organizations have led the quest to improve the professional lives of all teachers: the National Education Association (NEA) and the American Federation of Teachers (AFT). These two groups have had a long history of competition for the allegiance of teachers.

The National Education Association

Membership in the **National Education Association (NEA)**, the oldest and largest of the two organizations, includes both teachers and administrators. Originally called the National Teachers Association when it was founded in 1857, the group was started by 43 educators from a dozen states and the District of Columbia (Laurence, 2000).

The NEA has affiliates in every state plus Puerto Rico and the District of Columbia, and its local affiliates number more than 14,000. About two-thirds of the teachers in this country belong to the NEA. More than 78 percent of NEA's 3.2 million members are teachers; about 12 percent are guidance counselors, librarians, and administrators; almost 3 percent are university professors; about 2 percent are college and university students; about 3 percent are support staff (teacher aides, secretaries, cafeteria workers, bus drivers, and custodians); and about 2 percent are retired members (NEA, 2013).

To improve education in this country, the NEA has standing committees in the following areas: affiliate relationships, higher education, human relations, political action, teacher benefits, and teacher rights. These committees engage in a wide range of activities, among them preparing reports on important educational issues, disseminating the results of educational research, conducting conferences, working with federal agencies on behalf of children, pressing for more rigorous standards for the teaching profession, helping school districts resolve salary disputes, developing ways to improve personnel practices, and enhancing the relationship between the profession and the public.

Currently, more than two-thirds of states have passed some type of collective bargaining laws that apply to teachers. There is little uniformity among these laws, with most of the 31 states permitting strikes only if certain conditions have been met. The NEA has gone on record as supporting a federal statute that would set up uniform procedures for teachers to bargain with their employers.

The NEA continues today to focus on issues of concern to teachers, primarily in the area of professional governance. Efforts are being made to broaden teachers' decision-making powers related to curriculum, extracurricular responsibilities, staff development, and supervision. To promote the status of the profession, the NEA conducts annual research studies and opinion surveys in various areas, and publishes *NEA Today* and *Tomorrow's Teachers* for NEA student members.

The American Federation of Teachers

The **American Federation of Teachers (AFT)** was founded in 1916. Three teachers' unions in Chicago issued a call for teachers to form a national organization affiliated with organized labor. Teacher unions in Gary, Indiana; New York City; Oklahoma; Scranton, Pennsylvania; and Washington, D.C., joined the three Chicago unions to form the AFT.

The AFT differs from the NEA because it is open only to teachers and non-supervisory school personnel. The AFT is active today in organizing teachers, bargaining collectively, fostering public relations, and developing policies related to various educational issues. In addition, the organization conducts research in areas such as educational reform, bilingual education, teacher certification, and evaluation, and also represents members' concerns through legislative action and technical assistance.

The AFT has more than 1.5 million members who are organized through 43 state affiliates and more than 3,000 local affiliates (AFT, 2013). The AFT is affiliated with the American Federation of Labor–Congress of Industrial Organizations (AFL-CIO), which has over 13 million members. To promote the idea that teachers should have the right to speak for themselves on important issues, the AFT does not allow superintendents, principals, and other administrators to join. As an informational brochure on the AFT states, "Because the AFT believes in action—in 'getting things done' rather than issuing reports, letting someone else do the 'doing'—a powerful, cohesive structure is necessary."

Unlike the NEA, the AFT has been steadfastly involved throughout its history in securing economic gains and improving working conditions for teachers. Although the AFT has been criticized for being unprofessional and too concerned with bread-and-butter issues, none other than the great educator and philosopher John Dewey took out the first AFT membership card in 1916. After 12 years as a union member, Dewey (1955) made his stance on economic issues clear:

> It is said that the Teachers Union, as distinct from the more academic organizations, overemphasizes the economic aspect of teaching. Well, I never had that contempt for the economic aspect of teaching, especially not on the first of the month when I get my salary check. I find that teachers have to pay their grocery and meat bills and house rent just the same as everybody else. (pp. 60–61)

Traditionally, the AFT has been strongest in urban areas. Today, the AFT represents teachers not only in Chicago and New York but in Philadelphia; Washington, D.C.; Kansas City; Detroit; Boston; Cleveland; and Pittsburgh. NEA membership has tended to be suburban and rural. The NEA has always been the larger of the two organizations, and it is presently more than twice the size of its rival.

The NEAFT Partnership

For decades, many people within both the NEA and the AFT believed that the interests of teachers and students could best be served through a merger of the two organizations. One national teachers' union with enormous political strength, they believed, could do more to advance the teaching profession than two independent, often competing organizations. Until the turn of the century, however, differences between the two organizations thwarted periodic efforts to merge.

By the end of the 1990s, differences between the NEA and the AFT had become less apparent. Collective bargaining and the use of strikes, long opposed by the NEA, were now used by both organizations. Eventually, a "conceptual agreement" to merge the organizations was announced in 1998 by the presidents of the NEA and the AFT. The presidents cited an "assault" on public education in the form of voucher plans, charter schools, and other approaches to school privatization as a primary reason to merge (Bradley, 1998). In 2001, NEA and AFT Unity Discussion Teams and Advisory Committees forged the **NEAFT Partnership** and endorsed the following goals:

> **Building Relationships**—to increase knowledge, promote trust and collaboration and involve leaders and affiliates in both our unions at the national, state and local levels.
>
> **Making Collaboration Work**—to more effectively use our combined resources to focus on promoting the welfare of children, public education and our members.
>
> **Creating Value**—from the power of our collaboration to strengthen our ability to resist the challenges by the enemies of public education and collective bargaining.
>
> **Demonstrating Visibly**—our united strength and ability to improve the institutions in which our members work and further signal our commitment to public education and unionism. (NEAFT Partnership, 2002)

The NEA and AFT found additional common ground in their opposition to No Child Left Behind (NCLB). Both organizations maintained that the law was seriously flawed. In particular, NEAFT believed the NCLB's requirement that schools make adequate yearly progress (AYP) was harmful to public schools. NEAFT believed that NCLB did not give enough credit for schools that made academic progress but failed to reach NCLB's AYP standards. NEAFT is also working with other education associations to develop alternatives to what it views as punitive high-stakes testing programs. NEAFT supports high-stakes tests aligned with standards as one, but not the only, tool in student and school assessment. Currently, NEA state affiliates have merged with their AFT counterparts in Florida, Minnesota, Montana, and New York. As their attention focuses increasingly on issues of mutual concern, NEA and AFT groups in other states are considering similar mergers.

Other Professional Organizations

In addition to the NEA and AFT, teachers' professional interests are represented by more than 500 other national organizations. Several of these are concerned with improving the quality of education at all levels and in all subject areas. **Phi Delta Kappa (PDK)**, for example, is an international professional and honorary fraternity of educators concerned with enhancing quality education through research and leadership activities. Founded in 1906, Phi Delta Kappa has a membership of about 35,000. Members, who are graduate students, teachers, and administrators, belong to one of 250 chapters. To be initiated into Phi Delta Kappa, one must have demonstrated high academic achievement, have completed at least 15 semester hours of graduate work in education, and have made a commitment to a career of educational service. Phi Delta Kappa members receive *Phi Delta Kappan*, a journal of education published 10 times a year.

Another example is **ASCD** (formerly, the Association for Supervision and Curriculum Development), a professional organization of teachers, supervisors, curriculum coordinators, education professors, administrators, and others. ASCD is interested in school improvement at all levels of education. Founded in 1943, the association has a membership of about 170,000. ASCD provides professional development experiences in curriculum and supervision; disseminates information on educational issues; and encourages research, evaluation, and theory development. ASCD also conducts several National Curriculum Study Institutes around the country each year and provides a free research information service to members. Members receive *Educational Leadership*, a well-respected journal published eight times a year. ASCD also publishes a yearbook, with each edition devoted to a particular educational issue, and occasional books in the area of curriculum and supervision.

Many professional associations exist for teachers of specific subject areas, such as mathematics, English, social studies, music, physical education, and so on, as well as for teachers of specific student populations, such as exceptional learners, young children, and students with limited English proficiency.

HOW ARE TEACHER LEADERS TRANSFORMING THE PROFESSION OF TEACHING?

Teaching is changing in dramatic and exciting ways. Steadily, the **professionalization of teaching** is taking place in the United States. National board certification, state-sponsored teacher networks, shared decision making, peer review, teacher-mentor programs, and the growing influence of teacher researchers are among the changes that are providing unprecedented opportunities for teachers to assume leadership roles beyond the classroom. Along with these new opportunities for leadership, teaching as a profession is developing greater political influence and acquiring higher status in the public's eye. As a **NORTH CAROLINA** teacher told *The RESPECT Project: A National Conversation About the Teaching Profession* organized by the U.S. Department of Education: "It is time for sweeping changes to education" (U.S. Department of Education, April 2013, p. 1). Similarly, a **NEW MEXICO** teacher told the Project, "The time is ripe for teachers to reclaim our ideas and change our profession" (p. iv).

Perhaps the most dramatic change in teaching is how school administration is becoming more collaborative and participatory—throughout the nation, teachers are playing a key role in school governance. For example, in *Blueprint for Recognizing Educational Success, Professional Excellence and Collaborative Teaching* (RESPECT), the U.S. Department of Education identified shared, distributed leadership as a key element for the transformation of teaching:

> A culture of shared responsibility requires principals who bring together coalitions of teacher-leaders who have the skills to meet the school's objectives and create a culture of continuous learning and shared decision-making. Teams of teacher-leaders and principals work in partnerships to identify challenges, propose solutions, and share in distributed leadership and decision-making at all levels, including hiring, structuring the school day and school year, and designing professional learning (U.S. Department of Education, April 2013, p. 21).

Critical Components for Transforming Teaching

During 2012, more than 6,000 teachers presented their ideas for transforming teaching at more than 360 roundtables across the United States. These ideas were then analyzed at the conference on "Collaborating to Transform the Teaching Profession," held by the U.S. Department of Education, the National Education Association, the American Federation of Teachers, and five other national professional organizations. The conference identified the following seven "critical components" for transforming teaching, each based on teacher input:

1. **A Culture of Shared Responsibility and Leadership:** Teachers and principals together make the primary decisions about educator selection, assignment, evaluation, dismissal, and career advancement.
2. **Top Talent, Prepared for Success:** Aspiring educators must [demonstrate] strong knowledge in the content they teach; have mastered a repertoire of instructional strategies and know when to use each appropriately.
3. **Continuous Growth and Professional Development:** Effective teachers and principals are career-long learners.
4. **Effective Teachers and Principals:** Effective educators have high standards of professional practice and demonstrate their ability to improve student learning.
5. **A Professional Career Continuum with Competitive Compensation:** Educators [need] career pathways that provide opportunities for increasingly responsible roles, whether they choose to stay in the classroom, become instructional leaders or move into administration. And these roles must be coupled with compensation that is high enough to attract and retain a highly skilled workforce.
6. **Conditions for Successful Teaching and Learning:** School and district climates and cultures, use of time, approaches to staffing, use of technology, deployment of support services, and engagement of families and communities are optimized to continuously improve outcomes for the students they serve.
7. **Engaged Communities:** No school can be a strong pillar of a thriving community without deep community responsibility for and ownership of the school's academic success. (U.S. Department of Education, April 2013, pp. 5–8)

SUMMARY

Who Are Today's Teachers?

- Teachers teach in schools with different grade configurations, they teach in different subject-matter and specialized areas, and they teach students with different types of learning needs.
- Today's teachers are better educated and more qualified than ever.
- In addition to teachers who work in pre-K, elementary, middle, and high school programs, some teachers teach in nontraditional school settings, such as private schools, charter schools, alternative schools, and magnet schools.
- Some teachers teach in specialized areas such as art, vocational education, music, or physical education. Special education teachers specialize in teaching students with disabilities and/or special needs. Many teachers, whether they have specialized training or not, teach students whose first language

is not English (often called English language learners [ELLs]).

What Do Teachers *Do* in the Classroom?

- What teachers do goes beyond observable behaviors; the effective teacher understands that, simultaneously, he or she must be a role model for students, a spontaneous problem solver, and a reflective thinker.

What Knowledge and Skills Do Today's Teachers Need?

- Teachers need four kinds of knowledge: knowledge of self and students, knowledge of subject, knowledge of educational theory and research, and knowledge of how to integrate technology into teaching.
- Self-knowledge influences your ability to understand your students; ongoing reflection and a problem-solving orientation continue to guide your instruction.
- Teachers must know their students' aptitudes, talents, learning styles, stages of development, and readiness to learn new material so they can modify instructional strategies based on students' needs.
- Knowledge of educational theory and research enables teachers to know why certain strategies work and offers general guidelines for practice.
- Teachers also use craft knowledge, what they know about teaching as a result of reflecting on their classroom experiences.

To What Extent Is Teaching a Full Profession?

- Of the following nine criteria for a profession, teaching meets some more fully than others: (1) institutional monopoly of services; (2) teacher autonomy; (3) years of education and training; (4) provision of essential service; (5) degree of self-governance; (6) professional associations; (7) professional knowledge and skills; (8) level of public trust; and (9) prestige, benefits, and pay.
- A multistage career ladder for teaching proposed by the U.S. Department of Education consists of the following roles: *Resident* teacher, *Beginning* teacher, *Professional* teacher, *Master* teacher, and *Teacher Leader.*

To What Professional Organizations Do Teachers Belong?

- As the oldest and largest professional organization for educators, the National Education Association (NEA) has played a key role in addressing issues of concern to the 78 percent of its members who are teachers.
- Affiliated with organized labor and open only to teachers and nonsupervisory personnel, the American Federation of Teachers (AFT) has done much to secure greater financial rewards and improved working conditions for teachers.
- The NEA and AFT formed the NEAFT Partnership to work toward shared goals for improving the profession of teaching.
- Teachers are members of professional associations for specific subject areas and student populations.

How Are Teacher Leaders Transforming the Profession of Teaching?

- Today's teachers have unprecedented opportunities to assume leadership roles beyond the classroom.
- Teachers' ideas for transforming the profession of teaching were analyzed at the conference on "Collaborating to Transform the Teaching Profession," held by the U.S. Department of Education, the National Education Association, the American Federation of Teachers, and five other national professional organizations.
- Seven "critical components" of a transformed education profession are as follows: A Culture of Shared Responsibility and Leadership; Top Talent, Prepared for Success; Continuous Growth and Professional Development; Effective Teachers and Principals; A Professional Career Continuum with Competitive Compensation; Conditions for Successful Teaching; and Learning, and Engaged Communities.

PROFESSIONAL REFLECTIONS AND ACTIVITIES

Teacher's Journal

1. Do you plan to join a professional organization for teachers, such as the NEA, AFT, Phi Delta Kappa, or ASCD? What are your reasons? What advantages and disadvantages of joining are most important to you?
2. Regarding the grade level and subject area for which you are preparing to teach, what do you find most appealing, and why? What do you find least appealing, and why?

Teacher's Research

1. On the Internet, use your favorite search engine to search for information by keywords or topics such as *teachers' working conditions, teacher accountability,* and *teacher professional development.* Report your findings to the rest of your class.
2. Review several recent issues of the NEA publication *NEA Today,* and the AFT publication *American Teacher.* Compare and contrast concerns or issues that each publication addresses. What overall differences do you find between the NEA and AFT publications?

Observations and Interviews

1. Interview a few adults who are not involved in education to get their views on teaching as a

profession. What image do these adults have of teaching? What are their suggestions for improving the profession?

2. Interview a teacher about the knowledge and skills he or she thinks teachers must have. Which of the knowledge and skills discussed in this chapter does the teacher mention? Does he or she mention knowledge and skills not discussed in this chapter? If so, explain.

Professional Portfolio

Get on the Internet and begin to gather materials from teacher organizations that are relevant to the grade level and subject area for which you are preparing to teach. The following is a partial list of professional organizations. For information about these and other professional associations, see the *Encyclopedia of Associations: National Organizations of the U.S., 53rd Edition.* (Gale, 2014).

- American Alliance for Health, Physical Education, Recreation and Dance (AAHPERD)
- American Alliance of Teachers of French (AATF)
- American Association of Teachers of German (AATG)
- American Association of Teachers of Spanish and Portuguese (Hispanic) (AATSP)
- American Classical League (Language) (ACL)
- American Council on the Teaching of Foreign Languages (ACTFL)
- Council for Exceptional Children (CEC)
- Foundation for Exceptional Children (FEC)
- International Reading Association (IRA)
- Music Teachers National Association (MTNA)
- National Art Education Association (NAEA)
- National Association for Bilingual Education (Bilingualism) (NABE)
- National Association of Biology Teachers (NABT)
- National Association for the Education of Young Children (NAEYC)
- National Association for Gifted Children (NAGC)
- National Association for Trade and Industrial Education (NATIE)
- National Business Education Association (NBEA)
- National Council for the Social Studies (NCSS)
- National Council of Teachers of English (NCTE)
- National Council of Teachers of Mathematics (NCTM)
- National Middle School Association (NMSA)
- National Science Teachers Association (NSTA)
- Speech Communication Association (SCA)
- Teachers of English to Speakers of Other Languages (TESOL)

CHAPTER QUIZ

Take this quiz to check your understanding of the content covered in this chapter.

CHAPTER THREE
Today's Schools

learning outcomes

After reading this chapter, you will be able to do the following:

1. Explain the role of schools in today's society.
2. Explain how schools can be described.
3. Explain how schools function as social institutions.
4. Describe the characteristics of successful schools.
5. Identify and discuss social problems that affect schools and place students at risk.
6. Describe how schools are addressing societal problems.
7. Explain how community-based partnerships can help students learn.

What is the role of schools in today's society?

The role of today's schools is to prepare students for life in the 21st Century. At their schools, students acquire the knowledge and skills needed to live in an increasingly complex and competitive world.

—SHAWNDRA, Teacher Education program, first year

Schools do not exist in a vacuum. Schools must respond to the changing expectations of students, parents, teachers, communities, and the public at large. As the following section shows, today's schools have a complex, multifaceted role in today's society.

WHAT IS THE ROLE OF SCHOOLS IN TODAY'S SOCIETY?

Among the different perspectives on the role of schooling in U.S. society, the achievement of academic goals is the most universally agreed upon. Most people believe that the primary purpose of schools is to provide students with the academic knowledge and skills needed for schooling beyond high school or for the world of work. Philosophical, political, religious, and cultural beliefs and ideologies aside, people believe that schools should teach academic content; however, disagreement exists regarding the overall *purpose* for learning academic content.

Some people believe that the primary purpose of learning should be to promote the personal growth and development of students. Others, such as the leading policymakers, elected officials, educators, business CEOs, and community leaders featured in the NBC News Education Nation Summit during 2013 believe that the primary purpose of schooling is to ensure the success of the United States in a global economy and to prepare students for jobs of the future. For example, the theme of the 2013 Summit focused on "'What It Takes' for us as a nation, to ensure students are successfully prepared for college, career and beyond" (NBC News, Education Nation, October 1, 2013). President Barack Obama made the same point in his introduction to the *Blueprint for Reform: The Reauthorization of the Elementary and Secondary Education Act:*

> Today, more than ever, a world-class education is a prerequisite for success. America was once the best educated nation in the world. A generation ago, we led all nations in college completion, but today, 10 countries have passed us. It is not that their students are smarter than ours. It is that these countries are being smarter about how to educate their students. And the countries that out-educate us today will out-compete us tomorrow. (U.S. Department of Education, March 2010, p. 1)

TECHNOLOGY in ACTION
Using Video-Editing Software in Sixth Grade

A study skills unit has been a mainstay of Rachael Yelmin's sixth-grade language arts class for years. When her students enter middle school from elementary school, they seem to struggle to keep up with the pace of middle school. Two years ago, she experimented with a new way to teach study skills. Instead of telling her students about the things they need to do to be successful in middle school—like time management, social responsibility, reading for comprehension, and so on—she decided to let them tell her.

Ms. Yelmin now divides her students into groups of four and asks each group to create a high-definition video for fifth-grade students that highlights the study skills necessary to be successful in middle school. Each group checks out a video camera and accesses a free video-editing software program online. They are also given a DVD on which to burn their video.

The project begins with each group writing a storyboard for their video. At this point, students conduct research, select topics, and decide on their video sequence. This stage allows students to make important development decisions (with Ms. Yelmin's help) prior to the actual shooting and editing of their videos. After the storyboard is written, students perform in front of the camera, take video of important locations in the school, interview students and staff, develop graphics, select music, and write text. Then they edit the raw footage using the video-editing software program.

When the project is complete, Ms. Yelmin sends DVDs of the completed videos to fifth-grade classrooms at schools in the community. Ms. Yelmin has found that students who create a study skills video retain the study skills information much better than students to whom she merely lectures about study skills. She has also found that her incoming students (the fifth-graders who watch the videos created by "upperclassmen") have a good foundation from which to begin their middle school years.

VIDEO EDITING: Several free and open-source video-editing software programs are available on the Internet. A few sites allow you to compare video-editing options and features. You need a computer, a video source (such as a camera or already-captured video), enough hard drive space on which to store the raw video, video-editing software, and creativity.

POSSIBLE USES: Teachers use edited video in many ways. They use video to present information to students, create virtual field trips to historical sites, create compilations of student work, and allow students to submit research reports in video format—to name a few.

TRY IT OUT: Go online and locate the video-editing software program you want to use. After installing the program, upload your video clip(s). You can attach your video camera and upload from it, or you can import an already-captured video clip. Once you have your clip(s) in your workspace, you can begin editing. Here, you can add music, background textures, transition affects, titles, and so on. When you have finished your editing work, save your video. You can now showcase your masterpiece in your classroom, on the web, or through e-mail.

Schools and Prosocial Values

Although debate continues about the primary purpose of schooling in the United States, the public does agree that schools should teach **prosocial values** such as honesty, patriotism, fairness, and civility. The well-being of any society requires support of such values; they enable people from diverse backgrounds to live together peacefully. For example, U.S. Department of Education provides the following advice in response to a parent or guardian who wants to know "What can I do to help my child to develop good values and to learn right from wrong?"

> We want our children to develop respect and compassion for others. We want them to be honest, decent and thoughtful—to stand up for their principles, to cooperate with others and to act responsibly. We want them to make sound moral choices. The payoffs for encouraging a child's values are enormous: those who grow up with strong, consistent and positive values are happier, do better in school and are more likely to contribute to society (U.S. Department of Education, December 3, 2013).

Support for prosocial values reflects the public's belief that schools should play a key role in promoting the democratic ideal of equality for all. As President George W. Bush stated when he announced the No Child Left Behind Act three days after taking office in January 2001, "[I have a] deep belief in our public schools and their mission to build the mind and character of every child, from every background, in every part of America" (U.S. Department of Education, January 2001). The Technology in Action feature for this chapter explains how teachers can use video editing to teach students the importance of study skills and social responsibility.

Schools and Socialization of the Young

Through their experiences in schools, children and youth become socialized—they learn to participate responsibly in our nation's society. The goal of socializing students is evident in countless local schools whose mission statements focus on preparing students for responsible citizenship, further learning, and productive employment in our nation's economy. In effect, schools reflect or mirror society; they reproduce the knowledge, skills, values, and attitudes that society has identified as essential.

Education is the primary means of producing enlightened citizens. Without such a citizenry to hold it together, a society, especially a democratic society, is at risk. The need for each nation to socialize its children and youth was recognized by Emile Durkheim (1858–1917), the great French sociologist and philosopher, when he stated in *Education and Sociology* that "society can survive only if there exists among its members a significant degree of homogeneity; education perpetuates and reinforces this homogeneity by fixing in the child, from the beginning, the essential similarities collective life demands" (Durkheim, 1956, p. 70).

More than any other institution in our society, schools also assimilate persons from different ethnic, racial, religious, linguistic, and cultural backgrounds and pass on the values and customs of the majority. For example, one in every five students today speaks a language other than English at home, and nearly one-fourth of these students have difficulty speaking English (Aud et al., 2013). Through the schools, children and youth from such diverse backgrounds learn English and learn about the importance of U.S. holidays such as the Fourth of July and Memorial Day; the contributions of Thomas Jefferson, Abraham Lincoln, and Dr. Martin Luther King Jr.; and the importance of citizenship in a democracy.

Schools and Social Change

Schools also provide students with the knowledge and skills to improve society and to adapt to rapid social change. Thus, "education and social change [are] inextricably tied to one another" (Rury, 2002, p. ix). Not everyone agrees, however, that schools *should* attempt to improve society—as one observer of education in the United States noted: "The school continues to be used in efforts to solve social, political, and economic problems. It is easier for politicians to blame schools for social and economic problems than to try to directly correct these problems. . . . 'Reform the individual rather than society' is the message of those who trust the school to end crime, poverty, broken families, drug and alcohol abuse, and myriad other social problems" (Spring, 2008b, p. 32).

Less controversial have been service-learning activities that prepare students to serve others through volunteerism and to participate actively in the political life of the nation. During the late 1990s, some high schools began to require that every student complete a service requirement to help students understand that they are members of a larger community to which they are accountable. The Service-Learning Initiative of the Chicago Public Schools, the third largest school system in the United States, currently requires that each high school choose one of the following options as a requirement for graduation:

- One classroom-integrated service-learning project + 25 individual service hours
- Two classroom-integrated service-learning projects + 15 individual service hours
- Three classroom-integrated service-learning projects (Chicago Public Schools, 2013)

Service learning provides students with opportunities to deliver service to their communities while engaging in reflection and study on the meaning of those experiences. Service learning brings young people into contact with the elderly, the sick, the poor, and the homeless, and it acquaints them with neighborhood and governmental issues.

FOCUS ON DIVERSITY: SCHOOLS AND EQUAL EDUCATIONAL OPPORTUNITY

Ample evidence exists that certain groups in U.S. society are denied equality of opportunity economically, socially, and educationally. For example, if we look at the percentage of children 3 to 4 years old who participate in early childhood programs such as Head Start, nursery school, and prekindergarten—experiences that help children from less advantaged backgrounds start elementary school on an equal footing with other children—we find that children from lower-income families are less likely to have such opportunities (Aud et al., 2013). In addition, there is a positive relationship between parents' educational attainment and their children's enrollment in early childhood programs; also, Latino children are less likely to be enrolled than White or African American children (Aud et. al., 2013).

The United States has always derived strength from the diversity of its people, and all students should receive a quality education so that they may make their unique contributions to society. To reach this goal, extensive programs at the federal, state, and local levels have been developed to provide equity for all in the United States—regardless of race, ethnicity, language, gender, sexual orientation, or religion. For example, the *Blueprint for Reform: The Reauthorization of the Elementary and Secondary Education Act* states:

> Schools must support all students, including by providing appropriate instruction and access to a challenging curriculum along with additional supports and attention where needed. From English Learners and students with disabilities to Native American students, homeless students, migrant students, rural students, and neglected or delinquent students, [we must] support and strengthen programs for these students and ensure that schools are helping them meet college- and career-ready standards.
>
> To give every student a fair chance to succeed, and give principals and teachers the resources to support student success, we will call on school districts and states to take steps to ensure equity, by such means as moving toward comparability in resources between high- and low-poverty schools. (U.S. Department of Education, March 2010, p. 5)

The goal of providing equal educational opportunity for all has long distinguished education in the United States from that found in most other countries. Since the 1850s, schools in the United States have been particularly concerned with providing children from diverse backgrounds with the education they need to succeed in our society. As James Banks (2014, p. 6) suggests, "Education within a pluralistic society should affirm and help students understand their home and community cultures. [To] create and maintain a civic community that works for the common good, education in a democratic society should help students acquire the knowledge, attitudes, and skills needed to participate in civic action to make society more equitable and just."

HOW CAN SCHOOLS BE DESCRIBED?

Given the wide variation in schools and their cultures, many models have been proposed for describing the distinguishing characteristics of schools. Schools can be categorized according to the focus of their curricula; for example, high schools may be college prep, vocational, or general. Another way to view schools is according to their organizational structure, for example, alternative schools, charter schools, or magnet schools. Other models, such as those addressed in the following section, view schools metaphorically; that is, what is a school like?

Metaphors for Schools

Some schools have been compared to factories; students enter the school as raw material, move through the curriculum in a systematic way, and exit the school as finished products. Terrence Deal and Kent Peterson (2009, p. 31) have suggested that exemplary schools "offer, like tribes and clans, deep ties among people, and the values and traditions that give meaning to everyday life." Others have suggested that schools are like banks, gardens, prisons, mental hospitals, homes, churches, families, and teams.

In the school-as-family metaphor, for example, the effective school is a caring community of adults who attend to the academic, emotional, and social needs of the children and youth entrusted to their care. In schools that have a family-like atmosphere, students realize that teachers care about them. They know that teachers teach not only content; they help students solve problems, plan for the future, and live up to their potential.

FOCUS ON DIVERSITY: SCHOOLS AND SOCIAL CLASS

In spite of a general consensus that schools should promote social change and equal opportunity, some individuals believe that schools "reproduce" the existing society by presenting different curricula and educational experiences to students from different socioeconomic classes. Students at a school in an affluent suburb, for example, may study chemistry in a well-equipped lab and take a field trip to a high-tech industry to see the latest application of chemical research, whereas students at a school in an impoverished inner-city neighborhood learn chemistry from out-of-date texts, have no lab in which to conduct experiments, and take no field trips because the school district has no funds.

In effect, schools preserve the stratification within society and maintain the differences between the haves and the have-nots. As Joel Spring (2008b, p. 75) explains: "[T]he economic level of the family determines educational attainment. Children from low-income families do not attain so high a level of education as children from rich families. From this standpoint the school reinforces social stratification and contributes to intergenerational immobility." Moreover, rich families can afford to live in affluent school districts or send their children to private schools. This, in turn, increases the chances that their children will attend the "best" colleges and universities and ultimately maintain or increase the family's social-class status.

In addition, children from lower-income families tend to develop "restricted" language patterns with their use of English, whereas children from more affluent backgrounds tend to develop more "elaborated" language patterns (Bernstein, 1996; Heath, 1983). In many cases, children from lower-income families encounter a mismatch between the language patterns used in the home and those they are expected to use in school. This mismatch can be "a serious stumbling block for working class and nonwhite pupils" (MacLeod, 1995, p. 18). Therefore, it is important for teachers to understand the different types of knowledge students bring with them into the classroom and how this knowledge can conflict with the norms and values of schools and teachers.

FOUR TYPES OF SCHOOLS

A useful way to talk about the relationship between schooling and social class in the United States is suggested by the four categories of schools that Jean Anyon (1996) described in her study of several elementary schools in urban and suburban **NEW JERSEY**. Anyon maintains that schools "reproduce" the existing society by presenting different curricula and educational experiences to students from different socioeconomic classes. As a result of their experiences at school, students are prepared for particular roles in the dominant society.

The first kind of school she calls the *working-class school*. In this school, the primary emphasis is on having students follow directions as they work at rote, mechanical activities such as completing mimeographed worksheets. Students are given little opportunity to exercise their initiative or to make choices. Teachers may make negative, disparaging comments about students' abilities and, through subtle and not-so-subtle means, convey low expectations to students. Additionally, teachers at working-class schools may spend much of their time focusing on classroom management, dealing with absenteeism, and keeping extensive records.

The *middle-class school* is the second type identified by Anyon. Here, teachers emphasize to students the importance of getting right answers, usually in the form of words, sentences, numbers, or facts and dates. Students have slightly more opportunity to make decisions, but not much. Most lessons are textbook-based. Anyon points out that "while the teachers spend a lot of time explaining and expanding on what the textbooks say, there is little attempt to analyze how or why things happen. . . . On the occasions when creativity or self-expression is requested, it is peripheral to the main activity or it is 'enrichment' or 'for fun'" (Anyon, 1996, p. 191).

Unlike the previous two types of schools, the *affluent professional school* gives students the opportunity to express their individuality and to make a variety of choices. Fewer rules govern the behavior of students in affluent professional schools, and teacher and students are likely to negotiate about the work the students will do.

Anyon provides the following definition of the fourth type of school she identified, the *executive elite school:*

> In the executive elite school, work is developing one's analytical intellectual powers. Children are continually asked to reason through a problem, to produce intellectual products that are both logically sound and of top academic quality. (Anyon, 1996, p. 196)

In the affluent professional and executive elite schools, teacher–student relationships are more positive than those in the working-class and middle-class schools. Teachers are polite to their students, seldom give direct orders, and almost never make sarcastic or nasty remarks.

In applying Anyon's categories to schools in the United States, keep in mind that few schools are one type exclusively and that few schools actually fit the categories in all ways. Instead, most schools probably contain individual classrooms that represent all four types. Also, it is possible for one type of school to exist within a school of another type—for example, an advanced-placement program (essentially an affluent professional or executive elite school) within an urban working-class school.

Also keep in mind that Anyon studied a small group of schools in one metropolitan area, and her criteria are linked almost exclusively to socioeconomic status. There are many schools in poor urban areas, for example, whose culture is more like the affluent professional school Anyon describes than the working-class school, and vice versa. Nevertheless, regardless of how schools in the United States are categorized, it seems they do reflect the socioeconomic status of the communities they serve.

WHAT ARE SCHOOLS LIKE AS SOCIAL INSTITUTIONS?

Schools are social institutions. An institution is an organization established by society to maintain and improve its way of life. Schools are the institutions our society has established for the purpose of educating the young. For the last 200 years, schools in the United States have developed complex structures, policies, and curricula to accomplish this mission.

The School as a Reflection of Society

As the first part of this chapter has pointed out, schools mirror the national culture and the surrounding local culture and other special interests. Private, parochial, and religious schools, for example, are often maintained by groups that see the school as a means of perpetuating their preferred way of life. Schools also reflect their location. As Durkheim (1956, p. 68) observed: "do we not see education vary with . . . locality? That of the city is not that of the country." As the following sections illustrate, schools in rural, urban, and suburban settings often have significantly different cultures.

RURAL SCHOOL SETTINGS

Rural schools are often the focal point for community life and reflect values and beliefs that tend to be more conservative than those associated with urban and suburban schools. While the small size of a rural school may contribute to the development of a family-like culture, its small size may also make it difficult to provide students with an array of curricular experiences equal to that found at larger schools in more populated areas. In contrast, large suburban or urban schools may provide students with more varied learning experiences, but these schools may lack the cohesiveness and community focus of rural schools.

URBAN AND SUBURBAN SCHOOL ENVIRONMENTS

The differences among the environments that surround schools can be enormous. Urban schools found in or near decaying centers of large cities often reflect the social problems of the surrounding area, such as drug abuse, crime, and poverty. One of the most serious problems confronting education in the United States is the quality of such schools. Across the country—in Chicago, New York, Los Angeles, St. Louis, Detroit, and Cleveland—middle-class families who can afford to do so move away from urban centers or place their children in private schools. As a result, students in urban school districts are increasingly from low-income backgrounds.

In what ways do schools reflect their communities and the wider U.S. society? How might the surrounding neighborhood influence this school? The students who attend it? The teachers who work there?

In *Shame of the Nation*, Jonathan Kozol (2005) documents the startling contrast between the neighborhoods that surround impoverished inner-city schools and those that surround affluent suburban schools. He also examines the significant discrepancy between per-pupil spending for students at the two types of schools. For example, during 2002–2003, per-pupil funding for the Highland Park/Deerfield, **ILLINOIS**, School District, an affluent suburb north of Chicago, was $17,291. Ninety percent of students in the district were White or "other," and 10 percent were Black and Hispanic. On the other hand, per-pupil funding for Chicago Public Schools was $8,482. In Chicago, 87 percent of students were Black and Hispanic, and 18 percent were White or "other" (Kozol, 2005, p. 321).

In Kozol's earlier book, *Savage Inequalities*, he compares New Trier High School in affluent Winnetka, Illinois, and Chicago's DuSable High School, an inner-city school at which the author of this text taught for 8 years. Kozol (1991) points out that New Trier is in a neighborhood of "circular driveways, chirping birds and white-columned homes" (p. 62). In contrast, DuSable's surroundings are "almost indescribably despairing"; across the street from the school is "a line of uniform and ugly 16-story buildings, the Robert Taylor Homes, which constitute . . . the city's second-poorest neighborhood" (1991, pp. 68, 71).

FOCUS ON DIVERSITY: OVERCOMING THE EFFECTS OF POVERTY

As my description of Du Sable in *White Teacher, Black School* suggests, the extreme poverty found in some communities can affect schools in undesirable ways:

> The largest housing project in the world, Robert Taylor Homes overshadowed Du Sable High School both physically and spiritually . . . . In many buildings of the project, children outnumbered adults three to one. Gang violence was a way of life . . . (1983, p. 4).

In spite of grim conditions surrounding the school, many Du Sable teachers made students feel "rich" in ways that went beyond material wealth. Two teachers share how they saw students not as living in poverty, but as young people whom they could help to realize their full potential.

We get along very well. I don't have any discipline problems . . . . I don't really pat them on the back too much, but underneath I'm really proud of them, and I think they feel this (pp. 102-103).

I have confidence in my students, and I feel that the students have confidence in me. I have, I don't know why, a certain kind of idealistic view toward the young generation (p. 111).

And, three Du Sable students comment on how caring, supportive teachers help them learn:

I feel that this teacher has helped me a lot. He is not as impersonal as some of the teachers in our school, and he makes learning very enjoyable (p. 107).

I feel very relaxed in class. She doesn't front you off or get smart with you like other teachers often do. She tries to help you with your problems if there's some reason why you can't make it on time (p. 108).

She is a really nice and down-to-earth person, and I like her a lot. She is my favorite teacher this year and is very nice to talk to. She is also very warm, understanding, and considerate toward her students. I like her method teaching very much. I also have to say I learn a lot out of her class the short time I've been there (p. 108).

TEACHERS' VOICES
Walk in My Shoes
"I hold the potential to change a child's life."
Cheryl Beene
Center Hill High School,
Olive Branch, Mississippi

Another teacher similar to those who positively influenced the above three students is Cheryl Beene, who is featured in this chapter's Teachers' Voices: Walk in My Shoes. Beene is a family and consumer sciences teacher at Center Hill High School in Olive Branch, **MISSISSIPPI**. Beene, certified by the National Board for Professional Teaching Standards, was selected Mississippi Teacher of the Year for 2008. She has had numerous leadership roles in professional organizations, and she was state president of the Mississippi Association of Teachers of Family and Consumer Sciences. The phrase "It takes a village to raise a child" inspires her, and she believes that "Teachers represent one of the strongest links in that wonderful village."

The Culture of the School

Although schools are very much alike, each school is unique. Each has a culture of its own—a network of beliefs, values and traditions, and ways of thinking and behaving that distinguishes it from other schools.

Much like a community, a school has a distinctive culture—a collective way of life. Terms that have been used to describe **school culture** include *climate*, *ethos*, *atmosphere*, and *character*. Some schools may be characterized as community-like places where there is a shared sense of purpose and commitment to providing the best education possible for all students. Other schools lack a unified sense of purpose or direction and drift, rudderless, from year to year. Still others are characterized by internal conflict and divisiveness and may even reflect what Deal and Peterson (2009) term a "toxic" school culture; students, teachers, administrators, and parents may feel that the school is not sufficiently meeting their needs.

Schools with a community-like culture are characterized by open, two-way communication between teachers and administrators. Teachers feel free to make suggestions to the school's leadership team; and, in turn, teachers welcome feedback from members of the leadership team. In contrast, schools that have a negative or "toxic" culture are often characterized by low teacher morale and high teacher turnover. Such schools frequently have a succession of new principals.

The following sections discuss three dimensions of schools that have a significant influence on a school's culture: the physical environment, formal practices, and traditions.

THE PHYSICAL ENVIRONMENT

The physical environment of the school both reflects and helps to create the school's overall culture. "Whether school buildings are squeezed between other buildings or located on sprawling campuses, their fenced-in area or other physical separation distinguishes them from the community-at-large" (Ballantine, 1997, p. 210). Some schools are dreary places or, at best, aesthetically bland. The tile floors; concrete block walls; long, straight corridors; and rows of fluorescent lights often found in these schools contribute little to their inhabitants' sense of beauty, concern for others, or personal comfort.

Other schools are much more attractive. They are clean, pleasant, and inviting, and teachers and students take pride in their building. Overall, the physical environment has a positive impact on those who spend time in the school; it encourages learning and a spirit of cohesiveness.

PROFESSIONAL REFLECTION
Watch how educators help meet students' needs through the School Health Advisory Council grant.

FORMAL PRACTICES OF SCHOOLS

The formal practices of schools are well known to anyone who has been educated in U.S. schools. With few exceptions, students attend school from 5 or 6 years of age through 16 at least, and usually to 18, Monday through Friday, September through May, for 12 years. For the most part, students are assigned to a grade level on the basis of age rather than ability or interest. Assignment to individual classes or teachers at a given grade level, however, may be made on the basis of ability or interest.

The **self-contained classroom** is the most traditional and prevalent arrangement in elementary through secondary schools. In open-space schools, however, students are free to move among various activities and learning centers. Instead of self-contained classrooms, **open-space schools** have large instructional areas with movable walls and furniture that can be rearranged easily. Grouping for instruction is much more fluid and varied. Students do much of their work independently, with a number of teachers providing individual guidance as needed.

In middle schools and junior and senior high schools, students typically study four or five academic subjects taught by teachers who specialize in them. In this organizational arrangement, called **departmentalization**, students move from classroom to classroom for their lessons. High school teachers often share their classrooms with other teachers and use their rooms only during scheduled class periods.

SCHOOL TRADITIONS

School traditions are those elements of a school's culture that are handed down from year to year. The traditions of a school reflect what students, teachers, administrators, parents, and the surrounding community members believe is important and valuable about the school. One school, for example, may have developed a tradition of excellence in academic programs; another school's traditions may emphasize the performing arts; and yet another may focus on athletic programs. Whatever a school's traditions, they are usually a source of pride for members of the school community.

Ideally, traditions are the glue that holds together the diverse elements of a school's culture. They combine to create a sense of community, identity, and trust among people affiliated with a school. Traditions are maintained through stories that are handed down, rituals and ceremonial activities, student productions, and trophies and artifacts that have been collected over the years. For example, Joan Vydra, formerly principal of Briar Glen Elementary School in Wheaton, **ILLINOIS**, initiated Care Week as part of the fall tradition at her former school, Hawthorne Elementary. Vydra believed that a tradition of care would nurture student success. On the first day of Care Week, students learned the importance of caring for themselves; on Tuesdays, caring for their families; on Wednesdays, caring for each other; on Thursdays, caring for the school; and on Fridays, caring for those served by local charities (Deal & Peterson, 2009, p. 139).

The Culture of the Classroom

Just as schools develop their unique cultures, each classroom develops its own culture or way of life. **Classroom culture** is determined in large measure by the manner in which teachers and students interact and participate in common activities.

These students are participating in the culture of their school. What other behaviors, formal practices, and school traditions are probably part of their school culture?

The quality of teacher–student interactions is influenced by the physical characteristics of the setting (classroom, use of space, materials, resources, etc.) and the social dimensions of the group (norms, rules, expectations, cohesiveness, distribution of power and influence). These elements interact to shape classroom culture. Teachers who appreciate the importance of these salient elements of classroom culture are more likely to create environments that they and their students find satisfying and growth-promoting.

Students believe that effective teachers develop positive, task-oriented classroom cultures, whereas ineffective teachers develop negative cultures. One inner-city school, for example, provides an illustration of these two very different classroom cultures:

> [Sixth-grade] students saw their social studies/language arts teacher as someone they could learn from and relate to well, while they seemed to constantly do battle with their math and science teacher. Students portrayed [the math and science teacher] as overdemanding, impatient, and insensitive; [the social studies/language arts teacher] seemed to be just the opposite. [The math and science teacher], according to one student, "has an attitude problem. She wants us to be so good the first time. She wants us to always be perfect. She has us walk in a line in the hallway. We are the only class in the school to do that. . . . She is the only [teacher] who won't go over things. She never comes in with a smile; she is always evil. By not going over it, we got a bad attitude. I haven't learned nothing in her class." (Wilson & Corbett, 2001, pp. 54–55)

Clearly, the math and science teacher has developed an adversarial, counterproductive relationship with students. The social studies/language arts teacher, on the other hand, recognizes the importance of developing positive relationships with students and understands how such relationships pave the way for student learning.

WHAT ARE THE CHARACTERISTICS OF SUCCESSFUL SCHOOLS?

You may be uncertain at this point in your professional education of your ability to develop a positive classroom climate at a school. However, a great many schools in all settings and with all kinds of students are highly successful, including inner-city and isolated rural schools and schools that serve pupils of all socioeconomic, racial, and ethnic backgrounds. What are the characteristics of these schools? Do they have commonalities that account for their success?

Measures of Success

First, we must define what we mean by a *successful school*. One measure of success, naturally, is that students at these schools achieve at a high level and complete requirements for graduation. Whether reflected in scores on standardized tests or other documentation of academic learning gains, students at these schools are learning. They are achieving literacy in reading, writing, computation, and computer skills. They are learning to solve problems, think creatively and analytically, and, most important, they are learning to learn.

Another valid measure of success for a school is that it achieves results that surpass those expected from comparable schools in comparable settings. The achievement of students goes beyond what one would expect. In spite of surrounding social, economic, and political forces that impede the educative process at other schools, these schools are achieving results.

Finally, successful schools are those that are improving, rather than getting worse. School improvement is a slow process, and schools that are improving—moving in the right direction rather than declining—are also successful.

Research on School Effectiveness and School Improvement

During the 1980s and early 1990s, much research was conducted to identify the characteristics of successful (or effective) schools. The characteristics of successful schools were described in different ways in several research projects. The following is a synthesis of those findings.

- **Strong leadership**—Successful schools have strong leaders—individuals who value education and see themselves as educational leaders, not just as managers or bureaucrats. They monitor the performance of everyone at the school—teachers, staff, students, and themselves. These leaders have a vision of the school as a more effective learning environment, and they take decisive steps to bring that about.
- **High expectations**—Teachers at successful schools have high expectations of students. These teachers believe that all students, rich or poor, can learn, and they communicate this to students through realistic yet high expectations.
- **Emphasis on basic skills**—Teachers at successful schools emphasize student achievement in the basic skills of reading, writing, and mathematical computation.
- **Orderly school environment**—The environments of successful schools are orderly, safe, and conducive to learning. Discipline problems are at a minimum, and teachers can devote greater amounts of time to teaching.
- **Frequent, systematic evaluation of student learning**—The learning of students in successful schools is monitored closely. When difficulties crop up, appropriate remediation is provided quickly.
- **Sense of purpose**—Those who teach and those who learn at successful schools have a strong sense of purpose. From the principal to the students, everyone at the school is guided by a vision of excellence.
- **Collegiality and a sense of community**—Teachers, administrators, and staff at successful schools work well together. They are dedicated to creating an environment that promotes not only student learning but also their own professional growth and development.

Since the 1990s, researchers have focused, increasingly, on the characteristics of schools that improve over time. A key finding of **school improvement research** is that teachers must play a significant role in providing leadership for the improvement process. In other words, "If real reform is to occur, classroom teachers must be active in defining its objectives, design, implementation, and assessment. Reform as a product handed down to teachers must be redesigned to be a process in which teachers are vital contributors" (Armstrong, 2008, p. 142).

Schools that are improving are made up of collaborative teams of teachers, school administrators, and other stakeholders who are committed to working together to increase student learning. Teacher leadership teams; parent and community representation on school councils; and open, two-way communication with all stakeholders are examples of shared leadership. In short, the culture of a school that is improving encourages teachers to grow and to develop in the practice of their profession. It encourages them to develop knowledge and skills to respond to social problems such as those described in the following sections.

WHAT SOCIAL PROBLEMS AFFECT SCHOOLS AND PLACE STUDENTS AT RISK?

A complex and varied array of social issues affects schools. These problems often detract from the ability of schools to educate students. Furthermore, schools are often charged with the difficult (if not impossible) task of providing a frontline defense against such problems. Nevertheless, effective teachers understand how social issues influence student learning, and they are able to reduce the negative impact of those issues.

One of the most vocal advocates of the role of schools in solving social problems was George S. Counts, who said in his 1932 book *Dare the School Build a New Social Order?* that "if schools are to be really effective, they must become centers for the building, and not merely the contemplation, of our civilization" (Counts, 1932, p. 12). Many people, however, believe that schools should not try to build a new social order. They should be concerned only with the academic and social development of students—not with solving society's problems. Nevertheless, the debate over the role of schools with regard to social problems will continue to be vigorous. The following sections examine several societal problems that directly influence schools, teachers, and students.

Identifying Students at Risk

Increasing numbers of young people live under conditions characterized by extreme stress, chronic poverty, crime, and lack of adult guidance. For example, a few days after a gunman fatally shot 20 children and 6 adults at Sandy Hook Elementary School in Newton, Connecticut, on December 14, 2012, James Garbarino, author of Lost Boys: Why Our Sons Turn Violent and How We Can Save Them (1999) suggested that some youth have developed a "war zone mentality." This view, according to Garbarino, can lead a disturbed young person to imagine that their world is filled with "enemies" who, ultimately, must be destroyed. In addition, Garbarino believes that American culture desensitizes some youth to violence. The easy availability of guns and the popularity of video games in which the player shoots and kills others, he maintains, can lead some youth to think that violence is a justified way of achieving their version of justice in a dangerous world (Garbarino, 2012).

Frustrated, lonely, and feeling powerless, many youth escape into music with violence-oriented and/or obscene lyrics, violent video games, cults, movies and television programs that celebrate gratuitous violence and sex, and cruising shopping malls or hanging out on the street. Others turn also to crime, gang violence, promiscuous sex, or substance abuse. Not surprisingly, these activities place many young people at risk of academic failure and eventually dropping out of school.

Many children in the United States live in families that help them grow up healthy, confident, and skilled, but many do not. Instead, their life settings are characterized by problems of alcoholism or other substance abuse, family or gang violence, unemployment, poverty, poor nutrition, teenage parenthood, and a history of school failure. Such children live in communities and families that have many problems and frequently become dysfunctional, unable to provide their children with the support and guidance they need. According to the *2013 Kids Count Data Book,* "the number of low-income children continues to increase, and the gap between their well-being and that of their middleclass and affluent peers continues to widen . . . because children in low-income households often experience multiple risks—for example, living in poverty, having a single parent, and lacking access to quality early care and education programs and well-resourced public schools" (Annie E. Casey Foundation, 2013, p. 7).

It is important to remember that at-risk factors are only an indication of *potential* academic problems. The majority of children and youth who live in environments affected by poverty, crime, and other social problems are academically successful.

FOCUS ON DIVERSITY: AMERICA'S DROPOUT PROBLEM

Every school day, about 7,000 students decide to drop out of school—a total of more than 1.2 million students each year—and only about 70 percent of entering high school freshman graduate every year (White House Press Release, March 1, 2010). Grouped by gender, race, ethnicity, family income, age, and region, students drop out of school at varying rates. Table 3.1, for example, shows that the dropout rate for Hispanic students in 2012 was higher than the rates for other groups. Also, African American students dropped out of school more frequently than their White peers. The data also reveal high dropout rates for students who are foreign born or have foreign-born parents. Students at risk of dropping out tend to get low grades, perform below grade level academically, are older than the average student at their grade level because of previous retention, and have behavior problems in school. **Students at risk** need teachers who can recognize

TABLE 3.1 Dropout Rates,[1] and number and percentage distribution of Dropouts Ages 16 to 24, by selected characteristics: October 2012

	Dropout rate (percent)	Number of dropouts (thousands)	Percent of all dropouts	Percent of population
Total	6.6	2,563	100.0	100.0
Gender				
Male	7.3	1,427	55.7	50.4
Female	5.9	1,134	44.2	49.6
Age				
16–17	2.9	243	9.5	21.7
18–19	7.1	605	23.6	21.9
20–21	6.6	584	22.8	22.9
22–24	8.7	1,131	44.1	33.6
Race/Hispanic Origin[2]				
White, non-Hispanic	4.3	931	36.3	55.9
Black	8.6	516	20.1	15.4
Hispanic	12.7	1,039	40.5	21.1
Asian	3.0	59	2.3	5.1
Immigration status				
Foreign-Born	15.5	581	22.7	9.6
Children of Foreign-Born Parents	9.3	927	36.2	25.6
Children of Native-Born Parents	4.2	1,055	41.2	64.7

[1] This indicator uses the status dropout rate, which measures the percentage of young adults aged 16 to 24 who were not enrolled in a high school program and had not received a high school diploma or obtained an equivalency certificate.

[2] Due to relatively small sample sizes, American Indians/Alaskan Natives are included in the total but not shown separately. Hispanics may be of any race.

Note: Percentages may not add up to 100.0 due to rounding. Details may not add to totals due to rounding.

Source: Child Trends' calculations of U.S. Census Bureau, School Enrollment—Social and Economic Characteristics of Students: October 2012: Detailed Tables: Table 1. http://www.census.gov/hhes/school/data/cps/index.html. Child Trends Data Bank (September 2013). *High School Dropout Rates,* p. 9.

opportunities in the classroom to build up their confidence as learners, as Cynthia Gibson illustrates in the Teaching on Your Feet feature for this chapter.

Many youth take more than the typical 4 years to complete high school, or they eventually earn a high school graduate equivalency diploma (GED). If these alternative routes to high school completion are considered, however, there are still significant differences among racial/ethnic groups. For example, U.S. Census Bureau data indicate that 88.9 percent of Asians 25 years and over have completed high school, compared to 88.1 percent of Whites, 85.0 percent of African Americans, and 65.0 percent of Hispanics (U.S. Census Bureau, December 2013).

The life experiences of students who are at risk of dropping out can be difficult for teachers to imagine. Encountering the realities of poverty for the first time can be upsetting. For students living in poverty, lunch at school may be the main meal of the day. For several days in a row, they may wear the same clothes to school. At home, they may not have paper, pencils, crayons, or scissors to complete homework assignments. Day in and day out, it may be hard for teachers to witness how poverty can prevent a child from living up to his or her potential.

TEACHING ON YOUR FEET
Lies Our Students Tell Themselves

"I'm too poor and too black."

That's what one student told me not long after I started teaching here in Selma, Alabama. He didn't beat around the bush, and I wasn't just reading some subtle message into his behavior. He said it plainly—that he was "too poor and too black" to make it in this world.

I hear statements like that from my students far too often. They have opened my eyes to the battle I face every day. As teachers, each time we step into the classroom we vow to fight the lies that hold our students down.

I've been immersed in the culture of Selma for the past 15 months. The world knows Selma as a focal point of the civil rights movement. Presidents and presidents-to-be have come here to commemorate the city's role in the struggle for equal voting rights.

Despite the city's prominence in the public eye, progress in Selma is slow. This racially and economically divided town exemplifies the need for change, the need for social justice, and the need for healing.

I teach in a rural, all-Black school just outside of town. My students are hopeful yet disillusioned, free yet held down, youthful yet already grown. Many live at or below the national poverty line, have faced racial struggles, and can relate to at least one of Langston Hughes's deferred dreams. On the way to work I pass a golf course, one that even in the year 2008 is closed to Blacks, and therefore to all of my students.

Yet it's not so much the racist minority in the community that disturbs me. What disturbs me is the mindset I see in many of my students who—subtly—seem to believe that they are inferior, that their life options are limited, that they are unworthy of their own hopes and dreams. Statements like "too poor and too black" hint at a belief in the lie.

Here, the enemy comes in the form of that mindset. In your neighborhood, students may suffer from other toxic lies, ones no less damaging—lies of sexism, economic power, religious bigotry or intolerance toward anyone or anything different. No matter what their form, there's only one way to counter these lies: by changing lives, one mindset at a time.

On a recent field trip to the Civil Rights Memorial Center in Montgomery, I saw an immediate change in the mindset of many of my students.

Take "Jack," for example. Just a few days earlier, Jack had made a derogatory comment about gays. As we walked the hall dedicated to contemporary issues, however, he was the first to announce, "We have to treat everyone right, no matter what!" This unexpected remark came as a response to a story about a hate crime directed at a gay man.

Then there's "Alfred," a student with a sweet smile who tries to put on a rough exterior. On the ride home, I looked at him and stated, "You are *not* the thug you pretend to be." We talked candidly, and he said he realized that he is a better person than the tough-guy act he had created. I saw that spark in him and a big, soft heart. Since the trip, Alfred has been one of the best-behaved and most motivated students in class.

There's also "Daneka," who talked about her commitment to being different, to going to college and to helping others.

But the deepest change I feel personally is in me. I have grown to love the kids as family. Sharing a piece of their lives has renewed my commitment to breaking down barriers and challenging misguided mindsets. Teaching is about creating change and giving hope. When you give hope, I've found, you receive hope. I can't think of a better reason to teach.

ANALYZE & REFLECT

Click here to analyze and reflect on this scenario you have just read.

CYNTHIA GIBSON
Teacher Selma, ALABAMA

Note: The preceding is excerpted from Gibson's article that appeared in *Teaching Tolerance*, Number 35, Spring 2009, pp. 16–17.

Children and Poverty

Although the United States is one of the wealthiest countries in the world, by no means has it achieved an enviable record with regard to poverty among children (see Figure 3.1). According to the *2013 Kids Count Data Book: State Trends in Child Well-being,* the child poverty rate rose from 19 to 23 percent from 2005 to 2011, an increase of 3 million children. The states with the highest rates of child poverty are Mississippi (32 percent), New Mexico (31 percent), Louisiana (29 percent), Alabama (28 percent), Arkansas (28 percent), and South Carolina (28 percent) (Annie E. Casey Foundation, 2013, p. 42).

Despite the overall high standard of living, homelessness in the United States is a major social problem. Prior to the 1980s, homelessness was largely confined to the poorest areas of the nation's largest cities. Since then, changes in social policies such as welfare, minimum wages, and affordable housing—coupled with economic upheavals and continued unequal distributions of wealth—have swelled the number of homeless people. In addition, homelessness is moving beyond cities to rural areas where single mothers (often migrant farm workers) and their children make up the largest percentage of the homeless population (National Coalition for the Homeless, 2013a).

FIGURE 3.1 National trends in 16 key indicators of child well-being by race and Hispanic origin

ECONOMIC WELL-BEING	National Average	African American	American Indian	Asian and Pacific Islander	Hispanic	Non-Hispanic White	Two or More Races
Children in poverty: 2011	23%	39%	37%	14%	34%	14%	24%
Children whose parents lack secure employment: 2011	32%	49%	51%	22%	39%	25%	37%
Children living in households with a high housing cost burden: 2011	40%	53%	36%	40%	52%	31%	43%
Teens not in school and not working: 2011	8%	13%	15%	4%	11%	7%	9%
EDUCATION							
Children not attending preschool: 2009–11	54%	51%	58%	48%	63%	50%	53%
Fourth graders not proficient in reading: 2011	68%	84%*	81%*	51%*	82%	58%	63%*
Eighth graders not proficient in math: 2011	66%	87%*	83%*	45%*	80%	57%	63%*
High school students not graduating on time: 2009/10†	22%	34%*	31%*	6%*	29%	17%	N.A.
HEALTH							
Low-birthweight babies: 2010	8.1%	13.2%	7.6%	8.5%	7.0%	7.1%	N.A.
Children without health insurance: 2011	7%	6%	17%	8%	13%	5%	6%
Child and teen deaths per 100,000: 2010	26	36	30	14	21	25	N.A.
Teens who abuse alcohol or drugs: 2011^	7%	6%*	13%*	3%*+	7%	7%	9%
FAMILY AND COMMUNITY							
Children in single-parent families: 2011	35%	67%	53%	17%	42%	25%	42%
Children in families where the household head lacks a high school diploma: 2011	15%	14%	20%	12%	37%	6%	11%
Children living in high-poverty areas: 2007–11	12%	28%	27%	7%	21%	4%	10%
Teen births per 1,000: 2010	34	51	39	11	56	23	N.A.

* Data are for non-Hispanics only in each respective group. All other rates for these racial groups include both Hispanics and non-Hispanics.
† Provisional data.
^ These are single-year race data for 2011. Data in index are 2010–11 multiyear data.
+ Data results do not include Native Hawaiians/Pacific Islanders.
N.A. Data not available
Source: *2013 Data Book: State Trends in Child Well-being*. Baltimore: Annie E. Casey Foundation, 2013, p. 15.

About 75 percent of homeless or runaway children have dropped out or will drop out of school (National Coalition for the Homeless, 2013b). A host of barriers can make it difficult for them to attend school. First is the need to overcome health problems, hunger, and the difficulty of obtaining clothing and school supplies. Second, providing documentation for school enrollment is often almost impossible for homeless guardians. School districts are often reluctant to eliminate requirements for birth certificates, immunization records, and documentation of legal guardianship. Third, homeless shelters and other temporary housing may not be on regular school district bus routes, making it difficult for homeless children to get to and from school. And homeless children can be difficult to identify because they are often highly mobile and may not wish to be identified.

The nation's first law to provide assistance to homeless persons, particularly children, was passed in 1987. The McKinney Act (recently renamed the **McKinney-Vento Act**) requires states to provide homeless children with free public education. According to the McKinney-Vento Act, schools must remove obstacles to school registration for homeless students—requirements for residency, guardianship, immunization, and previous school records—as well as provide transportation to and from school. In addition, the act requires that each school district have a liaison whose responsibility is to help identify homeless students and to ensure their success in school.

Family Stress

The stress placed on families in a complex society is extensive and not easily handled. For some families, such stress can be overwhelming. The structure of families that are experiencing the effects of financial problems, substance abuse, or violence, for example, can easily begin to crumble. In this chapter's Teachers' Voices: Being an Agent of Change, I describe how a literary magazine I started gave my students opportunities to write about the stress in their lives.

The U.S. Department of Health and Human Services reported that Child Protective Services (CPS) agencies investigated 3.7 million reports of alleged child maltreatment in 2011. Of these children, CPS determined that about 681,000 were victims of child maltreatment. More than two-thirds of child victims (79 percent) suffered neglect (including medical neglect), 18 percent were physically abused, 9 percent were sexually abused, and 10 percent were victims of other types of maltreatment, including threatened abuse, parent's drug/alcohol abuse, or lack of supervision (U.S. Department of Health and Human Services, 2013). Clearly, the burden of having to cope with such abuse in the home environment does not prepare a child to come to school to learn. Such stress is often associated with health and emotional problems, failure to achieve, behavioral problems at school, and dropping out of school.

With the high rise in divorce and women's entry into the workforce, family constellations have changed dramatically. No longer is a working father, a mother who stays at home, and two or three children the only kind of family in the United States. The number of single-parent families, stepparent families, blended families, and extended families has increased dramatically during the last decade.

The composition of today's families is diverse, and so are the styles with which children are raised in families. Because of the number of working women and single-parent homes, an alarming number of children are unsupervised during much of the day. Between 3 P.M. and 8 P.M. is the most likely time for youth to engage in risk-taking or delinquent behaviors or to be victims of a crime (Cunningham, 2003). About one in nine children aged 5 to 14 spends time after school in a home without adult supervision, and about 4.5 million children are alone for an average of 6.5 hours a week (U.S. Census Bureau, May 3, 2013). To meet the needs of **latchkey children**, many schools offer before- and after-school programs.

In addition, many middle-class couples are waiting longer to have children. Although children of such couples may have more material advantages, they may be impoverished in regard to the reduced time they spend with their parents. To maintain their lifestyle, these parents are often driven to spend more time developing their careers. As a result, the care and guidance their children receive is inadequate, and such

TEACHERS' VOICES ➡ BEING AN AGENT OF CHANGE

FORREST W. PARKAY

STUDENTS COPE WITH STRESS THROUGH WRITING

I began my teaching career as a member of the English Department at Du Sable High School on Chicago's South Side. The school, located at 4934 S. Wabash, was designed for an enrollment of just over 2,000 students; however, during my first three years at the school, enrollment peaked at more than 3,000 students.

Severe overcrowding contributed to an environment that was, on occasion, stressful and chaotic. For example, while monitoring the first-floor lunchroom (part of my assignment as a beginning teacher) that first year, I was shocked on a few occasions when riots erupted and chairs went flying through the air.

All of the students at DuSable were African American, and most were from poor families. Many students lived just across the street in the Robert Taylor Homes, the largest housing project in the U.S. Gang violence occurred frequently in the surrounding neighborhood; on occasion, it spilled over into the school's long hallways.

In my Remedial English classes, I quickly realized that the curriculum developed by the Chicago Board of Education was not that relevant to many of my students. After school and on the weekends, I wondered, how can I teach my students the content of English in a way that will be meaningful and relevant to them?

Early on, I observed that students would often express themselves in writing not only on crumpled sheets of notebook paper, but on restroom walls and lockers. Perhaps, I thought, these personal expressions could be channeled in a more formal way. At that moment, I decided to launch *Write On: A Magazine of Student Writing*.

Write On was an immediate success! One hundred copies of the first edition sold out in a day. Two students and I photocopied the first two editions; after that, the magazine was offset printed by students in the school's print shop.

Word about the magazine spread quickly, and students began to stop me in the hallway to give me their stories and poems. Their writing focused on topics such as drugs, racism, violence, and the meaning of "true love." The following excerpts from *Write On* illustrate how students coped with stress through writing.

Top Secret, by Walter: "The Hater Gun is the key to all wars. There will not be another war with the Hater Gun. It knocks out all the hate in people. This gun works on a lever. In reverse, it will bring hate; forward, it brings on love."

Dialogue by a Locker, by Barbara: "*Debra*: Hey, girl, did you hear what happened? *Marchell*: Naw, girl. What happened? *Debra*: A girl got shot over by Beethoven School yesterday. She was coming out of the building and someone shot her in the head. *Marchell*: It is a pity people get shot for doing nothing. *Debra*: The police came and the ambulance took the girl away. *Marchell*: Did the police find who did it? *Debra*: Naw, girl. I'll see you tomorrow."

Hunger, by Cedric: "Hunger! Will change a man, brain a man, and sometimes even hang a man. Hunger! Will put a man to his last dime. Will make a man leave dreams behind. Hunger! Will make a man who cannot hide turn up committing suicide. Hunger! Will make a man a man no more."

QUESTIONS

1. What are the characteristics of teachers who help students from stressful home environments be successful, engaged learners while at school? Which of those characteristics do you possess?
2. Reflecting on your own experiences as a K-12 student, do you recall learning activities that helped you cope with stress in your life? Explain your answer.

Forrest W. Parkay taught English at DuSable High School for eight years and served as Chairman of the English Department for four years.

children may not develop adequate "internal controls, [a] sense of right and wrong or of responsibility" (Comer, 2009, p. 47). To fill the parenting void that characterizes the lives of an increasing number of children from all economic classes, schools and teachers are being called on to play an increased role in the socialization of young people.

Substance Abuse

One of the most pressing social problems confronting today's schools is the abuse of illegal drugs, tobacco, and alcohol. Although drug abuse by students moved from the top-ranked problem facing local schools according to the 1996 Gallup Poll of the Public's Attitudes toward the Public Schools to the sixth-ranked problem in the 2013 poll, drug use among students remains at alarming levels. A study sponsored by the National Institute on Drug Abuse (NIDA) found that 27.1 percent of students in grades 8, 10, and 12 had used illicit drugs during 2012, and 10.8 percent had used an illicit drug other than marijuana (see Table 3.2). In addition, the NIDA reported that the following percentages of eighth graders said it would be "fairly easily" or "very easy" to get the following drugs: marijuana (36.9 percent), crack (14.4 percent), and crystal methamphetamine (ice; 8.8 percent). For 10th graders,

TABLE 3.2 Trends in annual prevalence of use of various drugs for grades 8, 10, and 12 combined (entries are percentages.)

	1991	1992	1993	1994	1995	1996	1997	1998	1999	2000	2001	2002	2003	2004
Any Illicit Drug	20.2	19.7	23.2	27.6	31.0	33.6	**34.1**	32.2	31.9	31.4	31.8	30.2	28.4	27.6
Any Illicit Drug other than Marijuana	12.0	12.0	13.6	14.6	16.4	*17.0*	16.8	15.8	15.6	15.3‡	**16.3**	14.6	13.7	13.5
Any Illicit Drug including Inhalants	23.5	23.2	26.7	31.1	34.1	36.6	**36.7**	35.0	34.6	34.1	34.3	32.3	30.8	30.1
Marijuana/Hashish	15.0	14.3	17.7	22.5	26.1	29.0	**30.1**	28.2	27.9	27.2	27.5	26.1	24.6	23.8
Synthetic marijuana	—	—	—	—	—	—	—	—	—	—	—	—	—	—
Inhalants	7.6	7.8	8.9	9.6	**10.2**	9.9	9.1	8.5	7.9	7.7	6.9	6.1	6.2	6.7
Hallucinogens	3.8	4.1	4.8	5.2	6.6	*7.2*	6.9	6.3	6.1	5.4‡	**6.0**	4.5	4.1	4.0
LSD	3.4	3.8	4.3	4.7	5.9	**6.3**	6.0	5.3	5.3	4.5	4.1	2.4	1.6	1.6
Hallucinogens other than LSD	1.3	1.4	1.7	2.2	2.7	*3.2*	*3.2*	3.1	2.9	2.8‡	**4.0**	3.7	3.6	3.6
Ecstasy (MDMA)	—	—	—	—	—	3.1	3.4	2.9	3.7	5.3	**6.0**	4.9	3.1	2.6
Salvia	—	—	—	—	—	—	—	—	—	—	—	—	—	—
Cocaine	2.2	2.1	2.3	2.8	3.3	4.0	4.3	**4.5**	**4.5**	3.9	3.5	3.7	3.3	3.5
Crack	1.0	1.1	1.2	1.5	1.8	2.0	2.1	**2.4**	2.2	2.1	1.8	2.0	1.8	1.7
Other cocaine	2.0	1.8	2.0	2.3	2.8	3.4	3.7	3.7	**4.0**	3.3	3.0	3.1	2.8	3.1
Heroin	0.5	0.6	0.6	0.9	1.2	**1.3**	**1.3**	1.2	**1.3**	**1.3**	0.9	1.0	0.8	0.9
With a needle	—	—	—	—	**0.7**	**0.7**	**0.7**	**0.7**	**0.7**	0.5	0.5	0.5	0.5	0.5
Without a needle	—	—	—	—	0.9	0.9	1.0	0.9	1.0	**1.1**	0.7	0.7	0.6	0.7
OxyContin	—	—	—	—	—	—	—	—	—	—	—	2.7	3.2	3.3
Vicodin	—	—	—	—	—	—	—	—	—	—	6.0	**6.6**	5.8
Amphetamines	7.5	7.3	8.4	9.1	10.0	**10.4**	10.1	9.3	9.0	9.2	9.6	8.9	8.0	7.6
Ritalin	—	—	—	—	—	—	—	—	—	—	4.2	3.8	3.5	3.6
Adderall	—	—	—	—	—	—	—	—	—	—	—	—	—	—
Methamphetamine	—	—	—	—	—	—	—	—	—	4.1	3.5	3.4	3.2	3.0	2.6
Bath salts (synthetic stimulants)	—	—	—	—	—	—	—	—	—	—	—	—	—	—
Tranquilizers	2.8	2.8	2.9	3.1	3.7	4.1	4.1	4.4	4.4	4.5‡	**5.5**	5.3	4.8	4.8
OTC Cough/Cold Medicines	—	—	—	—	—	—	—	—	—	—	—	—	—	—
Rohypnol	—	—	—	—	—	*1.1*	*1.1*	*1.1*	0.8	0.7	0.9‡	0.8	0.8	**0.9**
GHB[b]	—	—	—	—	—	—	—	—	—	**1.4**	1.2	1.2	1.2	1.1
Ketamine[b]	—	—	—	—	—	—	—	—	—	**2.0**	1.9	**2.0**	1.7	1.3
Alcohol	67.4	66.3‡	59.7	60.5	60.4	60.9	**61.4**	59.7	59.0	59.3	58.2	55.3	54.4	54.0
Been drunk	35.8	34.3	34.3	35.0	35.9	36.7	**36.9**	35.5	36.0	35.9	35.0	32.1	31.2	32.5
Flavored alcoholic beverages	—	—	—	—	—	—	—	—	—	—	—	—	—	**44.5**
Alcoholic beverages containing caffeine	—	—	—	—	—	—	—	—	—	—	—	—	—	—
Dissolvable tobacco products	—	—	—	—	—	—	—	—	—	—	—	—	—	—
Snus	—	—	—	—	—	—	—	—	—	—	—	—	—	—
Steroids	1.2	1.1	1.0	1.2	1.3	1.1	1.2	1.3	1.7	1.9	**2.0**	**2.0**	1.7	1.6

	2006	2008	2010	2011	2011–2012 change	Peak year–2012 change		Low year–2012 change	
						Absolute change	Proportional change (%)[a]	Absolute change	Proportional change
Any Illicit Drug	25.8	24.9	27.3	27.6	−0.4	−6.9 sss	−20.3	+2.3 ss	+9.2
Any Illicit Drug other than Marijuana	12.7	11.9	11.8	11.3	−0.4	−5.5 sss	−33.6	—	—
Any Illicit Drug including Inhalants	28.7	27.6	29.7	29.8	−0.8	−7.7 sss	−21.0	+1.4	+5.0
Marijuana/Hashish	22.0	21.5	24.5	25.0	−0.2	−5.3 sss	−17.7	+3.4 sss	+15.8
Synthetic marijuana	—	—	—	—	—	—	—	—	—
Inhalants	6.9	6.4	6.0	5.0	−0.6 s	−5.7 sss	−56.2	—	—
Hallucinogens	3.6	3.8	3.8	3.7	−0.5 s	−2.7 sss	−46.0	—	—
LSD	1.4	1.9	1.8	1.8	−0.2	−4.7 sss	−74.9	+0.2	+13.0
Hallucinogens other than LSD	3.3	3.2	3.3	3.1	−0.4 s	−1.3 sss	−32.9	—	—
Ecstasy (MDMA)	2.7	2.9	3.8	3.7	−1.2 sss	−3.5 sss	−57.9	+0.2	+6.6
Salvia	—	—	3.5	3.6	−0.9 sss	−0.9 sss	—	—	—
Cocaine	3.5	2.9	2.2	2.0	−0.1	−2.5 sss	−57.0	—	—
Crack	1.5	1.3	1.1	1.0	−0.1	−1.5 sss	−64.2	—	—
Other cocaine	3.1	2.6	1.9	1.7	−0.1	−2.3 sss	−58.0	—	—
Heroin	0.8	0.8	0.8	0.7	−0.1 s	−0.7 sss	−55.1	—	—
With a needle	0.5	0.5	0.6	0.5	−0.1	−0.3 sss	−44.0	—	—
Without a needle	0.6	0.6	0.6	0.5	−0.2 s	−0.7 sss	−67.6	—	—
OxyContin	3.5	3.4	3.8	3.4	−0.6 s	−1.0 ss	−26.2	—	—
Vicodin	6.3	6.1	5.9	5.1	−0.9 s	−2.3 sss	−35.1	—	—
Amphetamines	6.8	5.8	6.2	5.9	−0.3	−4.7 sss	−45.5	—	—
Ritalin	3.5	2.6	2.2	2.1	−0.5	−2.5 sss	−60.1	—	—
Adderall	—	—	4.5	4.1	+0.4	−0.5 s	−10.3	+0.4	+9.2
Methamphetamine	2.0	1.3	1.3	1.2	−0.2	−3.1 sss	−75.3	—	—
Bath salts (synthetic stimulants)	—	—	—	—	—	—	—	—	—
Tranquilizers	4.6	4.3	4.4	3.9	−0.2	−1.8 sss	−32.2	—	—
OTC Cough/Cold Medicines	5.4	4.7	4.8	4.4	−0.1	−1.0 ss	−18.3	—	—
Rohypnol	0.7	0.7	0.8	0.9	−0.1	−0.2	−18.9	+0.1	+24.8
GHB[b]	0.9	0.9	0.8	0.8	—	—	—	—	—
Ketamine[b]	1.1	1.2	1.2	1.2	—	—	—	—	—
Alcohol	50.7	48.7	47.4	45.3	−1.0	−17.1 sss	−27.8	—	—
Been drunk	30.7	28.1	27.1	25.9	+0.5	−10.5 sss	−28.5	+0.5	+1.9
Flavored alcoholic beverages	42.4	39.0	35.9	33.7	−1.2	−11.9 sss	−26.9	—	—
Alcoholic beverages containing caffeine	—	—	—	19.7	−1.0	−1.0 s	−5.3	—	—
Dissolvable tobacco products	—	—	—	—	—	—	—	—	—
Snus	—	—	—	—	—	—	—	—	—
Steroids	1.3	1.1	0.9	0.9	−0.1	−1.1 sss	−56.7	—	—

[a] The proportional change is the percent by which the most recent year deviates from the peak year for the drug in question. So, if a drug was at 20% prevalence in the peak year and declined to 10% prevalence in the most recent year, that would reflect a proportional decline of 50%.
[b] Question was discontinued among 8th and 10th graders in 2012.

Note: Level of significance of difference between classes: s = .05, ss = .01, sss = .001. Values in bold equal peak levels since 1991. '—' indicates data not available. Any apparent inconsistency between the change estimate and the prevalence estimates for the two most recent years is due to rounding. '‡' indicates a change in the question text. Values in italics equal peak level before wording change. When a question change occurs, peak levels after that change are used to calculate the peak year to current year difference. Underlined values equal lowest level since recent peak level (value in bold).

Source: The Monitoring the Future study, the University of Michigan.

the percentages were marijuana (68.8 percent), crack (18.4 percent), and crystal methamphetamine (ice; 10.7 percent); and, for 12th graders, the percentages were marijuana (81.6 percent), crack (22.0 percent), and crystal methamphetamine (ice; 14.5 percent) (Johnston, O'Malley, Bachman, & Schulenberg, 2013, pp. 80–81, 83).

The use of drugs among young people varies from community to community and from year to year, but overall it is disturbingly high. Mind-altering substances used by young people include the easily acquired glue, white correction fluid, and felt marker, as well as marijuana, amphetamines, and cocaine. The abuse of drugs not only poses the risks of addiction and overdosing, but also is related to problems such as HIV/AIDS, teenage pregnancy, depression, suicide, automobile accidents, criminal activity, and dropping out of school. For an alarming number of young people, drugs are seen as a way of coping with life's problems.

Violence and Crime

According to *Indicators of School Crime and Safety, 2012,* jointly published by the Bureau of Justice Statistics and the National Center for Education Statistics, there were about 648,600 victims of theft and 597,500 victims of violence (ranging from "simple assault" to "serious violent crime") at schools during the previous year (Robers, Kemp, & Truman, 2013). Figure 3.2 shows the percentage of public schools, by level, that reported various types of crime to police during 2009–2010.

In addition, the U.S. Department of Justice's National Gang Center estimates that there were approximately 29,900 gangs and 782,500 gang members in the 50 states and the District of Columbia during 2011 (U.S. Department of Justice, September 2013). Figure 3.3 shows that 28.3 percent of public schools in cities reported gang activity, whereas the percentages for schools in towns, suburbs, and rural communities was much less—14.9, 13.9, and 9.1 percent, respectively.

Gang membership is perceived by many youth as providing them with several advantages: a sense of belonging and identity, protection from other gangs, opportunities for excitement, or a chance to make money through selling drugs or participating in other illegal activities. Although few students are gang members, a small number of gang-affiliated students can disrupt the learning process, create disorder in a school, and cause others to fear for their physical safety. Strategies for reducing the effect of gang activities on schools include identifying gang members, implementing dress codes that ban styles of dress identified with gangs, and quickly removing gang graffiti from the school.

Periodically, the nation's attention is riveted by a school shooting such as the one that took the lives of 20 children and 6 adults at Sandy Hook Elementary School in 2012. With each instance of horrific school violence, the recurring question is, Why? and there is a renewed effort to understand the origins of youth violence. After each shooting, the nation debates gun control measures; the influence of violence in television, movies, and point-and-shoot video games; and steps that parents, schools, and communities can take to curb school crime and violence. The belief that shooters are loners who "just snap" was contradicted by a U.S. Secret Service and U.S. Department of Education study of 37 school shootings that identified the following patterns:

- Incidents of targeted violence at school rarely were sudden, impulsive acts.
- Prior to most incidents, other people knew about the attacker's idea and/or plan to attack.
- Most attackers did not threaten their targets directly prior to advancing the attack.
- There is no accurate or useful "profile" of students who engaged in targeted school violence.
- Most attackers engaged in some behavior prior to the incident that caused others concern or indicated a need for help.
- Most attackers had difficulty coping with significant losses or personal failures. Moreover, many had considered or attempted suicide.

FIGURE 3.2   Percentage of public schools recording and reporting to police incidents of crime at school, by type of incident and school level: School year 2009–10

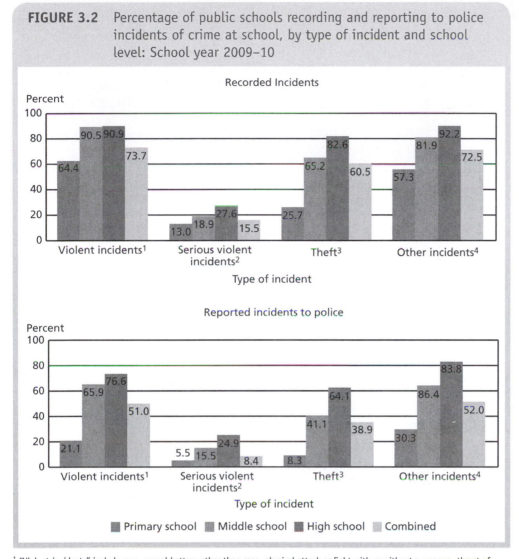

[1] "Violent incidents" include rape, sexual battery other than rape, physical attack or fight with or without a weapon, threat of physical attack with or without a weapon, and robbery with or without a weapon.

[2] "Serious violent incidents" include rape, sexual battery other than rape, physical attack or fight with a weapon, threat of physical attack with a weapon, and robbery with or without a weapon.

[3] "Theft or larceny" (taking things worth over $10 without personal confrontation) was defined for respondents as "the unlawful taking of another person's property without personal confrontation, threat, violence, or bodily harm." This includes pocket picking, stealing a purse or backpack (if left unattended or no force was used to take it from owner), theft from a building, theft from a motor vehicle or motor vehicle parts or accessories, theft of a bicycle, theft from a vending machine, and all other types of thefts.

[4] "Other incidents" include possession of a firearm or explosive device; possession of a knife or sharp object; distribution, possession, or use of illegal drugs or alcohol; vandalism; and inappropriate distribution, possession, or use of prescription drugs.

Note: Responses were provided by the principal or the person most knowledgeable about crime and safety issues at the school. "At school" was defined for respondents to include activities that happen in school buildings, on school grounds, on school buses, and at places that hold school-sponsored events or activities. Respondents were instructed to include incidents that occurred before, during, or after normal school hours or when school activities or events were in session.

Source: Robers, S., Kemp, J., and Truman, J. (2013). *Indicators of School Crime and Safety: 2012* (NCES 2013-036/NCJ 241446). National Center for Education Statistics, U.S. Department of Education, and Bureau of Justice Statistics, Office of Justice Programs, U.S. Department of Justice. Washington, DC, p. 29.

- Many attackers felt bullied, persecuted, or injured by others prior to the attack.
- Most attackers had access to and had used weapons prior to the attack.
- In many cases, other students were involved in some capacity.
- Despite prompt law enforcement responses, most shooting incidents were stopped by means other than law enforcement intervention. (Vossekuil, Fein, Reddy, Borum, & Modzeleski, 2002, pp. 11–12)

FIGURE 3.3   Percentage of public schools reporting selected discipline problems that occurred at school, by locale: School year 2009–10

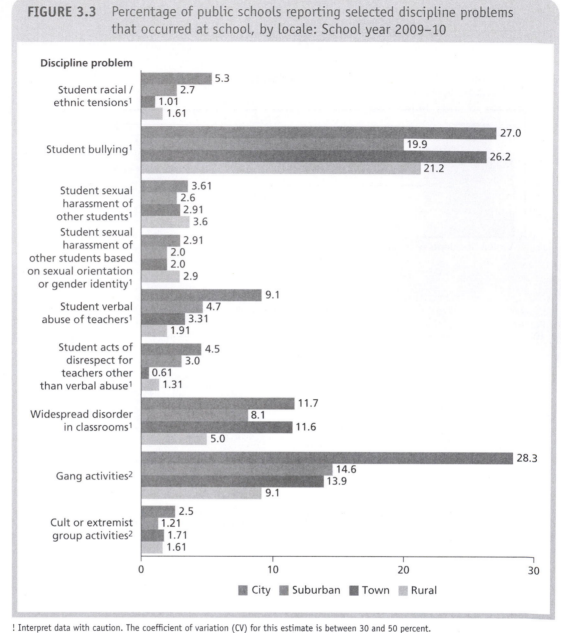

! Interpret data with caution. The coefficient of variation (CV) for this estimate is between 30 and 50 percent.

[1] Includes schools that reported the activity happens either at least once a week or daily.

[2] Includes schools that reported the activity happens at all at their school during the school year.

Note: Responses were provided by the principal or the person most knowledgeable about crime and safety issues at the school. "At school" was defined for respondents to include activities that happen in school buildings, on school grounds, on school buses, and at places that hold school-sponsored events or activities. Respondents were instructed to respond only for those times that were during normal school hours or when school activities or events were in session.

Source: Robers, S., Kemp, J., and Truman, J. (2013). *Indicators of School Crime and Safety: 2012* (NCES 2013-036/NCJ 241446). National Center for Education Statistics, U.S. Department of Education, and Bureau of Justice Statistics, Office of Justice Programs, U.S. Department of Justice. Washington, DC, p. 33.

Based on the results of their study, the two departments then issued *Threat Assessment in Schools: A Guide to Managing Threatening Situations and to Creating Safe School Climates* and recommended that schools take the following steps:

- Assess the school's emotional climate.
- Emphasize the importance of listening in schools.
- Adopt a strong, but caring stance against the code of silence.
- Prevent, and intervene in, cases of bullying.
- Involve all members of the school community in planning, creating, and sustaining a school culture of safety and respect.

- Develop trusting relationships between each student and at least one adult at school.
- Create mechanisms for developing and sustaining safe school climates. (Fein et al., 2002)

As a result of school shootings and the public's concern with school crime and violence, most schools have developed crisis management plans to cope with violent incidents on campus. Many schools use the "School Safety Checklist" (see Table 3.3), which is excerpted from the National School Safety Center's *School Safety Check Book*.

BULLYING

After the 1999 Columbine High School shootings left 14 students and a teacher dead, investigations of school violence brought the problem of bullying in schools to the forefront. Figure 3.4 shows that approximately one-fourth of public schools, regardless of location, report that bullying is a problem. In addition, about 32 percent of 12- to 18-year-old students reported having been bullied at school during the last year. Twenty-one percent of students said that the bullying involved being made fun of; 18 percent reported being the subject of rumors; 11 percent said they were pushed, shoved, tripped, or spit on; 6 percent said they were threatened with harm; 5 percent said they were excluded from activities on purpose; and 4 percent said that someone tried to make them do things they did not want to do and that their property was destroyed on purpose. Seventy-nine percent of students who were bullied said they were bullied inside the school, and 23 percent said they were bullied outside on school grounds (Bureau of Justice Statistics and the National Center for Education Statistics, December 2009, p. 40).

TABLE 3.3 School safety checklist

Give your school a thorough crime prevention inspection now. Use this checklist as a guideline to determine your school's strengths and weaknesses.

	Yes	No
1. Is there a policy for dealing with violence and vandalism in your school? (The reporting policy must be realistic and strictly adhered to.)		
2. Is there an incident-reporting system?		
3. Is the incident-reporting system available to all staff?		
4. Is statistical information about the scope of the problems at your school and in the community available?		
5. Have the school, school board, and administrators taken steps or anticipated any problems through dialogue?		
6. Does security fit into the organization of the school? (Security must be designed to fit the needs of the administration and made part of the site.)		
7. Are the teachers and administrators aware of laws that pertain to them? To their rights? To students' rights? Of their responsibility as to enforcement of and respect for rules, regulations, policies, and the law?		
8. Is there a working relationship with your local law enforcement agency?		
9. Are students and parents aware of expectations and school discipline codes?		
10. Are there any actual or contingency action plans developed to deal with student disruptions and vandalism?		
11. Is there a policy for restitution or prosecution of perpetrators of violence and vandalism?		
12. Is there any in-service training available for teachers and staff in the areas of violence and vandalism and other required reporting procedures?		
13. Is there a policy for consistent monitoring and evaluation of incident reports?		
14. Is the staff trained in standard crime-prevention behavior?		

Source: Excerpted from *The School Safety Check Book* by the National School Safety Center, Dr. Ronald D. Stephens, 141 Duesenberg Dr., Suite 11, Westlake Village, CA, 91362, http://www.nssc1.org

CYBERBULLYING

With the proliferation of personal computers and cell phones, bullying has gone on-line. **Cyberbullying** involves the use of information and communication technologies to harass or threaten an individual or group. Cyberbullies send harassing e-mails or instant messages; post obscene, insulting, and slanderous messages to online bulle-tin boards; or develop websites to promote and disseminate defamatory content. As Figure 3.4 shows, a survey of more than 4,400 students at 37 schools in one district

FIGURE 3.4 Cyberbullying

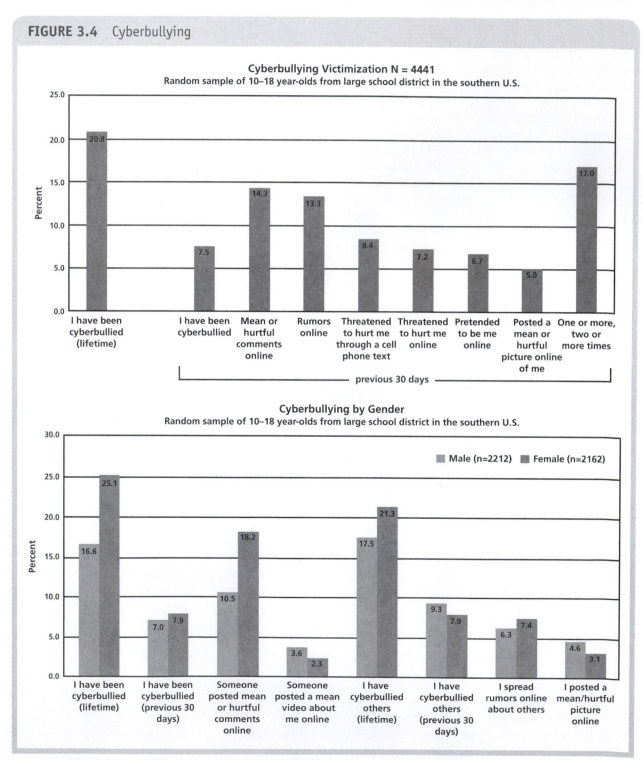

Source: Hinduja, S., and Patchin, J. W. "Cyberbullying research." Cyberbullying Research Center (www.cyberbullying.us). Retrieved September 1, 2010, from http://www.cyberbullying.us/research.php

revealed that almost 21 percent had experienced cyberbullying, and female students were more likely to have experienced cyberbullying (25.1 percent to 16.6 percent, respectively; Patchin & Hinduja, September 1, 2010).

Teen Pregnancy

In 2012, there were 29.4 births for every 1,000 adolescent females ages 15 to 19, or 305,420 babies born to females in this age group; about 89 percent of these births occurred outside of marriage (Hamilton, Martin, & Ventura, 2013). Indeed, most teachers of adolescents today may expect to have at least some students who are or have been pregnant.

Since peaking in 1990, the teenage pregnancy, birth, and abortion rates have declined, largely the result of more effective contraceptive practices among sexually active teenagers. However, the U.S. teen birth rate is higher than that of many other similar countries, including Canada and the United Kingdom, and teen pregnancies remain a serious problem in U.S. society. Because the physical development of girls in adolescence may not be complete, complications can occur during pregnancy and in the birthing process. Also, adolescents are less likely to receive prenatal care in the crucial first trimester; they tend not to eat well-balanced diets; and they are not free of harmful substances such as alcohol, tobacco, and drugs, which are known to be detrimental to a baby's development. "Children born to adolescents face particular challenges—they are more likely to have poorer educational, behavioral, and health outcomes throughout their lives, compared with children born to older parents" (U.S. Department of Health and Human Services, Office of Adolescent Health, 2013). Because most teen mothers drop out of school, forfeiting their high school diplomas and limiting their access to decent, higher-paying job opportunities, they and their children stay at the bottom of the economic ladder.

Suicide Among Children and Youth

The increase in individual and multiple suicides is alarming. After homicides and accidents, it is the third leading cause of death for young people ages 10 and 24 and accounts for approximately 4,600 lives lost each year (Centers for Disease Control and Prevention, 2012).

A survey of youth in grades 9–12 in public and private schools found that 16 percent reported seriously considering suicide, 13 percent reported creating a plan, and 8 percent reporting trying to take their own life in the 12 months preceding the survey. Each year, approximately 157,000 youth between the ages of 10 and 24 receive emergency medical care for self-inflicted injuries (Centers for Disease Control and Prevention, 2012).

Although female students are more likely than male students to have seriously considered attempting suicide during the preceding 12 months, about four times as many male students as females actually commit suicide. Latino students are about two times more likely than White students to attempt suicide, and students in grade 9 are about four times more likely than students in grade 12 to make a suicide attempt that requires medical attention (Centers for Disease Control and Prevention, 2009). Also, lesbian and gay youth are two to three times more likely to attempt suicide than their heterosexual peers, and they account for up to 30 percent of all completed suicides among youth (Besner & Spungin, 1995).

HOW ARE SCHOOLS ADDRESSING SOCIETAL PROBLEMS?

Responding to the needs of at-risk students is a crucial challenge for schools, families, and communities. The challenge is especially grave in light of a national economy that continues to be sluggish and widespread cutbacks in funding for social services. Because most children attend school, it is logical that this preexisting system be used for reaching large numbers of at-risk children (and, through them, their families). During the last decade, many school districts have taken innovative steps to address societal problems that affect students' lives.

Although programs that address social problems are costly, most of the public believes that schools should be used for the delivery of health and social services to students and their families. There has been disagreement, however, about the extent to which school facilities should be used for anything but meeting students' educational needs. In isolated instances, community groups and school boards have resisted school-based services such as family-planning clinics and mental health services. However, increases in state funding and foundation support to provide school-based health, mental health, and social services have tended to dissipate most of this resistance (Dryfoos, Quinn, & Barkin, 2005).

Under pressure to find solutions to increasing social problems among children and adolescents, educators have developed an array of intervention programs. In general, the aim of these programs is to address the behavioral, social, and academic adjustment of at-risk children and adolescents so they can receive maximum benefit from their school experiences.

The following sections describe seven strategies that have proven effective in addressing academic, social, and behavioral problems among children and adolescents: peer counseling/mentoring, peer mediation, full-service community schools, school-based case management, compensatory education, alternative schools and curricula, and expanded learning time (ELT) schools.

Peer Counseling/Mentoring

To address the social problems that affect students, some schools have initiated student-to-student **peer-counseling** or **peer-mentoring programs**—usually monitored by a school counselor or other specially trained adult. In peer-counseling/mentoring programs, students can address problems and issues such as low academic achievement, interpersonal problems at home and at school, substance abuse, and career planning. Evidence indicates that both peer counselor/mentors and students experience increased self-esteem and greater ability to deal with problems (Garringer & MacRae, 2008).

When peer counseling/mentoring is combined with cross-age tutoring, younger students can learn about drugs, alcohol, premarital pregnancy, delinquency, dropping out, HIV/AIDS, suicide, and other relevant issues. Here, the groups are often college-age students meeting with those in high school, or high school students meeting with those in junior high school or middle school. In these preventive programs, older students sometimes perform dramatic episodes that portray students confronting problems and model strategies for handling the situations presented.

FOCUS ON DIVERSITY: PEER MEDIATION TO PROMOTE TOLERANCE

Peer-mediation programs are similar to peer-counseling programs. The focus of **peer mediation** is on cultivating a classroom climate in which students influence one another to be more accepting of differences, not of solving problems per se. In some peer-mediation programs, students participate in role-plays and simulations to help them develop empathy, social skills, and awareness of prejudice.

An example of peer mediation can be found at John Marshall Middle School, in Long Beach, **CALIFORNIA**, where students increase their understanding of cultural differences by learning about peer mediation. Students become "diversity ambassadors" by attending workshops on peer mediation, cultural diversity, tolerance, and conflict resolution. The workshops focus on issues of racial and ethnic barriers for fellow students. The diversity ambassadors host a school assembly on school violence in partnership with the Long Beach Police Department's Gang Unit. Marshall School teachers and students report that the diversity ambassadors have improved the school climate (Learning in Deed, 2004).

Full-Service Community Schools

In response to the increasing number of at-risk students, many schools are serving their communities by integrating educational, medical, social, and/or human services.

Full-service community schools, also called community schools, operate in a public school building before, during, and after school; 7 days a week; all year long. Often located in low-income urban areas, community schools integrate educational, medical, social, and/or human services to meet the needs of children and their families.

Community schools involve collaborative partnerships among school districts, departments of public health, hospitals, and various nonprofit organizations. At full-service community schools, students and their families can receive health screening, psychological counseling, drug-prevention counseling, parent education, child-rearing tips, and family-planning information. Parents and community members also participate in adult education and job-training programs at the school, as well as use the school as a site to solve community problems.

Evaluations of community school programs indicate that they contribute to improved student achievement. They are also linked to increased attendance and reduced levels of high-risk behaviors (e.g., drug use and sexual activity). In addition, because community schools support families, family involvement in school programs increases and family functioning improves (Coalition for Community Schools, 2013).

Another benefit of community schools is that they encourage parents to view the school positively; thus, parents are more likely to support the school in maintaining high expectations for learning and behavior. Community schools also directly support the work of teachers in the classroom. As the Institute for Educational Leadership's Coalition for Community Schools (2002, p. 6) points out: "Teachers in community schools teach. They are not expected to be social workers, mental health counselors, or police officers. Partner organizations do this work, providing teachers with essential support, helping them recognize and respond effectively to student problems, and connecting students and their families with needed community services and opportunities."

School-Based Case Management

To respond to the needs of at-risk students, many schools have developed programs that draw from the resources of community organizations and public services. One such approach to forming new home, school, and community partnerships is known as **school-based case management**. The approach uses professionally trained case managers who work directly with teachers, the community, and the family to coordinate and deliver appropriate services to at-risk students and their families. The case management approach is based on a comprehensive service-delivery network of teachers, social agencies, and health-service agencies (Franklin, Harris, & Allen-Meares, 2006).

One of the first case management programs in the country is operated by the Center for the Study and Teaching of At-Risk Students (C-STARS) and serves 20 school districts in the Pacific Northwest. Center members include Washington State University, the University of Washington, a community-based organization, and **WASHINGTON** State's Department of Social and Health Services. Working with teachers and other school personnel, a case management team fulfills seven functions to meet the needs of at-risk students: assessment, development of a service plan, brokering with other agencies, service implementation and coordination, advocacy, monitoring and evaluation, and mentoring.

C-STARS also provides a combination of the following services customized to the specific needs of each community: after-school educational programs; summer school programs; recreational activities; social and health services; case management services for students and families; and parent resource centers offering educational opportunities such as English as a second language (ESL), computer literacy, and leadership training. Program evaluation data have shown significant measurable improvements in students' attendance, academic performance, and school behavior.

Compensatory Education

To meet the learning needs of at-risk students, several federally funded **compensatory education programs** for elementary and secondary students have been developed, the largest of which is Title I. Launched in 1965 as part of the Elementary and Secondary

Education Act (ESEA) and President Lyndon Johnson's Great Society education program, Title I (called Chapter I between 1981 and 1994) was designed to improve the basic skills (reading, writing, and mathematics) of low-ability students from low-income families. In 2010, the Obama administration began the process of reauthorizing ESEA; however, by early 2014, Congress had yet to act on the administration's call for reauthorization. To assist teachers in meeting the learning needs of students from low-income families, the proposed reauthorization would include provisions for supplemental educational services. Supplemental educational services (SES) give parents of eligible children the opportunity and the funding to choose private tutors or other academic support services to help their children succeed in school.

Students who participate in Title I programs are usually taught through pullout programs, in which they leave the regular classroom to receive additional instruction individually or in small groups. Title I teachers, sometimes assisted by an aide, often have curriculum materials and equipment not available to regular classroom teachers. Research on the effectiveness of Title I programs has been inconclusive, with some studies reporting achievement gains not found in other studies. Research has found positive effects on students' achievement in the early grades, but these gains tend to dissipate during the middle grades. However, *Title I Implementation—Update on Recent Evaluation Findings* (U.S. Department of Education, January 2009), reported that, across a sample of seven Title I school districts, students in supplemental educational services experienced gains in reading and mathematics achievement that were greater than the gains for nonparticipating students.

Some critics of Title I and other compensatory education programs, such as Head Start for preschool children, Success for All for preschool and elementary children, and Upward Bound for high school students, argue that they are stopgap measures at best. Instead, they maintain, social problems such as poverty, the breakdown of families, drug abuse, and crime that contribute to poor school performance should be reduced.

Alternative Schools and Curricula

To meet the needs of students at risk of education failure because of various social problems, many school districts have developed alternative schools and curricula. These programs are designed to minimize students' high-risk behavior and address concerns about violence, weapons, and drugs in schools. Despite the need for such programs, only about 64 percent of school districts have alternative programs for at-risk students (Carver & Lewis, 2010).

An **alternative school** is usually a small, highly individualized school separate from the regular school; in other cases, the alternative school is organized as a **school-within-a-school**. Alternative school programs usually provide remedial instruction, some vocational training, and individualized counseling. Because they usually have much smaller class sizes, alternative school teachers can monitor students' progress more closely and, when problems do arise, respond more quickly and with greater understanding of student needs.

One exemplary alternative school is the Union Alternative School in Tulsa, **OKLAHOMA**, serving 9th- through 12th-grade students. The atmosphere at Union is supportive. To increase students' success, the school provides extensive counseling services, and teachers use innovative teaching methods. Students can pursue an individualized course of study based on a flexible schedule, and the teacher-student ratio in classrooms is 1 to 15 or less.

During two class periods of each school day, students may attend elective classes at the regular high school, participate in a work/study program, perform school or community service projects, attend classes at Tulsa Technology Center, or receive tutorial or enrichment assignments (Union Alternative School, 2010).

Another exemplary alternative school is the William R. Beard School in Syracuse, **NEW YORK**. The school's "positive behavioral expectations" for students are: *Be here. Be safe. Act respectfully.* and *Act responsibly.* Students address important community issues such as hunger, domestic violence, the criminal justice system, racism, and gender issues. Students receive up to 24 points a day based on their daily performance in four categories: Attendance, Rules, Respect, and Effort. A minimum of 30 points is needed to participate in a weekly reward program. In partnership with the Center for Community Alternatives and Communities United to Rebuild Neighborhoods, students maintain a flower and vegetable garden on the city's southwest side. The students publish a biannual student newspaper that deals with topics relevant to students' lives. Students also participate in classroom learning experiences based on their volunteer activities (William R. Beard School, 2010).

OUT-OF-SCHOOL-TIME (OST) ACTIVITIES

One approach to reducing high-risk behaviors among youth is to involve them in **out-of-school-time (OST) activities** (often called *extracurricular activities*). OST activities support and promote youth's development because they (a) place youth in safe environments; (b) prevent youth from engaging in delinquent activities; (c) teach youth general and specific skills, beliefs, and behaviors; and (d) provide opportunities for youth to develop relationships with peers and mentors (Simpkins, 2003). OST programs provide opportunities for growth and development at times when youth are unsupervised and might be tempted to engage in risky behaviors.

Frequently, children living in poverty don't have the same opportunities as other children to participate in music and dance, sports programs, and other OST activities. Students who spend 1 to 4 hours in OST activities each week are 49 percent less likely to use drugs and 37 percent less likely to become teen parents than students who do not participate in such activities (Little & Harris, 2003).

An exemplary OST program is the 4-H Job Experience and Training Program (JET) located in a 4-H education center in Dayton, **OHIO**. JET is a work-based learning program at Adventure Central, an urban education center in Dayton. Extension educators from Ohio State University run the JET program. The program runs for 6 months and culminates in an 8-week summer work experience in collaboration with a local park district (Ferrari, Arnett, & Cochran, 2007; Job Experience and Training [JET] Program, 2010).

ALTERNATIVE CURRICULA

Although they don't work in alternative school settings, many highly effective regular teachers have developed alternative curricula to meet the unique learning needs of students at risk. Many teachers, for example, link students' learning to the business, civic, cultural, and political segments of their communities. The rationale is that connecting at-risk students to the world beyond their schools will enable them to see the relevance of education.

Expanded Learning Time (ELT) Schools

Increasingly, educational policymakers recognize that the traditional school year of approximately 180 days is not the best arrangement to meet students' learning needs. As President Obama explained in his first major education address in March 2009, "We can no longer afford an academic calendar designed when America was a nation of farmers who needed their children at home plowing the land at the end of each day. That calendar may have once made sense, but today, it puts us at a competitive disadvantage."

Proposals for year-round schools and educationally oriented weekend and after-school programs address the educational and developmental needs of students affected by social problems. According to the National Association for Year-Round Education, 1,646 year-round schools served 1.3 million students in 1992; by 2007, 2,764 year-round schools served more than 2 million students. In Austin, **TEXAS**, for example, schools can participate in an optional extended year (OEY) program that allows them to provide additional instruction in reading and mathematics to students at risk of being retained a grade. Schools participating in OEY can choose from among four school-day options: (1) extended day, (2) extended week, (3) intersession of year-round schools, and (4) summer school (Washington, 2009).

Another approach to increasing time for teaching and learning is to add time to the school day. For example, **MASSACHUSETTS** implemented the Expanded Learning Time (ELT) Initiative to increase student achievement, opportunities for enrichment, and partnerships with community organizations. In 2010, 22 **expanded learning time (ELT) schools** served over 12,000 students in the state; and, nationwide, over 650 ELT schools served 300,000 students in 36 states (Massachusetts Expanded Learning Time Initiative, 2010).

Boston's Clarence Edwards Middle School is an ELT success story. Nearly 90 percent of the school's students are from low-income families; 88 percent are minority; 32 percent receive special education services; and 24 percent are limited English proficiency. Before the ELT transformation, the school was on the verge of being shut down and had among the lowest math scores of any middle school in the city. Enrollment was falling, as neighborhood families sent their children to other schools. Faculty and student morale was low, and family involvement was very limited. Like other middle schools in Boston, students left the building at 1:30 P.M. every day.

In 2006, the school added 300 hours of learning and personalized instruction to the school calendar. The school also added enrichment activities, including a band, a football team, and student apprenticeships with Google and MIT. By 2009, the school had become one of the highest-performing middle schools in Boston. Test scores increased dramatically in all areas, including math, science, and English; and, today, the school has a waiting list.

HOW CAN COMMUNITY-BASED PARTNERSHIPS HELP STUDENTS LEARN?

The previous section looked at intervention programs that schools have developed to ensure the optimum behavioral, social, and academic adjustment of at-risk children and adolescents to their school experiences. This section describes innovative, community-based partnerships that some schools have developed recently to prevent social problems from hindering students' learning.

The Community as a Resource for Schools

To assist schools in addressing the social problems that affect students, many communities are acting in the spirit of a recommendation made by the late Ernest Boyer (1928–1995): "Perhaps the time has come to organize, in every community, not just a *school* board, but a *children's* board. The goal would be to integrate children's services and build, in every community, a friendly, supportive environment for children" (Boyer, 1995, p. 169). In partnerships between communities and schools, individuals, civic organizations, or businesses select a school or are selected by a school to work together for the good of students. The ultimate goals of such projects are to provide students with better school experiences and to assist students at risk.

CIVIC ORGANIZATIONS

To develop additional sources of funding, many local school districts have established partnerships with community groups interested in improving educational opportunities in the schools. Some groups raise money for schools. The American Jewish Committee and the Urban League raised funds for schools in Pittsburgh, **PENNSYLVANIA**, for example. Other partners adopt or sponsor schools and enrich their educational programs by providing funding, resources, or services.

One example of partnerships with community groups involved the Phenix City (**ALABAMA**) schools. Students worked with civic organizations to raise awareness among students and community members about important health issues. The Healthcare Science and Technology (HST) Department and the Western District medical/dental associations taught preventive health skills, including hand washing and oral hygiene, to all kindergarten, first-grade, and special education students in the Phenix City school system. Working with the civic organizations, the students developed and prepared all materials used in the training programs. In addition, students collaborated with the organizations to provide the community with educational programs on diabetes, and they offered blood sugar screenings to the community (Learning in Deed, 2004).

VOLUNTEER MENTOR PROGRAMS

Mentorship is a trend in community-based partnerships today, especially with students at risk. Parents, business leaders, professionals, and peers volunteer to work with students in neighborhood schools. Goals might include dropout prevention, high achievement, improved self-esteem, and healthy decision making. Troubleshooting on lifestyle issues often plays a role, especially in communities plagued by drug dealing, gang rivalry, casual violence, and crime. Mentors also model success.

Some mentor programs target particular groups. For instance, Concerned Black Men (CBM), a **WASHINGTON, D.C.**–based organization with 31 chapters around the country, targets inner-city African American male youth. African American men in diverse fields and from all walks of life participate as CBM mentors to students in area schools. Their goal is to serve as positive adult male role models for youth, many of whom live only with their mothers or grandmothers and lack male teachers in school. To date, CBM has given cash awards and scholarships to several thousand youth selected on the basis of high academic achievement, motivation, leadership in academic and nonacademic settings, and community involvement (Concerned Black Men, 2010).

CBM volunteer mentors receive training and attend class every day, working as teachers' aides, contributing materials, arranging field trips, and running an after-school program for latchkey children. Many volunteers started working with first- and second-graders and saw these same children all the way through their elementary school years. The program's good results have made it a model for mentorship programs in other schools.

CORPORATE–EDUCATION PARTNERSHIPS

Business involvement in schools has taken many forms, including, for example, contributions of funds or materials needed by a school, release time for employees to visit classrooms, adopt-a-school programs, cash grants for pilot projects and teacher development, educational use of corporate facilities and expertise, employee participation, student scholarship programs, and political lobbying for school reform. Extending beyond advocacy, private-sector efforts include job initiatives for disadvantaged youth, in-service programs for teachers, management training for school administrators, minority education and faculty development, and even construction of school buildings.

Business-sponsored school experiments focus on creating model schools, laboratory schools, or alternative schools that address particular local needs. In Minneapolis, **MINNESOTA**, for example, the General Mills Foundation provided major funding to create the Metropolitan Federation of Alternative Schools (MFAS), an alliance of 10 community-based organizations that operates 12 alternative schools. MFAS is designed to serve students who have not been successful in regular school programs. The goals for students who attend MFAS schools include returning to regular school when appropriate, graduating from high school, and/or preparing for postsecondary education or employment. MFAS schools have small class sizes, increased individual academic help, enhanced supplemental services, and strong parental involvement (MFAS, 2010).

In addition to contributing more resources to education, chief executive officers and their employees are donating more time; 83 percent of the top managers surveyed by a recent *Fortune* poll said they "participate actively" in educational reform, versus 70 percent in 1990. For example, IBM MentorPlace enables more than 6,000 IBM employees in more than 35 countries to provide students with online academic assistance and career counseling and to volunteer in schools. IBM mentors work with teachers to identify online activities they would like students to work on with their mentors. Online activities cover all core academic areas, including science and math (IBM MentorPlace, 2010).

21ST CENTURY COMMUNITY LEARNING CENTERS (CCLCS)

Established as part of the No Child Left Behind Act, the 21st Century Community Learning Center (CCLC) program provides federal funding for community learning centers that provide academic enrichment opportunities during nonschool hours for children, particularly those who attend high-poverty and low-performing schools. CCLCs are located in schools, community facilities, and/or faith-based facilities and provide services to support student learning and development. These services include tutoring and mentoring, homework assistance, academic enrichment (such as hands-on science or technology programs), community service opportunities, music, art, sports, and cultural activities. Centers also provide safe environments for students during nonschool hours.

Schools as Resources for Communities

A shift from the more traditional perspective of schools is the view that schools should serve as multipurpose resources for the community. By focusing not only on the development of children and youth, but on their families as well, schools ultimately enhance the ability of students to learn. As Ernest Boyer (1995, p. 168) put it, "No arbitrary line can be drawn between the school and life outside. Every [school] should take the lead in organizing a referral service—a community safety net for children that links students and their families to support agencies in the region—to clinics, family support and counseling centers, and religious institutions."

BEYOND THE SCHOOL DAY

Many schools and school districts are serving their communities by providing educational and recreational programs before and after the traditional school day and during the summers. After-school educational and recreational programs are designed to (1) provide children with supervision at times when they might become involved in antisocial activities, (2) provide enrichment experiences to widen children's perspectives and increase their socialization, and (3) improve the academic achievement of children not achieving at their potential during regular school hours. Ernest Boyer argued that schools should adapt their schedules to those of the workplace so that parents could become more involved in their children's education, and that businesses, too, should give parents more flexible work schedules. Drawing on the model of Japan, Boyer suggested that the beginning of the school year could be a holiday so that parents could attend opening-day ceremonies and celebrate the launching and continuation of education in the same way that we celebrate its ending.

For several years, the After-School Plus (A+) Program in **HAWAII** has operated afternoon enrichment programs from 2:00 to 5:00 for children in kindergarten through sixth grade. The children, who are free to do art, sports, drama, or homework, develop a sense of *ohana*, or "feeling of belonging." Currently, more than 59,000 K–12 students participate in after-school programs in Hawaii (Afterschool Alliance, 2010).

Some research indicates that extended school days and school calendars

What risk factors might affect these youth? What are some effective approaches for helping students succeed in school?

have a positive influence on achievement (Center for Research on Effective Schooling for Disadvantaged Students, 1992; Gandara & Fish, 1994), but the Center for Research on the Education of Students Placed at Risk (CRESPAR) at Johns Hopkins University concluded that "there is no straightforward answer to the question of what works best in after-school programs" (Fashola, 1999). According to CRESPAR, few studies of the effects of after-school programs on measures such as achievement or reduction of antisocial behavior meet minimal standards for research design. Nevertheless, CRESPAR found that after-school programs with stronger evidence of effectiveness had four elements: training for staff, program structure, evaluation of program effectiveness, and planning that includes families and children (Fashola, 1999).

SOCIAL SERVICES

In response to the increasing number of at-risk and violence-prone children and youth, many schools are also providing an array of social services to students, their families, and their communities. The following comments by three female students highlight the acute need for support services for at-risk youth who can turn to aggression and violence in a futile attempt to bolster their fragile self-esteem and to cope with the pain in their lives. All three girls have been involved in violent altercations in and around their schools, and all three frequently use alcohol and illegal drugs. Fifteen-year-old "Mary" has been physically abused by both her father and mother, and she was raped when she was 14. "Linda," also 15 years old, was sexually molested during a 4-year period by a family acquaintance, and she endures constant physical and psychological abuse from her father. Fourteen-year-old "Jenny" is obsessed with death and suicide, and she aspires to join a gang.

> When you're smoking dope, you just break out laughing, you don't feel like punching people because it's just too hard. It takes too much. . . . You're mellow. . . . You just want to sit there and trip out on everybody. . . . It's even good for school work. When I used to get stoned all the time last year, I remember, I used to sit in class and do my work because I didn't want the teacher to catch me, and this year I'm getting failing marks 'cause I'm not doing my work 'cause I'm never stoned [Mary].
>
> I just know I got a lot of hatred. . . . And there's this one person [Jenny], and it just kinda happened after she mouthed me off, I was just like totally freaked with her and now I just want to slam her head into something. I wanna shoot her with a gun or something. I wanna kill her. . . . If I could get away with it I'd kill her. I wouldn't necessarily kill her, but I'd get her good. I just want to teach her a lesson. I'd beat the crap out of her. She's pissed me off so badly. I just want to give her two black eyes. Then I'd be fine. I'd have gotten the last word in [Linda].
>
> I like fighting. It's exciting. I like the power of being able to beat up people. Like, if I fight them, and I'm winning, I feel good about myself, and I think of myself as tough. . . . I'm not scared of anybody, so that feels good. My friends are scared of a lot of people, and I go "Oh yeah," but I'm not scared of them. . . . All these people in grade eight at that junior high are scared of me, they don't even know me, and they're scared of me. It makes me feel powerful [Jenny]. (Artz, 1999, pp. 127, 136, 157)

Although some believe that schools should not provide social services, an increase in the number of at-risk students like Mary, Linda, and Jenny suggests that the trend is likely to continue. In Seattle, **WASHINGTON**, a referendum required that a percentage of taxes be set aside to provide services to elementary-age children. In **FLORIDA**, Palm Beach County officials created the Children's Services Council to address 16 areas, from reducing the dropout rate to better child care. From parent support groups, to infant nurseries, to programs for students with special needs, the council has initiated scores of projects to benefit the community and its children.

SUMMARY

What Is the Role of Schools in Today's Society?

- Although the debate about the role of schools continues, many people in the United States believe that schools have a responsibility to socialize students to participate intelligently and constructively in society.

How Can Schools Be Described?

- Schools can be categorized according to the focus of their curricula and according to their organizational structures.

What Are Schools Like as Social Institutions?

- As social institutions that contribute to the maintenance and improvement of society, schools mirror the national U.S. culture as well as the surrounding local culture. Schools often reproduce the existing social class structure, maintaining differences between the haves and have-nots.
- Elements of a school's physical environment such as self-contained classrooms, open-space arrangements, and departmentalization contribute to a school's character and culture. Similarly, each classroom develops its own culture, which is influenced by the physical setting and the social dimensions of the group.
- Three views of successful schools have been suggested: (1) their students manifest a high level of learning, (2) their results surpass those for comparable schools, and (3) they are improving rather than getting worse.

What Are the Characteristics of Successful Schools?

- Research has identified seven characteristics of effective schools: strong leadership, high expectations, emphasis on basic skills, orderly school environment, frequent and systematic evaluation of student learning, sense of purpose, and collegiality and a sense of community.

What Social Problems Affect Schools and Place Students at Risk?

- In response to life experiences characterized by extreme family stress, poverty, crime, and lack of adult guidance, growing numbers of youth are at risk of dropping out of school. Minority at-risk students may also have to contend with intangible obstacles such as language barriers, conflicts with fellow students and teachers, and racism and discrimination.

How Are Schools Addressing Societal Problems?

- Seven effective intervention and prevention programs that schools have developed to address social problems are peer counseling/mentoring, peer mediation, full-service community schools, school-based case management, compensatory education, alternative schools and curricula, and expanded learning time (ELT) schools.
- Since 1965, an array of federally funded compensatory education programs has provided educational services to improve the basic skills of low-ability students from low-income families.
- Many school districts have developed alternative schools or schools within a school that provide highly individualized instructional and support services for students who have not been successful in regular schools. Also, highly effective teachers modify their techniques and develop alternative curricula to meet the needs of students at risk.

How Can Community-Based Partnerships Help Students Learn?

- Schools serve as resources for their communities by providing educational and recreational programs before and after the school day, and by providing health and social services. In addition, community and corporate partnerships can help schools address social problems that hinder students' learning by providing various forms of support.

PROFESSIONAL REFLECTIONS AND ACTIVITIES

Teacher's Journal

1. Write a short paper based on your own high school experience, addressing the following:

   - Who comprised the at-risk population?
   - What percentage of the school population would you have considered at risk? How did this affect the overall school program?
   - What special considerations were made for at-risk students?
   - Describe the personalities or actions of any teachers or counselors who were dedicated to helping this population succeed.
   - Describe one success story involving an at-risk student from your school experience.
   - Describe one failure. What might have changed that failure to success?

2. What are the characteristics of teachers who effectively meet the needs of students placed at risk?

Which of those characteristics do you possess? How can you develop those characteristics more fully as you progress through your teacher education program?

Teacher's Research

1. Gather data on the Internet about children and/or adolescents that reflect issues of health, safety, and welfare in your state. State government databases are good places to start. Narrow your search to one of the following areas:

   - Childhood poverty and homelessness
   - Student nutrition and health
   - Teen pregnancy
   - Bullying in school
   - Child abuse and neglect
   - Student drug, alcohol, and tobacco abuse
   - School violence and crime
   - Truancy
   - Juvenile delinquency
   - Suicide among children and youth

2. Go to the home page for the National Education Association (NEA). From there, click on the link to NEA's Legislative Action Center. At that site, gather information about federal or state legislation that addresses meeting the educational needs of students at risk. Send an e-mail message to Congress or one of your state's legislators explaining your position regarding that legislation.

Observations and Interviews

1. Reflect on your experiences relating to social problems at the elementary, middle, or high school level. Then, visit a school to gather statistics and information about how the school is responding to the social problems you identified. Interview several teachers. How have the teachers responded to these social issues? From their point of view, what resources would enable them to respond more effectively to these issues?

2. Interview a social worker in your community. According to him or her, what kind of relationship should exist between the schools and social service agencies?

Professional Portfolio

Develop a case study of a school's culture. Visit a local school or base your study on a school you have attended. Organize your case in terms of the following categories of information:

- **Environment**—How would you describe the school facility or physical plant and its material and human resources? How is space organized? What is the climate of the school?
- **Formal Practices**—What grades are included at the school? How is the school year organized? How is time structured? How are students and teachers grouped for instruction?
- **Traditions**—What events and activities and products seem important to students, teachers, and administrators? What symbols, slogans, and ceremonies identify membership in the school? How do community members view and relate to the school?

Draw conclusions from your case study: What aspects of the school culture seem to support learning and academic achievement? On the basis of your case study, draft a position statement on the kind of culture you would like to create or promote in your classroom.

CHAPTER QUIZ

Take this quiz to check your understanding of the content covered in this chapter.

PART TWO
FOUNDATIONS OF TEACHING

▶ DEAR **MENTOR** I am in my final quarter of my freshman year at Otterbein University. I plan to major in early childhood education (ECE). I'll graduate in three years and begin my search for a teaching position in Columbus, **OHIO**, or surrounding area.

I have chosen the ECE program because I am comfortable in an early childhood environment. Such an environment is constantly changing, so being prepared and organized is key. When comparing careers that best fit my personality, I decided that this area of concentration suits me because of my ability to develop relationships with children; my organizational skills; and my caring nature as a peer, mentor, and teacher.

During this final freshman quarter at Otterbein, I student taught at various schools in Westerville, Ohio. During that time, I acquired knowledge about the constantly changing classroom and the individuality of each student.

Today, in these changing times, students are faced with many challenges. As a teacher, I must have a knowledgeable perspective on ethnic, cultural, and linguistic diversity among students. What guidance do you have for preparing to meet these challenges in today's diverse classrooms?

SINCERELY, ALISON THOMPSON

▶ DEAR **ALISON** Start with your own self-exploration. Be cognizant that diversity has many faces, and it does not just include ethnicity, gender, or socioeconomic levels. You must understand your own values, style of speaking and interacting, and response to the various forms of diversity. It is imperative that you are able to articulate your mores and traditions, as your values may be in conflict with some children's family cultures. Developing sensitivity to differences will help you to provide a richer social and learning environment for your students.

Furthermore, start researching the cultures and other forms of diversity presently represented in your area. Seek out people, experiences, and other resources that will help you understand the customs and way of life of other populations. Attend some community functions, ask questions, and be alert to classroom implications. Have discussions with classroom teachers as to the impact diversity has had on their teaching.

When you begin teaching, remember to always be respectful of the various types of families that are represented in your community. Also, be constantly aware that those parents may have different values and beliefs surrounding education that could be markedly different than your own. Include *all* families in the education-related decisions about their children. And lastly, it is important to always rely on school and district professional guidelines, standards, and ethics to inform decision making concerning your students.

EDUCATIONALLY YOURS, **LYNN HINES**

NBCT (National Board Certified Teacher) 1995, 2005
Western Kentucky University,
NBPTS (National Board for Professional Teaching Standards)
Program Faculty, NBPTS

CHAPTER FOUR
Philosophical Foundations of U.S. Education

learning outcomes

After reading this chapter, you will be able to do the following:

1. Explain why philosophy is important to teachers.
2. Explain the nature of philosophy.
3. Discuss the key elements of your educational philosophy.
4. Explain six branches of philosophy that are important to teachers.
5. Describe five modern philosophical orientations to teaching.
6. Explain three schools of psychological thought that can influence a teacher's philosophy.
7. Explain how you will develop an eclectic educational philosophy to guide your own teaching.

READERS' VOICES

Why is philosophy important to teachers?

Philosophy is important to teachers because it helps them understand how their beliefs and values influence the curriculum they present to students. Educational philosophy helps teachers focus on the true purpose of education—providing students with knowledge that is worthwhile and useful to them.

—ÁNGELITA, **Teacher Education program, first year**

If you think about your own teachers in elementary through high school, you no doubt recall that each of them had a different approach to teaching. Each had a different set of responses to the vital questions that all teachers must answer: What should the purpose(s) of education be? What knowledge is of most worth? What values should teachers encourage their students to develop? How should learning be evaluated? As difficult as these questions might be, teachers must answer them. To answer these and similar questions, teachers use philosophy.

WHY IS PHILOSOPHY IMPORTANT TO TEACHERS?

Today's schools reflect the philosophical foundations and the aspirations and values brought to this country by its founders and generations of settlers. Understanding the philosophical ideas that have shaped education in the United States is an important part of your education as a professional. This understanding will enable you "to think clearly about what [you] are doing, and to see what [you] are doing in the larger context of individual and social development" (Ozmon & Craver, 2007).

Still, you may wonder, what is the value of knowing about the philosophy of education? Will that knowledge help you become a better teacher? An understanding of the philosophy of education will enhance your professionalism in three important ways. First, knowledge of philosophy of education will help you understand the complex political forces that influence schools. When people act politically to influence schools, their actions reflect their educational philosophies. Second, knowledge of how philosophy has influenced our schools will help you evaluate more effectively current proposals for change. You will be in a better position to evaluate changes if you understand how schools have developed and how current proposals might relate to previous change efforts. Last, awareness of how philosophy has influenced teaching is a hallmark of professionalism in education.

In addition, philosophy can reveal principles that may be used as a guide for professional action. (Some teachers disagree and think that philosophical reflections have nothing to contribute to the actual act of teaching; this stance, of course, is itself a philosophy of education.) For example, when deciding how to present new information to students, a teacher with a well-thought-out philosophy of education might realize "that a particular approach to teaching is better to adopt than its alternative because it treats subject matter intellectually rather than as solely a store of facts, which means regarding students as human beings capable of thought rather than merely of absorption" (Hansen, 2007, p. 7). Without the benefit of an educational philosophy, the teacher might have focused exclusively on students merely "absorbing" the new information. Similarly, educational philosophy can help teachers make appropriate decisions in the middle of a lesson—for example, deciding to "ask a thoughtful question about the novel at hand when students are restless rather than automatically piling on more information about it" (Hansen, 2007, p. 7).

Philosophy is also important to schools. As the great educational philosopher John Dewey (1916, p. 383) put it, to be concerned with education is to be concerned with philosophy: "If we are willing to conceive education as the process of forming fundamental dispositions, intellectual and emotional, toward nature and fellow men, philosophy may even be defined as *the general theory of education*." Most schools have a statement of philosophy that serves to focus the efforts of teachers, administrators, students, and parents in a desired direction. A school's philosophy is actually a public statement of school values, a description of the educational goals it seeks to attain. So important is a school's philosophy that school accrediting agencies evaluate schools partially on the basis of whether they achieve the goals set forth in their statements of philosophy.

WHAT IS THE NATURE OF PHILOSOPHY?

Philosophy is concerned with identifying the basic truths about being, knowledge, and conduct. Whereas the religions of the world arrive at these truths based on supernatural revelations, philosophers use their reasoning powers to search for answers to the fundamental questions of life. Philosophers use a careful, step-by-step, question-and-answer technique to extend their understanding of the world. Through very exacting use of language and techniques of linguistic and conceptual analysis, philosophers attempt to describe the world in which we live.

The word *philosophy* may be literally translated from the original Greek as "love of wisdom." In particular, a philosophy is a set of ideas formulated to comprehend the world. Among the giants of Western philosophy have been Socrates, Plato, Aristotle, Saint Thomas Aquinas, Réné Descartes, John Locke, David Hume, Jean-Jacques Rousseau, Immanuel Kant, Georg Hegel, John Stuart Mill, Karl Marx, John Dewey, Jean-Paul Sartre, and Mortimer Adler. They devoted their lives to pondering the significant questions of life: What is truth? What is reality? What life is worth living?

WHAT DETERMINES YOUR EDUCATIONAL PHILOSOPHY?

Listen for the ways these teachers use their own philosophy to create and update their courses.

In simplest terms, your **educational philosophy** consists of what you believe about education—the set of principles that guides your professional action. Every teacher, whether he or she recognizes it, has a philosophy of education—a set of beliefs about how human beings learn and grow and what one should learn in order to live the good life. Professional teachers recognize that teaching, because it is concerned with *what ought to be*, is basically a philosophical enterprise.

Your behavior as a teacher is strongly connected to your beliefs about teaching and learning, students, knowledge, and what is worth knowing (see Figure 4.1). Regardless of where you stand in regard to these dimensions of teaching, you should be aware of the need to reflect continually on *what* you do believe and *why* you believe it. Taken together, your beliefs about different dimensions of teaching are the foundation of your educational philosophy.

The Teachers' Voices: Walk in My Shoes for this chapter profiles Paul Gray, who explains how his life experiences, including mentoring by a philosophy professor, helped him to clarify the beliefs that are part of his educational philosophy.

FIGURE 4.1   Educational beliefs and teaching behavior

TEACHERS' VOICES
Walk in My Shoes
"I get to shape America's future."
Paul Gray
**Russellville High School,
Russellville, Arkansas**

Beliefs About Teaching and Learning

One of the most important components of your educational philosophy is your beliefs about teaching and learning. In other words, what will be your primary role as a teacher? Will it be to transmit knowledge to students and then to guide their practice as they develop skills in using that knowledge? Or will it be to develop self-directed learners by building on students' interests, prior experiences, and current understandings? The first view emphasizes *transmission* of knowledge to students, whereas the second view emphasizes students' *construction* of knowledge.

The transmission view emphasizes changes in students' behavior. Learning involves making associations between various stimuli and responses. In other words, learning results from forces that are *external* to the individual. The constructivist view, on the other hand, emphasizes the individual student's experiences and cognitions. Learning occurs when personal experiences lead to changes in thoughts or actions. That is, learning is largely the result of *internal* forces within the individual. To assess your current beliefs about teaching and learning, complete the activity presented in Figure 4.2.

Beliefs About Students

Your beliefs about students will have a great influence on how you teach. Every teacher formulates an image in his or her mind about what students are like—their dispositions, skills, motivation levels, and expectations. What you believe students are like is based on your unique life experiences, particularly your observations of young people and your knowledge of human growth and development.

Negative views of students may promote teacher–student relationships based on fear and coercion rather than on trust and helpfulness. Extremely positive views may risk not providing students with sufficient structure and direction and not communicating sufficiently high expectations. In the final analysis, the truly professional teacher—the one who has a carefully thought-out educational philosophy—recognizes that, although children differ in their predispositions to learn and grow, they all *can* learn. In regard to beliefs about students, it is important that teachers convey positive attitudes toward their students and a belief that they *can* learn.

PROFESSIONAL REFLECTION

Watch the ways these teachers meet the needs of the students at this elementary school, based on their beliefs about students.

FIGURE 4.2 Where do you stand?

For each pair of statements about the teacher's role, circle the response that most closely reflects where you stand regarding the two perspectives. Remember, there are no correct responses, and neither perspective is better than the other.

Constructivist Perspective		*Transmission Perspective*
"I mainly see my role as a facilitator. I try to provide opportunities and resources for my students to discover or construct concepts for themselves."	*vs.*	"That's all nice, but students really won't learn the subject unless you go over the material in a structured way. It's my job to explain, to show students how to do the work, and to assign specific practice."

Definitely Prefer	Tend to Prefer	Cannot Decide	Tend to Prefer	Definitely Prefer

"It is a good idea to have all sorts of activities going on in the classroom. Some students might produce a scene from a play they read. Others might create a miniature version of the set. It's hard to get the logistics right, but the successes are so much more important than the failures."	*vs.*	"It's more practical to give the whole class the same assignment, one that has clear directions, and one that can be done in short intervals that match students' attention spans and the daily class schedule."

Definitely Prefer	Tend to Prefer	Cannot Decide	Tend to Prefer	Definitely Prefer

"The most important part of instruction is that it encourage 'sense-making' or thinking among students. Content is secondary."	*vs.*	"The most important part of instruction is the content of the curriculum. That content is the community's judgment about what children need to be able to know and do."

Definitely Prefer	Tend to Prefer	Cannot Decide	Tend to Prefer	Definitely Prefer

"It is critical for students to become interested in doing academic work—interest and effort are more important than the particular subject-matter they are working on."	*vs.*	"While student motivation is certainly useful, it should not drive what students study. It is more important that students learn the history, science, math, and language skills in their textbooks."

Definitely Prefer	Tend to Prefer	Cannot Decide	Tend to Prefer	Definitely Prefer

Source: Adapted from Jason L. Ravitz, Henry Jay Becker, and Yan Tien Wong. *Constructivist-Compatible Beliefs and Practices Among U.S. Teachers.* Center for Research on Information Technology and Organizations, University of California, Irvine; and University of Minnesota, July 2000.

FOCUS ON DIVERSITY: ACCEPTING ALL STUDENTS

As a teacher, you should guard against negative attitudes toward individual students or groups of students. Although you cannot eliminate the prejudice, inter-group hostility, and racism that are found in society at large, you will have an obligation to see that your actions in the classroom do not convey negative attitudes about students on the basis of factors such as gender, race, ethnicity, religion, sexual orientation, family lifestyle, manner of dress, language, or socioeconomic status. A teacher who models positive attitudes toward all students is Cathleen Cadigan, who teaches at Thomas

Jefferson High School in Dallas, **TEXAS**. Although her school has surveillance cameras in the hallways, a police officer assigned to the school, and a metal detector at the main entrance, Cadigan reports that "There is not a thug in this building. We have some who *think* they are. [There is no one] who wouldn't say, 'Miss Cadigan, can I carry that box for you? Can I hold the door for you?' They are just as sweet as sweet can be . . . they are probably the most polite kids I have ever met" (College Board and Phi Delta Kappa, 2009, p. 7).

Beliefs About Knowledge

How teachers view knowledge is directly related to how they go about teaching. If teachers view knowledge as the sum total of small bits of subject matter or discrete facts, students will most likely spend a great deal of time learning that information in a straightforward, rote manner. Recall your own school days; perhaps you had to memorize the capitals of the 50 states, definitions for the eight parts of speech, the periodic table in chemistry, and so on.

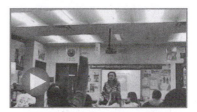

Watch the way this teacher uses her beliefs about knowledge and how students learn as she teaches a lesson.

Other teachers view knowledge more conceptually, that is, as consisting of the big ideas that enable us to understand and influence our environment. Such a teacher would want students to be able to explain how legislative decisions are made in the state capital, how an understanding of the eight parts of speech can empower the writer and enliven one's writing, and how chemical elements are grouped according to their atomic numbers.

Finally, teachers differ in their beliefs about whether students' increased understanding of their own experiences is a legitimate form of knowledge. Knowledge of self and one's experiences in the world is not the same as knowledge about a particular subject, yet personal knowledge is essential for a full, satisfying life. In addition, as Steven Crawford, a Spanish teacher at a Bellevue, **WASHINGTON**, high school points out, self-understanding is essential for teachers: "[Good teaching] is just having a center of yourself and an understanding of who you are in front of the kids and who they need you to be" (College Board and Phi Delta Kappa, 2009, p. 25). The Technology in Action feature for this chapter profiles a teacher who believes that study of a foreign language should go beyond knowledge of correct grammatical structures and rote memorization of vocabulary words. For this teacher, the personal knowledge a student gains from cross-national communication is a valid goal for foreign language study.

Beliefs About What Is Worth Knowing

Teachers have different ideas about what should be taught. One teacher, who tends to prefer a transmission view of teaching, believes it is most important that students learn the basic skills of reading, writing, computation, and oral communication. These are the skills they will need to be successful in their chosen occupations, and it is the school's responsibility to prepare students for the world of work. Another teacher believes that the most worthwhile content is to be found in the classics, or the Great Books. Through mastering the great ideas from the sciences, mathematics, literature, and history, students will be well prepared to deal with the world of the future. Still another teacher, one who tends toward a constructivist view of teaching, is most concerned with students learning how to reason, communicate effectively, and solve problems. Students who master these cognitive processes will have learned how to learn—and this is the most realistic preparation for an unknown future. And finally, another teacher is concerned with developing the whole child, teaching students to become self-actualizing persons. Thus, the content of the curriculum should be meaningful to the student, contributing as much as possible to the student's efforts to become a mature, well-integrated person. As you can see, there are no easy answers to the question, What knowledge is of most worth?

PROFESSIONAL REFLECTION
Watch the way this teacher uses her beliefs to share what is worth knowing during a lesson with her students.

TECHNOLOGY in ACTION
Web Conferencing in 11th-Grade Chinese Language Class

Louise Zhao has taught Advanced Chinese at Lincoln High School for the past 5 years. Her approach is part presentation of grammar and vocabulary—and lots and lots of practice. Whenever possible, she tries to bring in native Chinese speakers to speak to her class, but this usually takes the form of a presentation. However, these presentations don't give her students what she is really after—to have her students engage in extensive one-on-one conversations with Chinese speakers.

Mrs. Zhao was born in Shanghai and still has family living there. She communicates with them often using various online communication tools, but it was not until she walked in on her 13-year-old son carrying on a video phone call with his cousin in Shanghai that she realized she had the solution to her classroom dilemma. The next day she went to her principal and presented her idea. He agreed and she began to develop her lesson plan.

Through her family connections, she contacted Mr. Lee, who teaches English to students at a high school in Shanghai. The two teachers agreed that they would have their students meet once each week, for 1 hour, via Elluminate. Elluminate is web conferencing software that allows individuals or groups to conference via text, audio, and/or graphics online. The local community college had just purchased an Elluminate web conferencing license. As part of its community outreach, the community college allowed the local school district in its service area to use the tool. Each student in Mrs. Zhao's class would be paired with a student in Mr. Lee's class. During their 1-hour Elluminate session, they would speak Chinese for the first 30 minutes and then speak English for the next 30 minutes. The session would also be recorded so Mr. Lee and Mrs. Zhao could review the individual conversations at a later time and provide feedback to their students.

To make this happen, however, Mrs. Zhao realized she had a lot to do. She had to schedule the weekly events—adjusting for time-zone differences. She had to pair the students, ensure that they stayed on task, and create a setting conducive for one-on-one conversation.

Luckily for Mrs. Zhao, the school's computer lab was up to date, and each computer in the lab had been fitted with microphone headsets. The headset speakers would keep out external noise so that her 20-plus students seated in the computer lab could chat away and not disturb their neighbors. With the setting and technology taken care of, the next thing she had to deal with was timing. There was

no way that she could make the timing of this event coincide within the hours of the standard school day. What she decided to do was make these events voluntary. To her surprise, all of her students agreed to attend the first session. At 4:00 P.M. each Thursday, her students would meet in the computer lab, click on their Elluminate session proposal, and connect with their counterparts in Shanghai, who were seated at their computers at 7:00 A.M. the next day, their time. This novelty was the first thing the students discussed. Although they are only halfway through the semester, the students appear each week for their conversations with their friends on the other side of the world.

WEB CONFERENCING: Web conferencing allows individuals or groups to connect on the web via video and/or audio. This is usually a synchronous or live session in which individuals are seated at their computers and interact with others. Participants can be in the same building or in another country. To participate in a web videoconference, you will need a USB video input, a microphone, appropriate computer sound and video cards, the video conferencing software or plugin, and an Internet connection robust enough to handle a web conference.

VISIT: A few websites offer thorough reviews of free or inexpensive software options for web conferencing, such as Skype, iChat (for Macintosh), Windows Live Messenger, and VoIP (Voice over Internet). Reviews cover topics such as real-time web conferencing, desktop video conferencing, screen sharing, online meetings, web seminars, and host sites.

POSSIBLE USES: Teachers have used web conferencing for tutoring sessions, meeting with parents, bringing outside speakers into their classrooms, pursuing professional development opportunities, and connecting with colleagues around the country.

TRY IT OUT: There are many options to choose from if you would like to have your students participate in a web videoconference. You can try many of these options on a temporary basis for free. One easy web conferencing solution is Windows Messenger. Just open Messenger and click on Start Video Conversation. Type in the e-mail address of the person you want to conference with and you are connected.

WHAT ARE THE BRANCHES OF PHILOSOPHY?

To provide you with additional tools to use in formulating and clarifying your educational philosophy, this section presents brief overviews of six areas of philosophy that are of central concern to teachers: metaphysics, epistemology, axiology, ethics, aesthetics, and logic. Each of these areas focuses on one of the questions that have concerned the world's greatest philosophers for centuries: What is the nature of reality? What is the nature of knowledge, and is truth ever attainable? According to what values should one live life? What is good and what is evil? What is the nature of beauty and excellence? And finally, What processes of reasoning will yield consistently valid results?

Metaphysics

Metaphysics is concerned with explaining, as rationally and as comprehensively as possible, the nature of reality (in contrast to how reality *appears*). What is reality? What is the world made of? These are metaphysical questions. Metaphysics is also concerned with the nature of being and explores questions such as, What does it mean to exist? What is humankind's place in the scheme of things? Metaphysical questions such as these are at the very heart of educational philosophy. As one educational philosopher put it, "nothing short of the fullest awareness possible of 'man's place in the cosmos' is the constant problem of the philosopher of education" (Bertocci, 1960, p. 158). Or as two educational philosophers put it: "Our ultimate preoccupation in educational theory is with the most primary of all philosophic problems: metaphysics, the study of ultimate reality" (Morris & Pai, 1994, p. 28).

Metaphysics has important implications for education because the school curriculum is based on what we know about reality. And what we know about reality is driven by the kinds of questions we ask about the world. In fact, any position regarding what the schools should teach has behind it a particular view of reality, a particular set of responses to metaphysical questions. This chapter's Teachers' Voices: Being an Agent of Change feature profiles a teacher who encourages her students to grapple with metaphysical questions.

Epistemology

The next major set of philosophical questions that concerns teachers is called **epistemology**. These questions all focus on knowledge: What knowledge is true? How does knowing take place? How do we know what we know? How do we decide between opposing views of knowledge? Is truth constant, or does it change from situation to situation? And finally, What knowledge is of most worth?

How you answer the epistemological questions that confront all teachers will have significant implications for your teaching. First, you will need to determine what is true about the content you will teach, then you must decide on the most appropriate means of teaching this content to students. Even a casual consideration of epistemological questions reveals that there are many ways of knowing about the world, at least five of which are of interest to teachers.

1. **Knowing based on authority**—for example, knowledge from the sage, the poet, the priest, or the ruler. In schools, the textbook, the teacher, and the administrator are the sources of authority for students. In everyday conversations, we refer to unnamed experts as sources of authoritative knowledge: "*They* say we'll have a manned flight to Mars by the middle of the century."
2. **Knowing based on divine revelation**—for example, knowledge in the form of supernatural revelations from the sun god of early peoples, the many gods of the ancient Greeks, or the Judeo-Christian god.
3. **Knowing based on empiricism (experience)**—for example, knowledge acquired through the senses, the informally gathered empirical data that direct most of our daily behavior. When we state that "experience is the best teacher," we refer to this mode of knowing.
4. **Knowing based on reason and logical analysis**—for example, knowledge inferred from the process of thinking logically. In schools, students learn to apply rational thought to tasks such as solving mathematical problems, distinguishing facts from opinions, or defending or refuting a particular argument. Many students also learn a method of reasoning and analyzing empirical data known as the scientific method. Through this method, a problem is identified, relevant data are gathered, a hypothesis is formulated based on these data, and the hypothesis is empirically tested.
5. **Knowing based on intuition**—for example, knowledge arrived at without the use of rational thought. Intuition draws from our prior knowledge and experience and gives us an immediate understanding of the situation at hand. Our intuition convinces us that we know something, but we don't know how we know.

Axiology

The next set of philosophical problems concerns values. Teachers are concerned with values "because school is not a neutral activity. The very idea of school expresses a set of values" (Nelson, Carlson, & Palonsky, 2000, p. 304).

Among the axiological questions teachers must answer for themselves are: What values should teachers encourage students to adopt? What values raise humanity to our highest expressions of humaneness? What values does a truly educated person hold?

Axiology highlights the fact that the teacher has an interest not only in the *quantity* of knowledge that students acquire but also in the *quality* of life that becomes possible because of that knowledge. Extensive knowledge may not benefit the individual if he or she is unable to put that knowledge to good use. This point raises additional questions: How do we define quality of life? What curricular experiences contribute most to that quality of life? All teachers must deal with the issues raised by these questions.

ETHICS

Whereas axiology addresses the question, What is valuable? **ethics** focuses on, What is good and evil, right and wrong, just and unjust?

TEACHERS' VOICES ➡ BEING AN AGENT OF CHANGE

KAREN TOAVS

EVERY DAY IS FILLED WITH DEEP THINKING AND CONTEMPLATION

I teach because I want to help students figure out what they are going to do in the world. I want students to realize that they have the power and the imagination to help change where we're going to go.

The students I see every day in my classroom are very different from students of the past. Their world is full of technology and full of insights, and they need to have direction with where they want to go with that.

When I have students in my room, one of the most important things we do is engage in conversation. So I share with them what I know about human knowledge and where we've been. Part of my challenge to them is: Where do you want to take this? Where is our future going to go? Because it's that future that's so important.

For me, teaching is a gift because every day is filled with laughter and filled with deep thinking and contemplation—sometimes arguments, sometimes debates—but that's all part of the magic of helping kids understand the world and helping kids develop their own opinions about where we should go in the future.

In my classroom, part of helping students record that is a technique called visual mapping. When students walk in my classroom every day, they create one page per day as a visual map, a graphic organizer. We use all sorts of colors, images, texts, key words, and deep reflections. Students record the entire time that we are talking or learning everything that goes on in the classroom that hour.

As a result of that, we have a database, a place to start the next day. Every day we move forward, and our discussions get deeper and deeper, and the kids realize great things about the world. I love watching them grow in that depth.

As a Teacher of the Year, one of the things that I've enjoyed the most is the deep discussions that we have as colleagues about where we come from in education, what we hope for our students; and, universally, it's all the same . . . we teach because we want students to believe that they *can* change the world. We teach inspiration, and, unfortunately, that's not something that's easily tested; that's not something that's easily measured.

Yes, I believe what students learn in my classroom for content and the things that they do on their visual maps are so important to help them understand the world, but it's not nearly as important as what they do when they walk out of my classroom. I want students to know that they have the power to go out there and do all the great things that they want to accomplish. I teach because I want to help students change the world.

QUESTIONS

1. Toavs uses "visual mapping" to stimulate her students' "deep thinking and contemplation." With reference to the subject area and grade level for which you are preparing to teach, how might you use visual mapping with your students? What are some examples of possible "deep thinking" by your students?

2. Based on Toavs's comments, what do you think are her beliefs about teaching and learning? Beliefs about students? Beliefs about knowledge? Beliefs about what is worth knowing?

3. Toavs says that teachers "teach inspiration." Reflecting on your own teachers, have any of them "taught" you inspiration? How did they do that? How might you "teach" inspiration to your future students?

Karen Toavs was the 2011 North Dakota State Teacher of the Year. This feature is adapted from her Council of Chief State School Officers Teacher of the Year video retrieved February 2, 2014, from http://www.pearsonfoundation.org/ccsso-toy/2011/nd/autoplay.

Knowledge of ethics can help the teacher solve many of the dilemmas that arise in the classroom. Frequently, teachers must take action in situations where they are unable to gather all the relevant facts and where no single course of action is totally right or wrong. For example, a student whose previous work was above average plagiarizes a term paper: Should the teacher fail the student for the course if the example of swift, decisive punishment will likely prevent other students from plagiarizing? Or should the teacher, following her hunches about what would be in the student's long-term interest, have the student redo the term paper and risk the possibility that other students might get the mistaken notion that plagiarism has no negative consequences? Another ethical dilemma: Is an elementary mathematics teacher justified in trying to increase achievement for the whole class by separating two disruptive girls and placing one in a mathematics group beneath her level of ability?

Ethics can provide the teacher with ways of thinking about problems for those situations where it is difficult to determine the right course of action. Ethics also helps teachers to understand that "ethical thinking and decision making are not just following the rules" (Strike & Soltis, 1985, p. 3).

AESTHETICS

The branch of axiology known as **aesthetics** is concerned with values related to beauty and art. Although we expect that teachers of music, art, drama, literature, and writing regularly have students make judgments about the quality of works of art, we can easily overlook the contributions that the arts can make to *all* areas of the curriculum. For example, "participating in plays, songs, and dances fills children with joy, and this joy carries over into the rest of their education" (Nussbaum, 2009, p. 58). Clearly, educational philosopher Harry Broudy (1979) was correct when he made his often-quoted statement that "the arts are necessary, not 'just nice'" (pp. 347–350).

Aesthetics can also help the teacher increase his or her effectiveness. Because it may be viewed as a form of artistic expression, teaching can be judged according to artistic standards of beauty and quality. In this regard, the teacher is an artist whose medium of expression is the spontaneous, unrehearsed, and creative encounter between teacher and student.

LOGIC

Logic is the area of philosophy that deals with the process of reasoning and identifies rules that will enable the thinker to reach valid conclusions. The public is nearly unanimous in its belief that a key goal of education is to teach students how to think. The two kinds of logical thinking processes that teachers most frequently have students master are *deductive* and *inductive* thinking. The deductive approach requires the thinker to move from a general principle or proposition to a specific conclusion that is valid. By contrast, inductive reasoning moves from the specific to the general. Here, the student begins by examining particular examples that eventually lead to the acceptance of a general proposition. Inductive teaching is often referred to as discovery teaching—by which students discover, or create, their own knowledge of a topic.

How might this teacher be helping his students develop their logical thinking skills? With reference to the level and subject area for which you are preparing to teach, what activities can help students develop their ability to think logically?

Perhaps the best-known teacher to use the inductive approach to teaching was the Greek philosopher Socrates (ca. 470–399 B.C.). His method of teaching, known today as the Socratic method, consisted of holding philosophical conversations (dialectics) with his pupils. **Socratic questioning** is a discussion that is characterized by the following:

- The discussion leader only asks questions.
- The discussion is systematic (not a free-for-all).
- The leader's questions direct the discussion.
- Everyone participates in an effort to "go beneath the surface" and to explore the complexities of the topic or issue under discussion.

The legacy of Socrates lives on in all teachers who use Socratic questioning to encourage students to think for themselves. Figure 4.3 presents "The Art of Socratic Questioning Checklist."

The next section examines philosophical orientations to teaching that have been developed in response to the branches of philosophy we have just examined.

FIGURE 4.3   Eight guidelines for facilitating a Socratic discussion

The following guidelines can be used to facilitate a Socratic discussion with students. After some experience with the approach, students could even take turns leading a Socratic discussion in small groups of 5-6 students. In addition to a student who acts as discussion leader, one student should be an observer and provide feedback to the group about how well it followed the guidelines. After each guideline, suggested comments for the discussion leader are presented in italics. Each student should have a copy of the guidelines to use during the discussion.

1. At the beginning of the discussion, did the discussion leader clarify the goal(s) of the discussion?
    (The goal(s) of this discussion is (are) . . . . . .

2. Each time a student answered a question, did the discussion leader respond with another question?
    (Based on your comment, I'd like you to respond to the following question . . . .)

3. As the discussion proceeded, did the discussion leader ask for additional relevant information, evidence, or data?
    (On what information, evidence, or data is your comment based?)

4. As appropriate, did the discussion leader question the conclusions, interpretations, and/or inferences made by participants in the discussion?
    (What evidence led you to draw that conclusion? Can you explain your thinking? Might there be another possible explanation?)

5. Did the discussion leader keep the discussion focused on topics related to the goal(s) of the discussion?
    (Can you explain how your comment is related to the goal(s) of our discussion?)

6. Did the discussion leader ask participants to explain unwarranted assumptions?
    (What leads you to make that assumption?)

7. As appropriate, did the discussion leader ask for the implications and/or consequences of statements made by participants?
    (What are the implications of your statement? What might be the consequences if people did as you are suggesting?)

8. Did the discussion leader ask participants to consider the point(s) of view reflected in comments?
    (What would someone who has a different point of view think about your comment? What would you say to that person?)

Adapted from Richard Paul and Linda L. Elder. (2006). *The Thinker's Guide to the Art of Socratic Questioning*. Dillon Beach, CA: Foundation for Critical Thinking, p. 10.

WHAT ARE FIVE MODERN PHILOSOPHICAL ORIENTATIONS TO TEACHING?

Five major coherent philosophical orientations to teaching have been developed in response to the questions concerning metaphysics, epistemology, axiology, ethics, aesthetics, and logic, with which all teachers must grapple. These orientations, or schools of thought, are perennialism, essentialism, progressivism, existentialism, and social reconstructionism. The following sections present a brief description of each orientation, moving from those that are teacher-centered to those that are student-centered (see Figure 4.4). Each description concludes with a sample portrait of a teacher whose behavior, to a considerable extent, illustrates that philosophical orientation in action. Remember, though, that most teachers develop an approach to teaching that reflects an *eclectic blend* of two or more orientations to teaching. Figure 4.5 presents a matrix for comparing the underlying belief systems of these five orientations. After reading the description of each teacher, what words or phrases would fit the cells that apply to that teacher?

FIGURE 4.4   Five philosophical orientations to teaching

FIGURE 4.5   A matrix for comparing the underlying belief systems of five philosophical orientations to teaching

Educational Beliefs	Philosophical Orientations to Teaching				
	Perennialist Teacher	Essentialist Teacher	Progressive Teacher	Existentialist Teacher	Social Reconstructionist Teacher
Beliefs about Teaching and Learning					
Beliefs about Students					
Beliefs about Knowledge					
Beliefs about What is Worth Knowing					
Personal Beliefs in Philosophical Areas					

TEACHING ON YOUR FEET
Reluctant Readers

I have over 400 book titles in my classroom library. There is a wide range of genres and reading levels. I've read nearly all of them. Within our literacy block I make sure there is time for my students to read their self-selected books. We confer and I note their progress. I've implemented ideas based on books I've read and workshop sessions I've attended. There is a 40-book goal each year for the students. Student as well as teacher book chats take place frequently. Students have a "someday list" in their reading and writing logs, and add books to this list during book chats if the book interests them. I let them know that the most important thing they can do for me is read. They are to read at least 20 minutes each night for homework, and I let them know I trust them to do this; no logs are used. As a class rule, students may not abandon a book until they have read at least 50 pages minus their age. I check in with them and note what they are reading, the page number and their insights. This all builds accountability.

Sometimes a read aloud can help. *Indian in the Cupboard* by Lynn Reid Banks is a favorite, and I find even my reluctant readers want me to read more. This book touches on history, fantasy, and realistic fiction with beautiful imagery and humor. *Flying Solo* by Ralph Fletcher is another book that engages even my most reluctant readers.

Once they connect with an author or genre, having them read on their own is a risk they are willing to step into.

As a teacher, students need to know you are a reader too. They need to understand that you will support them, that you have high expectations, that you won't give up on them. I find books that relate to their interests and suggest them to students. Providing this scaffolding can move them from reluctant to more engaged.

I have a student this year who has already made great progress. He now asks me for book recommendations and is reading. He may have only read three books so far eight weeks into the year, but that's two more than he did over the same period last year. I consider that success. Giving up on reluctant readers is not an option.

ANALYZE & REFLECT

Click here to analyze and reflect on this scenario you have just read.

"DANDRE"

Perennialism

As the term implies, **perennialism** views truth as constant, or perennial. The aim of education, according to perennialist thinking, is to ensure that students acquire knowledge of these unchanging principles or great ideas, and "the function of the school is to educate the intellect" (Leahy, 2009, p. 44). Perennialists also believe that the natural world and human nature have remained basically unchanged over the centuries; thus, the great ideas continue to have the most potential for solving the problems of any era. Furthermore, the perennialist philosophy emphasizes the rational thinking abilities of human beings; it is the cultivation of the intellect that makes human beings truly human and differentiates them from other animals.

The curriculum, according to perennialists, should stress students' intellectual growth in the arts and sciences. To become culturally literate, students should encounter in these areas the best, most significant works that humans have created. In regard to any area of the curriculum, only one question needs to be asked: Are students acquiring content that represents humankind's most lofty accomplishments in that area? Thus, a high school English teacher would require students to read Melville's *Moby Dick* or any of Shakespeare's plays rather than a novel on the current best-seller list. Similarly, science students would learn about the three laws of motion or the three laws of thermodynamics rather than build a model of the space shuttle.

PERENNIALIST EDUCATIONAL PHILOSOPHERS

Two of the best-known advocates of the perennialist philosophy are Robert Maynard Hutchins (1899–1977) and Mortimer Adler (1902–2001). As president of the University of Chicago, Hutchins developed an undergraduate curriculum based on the study of the great books and discussions of these classics in small seminars (Hutchins & Adler, 1963). Hutchins's perennialist curriculum was based on three assumptions about education:

1. Education must promote human-kind's continuing search for truth. Whatever is true will always, and everywhere, be true; in short, truth is universal and timeless.

2. Because the mind's work is intellectual and focuses on ideas, education must also focus on ideas. The cultivation of human rationality is the essential function of education.

3. Education should stimulate students to think thoughtfully about significant ideas. Teachers should use correct and critical thinking as their primary method, and they should require the same of students.

Perennialist teachers often inspire students to seek truth, discover universalities in human experience, and celebrate the achievements of human civilization. How might this art lesson reflect perennialist ideas? How might the lesson be different if it were based on the essentialist educational philosophy?

Noted educational philosopher Mortimer Adler, along with Hutchins, was instrumental in organizing the Great Books of the Western World curriculum. Through the study of over 100 enduring classics, from Plato to Einstein, the Great Books approach aims at the major perennialist goal of teaching students to become independent and critical thinkers. It is a demanding curriculum, and it focuses on the enduring disciplines of knowledge rather than on current events or student interests.

PORTRAIT OF A PERENNIALIST TEACHER

Mrs. Bernstein has been teaching English at the high school level since the late 1980s. Among students and teachers as well, she has a reputation for demanding a lot. As one student put it, "You don't waste time in Mrs. Bernstein's classes. Turn off your cell phone, no texting, no multitasking—you pay attention to what she says."

From time to time, she encounters students who insist on being taught subjects that they call "relevant." A graduate of a top-notch university in the East, where she received a classical, liberal education, Mrs. Bernstein refuses to lessen the emphasis in her classes on great works of literature that she believes students need to know—*Beowulf* and the works of Chaucer, Dickens, and Shakespeare, for example.

As far as her approach to classroom management is concerned, another student sums it up this way: "She doesn't let you get by with a thing; she never slacks off on the pressure. She lets you know that she's there to teach and you're there to learn." Mrs. Bernstein believes that hard work and effort are necessary if one is to get a good education. As a result, she gives students very few opportunities to misbehave, and she appears to be immune to the grumbling of students who do complain openly about the workload.

She becomes very animated when she talks about the value of the classics to students who are preparing to live as adults in the 21st century:

> The classics are unequaled in terms of the insights they can give students into the major problems that they will have to deal with during their lifetimes. Though our civilization has made impressive technological advances during the last two centuries, we have not really progressed that much in terms of improving the quality of our lives as human beings. The observations of a Shakespeare or a Dickens on the human condition are just as relevant today as they were when they were alive.

Essentialism

Essentialism, which has some similarities to perennialism, is a conservative philosophy of education originally formulated as a criticism of progressive trends in schools by William C. Bagley (1874–1946), a professor of education at Teachers College, Columbia University. Bagley founded the Essentialistic Education Society and, to promote the society's views, the educational journal *School and Society*.

Essentialism holds that our culture has a core of common knowledge that the schools are obligated to transmit to students in a systematic, disciplined way. Unlike perennialists, who emphasize a set of external truths, essentialists stress what they believe to be the essential knowledge and skills (often termed "the basics") that productive members of our society need to know.

According to essentialist philosophy, schooling should be practical and provide children with sound instruction that prepares them for life; schools should not try to influence or set social policies. Critics of essentialism, however, charge that such a tradition-bound orientation to schooling will indoctrinate students and rule out the possibility of change. Essentialists respond that, without an essentialist approach, students will be indoctrinated in humanistic and/or behavioral curricula that run counter to society's accepted standards and need for order.

PORTRAIT OF AN ESSENTIALIST TEACHER

Mr. Samuels teaches mathematics at a junior high school in a poor section of a major urban area. Prior to coming to this school six years ago, he taught at a rural elementary school.

Middle-aged and highly energetic, Mr. Samuels is known around the school as a hardworking, dedicated teacher. His commitment to children is especially evident when he talks about preparing "his" children for life in high school and beyond. "A lot of teachers nowadays have given up on kids," he says with a touch of sadness to his voice. "They don't demand much of them. If we don't push kids now to get the knowledge and skills they're going to need later in life, we've failed them. My main purpose here is to see that my kids get the basics they're going to need."

Mr. Samuels has made it known that he does not approve of the methods used by some of the younger, more humanistic-oriented teachers in the school. At a recent faculty meeting, for example, he was openly critical of some teachers' tendency to "let students do their own thing" and spend time "expressing their feelings." He called for all teachers to focus their energies on getting students to master subject-matter content, "the things kids will need to know," rather than on helping students adjust to the interpersonal aspects of school life. He also reminded everyone that "kids come to school to learn." All students would learn, he pointed out, if "teachers based their methods on good, sound approaches that have always worked—not on the so-called innovative approaches that are based on fads and frills."

Mr. Samuels's students have accepted his no-nonsense approach to teaching. With few exceptions, his classes are orderly and businesslike. Each class period follows a standard routine. Students enter the room quietly and take their seats with a minimum of the foolishness and horseplay that mark the start of many other classes in the school. As the first order of business, the previous day's homework is returned and reviewed. Following this, Mr. Samuels presents the day's lesson, usually a 15- to 20-minute explanation of how to solve a particular kind of math problem. His mini-lectures are lively, and his wide-ranging tone of voice and animated, spontaneous delivery convey his excitement about the material and his belief that students can learn. During large-group instruction, Mr. Samuels also makes ample use of a whiteboard, software such as Geometer's Sketchpad, and manipulatives such as a large abacus and colored blocks of different sizes and shapes.

Progressivism

Progressivism is based on the belief that education should be child-centered rather than focused on the teacher or the content area. The writing of John Dewey

(1859–1952) in the 1920s and 1930s contributed a great deal to the spread of progressive ideas. Briefly, Deweyan progressivism is based on the following three central assumptions:

1. The content of the curriculum ought to be derived from students' interests rather than from the academic disciplines.
2. Effective teaching takes into account the whole child and his or her interests and needs in relation to cognitive, affective, and psychomotor areas.
3. Learning is essentially active rather than passive.

PROGRESSIVE STRATEGIES

The progressive philosophy also contends that knowledge that is true in the present may not be true in the future. Hence, the best way to prepare students for an unknown future is to equip them with problem-solving strategies that will enable them to discover meaningful knowledge at various stages of their lives. Teachers with a progressive orientation give students considerable freedom to determine their school experiences. "They guide students in various projects and discoveries, relying in part, on the child's natural curiosity" (Leahy, 2009, p. 34). Contrary to the perceptions of many, however, progressive education does not mean that teachers do not provide structure or that students are free to do whatever they wish. Progressive teachers begin with where students are and, through the daily give-and-take of the classroom, lead students to see that the subject to be learned can enhance their lives.

In a progressively oriented classroom, the teacher serves as a guide or resource person whose primary responsibility is to facilitate student learning. The teacher helps students learn what is important to them rather than passing on a set of so-called enduring truths. Toward this end, the progressive teacher tries to provide students with experiences that replicate everyday life as much as possible. Students have many opportunities to work cooperatively in groups, often solving problems that the group, not the teacher, has identified as important.

PORTRAIT OF A PROGRESSIVE TEACHER

Mr. Barkan teaches social studies at a middle school in a well-to-do part of the city. Boyishly handsome and in his mid-30s, Mr. Barkan usually works in casual attire—khaki pants, soft-soled shoes, and a sports shirt. He seems to get along well with students. Mr. Barkan likes to give students as much freedom of choice in the classroom as possible. Accordingly, his room is divided into interest and activity centers, and much of the time students are free to choose where they want to spend their time. One corner at the back of the room has a library collection of paperback and hardcover books, an easy chair, and an area rug; the other back corner of the room is set up as a project area and has a worktable on which are several globes, maps, large sheets of newsprint, and assorted drawing materials. At the front of the room in one corner is a small media center with a computer and flat-screen monitor, laser printer, and DVD/VCR.

Mr. Barkan makes it a point to establish warm, supportive relationships with his students. He is proud of the fact that he is a friend to his students. "I really like the kids I teach," he says in a soft, gentle voice. "They're basically good kids, and they really want to learn if we teachers, I mean, can just keep their curiosity alive and not try to force them to learn. It's up to us as teachers to capitalize on their interests."

The visitor to Mr. Barkan's class today can sense his obvious regard for students. He is genuinely concerned about the growth and nurturance of each one. As his students spend most of their time working in small groups at the various activity centers in the room, Mr. Barkan divides his time among the groups. He moves from group to group and seems to immerse himself as an equal participant in each group's task. One group, for example, has been working on making a papier-mâché globe. Several students are explaining animatedly to him how they plan to transfer the flat map of the world they have drawn to the smooth sphere they have fashioned out of the papier-mâché. Mr. Barkan listens carefully to what his students have to say and then congratulates the group on how cleverly they have engineered the project. When he speaks to his students, he does so in a matter-of-fact, conversational tone, as though speaking to other adults.

As much as possible he likes to bring textbook knowledge to life by providing his students with appropriate experiences—field trips, small-group projects, simulation activities, role-playing, Internet explorations, and so on. Mr. Barkan believes that his primary function as a teacher is to prepare his students for an unknown future. Learning to solve problems at an early age is the best preparation for this future, he feels.

> The increase in the amount of knowledge each decade is absolutely astounding. What we teach students as true today will most likely not be true tomorrow. Therefore, students have to learn how to learn and become active problem-solvers. In addition, students need to learn how to identify problems that are meaningful to them. It doesn't make much sense to learn to solve problems that belong to someone else. To accomplish these things in the classroom, teachers have to be willing to take the lead from the students themselves—to use their lives as a point of departure for learning about the subject. What this requires of the teacher is that he or she be willing to set up the classroom along the lines of a democracy, a close community of learners whose major purpose for being there is to learn. You can't create that kind of classroom atmosphere by being a taskmaster and trying to force kids to learn. If you trust them and let them set their own directions, they'll respond.

Existentialism

Existential philosophy is unique because it focuses on the experiences of the individual. Other philosophies are concerned with developing systems of thought for identifying and understanding what is common to *all* reality, human existence, and values. **Existentialism**, on the other hand, offers the individual a way of thinking about *my* life, what has meaning for *me,* what is true for *me.* "The purpose of life, for the existentialists, is to define oneself" (Leahy, 2009, p. 38). In general, existentialism emphasizes creative choice, the subjectivity of human experiences, and concrete acts of human existence over any rational scheme for human nature or reality.

The writings of Jean-Paul Sartre (1905–1980), a well-known French philosopher, novelist, and playwright, have been most responsible for the widespread dissemination of existential ideas. According to Sartre (1972), every individual first exists, and then he or she must decide what that existence is to mean. The task of assigning meaning to that existence is the individual's alone; no pre-formulated philosophical belief system can tell one who one is. It is up to each of us to decide who we are. According to Sartre (1972), "Existence precedes essence. . . . First of all, man exists, turns up, appears on the scene, and, only afterwards, defines himself" (p. 98).

Life, according to existential thought, has no meaning, and the universe is indifferent to the situation humankind finds itself in. Moreover, "existentialists [believe] that too many people wrongly emphasize the optimistic, the good, and the beautiful—all of which create a false impression of existence" (Ozmon & Craver, 2007). With the freedom that we have, however, we must commit ourselves to assign meaning to our *own* lives. As Maxine Greene, who has been described as "the preeminent American philosopher of education today" (Ayers & Miller, 1998, p. 4), stated: "We have to know about our lives, clarify our situations if we are to understand the world from our shared standpoints" (Greene, 1995a, p. 21). The human enterprise that can be most helpful in promoting this personal quest for meaning is the educative process. Therefore, teachers must allow students freedom of choice and provide them with experiences that will help them find the meaning of their lives. This approach, contrary to the belief of many, does not mean that students may do whatever they please; logic indicates that freedom has rules, and respect for the freedom of others is essential.

Existentialists judge the curriculum according to whether it contributes to the individual's quest for meaning and results in a level of personal awareness that Greene terms "wide-awakeness." As Greene (1995b, pp. 149–150) suggests, the ideal curriculum is one that provides students with extensive individual freedom and requires them to ask their own questions, conduct their own inquiries, and draw their own conclusions: "To feel oneself en route, to feel oneself in a place where there are always possibilities of clearings, of new openings, this is what we must communicate to the young if we want to awaken them to their situation and enable them to make sense of and to name their worlds."

EXISTENTIALISM AND POSTMODERNISM

A philosophical orientation that has received increased attention since the 1980s, **postmodernism** has many similarities with existentialism. Postmodern thinking influences the curriculum content and instructional strategies some teachers use.

Postmodernists challenge the metaphysical views—or explanations of "reality"— that are presented in many textbooks. These books, they claim, present a "historically constructed" view of reality that gives advantages to some persons and groups in our society (White males, for example), whereas it marginalizes others (people of color, women, and unskilled workers, for example).

Postmodernist educators are critical of school curricula that advance the perspectives of dominant groups and ignore other "voices." They point out, for example, that some history books, written from a Eurocentric perspective, state that Columbus "discovered" a "New World." The people who lived in what is now the United States centuries before the arrival of Columbus, of course, have a very different perspective because their native cultures endured disease, genocide, and forced assimilation at the hands of the Europeans.

Similarly, English teachers with a postmodern orientation point out that most of the literature students are required to read has been written by "dead White males" (Shakespeare, Melville, and Hawthorne, for example). Students seldom have opportunities to read the "voices" of authors who represent women, people of color, and writers from developing countries.

In general, postmodernists believe there are no absolute truths. Postmodernism disputes the certainty of scientific, or objective, explanations of reality. In addition, postmodernism is skeptical of explanations that claim to be true for all groups, cultures, traditions, or races. Similar to existentialists, postmodernists emphasize what is true for the individual. Reality is based on our interpretations of what the world means to us individually. Postmodernism emphasizes concrete experience over abstract principles.

Postmodernism is "post" because it rejects the "modern" belief that there are scientific, philosophical, and religious truths. Postmodernists believe there are many truths, and many different voices that need to be heard.

Postmodernists maintain that knowledge is invented or constructed in the minds of people, not discovered as modernists claim. Thus, the knowledge that teachers teach and students learn does not necessarily correspond to reality. Instead, that knowledge is a human construction. Knowledge, ideas, and language are created by people, not because they are true but because they are useful.

According to postmodernists, reality is a "story." Reality exists only in the minds of those who perceive it. As a result, no version of reality can claim to be the truth because versions of reality are merely human creations.

PORTRAIT OF AN EXISTENTIALIST TEACHER

After he started teaching English eight years ago at a suburban high school, Algernon Gates began to have doubts about the value of what he was teaching students. Although he could see a limited, practical use for the knowledge and skills he was teaching, he felt he was doing little to help his students answer the most pressing questions of their lives. Also, Algernon had to admit to himself that he had grown somewhat bored with following the narrow, unimaginative Board of Education curriculum guides.

During the next eight years, Algernon gradually developed a style of teaching that placed emphasis on students finding out who they are. He continued to teach the knowledge covered on the achievement test mandated by his state, but he made it clear that what students learned from him, they should use to answer questions that were important to them. Now, for example, he often gives writing assignments that encourage students to look within in order to develop greater self-knowledge. He often uses assigned literature as a springboard for values clarification discussions. And whenever possible, he gives his students the freedom to pursue individual reading and writing projects. His only requirement is that students be meaningfully involved in whatever they do.

Algernon is also keenly aware of how the questions his students are just beginning to grapple with are questions that he is still, even in his mid-30s, trying to answer for himself. Thoughtfully and with obvious care for selecting the correct words, he sums up the goals that he has for his students:

> I think kids should realize that the really important questions in life are beyond definitive answers, and they should be very suspicious of anyone— teacher, philosopher, or member of organized religion—who purports to have the answers. As human beings, each of us faces the central task of finding *our own* answers to such questions. My students know that I'm wrestling with the same questions they're working on. But I think I've taught them well enough so that they know that my answers can't be their answers.

Algernon's approach to teaching is perhaps summed up by the bumper sticker on the sports car he drives: "Question authority." Unlike many of his fellow teachers, he wants his students to react critically and skeptically to what he teaches them. He also presses them to think thoughtfully and courageously about the meaning of life, beauty, love, and death. He judges his effectiveness by the extent to which students are able and willing to become more aware of the choices that are open to them.

Social Reconstructionism

As the term implies, **social reconstructionism** holds that schools should take the lead in changing or reconstructing the current social order. Theodore Brameld (1904–1987), acknowledged as the founder of social reconstructionism, based his philosophy on two fundamental premises about the post–World War II era: (1) We live in a period of great crisis, most evident in the fact that humans now have the capability of destroying civilization overnight, and (2) humankind also has the intellectual, technological, and moral potential to create a world civilization of "abundance, health, and humane capacity" (Brameld, 1956, p. 19). In this time of great need, then, the schools should become the primary agent for planning and directing social change. In short, schools should not only *transmit* knowledge about the existing social order; they should seek to *reconstruct* it as well.

SOCIAL RECONSTRUCTIONISM AND PROGRESSIVISM

Social reconstructionism has clear ties to progressive educational philosophy. Both provide opportunities for extensive interaction between teacher and students and among students themselves. Furthermore, both place a premium on bringing the community, if not the entire world, into the classroom. Student experiences often include field trips, community-based projects of various sorts, and opportunities to interact with persons beyond the four walls of the classroom.

A social reconstructionist curriculum is arranged to highlight the need for various social reforms and, whenever possible, allow students to have firsthand experiences in reform activities. Teachers realize that they can play a significant role in the control and resolution of these problems, that they and their students need not be buffeted about like pawns by these crises.

According to Brameld and social reconstructionists such as George Counts, who wrote *Dare the School Build a New Social Order?* (1932), schools should provide students with methods for dealing with the significant crises that confront the world: war, economic depression, international terrorism, hunger, natural disasters, inflation, and ever-accelerating technological advances. The logical outcome of such education would be the eventual realization of a worldwide democracy (Brameld, 1956). Unless we actively seek to create this kind of world through the intelligent application of present knowledge, we run the risk that the destructive forces of the world will determine the conditions under which humans will live in the future.

PORTRAIT OF A SOCIAL RECONSTRUCTIONIST TEACHER

At the urban high school where she teaches social studies and history, Martha Hernandez has the reputation for being a social activist. On first meeting her, she presents a casual and laid-back demeanor. Her soft voice and warm smile belie the intensity of her convictions about pressing world issues, from international terrorism and hunger to peaceful uses of space and the need for all humans to work toward a global community.

During the early 1970s, Martha participated as a high school student in several protests against the war in Vietnam. This also marked the beginning of her increased awareness of the need for social justice in society. Like many young people of that era, Martha vigorously supported a curriculum that focused on students understanding these inequities and identifying resources that might eliminate them from society. Before she graduated from high school, Martha had formulated a vision of a healthier, more just society, and she vowed to do what she could to make that vision become a reality during her lifetime.

Martha feels strongly about the importance of having students learn about social problems as well as discovering what they can do about them. "It's really almost immoral if I confront my students with a social problem and then we fail to do anything about it," she says. "Part of my responsibility as a teacher is to raise the consciousness level of my students in regard to the problems that confront all human beings. I want them to leave my class with the realization that they can make a difference when it comes to making the world a more humane place."

For Martha to achieve her goals as a teacher, she frequently has to tackle controversial issues—issues that many of her colleagues avoid in the classroom. She feels that students would not learn how to cope with problems or controversy if she were to avoid them.

> I'm not afraid of controversy. When confronted with controversy, some teachers do retreat to the safety of the more "neutral" academic discipline. However, I try to get my students to see how they can use the knowledge of the discipline to work for social justice. So far, I've gotten good support from the principal. She's backed me up on several controversial issues that we've looked at in class: the nuclear energy plant that was to be built here in this county, the right to die, and absentee landlords who own property in the poorer sections of the city.

Two additional philosophical orientations may be placed under the broad umbrella of social reconstructionism—critical pedagogy and feminist pedagogy. These orientations have a significant influence on the curriculum content some teachers emphasize and the instructional strategies they use. The following sections provide brief descriptions of these orientations.

FOCUS ON DIVERSITY: CRITICAL PEDAGOGY

Much like social reconstructionism, **critical pedagogy** focuses on how education can promote **social justice**, especially for underrepresented groups that often do not enjoy positions of power and influence in society. Critical pedagogy teaches students how to identify and to understand the complexities of social injustice. It gives them "the tools to better themselves and strengthen democracy, to create a more egalitarian and just society, and thus to deploy education in a process of progressive social change" (Kellner, 2000).

One educator who advocated critical pedagogy was Paulo Freire (1921–1997). He spent his childhood in the comfort of the Brazilian middle class. However, he encountered poverty when his father lost his job as a military officer during the economic crisis of 1929 (Smith & Smith, 1994). That experience "led him to make a vow, at age eleven, to dedicate his life to the struggle against hunger, so that other children would not have to know the agony he was then experiencing." It also led him to understand what he described as "'the culture of silence' of the dispossessed" (Freire, 1970, p. 10). The difficulty poor people encountered when they tried to improve the quality of their lives he attributed to the physical conditions of poverty and to a deep sense that they were not entitled to move beyond their plight. Freire also believed that paternalism embedded in the political and educational systems led to inequality of opportunity. "Rather than being encouraged and equipped to know and respond to the concrete realities of their world, they (poor students) were kept 'submerged' in a situation in which such critical awareness and response were practically impossible" (Freire, 1970, p. 11).

Freire regarded education, and particularly literacy, as the best way to improve the quality of one's life. Influenced by numerous philosophers, psychologists, and political thinkers, including Sartre, Mahatma Gandhi, and Martin Luther King, Jr., he developed a philosophy of education for his doctoral dissertation in 1959. His dissertation provided the basis for his now internationally famous book *Pedagogy of the Oppressed*. The key premise of his book is that "human interaction rarely escapes oppression of one kind or another; by reason of class, race, or gender, people tend to be victims and/ or perpetrators of oppression" (Torres, 1994, p. 181). His approach to education "calls for dialogue and ultimately conscientization—critical consciousness or awareness—as a way to overcome relationships of domination and oppression" (Torres, 1994, p. 187).

Freire contrasted his pedagogy with what he described as a "banking" concept of education—teachers "deposit" their knowledge into empty "accounts" (their students). Freire's success in working with poor, illiterate adults in northern Brazil was so great that he was regarded as a threat to the existing political order. He was imprisoned and eventually exiled.

FOCUS ON DIVERSITY: FEMINIST PEDAGOGY

According to an advocate of **feminist pedagogy** and a teacher at an elementary school in **INDIANA**, schools "serve the power of dominant ideologies and beliefs" (Scering, 1997, p. 62). To ensure the growth and well-being of *all* students in a society dominated by the beliefs and perspectives of White males, then, "feminist pedagogy challenges the emphasis on efficiency and objectivity that perpetuate the domination of masculine rationality. . . . The role of schools in perpetuating unequal social, cultural, political, and economic realities is a central theme of [feminist pedagogy]" (Scering, 1997, p. 62). Thus, the goal of feminist pedagogy is to create caring communities of engaged learners who respect differences and work collaboratively to make democracy a reality for all classes of people.

A leading advocate for feminist pedagogy is bell hooks (she does not use capital letters in her name). According to hooks,

> Feminist education—the feminist classroom—is and should be a place where there is a sense of struggle, where there is a visible acknowledgment of the union of theory and practice, where we work together as teachers and students to overcome the estrangement and alienation that have become so much the norm. . . . Most importantly, feminist pedagogy should engage students in a learning process that makes the world "more real than less real." (hooks, 1989, p. 51)

In *Teaching to Transgress: Education as the Practice of Freedom*, hooks (1994, p. 12) states that education should be viewed as "the practice of freedom, [and] more than ever before . . . educators are compelled to confront the biases that have shaped teaching practices in our society and to create new ways of knowing, different strategies for the sharing of knowledge." hooks (2003, p. xv) also maintains that the classroom should be "a place that is life-sustaining and mind-expanding, a place of liberating mutuality where teacher and student together work in partnership."

Advocates of feminist pedagogy point out that different voices and different ways of knowing tend not to be acknowledged in classrooms dominated by Eurocentric, patriarchal curricula. hooks (2003, p. 3), for example, calls for the "decolonisation of ways of knowing."

Another well-known advocate of feminist pedagogy and a scholar instrumental in developing the legal definition of sexual harassment, Catharine MacKinnon (1994), explains how what is viewed as *the truth* in our society is determined by those in positions of power: "Having power means, among other things, that when someone says, 'this is how it is,' it is taken as being that way. . . . Powerlessness means that when you say, 'this is how it is,' it is not taken as being that way. This makes articulating silence, perceiving the presence of absence, believing those who have been socially stripped of credibility, critically contextualizing what passes for simple fact, necessary to the epistemology of a politics of the powerless."

WHAT PSYCHOLOGICAL ORIENTATIONS HAVE INFLUENCED TEACHING PHILOSOPHIES?

In addition to the five philosophical orientations to teaching described in previous sections of this chapter, several schools of psychological thought have formed the basis for teaching philosophies. These psychological theories are comprehensive worldviews that serve as the basis for the way many teachers approach their teaching. Psychological orientations to teaching are concerned primarily with understanding the conditions that are associated with effective learning. In other words, what motivates students to learn? What environments are most conducive to learning?

Chief among the psychological orientations that have influenced teaching philosophies are humanistic psychology, behaviorism, and constructivism. The following sections present a brief description of each orientation. Following each description is a sample portrait of a teacher whose behavior, to a considerable extent, illustrates that psychological orientation in action. Figure 4.6 presents a matrix for comparing the underlying belief systems of these three psychological orientations. After reading the description of each teacher, what words or phrases would fit the cells that apply to that teacher?

FIGURE 4.6　A matrix for comparing the underlying belief systems of three psychological orientations to teaching

Educational Beliefs	Psychological Orientations to Teaching		
	Humanist Teacher	Behaviorist Teacher	Constructivist Teacher
Beliefs about Teaching and Learning			
Beliefs about Students			
Beliefs about Knowledge			
Beliefs about What is Worth Knowing			
Personal Beliefs in Philosophical Areas			

Humanistic Psychology

Humanistic psychology emphasizes personal freedom, choice, awareness, and personal responsibility. As the term implies, it also focuses on the achievements, motivation, feelings, actions, and needs of human beings. The goal of education, according to this orientation, is individual self-actualization.

Humanistic psychology is derived from the philosophy of **humanism**, which developed during the European Renaissance and Protestant Reformation and is based on the belief that individuals control their own destinies through the application of their intelligence and learning. People "make themselves." The term *secular humanism* refers to the closely related belief that the conditions of human existence relate to human nature and human actions rather than to predestination or divine intervention.

In the 1950s and 1960s, humanistic psychology became the basis of educational reforms that sought to enhance students' achievement of their full potential through self-actualization (Maslow, 1954, 1962; Rogers, 1961). According to this psychological orientation, teachers should not force students to learn; instead, they should create a climate of trust and respect that allows students to decide what and how they learn, to question authority, and to take initiative in "making themselves." Teachers should be what noted psychologist Carl Rogers (1982) calls facilitators, and the classroom should be a place "in which curiosity and the natural desire to learn can be nourished and enhanced" (p. 31). Through their nonjudgmental understanding of students, humanist teachers encourage students to learn and grow.

PORTRAIT OF A HUMANIST TEACHER

Ten years ago, Ramerra Alexander began teaching at a small rural middle school—a position she enjoys because the school's small size enables her to develop close relationships with her students and their families. Her teaching style is based on humane, open interpersonal relationships with her students, and she takes pride in the fact that students trust her and frequently ask her advice on problems common to children in early adolescence. The positive rapport Ramerra has developed with her students is reflected in the regularity with which former students return to visit or to seek her advice.

These children are active learners in a real or relevant context, and they are constructing their own meanings through direct experience. How might this lesson be seen as an eclectic blend of progressive, existential, and constructivist ideals?

Ramerra is also committed to empowering her students, to giving them opportunities to shape their learning experiences. As she puts it: "I encourage students to give me feedback about how they feel in my classroom. They have to feel good about themselves before they can learn. Also, I've come to realize that students should help us (teachers) plan. I've learned to ask them what they're interested in. 'What do you want to do?' 'How do you want to do it?'"

Much of Ramerra's teaching is based on classroom discussions in which she encourages students to share openly their ideas and feelings about the subject at hand. Ramerra's interactions with students reveal her skill at creating a conversational environment that makes students feel safe and willing to contribute. During discussions, Ramerra listens attentively to students and frequently paraphrases their ideas in a way that acknowledges their contributions. She frequently responds with short phrases that indicate support and encourage the student to continue the discussion, such as the following: "I see. Would you say more about that?" "That is an interesting idea; tell us more."

When Ramerra is not facilitating a whole-group discussion, she is more than likely moving among the small cooperative-learning groups she has set up. Each group decided how to organize itself to accomplish a particular learning task—developing a strategy for responding to a threat to the environment or analyzing a poem about brotherhood, for example. "I think it's important for students to learn to work together, to help one another, and to accept different points of view," says Ramerra.

Behaviorism

Behaviorism is based on the principle that desirable human behavior can be the product of design rather than accident. According to behaviorists, it is an illusion to say that humans have a free will. Although we may act as if we are free, our behavior is really determined by forces in the environment that shape our behavior. "We are what we are and we do what we do, not because of any mysterious power of human volition, but because outside forces over which we lack any semblance of control have us caught in an inflexible web. Whatever else we may be, we are not the captains of our fate or the masters of our soul" (Power, 1982, p. 168).

FOUNDERS OF BEHAVIORISTIC PSYCHOLOGY

John B. Watson (1878–1958) was the principal originator of behavioristic psychology and B. F. Skinner (1904–1990) its best-known promoter. Watson first claimed that human behavior consisted of specific stimuli that resulted in certain responses. In part, he based this new conception of learning on the classic experiment conducted by Russian psychologist Ivan Pavlov (1849–1936). Pavlov had noticed that a dog he was working with would salivate when it was about to be given food. By introducing the sound of a bell when food was offered and repeating this several times, Pavlov discovered that the sound of the bell alone (a conditioned stimulus) would make the dog salivate (a conditioned response). Watson was so confident that all learning conformed to this basic stimulus–response model (now termed classical or type S conditioning) that he once boasted, "Give me a dozen healthy infants, well-formed, and my own specified world to bring them up in, and I'll guarantee to take any one at random and train him to become any type of specialist I might select—doctor, lawyer, artist, merchant-chief and, yes, even beggarman and thief, regardless of his talents, penchants, tendencies, abilities, vocations, and race of his ancestors" (Watson, 1925, p. 82).

Skinner went beyond Watson's basic stimulus–response model and developed a more comprehensive view of conditioning known as operant (or type R) conditioning. Operant conditioning is based on the idea that satisfying responses are conditioned, unsatisfying ones are not. In other words, "The things we call pleasant have an energizing or strengthening effect on our behaviour" (Skinner, 1972, p. 74). Thus, the teacher can create learners who exhibit desired behaviors by following four steps:

1. Identify desired behaviors in concrete (observable and measurable) terms.
2. Establish a procedure for recording specific behaviors and counting their frequencies.
3. For each behavior, identify an appropriate reinforcer.
4. Ensure that students receive the reinforcer as soon as possible after displaying a desired behavior.

PORTRAIT OF A BEHAVIORIST TEACHER

Ramona Day teaches fourth grade at a school with an enrollment of about 500 in a small midwestern town. Now in her fifth year at the school, Ramona has spent the last 3 years developing and refining a systematic approach to teaching. Last year, the success of her methods was confirmed when her students received the highest scores on the state's annual basic skills test.

Her primary method is individualized instruction, wherein students proceed at their own pace through modules she has put together. The modules cover five major areas: reading, writing, mathematics, general science, and spelling. She is working on a sixth module, geography, but it won't be ready until next year. She has developed a complex point system to keep track of students' progress and to motivate them to higher levels of achievement. The points students accumulate entitle them to participate in various in-class activities: free reading, playing with the many games and puzzles in the room, drawing or painting in the art corner, or playing video games on one of the two personal computers in the room.

Ramona has tried to convert several other teachers at the school to her behavioristic approach, and she is eager to talk to anyone who will listen about the effectiveness of her systematic approach to instruction. When addressing this topic, her exuberance is truly exceptional: "It's really quite simple. Students just do much better if you tell them exactly what you want them to know and then reward them for learning it."

In regard to the methods employed by some of her colleagues, Ramona can be rather critical. She knows some teachers in the school who teach by a trial-and-error method and "aren't clear about where they're going." She is also impatient with those who talk about the "art" of teaching; in contrast, everything that she does as a teacher is done with precision and a clear sense of purpose. "Through careful design and management of the learning environment," she says, "a teacher can get the results that he or she wants."

Constructivism

In contrast to behaviorism, constructivism focuses on processes of learning rather than on learning behavior. According to **constructivism**, students use cognitive processes to *construct* understanding of the material to be learned—in contrast to the view that they *receive* information transmitted by the teacher. Constructivist approaches support student-centered rather than teacher-centered curriculum and instruction. The student is the key to learning.

Unlike behaviorists who concentrate on directly observable behavior, constructivists focus on the mental processes and strategies that students use to learn. Our understanding of learning has been extended as a result of advances in **cognitive science**—the study of the mental processes students use in thinking and remembering. By drawing from research in linguistics, psychology, anthropology, neurophysiology, and computer science, cognitive scientists are developing new models for how people think and learn.

Teachers who base classroom activities on constructivism know that learning is an active, meaning-making process, that learners are not passive recipients of information. In fact, students are continually involved in making sense out of activities around them. Thus, the teacher must *understand students' understanding* and realize that students' learning is influenced by prior knowledge, experience, attitudes, and social interactions.

PORTRAIT OF A CONSTRUCTIVIST TEACHER

Lisa Sanchez teaches English at a middle school in a large city on the East Coast. The walls of her classroom are decorated with students' work—poetry, drawings, and students' writing reflecting various stages of the writing process: prewriting, revising, and final drafts.

Working in five groups, four students in each group, Lisa's eighth-grade students are translating *Romeo and Juliet* into modern English. Each group is translating a different act. Later, each group of students will choose a scene to enact, after designing a set and contemporary costumes. Lisa points out that her students will have to make decisions regarding the most appropriate costumes for each character based on their understanding of Shakespeare's play. "I want them to understand how *Romeo and Juliet* is relevant even today."

As students discuss the most appropriate translation line by line, Lisa moves from group to group. She asks clarifying questions and provides encouragement as students work to understand the meaning of Shakespeare's words.

At the end of class, Lisa explains her approach to teaching: "My teaching is definitely student-centered. I try to create a democratic classroom environment. My students are actively involved in creating meaning and knowledge for themselves. They do a lot of work in small groups, and they learn to question, investigate, hypothesize, and invent. They have to make connections between what they already know and new knowledge."

HOW CAN YOU DEVELOP YOUR EDUCATIONAL PHILOSOPHY?

As you read the preceding brief descriptions of five educational philosophies and three psychological orientations to teaching, perhaps you felt that no single philosophy fit perfectly with your idea of the kind of teacher you want to become. Or there may have been some element of each approach that seemed compatible with your own emerging philosophy of education. In either case, don't feel that you need to identify a single educational philosophy around which you will build your teaching career. In reality, few teachers follow only one educational philosophy, and as Figure 4.7 shows, educational philosophy is only one determinant of a teacher's behavior in the classroom. A teacher's behavior is also influenced by factors such as student's needs and interests, economic conditions, the culture of the school, political dynamics, family expectations, social forces, and community expectations.

Most teachers develop an *eclectic* philosophy of education, which means they develop their own unique blending of two or more philosophies. To help you identify the philosophies most consistent with your beliefs and values about educational goals, curriculum, and teachers' and students' roles in learning, complete the philosophic inventory in Figure 4.8. The self-knowledge you glean from completing the inventory

FIGURE 4.7 Factors that shape an eclectic philosophy of education and teaching behaviors

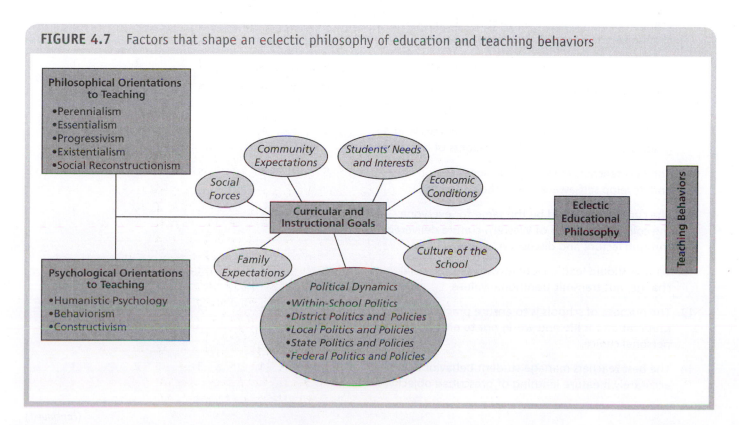

and the philosophical constructs presented in this chapter provide a useful framework for understanding various periods of our nation's educational history. For example, philosophical orientations to education waxed and waned during different periods— whether it was the perennialism and essentialism that characterized colonial schools, the progressivism of the 1920s and 1930s, the essentialism of the 1950s and 1980s, the humanism and social reconstructionism of the 1960s, or the constructivism of the 1990s and the first decade of the new century.

FIGURE 4.8 Philosophic inventory

The following inventory is to help identify your educational philosophy. Respond to the statements on the scale from 5, "Strongly Agree," to 1, "Strongly Disagree," by circling the number that most closely fits your perspective.

	Strongly Agree				Strongly Disagree
1. The curriculum should emphasize essential knowledge, *not* students' personal interests.	5	4	3	2	1
2. All learning results from rewards controlled by the external environment.	5	4	3	2	1
3. Teachers should emphasize interdisciplinary subject matter that encourages project-oriented, democratic classrooms.	5	4	3	2	1
4. Education should emphasize the search for personal meaning, *not* a fixed body of knowledge.	5	4	3	2	1
5. The ultimate aim of education is constant, absolute, and universal: to develop the rational person and cultivate the intellect.	5	4	3	2	1
6. Schools should actively involve students in social change to reform society.	5	4	3	2	1
7. Schools should teach basic skills, *not* humanistic ideals.	5	4	3	2	1
8. Eventually, human behavior will be explained by scientific laws, proving there is no free will.	5	4	3	2	1
9. Teachers should be facilitators and resources who guide student inquiry, *not* be managers of behavior.	5	4	3	2	1
10. The best teachers encourage personal responses and develop self-awareness in their students.	5	4	3	2	1
11. The curriculum should be the same for everyone: the collective wisdom of Western culture delivered through lecture and discussion.	5	4	3	2	1
12. Schools should lead society toward radical social change, *not* transmit traditional values.	5	4	3	2	1
13. The purpose of schools is to ensure practical preparation for life and work, *not* to encourage personal choice.	5	4	3	2	1
14. The best teachers manage student behavior and accurately measure learning of prescribed objectives.	5	4	3	2	1

(continued)

FIGURE 4.8 (continued)

	Strongly Agree				Strongly Disagree
15. Curriculum should emerge from students' needs and interests: therefore, it *should not* be prescribed in advance.	5	4	3	2	1
16. Helping students develop personal values is more important than transmitting traditional values.	5	4	3	2	1
17. The best education consists primarily of exposure to great works in the humanities.	5	4	3	2	1
18. It is more important for teachers to involve students in activities to criticize and transform society than to teach the "Great Books."	5	4	3	2	1
19. Schools should emphasize discipline, hard work, and respect for authority, *not* reform society.	5	4	3	2	1
20. Human learning can be controlled: anyone can be taught to be a scientist or a thief; therefore, personal choice is a myth.	5	4	3	2	1
21. Education should enhance personal growth through problem solving in the present, *not* emphasize preparation for a distant future.	5	4	3	2	1
22. Because we are born with an unformed personality, personal growth should be the focus of education.	5	4	3	2	1
23. The universal constant in human nature is the ability to reason; therefore, the sole focus of education should be to develop reasoning ability.	5	4	3	2	1
24. Schools perpetuate racism and sexism camouflaged as traditional values.	5	4	3	2	1
25. Teachers should efficiently transmit a set fixed body of knowledge, *not* experiment with curriculum.	5	4	3	2	1
26. Teaching is primarily management of student behavior to achieve the teacher's objectives.	5	4	3	2	1
27. Education should involve students in democratic activities and reflective thinking.	5	4	3	2	1
28. Students should have significant involvement in choosing what and how they learn.	5	4	3	2	1
29. Teachers should promote the permanency of the "classics," *not* practical preparation for life.	5	4	3	2	1
30. Learning should lead students to involvement in social reform.	5	4	3	2	1
31. On the whole, school should and must indoctrinate students with traditional values.	5	4	3	2	1
32. If ideas cannot be proved by science, they should be ignored as superstition and nonsense.	5	4	3	2	1

(continued)

FIGURE 4.8 Philosophic inventory (continued)

	Strongly Agree				Strongly Disagree
33. The major goal for teachers is to create an environment where students can learn on their own by guided reflection on their experiences.	5	4	3	2	1
34. Teachers should create opportunities for students to make personal choices, *not* shape their behavior.	5	4	3	2	1
35. The aim of education should be the same in every age and society, *not* differ from teacher to teacher.	5	4	3	2	1
36. Education should lead society toward social betterment, *not* confine itself to essential skills.	5	4	3	2	1

Philosophic Inventory Score Sheet

Record the number you circled for each statement (1–36). Total the number horizontally and record it in the space on the far right of the score sheet. The highest total indicates your educational philosophy.

Essentialism

Essentialism was a response to progressivism. It advocates a conservative philosophic perspective. The emphasis is on intellectual and moral standards that should be transmitted by the schools. The core of the curriculum should be essential knowledge and skills. Schooling should be practical and not influence social policy. It is a "back-to-basics" movement that emphasizes facts. Students should be taught discipline, hard work, and respect for authority. Influential essentialists: William C. Bagley, H. G. Rickover, Arthur Bestor, and William Bennett; E. D. Hirsch's *Cultural Literacy* could fit this category.

_____	+	_____	+	_____	+	_____	+	_____	+	_____	=	_____
1		7		13		19		25		31		Total

Behaviorism

Behaviorism denies free will and maintains that behavior is the result of external forces, which cause humans to behave in predictable ways. Behaviorism is linked with empiricism, which stresses scientific experiment and observation. Behaviorists are skeptical about metaphysical claims. Behaviorists look for laws governing human behavior the way natural scientists look for empirical laws governing natural events. The role of the teacher is to identify behavioral goals and establish a reward system to achieve goals. Influential behaviorists: B. F. Skinner, Ivan Pavlov, J. B. Watson, and Benjamin Bloom.

_____	+	_____	+	_____	+	_____	+	_____	+	_____	=	_____
2		8		14		20		26		32		Total

Progressivism

Progressivism focuses more on the child than the subject matter. The students' interests and personal growth are important. Learners should be active and learn to solve problems by reflecting on their experiences. The school should help students develop democratic personal and social values. Because society is always changing, new ideas are important to make the future better than the past. Influential progressivists: John Dewey, William Kilpatrick, and Francis Parker.

_____	+	_____	+	_____	+	_____	+	_____	+	_____	=	_____
3		9		15		21		27		33		Total

Existentialism

Existentialism is a highly subjective philosophy that stresses the importance of the individual and emotional commitment to living authentically. It emphasizes individual choice over the importance of rational theories, history, and social institutions. Jean Paul Sartre, the French philosopher, claimed "existence precedes essence." Sartre meant that people are born and must define themselves through personal choices. Influential existentialists: Jean Paul

(continued)

FIGURE 4.8 (continued)

Sartre, Soren Kierkegaard, Martin Buber, Martin Heidegger, Gabriel Marcel, Friedrich Nietzsche, Albert Camus, Carl Rogers, A. S. Neill, and Maxine Greene.

_____ + _____ + _____ + _____ + _____ + _____ = _____
   4   10   16   22   28   34   Total

Perennialism

Perennialists advocates that the aim of education is to ensure that students acquire knowledge about the great ideas of Western culture. Human beings are rational, and it is this capacity that needs to be developed. Cultivation of the intellect is the highest priority of an education worth having. The highest level of knowledge in each field should be the focus of curriculum. Influential perennialists: Robert Maynard Hutchins, Mortimer Adler, and Allan Bloom.

_____ + _____ + _____ + _____ + _____ + _____ = _____
   5   11   17   23   29   35   Total

Reconstructionism

Reconstructionists advocate that schools should take the lead to reconstruct society. Schools have more than a responsibility to transmit knowledge; they have the mission to transform society as well. Reconstructionists go beyond progressivists in advocating social activism. Influential reconstructionists: Theodore Brameld, George Counts, Paulo Freire, and Henry Giroux.

_____ + _____ + _____ + _____ + _____ + _____ = _____
   6   12   18   24   30   36   Total

Source: Originally prepared by Robert Leahy for *Becoming a Teacher: Accepting the Challenge of a Profession*, 3d ed., 1995. Revised by the author for inclusion in *Authentic Educating*, 2009, Lanham, MD: University Press of America, Inc., pp. 17–21. Used by permission of the author.

SUMMARY

Why Is Philosophy Important to Teachers?

- Knowledge of educational philosophy enables teachers to understand the complex political forces that influence schools, to evaluate more effectively current proposals for change, and to grow professionally. Professional teachers continually strive for a clearer, more comprehensive answer to basic philosophical questions.
- Most schools have a statement of philosophy that describes educational values and goals.

What Is the Nature of Philosophy?

- Philosophy, which means "love of wisdom," is concerned with pondering the fundamental questions of life: What is truth? What is reality? What life is worth living?

What Determines Your Educational Philosophy?

- An educational philosophy is a set of beliefs about education, a set of principles to guide professional action.
- A teacher's educational philosophy is made up of personal beliefs about teaching and learning, students, knowledge, and what is worth knowing.

What Are the Branches of Philosophy?

- The branches of philosophy and the questions they address are (1) metaphysics (What is the nature of reality?), (2) epistemology (What is the nature of knowledge and is truth attainable?), (3) axiology (What values should one live by?), (4) ethics (What is good and evil, right and wrong?), (5) aesthetics (What is beautiful?), and (6) logic (What reasoning processes yield valid conclusions?).

What Are Five Modern Philosophical Orientations to Teaching?

- **Progressivism**—The aim of education should be based on the needs and interests of students.
- **Perennialism**—Students should acquire knowledge of enduring great ideas.
- **Essentialism**—Schools should teach students, in a disciplined and systematic way, a core of "essential" knowledge and skills.
- **Existentialism**—In the face of an indifferent universe, students should acquire an education that will enable them to assign meaning to their lives. Postmodernism, which is similar to existentialism, maintains that there

are no absolute truths and disputes the certainty of scientific, or objective, explanations of reality.

- **Social reconstructionism**—In response to the significant social problems of the day, schools should take the lead in creating a new social order. Critical pedagogy, much like social reconstructionism, focuses on how education can promote social justice, especially for those who do not enjoy positions of power and influence in society. Feminist pedagogy, also similar to social reconstructionism, maintains that different voices and different ways of knowing tend not to be acknowledged in classrooms that are dominated by Eurocentric, patriarchal curricula.

What Psychological Orientations Have Influenced Teaching Philosophies?

- **Humanism**—Children are innately good, and education should focus on individual needs, personal freedom, and self-actualization.

- **Behaviorism**—By careful control of the educational environment and with appropriate reinforcement techniques, teachers can cause students to exhibit desired behaviors.
- **Constructivism**—Teachers should "understand students' understanding" and view learning as an active process in which learners construct meaning.

How Can You Develop Your Educational Philosophy?

- Instead of basing their teaching on only one educational philosophy, most teachers develop an eclectic educational philosophy.
- Professional teachers continually strive for a clearer, more comprehensive answer to basic philosophical questions.

PROFESSIONAL REFLECTIONS AND ACTIVITIES

Teacher's Journal

1. To illustrate educational philosophies in action, this chapter presents "portraits" of eight different teachers. Imagine that you are a colleague of one of these teachers—a teacher whose educational philosophy is very different from your own. Write that teacher a letter in which you react to his or her philosophical orientation to teaching. Your letter might include questions or concerns about the teacher's educational philosophy, as well as an explanation of why your educational philosophy is more appropriate for today's students.

2. Review the five philosophical and three psychological orientations discussed in this chapter. With reference to today's schools, what is the current status of each—that is, is it widespread or not? Which orientation do you think is most popular among teachers? Least popular?

3. Recall one of your favorite teachers at the elementary, middle, or high school levels. Which of the educational philosophies or psychological orientations to teaching described in this chapter best capture that teacher's approach to teaching? Write a descriptive sketch of that teacher in action. How has this teacher influenced your educational philosophy?

Teacher's Research

1. Numerous organizations influence educational policy and practice in the United States. Visit the websites of two or more of the following organizations and compare the educational philosophies that are reflected in their goals, position statements, and political activities with regard to education:

   Alternative Public Schools Inc. (APS)
   American Federation of Teachers (AFT)
   National Education Association (NEA)
   Chicago Teachers Union (or other municipal teachers' organization)
   National Congress of Parents and Teachers (PTA)
   Parents as Teachers (PAT)
   Texas State Teachers Association (or other state teachers' organization)

2. Explore encyclopedias, bibliographies, periodicals, news sources, and other online reference works to research in greater detail the contributions of one of the educational philosophers included in their chapter. In a brief oral report, present your findings to the rest of your class.

Observations and Interviews

1. Interview a teacher for the purpose of understanding his or her educational philosophy. Formulate your interview questions in light of the philosophical concepts discussed in this chapter and the questions posed at the beginning of this chapter. What should the purpose(s) of education be? What knowledge is of most worth? What values should teachers encourage their students to develop? How should learning be evaluated? Discuss your findings with classmates.

2. Observe the class of a teacher at the level at which you plan to teach. Which of the five philosophies or three psychological orientations to teaching discussed in this chapter most characterizes this teacher? Describe the teacher–student interactions that result in your response.

Professional Portfolio

Each month, prepare a written (or videotaped) statement in which you explain one of the following key elements of your educational philosophy (see Figure 4.1, on page 115). At the end of 5 months, you should have a statement for each set of beliefs.

- Beliefs about teaching and learning
- Beliefs about students
- Beliefs about knowledge
- Beliefs about what is worth knowing
- Personal beliefs in philosophical areas

As appropriate, revise your belief statements throughout the course and during the remainder of your teacher education program. On completion of your teacher education program, review your portfolio entry and make any appropriate revisions. The ability to provide a full explanation of your philosophy of education will be a definite advantage when you begin to look for your first job as a teacher.

CHAPTER QUIZ

Take this quiz to check your understanding of the content covered in this chapter.

CHAPTER FIVE

Historical Foundations of U.S. Education

learning outcomes

After reading this chapter, you will be able to do the following:

1. Explain why educational history is important for teachers.
2. Describe the European antecedents of American education.
3. Describe teaching and schools in the American colonies (1620–1750).
4. Identify the goals of education during the Revolutionary period (1750–1820).
5. Explain how the struggle for state-supported common schools was won (1820–1865).
6. Explain how compulsory education changed schools and the teaching profession (1865–1920).
7. Describe the aims of education during the progressive era (1920–1945).
8. Explain how education changed during the modern postwar era (1945–2000).
9. Explain the educational priorities of the new century (2000 to the present).

READERS' VOICES

Why is educational history important?

Educational history helps us understand how schools have evolved—how our country has continuously sought to improve schools. Also, educational history serves as a guide for what we must do today to continue that improvement and to provide a quality education for all students.

—ALIANNA, Teacher Education program, first year

WHY IS EDUCATIONAL HISTORY IMPORTANT?

In *The Life of Reason*, George Santayana said, "Those who cannot remember the past are condemned to repeat it." Similarly, Adlai Stevenson, presidential candidate in 1952 and 1956, said, "We can chart our future clearly and wisely only when we know the path which has led us to the present." For teachers, the implication of these statements is clear—the past has an impact on teaching and schools today. Accomplished teachers learn from our nation's educational past. They know that educational practices from the past have not disappeared—they continue to evolve, and they shape the present, as well as the future. As Hal Adams, the **UTAH** Teacher of the Year profiled in this chapter's Teachers' Voices: Walk in My Shoes feature points out, "understanding the past is the best compass for the future."

We cannot understand schools today without a look at what they were yesterday. Today's teachers must be students of our educational past so that they may provide leadership to improve our educational future. For example, the history of education in the United States reveals countless examples of how political forces, social class, special-interest groups, religion, and cultural and ethnic diversity have influenced schools; and professional teachers understand these influences.

The current system of public and private education in the United States is an ongoing reflection of its historical foundations and of the aspirations and values brought to this country by its founders and generations of settlers. Thus, it is impossible to understand schools today without a look at what they were yesterday. Becoming familiar with events that have shaped the quest for educational quality and equity in the United States is an important part of your education as a professional.

Still, you may wonder, what is the value of knowing about the history of U.S. education? Will that knowledge help you to be a better teacher? First, knowledge of the events that have influenced our schools will help you evaluate more effectively current proposals for change. You will understand how schools have developed and how current proposals might relate to previous change efforts. As a first-year teacher education student, Thomas, puts it: "Educational history helps us understand the 'flaws' of previous approaches to schooling, and it allows us to reform today's system of schooling based on that understanding."

Second, awareness of events that have influenced teaching is a hallmark of professionalism in education. Just as an effective democracy demands enlightened, aware citizens, so, too, does a profession require knowledgeable professionals. For teachers, the study of educational history is an important part of professional knowledge.

This chapter begins with a brief description of some of the European influences on U.S. education. Next, the chapter presents brief overviews of seven periods of education in the United States. Each section examines the individuals, social forces, and events that, in the author's judgment, have had the greatest impact on schools in our country.

WHAT WERE THE EUROPEAN ANTECEDENTS OF AMERICAN EDUCATION?

Many practices in today's schools originated in much earlier societies throughout the world. Non-Western civilizations in ancient Egypt, China, and India, for example, emphasized the need for practical education in mathematics, astronomy, medicine, engineering, agriculture, and geography. Similarly, early Western civilizations emphasized the role of education in preparing children and youth for their roles as adults in society. The timeline in Figure 5.1 shows major events and individuals in Europe that had an impact on the development of education in 17th-century colonial America. This section presents (1) an overview of education in Greece and Rome, (2) a brief glimpse of the kaleidoscope of European history from the fall of Rome to the start of the 18th century, and (3) a review of how four 18th-century European thinkers influenced education in colonial America.

FIGURE 5.1   European influences on American Education, 5000 B.C. – 1900 A.D.

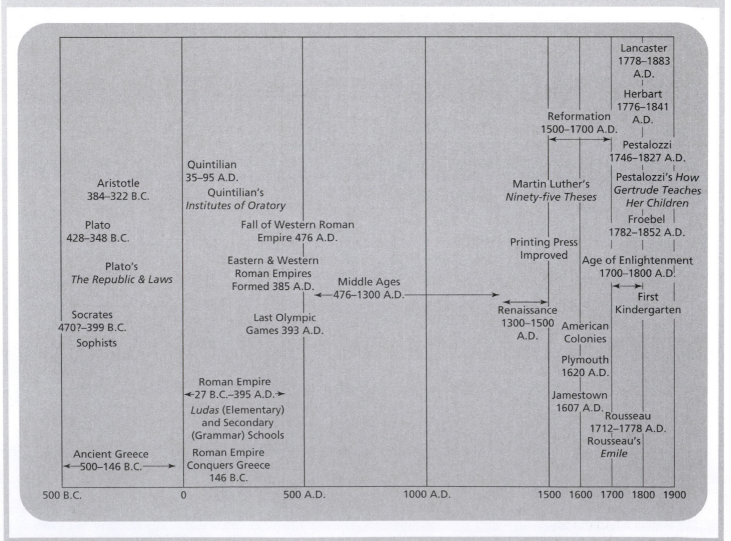

Education in Ancient Greece

Education in ancient Greece (500–146 B.C.) has had an enduring impact on today's schools. The Greeks believed that people should use leisure time to reflect on the practical and aesthetic values of life. Based on principles of moderation and balance, the goal of Greek education was the well-rounded development of mind and body.

Although the pursuit of knowledge by the ancient Greeks is worthy of imitation, other facets of this ancient civilization conflict with the values and goals of today's society. For example, the leisure enjoyed by the small middle and upper classes in ancient Greece was made possible by a vast population of slaves, and women were not eligible to become citizens.

Several philosophers in ancient Greece shaped ideas about the relationship between education and life. Perhaps the greatest contributions were made by Socrates (ca. 470–399 B.C.), Plato (428–348 B.C.), and Aristotle (384–322 B.C.).

SOCRATES

What little we know about Socrates comes to us from his portrayal in the *Dialogues* written by his student, Plato. Socrates' questioning strategies, his emphasis on discussion to promote inquiry, and his quest for virtue are reflected in today's teaching practices. Socrates questioned his pupils in a manner that led them to see errors and inconsistencies in their thinking. By using an inductive approach, Socrates believed that the truth could be discovered. **Socratic questioning**, according to contemporary educational philosopher Mortimer Adler (1982), is essential for the study of six great ideas: truth, beauty, goodness, liberty, equality, and justice. By questioning students repeatedly, Socrates led his students to these eternal truths.

PLATO AND ARISTOTLE

A student and disciple of Socrates, Plato believed that the individual's abilities should be developed through education for the good of society. To promote his views among Athenians, Plato founded the free, coeducational Academy, often referred to as the world's first university.

Plato believed that boys and girls should be educated from age 6 to 18, with music, mathematics, and gymnastics the main areas of study. Music was a source of "noble" emotions and included the study of literature and history. Mathematics linked the powers of reason with the processes of nature and enabled one to influence the environment. And gymnastics, which emphasized physical and mental well-being, included the study of dance, rhythm, athletics, and military arts. Taken together, the aim of this three-part curriculum was to improve the soul and enable the individual to achieve moral excellence and to realize the ultimate good.

Aristotle, Plato's most famous student, studied and taught at the Academy for 20 years. Whereas Plato was an idealist and believed that ideas are the ultimate reality, Aristotle was a realist and believed that reality, knowledge, and value exist in the physical world independent of the mind. Goodness and virtue depend upon deeds, not knowledge.

Like Plato, Aristotle believed that society needed a strong system of education. Aristotle supported education for all Athenian citizens; however, the majority of Athens' inhabitants were not citizens. Women, for example, were ineligible for citizenship because it was felt they lacked the rational capacities for citizenship and wisdom.

Education in Ancient Rome

In 146 B.C., Greece was conquered by a Roman army. In 27 B.C., Augustus established the Roman Empire, which continued until A.D. 395, when it was divided into the Western Roman Empire, with the capital at Rome, and the Eastern Roman Empire, with the capital at Constantinople. In A.D. 476, the Roman Empire fell.

Roman education was heavily influenced by Greek education. The Roman school system consisted of the *ludus,* or elementary school, and a secondary or grammar school. Boys and girls aged 7 to 12 attended the ludi, where they learned to read, write, and compute. The education of girls seldom went beyond the ludus. Upper-class boys aged 12 to 16 attended grammar schools, where they studied Greek or Latin grammar and literature. Boys aged 16 to 20 attended a school of rhetoric, where they studied grammar, rhetoric, dialectic, music, arithmetic, geometry, and astronomy.

From the Middle Ages to the Age of Enlightenment

The period from the fall of the Roman Empire to the 14th century is known as the Middle Ages. During the medieval period, the Roman Catholic Church came to have the greatest influence on education in Europe. For the most part, the prevailing class structure based on feudalism was not fertile ground for the growth of schools during the Middle Ages. However, the clergy received instruction in the monasteries and at cathedral schools, and medieval universities were established in Spain, France, and England.

A rebirth of interest in Greco-Roman traditions of art, literature, and learning began in the 14th century and reached a peak in the 15th century. This period, known as the Renaissance, began in northern Europe and Italy and spread throughout Europe.

The key to improving the human condition, according to Renaissance humanists, was to transfer wealth and power from the Church to the people. In addition, humanists believed that an educational system similar to ancient Rome's should be created. They also believed that instruction should consist of the study of ancient classical literature, particularly the work of Plato and Aristotle. The ideal curriculum of the time was based on the seven liberal arts: the *trivium* of grammar, logic, and rhetoric, and the *quadrivium* of arithmetic, geometry, astronomy, and music. Figure 5.2 illustrates the seven liberal arts, with Socrates and Plato in the inner circle.

Educational Thought in 18th-Century Europe

The Reformation, with its questioning of religious doctrines, revived interest in the scientific understanding of nature. The 18th century came to be known as the Age of Enlightenment or the Age of Reason because reasoning and scientific inquiry were being used to improve society. European thinkers of the 1700s have had a lasting impact on education in the United States.

Jean-Jacques Rousseau (1712–1778), considered by some to be the "father of modern child psychology" (Mayer, 1973), believed that children progressed through stages of growth and development. According to Rousseau, knowledge of these stages should guide the development of instructional strategies. Rousseau also believed in the innate goodness of children—a natural goodness that society corrupts. Rousseau's child-centered educational theories influenced many educators in France and beyond. For example, John Dewey, whose educational philosophy shaped the progressive education movement in the United States from 1920–1945, was influenced by Rousseau.

Johann Heinrich Pestalozzi (1746–1827) was a Swiss educator who implemented many of Rousseau's ideas. Noted educators worldwide, including Horace Mann from the United States, traveled to Pestalozzi's experimental school in Yverdun, Switzerland, to observe his methods and learn from him. His 1826 book, *How Gertrude Teaches Her Children,* contributed greatly to the development of elementary schools.

Like Rousseau, Pestalozzi believed that the innate goodness of children was corrupted by society, and that instructional practices and curriculum materials should be selected in light of students' natural abilities and readiness to learn. Effective instruction, Pestalozzi believed, moved from concrete experiences to abstract concepts, from the simple to the complex.

Pestalozzi also recognized that children's learning was enhanced by a healthy self-esteem and feelings of emotional security. He was particularly concerned about poor children whom he believed needed to feel loved by their teachers, as Ulich (1950, p. 264) points out: "In the studies of Old Swiss and German schoolmasters one could often find a reproduction of a painting of Pestalozzi, in which we see him, with a

FIGURE 5.2   The Seven Liberal Arts

Source: http://www.rgle.org.uk/RGLE_Liberal_arts.htm

profound expression of love on his ugly and wrinkled face, embracing the children of peasants who, clad in rags, enter the simple schoolroom."

Johann Friedrich Herbart (1776–1841) was a student of Pestalozzi's and became known as the father of the science of education and of modern psychology (Schubert, 1986). Herbart believed that education should focus primarily on developing moral character. His five-step systematic approach for presenting new material to students is still in use today:

1. Preparation: helping students make connections between what they know and what they are about to learn.
2. Presentation: introducing material in a manner that is appropriate for the psychological development of the student.

3. Association: combining new and previously learned material.
4. Generalization: moving from concrete examples to abstract principles.
5. Application: using recently acquired knowledge to learn more.

The development of schools in the 18th and 19th centuries was related to European industrialization, urbanization, and population growth. For example, in England, Joseph Lancaster (1778–1838) developed a **monitorial system** for crowded schools in which older students taught younger students. According to the Lancasterian system, one teacher instructed hundreds of pupils through the use of student monitors—older students selected for their academic abilities. Lancaster eventually emigrated to America, where monitorial schools spread rapidly in urban areas after the first school opened in New York City in 1806.

WHAT WERE TEACHING AND SCHOOLS LIKE IN THE AMERICAN COLONIES (1620–1750)?

Education in colonial America had its primary roots in English culture. The settlers of our country initially tried to develop a system of schooling that paralleled the British two-track system. If students from the lower classes attended school at all, it was at the elementary level for the purpose of acquiring practical skills in reading, writing, and computation and receiving religious instruction. Students from the upper classes had the opportunity to attend Latin grammar schools, where they were given a college-preparatory education that focused on subjects such as Latin and Greek classics.

Above all, the colonial curriculum stressed religious objectives. Generally, no distinction was made between secular and religious life in the colonies. The religious motives that impelled the Puritans to endure the hardships of settling in a new land were reflected in the schools' curricula. The primary objective of elementary schooling was to learn to read so that one might read the Bible and religious catechisms and thereby receive salvation and spend eternity in heaven.

What textbooks might students have used in this early classroom? What educational beliefs and values were reflected in the curriculum and instruction of this period?

The Status of Teachers

Because those who taught in colonial schools could do so with minimal qualifications—and for little pay—their status was relatively low. Respect increased with grade level and the amount of education required for the position. Elementary school teachers, the majority of whom had no more than an elementary education themselves, were given the least respect, and teachers in the few secondary schools were accorded the highest status.

Colonial teachers were "special but shadowed," according to Dan Lortie (1975). Because teachers, and members of the clergy, were educated, they were "special" and expected to have high moral character. On the other hand, teachers were "shadowed" because they were subordinate to the clergy, the power elite in the community. Teachers' extra duties reflected their marginal status: "Teachers rang the church bells, . . . swept up . . . taught Bible lessons, and occasionally substituted for the ailing pastor. Those who wished to teach had to accept stern inspection of their moral behavior" (Lortie, 1975, p. 11).

Teaching was also shadowed by what was seen as the "real" work of the community—farming. "Farming was the vital preoccupation. And though males were preferred as teachers, in the summer months, when men were needed to work the land, women were recruited to take their places" (Lightfoot, 1978, p. 47).

Colonial Schools

In the New England colonies (Massachusetts Bay, New Hampshire, and Connecticut), there was a general consensus that church, state, and schools were interrelated. As a result, town schools were created throughout these colonies to teach children the basics of reading and writing so they could learn the scriptures. These schools were heavily influenced by the Puritans, a group of Protestants who believed in strict religious discipline and simplified religious ceremonies.

The Puritan view of the child included the belief that people are inherently sinful. Even natural childhood play was seen as devil-inspired idleness. The path to redemption lay in learning to curb one's natural instincts and behave like an adult as quickly as possible.

To bring about this premature growth, the teacher had to correct the child constantly and try to curb his or her natural instincts. As one historian put it, "In colonial New England the whole idea of education presumed that children were miniature adults possessed of human degeneracy. The daily school routine was characterized by harshness and dogmatism. Discipline was strict, and disobedience and infractions of rules were often met with severe penalties meted out by quick-tempered, poorly qualified instructors" (Rippa, 1997, p. 30).

The middle colonies (New York, New Jersey, Pennsylvania, and Delaware) were more diverse, and groups such as the Irish, Scots, Swedes, Danes, Dutch, and Germans established **parochial schools** based on their religious beliefs. Anglicans, Lutherans, Quakers, Jews, Catholics, Presbyterians, and Mennonites in the middle colonies tended to establish their own schools. In the largely Protestant southern colonies (Virginia, Maryland, Georgia, and North and South Carolina), wealthy plantation owners believed the primary purpose of education was to promote religion and to prepare their children to attend colleges and universities in Europe. The vast majority of small farmers received no formal schooling, and the children of African slaves received only the training they needed to serve their masters.

No one type of schooling was common to all the colonies. The most common types, however, were the dame schools, the reading and writing schools, and the Latin grammar schools.

THE DAME SCHOOLS

Dame schools provided initial instruction for boys and often the only schooling for girls. These schools were run by widows or housewives in their homes and supported by modest fees from parents. At **dame schools**, classes were usually held in the kitchen, where children learned only the barest essentials of reading, writing, and arithmetic during instruction lasting for a few weeks to 1 year. Females might also be taught sewing and basic homemaking skills. Students often began by learning the alphabet from a horn book. Developed in medieval Europe, the **horn book** was a copy of the alphabet covered by a thin transparent sheet made from a cow's horn. "The layer of horn protected the parchment from the wear and tear and smudges of little hands" (Urban & Wagoner, 2009, p. 46). The alphabet and the horn covering were attached to a paddle-shaped piece of wood. Students often hung their hornbooks around their necks with a leather cord threaded through a hole in the paddle.

TEACHERS' VOICES
Walk in My Shoes
"Understanding the Past is the Best Compass for the Future."
Hal Adams
Grand County High School
Moab, Utah

READING AND WRITING SCHOOLS

At **reading and writing schools**, boys received an education that went beyond what their parents could teach them at home or what they could learn at a dame school. Reading lessons were based on the Bible, various religious catechisms, and the *New England Primer*, first printed in 1690. The *Primer* introduced children to the letters of the alphabet through the use of illustrative woodcuts and rhymed couplets. The first couplet began with the pronouncement that

> *In Adam's fall*
> *We sinned all.*

And the final one noted that

> *Zaccheus be*
> *Did climb the Tree*
> *His Lord to see.*

The *Primer* also presented children with large doses of stern religious warnings about the proper conduct of life.

LATIN GRAMMAR SCHOOLS

The Boston Latin School was founded in 1635 to provide a pre-college education for the new country's future leaders. At a mass meeting that April, the residents of Boston decided to hire Philemon Pormont "for the teaching and nurturing of children with us" (Urban & Wagoner, 2009, p. 44). The **Latin grammar school**, comparable to today's secondary school, was patterned after the classical schools of Europe. Boys enrolled in the Latin grammar schools at the age of 7 or 8, whereupon they began to prepare to enter Harvard College (established in 1636). Following graduation from Harvard, they would assume leadership roles in the church.

At first, grammar schools were 7-year schools; later, they were made into 4-year schools. The quality of teaching in the Latin grammar schools was higher than that found in the dame schools or reading and writing schools. In addition, grammar school teachers assumed that students had learned to read and write, either at home or in dame schools.

Latin and Greek were the principal studies in these schools, although arithmetic was introduced in 1745. Students were required to read Latin authors and to speak Latin in poetry and prose as well as conjugate Greek verbs. As the following description indicates, both the curriculum and the mode of instruction were rigorous:

> In most of the Latin schools, the course of study lasted for seven years. Apparently school was in session six days a week and continued throughout the winter and summer. The school day was usually from six to eleven o'clock in the morning and from one to four or five o'clock in the afternoon. The boys sat on benches for long hours. Great faith was placed in the *memoriter* method of drill and rote learning. Through repeated recitations the students were conditioned to respond with a definite answer to a particular question. Class discussions were not permitted. The Latin schools inherited the English tradition of severe discipline. It was not unusual for a quick-tempered schoolmaster to hit a pupil for an unsatisfactory recitation. School regulations designated the punishments which should be meted out for fighting, lying, cursing, and playing cards or dice. (Rippa, 1984, p. 43)

Contrast how students were treated in Latin grammar schools during the colonial era with how the teacher profiled in this chapter's Teaching on Your Feet feature treats her unmotivated, emotionally troubled student, Frank.

SCHOOLS FOR AFRICAN AMERICANS AND NATIVE AMERICANS

One of the first schools for African Americans and Native Americans was started by Elias Neau in New York City in 1704. Neau spoke out against slavery and the lack of education for the children of the slaves. When he asked the Church of England to provide a teacher, church leaders appointed him to teach African Americans and Native Americans how to read as part of the church's efforts to convert students (Pierre, 1916).

The Origins of Mandated Education

As today's citizens know, compulsory education laws require that parents, or those who have custody of children between certain ages, send their children to school. During the colonial era, however, this was not the case.

Universal compulsory education had its origins in the **Massachusetts Act of 1642**, viewed by some as the first school law in the colonies (Urban & Wagoner, 2013). Prior to this date, parents could decide whether they wished their children to be educated at home or at a school. Church and civic leaders in the colonies, however, decided that education could no longer remain voluntary. They saw that many children were receiving inadequate occupational training. Moreover, they realized that organized schools would serve to strengthen and preserve Puritan religious beliefs.

The Puritans decided to make education a civil responsibility of the state. The Massachusetts General Court passed a law in 1642 that required each town to determine whether young people could read and write. Parents and apprentices' masters whose children were unable "to read and understand the principles of religion and the capital laws of the country" (Spring, 2008b, p. 15) could be fined and possibly lose custody of their children.

Although the Massachusetts Act of 1642 did not mandate the establishment of schools, it did make it clear that the education of children was a direct concern of the local citizenry. In 1648, the court revised the 1642 law, reminding town leaders that "the good education of children is of singular behoof and benefit to any commonwealth" and that some parents and masters were still "too indulgent and negligent of their duty"

TEACHING ON YOUR FEET
Worth the Struggle

"If there is no struggle, there is no progress." Frederick Douglass's words apply not only to history but also to teaching. When I first became a teacher, I thought I would enter the classroom and instantly inspire all of my students to fall in love with American history. Although I have taught many students who eventually come to appreciate history, I have also struggled with student issues that transcend academic subject matter; indeed, the biggest challenge most teachers encounter is unmotivated students.

I remember one unmotivated student especially well. Frank (not his real name) arrived in the middle of the year, when my classroom was running smoothly and all of my students were accustomed to my classroom policies and procedures. Frank had long hair that nearly covered his face, kept his head down, and rarely looked me in the eye. I quickly realized that Frank was not just unmotivated; he was also emotionally troubled. He was moody and frequently missed school, and when I asked him a question, he would usually shrug his shoulders and whisper, "I don't care." He was falling behind in his schoolwork and was unresponsive to the motivational speeches I often gave when students failed to turn in a homework assignment. Despite his behavior, I wanted to help Frank. I offered him individual attention through after-school tutoring.

To ensure that Frank received proper help, I shared my concerns with the school psychologist. She met with Frank and suggested that I could best help Frank by listening to him and showing a genuine interest in him and his life. I decided to ignore his antisocial behavior and treat him as if he were the most interesting student in class.

The tutoring sessions turned out to be the perfect environment to get to know Frank well. Initially, Frank was very quiet and withdrawn. The first few tutoring sessions were very mechanical: I reviewed a lesson with him, then he would work on the homework. During lessons, I tried to relate the material to his life. I tried to connect history with his life in the here and now. Although it took some time, he slowly began to open up and to talk to me about his life and family. I took the time to listen and to relate his experiences to a lesson.

After 2 months of tutoring sessions, I began to see an improvement in Frank's mood. He was still shy, but he started answering questions in class and showing an interest in American history. At the end of the school year, Frank participated in the eighth-grade promotion ceremony. Afterward, to my surprise, he handed me a card. I read the card later that evening. It was a simple message thanking me for being kind to him.

ANALYZE & REFLECT

Click here to analyze and reflect on this scenario you have just read.

ELIZABETH GUBBINS
Las Palmas Middle School
Covina, **CALIFORNIA**

(Cohen, 1974, pp. 394–395). As the first educational law in this country, the Massachusetts Act of 1642 was a landmark.

The **Massachusetts Act of 1647**, often referred to as the Old Deluder Satan Act (because education was seen as the best protection against the wiles of the devil), mandated the establishment and support of schools. In particular, towns of 50 households or more were to appoint a person to instruct "all such children as shall resort to him to write and read." Teachers were to "be paid either by the parents or masters of such children, or by the inhabitants in general" (Rippa, 1997, p. 36). This act also required towns of 100 households or more to establish a Latin grammar school to prepare students for Harvard College. A town that failed to satisfy this law could be assessed a fine of 5 pounds.

Support for mandated education was later expanded by passage of the Northwest Ordinance in 1785, which gave federal land to the states for educational purposes. The Ordinance divided the Northwest Territories (now Illinois, Indiana, Michigan, Ohio, Wisconsin, and part of Minnesota) into 36-square-mile sections, with the 16th square mile designated for public schools.

WHAT WERE THE GOALS OF EDUCATION DURING THE REVOLUTIONARY PERIOD (1750–1820)?

Education in the United States during the Revolutionary period was characterized by a general decline of European influences on schools. Religious traditions that had their origins in Europe continued to affect the curriculum; however, the young country's need to develop agriculture, shipping, and commerce also exerted an influence on the curriculum. By this time, the original settlers who had emigrated from Europe had been replaced by a new generation whose most immediate roots were in the new soil of the United States. This new, exclusively American identity was enhanced by the rise of civil town governments, the great increase in books and newspapers that addressed life in the new country, and a turning away from Europe toward the unsettled West. The colonies' break with Europe was most potently demonstrated in the American Revolution of 1776.

Following independence, many leaders were concerned that new disturbances from within could threaten the well-being of the new nation. Among these leaders were Benjamin Franklin, Sarah Pierce, Thomas Jefferson, and Noah Webster. To preserve the freedoms that had been fought for, a system of education became essential. Through education, people would become intelligent, participating citizens of a constitutional democracy.

Benjamin Franklin's Academy

Benjamin Franklin (1706–1790) designed and promoted the Philadelphia Academy, a private secondary school, which opened in 1751. This school, which replaced the old Latin grammar school, had a curriculum that was broader and more practical and also focused on the English language rather than Latin. The academy was also a more democratically run institution than previous schools had been. Although **academies** were largely privately controlled and privately financed, they were secular and often supported by public funds. Most academies were public because anyone who could pay tuition could attend, regardless of church affiliation (Rippa, 1997, p. 65).

In his *Proposals Relating to the Education of Youth in Pennsylvania*, written in 1749, Franklin noted that "the good Education of youth has been esteemed by wise men in all ages, as the surest foundation of the happiness both of private families and of commonwealths" (Franklin, 1931, p. 151).

Franklin's proposals for educating youth called for a wide range of subjects that emphasized the classics as well as practical knowledge and skills: English grammar, composition, and literature; classical and modern foreign languages; science; writing and drawing; rhetoric and oratory; geography; various kinds of history; agriculture and gardening; arithmetic and accounting; and mechanics.

Sarah Pierce's Female Academy

English academies, often called people's colleges, multiplied across the country, reaching a peak of 6,185 in 1855, with an enrollment of 263,096 (Spring, 2008b, p. 35). Usually, these academies served male students only; a notable exception was Sarah Pierce's Litchfield Female Academy in Litchfield, Connecticut. Pierce (1767–1852) began her academy in the dining room of her home with two students; eventually, the academy grew to 140 female students from nearly every state and from Canada (Button & Provenzo, 1989, p. 87).

For the most part, however, girls received little formal education in the 17th and 18th centuries and were educated for entirely different purposes than were boys. As the following mission statement for Pierce's Academy suggests, a curriculum that emphasized practical knowledge and skills, rather than the classics, was appropriate for girls:

> Our object has been, not to make learned ladies, or skillful metaphysical reasoners, or deep read scholars in physical science: there is a more useful, tho' less exalted and less brilliant station that woman must occupy, there are duties of incalculable importance that she must perform: that station is home; these duties are the alleviation of the trials of her parents; the soothing of the labours & fatigues of her partner; & the education for time and eternity of the next generation of immortal beings. (Button & Provenzo, 1989, p. 88)

Some women enrolled in **female seminaries**, first established in the early 19th century to train women for higher education and public service outside the home. Educational opportunities for women expanded in conjunction with social reform movements that gradually led to greater political equality for women, including the right to vote in the 20th century. For example, Troy Seminary, founded in 1821 by educator and poet Emma Willard (1787–1870), became one of the first women's colleges in the country.

Thomas Jefferson's Philosophy

Thomas Jefferson (1743–1826), author of the Declaration of Independence, viewed the education of common people as the most effective means of preserving liberty. Providing basic education to citizens, he believed, was necessary in order "to raise the mass of the people to the high ground of moral respectability necessary to their own safety, and to orderly government" (quoted in Urban & Wagoner, 2009, p. 83).

Jefferson was born at Shadwell, Virginia, to a father who was a member of Virginia's landed gentry. Educated at the College of William and Mary, the second college to open in America, Jefferson went on to become one of this country's most influential leaders. Author of the Declaration of Independence at age 33, he also served the public as a member of the Virginia legislature, governor of Virginia, minister to France, secretary of state, vice president, and two-term president of the United States. His life demonstrated his wholehearted dedication to education. He was fluent in Latin, Greek, and many modern languages. He was strongly influenced by the work of the English philosopher John Locke, various British ideas on constitutional law, and the writings of French educators.

Jefferson was dedicated to human freedom and repulsed by any form of tyranny or absolutism. "I have sworn," he once said, "eternal hostility against every form of tyranny over the mind of man" (Rippa, 1984, p. 68). Toward this end, Jefferson was decidedly influential in the intellectual and educational circles of his day. He was a member of the American Academy of Arts and Sciences and president of the American Philosophical Society.

For a society to remain free, Jefferson felt, it must support a continuous system of public education. He proposed to the Virginia legislature in 1779 his Bill for the More General Diffusion of Knowledge. This plan called for state-controlled elementary schools that would teach, with no cost to parents, 3 years of reading, writing, and arithmetic to all White children. In addition, 20 state grammar schools would be created in which selected poor students would be taught free for a maximum period of 6 years. Jefferson's plan departed somewhat from the practical orientation of Franklin because the grammar schools would teach boys a more academic curriculum: English grammar, Greek, Latin, geography, and advanced arithmetic.

Jefferson was unsuccessful in his attempt to convince the Virginia House of Burgesses of the need for a uniform system of public schools as outlined in his bill. Jefferson was able to implement many of his educational ideas, however, through his efforts to found the University of Virginia. He devoted the last years of his life to developing the university, and he lived to see the university open with 40 students in March 1824, a month before his 81st birthday.

Noah Webster's Speller

In the years following the Revolution, several textbooks were printed in the United States. Writers and publishers saw the textbook as an appropriate vehicle for promoting democratic ideals and cultural independence from England. Toward this end, U.S. textbooks were filled with patriotic and moralistic maxims. Among the most widely circulated books of this type were Noah Webster's *Elementary Spelling Book* and *The American Dictionary*.

Born in Connecticut, Noah Webster (1758–1843) had successful careers as a lawyer, writer, politician, and schoolmaster. He first introduced his speller in 1783 under the cumbersome title *A Grammatical Institute of the English Language*. Later versions were titled the *American Spelling Book* and the *Elementary Spelling Book*. Webster's speller earned the nickname "the old blue-back" because early copies of the book were covered in light blue paper and later editions were covered with bright blue paper.

In the introduction to his speller, Webster declared that its purpose was to help teachers instill in students "the first rudiments of the language, some just ideas of religion, morals and domestic economy" (Button & Provenzo, 1989, p. 65). Throughout, the little book emphasized patriotic and moralistic virtues. Short, easy-to-remember maxims taught pupils to be content with their lot in life, to work hard, and to respect the property of others. Readers were cautioned to "prefer solid sense to vain wit" and to "let no jest intrude to violate good manners." Webster also gave readers extensive instructions on how to behave in school:

> He that speaks loud in school will not learn his own book well, nor let the rest learn theirs; but those that make no noise will soon be wise, and gain much love and good will.
>
> Shun the boy that tells lies, or speaks bad words; for he would soon bring thee to shame. (Commager, 1962, pp. 61–63)

Webster's speller was so popular that it eventually sold over 24 million copies. Historian Henry Steele Commager (1958) said of the book, "The demand was insatiable. . . . No other secular book had ever spread so wide, penetrated so deep, lasted so long" (p. 12). It has been estimated that more than 1 billion people have read Webster's book.

Webster's speller addressed so many topics that it has been called one of the first curriculum guides for the elementary grades (Johanningmeier, 1980, p. 65). Webster was a post-Revolutionary educational leader who had a profound impact on the American language and culture, and he "did much to help define the new nation" (Urban & Wagoner, 2004, p. 79).

Education for African Americans and Native Americans

At the close of the American Revolution, nearly all of the half million African Americans were slaves who could neither read nor write (Button & Provenzo, 1989). In most cases, those who were literate had been taught by their masters or through small, church-affiliated programs. Literate Native Americans and Mexican Americans usually had received their training at the hands of missionaries.

Other schools for African and Native Americans were started by the Quakers, who regarded slavery as a moral evil. One of the best known schools for African Americans was founded in Philadelphia in 1770 by Anthony Benezet, who believed that African Americans were "generously sensible, humane, and sociable, and that their capacity is as good, and as capable of improvement as that of White people" (Button & Provenzo, 1989, p. 45). Schools modeled on the Philadelphia African School opened elsewhere in the Northeast, and so-called Indian schools were also founded as philanthropic enterprises.

The Quakers also founded Indian schools as philanthropic enterprises. In 1819, federal funds for reservation schools were first granted through the newly created Office of Indian Affairs. Federal involvement brought little improvement in programs and enrollments, however. In 1901, for instance, only 300 of the 4,000 to 5,000 school-age Navajos attended school (Button & Provenzo, 1989, p. 276).

HOW WAS THE STRUGGLE WON FOR STATE-SUPPORTED COMMON SCHOOLS (1820–1865)?

The first state-supported high school in the United States was the Boston English Classical School, established in 1821. The opening of this school, renamed English High School in 1824, marked the beginning of a long, slow struggle for state-supported **common schools** in this country. Those in favor of free common schools tended to be city residents and nontaxpayers, democratic leaders, philanthropists and humanitarians, members of various school societies, and working people. Those opposed were rural residents and taxpayers, members of old aristocratic and conservative groups, owners of private schools, members of conservative religious sects, Southerners, and non-English-speaking residents. By far the most eloquent and effective spokesperson for the common school was Horace Mann.

Horace Mann's Contributions

Horace Mann (1796–1859) was a lawyer, Massachusetts senator, and the first secretary of a state board of education. He is best known as the champion of the common school movement, which has led to the free, public, locally controlled elementary schools we know today. Mann worked tirelessly to convince people that their interests would be well served by a system of universal free schools for all:

> [A free school system] knows no distinction of rich and poor, of bond and free, or between those, who, in the imperfect light of this world, are seeking, through different avenues, to reach the gate of heaven. Without money and without price, it throws open its doors, and spreads the table of its bounty, for all the children of the State. (Mann, 1868, p. 754)

IMPROVING SCHOOLS

In 1837, Mann accepted the position of Secretary of the Massachusetts State Board of Education. At the time, conditions in Massachusetts schools were deplorable, and Mann immediately began to use his new post to improve the quality of schools. Through the 12 annual reports he submitted while secretary and through *The Common School Journal*, which he founded and edited, Mann's educational ideas became widely known in this country and abroad.

In his widely publicized *Fifth Report* (published in 1841), Mann told the moneyed conservative classes that support of common public schools would provide them "the cheapest means of self-protection and insurance." Where could they find, Mann asked, "any police so vigilant and effective, for the protection of all the rights of person, property and character, as such a sound and comprehensive education and training, as our system of Common Schools could be made to impart?" (Rippa, 1997, p. 95).

In his *Seventh Report* (published 1843), Mann extolled the virtues of schools he had visited in Prussia that implemented the humanistic approaches of noted Swiss educator Johann Heinrich Pestalozzi (1746–1827). He was impressed by "the harmonious relationship that existed between the Pestalozzian teachers and their charges, [and he] advocated a similar approach in Massachusetts' schools, one that valued children and their interests" (Urban & Wagoner, 2009, p. 125).

THE NORMAL SCHOOL

During the late 1830s, Mann put forth a proposal that today we take for granted. Teachers, he felt, needed more than a high school education to teach; they should be trained in professional programs. The French had established the *école normale* for preparing teachers, and Mann and other influential educators of the period, such as Catherine Beecher (1800–1878), whose sister, Harriet Beecher Stowe (1811–1896), wrote *Uncle Tom's Cabin*, believed that a similar program was needed in the United States. Through her campaign to ensure that women had access to an education equal to that of men and her drive to recruit women into the teaching profession, Beecher contributed significantly to the development of publicly funded schools for training teachers (Holmes & Weiss, 1995).

The first public **normal school** in the United States opened in Lexington, Massachusetts, on July 3, 1839. The curriculum consisted of general-knowledge courses plus courses in pedagogy (or teaching) and practice teaching in a model school affiliated with the normal school. In 1849, Electa Lincoln Walton (1824–1908), an 1843 graduate of the normal school, became acting head administrator and the first woman to administer a state normal school. Walton was energetic and determined to succeed, as her journal reveals:

> Many people think women can't do much. I'd like to show them that they can keep a Normal School and keep it well too. . . . I will succeed. . . . I will never be pointed at as an example of the incompetency of woman to conduct a large establishment well." (Holmes & Weiss, 1995, p. 42)

When Mann resigned as secretary in 1848, his imprint on education in the United States was broad and deep. As a result of his unflagging belief that education was the "great equalizer of the conditions of men—the balance wheel of the social machinery" (Mann, 1957, p. 87), Massachusetts had a firmly established system of common schools and led the way for other states to establish free public schools.

Reverend W. H. McGuffey's Readers

Reverend William Holmes McGuffey (1800–1873) had perhaps the greatest impact on what children learned in the new school. Far exceeding Noah Webster's speller in sales were the famous **McGuffey readers**. Between 1836, when the book first appeared, and 1860, approximately 120 million copies of the six-volume series were sold (Urban & Wagoner, 2009, p. 113). The six readers ranged in difficulty from the first-grade level to the sixth-grade level. Through such stories as "The Wolf," "Meddlesome Matty," and "A Kind Brother," the readers emphasized virtues such as hard work, honesty, truth, charity, and obedience.

Absent from the McGuffey readers were the dour, pessimistic views of childhood so characteristic of earlier primers. Nevertheless, they had a religious, moral, and ethical influence over millions of American readers. Through their reading of the "Dignity of Labor," "The Village Blacksmith," and "The Rich Man's Son," for example, readers learned that contentment outweighs riches in this world.

OF THE ECLECTIC SEREIS.   15

LESSON VIII.

his	this	bite	keep	wants
can	four	play	moon	watch
hog	cow	kind	sheep	stands
how	dark	most	chase	shines

SEE how this dog stands on his feet. He wants to play with John.

A dog has four feet. A dog and a cat can see in the dark.

Dogs keep watch at night, and bark. They bark most when the moon shines.

A dog will chase a sheep, or a hog, or a cow, and bite it. If you are kind to the dog, he will not bite you.

What did children learn from typical lessons in 19th century textbooks like this one, the story of "The Boy and Dog" from McGuffey's *The Eclectic First Reader*?

In addition to providing explicit instructions on right living, the McGuffey readers also taught countless children and adults how to read and study.

Justin Morrill's Land-Grant Schools

The common school movement and the continuing settlement of the West stimulated the development of public higher education. In 1862, the **Morrill Land-Grant Act**, sponsored by Congressman Justin S. Morrill (1810–1898) of Vermont, provided federal land for states either to sell or to rent in order to raise funds for the establishment of colleges of agriculture and mechanical arts. Each state was given a land subsidy of 30,000 acres for each representative and senator in its congressional delegation.

Eventually, $7.5 million from the sale of over 17 million acres was given to land-grant colleges and state universities. The Morrill Act of 1862 set a precedent for the federal government to take an active role in shaping higher education in the United States. A second Morrill Act in 1890 provided even more federal funds for land-grant colleges.

Segregation of Schools

From the 17th to the late 20th centuries, schools were segregated by race. The first recorded official ground for school segregation dates back to a decision of the Massachusetts Supreme Court in 1850. When the Roberts family sought to send their daughter Sarah to a White school in Boston, the court ruled that "equal, but separate" schools were being provided and that the Roberts therefore could not claim an injustice (*Roberts v. City of Boston,* 1850). From the beginning, however, schools were not equal, and students did not have equal educational opportunity.

As the nation moved toward civil war, positions on the institution of slavery and the education of slaves hardened. While abolitionists established schools for free and escaped blacks, some Southern states made the teaching of reading and writing to slaves a crime.

HOW DID COMPULSORY EDUCATION CHANGE SCHOOLS AND THE TEACHING PROFESSION (1865–1920)?

From the end of the Civil War to the end of World War I, publicly supported common schools steadily spread westward and southward from New England and the Middle Atlantic states. Beginning with Massachusetts in 1852, compulsory education laws were passed in 32 states by 1900 and in all states by 1930.

Because of compulsory attendance laws, an ever-increasing proportion of children attended school. In 1869–1870, only 64.7 percent of 5- to 17-year-olds attended public school. By 1919–1920, this proportion had risen to 78.3 percent; and in 2006–2007, it was 92.8 percent (Snyder & Dillow, 2010). The growth in enrollment on the high school level was exceptional. Historical data from the National Center for Education Statistics (Snyder & Dillow, 2010) show that the population in the United States increased 108 percent between 1880 and 1920, whereas high school enrollment increased 1,900 percent!

As common schools spread, school systems began to take on organizational features associated with today's schools: centralized control; increasing authority for state, county, and city superintendencies; and a division of labor among teachers and administrators at the individual school site. Influenced by the work of Frederick W. Taylor (1856–1915), an engineer and the founder of **scientific management**, school officials undertook reforms based on management principles and techniques from big business. For example, they believed that top-down management techniques should be applied to schools as well as factories.

The Kindergarten

Early childhood education also spread following the Civil War. Patterned after the progressive, humanistic theories of the German educator Friedrich Froebel (1782–1852), the **kindergarten**, or "garden where children grow," stressed the motor development and self-activity of children before they began formal schooling at the elementary level. Through play, games, stories, music, and language activities, a foundation beneficial to the child's later educational and social development would be laid. After founding the first kindergarten in 1837, Froebel developed child-centered curriculum materials that were used in kindergartens in the United States and throughout the world.

Margarethe Schurz (1832–1876), a student of Froebel, opened the first U.S. kindergarten in her home at Watertown, Wisconsin, in 1855. Her small neighborhood class was conducted in German. In 1860, Elizabeth Palmer Peabody (1804–1891), sister-in-law of Horace Mann and the American writer Nathaniel Hawthorne, opened the first private English-speaking kindergarten in this country in Boston.

Initially, kindergartens were privately supported, but in St. Louis in 1873, Susan Blow (1843–1916) established what is commonly recognized as the first successful public kindergarten in the United States. She patterned her kindergarten after one she visited while in Germany. She was a fierce advocate for public kindergartens, and in 1873 she stated that "we shall see the day when [the kindergarten] will have grown into a mighty tree, and I am more than ever anxious to see the system introduced into our Public schools." So successful was her program that by 1879, a total of 131 teachers were working in 53 kindergarten classes (Button & Provenzo, 1989, p. 169).

The U.S. Bureau of Education recorded a total of 12 kindergartens in the country in 1873, with 72 teachers and 1,252 students. By 2012, enrollments had mushroomed to 2,681,000 in public kindergartens and 289,000 in private kindergartens (Snyder & Dillow, 2014).

Schooling for African Americans

After the Civil War and emancipation, schools for former slaves were opened throughout the South by African American communities. Approximately 500 of these schools operated in the South shortly after the war ended (Urban & Wagoner, 2013). In 1865, African American leaders in Georgia formed an education association to raise money and to supervise their own schools. That same year, an editorial in the *New Orleans Black Republican* stated that "Freedom and school books and newspapers go hand in hand. Let us secure the freedom we have received by the intelligence that can maintain it" (Urban & Wagoner, 2009, p. 164).

In addition to schools operated by African Americans, Congress established the **Freedmen's Bureau** to provide the "foundations for education" for former slaves. Throughout the South, the Freedmen's Bureau operated "a vast network of reading, writing, and industrial schools that operated by day, night, and on Sundays" (Urban & Wagoner, 2009, p. 161). By 1869, more than 9,500 teachers taught at freedmen's schools. In 1870, when the Bureau ended, 4,329 freedmen's schools had been established, with a total enrollment of more than 247,000 students (Franklin, 1947, p. 308).

Higher Education for African Americans

In *Up from Slavery*, Booker T. Washington (1856–1915) recounts how he walked part of the 500 miles from his home in West Virginia to attend the Hampton Normal and Agricultural Institute of Virginia, one of the country's first institutions of higher education for African Americans. Four years after graduating from Hampton, Washington returned to be the school's first African American instructor.

Washington had a steadfast belief that education could improve the lives of African Americans, just as it had for White people: "Poverty and ignorance have affected the black man just as they affect the white man. But the day is breaking, and education will bring the complete light" (Rippa, 1997, p. 122). In 1880, Washington helped to found the Tuskegee Institute, an industrial school for African Americans in rural Alabama. According to Washington, the institute would play a key role in bringing about racial equality:

> The Tuskegee idea is that correct education begins at the bottom, and expands naturally as the necessities of the people expand. As the race grows in knowledge, experience, culture, taste, and wealth, its wants are bound to become more and more diverse; and to satisfy these wants there will be gradually developed within our ranks—as already has been true of the whites—a constantly increasing variety of professional and business men and women. (Button & Provenzo, 1989, p. 274)

Not all African Americans shared Washington's philosophy and goals. William E. Burghardt DuBois (1868–1963), the first African American to be awarded a Ph.D. and one of the founders of the National Association for the Advancement of Colored People (NAACP), challenged Booker T. Washington's views on education. In his book *The Souls of Black Folks*, DuBois criticized educational programs that seemed to imply that African Americans should accept inferior status and develop manual skills. DuBois called for the education of the most "talented tenth" of the African American population to equip them for leadership positions in society as a whole.

The Professionalization of Teaching

During the later 1800s, professional teacher organizations began to have a great influence on the development of schools in America. The National Education Association (NEA), founded in 1857, and the American Federation of Teachers (AFT), founded in 1916, labored diligently to professionalize teaching and to increase teachers' salaries and benefits. The NEA also appointed its Committee of Ten in 1892 and its Committee of Fifteen in 1893 to make recommendations for secondary and elementary curricula, respectively. In 1913, the NEA appointed the Commission on the Reorganization of Secondary Education to reexamine the secondary curriculum in regard to students' individual differences.

COMMITTEE OF TEN

During 1892–1893, the directors of the National Education Association appropriated $2,500 for a **Committee of Ten** to hold nine conferences that focused on the following subjects in the high school curriculum: (1) Latin; (2) Greek; (3) English; (4) other modern languages; (5) mathematics; (6) physics, astronomy, and chemistry; (7) natural history (biology, botany, and zoology); (8) history, civil government, and political science; and (9) geography (physical geography, geology, and meteorology). The group's members decided that the primary function of high schools was to take intellectually elite students and prepare them for life. Their recommendations stressed mental discipline in the humanities, languages, and science.

COMMITTEE OF FIFTEEN

The report of the Committee of Ten sparked such discussion that in 1893 the National Education Association appointed the **Committee of Fifteen** to examine the elementary curriculum. In keeping with the view that high schools were college preparatory institutions, the committee's report, published in 1895, called for the introduction of Latin, the modern languages, and algebra into the elementary curriculum. In addition, the curriculum was to be organized around five basic subjects: grammar, literature, arithmetic, geography, and history.

REORGANIZATION OF SECONDARY EDUCATION

In 1913 the National Education Association appointed the **Commission on the Reorganization of Secondary Education**. The commission's report, *Cardinal Principles of Secondary Education*, was released in 1918 and called for a high school curriculum designed to accommodate individual differences in scholastic ability. Seven educational goals, or "cardinal principles," were to provide the focus for schooling at all levels: health, command of fundamental processes (reading, writing, and computation), worthy home membership, vocation, citizenship, worthy use of leisure time, and ethical character.

WOMEN'S INFLUENCE ON TEACHING

By the early 1900s, the demand for teachers had grown dramatically. Because of greater demand for teachers, greater job mobility, and more and more women becoming teachers, the character of teaching changed. Both respected and regarded with suspicion, teachers became distanced from the communities they served. In his classic book *The Sociology of Teaching,* Willard Waller (1932) refers to this distancing as an "impenetrable veil" between the teacher and the rest of the community. Nevertheless, "women, as . . . vessels of virtue, were considered the ideal teachers for a system of schooling that emphasized moral development" (Spring, 2005, p. 145).

In spite of their "second-class citizenship" (Spring, 2005, p. 145), women became influential in shaping educational policies during the early 1900s, in part through the women's suffrage movement that led to the right to vote. Women such as Ella Flagg Young (1845–1918), superintendent of Chicago schools from 1909 to 1915, and Catherine Goggin and Margaret Haley, leaders of the Chicago Teachers Federation, played important roles in the governance of Chicago schools (Spring, 2008b). Another Chicagoan and visionary educational leader, Jane Addams (1860–1935), founded Hull House, a social and educational center for poor immigrants. In *Democracy and Social Ethics* (published in 1902), Addams drew from her training as a social worker and developed a philosophy of socialized education that linked schools with other social service agencies and institutions in the city. At the ceremony to present her the Nobel Peace Prize in 1931, Addams was described as "the foremost woman of her nation" (Rippa, 1997, p. 142).

WHAT WERE THE AIMS OF EDUCATION DURING THE PROGRESSIVE ERA (1920–1945)?

From the end of World War I to the end of World War II, education in the United States was influenced significantly by the philosophy of progressivism. **Progressivism** is a philosophical orientation based on the belief that life is evolving in a positive direction, that people may be trusted to act in their own best interest, and that education should focus on children's interests and practical needs.

During the late 19th and early 20th centuries, supporters of the **progressive movement** were intent on social reform to improve the quality of American life. In 1919, the Progressive Education Association was founded and went on to devote the next two decades to implementing progressive theories in the classroom that they believed would lead to the improvement of society.

Progressives were not united by a single educational philosophy. For the most part, they were opposed to autocratic teaching methods; teaching styles that relied almost exclusively on textbooks, recitations, and rote memorization; the relative isolation of the classroom from the real world; and classroom discipline based on fear or physical punishment.

Teachers in progressive schools functioned as guides rather than taskmasters. They first engaged students through providing activities related to their natural interests, and then they moved students to higher levels of understanding. To teach in this manner was demanding: "Teachers in a progressive school had to be extraordinarily talented and well educated; they needed both a perceptive understanding of children and a wide knowledge of the disciplines in order to recognize when the child was ready to move through an experience to a new understanding, be it in history or science or mathematics or the arts" (Ravitch, 1983, p. 47).

JOHN DEWEY'S LABORATORY SCHOOL

Progressive educational theories were synthesized most effectively and eloquently by John Dewey (1859–1952). Born in the year that Darwin's *Origin of Species* was published, Dewey graduated from the University of Vermont when he was 20. He later earned a doctorate at Johns Hopkins University, where his thinking was strongly influenced by the psychologist William James.

From 1894 to 1904, Dewey served as head of the departments of philosophy, psychology, and pedagogy at the University of Chicago. From 1904 until he retired in 1930, Dewey was a professor of philosophy at Columbia University. Dewey's numerous writings have had a profound impact on U.S. schools. In his best-known works, *The School and Society* (1900) and *The Child and the Curriculum* (1902),

What hallmarks of progressive education are evident in this photograph of one of the first classrooms in the country operated according to Dewey's philosophy? How would a progressive classroom look today?

Dewey states that school and society are connected and that teachers must begin with an understanding of the child's world, the psychological dimension, and then progress to the logical dimension represented by the accumulated knowledge of the human race.

While at the University of Chicago, Dewey and his wife, Alice, established the Laboratory School for testing progressive principles in the classroom. The school opened in 1896 with two instructors and 16 students and, by 1902, had grown to 140 students with 23 teachers and 10 university graduate students as assistants. The children, 4 to 14 years old, learned traditional subjects by working cooperatively in small groups of 8 to 10 on projects such as cooking, weaving, carpentry, sewing, and metalwork (Rippa, 1997).

With Dewey as director and his wife as principal, the school became a virtual laboratory for testing Dewey's ideas. The school was so unique that historian Lawrence Cremin (1961) referred to it as "the most interesting experimental venture in American education" (p. 136). In addition to giving students a meaningful, relevant education, Dewey's school had two purposes: "(1) to exhibit, test, verify, and criticize [Dewey's] theoretical statements and principles; and (2) to add to the sum of facts and principles in its special line with question marks, rather than fixed rules" (Mayhew & Edwards, 1936, p. 3).

What made Dewey's Laboratory School unique was that it was thoroughly child-centered. The curriculum was a natural outgrowth of the children's interests. The faculty was committed to following the lead set by students. For example, "a student or students might express an interest in milk. The teacher would guide the students to sources of the production, chemistry, and distribution of milk. Groups of students might visit the local dairy and develop a group project on milk for the classroom. During this group study of milk, students might learn chemistry, economics, arithmetic, social history, and cooperation" (Spring, 2008b, pp. 300–301).

Maria Montessori's Method

While Dewey's ideas provided the basis for the development of progressive education in the United States, progressive educators in Europe were similarly developing new approaches that would also affect U.S. education. Chief among these was Maria Montessori (1870–1952), an Italian physician who was influenced by Rousseau and believed that children's mental, physical, and spiritual development could be enhanced by providing them with developmentally appropriate educational activities.

At Montessori's school for poor preschool-age children in Rome, teachers created learning environments based on students' levels of development and readiness to learn new material. According to the **Montessori method**,

> [C]hildren pass through "sensitive periods" for particular intellectual, social, and moral awakenings. These are sensitive periods for language, movement, music, order, and so on. The central role of the adult . . . is to recognize these sensitive periods and direct the child to work designed to foster those awakenings. (Cossentino & Whitcomb, 2007, p. 117)

Montessori teachers use prescribed sets of materials and physical exercises to develop students' knowledge and skills, and students are allowed to use or not use the materials as they see fit. The materials arouse students' interest, and the interest motivates them to learn. Through highly individualized instruction, students develop self-discipline and self-confidence. Montessori's ideas spread throughout the world; by 1915, almost 100 Montessori schools were operating in the United States (Webb, Metha, & Jordan, 2010). Today, Montessorian materials and activities are a standard part of the early childhood and elementary curricula in public schools throughout the nation.

The Decline of Progressive Education

By the start of World War II, the progressive education movement, faced with rising public criticism, began a rapid decline. "All sorts of people seemed to believe that the U.S. system of public education was woefully out of step with the needs of the nation. As a result, an undifferentiated fury was directed at progressive education" (Hartman, 2008, p. 1). Many of the schools' deficiencies were blamed on progressive approaches that were seen as soft and lacking the structure and discipline children needed. In 1955, the Progressive Education Association ceased operation. According to one historian, when the association began in 1919, "progressive education meant all that was good in education; 35 years later nearly all the ills in American education were blamed on it" (Graham, 1967, p. 145).

In spite of its short life, the progressive education movement had an unmistakable impact on American education. Many current practices in schools have their origins in the experimentation of the progressive era: inquiry or discovery learning, self-paced instructional approaches, field trips, flexible scheduling, open-concept classrooms, non-graded schools, small-group activities, and school-based counseling programs, to name a few.

FOCUS ON DIVERSITY: EDUCATION OF IMMIGRANTS AND MINORITIES

The diversity of America's school population increased dramatically during the late 19th and early 20th centuries. Latin Americans, eastern Europeans, and southern Europeans followed earlier waves of western and northern European immigrants such as the Irish and Germans. As with Native American education, the goal of immigrant education was rapid

American Indian children who attended boarding schools were not allowed to speak their native languages. Why is it important for school curricula to reflect and honor students' cultural backgrounds?

assimilation into an English-speaking Anglo-European society that did not welcome racially or ethnically different newcomers.

Also at stake was the preservation or loss of traditional culture. In some areas, school policies included the punishment of Cuban and Puerto Rican children, for example, for speaking Spanish in school, and children learned to mock their unassimilated parents. In other areas, efforts were made to exclude certain groups, such as Asians, and ethnic enclaves established separate schools for the purpose of preserving, for example, traditional Chinese culture.

By the time Native Americans were granted U.S. citizenship in 1924, confinement on reservations and decades of forced assimilation had devastated Native American cultures and provided few successful educational programs. "The federal government forcibly placed tribal children in the harsh, military-like institutions in an effort to assimilate them into the dominant culture" (King, 2008). Boarding school children who spoke their native language were beaten with a strap, while other children were forced to watch. By the early 1930s, an estimated two-thirds of Native Americans had attended boarding schools. The emotional scars from the boarding school experience continue into the present, and the national Boarding School Healing Project was launched in South Dakota in 2002 by Indians from various states (King, 2008).

In 1928, a landmark report titled *The Problem of Indian Administration* recommended that Native American education be restructured. Recommendations included building day schools in Native American communities and the reform of boarding schools for Native American children. In addition, the report recommended that school curricula be revised to reflect tribal cultures and the needs of local tribal communities. In the Teachers' Voices feature for this chapter, a Native American teacher stresses the importance of curricula that affirm the identity of Native American students.

An early champion of the educational rights of African Americans was Mary McLeod Bethune (1875–1955). The 15th child of former slaves in South Carolina, Bethune attended a school operated by the Presbyterian Board of Missions for Freedmen and Barber-Scotia College in Concord, North Carolina. She then went on

TEACHERS' VOICES ➧ BEING AN AGENT OF CHANGE

KRISTINE SHOTLEY

NATIVE AMERICAN TEACHERS NEED SUPPORT

When I was studying to be a teacher, a White female student in the same program asked me what I thought my chances were of finding a job after graduation. I replied that, because I am Native American, and a woman, I thought I would have excellent opportunities for immediate employment. "How nice," she said, "to turn two negatives into two positives!" I was taken aback. It had not occurred to me that in this day and age, I would still have to defend my identity.

In the United States, most Native American children are still taught by non-Native teachers. There are fewer than 18,000 Native American teachers working today.

To recruit more teachers, we need to develop curricula that affirm our Native American identity. For example, elementary school kids need to learn an accurate and truthful account of American history. How many times do we have to reiterate that Christopher Columbus did not "discover" America?

When I was growing up, Native American history was not taught. I endured the appalled looks of my White classmates

when our teachers presented a one-sided account of American history. I felt apologetic for my ancestors who tried to defend their lands from White settlers.

The United States [must address] the lack of Native American teachers. I want my son and other Native American sons and daughters to realize they can become anything they choose because they have the educational background they need.

QUESTIONS

1. Shotley says teachers should develop curricula that "affirm" Native American identity. What are the characteristics of curricula that "affirm" the diverse identities of today's students?

2. What should a teacher do if the only instructional materials available present outdated, perhaps even distorted, interpretations of American history?

Kristine Shotley is a member of the Fond Du Lac Tribe of Ojibwe in Minnesota, and she writes for *The Circle*, a Native American news and arts paper published in Minneapolis. This article is from Progressive Media Project, January 12, 2000.

to study at the Moody Bible Institute in Chicago. She went to Daytona Beach in 1904 where, with only $1.50 in savings, she founded the Daytona Normal and Industrial School for Training Negro Girls.

The school was in a rundown building Bethune rented. At first, she had only six students, including her son. To keep the school open, Bethune and her students sold sweet potato pies and fried fish and gave concerts in nearby resort hotels. In 1923, the school merged with a boys' school in Jacksonville, Florida, and became Bethune-Cookman College a year later.

Bethune was an eloquent spokesperson for the educational rights of African American youth. During the Great Depression of the 1930s, she was appointed to the Advisory Board of the National Youth Administration (NYA). That year, almost 24 percent of the 21 million youth between 16 and 24 years of age were out of school and jobless. When Bethune spoke eloquently about the needs of African American youth, President Franklin Roosevelt added an office of minority affairs to the NYA and asked Bethune to direct it.

The level of Bethune's commitment to education is reflected in a comment she made in the *Journal of Negro Education* (Collier-Thomas, 1982): "I cannot rest while there is a single Negro boy or girl lacking a chance to prove his worth." As director of the NYA, she made it possible for 150,000 African American young people to attend high school and for 60,000 to graduate from college.

World War II and Increasing Federal Involvement in Education

World War II created conditions in this country that led the federal government to fund several educational programs. One of these, the **Lanham Act** (1941), provided funding for (1) the training of workers in war plants by U.S. Office of Education personnel, (2) the construction of schools in areas where military personnel and workers on federal projects resided, and (3) the provision of child care for the children of working parents.

Another influential and extensive federal program in support of education was the Servicemen's Readjustment Act, popularly known as the **G.I. Bill of Rights**. Signed into law by President Franklin D. Roosevelt in 1944, the G.I. bill has provided millions of veterans with payments for tuition and room and board at colleges and universities and at special schools. Similar legislation was later passed to grant educational benefits to veterans of the Korean and Vietnam conflicts. Not only did the G.I. bill stimulate the growth of American colleges and universities, it also changed the character of the higher education student population. Generally, the returning veterans were older and more serious than students who had not served in the military.

HOW DID EDUCATION CHANGE DURING THE MODERN POSTWAR ERA (1945–2000)?

Throughout the 20th century, many long-standing trends in U.S. education continued. These trends may be grouped and summarized in terms of three general patterns, shown in Figure 5.3. At the same time, the decades since the end of World War II have seen a series of profound changes in U.S. education. These changes have addressed three as-yet unanswered questions: (1) How can full and equal educational opportunity be extended to all groups in our culturally pluralistic society? (2) What knowledge and skills should be taught in our nation's schools? (3) How should knowledge and skills be taught? The importance of these questions was captured well by a first-year teacher education student who told the author that "It is important for teachers to understand how American education has, over the years, worked to provide equal educational opportunity to all students. Also, teachers need to understand how views of what should be taught in schools have changed, and how they continue to change even today."

FIGURE 5.3   Three general patterns of trends in U.S. education

Americanization
- Americanizing of European educational institutions and instructional models
- Americanizing of English language textbooks and curriculum
- Cultural assimilation of immigrants and others through education
- Aims of education based on moral didacticism and pragmatism
- Aims of education relating to child development and child welfare
- Aims of education relating to success in a society based on capitalism
- Aims of education relating to citizenship in a democracy

Democratization
- Steady growth of compulsory, free, secular, publicly funded education
- Preservation of state, local, and parental control of schooling and schools
- Protection of teachers' and students' rights under the U.S. Constitution
- Shifts in educational reform initiatives that reflect a two-party electoral system
- Continual expansion of early childhood education
- Continual expansion of opportunities for higher education and adult education
- Traumatic periodic extensions of educational opportunity to "other" Americans (women; racial, ethnic, and language minorities; people with disabilities)

Professionalization
- Professionalizing of teaching as an occupation
- Professionalizing of teacher organizations and associations
- Growth in scientific and bureaucratic models for the management of schools
- Rising standards for qualifications to teach
- Continual development of institutions and programs for teacher education
- Greater application of theory and research on teaching and learning
- Generally rising status and salaries for teachers as members of a profession

The 1950s: Defense Education and School Desegregation

Teachers and education were put in the spotlight in 1957 when the Soviet Union launched the first satellite, *Sputnik*, into space. Stunned U.S. leaders immediately blamed the space lag on inadequacies in the education system. The Soviet Union was first into space, they maintained, "because the schools had long been under the sway of progressive education, which de-emphasized intellectual values" (Hartman, 2008, p. 176). U.S. students, for example, were taught less science and mathematics, and fewer foreign languages, than their European counterparts. Students, not just teachers, felt the impact of *Sputnik*, as the following reflections illustrate:

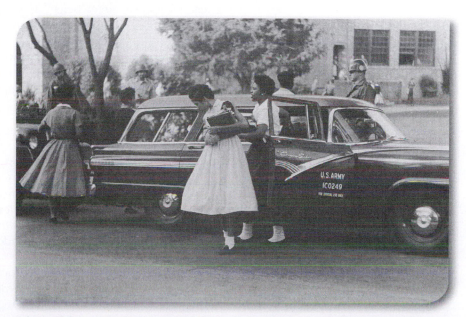

When African American students desegregated Little Rock Central High School in 1957, they were protected by the National Guard. What is the legacy of school desegregation today?

> As a fifth-grade student, it seemed to me that the Russian space success was perceived as American educational failure; the result was a monumental effort to revise school curriculum to emphasize patriotic involvement in math and science. [It was] important to have American students dedicated to defeating Russian students in a core curriculum of math and science, in order to assure the survival of our society. (Leahy, 2009, p. 28)

From our perspective today, "the 1950s can be characterized as a war between U.S. and Soviet school systems—each trying to educate the best scientists and engineers for development of military technology" (Spring, 2008b, p. 221). In the public's mind, the ability of America to defend itself was directly related to the quality of its schools. As the title of the first chapter of Vice Admiral H. G. Rickover's (1959) book *Education and Freedom* put it: "Education is our first line of defense."

The federal government appropriated millions of dollars over the next decade for educational reforms that reflected the importance of teaching knowledge and skills that were viewed as essential for adult life. Through provisions of the **National Defense Education Act of 1958**, the U.S. Office of Education sponsored research and innovation in science, mathematics, modern foreign languages, and guidance. Out of their work came the new math; new science programs; an integration of anthropology, economics, political science, and sociology into new social studies programs; and renewed interest and innovations in foreign language instruction. Teachers were trained in the use of new methods and materials at summer workshops, schools were given funds for new equipment, and research centers were established. In 1964, Congress extended the act for 3 years and expanded Title III of the act to include money for improving instruction in reading, English, geography, history, and civics.

During the reform activity of the 1960s, public school enrollments rose dramatically. In 1950, about 25 million children were enrolled; in 1960, about 36 million; and in 1970, about 50 million. As a result of a decline in births, however, this trend stopped abruptly in the late 1970s. In the fall of 1979, for example, 41.5 million students were enrolled in K–12 classes, a decrease of 1,069,000, or 2.5 percent, from the year before (Rippa, 1984).

The curriculum reform movement of the 1960s did not bear the positive results that its supporters hoped for. The benefits of the new federally funded programs reached only a small percentage of teachers. In regard to some of the new materials—those related to the new math, for example—teachers complained that the recommended approaches failed to take into account the realities of classroom life. Many of the materials, it turned out, were developed by persons who had little or no classroom experience. Thus, many teachers of the 1960s ignored the innovations and continued teaching as they had always done. Educational historian, and former United States Assistant Secretary of Education, Diane Ravitch (1985) describes the tendency for teachers to resist educational reforms during this era:

> A teacher whose career began in 1960 has lived through an era of failed revolutions. One movement after another arrived, peaked, and dispersed. Having observed the curriculum reform movement, the free school movement, the minimum competency movement, and, more recently, the back-to-basics movement, a veteran teacher may be excused for secretly thinking, when confronted by the next campaign to "save" the schools, "This too shall pass." (p. 303)

The end of World War II also saw the beginning of school **desegregation**. On May 17, 1954, the U.S. Supreme Court rejected the "separate but equal" doctrine that had been used since 1850 as a justification for excluding African Americans from attending school with Whites. In response to a suit filed by the NAACP on behalf of a Kansas family, Chief Justice Earl Warren declared that to segregate school children "from others of similar age and qualifications solely because of their race generates a feeling of inferiority as to their status in the community that may affect their hearts and minds in a way unlikely ever to be undone" (***Brown v. Board of Education of Topeka, 1954***).

The Supreme Court's decision did not bring an immediate end to segregated schools. Although the court 1 year later ordered that desegregation proceed with "all deliberate speed," opposition to school integration arose in school districts across the country. Some districts, whose leaders modeled restraint and a spirit of cooperation, desegregated peacefully. Other districts became battlegrounds, characterized by boycotts, rallies, and violence.

The 1960s: The War on Poverty and the Great Society

The 1960s, hallmarked by the Kennedy administration's spirit of action and high hopes, provided a climate that supported change. Classrooms were often places of pedagogical experimentation and creativity reminiscent of the progressive era. The open-education movement, team teaching, individualized instruction, the integrated-day concept, flexible scheduling, and non-graded schools were some of the innovations that teachers were asked to implement. These structural, methodological, and curricular changes implied the belief that teachers were capable professionals.

The image of teachers in the 1960s was enhanced by the publication of several books by educators who were influenced by the progressivist educational philosophy and humanistic psychology. A. S. Neill's *Summerhill* (1960), Sylvia Ashton-Warner's *Teacher* (1963), John Holt's *How Children Fail* (1964), Herbert Kohl's *36 Children* (1967), James Herndon's *The Way It Spozed to Be* (1969), and Jonathan Kozol's *Death at an Early Age* (1967)—a few of the books that appeared at the time—gave readers inside views of teachers at work and teachers' perceptions of how students learn.

The administrations of Presidents Kennedy and Johnson funneled massive amounts of money into a War on Poverty. Education was seen as the key to breaking the transmission of poverty from generation to generation. The War on Poverty developed methods, materials, and programs such as subsidized breakfast and lunch programs, Head Start, Upward Bound, and the Job Corps that would be appropriate to children who had been disadvantaged due to poverty.

The War on Poverty President Johnson announced during his State of the Union address on January 8, 1964, has proved much more difficult to win than imagined, and the results of such programs 50 years later have been mixed. The 3- to 6-year-olds who participated in Head Start did much better when they entered public schools; however, academic gains appeared to dissolve over time. Although the Job Corps enabled scores of youth to avoid a lifetime of unemployment, many graduates returned to the streets, where they eventually became statistics in unemployment and crime records. The education of low-income children received a boost in April 1965 when Congress passed the **Elementary and Secondary Education Act**. As part of President Johnson's Great Society program, the act allocated funds on the basis of the number of poor children in school districts. Thus, schools in poverty areas that frequently had to cope with problems such as low achievement, poor discipline, truancy, and high teacher turnover rates received much-needed assistance in addressing their problems.

In 1968, the Elementary and Secondary Education Act was amended with Title VII, the Bilingual Education Act. This act provided federal aid to low-income children "of limited English-speaking ability." The act did not spell out clearly what bilingual education might mean other than to say that it provided money for local school districts to "develop and carry out new and imaginative elementary and secondary school programs" to meet the needs of non-English-speaking children. Since the passing of Title VII, debate over the ultimate goal of bilingual education has been intense: Should it help students make the transition to regular English-speaking classrooms, or should it help such students maintain their non-English language and culture?

The 1970s: Accountability and Equal Opportunity

The 1970s saw drops in enrollment, test scores, and public confidence in our nation's schools. At the same time, new educational policies called for equality of education for all in the United States. Troubled by the continued low academic performance of many U.S. students, parents, citizens groups, and policymakers initiated a back-to-basics movement and called for increased teacher accountability.

Many school systems had to cope with financial crises during the 1970s. Public and private elementary school enrollments, instead of increasing as they had

What impact has Title IX had on the education of females? What does equal educational opportunity for female and male students really mean?

since 1940, declined by nearly 5 million during the 1970s (National Center for Education Statistics, March 25, 2008). As a result of declining enrollments, schools received less state aid. Moreover, voters frequently failed to support referendums to increase school funding because they lacked confidence in the schools.

Many parents responded to the crisis by becoming education activists, seeking or establishing alternative schools, or joining the home education movement led by John Holt, who by then had given up on reforming schools. These parents believed they could provide a better education for their children than public school teachers. Those who kept their children in the public schools demanded teacher **accountability**, which limited teachers' instructional flexibility and extended their evaluation paperwork. Basal readers and teacher-proof curricular packages descended on teachers, spelling out with their cookbook directions the deeper message that teachers were not to be trusted to teach on their own. Confidence in teachers reached a low point.

In addition, during the late 1960s and early 1970s, increasing numbers of young people questioned what the schools were teaching and how they were teaching it. Thousands of them mobilized in protest against an establishment that, in their view, supported an immoral, undeclared war in Vietnam and was unconcerned with the oppression of minorities at home. In their search for reasons why these and other social injustices were allowed to exist, many militant youth groups singled out the schools' curricula. From their perspective, the schools taught subjects irrelevant to finding solutions to pressing problems.

Responding in good faith to their critics' accusations, schools greatly expanded their curricular offerings and instituted a wide variety of instructional strategies. In making these changes, however, school personnel gradually realized that they were alienating other groups: taxpayers who accused schools of extravagant spending; religious sects that questioned the values that children were being taught; **back-to-basics** advocates who charged that students were not learning how to read, write, and compute; and citizens who were alarmed at steadily rising school crime, drugs, and violence.

Despite the siege on teachers and schools, however, the reforms of the 1960s and 1970s did result in a number of improvements that have lasted into the present. More young people graduate from high school now than in previous decades, more teachers have advanced training, school buildings are better equipped, and instructional methods and materials are both more relevant to learners and more diverse.

For those people who had been marginalized by the educational system, the federal acts that were passed in the 1970s brought success and encouragement: the Title IX Education Amendment prohibiting sex discrimination (1972), the Indian Education Act (1972), the Education for All Handicapped Children Act (1975), and the Indochina Migration and Refugee Assistance Act (1975).

Title IX of the Education Amendments Act, which took effect in 1975, stated that "no person in the United States shall, on the basis of sex, be excluded from participation in, be denied the benefits of, or be subjected to discrimination under any education program or activity receiving Federal financial assistance."

The **Education for All Handicapped Children Act (Public Law 94–142)**, passed by Congress in 1975, extended greater educational opportunities to children with disabilities. This act (often referred to as the **mainstreaming** law) specifies extensive due process procedures to guarantee that children with special needs will receive a free, appropriate education in the least restrictive educational environment. Through the act's provisions, parents are involved in planning educational programs for their children.

The 1980s: A Great Debate

The first half of the 1980s saw a continuation, perhaps even an escalation, of the criticisms aimed at the schools during the two previous decades. In fact, Lee Shulman (1987) characterized much of the 1980s as an era of "teacher bashing." With the publication in 1983 of the report by the National Commission on Excellence in Education, **A Nation at Risk: The Imperative for Educational Reform**, a great national debate was begun on how to improve the quality of schools. *A Nation at Risk* and dozens of other national reports on U.S. schools gave evidence to some that the schools were failing miserably to achieve their goals. The following excerpt from the first paragraph of *A Nation at Risk* exemplifies the tone of the **educational reform movement**:

> Our Nation is at risk. Our once unchallenged preeminence in commerce, industry, science, and technological innovation is being overtaken by competitors throughout the world . . . the educational foundations of our society are presently being eroded by a rising tide of mediocrity that threatens our very future as a Nation and a people. (National Commission on Excellence in Education, 1983)

Responses included more proposals for curriculum reform. Mortimer Adler's **Paideia Proposal** (1982) called for a perennialist core curriculum based on the Great Books. **High School: A Report on Secondary Education in America** (1983), written by Ernest Boyer (1928–1995) for the Carnegie Foundation for the Advancement of Teaching, suggested strengthening the academic core curriculum in high schools, a recommendation that was widely adopted. In 1986, former secretary of the U.S. Department of Education William Bennett advocated an intellectually rigorous high school curriculum that he described in *James Madison High* (1987). Educators at the middle school level began to create small learning communities, eliminate tracking, and develop new ways to enhance student self-esteem as a result of the Carnegie Council on Adolescent Development report *Turning Points: Preparing American Youth for the 21st Century* (1989). These and other reform reports that swept the nation during the 1980s made a lasting imprint on education in the United States.

The 1990s: Teacher Leadership

The push to reform schools begun in the 1980s continued throughout the 1990s, and teaching was transformed in dramatic ways. In response to challenges such as greater diversity, greater international competition, less support for public education, and decentralization and deregulation of schools, innovative approaches to teaching and learning were developed throughout the United States (see Figure 5.4). Teachers went beyond the classroom and assumed leadership roles in school restructuring and educational reform. Through collaborative relationships with students, principals, parents, and the private sector, teachers changed the nature of their profession. As one high school teacher said in the late 1990s: "I see it [change] happening. Not overnight, but I think it's going to. When I first started teaching in the early sixties, I would never have envisioned things changing as much as they have" (Grant & Murray 1999, p. 212).

FIGURE 5.4   The 1990s: A sample of trends in education

WHAT ARE THE EDUCATIONAL PRIORITIES OF THE NEW CENTURY (2000–THE PRESENT)?

Without a doubt, the world of teaching during the second decade of the new century is characterized by rapid, complex changes. Among the major trends influencing teaching are increasing ethnic and cultural diversity, new leadership roles for teachers, and the continuing influence of new technologies on education. The Technology in Action feature for this chapter illustrates how one teacher's understanding of this technologically rich, complex teaching environment enables him to develop an effective teaching strategy.

When you become a teacher, your work will be enhanced also if you understand and appreciate the historical context for U.S. education, as presented in Figure 5.5. The left-hand column of the timeline identifies three trends that will continue to be educational priorities throughout this century: *equity* for all students, *excellence* and high standards, and *accountability* for schools and teachers.

FOCUS ON DIVERSITY: EQUITY FOR ALL STUDENTS

Although reform efforts during the 1950s through the 1990s resulted in significant improvements in education, in the new century, minority-group students continue to be disproportionately represented among those who fail to master minimum competencies in reading, writing, and mathematics. Moreover, it is estimated that they are two to four times more likely than others to drop out of high school (Bennett, 2011). In 2012, 3 percent of Asian youth and 4 percent of Whites ages 16 to 24 were not enrolled in school and had not completed high school, compared with 9 percent of Blacks and 13 percent of Hispanics (U.S. Census Bureau, October 2012).

Data gathered during the first two decades of the new century indicate that an **achievement gap** continues to exist between White students and Hispanic, Black, and American Indian/Alaska Native students on many measures of educational achievement. For example, on the 2013 National Assessment of Educational Progress (NAEP) reading and mathematics assessments, higher percentages of Asian/Pacific Islander and White fourth graders and eighth graders scored at or above "Proficient" than did

FIGURE 5.5 Historical timeline for U.S. education

Religious Emphasis	1620	1620 — Emphasis on basic skills needed to learn religious catechisms and read prayers. Curriculum also includes surveying, navigation, and bookkeeping. Education primarily for the elite.
	1640	1636 — Latin grammar (college-prep) schools established and, like Harvard and Yale Colleges, emphasize Latin, Greek, theology, and philosophy for those preparing to enter law or religion.
	1660	1647 — Massachusetts Law of 1647 mandates a reading and writing teacher for towns of 50 or more families; a Latin teacher for towns of 100 or more. Females taught basics to enable them to carry out religious and family responsibilities.
	1680	
	1700	1700s — Public schools teach reading, writing, and basic mathematics (counting, adding, and subtracting) to prepare students for jobs and apprenticeships.
	1720	
	1740	
Political Emphasis	1760 / 1780	Early 1750s — Academies teach secondary students a practical curriculum (drawing, surveying, navigation, merchant's accounting, etc.) to become tradesmen and workers.
	1800	
Utilitarian Emphasis	1820 / 1840	1821 — First public high school teaches basic skills and history, geography, health, and physical training.
	1860	1860 — First English-speaking kindergarten emphasizes growth, activity, play, songs, and stories.
		1874 — Free public schooling now includes high schools that place strong emphasis on vocational education and reading, writing, and mathematics.
	1880	1893 — Committee of Ten asserts that high schools are for college-bound and curriculum should emphasize mental disciplines in humanities, language, and science.
Education for Masses	1900	1918 — Commission on Reorganization of Secondary Education focuses on individual differences. Curriculum to stress Seven Cardinal Principles.
	1920	1930s & 1940s — Progressive education movement stresses curriculum based on student's needs and interests. Home economics, health, family living, citizenship, and woodshop added to the curriculum.
	1940	1957 — Soviet *Sputnik* sparks emphasis on science, mathematics, and languages.
The Excellence Movement	1960	1960s — Calls for relevancy result in expanded course offerings and electives. Mid. 1970s — Back-to-basics movement emphasizes reading, writing, mathematics, and oral communication.
	1980	1983 — *Nation at Risk* report calls for "five new basics"—English, mathematics, science, social studies, and computer science.
		1985 — Rigorous core curricula advocated at all levels in an effort to increase standards and to ensure quality.
		1989 — The Carnegie Council on Adolescent Development report, *Turning Points*, recommends the creation of learning communities and a core academic program for middle-level students. President George H. W. Bush convenes education summit meeting for 50 state governors.
		1990 — President George H. W. Bush unveils Goals 2000, identifying six educational goals: readiness for school; high school completion; student achievement and citizenship: science and mathematics; adult literacy and lifelong learning; and safe, disciplined, and drug-free schools.
		1994 — President Bill Clinton signs into law Goals 2000: Educate America Act.
		1995 — President Bill Clinton creates the National Information Infrastructure (NII) to encourage schools to become connected to the "information superhighway."
		1996 — President Bill Clinton launches the President's Educational Technology Initiative.
		1999 — President Bill Clinton signs into law the Educational Excellence for All Children Act, reauthorizing the Elementary and Secondary Education Act (ESEA).
High-Stakes Testing; School and Teacher Accountability	2000	2002 — President George W. Bush signs into law the No Child Left Behind (NCLB) Act of 2001, reauthorizing ESEA and calling for all students to make "adequate yearly progress" (AYP).
		2009 — National Governors Association (NGA) and Council of Chief State School Officers (CCSSO) organize the Common Core State Standards Initiative (CCSSI). Forty-eight states participate in developing the Standards.
	2010	2010 — President Barack Obama proposes broad changes to NCLB and releases *A Blueprint for Reform*, calling for the reauthorization of ESA. Schools will no longer be singled out for not making "adequate yearly progress." Race to the Top and the Teacher and Leader Innovation Fund are key elements of *A Blueprint*. Common Core State Standards for K–12 English-language arts and mathematics released.
		2011 — Congress fails to act on the call to reauthorize ESEA; the Obama administration announces that states can voluntarily seek "ESEA flexibility" and be exempt from certain requirements of NCLB by submitting comprehensive plans to improve education for all students.
		2012 — Race to the Top expanded to include competition for school districts; 55 districts receive a total of $400 million.
		2013 — Forty-five states submit plans for ESEA flexibility, and 42 are approved. More than $4 billion in Race to the Top funds are awarded to 19 states. Forty-five states adopt Common Core Standards; a few states pass legislation to delay or withdraw from using the Common Core Standards.
		2014 — By 2014, all students will leave high school "college or career ready."
	2015	2015 — States collaborate to develop common assessments aligned to Common Core Standards; assessments to begin during the 2014–2015 school year.

American Indian/Alaska Native, Black, and Hispanic students at the same grade levels (National Assessment of Educational Progress, 2013).

Promoting the achievement of students from diverse racial, cultural, and social-class groups continues to be a challenge for U.S. education. In *The Black-White Achievement Gap: Why Closing It Is the Greatest Civil Rights Issue of Our Time,* Rod Paige, former U.S. Secretary of Education (2001–2005) and his sister, Elaine Witty, former education dean at Norfolk State University, make this point very clear:

> Now, the primary barrier impeding progress toward our twin goals of racial equality and social justice isn't the clearly visible objects of oppression of yesteryear. Today's primary barrier appears much more innocuous and much more subtle. In a way, it's almost invisible to society at large, and unlike segregation, slavery, and discrimination, which were imposed intentionally by a racist society, no one is forcing this barrier to exist—yet it's there. Today's primary barrier is the black-white achievement gap. (Paige & Witty, 2010, p. 2)

Excellence

In spite of the historic nationwide recession that began in 2008, states continued to develop new, cost-effective ways to promote excellence during the new century. They implemented comprehensive strategies to ensure that teachers have the skills, knowledge, and support required to raise achievement for all students. At least 23 states enacted 43 laws during the 2009 legislative sessions to promote excellence (National Conference of State Legislatures, 2010, p. 4). For example, **WEST VIRGINIA** created a process for designating schools as "innovation zones." This ensures that, in exchange for greater accountability, schools approved by the State Board of Education would have greater control over curriculum, personnel, organization of the school day and year, technology use, and delivery of educational services to improve student learning (National Conference of State Legislatures, 2010).

States also promoted excellence by participating in the **Common Core State Standards Initiative (CCSSI)**. To bring uniformity to a "patchwork quilt" of state standards, the Council of Chief State School Officers (CCSSO) and the National Governors Association Center for Best Practices (NGA Center) organized the CCSSI during 2009. Forty-eight states, not including Texas and Alaska, participated in developing K–12 standards in English language arts and mathematics that were released the following year.

At first, reactions to the Standards were largely positive; however, a heated national debate over the Standards emerged. Although the CCSSI made it clear that the standards were "voluntary"—they *were not* a federal initiative—many observers claimed that the Standards amounted to a federal "takeover" of school curricula. By 2013, 45 states had formally adopted the Standards, whereas a few states passed legislation to delay or withdraw from using the Standards. States also collaborated to develop common assessments aligned to the Common Core Standards, and assessments were to begin during the 2014–2015 school year.

After the turn of the century, the U.S. Department of Education promoted excellence on many fronts. The Obama administration released *A Blueprint for Reform* in 2010, calling for the reauthorization of the Elementary and Secondary Education Act (ESEA) and proposing broad changes to No Child Left Behind (NCLB). According to the *Blueprint,* schools would no longer be singled out for not making "adequate yearly progress" (AYP), and, by 2014, all students would leave high school "college or career ready." To promote excellence and innovation at the state level, the Blueprint included a competitive $4 billion Race to the Top program and the Teacher and Leader Innovation Fund. Race to the Top was expanded in 2012 to include competition for school districts, and 55 districts subsequently received $400 million.

By 2011, Congress had failed to act on the call to reauthorize ESEA, which led the Obama administration to announce that states could voluntarily seek "ESEA flexibility"

PROFESSIONAL REFLECTION
These educators share how the needs of students are met under No Child Left Behind.

and be exempt from certain requirements of NCLB by submitting comprehensive plans to improve education for all students. Forty-five states submitted such plans by 2013, and 42 were approved.

Accountability

Politicians, business leaders, and citizens continued to hold schools, teachers, and administrators accountable for student learning during the first two decades of the new century. For example, one teacher describes the biggest change she experienced in 10 years of teaching—being accountable for monitoring student progress in mathematics on a daily basis:

> Before, you didn't have four or five groups going in math . . . You didn't give an exit card [formative assessment] at the end of every lesson to see who got it, who didn't, who needs re-teaching. And that's a daily thing now, to figure out where you're gonna go tomorrow, who's going on, who's staying here, who's going backwards.
>   . . . . Before, you taught a lesson to everybody, and hopefully, everybody got it. (Valli & Buese, 2007, p. 541)

To hold educators accountable for student learning, some states linked test results to merit rewards, increased funding, or sanctions; others provided additional funds for high-performing schools or bonuses for educators at those schools. For example, **CALIFORNIA** implemented several merit-based incentive programs for teachers, schools, and administrators, including the "Governor's Performance Awards" that gave money to schools based on their "academic performance index." Similarly, in New York City, **NEW YORK**, the school system gave bonuses to principals and other administrators whose schools showed significant gains on test scores. School system administrators grouped schools into three performance categories—low, middle, and high—taking into account students' economic circumstances. For high schools, factors such as dropout rates were also used.

Watch how these educators are held accountable and hold students accountable.

Continuing the Quest for Excellence and Equity

In spite of the challenges that confront the U.S. system of education, ours is one of the few countries in the world to offer a free public education to *all* of its children. When we look to the future and consider ways to make our educational system even stronger, we must acknowledge the debt we owe to those who have shaped the history of U.S. education up to the present moment. We must be students of our past if we are to improve education in the future.

The United States has set for itself an education mission of truly ambitious proportions. To realize fully this mission during the decades to come will be difficult, but an examination of our history shows that it is not impossible. In little more than 380 years, our education system has grown from one that provided only a minimal education to an advantaged minority to one that now provides maximal educational opportunity to the majority. Clearly, the first decade of the new century provides ample evidence that our nation will not waver from its long-standing commitment to ensuring that all children have equal access to educational excellence.

PROFESSIONAL REFLECTION
Watch how this bilingual world history teacher implements her quest for excellence and equity with her students.

TECHNOLOGY in ACTION
Screen-Recorder Software in 12th-Grade Calculus

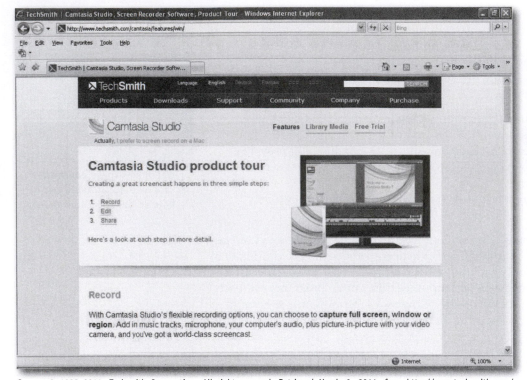

After a brief conversation with Jenny Seasam, the building instructional technology (IT) person, Mr. DeWilt had a copy loaded onto his office computer. Now, when a student comes to him with a calculus problem, he opens the free web-based calculus tool, puts on his headset microphone, launches Camtasia, and walks the student through the application. When he finishes, he saves the file as a web file and publishes it on his class website. Students can access it anytime, anywhere. This solution not only helps his students with their technical issues, it also helps reinforce the calculus concepts he wants students to learn.

SCREEN RECORDER: A screen recorder is a tool that allows you to record your movements on a computer screen while adding voice, text, and graphics. This is an easy-to-use, cost-effective way to create custom, just-in-time tutorials, examples, and navigation on your computer screen. To use this tool, you will need at least 1 GB of RAM, a sound card, a video card, microphone, and speakers.

POSSIBLE USES: Screen-recorder software can be used to record website navigation, software tutorials, or any other computer-based activity that you want to demonstrate to an audience. Teachers have used screen-recorder software to help students understand how to navigate a complex website. Teachers have also used screen recorder software to develop tutorials to help their students use a specific piece of software. For example, see the following Try It Out section of this feature. Instead of presenting this material to you as text, I could use the software tool to record the instructions presented below; then, at your convenience, you could watch me demonstrate how to use the Camtasia software.

TRY IT OUT: As a teacher, you have several screen-recorder options available. The tool highlighted in this feature is just one example you can use. If you want to demo Camtasia, you can download a free trial version (Windows or Mac) from the Internet. Once you have downloaded the software and installed it, merely click on the Camtasia icon on your desktop or the Camtasia link in your Start menu. Next, you will be prompted to open an existing project or start a new one.

Let's start a new one. As you set up your project, you will need to make some decisions. First, will you record a region of your computer screen, a specific window, or the entire screen? The answer will depend on the project you want to create. You

Some students struggle in Mr. DeWilt's 12th-grade calculus class. The textbook, his teaching, and the text's website are good, but he needs something more. He needs to supplement his in-class explanations of calculus with something that is flexible and personal. Most of his students understand the material most of the time. However, when he "does the math" over the course of a school year, Mr. DeWilt realizes that a number of students don't "get it."

The textbook he uses has a supplemental DVD that allows students to view video examples of solutions to calculus problems—in his opinion, these are very effective. During a web search for additional similar support for his teaching, Mr. DeWilt located a free web-based calculus tool. The tool allows students to plug in a problem and complete the equation. However, this free tool was not user-friendly and had little technical help and documentation. When he used it with his students, he spent more time explaining how to use the tool than how to understand the calculus concepts he wanted his students to learn. He needed something that students could access any time they ran into trouble, something they could return to again and again.

At first, he tried videotaping his work on the computer screen, but that did not work. The audio was poor, and the image quality was worse. Also, it was extremely time-consuming to set up the video equipment for each concept he wished to provide students with additional support for their learning.

Frustrated, Mr. DeWilt sent an e-mail to the textbook's publisher asking how the computer screen recordings on the DVD were made so clear. He learned that the publisher used a screen-recorder software program called Camtasia Studio.

will also need to determine the size of your video image. Larger images are easier to watch, but they result in a larger file size, which can be problematic for web delivery of the screen capture. After you determine the type of audio for the project, you are ready to continue.

Now, click on the part of your computer screen you want to record—a highlighted box will surround the section that will be recorded. If the highlighted section is accurate, click "Record" from your Camtasia Recorder prompt. From this point, everything you do on your computer will be recorded. When you are done recording, hit "Stop Recording" and save the file. If you like what you did, you can render (re-create) the file to an appropriate file format, like Quicktime or Flash. If you do not like it, place your unrendered file on the editing timeline, edit it, and then render it.

SUMMARY

Why Is Educational History Important?

- An understanding of educational history is necessary so teachers can provide leadership to improve our educational future.
- Educational history is an important part of professional knowledge.

What Were the European Antecedents of American Education?

- Many practices in today's schools had their origins in Europe, where the role of education was to prepare children and youth for adulthood.
- Ancient Greeks believed that leisure should be used to reflect on practical and aesthetic values and to develop a well-rounded mind and body.
- Socrates questioned pupils to reveal errors in their thinking and to lead them to eternal truths.
- Plato, a student of Socrates, founded the Academy, often called the world's first university.
- Aristotle, a student of Plato, was a realist who believed that reality, knowledge, and value exist independent of the mind.
- Roman education, patterned after Greek education, consisted of the *ludus,* or elementary school, and a secondary or grammar school.
- Education in the European Middle Ages was mediated through the Roman Catholic Church. The Renaissance marked a rebirth of interest in Greco-Roman art, literature, secular learning, and humanism.
- Four 18th-century European thinkers who influenced American education are Rousseau, Pestalozzi, Herbart, and Lancaster.

What Were Teaching and Schools Like in the American Colonies (1620–1750)?

- Colonial education was patterned after the British two-track system, and its primary objective was to promote religion.
- Colonial teachers had low status, although respect increased with the grade level taught.
- Puritans believed children were naturally corrupt and sinful and should be disciplined sternly at the dame schools, reading and writing schools, and Latin grammar schools common to the colonies.

- One of the first schools for African Americans and Native Americans was started in 1704.
- Mandated education in the United States had its origins in two colonial laws: the Massachusetts Acts of 1642 and 1647.

What Were the Goals of Education During the Revolutionary Period (1750–1820)?

- During the Revolutionary period, characterized by a declining European influence on American education, education in the new democracy was shaped by the ideas of Benjamin Franklin, Sarah Pierce, Thomas Jefferson, and Noah Webster.
- At the end of the American Revolution, the few African and Native Americans who were literate were taught at church-sponsored schools that were segregated by race.
- Educational opportunities for women were often limited to preparing them for family life.

How Was the Struggle Won for State-Supported Common Schools (1820–1865)?

- Horace Mann, a strong advocate for state-supported, free common schools, believed that teachers should receive postsecondary training in normal schools.
- The six-volume McGuffey reader, with its moral lessons and emphasis on virtue, determined much of what children learned at school.
- The Morrill Land-Grant Act, passed in 1862, provided federal land for colleges and set a precedent for federal involvement in education.
- A Massachusetts Supreme Court ruling in 1850 supported "equal, but separate" schools for African Americans.

How Did Compulsory Education Change Schools and the Teaching Profession (1865–1920)?

- The spread of common schools and dramatic increases in their enrollments led to the use of scientific management techniques for their operation.
- Booker T. Washington, founder of the Tuskegee Institute, believed education could prepare African Americans to live peaceably with Whites, whereas W. E. B. DuBois believed African Americans should educate

themselves for leadership positions and not accept inferior status.

- Kindergartens became common and used child-centered curricula patterned after German educator Friedrich Froebel's ideas.
- After the Civil War and emancipation, schools for former slaves were opened throughout the South by African American communities; the Freedmen's Bureau also operated schools for former slaves and their children.
- The National Education Association (NEA) and the American Federation of Teachers (AFT) were founded to professionalize teaching and increase teachers' salaries and benefits.
- The NEA appointed the Committee of Ten and the Committee of Fifteen to make recommendations for the secondary and elementary school curricula, respectively.
- The Commission on the Reorganization of Secondary Education, appointed by the NEA to reexamine the secondary curriculum in regard to students' individual differences, developed "seven cardinal principles" for schooling at all levels: health, command of fundamental processes (reading, writing, and computation), worthy home membership, vocation, citizenship, worthy use of leisure time, and ethical character.

What Were the Aims of Education During the Progressive Era (1920–1945)?

- John Dewey's Laboratory School at the University of Chicago, a model of progressive education, offered a curriculum based on children's interests and needs.
- Progressive educator Maria Montessori developed age-appropriate materials and teaching strategies that were implemented in the United States and throughout the world.
- Public criticism of progressive education led to its decline at the start of World War II.

- School enrollments became increasingly diverse as a result of immigration, and a goal of education was the rapid assimilation of all groups into an English-speaking Anglo-European culture.

How Did Education Change During the Modern Postwar Era (1945–2000)?

- The Soviet Union's launching of *Sputnik* in 1957 sparked educational reform, particularly in science, mathematics, and foreign language education. Schools were ordered to desegregate with "all deliberate speed" as a result of a 1954 decision by the Supreme Court in *Brown v. Board of Education of Topeka*.
- Innovative curricula and instructional strategies were used in many classrooms of the 1960s. The Elementary and Secondary Education Act of 1965, part of President Johnson's Great Society and War on Poverty programs, provided federal money to improve the education of poor children.
- Alarmed by declining test scores, the public became critical of schools during the 1970s and demanded accountability. An array of federal legislation was passed to provide equal educational opportunity for all students.
- *A Nation at Risk* and other reports during the 1980s addressed weaknesses in U.S. schools and sparked debate on how to improve U.S. education.
- In response to continuing challenges to education today, teachers are taking leadership roles in school restructuring, school governance, curriculum change, and other aspects of educational reform.

What Are the Educational Priorities of the New Century (2000–the Present)?

- Three trends will continue to be educational priorities during this century: *equity* for all students, *excellence* and high standards, and *accountability* for schools and teachers.

PROFESSIONAL REFLECTIONS AND ACTIVITIES

Teacher's Journal

1. Benjamin Franklin suggested that education is "the surest foundation" for happiness. To what extent do you agree or disagree with Franklin's statement?
2. What remnants remain of the Puritan influence on American education? Of the progressive influence?
3. Reflect on the "daily school routine" you experienced as an elementary school child. How does that routine differ from that experienced by children in colonial schools? Recall how your teachers handled classroom discipline; how do those approaches differ from those used by colonial teachers?

Teacher's Research

1. Examine several textbooks currently in use at the level of education that interests you the most. Then, locate some texts that were used at that level several decades ago. What differences do you notice? Report your findings to your classmates.
2. Use online references to research in greater detail the contributions of a pioneer in education whose work is summarized in this chapter.

Observations and Interviews

1. Interview veteran teachers and administrators at a local school and ask them to comment on the changes in education that they have observed and experienced during their careers. In particular, compare their remarks to this chapter's discussion of education during the post–World War II era, using this chapter's descriptions of the era to guide your questions. What events do respondents identify as having had the greatest impact on their teaching?

2. Visit a museum in your area for the purpose of examining some artifacts from early U.S. educational history. Take notes on what you find and describe several of the artifacts to the rest of your class.

3. Interview several elderly people, at a nursing home perhaps, about their school experiences. Do any of their recollections coincide with the descriptions of the time periods discussed in this chapter?

Professional Portfolio

Prepare a videotaped oral history that focuses on the changes that have occurred over the years in local schools or an interest of local concern. You may decide to interview experienced teachers, administrators, or school board members, or you may decide to interview older members of the community.

Prior to conducting your interviews, prepare several interview questions that focus on your area of interest. At the conclusion of each interview, invite the interviewee to provide any other relevant information he or she might have.

CHAPTER QUIZ

Take this quiz to check your understanding of the content covered in this chapter.

CHAPTER SIX

Governance and Finance of U.S. Schools

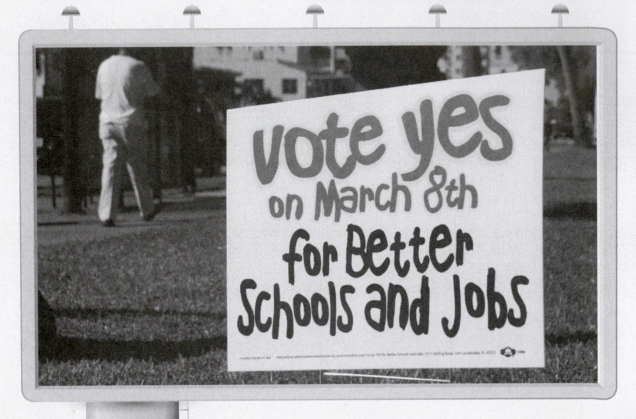

learning outcomes

After reading this chapter, you will be able to do the following:

1. Explain why teachers must understand educational politics.
2. Explain how local communities influence schools.
3. Describe the powers and the influence of states related to school governance.
4. Explain how regional education agencies assist schools.
5. Explain how the federal government influences education.
6. Describe the role of teacher leaders in school governance.
7. Explain how schools are financed in the United States.
8. Describe trends in funding for educational equity and excellence.
9. Explain how the privatization movement is affecting equity and excellence in education.

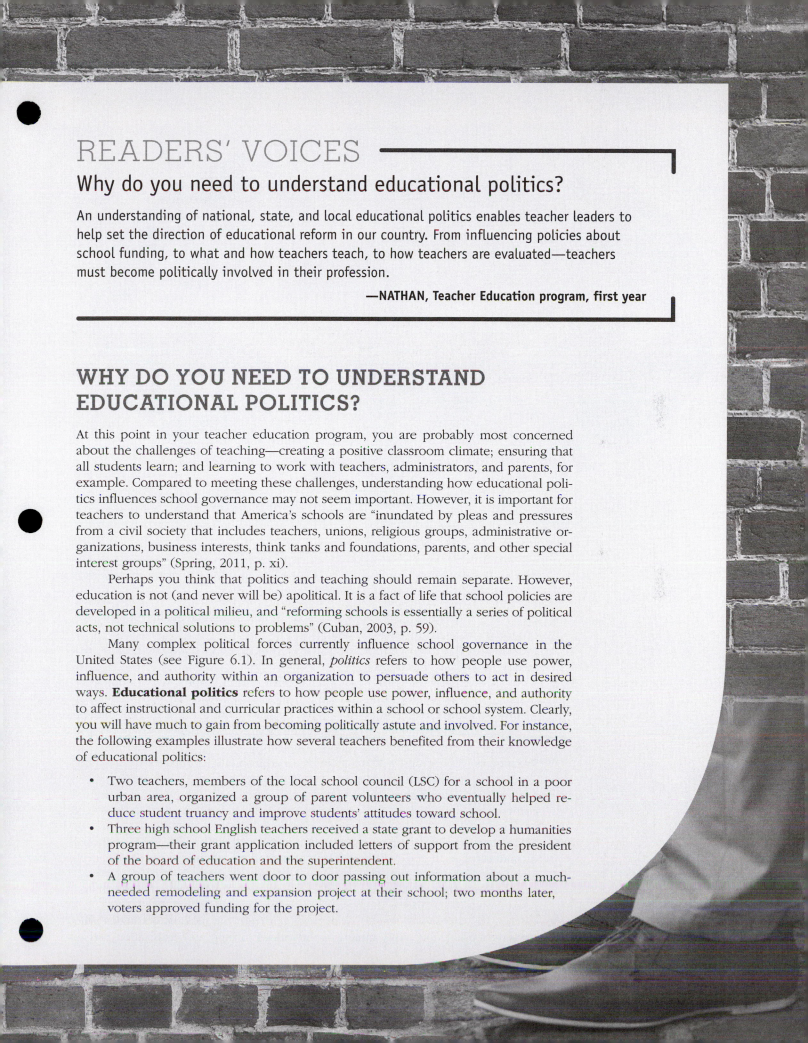

Why do you need to understand educational politics?

An understanding of national, state, and local educational politics enables teacher leaders to help set the direction of educational reform in our country. From influencing policies about school funding, to what and how teachers teach, to how teachers are evaluated—teachers must become politically involved in their profession.

—NATHAN, Teacher Education program, first year

WHY DO YOU NEED TO UNDERSTAND EDUCATIONAL POLITICS?

At this point in your teacher education program, you are probably most concerned about the challenges of teaching—creating a positive classroom climate; ensuring that all students learn; and learning to work with teachers, administrators, and parents, for example. Compared to meeting these challenges, understanding how educational politics influences school governance may not seem important. However, it is important for teachers to understand that America's schools are "inundated by pleas and pressures from a civil society that includes teachers, unions, religious groups, administrative organizations, business interests, think tanks and foundations, parents, and other special interest groups" (Spring, 2011, p. xi).

Perhaps you think that politics and teaching should remain separate. However, education is not (and never will be) apolitical. It is a fact of life that school policies are developed in a political milieu, and "reforming schools is essentially a series of political acts, not technical solutions to problems" (Cuban, 2003, p. 59).

Many complex political forces currently influence school governance in the United States (see Figure 6.1). In general, *politics* refers to how people use power, influence, and authority within an organization to persuade others to act in desired ways. **Educational politics** refers to how people use power, influence, and authority to affect instructional and curricular practices within a school or school system. Clearly, you will have much to gain from becoming politically astute and involved. For instance, the following examples illustrate how several teachers benefited from their knowledge of educational politics:

- Two teachers, members of the local school council (LSC) for a school in a poor urban area, organized a group of parent volunteers who eventually helped reduce student truancy and improve students' attitudes toward school.
- Three high school English teachers received a state grant to develop a humanities program—their grant application included letters of support from the president of the board of education and the superintendent.
- A group of teachers went door to door passing out information about a much-needed remodeling and expansion project at their school; two months later, voters approved funding for the project.

FIGURE 6.1   Political influences on the schools

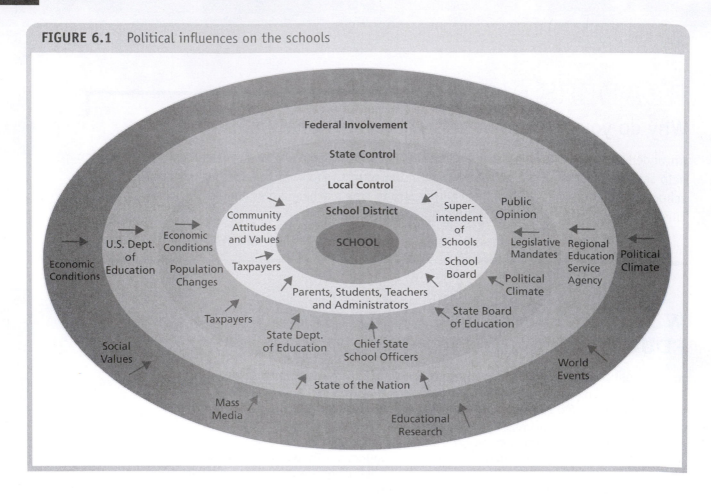

Among the groups who will compete to shape educational policies during your teaching career, at least ten can be identified:

1. **Parents**—concerned with controlling local schools so that quality educational programs are available to their children.
2. **Students**—concerned with policies related to freedom of expression, dress, behavior, and curricular offerings.
3. **Teachers**—concerned with their role in school reform, improving working conditions, terms of employment, and other professional issues.
4. **Administrators**—concerned with providing leadership so that various interest groups, including teachers, participate in the shared governance of schools and the development of quality educational programs.
5. **Taxpayers**—concerned with maintaining an appropriate formula for determining local, state, and federal financial support of schools.
6. **Federal, state, and local authorities**—concerned with the implementation of court orders, guidelines, and legislative mandates related to the operation of schools.
7. **Ethnic and racial groups**—concerned with the availability of equal educational opportunity for all and with legal issues surrounding administrative certification, terms of employment, and evaluation.
8. **Educational theorists and researchers**—concerned with using theoretical and research-based insights as the bases for improving schools at all levels.
9. **Corporate sector**—concerned with receiving from the schools graduates who have the knowledge, skills, attitudes, and values to help an organization realize its goals.
10. **Special-interest groups**—concerned with advancing educational reforms that reflect particular religious, philosophical, and economic points of view.

FIGURE 6.2   Five dimensions of educational politics that influence teachers

Five Dimensions of Educational Politics

Figure 6.2 illustrates five dimensions of educational politics that influence teachers. First, whether it is federal legislation such as Race to the Top or a local school bond issue, politics at the federal, regional, state, and local levels influence teachers. Second, educators, citizens, and policymakers use politics to lobby for the development of educational programs that reflect their beliefs about what should be taught and how it should be taught. Third, the allocation of resources to schools can easily become a political issue in a community, as anyone who has voted on a school bond issue knows. Fourth, the legal rights and responsibilities of teachers and students are continuously changing, often as a result of conflicting political views about education. And fifth, one of the "hottest," politically charged issues in education today involves the push for higher standards; mandated testing to ensure that students have mastered those standards; and calls for **accountability** to ensure that schools, teachers, and administrators produce results.

Indeed, it is no exaggeration to say that educational politics can place a teacher "in the line of fire." For example, the following statement by a teacher illustrates how teachers can come into "the line of fire" if they publicly express their ideas about what should be taught and how it should be taught.

> *I have to be very careful about what I say about* _____ *[a commercial reading program adopted by my school]* because it's almost heresy to suggest that something else might work as well or even better. *I don't know why these teachers won't say what they believe.* They are frustrated with it but they won't say anything against it. If they do, it's reported to the principal and he reprimands them for "being against [the reading program]." (Garan, 2004, p. 84, words emphasized in original)

In this chapter's Teachers' Voices: Being an Agent of Change feature, Ariel Sacks, a middle school teacher in Brooklyn, encourages teachers to speak out and to become involved in developing educational policies.

The next four sections of this chapter examine how educational politics at the local, state, regional, and national levels influence schools and teachers.

HOW DOES THE LOCAL COMMUNITY INFLUENCE SCHOOLS?

Although the Constitution does not address public education, the 10th Amendment is used as the basis for giving states the legal authority to create and manage school

TEACHERS' VOICES ➡ BEING AN AGENT OF CHANGE

ARIEL SACKS

TEACHERS NEED TO BE HEARD

Ariel Sacks teaches eighth-grade English at a middle school in Brooklyn, **NEW YORK**. Previously, she was team leader and English department chair at a public secondary school in Crown Heights, Brooklyn, and she taught English to transitional English language learners in a bilingual middle school in East Harlem. She has published articles about her work in *Teacher Magazine* and is a co-author of *Teaching 2030: What We Must Do for Our Students and Our Public Schools—Now and in the Future*, Teachers College Press, 2011.

Committed to implementing student-centered methods in high-needs public schools and promoting teacher leadership, Sacks has presented her ideas at Bank Street College of Education, the National Council of Teachers of English, the Ford Foundation, and Great Teachers for Great City Schools. She is passionate about the need for teachers to become involved in developing educational policy. The following is excerpted from her Teacher Leaders Network (TNL) featured blog titled "On the Shoulders of Giants."

Recently on the Teacher Leaders Network, I landed in a discussion about the many great teachers we know who, for a variety of reasons, stay far away from education policy. In this post, I respond to what I see as the top [three] reasons teachers tend not to get involved.

One: *It's not my job to be involved in education policy.*

My Response: *While it's not in our job description to be involved in education policy, it is in our best interest to voice our perspectives, because policies directly affect the conditions of our work, our ability to do our best for our students, and our willingness to stay in teaching. Historically, teachers have been the recipients of policies written by outsiders, higher up on the ladder than we are. We experience the results of decisions and usually have plenty to say about how they play out in our schools. How many times have you issued some choice words about the latest education legislation at lunch with a group of colleagues? Why not hone that message and share it with a wider audience? Also, if the policymakers are at the top of the education pyramid, who does that leave at the bottom? Students and parents. And that's just not right. We need to challenge the current hierarchy so that the people who matter most in American public education, students, parents, and teachers, have a bigger voice. Teachers, especially, who are most directly responsible for the education of students, need to be heard on the issues.*

Two: *Nobody wants to listen to teachers.*

My Response: *There is now ample research that says that the single most important factor in a child's education is the quality of his or her teachers. This is causing policymakers, media, and the general public to focus a lot of attention on teachers. Some of that attention has been in the form of negative attacks (wholly unproductive), but there are a lot of policymakers and influential organizations that are very interested in what teachers bring to the policy conversation.*

Center for Teaching Quality and Teacher Leaders Network have been at the forefront of the movement for getting teachers involved in education policy, and the progress over the last 10 to 15 years has been huge, according to those who've been involved longer than I. Even in the 7 years I've been a public school teacher, the idea of teacher leadership has gone from a pretty much unknown concept to an on-the-ground reality for many teachers and many schools.

Three: *I don't have time for education policy.*

My Response: *OK, this one becomes a little harder for me to argue with. I get it; certainly, I do. At the end of a busy, tiring day, the last thing you need is more work. But I would ask, do you read the newspaper or watch the news? If so, you are getting some information on education policy, but from too limited a source. Round out your education reading a little bit.*

Spend 10 minutes, after you do your regular reading of the paper, reading about education policy from educators who follow it closely and speak from their experiences. Try the blogs at Edweek Teacher (Teacher Magazine), or Public School Insights, or any of my colleagues' Teacher Leader Network blogs, or the new teacher blogs at the Huffington Post Education section.

Join the conversation by leaving ONE comment. Additionally, you can be involved by forwarding an article or blog post to one colleague or interested friend. Finally, you can follow most of these bloggers on Twitter and get a multitude of interesting and quick thoughts and links to news. Sometimes, believe it or not, after a long day, some sane words from a thoughtful educator about the big picture of what's going on in our profession and in our schools is exactly what you need!

Whatever your level of involvement is or will be, the most important thing is to realize how much each of us, as teachers, actually matters in the world of education policy. We do our work in the spaces where education policymakers intend to make change. The more we can know about these policies and make our voices and positions known, the more sensible the changes will become.

PERSONAL REFLECTION

1. Thinking ahead to your future as a teacher, what steps can you take to influence the development of educational policies?

2. If the majority of teachers in a school or district are opposed to an educational policy adopted by their school board, what should they do?

3. Read one of the featured blogs at the Teacher Leaders Network (http://www.teacherleaders.org/featured-bloggers). Post a short response to the author of the blog. Your response should explain why you agree, or disagree, with the author's ideas.

The preceding is excerpted from Ariel Sacks's December 31, 2010, blog, "Responses to the Top 5 Reasons Teachers Stay Away from Education Policy," retrieved February 13, 2011, from http://teacherleaders.typepad.com/shoulders_of_giants/2010/12/responses-to-the-top-5-reasons-teachers-stay-away-from-in-education-policy-.html.

systems. In addition, as illustrated in Figure 6.1, various individuals and groups, although not legally empowered, compete vigorously to influence those legally entitled to operate the schools.

The 10th Amendment gives to the states all powers not reserved for the federal government and not prohibited to the states. The states, in turn, have created local school districts, giving them responsibility for the daily operation of public schools. As a result of efforts to consolidate districts, the number of local public school districts declined from 117,108 in 1939–1940 to 13,588 in 2010–2011 (Snyder & Dillow, 2013, p. 145).

Local School District

Local school districts vary greatly in regard to demographics such as number of school-age children; educational, occupational, and income levels of parents; operating budget; number of teachers; economic resources; and number of school buildings. Some serve extremely wealthy communities; others serve impoverished ghetto neighborhoods or rural areas. Their operations include approximately 300 one-teacher elementary schools in this country (Snyder & Dillow, 2014) as well as scores of modern, multi-building campuses in heavily populated areas.

The largest school districts are exceedingly complex operations. The largest—the New York City school system—has 1.1 million pupils (from 190 countries), 75,000 classroom teachers (a number that exceeds the number of students in Cincinnati; Minneapolis; Portland, Oregon; Sacramento; Seattle; and St. Louis), 1,800 schools, and an annual budget of $24 billion (New York City Department of Education, 2014). The New York system, overseen by a schools chancellor, consists of 32 community school districts, each with its own superintendent. Table 6.1 shows selected statistics for the 10 largest school districts in the United States and jurisdictions for the 2008–2009 school year.

TABLE 6.1 Selected statistics for 10 largest public school districts

Name of district	Enrollment, fall 2010	Number of English language learners, 2010	Percent eligible for free or reduced-price lunch, 2010	Number of classroom teachers, 2010	Percent dropping out of grades 9–12, 2008–2009	Number of schools, fall 2010
New York City	995,336	146,207	74.3	68,458	7.4	1,552
Los Angeles Unified	667,273	—	62.2	31,092	—	914
City of Chicago	405,644	56,993	85.4	23,146	15.0	638
Dade County, FL	347,366	61,944	70.2	21,195	4.7	515
Clark County, NV	314,059	67,877	53.6	15,269	—	364
Broward County, FL	256,472	24,316	54.5	15,573	2.4	320
Houston Independent School District	204,245	56,067	50.9	11,811	4.6	302
Hillsborough, FL	194,525	23,291	55.9	13,470	1.1	298
Hawaii Department of Education	179,601	19,092	46.8	11,396	4.9	289
Orange County, FL	176,008	28,370	57.0	11,115	1.2	240

—Not available

Adapted from Snyder, T. D., and Dillow, S. A. (2013). *Digest of Education Statistics 2012* (NCES 2014-015). National Center for Education Statistics, Institute of Education Sciences, U.S. Department of Education. Washington, DC., pp. 148–158.

The organizational structures of school districts also differ. Large urban systems, which may contain several districts, tend to have a more complex distribution of roles and responsibilities than do smaller districts. Figure 6.3 shows the organizational chart for a school district of about 20,000 pupils.

School Board

A **school board**, acting as a state agent, is responsible for the following: approving the teachers, administrators, and other school personnel hired by the superintendent; developing organizational and educational policies; and determining procedures for evaluating programs and personnel.

In most communities, school board members are elected in general elections. In some urban areas, however, board members are selected by the mayor. Board members typically serve a minimum of 3 to 5 years, and their terms of office are usually staggered. School boards usually range from 5 to 15 members, with 5 or 7 frequently suggested as the optimum size. Board members in urban areas usually are paid, but in most other areas they are not.

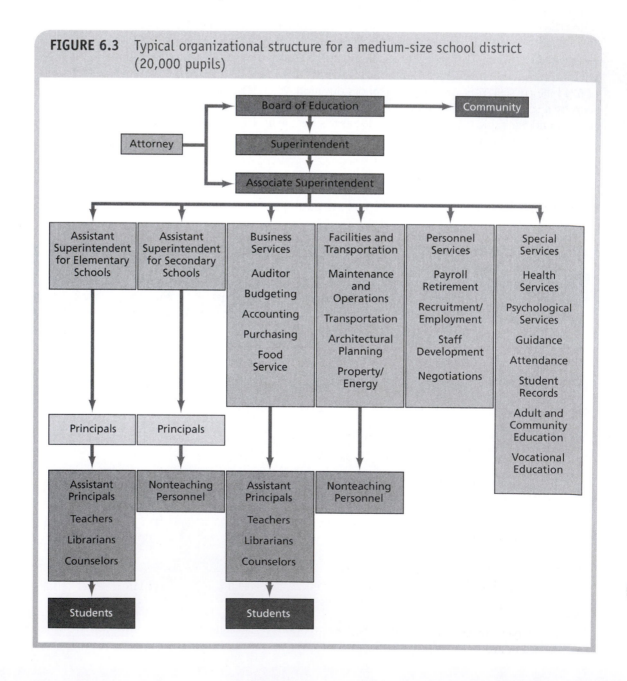

FIGURE 6.3 Typical organizational structure for a medium-size school district (20,000 pupils)

Nearly all school board meetings are open to the public; in fact, many communities even provide radio and television coverage. Open meetings allow parents and interested citizens an opportunity to express their concerns and to get more information about problems in the district.

A national survey of school board members (Hess & Meeks, 2010) revealed the following characteristics of board members:

- White, 80.7 percent; African American, 12.3 percent; and Hispanic, 3.1 percent. Large districts (15,000 or more students), however, have more minority-group board members: African American, 21.8 percent, and Latinos, 6 percent.
- Nearly three-fourths of board members have at least a bachelor's degree, far exceeding the 29 percent of American adults over age 25 who hold at least a B.A. In large districts, 85 percent of board members have at least a B.A., and more than half report that they have earned an advanced degree.
- Politically, 47.3 percent view themselves as moderates, 32.3 percent as conservatives, and 20.4 percent as liberals.
- Fifty-six percent are male, and 44 percent are female. Nearly two-thirds of board members in small districts (1,000–2,499 students) are male, whereas less than half are male in large and medium-size (2,500–14,999 students) districts.
- The most common occupations for board members are education (27.1 percent), business or commerce (18.1 percent), nonprofit organizations and government (14.4 percent), and professional services like law and medicine (14 percent).

School boards play a critical role in the U.S. education system. However, school boards have been criticized for not educating themselves about educational issues, being reluctant to seek input from their communities, not communicating a vision of educational excellence to their communities, and not developing positive relationships with superintendents. For example, a nonprofit education policy organization that co-sponsored a national school board survey suggested that education would better meet the nation's needs if school districts were led by visionary leaders rather than members of the local community (Hess & Meeks, 2010).

Some states have taken steps to reform school boards. For example, ARKANSAS provides board members with training in developing partnerships with their communities, creating a vision of educational excellence, and team building. WEST VIRGINIA restructured school boards, and board members must complete training that focuses on "boardmanship and governing effectiveness." One study of school boards found that effective boards

- focus on student achievement,
- allocate resources to needs,
- watch the return on investment,
- use data, and
- engage the communities they serve (Ward & Griffin, 2006).

Superintendent of Schools

Although school boards operate very differently, the **superintendent** is the key figure in determining a district's educational policy. The board of education delegates broad powers to the superintendent, but his or her policies require board approval. The specific responsibilities of the superintendent are many. Among the most important are the following:

- To serve as professional adviser to the board of education and to make policy recommendations for improving curricular and instructional programs.
- To act as employer and supervisor of professional and nonteaching personnel (janitors, cafeteria workers, etc.).
- To represent the schools in their relations with the community and to explain board of education policies to the community.
- To develop policies for the placement and transportation of students within the district.
- To prepare an annual school budget and adhere to the budget adopted by the school board.

How the superintendent and his or her board work together is related to the size of the school district, with superintendents and school boards in larger districts more likely to be in conflict. School boards in smaller districts are more effective, however, when they do oppose the superintendent. In large districts, the board's own divisiveness makes it less likely that the board will successfully oppose the superintendent (Wirt & Kirst, 2009).

Superintendents must have great skill to respond appropriately to the many external political forces that demand their attention, and conflict is inevitable. Effective superintendents demonstrate that they are able to play three roles simultaneously: politician, manager, and teacher. It is a demanding position, and turnover is high; for example, between 1980 and 1995, the New York City school system had 10 chancellors (Hurwitz, 1999).

The Role of Parents

Parents may not be involved legally in the governance of schools, but they do play an important role in education. One characteristic of successful schools is that they have developed close working relationships with parents. Children whose parents or guardians support and encourage school activities have a definite advantage in school.

Through participation on school advisory and site-based councils, parents are making an important contribution to restructuring and school reform efforts around the country. In addition, groups such as the parent-teacher association (PTA), parent-teacher organization (PTO), or parent advisory council (PAC) give parents the opportunity to communicate with teachers on matters of interest and importance to them. Through these groups, parents can become involved in the life of the school in a variety of ways—from making recommendations regarding school policies to providing much-needed volunteer services, or to initiating school-improvement activities such as fundraising drives.

One example of how parents can serve as advocates for their children's education is Zakiyah Ansari, a parent activist with the New York City Coalition for Educational Justice (CEJ), a parent-led collaborative whose mission is to address education inequities, and the **NEW YORK** state chapter of the Alliance for Educational Justice (AEJ). The mother of eight children who graduated from or now attend New York City public schools, Ansari has organized parents, teachers, and community members to work for increased school funding, more support services for students, and coaching and mentoring programs to promote teachers' professional growth (Ansari, February 2011).

Many parents are also influencing the character of education through their involvement with the growing number of private, parochial, for-profit, and charter schools. In addition, many parents are activists in promoting school choice, voucher systems, and the home schooling movement.

Some parents even join well-funded conservative think tanks that launch sophisticated national campaigns to remove from public schools practices and materials that they find objectionable. People for the American Way (2008) reported that, between 1990 and 2000, there were 6,364 censorship challenges, 71 percent of which were to materials in schools or school libraries. The bases of challenge are as follows:

Learn about ways that educators can have a welcoming school environment for parents.

- 1,607 were challenges to "sexually explicit" material
- 1,427 were challenges to material considered to use "offensive language"
- 1,256 were challenges to material considered non-age-appropriate or "unsuited to age group"
- 842 were challenges to material with an "occult theme or promoting the occult or Satanism"
- 737 were challenges to material considered to be "violent"
- 515 were challenges to material with a homosexual theme or "promoting homosexuality"
- 419 were challenges to material "promoting a religious viewpoint"
- 317 were challenges to materials that included "nudity"

School Restructuring

At many schools across the country, exciting changes are taking place in how schools are controlled locally. To improve the performance of schools, to decentralize the system of governance, and to enhance the professional status of teachers, some districts are **restructuring** their school systems. Restructuring goes by several names: shared governance, administrative decentralization, teacher empowerment, professionalization, bottom-up policymaking, school-based planning, school-based management, distributed leadership, and shared decision making. What all these approaches have in common is allowing those who know students best—teachers, principals, aides, custodians, librarians, secretaries, and parents—greater freedom in deciding how to meet students' needs.

The *Handbook on Restructuring and Substantial School Improvement,* developed by the Academic Development Institute with support from the U.S. Department of Education, includes the following among the "indicators" at successfully restructured schools:

What are the goals of school restructuring? In school-based management, who participates in the governance and management of schools? How is school-based management different from the school board model of local governance?

- A team structure is officially incorporated into the school improvement plan and school governance policy.
- A leadership team consisting of the principal, teachers who lead the instructional teams, and other key professional staff meets regularly (twice a month or more for an hour each meeting).
- The leadership team regularly looks at school performance data and aggregated classroom observation data and uses that data to make decisions about school improvement and professional development needs.
- Professional development of individual teachers includes an emphasis on indicators of effective teaching.
- Parent policies, activities, and programs cultivate the "curriculum of the home."
- The school maintains a central database that includes each student's test scores, placement information, demographic information, attendance, behavior indicators, and other variables useful to teachers. (Walberg, 2007, pp. 119–120, 122–123, 127)

The Technology in Action feature for this chapter describes how a leadership team of teachers increased students' access to the latest technology by working with their principal to purchase a Second Life "island," a 3D virtual world where students can interact with other students and build virtual environments.

School-Based Management

A frequently used approach to restructuring schools is **school-based management (SBM)**. Most SBM programs have three components in common:

1. Power and decisions formerly made by the superintendent and school board are delegated to teachers, principals, parents, community members, and students at local schools. At SBM schools, teachers can become involved directly in decisions about curriculum, textbooks, standards for student behavior, staff development, promotion and retention policies, teacher evaluation, school budgets, and the selection of teachers and administrators.

TEACHING ON YOUR FEET
"We Are All Responsible for One Another...."

LISA M. WEINBAUM was awarded a $2,000 grant for a "Homeless but Not Hopeless" project for her students at a Las Cruces, **NEW MEXICO**, middle school. She applied for the grant after her students made fun of the homeless. According to Weinbaum, they thought homeless people were lazy and might be "faking it."

"We are all responsible for one another and not just ourselves," Weinbaum wrote in her grant application. "The dispossessed still starve, and no one knows or cares to know."

She used the grant money to buy reading material about the homeless, take her students to a homeless shelter, and print a student-written anthology of oral histories, essays, poems, and stories honoring the homeless of Las Cruces.

In the following, Weinbaum describes how a field trip to a pauper's cemetery increased her students' understanding of how homelessness and poverty affect death as was well as life. Her students also "learned they have political power, the ability to help eradicate injustice."

A no-name cemetery containing about 100 unmarked graves was located about five blocks from our school, but few of my students knew it existed. . . .

Even for Las Cruces it was an unseasonably warm late September day and perhaps too hot for a walking field trip. I decided to escort my students anyway, but not all were enthused about making an uphill trek to an abandoned paupers' graveyard in the blistering sun. "What could this cemetery possibly have to do with us?" they demanded.

About 70 percent of my school's students receive free or reduced-price lunch, and many families are relegated to low-paying jobs. Because we were studying the societal causes of homelessness within a unit titled "Homeless but Not Hopeless," I wanted to illustrate that poverty affects life as well as death. In short, this cemetery had everything to do with them. Moreover, I knew that middle school students possess a profound regard for justice.

Once in sight of the cemetery, the students' complaining ceased, replaced with a sudden flurry of note-taking. They stared at the small earthen mounds, at the unkempt, overgrown gravesites. Single cinder-block headstones adorned some graves, while others sprouted misshapen mesquite shrubs or prickly pear cacti. Rough, weather-worn crosses lay haphazardly on the ground, nails protruding. Remnants of windblown Wal-Mart bags, broken Budweiser bottles and faded pink plastic roses littered the landscape. But the final disgrace was the presence of tiny American flags, obviously planted decades ago, perhaps to honor fallen veterans. Tattered and torn, they were threadbare and colorless. Clearly, the souls buried within the cemetery had long since been abandoned by our community.

Totally disgusted, my students vowed to clean the graveyard. They were willing to return on their own, beyond school hours, to complete the job if necessary. But upon contacting a government official, I was told that because the cemetery was located on Doña Ana County property, approval must first be granted from government attorneys, which could take months.

Incensed by the county's bureaucratic run-around and the apparent indifference toward the plight of the cemetery and those interred there, my students wrote protest letters to our local newspapers. Intrigued by the students' concerns, the Las Cruces Sun-News *featured a front-page exposé about the cemetery, followed the next day by an editorial chastising the county for abandoning the dead. Later, the cemetery story aired on the TV news in El Paso, 45 miles to our south, and Albuquerque, 250 miles to our north.*

Embarrassed by the unflattering publicity initiated by my students, the county quickly sponsored a community cleanup at the cemetery. Early on a November Saturday morning, led by my students and their parents with help from other teachers from our school, county employees and local residents, we cleaned the graveyard. Doña Ana County provided heavy machinery, water bottles, gloves, shovels, rakes, and trash bags, while a local restaurateur supplied breakfast burritos. In addition, a recreational vehicle dealership made available an RV rest station. One gentleman, so moved by my students' letters, donated a granite monument engraved not only with the names of the departed, but also with the inscription, "For the Forgotten of Doña Ana County, Both Living and Deceased."

My students were so proud of themselves. Through the strength of their collective speech, they learned their voices are valued. They learned they have political power, the ability to help eradicate injustice. Through their passion, perseverance, and eloquence, they captured our attention. And perhaps for the first time in their educational lives, they were taken seriously. No longer were they labeled as "at-risk" kids relegated to remedial reading; they were the kids who forced our community to look. They were the kids who forced our community to act.

They are writers. They are activists. They are heroes.
They are my students.

ANALYZE & REFLECT

Click here to analyze and reflect on this scenario you have just read.

LISA M. WEINBAUM
Seventh-Grade Literature, Lynn Middle School
Las Cruces, NEW MEXICO

The preceding is excerpted from Weinbaum's article that appeared in *Teaching Tolerance,* "'At Risk' of Greatness," Spring 2007. Retrieved February 20, 2011, from http://www.tolerance.org/magazine/number-31-spring-2007/risk-greatness.

TECHNOLOGY in ACTION
Virtual Worlds and an Interdisciplinary Curriculum

Candis Randall knew her students loved videogames. In fact, she had incorporated a few videogames into her 11th-grade history classroom, and her students really enjoyed them. However, the free or less expensive videogames she could access were quite prescriptive. That is, the variables programmed into the games only allowed for specific actions and reactions. This was fine for basic lessons, but she wanted applications that emphasized more in-depth concepts and critical thinking. After research on the Internet, she found an alternative approach, something different than videogames—virtual worlds. Virtual worlds allow students to explore interesting places alone or in groups; to interact with other students; and to build structures, environments, and/or organisms.

She began to explore Second Life, ActiveWorlds, and There, three of several 3D virtual worlds available on the Internet. Eventually, she decided to set up her avatar (a 3D representation of herself) at Second Life. She found several islands that she could use in her lessons, but the real benefit occurred after she demonstrated Second Life (SL) to her fellow teachers. After the demo and a series of in-depth conversations, the teachers convinced their principal to purchase an island for the school. They also decided that the English teacher, Mr. Lee; the math teacher, Mrs. Sanchez; the art teacher, Mr. Hummer; the technology teacher, Ms. Sushak; and Ms. Randall would participate in a pilot activity.

They agreed that they would spend the next month using SL as their virtual classroom. They and their students would participate in SL activities that would cover the concepts and learning outcomes normally addressed for that month in each of their classes. They created a new form of combined or blended classroom, which allows individual teachers to address specific academic disciplines using connected subject matter or a common theme.

The teachers agreed that the first activity would be a lesson on medieval England. The students in Mrs. Sanchez's math class were asked to build a castle on the school's SL island. Mr. Hummer's students created thematic graphics, such as family crests, portraits, and landscapes. Mr. Lee's students set prose requirements on the island; that is, students could not speak to one another unless they "speaketh correctly." And Ms. Randall's students researched the type of activities that might take place around a medieval castle.

Then they set up a series of roles that individual students would assume. There were a lord and his lady, groomsmen, knights, a constable, and more. Each student was assigned a role to play and was required to interact appropriately.

The activity was a tremendous success. As word got out about the fun these students were having in math, history, English, and art, other students and teachers in the school began visiting the school's medieval community. A rumor started that a student from a neighboring high school heard about the activities taking place and was trying to raise an army to storm the castle.

VIRTUAL WORLDS: Virtual worlds, such as Second Life, are online, three-dimensional spaces in which participants can explore, interact, and create. In addition to their stunning visual effects, the social interactions fostered in these worlds can have a great impact on students' learning. Unlike videogames like those for X-box or Play Station, virtual worlds have no pre-programmed variables—no objectives, no action/reactions programmed into them. Instead, students create the rules and objectives, and they create some of the buildings. They determine what they look like and how they will communicate.

POSSIBLE USES: Teachers have used virtual worlds to have students visit active volcanoes, experience schizophrenia, walk through the scene of a Van Gogh painting, and explore the solar system. Students have experienced life in a post–Civil War western town, responded to a natural disaster as a medical provider, seen artificial intelligence at work, and been granted citizenship in Athens.

TRY IT OUT: Currently, the most popular virtual world is Second Life. To try it out, visit the Second Life website and download the software. You will create a user account that will eventually become a 3D representation of yourself, known as an avatar. Choose your name carefully because it will remain with you for all time in SL. Once you have your name, decide what you will look like—your gender, race, body type, hair (or no), clothing, and gestures. Once your avatar is complete, you will walk through a tutorial, where you learn how to walk, shop, fly, and talk. Once the tutorial is completed, you are free to live your second life.

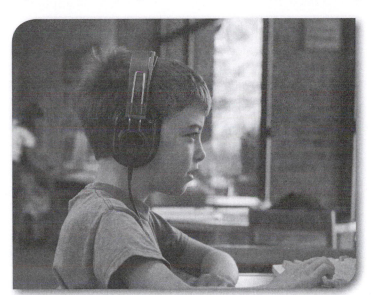

Virtual worlds enable students to visit three dimensional spaces located in the past, present, or future. With reference to the level and subject area for which you are preparing to teach, how can virtual worlds be used to help students acquire important knowledge and skills?

2. At each school, a decision-making body (known as a board, cabinet, site-based team, or council)—made up of teachers, the principal, and parents—implements the SBM plan.
3. SBM programs operate with the full support of the superintendent of schools.

STRUGGLE FOR CONTROL OF CHICAGO SCHOOLS

One of the nation's longest running struggles for control of local schools has taken place in Chicago, Illinois. For years, the Chicago Public Schools have faced an array of problems: low student achievement, periodic teacher strikes, budget crises, a top-heavy central bureaucracy, gang violence, and schools in the decaying inner city that seemed beyond most improvement efforts. In response to these problems, a 55-member committee of business, education, and community leaders developed a school reform proposal. Among the group's recommendations was the creation of a **local school council (LSC)** for each of the city's more than 600 schools, with the majority of council members being parents of schoolchildren.

The Illinois state legislature passed the Chicago School Reform Act, "a series of bold, original reforms [that] attracted intense nationwide interest, particularly because many of the problems faced by Chicago's schools are shared by schools throughout the nation" (Russo, 2004, p. v). Among the provisions of the act were the following:

- School budgets would be controlled by a local school council made up of six parents, two community members, two school employees, and the principal.
- The council had the authority to hire and fire the principal.
- The council, with input from teachers and the principal, had the authority to develop an improvement plan for the local school.
- New teachers would be hired on the basis of merit, not seniority.
- Principals could remove teachers 45 days after serving them official notice of unsatisfactory performance.
- A professional personnel advisory committee of teachers would have advisory responsibility for curriculum and instruction.

The Chicago Reform Act produced few concrete improvements. Frustrated with the district's chronic fiscal problems and inability to increase student achievement, the Illinois legislature gave Mayor Richard M. Daley control over Chicago's schools in 1995. Daley created a five-member "reform board of trustees" and appointed a chief executive officer (CEO) who advocated "a balance between local control and central-office control" (Hendrie, 1999).

The program resulted in modest increases in student achievement. In 1990, less than one-quarter of the city's third through eighth graders read at the national norm; by 2000, more than one-third (36.4 percent) did so (Hess, 2004). Mathematics scores improved even more—from just over one-quarter of elementary students at the national norm in 1990 to just under half in 2000 (Hess, 2004). At the high school level, graduation rates for 19-year-olds increased slightly, and dropout rates for 19-year-olds decreased slightly (Miller, Allensworth, & Kochanek, 2002).

The preceding gains, however, were not uniform in schools across the city; for example, the city's lowest-performing schools showed little improvement (Rosenkranz, 2002). In addition, the Chicago Reform Act's goal for Chicago schools to reach national norms within five years was not reached.

Struggles between the mayor's management team and the parent-dominated LSCs continue to the present day, with both sides from time to time accusing the other of acting in ways that block meaningful reform. Periodically, conflicts erupt over school governance. The 2012 academic year began with a teacher's strike that lasted seven days (Sawchuk, 2012). At the beginning of the 2013–2014 school year, protesters marched from the district's offices to City Hall to voice their disapproval that 49 schools were closed, resulting in more than 12,000 students attending different schools from last year, and 1,600 teachers and staff were laid off to deal with a $1 billion budget deficit

(Zubrzycki, 2013). Protesters also renewed their demand that an elected school board run the school district rather than Mayor Rahm Emanuel.

Also, protesters called for the district to ensure the safety of students, as school closings required many of them to pass through gang-impacted neighborhoods to reach their new schools. A surge in violence in these neighborhoods received international attention when 500 people were shot to death in 2012 and 329 in 2013. In response to parental concern, school district officials expanded the Safe Passage program started in 2009 and lined more than 57 miles of streets with yellow "Safe Passage" signs and dispatched 1,200 Safe Passage workers to ensure that students got to and from school safely (Zubrzycki, 2013). The district also had 41 vacant buildings demolished along the routes, 4,900 trees trimmed, 2,800 instances of graffiti removed, and hundreds of streetlights repaired (Davey, 2013).

After many years, Chicago's approach to school governance has yet to produce significant results. Nevertheless, Chicago has provided the nation with one of the more dramatic efforts to empower parents and to make them full partners in school governance.

INNOVATIVE APPROACHES TO SCHOOL GOVERNANCE

Although traditionally organized school districts govern most schools in the United States, "districts are remaking themselves in a variety of creative and sometimes unprecedented ways as they seek to cope with fiscal, academic, and social pressures that complicate the job of educating America's students" (*Education Week*, 2014). Among the large-city school districts experimenting with innovative approaches to school governance similar to Chicago's are New York City; Washington, D.C.; Memphis; and New Orleans.

Schools in New York, **NEW YORK**, like Chicago schools, switched to a mayoral control system of governance when Mayor Michael Bloomberg won the right in 2002 to replace an elected school board with a board he appointed. Mayor Bloomberg also appointed a chancellor to head the city's school system. Similarly, in 2007, Mayor Adrian Fenty won the right to appoint the chancellor of **WASHINGTON, D.C.**, schools.

After decades of financial strife and low academic performance, the Memphis, **TENNESSEE**, school system changed from a traditional district of 205 schools to a system comprised of different approaches to governance. In 2010, the state created the Achievement School District, which took over 15 low-performing schools, with plans to take over more than 50 schools during subsequent years. In addition, the former 104,000-student Memphis district, which served a high-poverty, majority African American student body, merged during summer 2013 with the neighboring, wealthier Shelby County school system. The merged district also authorized more than 40 charter schools that would be governed under a "charter-management organization." However, by the end of the year, six suburban municipalities began the process of withdrawing from the merged district to form their own school districts for the 2014–2015 school year. Shelby County and the Memphis City Council filed a lawsuit against the suburban districts, claiming that the new districts would re-segregate the county's schools and violate the equal protection clause of the 14th Amendment. In response, the suburbs said they wanted a system with more local control (Zubrzycki, 2014). New Orleans, **LOUISIANA** provides a final example of innovative approaches to school governance. After Hurricane Katrina in 2005, most schools in New Orleans became charter schools operated by the privately run Recovery School District (RCD). The RCD empowers teachers, principals, and parents by providing them the following roles in school governance:

- Teachers, rather than the district, select the methods and materials they use to teach students.
- Principals, rather than the district office, hire teachers and manage a school's budget.
- Parents choose the schools their children attend; previously, children's home addresses determined the schools they attended (Recovery School District, 2014).

WHAT POWERS AND INFLUENCE DO STATES HAVE IN GOVERNING SCHOOLS?

Above the level of local control, states have a great influence on schools. Since the 1990s, the influence of the state on educational policy has increased steadily. For example, every state has statewide academic standards, and every state has mandated a standardized test to assess students' mastery of academic standards. Currently, 26 states require students to attain minimum scores on state assessments to graduate from high school (Education Commission of the States, 2011). In addition, more than 20 states give state boards of education the authority to intervene in academically "bankrupt" schools whose students score too low as a group.

In response to criticisms of U.S. education, many states launched extensive initiatives to improve education, such as the following:

- Increased academic standards
- Greater accountability for teachers
- Testing students in teacher education programs prior to graduation
- Frequent assessments of students' mastery of basic skills
- Professional development as a criterion for continued employment of teachers
- Recertification of experienced teachers

As mentioned previously, the 10th Amendment to the Constitution allows the states to organize and to administer education within their boundaries. To meet the responsibility of maintaining and supporting schools, the states have assumed several powers:

- The power to levy taxes for the support of schools and to determine state aid to local school districts
- The power to set the curriculum and, in some states, to identify approved textbooks
- The power to determine minimum standards for teacher certification
- The power to establish standards for accrediting schools
- The power to pass legislation necessary for the proper maintenance and support of schools

To carry out the tasks implied by these powers, the states have adopted a number of different organizational structures. Most states, however, have adopted a hierarchical structure similar to that presented in Figure 6.4.

The Roles of State Government in Education

Various people and agencies play a role in operating the educational system within each state. Although state governments differ, the state legislature, the state courts, and the governor have a direct, critical impact on education in each state.

THE LEGISLATURE

In nearly every state, the legislature is responsible for establishing and maintaining public schools and for determining basic educational policies within the state. Among the policies that the state legislature may determine are the following:

- How the state boards of education will be selected and what their responsibilities will be
- How the chief state school officer will be selected and what his or her duties will be
- How the state department of education will function
- How the state will be divided into local and regional districts
- How higher education will be organized and financed
- How local school boards will be selected and what their powers will be

In addition, the legislature may determine how taxes will be used to support schools, what will or will not be taught, the length of the school day and school

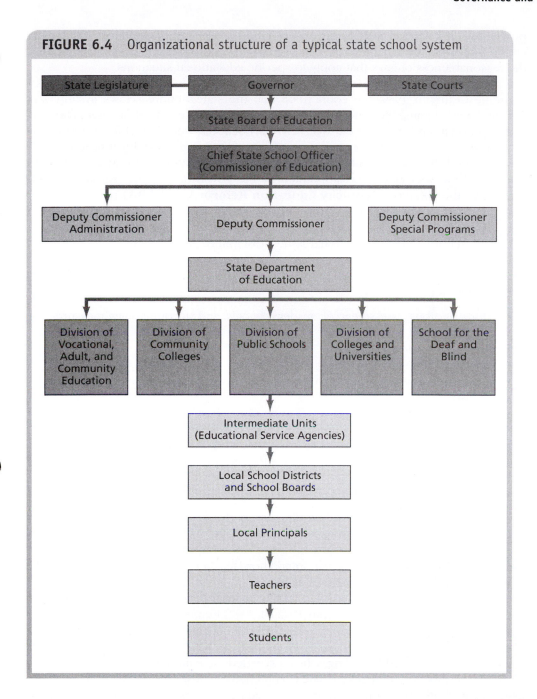

FIGURE 6.4   Organizational structure of a typical state school system

year, how many years of compulsory education will be required, and whether or not the state will have community colleges and/or vocational/technical schools. Legislatures may also make policies that apply to matters such as pupil attendance, admission, promotion, teacher certification, teacher tenure and retirement, and collective bargaining.

Other policies developed by the state legislature may also apply to nonpublic schools in the state—policies related to health services, building construction, safety, school lunch services, textbooks, and testing of pupils, for example. In general, state legislatures may pass laws that provide for the reasonable supervision of nonpublic educational institutions.

THE STATE COURTS

From time to time, state courts are called on to uphold the power of the legislature to develop laws that apply to schools. The state courts must determine, however, that this power does not conflict with the state constitution or the U.S. Constitution. It is important to remember, too, that the role of state courts is not to develop laws but to rule on the reasonableness of laws that apply to specific educational situations.

Perhaps no state court has had a greater impact on education than the Kentucky Supreme Court. In 1989, the court ruled that the state's entire school system was "inadequate." Naming the state superintendent and the state education agency as part of the problem and pointing out that **KENTUCKY** schools were ineffective and inequitable, the court labeled the school system "unconstitutional." The court called on the governor and the legislature to develop an entirely new system of education for the state. A 22-member task force, appointed by the governor and the legislature, then developed the 906-page **Kentucky Education Reform Act (KERA)** passed in 1990. KERA required each school to form a school-based management council by 1996 with authority to set policy in eight areas: curriculum, staff time, student assignment, schedule, school space, instructional issues, discipline, and extracurricular activities. Each council comprised three teachers, two parents (elected by their peers), and the principal. In addition, KERA included the following major changes to the state's education system:

- More rigorous assessment of academic goals and accountability measures for reaching those goals
- Reforms in school governance
- More equitable school funding
- A corps of trained educators to assist or take over underperforming schools and/ or districts
- Changes in the training and certification of teachers and administrators
- Expanded inclusion of children with special needs in regular classrooms
- A comprehensive program of tutorial/remedial services for students
- Family Resource/Youth Service Centers to serve preschool and K–12 students and their families
- Multiage environments for K–3 students

KERA dramatically equalized funding across the state, and some school districts made substantial gains in funding for students. "Districts with low incomes or little property value per student [were] just as likely to have high educational spending as are wealthy districts" (Hoyt, 1999, p. 36). In addition, teacher salaries and student/teacher ratios improved compared to national averages.

Evidence suggests that KERA led to significant improvements in Kentucky's system of education. For example, from 1992 to 2002, Kentucky increased six points in reading on the 4th Grade National Assessment of Educational Progress (NAEP); only five other states showed larger gains. From 1998 to 2002, Kentucky increased three points on 8th Grade NAEP reading, which exceeded the national average increase. Furthermore, results from Kentucky's 2002 Comprehensive Test of Basic Skills Test (CTBS) assessment showed sustained progress in reading, language arts, and mathematics, with Kentucky above the national average at all three testing stages: grades 3, 6, and 9. Last, in 2000, Kentucky *led* the nation in the percentage increase in the high school completion rate for 25- to 34-year-olds (Haselton & Davis, 2004, p. 7).

KERA also resulted in positive changes that were beyond numerical measurement. For example, two Kentucky educators noted that "We [have seen] a potent, though hard to quantify, change in the culture of our schools. This is visible in the strong record of local revenue efforts since the reform began, in the clear decline in hiring based on family and political ties, and in the strong achievement emphasis now heard among the rising leadership among school boards, superintendents, and other educators" (Weston & Sexton, December 2009, p. 32).

Many other observers, such as the following, came to a different conclusion about the impact of KERA: "In its 20 years of existence, a large number of KERA's major efforts have proven unsuccessful. This despite the fact that educators assured citizens time and again—often using terms like 'the research shows'—that their fad ideas were succeeding" (Innes, 2010, p. 2).

The debate about the impact of KERA notwithstanding, there is a mutually agreed-upon lesson from KERA. Improving a statewide system of education is a complex, political process. As Kentucky, like most other states, continues its efforts to improve education by implementing more rigorous standards, developing better approaches to assessing students' learning, and considering innovative to governance such as charter schools, these efforts must be driven by a strong desire to improve education for all students.

THE GOVERNOR

Although the powers of governors vary greatly from state to state, a governor can, if he or she chooses, have a great impact on education within the state. The governor may appoint and/or remove educators at the state level, and in some states the governor may even appoint the chief state school officer. Furthermore, in every state except North Carolina, the governor may use his or her veto power to influence the legislature to pass certain laws related to education.

Governors are also extremely influential because they make educational budget recommendations to legislatures and, in many states, they may elect to use any accumulated balances in the state treasury for education. Governors can also have a significant impact on matters related to curriculum and instruction within the state and, indeed, across the nation. For example, Roy Romer, former governor of **COLORADO**, was instrumental in organizing ACHIEVE, an effort by U.S. governors and corporate leaders to raise academic standards and develop accountability systems for schools. In addition, the **National Governors' Association (NGA)** is active in teacher education and school reforms.

STATE TAKEOVER OF SCHOOLS

Since passage of the No Child Left Behind Act of 2001, **state takeover** is an intervention that can be applied to chronically low-achieving schools and districts. The School District of Philadelphia, **PENNSYLVANIA**, has been the site of the nation's largest takeover of schools. In 2002, the state of Pennsylvania, frustrated by years of low achievement and a decade of budget crises in the School District of Philadelphia, took charge of the city's 200,000-pupil system. The state replaced Philadelphia's nine-member school board with an appointed school reform commission (SRC) composed of three members appointed by the governor and two appointed by the city's mayor. The SRC then hired a new CEO who immediately instituted sweeping changes, including the implementation of districtwide common curricula and a system of frequent benchmark assessments to be used for diagnostic purposes.

More controversially, the SRC adopted a "diverse provider" model as it turned over management of 45 of the district's lowest-performing elementary and middle schools to seven for-profit and nonprofit organizations, including two local universities. The private managers were given additional per-pupil funding to support their work.

During 2002–2006, achievement gains at Philadelphia schools managed privately did not exceed achievement gains at schools in the rest of the district. "With respect to state takeover, results are ambiguous: Subsequent to the state's takeover of the district, proficiency percentages increased district-wide, but the total increase over four years was not substantially greater than the increase of other low-achieving schools in the state, in most cases" (Gill, Zimmer, Christman, & Blanc, 2007).

By 2013, the nation had recovered somewhat from the Great Recession of 2008; however, Philadelphia schools faced a financial crisis. In response to the $304 million shortfall the district faced, the president of the American Federation of Teachers asked the U.S. Secretary of Education to intervene. In response, the U.S. Secretary of Education stated:

> There's no excuse for a public school system anywhere in the U.S. to be in this situation in the 21st century, and it's even worse to see it in Philadelphia, the cornerstone of this great country and the cradle for our founding principles. I strongly urge everyone involved to continue working together to avert this educational crisis. . . . The bottom line is that doing what's

right for Philadelphia students will not only benefit the city, but the commonwealth of Pennsylvania and the country. Philadelphia's children didn't create these problems or ask for them—our responsibility as adults is to do everything we can to provide students in Philadelphia the world class education they deserve. Without courage and leadership, I worry greatly that Philadelphia's children will be shortchanged. We must invest in public education, not abandon it. (U.S. Department of Education, July 2, 2013)

State Board of Education

The **state board of education**, acting under the authority of the state legislature, is the highest educational agency in a state. Every state, with the exception of Wisconsin, has a state board of education. Most states have two separate boards, one responsible for elementary through secondary education, the other for higher education.

The method of determining board members varies from state to state. In some states, the governor appoints members of the state board; in other states, members are selected through general elections. People disagree on which is better: electing or appointing board members. Some believe that election to the state board may cause members to be more concerned with politics than with education. Others argue that elected board members are more aware of the wishes of the public, whom the schools are supposed to serve. People in favor of appointing members to the state board suggest that appointment increases the likelihood that individuals will be chosen on the basis of merit rather than politics.

The regulatory and advisory functions generally held by state boards are as follows:

- Ensuring that local school districts adhere to legislated educational policies, rules, and regulations
- Setting standards for issuing and revoking teaching and administrative certificates
- Establishing standards for accrediting schools
- Managing state monies appropriated for education
- Developing and implementing a system for collecting educational data needed for reporting and program evaluation
- Advising the governor and/or the state legislature on educational issues
- Identifying both short- and long-range educational needs in the state and developing plans to meet those needs
- Hearing all disputes arising from the implementation of its educational policies

In addition, a few state boards of education have instituted a statewide textbook adoption system. In the adoption system, boards choose a small number of titles for each subject area and grade level for all the state's schools. Individual schools and teachers then select their textbooks from this list. **NORTH CAROLINA**, for example, has created a 23-member textbook commission made up of teachers, principals, parents, and a local superintendent. Textbooks are evaluated using criteria based on the North Carolina Standard Course of Study, and adopted textbooks are placed on the statewide textbook list for five years.

State Department of Education

The educational program of each state is implemented by the state's department of education, under the leadership of the chief state school officer. State departments of education have a broad set of responsibilities, and they affect literally every school, school district, and teacher education program in a state. In general, the state board of education is concerned with policymaking, the **state department of education** with the day-to-day implementation of those policies.

A great boost for the development of state departments of education came with the federal government's Elementary and Secondary Education Act of 1965. This act and its subsequent amendments required that local applications for federal funds to be used for innovative programs and for the education of disadvantaged, disabled, bilingual, and migrant students first receive approval from state departments of education.

Today, the responsibilities of state departments of education include (1) certifying teachers, (2) distributing state and federal funds to school districts, (3) reporting to the public the condition of education within the state, (4) ensuring that school districts adhere to state and federal guidelines, (5) accrediting schools, (6) monitoring student transportation and safety, and (7) sponsoring research and evaluation projects to improve education within the state.

Perhaps the most significant index of the steady increase in state control since the 1980s is the fact that the states now supply the majority of funding for schools. Clearly, the power and influence of state departments of education will continue to be extensive.

Chief State School Officer

The **chief state school officer** (known as the commissioner of education or superintendent of public instruction in many states) is the chief administrator of the state department of education and the head of the state board of education. In 25 states, the state board of education appoints the chief state school officer; in 15 states, the office is filled through a general election; and in the remaining ten, the governor appoints an individual to that position (Council of Chief State School Officers, 2008).

Although the specific responsibilities of the chief state school officer vary from state to state, most individuals in this position hold several responsibilities in common:

1. Serving as chief administrator of the state department of education and state board of education
2. Selecting state department of education personnel
3. Recommending educational policies and budgets to the state board
4. Interpreting state school laws and state board of education policies
5. Ensuring compliance with state school laws and policies
6. Mediating controversies involving the operation of schools within the state
7. Arranging for studies, committees, and task forces to address educational problems and recommend solutions
8. Reporting on the status of education to the governor, legislature, state board, and public

HOW DO REGIONAL EDUCATION AGENCIES ASSIST SCHOOLS?

When you think about how schools are governed and the sources of political pressure applied to them, you probably think of influences originating at three levels: local, state, and federal. There is, however, an additional source of control—the regional, or intermediate, unit. The intermediate unit of educational administration, or the **regional educational service agency (RESA)**, is the least understood branch of the state public school system. Through the intermediate unit, local school districts can receive supportive services that, economically and logistically, they could not provide for themselves.

Today, about half of the states have some form of intermediate or regional unit. The average unit is made up of 20 to 30 local school districts and covers a 50-square-mile area. The intermediate or regional unit has many different names: educational service district (in Washington), county education office (in California), education service center (in Texas), intermediate school district (in Michigan), multicounty educational service unit (in Nebraska), and board of cooperative educational services (in New York).

The primary role of the intermediate unit is to provide assistance directly to districts in the areas of staff development, curriculum development, instructional media, and program evaluation. Intermediate or regional units also help school districts with their school improvement efforts in targeted areas such as bilingual education, vocational education, educational technology, and the education of gifted and talented students and students with disabilities. Although intermediate units monitor local school districts to see that they follow state educational guidelines, local districts, in fact, exert great influence over RESAs by identifying district-level needs that can be met by the intermediate unit.

HOW DOES THE FEDERAL GOVERNMENT INFLUENCE EDUCATION?

Since the birth of the United States, the federal government has played a major role in shaping the character of schools. This branch of government has always recognized that the strength and well-being of the country are directly related to the quality of its schools. The importance of a quality education, for example, has been highlighted by many U.S. Supreme Court rulings supporting the free speech rights of teachers and students under the 1st Amendment and the right of all citizens to equal educational opportunity under the 14th Amendment.

Federal Initiatives

The federal government has taken aggressive initiatives to influence education at several points in U.S. history, such as the allocation of federal money to improve science, mathematics, and foreign language education after the former Soviet Union launched *Sputnik*, the world's first satellite. During World War II, the federal government funded several new educational programs. One of these, the Lanham Act (1941), provided funding for (1) the training of workers in war plants by U.S. Office of Education personnel, (2) the construction of schools in areas where military personnel and workers on federal projects resided, and (3) the provision of child care for the children of working parents.

Another influential and extensive federal program in support of education was the Servicemen's Readjustment Act, popularly known as the **G.I. Bill of Rights**. Signed into law by President Franklin D. Roosevelt in 1944, the G.I. bill has provided millions of veterans with payments for tuition and room and board at colleges and universities and at technical schools. Similar legislation was later passed to grant educational benefits to veterans of the Korean and Vietnam conflicts. Not only did the G.I. bill stimulate the growth of colleges and universities in the United States, it also opened higher education to an older and nontraditional student population.

The executive, legislative, and judicial branches of the federal government influence education in four ways:

1. **Exert moral suasion**—develop a vision and promote educational goals for the nation; for example, U.S. Secretary of Education Arne Duncan convened a February 2011 conference, "Advancing Student Achievement Through Labor-Management Collaboration," for 150 school district leaders to discuss how labor and management could work together to improve student learning.
2. **Provide categorical aid**—assist school systems with funding if they adopt federally endorsed programs, methods, or curricula.
3. **Regulate**—withhold federal funds if a school system fails to follow legal statutes related to equal educational opportunity.
4. **Fund educational research**—identify and then fund research projects related to federal goals for education.

The Teachers' Voices: Walk in My Shoes feature in this chapter profiles Derek Boucher, a teacher who is critical of a federally mandated approach to reading instruction.

THE IMPACT OF PRESIDENTIAL POLICIES

Presidential platforms on education can have a profound effect on education. Presidents Reagan and George H. W. Bush, for example, scaled back federal involvement in education. President Clinton's administration, on the other hand, assumed a more active role in ensuring equal educational opportunity. And the No Child Left Behind (NCLB) Act developed and implemented during President George W. Bush's two terms

TEACHERS' VOICES
Walk in My Shoes
Derek Boucher
Roosevelt High School, Fresno, California

The preceding is adapted from "The Sordid Legacy of Reading First," an article Boucher wrote and uploaded at his Roosevelt High School "About Me" website. The article also appeared as an editorial in the *Fresno Bee*. Retrieved February 19, 2011, from http://www.boucherclass.com/opinions.

continues to have a significant impact on our nation's schools.

In March 2010, President Barack Obama's administration and the U.S. Department of Education released **A Blueprint for Reform: The Reauthorization of the Elementary and Secondary Education Act.** The *Blueprint* eliminated NCLB's 2014 deadline for all students to attain academic proficiency; instead, they would leave high school "college or career ready." In addition, schools no longer would be singled out for not making "adequate yearly progress" as evidenced by students' test scores. The *Blueprint* also emphasized four key areas of educational reform: (1) improving teacher and principal effectiveness, (2) providing information to families to help them evaluate and improve their children's schools, (3) implementing college- and career-ready standards, and (4) improving student learning and achievement in America's lowest-performing schools by providing intensive support and effective interventions.

How do federal education initiatives influence schools at the local level? How does federal funding help reduce inequities among schools?

In his 2014 State of the Union Address, President Obama made the following comments about the influence of his administration on education in our nation:

Race to the Top, with the help of governors from both parties, has helped states raise expectations and performance. Teachers and principals in schools from Tennessee to Washington, D.C. are making big strides in preparing students with skills for the new economy—problem solving, critical thinking, science, technology, engineering, and math. Some of this change is hard. It requires everything from more challenging curriculums and more demanding parents to better support for teachers and new ways to measure how well our kids think, not how well they can fill in a bubble on a test. But it's worth it—and it's working.

The problem is we're still not reaching enough kids, and we're not reaching them in time. That has to change.

Research shows that one of the best investments we can make in a child's life is high-quality early education. Last year, I asked this Congress to help states make high-quality pre-K available to every four year-old. As a parent as well as a President, I repeat that request tonight. But in the meantime, thirty states have raised pre-k funding on their own. They know we can't wait. So just as we worked with states to reform our schools, this year, we'll invest in new partnerships with states and communities across the country in a race to the top for our youngest children. And as Congress decides what it's going to do, I'm going to pull together a coalition of elected officials, business leaders, and philanthropists willing to help more kids access the high-quality pre-K they need.

Last year, I also pledged to connect 99 percent of our students to high-speed broadband over the next four years. Tonight, I can announce that with the support of the FCC and companies like Apple, Microsoft, Sprint, and Verizon, we've got a down payment to start connecting more than 15,000 schools and twenty million students over the next two years, without adding a dime to the deficit.

We're working to redesign high schools and partner them with colleges and employers that offer the real-world education and hands-on training that can lead directly to a job and career (White House Press Release, January 28, 2014).

U.S. Department of Education

In addition to supporting educational research, disseminating the results of research, and administering federal grants, the U.S. Department of Education advises the president on setting a platform for national education policy. For example, in February 2011, U.S. Secretary of Education Arne Duncan announced the formation of the Equity and Excellence Commission. The Commission comprises 28 education advocates, civil rights leaders, scholars, lawyers, and corporate leaders who will recommend policies for closing the achievement gap and recommend ways to improve school finance to increase equity and achievement (U.S. Department of Education, February 17, 2011).

WHAT ROLE DO TEACHER LEADERS PLAY IN SCHOOL GOVERNANCE?

Today's professional teachers willingly respond to the call to leadership, and they become involved at the local, state, and federal levels in the quest to improve our nation's schools. They understand that teachers must play a vital role in school governance and that their roles will continue to change in fundamental and positive ways during the future. Furthermore, they understand that "to create real and lasting change in schools, leadership must come from all members of [the] school community. We can no longer rely on the principal and leadership teams to make important changes. Thus, teacher leadership must be valued and cultivated within the four walls of [a] school" (Yendol-Hoppey & Dana, 2010, p. xiv).

Greater autonomy and an expanded role in school governance will provide you with opportunities to extend your leadership roles beyond the classroom. To prepare for this future, you will need to develop leadership skills to a degree not needed in the past.

Teacher Involvement in Teacher Education, Certification, and Staff Development

Teacher input into key decisions about teacher preparation, certification, and staff development is on the rise. Through their involvement with professional development schools and the National Board for Professional Teaching Standards (NBPTS); state professional standards boards; and scores of local, state, and national education committees, teachers are changing the character of pre- and in-service education. For example, in the evaluation of the NBPTS authorized by the U.S. Congress, the prestigious National Research Council noted that "board-certified teachers are used as mentors, team leaders, and organizers of professional development activities; board certification is viewed as part of a broader commitment to improving professional development and meeting higher standards for teachers" (National Research Council, 2008, p. S-8).

In addition, the NBPTS established a network designed to allow nearly seven percent of the nation's 2.5 million teachers to participate in field-testing various components of the NBPTS certification system. The NBPTS allocated $1 million to teachers, in the form of honoraria, for helping to field-test the NBPTS assessment materials. One of the first participants in the field test reflects on how teacher participation in the NBPTS can positively influence the profession of teaching:

> At its best, NBPTS can help us validate our skills as teachers; it can help us focus on areas of needed improvement; it can encourage a core of committed teacher-thinkers. (Hletko, 1995, p. 36)

Since the NBPTS certification program began, in 1993, through 2013, more than 100,000 teachers have earned board certification (National Board for Professional Teaching Standards, January 8, 2013). Teachers who have received National Board Certification are recognized as professionals not only in their schools, but also in their districts and beyond. For example, after receiving board certification, these teachers had the following professional opportunities:

- Helene Alolouf (Early Adolescence/English Language Arts certificate) of Yonkers, **NEW YORK**, was invited to teach at the Manhattanville Graduate School of Education as an adjunct professor.
- Sandra Blackman (Early Adolescence/English Language Arts certificate) of San Diego, **CALIFORNIA**, was promoted to resource teacher for the humanities departments for 55 schools, where she provides staff development for a standards-based system.
- Edward William Clark Jr. (Early Childhood/Generalist certificate) of Valley, **ALABAMA**, helped the State Department of Education and the Alabama Education Association develop National Board Certification training modules to assist Alabama teachers with National Board Certification.
- Linda Lilja (Middle Childhood/Generalist certificate) of Scranton, **KANSAS**, was invited to serve as a member of the task force for the National Teachers Hall of Fame.
- Donna W. Parrish (Early Adolescence/Generalist certificate) of Shelby, **NORTH CAROLINA**, was appointed curriculum specialist at a middle school.

Teacher Leaders

Throughout the nation, teacher leaders are reshaping the profession and transforming schools. "Teacher leaders fulfill coordinating and managing responsibilities, such as planning events, coordinating schedules, and preparing materials; engage in school- and district-level curriculum work; engage in professional development, including mentoring, peer coaching, and leading workshops; promote organizational change; secure resources and support; nurture supportive collegial relationships; and advocate for children" (Grenda & Hackmann, 2014, p. 56). As the titles of a few of the many books on teacher leadership published during 2014 suggest, the term **teacher leader** has become part of the vocabulary of educational reform:

- *The Power of Teacher Leaders: Their Roles, Influence, and Impact* (Bond, 2014)
- *The Teacher Leader: Core Competencies and Strategies for Effective Leadership* (Tomal, Schilling, & Wilhite, 2014)
- *Teacher Leadership* (Lieberman & Miller, 2014)
- *Teacher Leadership: New Conceptions for Autonomous Student Learning in the Age of the Internet* (Katyal & Evers, 2014)
- *Pathways to Teacher Leadership: Emerging Models, Changing Roles* (Levenson, 2014)
- *Schools Where Teachers Lead: What Successful Leaders Do* (Bell, Schargel, & Thacker, 2014)

A brief look at the professional activities of Sandra MacQuinn, a teacher leader who worked with the author on a major restructuring effort at Rogers High School in Spokane, **WASHINGTON**, illustrates the critical role that a teacher leader can play in school governance. In addition to teaching, here are just a few of MacQuinn's leadership activities while serving as liaison and on-site coordinator of a school–university partnership between Rogers High School and Washington State University's College of Education:

- Writing grant proposals for teacher-developed projects
- Helping other teachers write grant proposals
- Facilitating the development of an integrated school-to-work curriculum
- Preparing newsletters to keep faculty up-to-date on restructuring
- Organizing and facilitating staff development training
- Developing connections with area businesses and arranging job-shadowing sites for students
- Working with a community college to create an alternative school for Rogers High School students at the college
- Scheduling substitute teachers to provide Rogers High School teachers with release time to work on restructuring

- Making presentations on the Rogers High School restructuring at state and regional conferences
- Arranging for Rogers High School students to visit Washington State University (WSU)
- Meeting with the principal, assistant principals, WSU professors, and others to develop short- and long-range plans for implementing site-based management
- Chairing meetings of the site-based council, the restructuring steering committee, and other restructuring-related committees

Among the nation's thousands of teacher leaders are the eight teachers selected by the U.S. Department of Education to be Teaching Ambassador Fellows for 2013–2014. The following three spent that year as full-time employees at the Department of Education's headquarters in Washington, D.C.:

- Lisa Clarke, a social studies teacher from Kent-Meridian High School in Kent, **WASHINGTON**, [served] as the program's inaugural Team Leader and [worked] in the Office of Elementary and Secondary Education.
- Joiselle Cunningham, a fifth-grade reading teacher at KIPP Infinity Middle School in Harlem, **NEW YORK**, [worked] on teacher quality issues in the Office of the Secretary.
- Emily Davis, a seventh- and eighth-grade Spanish teacher at Pacetti Bay Middle School, an International Baccalaureate school in St. Augustine, **FLORIDA**, [worked] in the Office of Educational Technology. (U.S. Department of Education, August 7, 2013)

HYBRID TEACHERS

As more teachers assume important leadership roles in their schools and districts, the role of the *hybrid teacher* has emerged. A **hybrid teacher** combines part-time classroom teaching with leadership roles in a school or district. A *MetLife Survey of the American Teacher* found that more than half of teachers (51 percent) were "interested in a hybrid role that combines classroom teaching with other responsibilities" (Harris Interactive, Inc., 2013, p. 49). Hybrid teaching roles are particularly appealing to mid-career teachers (57 percent). Additionally, more than half of the teachers (51 percent) surveyed reported that they "currently have a formal leadership role in their school, such as department chair, instructional resource, teacher mentor, or leadership team member" (Harris Interactive, Inc., 2013, p. 50).

Hybrid teaching is further described by the 12 teacher leaders who co-authored *Teaching 2030: What We Must Do for Our Students and Our Public Schools—Now and in the Future*: "We imagine a profession based on the concept of hybridization, with many expert teacher-leaders who are specially prepared and paid as change agents, both working closely with students and playing other roles that advance learning" (Berry et al., 2011, p. 18).

Dimensions of Teacher Leadership Beyond the Classroom

Currently, many states have incentives for teachers to assume leadership roles outside the classroom. These incentives are based on a realization that "leadership roles are fluid . . . as a result, teachers—who have the greatest school influence on student achievement—[must be] empowered to engage in leadership roles and transfer their knowledge and skills throughout the school organization" (Grenda & Hackmann, 2014, pp. 55–56).

Figure 6.5 illustrates 11 dimensions of teacher leadership beyond the classroom. The many teachers with whom I have worked on school restructuring projects during the last few years have used these skills to reach an array of educational goals. At schools around the country, teachers and principals are using a "collaborative, emergent" approach to leadership; that is, the person who provides leadership for a particular school-wide project or activity may or may not be the principal or a member of the administrative team (Parkay, Shindler, & Oaks, 1997). A middle school social studies teacher describes how a collaborative approach to leadership works at her school:

> It's part of [principal's name]'s philosophy . . . . You will hear him say "Many hands make light work," and it is true. Everybody at Blue Trail

FIGURE 6.5   Eleven dimensions of teacher leadership beyond the classroom

[Middle School] hears that over and over. It's the expectation in the building. That's the way the administrative team functions, and so does the teaching staff. Everybody has different things they are better at, so they use their strengths and help each other. If you asked the kids, they're not sure who runs the building. Some kids know that [principal's name] is actually the principal, but they're not sure, because everyone runs this building. (Grenda & Hackmann, 2014, p. 63)

TEACHERPRENEURS

Aware that more teachers are assuming leadership roles beyond the classroom and that many of them are influencing educational policies in entrepreneurial ways, Ariel Sacks, an English teacher in Brooklyn, **NEW YORK**, and a co-author of *Teaching 2030*, coined the term *teacherpreneur*. A **teacherpreneur** "is always engaged with students, while also investing know-how and energy into important projects, including those supported by the district, the state, or a partnering organization" (Berry et al., 2011, p. 138). The team of teacher leaders who wrote *Teaching 2030* presents a compelling portrait of how teacherpreneurs will influence the teaching profession in 2030:

In 2030, teaching has come to be seen as complex professional work. . . . About 15 percent of the nation's teachers—more than 600,000—have been prepared in customized residency programs designed to fully train them in the cognitive science of teaching and to also equip them for new leadership roles. Most now serve in hybrid positions as teacherpreneurs, teaching students part of the day or week, and also have dedicated time to lead as student support specialists, teacher educators, community organizers, and virtual mentors in teacher networks. Some spend part of their nonteaching time working closely with university- and think tank-based researchers on studies of teaching and learning—or conducting policy analyses that are grounded in their everyday pedagogical experiences. In some school districts, teachers in these hybrid roles earn salaries comparable to, if not higher than, the highest paid administrators. (Berry et al., 2011, p. 7)

HOW ARE SCHOOLS FINANCED IN THE UNITED STATES?

To provide free public education to all school-age children in the United States is a costly, complex undertaking. Today's school districts are big-business enterprises and must provide services and facilities to students from many ethnic, racial, social, cultural, linguistic, and individual backgrounds.

Education Funding and the Great Recession

In 2008, the nation entered the worst financial crisis since the Great Depression of the 1930s. Nationwide, the unemployment rate rose from less than 5 percent at the end of 2007 to about 10 percent by the end of 2009, before dropping to about 7.5 percent by early 2014. State funding for education dropped dramatically, and many school districts, facing large budget deficits, had to lay off teachers and close schools. To keep layoffs to a minimum, school districts trimmed their budgets in other areas—eliminating summer school programs, after-school programs, bus routes, and days from the school calendar, for example.

In response to the Great Recession, the American Recovery and Reinvestment Act of 2009 included $100 billion for education. That stimulus money enabled school districts to avoid thousands of scheduled teacher layoffs and to rehire teachers previously laid off. At the beginning of the 2010–2011 school year, the federal government provided another $10 billion for school districts to retain or rehire teachers and other educational staff. However, the real estate meltdown, high unemployment, and severe shortfalls in state and federal budgets are continuing to have a great impact on school funding. "School districts are learning to make do with less—and, in some cases, dramatically changing how they spend their money and deploy their teaching staffs" (McNeil, 2014).

The Great Recession resulted in a decline in total expenditures for public elementary and secondary education of nearly $75 billion between fiscal years 2008 and 2011. However, total expenditures are expected to rise from 2011 through 2022–2023 (see Figure 6.6). Total expenditures for public elementary and secondary schools during fiscal year 2011 were $527.17 billion, and the total **expenditure per pupil** was $10,6587 (Cornman, 2013, pp. 10, 12). Figure 6.7 shows how the education dollar for public schools is allocated.

The Challenge of Equitable Funding

Financing an enterprise as vast and ambitious as the U.S. system of free public schools has not been easy. It has proved difficult both to devise a system that equitably distributes the tax burden for supporting schools and to provide equal educational services and facilities for all students.

An additional funding challenge is that, rather than one national education system, there are 50 state systems that raise revenues from local, state, and federal sources. Dollars are distributed quite unequally across the states, districts, and schools. And as Figure 6.6 shows, about 71.5 percent of education dollars is available for instruction and instruction-related services, and a significant proportion (about 28.6 percent) goes to operations and administration.

Moreover, financial support of schools tends to be outpaced by factors that continually increase the cost of operating schools—inflation, rising enrollments, and the need to update aging facilities, for example. Not surprisingly, "lack of financial support" was the number one problem confronting local schools from 2002 to 2013, according to Gallup polls of the public's attitudes toward public schools (Bushaw & Lopez, 2013, p. 20).

FIGURE 6.6 Actual and projected current expenditures for public elementary and secondary schools (in constant 2011–12 dollars): School years 1997–98 through 2022–23

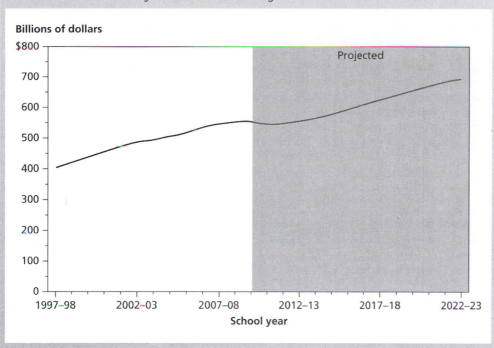

Note: Numbers were placed in constant dollars using the Consumer Price Index (CPI) for all urban consumers, Bureau of Labor Statistics, U.S. Department of Labor.

Source: Hussar, W. J., and Bailey, T. M. (2013). *Projections of Education Statistics to 2022* (NCES 2014-051). U.S. Department of Education, National Center for Education Statistics. Washington, DC: U.S. Government Printing Office, p. 17.

FIGURE 6.7 Percentage distribution of current expenditures for public elementary and secondary education in the United States, by function: Fiscal year 2011

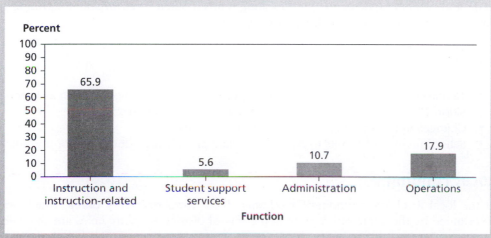

Note: Current expenditures include instruction, instruction-related, support services, and other elementary/secondary current expenditures, but exclude expenditures on capital outlay, other programs, and interest on long-term debt. Instruction and instruction-related expenditures include current expenditures for classroom instruction (including teachers and teaching assistants), libraries, in-service teacher training, curriculum development, student assessment, and instruction technology. Administration includes general administration, school administration, and other support services. Operations include operations and maintenance, student transportation, food services, and enterprise operations. Student support services include attendance and social work, guidance, health, psychological services, speech pathology, audiology, and other student support services. Data include the 50 states and the District of Columbia. Detail may not sum to totals because of rounding.

Source: Cornman, S. Q. (2013). *Revenues and Expenditures for Public Elementary and Secondary Education: School Year 2010–11 (Fiscal Year 2011)* (NCES 2013-342). U.S. Department of Education. Washington, DC: National Center for Education Statistics, p. 7.

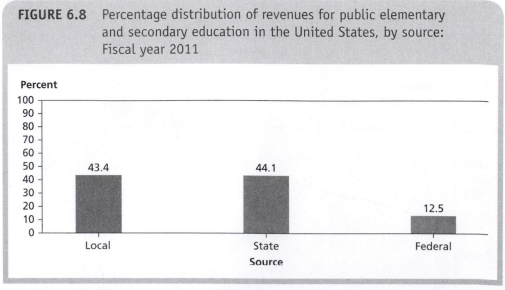

FIGURE 6.8   Percentage distribution of revenues for public elementary and secondary education in the United States, by source: Fiscal year 2011

Note: Data include the 50 states and the District of Columbia.

Source: Cornman, S. Q. (2013). *Revenues and Expenditures for Public Elementary and Secondary Education: School Year 2010–11 (Fiscal Year 2011)* (NCES 2013-342). U.S. Department of Education. Washington, DC: National Center for Education Statistics, p. 6.

Sources of Funding

A combination of revenues from local, state, and federal sources is used to finance public elementary and secondary schools in the United States. As Figure 6.8 shows, schools received 44.1 percent of fiscal year 2011 funding from the state, 43.4 percent from local sources, and 12.5 percent from the federal government. Since 1980, schools have received almost equal funding from local and state sources. Prior to that date, however, schools received most of their revenues from local sources, and early in the 20th century, nearly all school revenues were generated from local property taxes.

Revenues for education are influenced by many factors, including the apportionment of taxes among the local, state, and federal levels; the size of the tax base at each level; and competing demands for allocating funds at each level. In addition, funding for education is influenced by the following factors:

- The rate of inflation
- The health of the national economy
- The size of the national budget deficit
- Taxpayer revolts to limit the use of property taxes to raise money, such as Proposition 13 in California and Oregon's property tax limitation
- Changes in the size and distribution of the population
- School-financed lawsuits to equalize funding and ensure educational opportunity

Local Funding

At the local level, most funding for schools comes from **property taxes**, which are determined by the value of property in the school district. Property taxes are assessed against real estate and, in some districts, also against personal property such as cars, household furniture and appliances, and stocks and bonds. Increasing taxes to meet the rising costs of operating local schools or to fund needed improvements is often a heated issue in many communities.

Although property taxes provide a steady source of revenue for local school districts, there are inequities in how taxes are determined. By locating in areas where taxes are lowest, for example, businesses and industries often avoid paying higher taxes while continuing to draw on local resources and services. In addition, the fair market value of property is often difficult to assess, and groups within a community sometimes pressure assessors to keep taxes on their property as low as possible. Most states specify by law the minimum property tax rate for local school districts to set. In many districts, an increase in the tax rate must have the approval of voters. Some states place no cap, or upper limit, on tax rates, and other states set a maximum limit.

State Funding

Most state revenues for education come from sales taxes and income taxes. Sales taxes are added to the cost of items such as general goods, gasoline, amusements, alcohol, and insurance. Income taxes are placed on individuals (in many states) and on business and industry.

As mentioned previously, states contribute nearly 50 percent of the resources needed to operate the public schools. The money that a state gives to its cities and towns is known as **state aid**. Table 6.2 compares selected states on the percentage of education funds received from local, state, and federal sources in relation to total revenues for 2010–2011. The table also shows that the greatest percentage of local funds comes from property taxes, whereas a small percentage come from private sources such as gifts and tuition and fees.

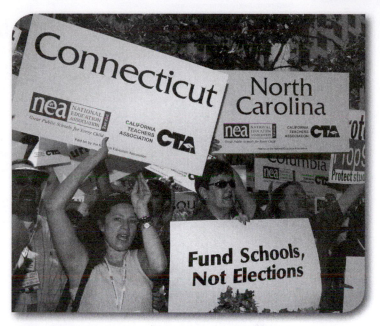

About 50 percent of funding for schools comes from the state level. What steps have citizens in your state taken to increase state funding for education? How successful have those steps been?

Federal Funding

The role of the federal government in providing resources for education has been limited. The federal share of funding for public elementary and secondary schools peaked in 1979–1980 at 9.8 percent, and, as Figure 6.8 shows, it was 12.5 percent in fiscal year 2011. Prior to 1980, the federal government had in effect bypassed the states and provided funding for local programs that were administered through various federal agencies, such as the Office of Economic Opportunity (Head Start, migrant education, and Follow Through) and the Department of Labor (Job Corps and the Comprehensive Employment Training Act [CETA]).

Since the Reagan administration (1980–1988), federal aid has increasingly been given directly to the states in the form of **block grants**, which a state or local education agency may spend as it wishes, with few limitations. The 1981 **Education Consolidation and Improvement Act (ECIA)** gave the states a broad range of choices in spending federal money. The ECIA significantly reduced federal aid to education, however, thus making state aid to education even more critical.

Although a small proportion of the funds for schools comes from the federal level, the federal government has enacted supplemental programs to help meet the educational needs of special student populations. Such programs are often referred to collectively as **entitlements**. The most significant entitlement is the Elementary and Secondary Education (ESEA) Act of 1965, which President George W. Bush reauthorized in 2002 as the No Child Left Behind Act. To begin the next reauthorization of ESEA, the Obama administration issued the *A Blueprint for Reform: The Reauthorization of the Elementary and Secondary Education Act* in 2010. Title I of the act allocates $1 billion annually to school districts with large numbers of students from low-income families. Among the other funded entitlement programs are the Vocational Education Act (1963), the Manpower Development and Training Act (1963), the Economic Opportunity Act (1964), the Bilingual Education Act (1968), the Indian Education Act (1972), and the Education for All Handicapped Children Act (1975).

TABLE
6.2   Revenues for public elementary and secondary schools, by source of funds and state or jurisdiction: 2010–11

[In current dollars]

State or jurisdiction	Total (in thousands)	Federal			State		Local (including intermediate sources below the state level)		Property taxes		Private[2]	
		Amount (in thousands)	Per pupil	Percent of total	Amount (in thousands)	Percent of total	Amount (in thousands)[1]	Percent of total	Amount (in thousands)	Percent of total	Amount (in thousands)	Percent of total
1	2	3	4	5	6	7	8	9	10	11	12	13
United States	**$604,293,209**	**$75,541,475**	**$1,527**	**12.5**	**$266,786,402**	**44.1**	**$261,965,331**	**43.4**	**$211,651,391**	**35.0**	**$11,835,394**	**2.0**
Alabama	7,386,471	1,250,581	1,655	16.9	3,827,907	51.8	2,307,983	31.2	1,070,276	14.5	305,976	4.1
California	67,864,062	9,248,710	1,470	13.6	38,411,425	56.6	20,203,927	29.8	16,065,777	23.7	445,791	0.7
District of Columbia	1,925,824	227,198	3,187	11.8	†	†	1,698,626	88.2	553,482	28.7	10,651	0.6
Florida	26,358,355	4,796,329	1,814	18.2	9,069,113	34.4	12,492,913	47.4	10,549,648	40.0	945,427	3.6
Illinois	28,895,633	2,900,110	1,387	10.0	9,304,471	32.2	16,691,051	57.8	14,482,300	50.1	494,189	1.7
Massachusetts	15,357,042	1,271,995	1,331	8.3	5,797,874	37.8	8,287,173	54.0	7,801,657	50.8	203,619	1.3
Minnesota	10,938,581	905,392	1,080	8.3	6,397,541	58.5	3,635,648	33.2	2,498,019	22.8	321,762	2.9
Mississippi	4,483,191	1,006,453	2,052	22.4	2,071,471	46.2	1,405,267	31.3	1,132,742	25.3	113,009	2.5
New York	57,538,128	5,368,090	1,963	9.3	23,097,859	40.1	29,072,179	50.5	26,342,464	45.8	348,905	0.6
North Carolina	13,228,999	2,139,214	1,435	16.2	7,688,360	58.1	3,401,425	25.7	2,737,195	20.7	245,351	1.9
Pennsylvania	27,174,139	3,318,881	1,851	12.2	9,378,294	34.5	14,476,964	53.3	11,633,093	42.8	427,746	1.6
Rhode Island	2,278,564	250,194	1,740	11.0	830,217	36.4	1,198,154	52.6	1,166,220	51.2	19,890	0.9
Tennessee	8,915,680	1,312,271	1,329	14.7	3,995,291	44.8	3,608,119	40.5	1,754,306	19.7	437,477	4.9
Texas	50,874,695	7,968,095	1,614	15.7	20,430,187	40.2	22,476,413	44.2	20,382,782	40.1	967,193	1.9
Utah	4,597,983	577,903	987	12.6	2,340,850	50.9	1,679,229	36.5	1,263,423	27.5	193,309	4.2
Vermont	1,641,955	175,721	1,814	10.7	1,340,743	81.7	125,491	7.6	1,276	0.1	21,928	1.3
Virginia	14,444,511	1,427,295	1,141	9.9	5,349,193	37.0	7,668,024	53.1	4,655,902	32.2	271,692	1.9
Washington	11,801,402	1,365,968	1,309	11.6	6,757,950	57.3	3,677,484	31.2	3,058,791	25.9	317,048	2.7
Wisconsin	11,429,211	1,045,227	1,208	9.1	5,246,795	45.9	5,137,189	44.9	4,714,226	41.2	225,258	2.0

—Not available.
†Not applicable.
#Rounds to zero.
[1] Includes other categories of revenue not separately shown.
[2] Includes revenues from gifts, and tuition and fees from patrons.
Excludes revenues for state education agencies. Detail may not sum to totals because of rounding.

Source: U.S. Department of Education, National Center for Education Statistics, Common Core of Data (CCD), "National Public Education Financial Survey," 2010–11. *Digest of Education Statistics,* July 2013. Retrieved February 22, 2014, from http://nces.ed.gov/programs/digest/d13/tables/dt13_235.20.asp

The federal government also provides funding for preschool programs such as Project Head Start. **Head Start** promotes the school readiness of children ages birth to five from low-income families by enhancing their cognitive, social, and emotional development. Head Start services, many of which are delivered by parents and volunteers, focus on education, socio-emotional development, physical and mental health, and nutrition. The Head Start Act Amendments of 1994 also established the Early Head Start program, designed to serve pregnant women and children under age three from low-income families.

Since the program began in 1965, Head Start has served almost 30 million children, and more than 1 million children are served each year. In 2012, more than 130,000 children were enrolled in Early Head Start, and almost 910,000 in Head Start (Children's Defense Fund, 2012). Funding for Head Start, Early Head Start, American Indian and Alaska Native Head Start, and Migrant and Seasonal Head Start was more than $7.5 billion for fiscal year 2013 (U.S. Department of Health and Human Services, April 26, 2013).

WHAT ARE SOME TRENDS IN FUNDING FOR EQUITY AND EXCELLENCE?

The fact that schools rely heavily on property taxes for support has resulted in fiscal inequities for schools. Districts with higher property wealth can generate more money per pupil than can districts with lower property values. The degree of inequity between the wealthiest and the poorest districts, therefore, can be quite large. In some states, the ability of one district to generate local property tax revenues may be several times greater than another district's.

FOCUS ON DIVERSITY: INEQUITABLE FUNDING OF SCHOOLS IN POOR COMMUNITIES

The degree of inequity between the wealthiest and the poorest school districts in the United States can be quite large. In addition, "[W]ealthy African Americans, whites, Asians, and Hispanics can choose to live in school districts with adequate and exceptional public schools" (Spring, 2008a, p. 95), whereas poor families do not have that option. Therefore, students from poor families are less likely to have access to educational opportunities and resources such as the following:

- Preschool programs
- High-quality teachers
- Challenging curricula
- High standards
- Up-to-date technology
- Modern facilities (Spring, 2008a, pp. 95–96)

In *The Shame of the Nation: The Restoration of Apartheid Schooling in America*, Jonathan Kozol (2005) presents a compelling analysis of inequities in school funding. For example, the following compares per-pupil spending in five major U.S. cities with spending in wealthy nearby suburbs (Black and Hispanic enrollments ranged from 72 to 95 percent in the cities and 8 to 20 percent in the suburbs):

- Chicago ($8,483)   Highland Park and Deerfield, IL ($17,291)
- Philadelphia ($9,299)   Lower Merion, PA ($17,261)
- New York City ($11,627)   Manhasset, NY ($22,311)
- Detroit ($9,576)   Bloomfield Hills, MI ($12,825)
- Milwaukee ($10,874)   Maple Dale–Indian Hill, WI ($13,955) (Kozol, 2005, pp. 321–324)

Such discrepancies in per-pupil funding led one critic to claim that "[S]tatistics on school spending demonstrate a virulent form of institutional racism" (Spring, 2008a, p. 94).

Politics also contribute to funding inequities among schools. The following political factors have made it difficult for school reform efforts to reach students in resource-poor schools, according to the Center on Reinventing Education:

- Local school boards are political bodies pursuing many agendas, of which educational effectiveness is only one.
- School districts allow money and other resources to follow political influence, so that poor students end up receiving the least money and the worst facilities and equipment.
- Teachers with seniority, superior preparation, and other attributes that make them attractive to "nice" schools can usually avoid teaching the most disadvantaged children in a school district (Hill, May 12, 2003, A11).

Tax Reform and Redistricting

To correct funding inequities, several court suits were initiated during the 1970s. In the 1971 *Serrano v. Priest* case in California, it was successfully argued that the relationship between spending and property wealth violated the state's obligation to provide equal protection and education. The California Supreme Court ruled that the quality of a child's education should not depend on the "wealth of his parents and neighbors." The court also recognized that communities with a poor tax base could not be expected to generate the revenues of more affluent districts. Nevertheless, the court did not forbid the use of property taxes to fund education.

Then, in 1973, the U.S. Supreme Court decided in *San Antonio Independent School District v. Rodriguez* that fiscal inequities stemming from unequal tax bases did not violate the Constitution. That Court's decision reversed a lower court's ruling claiming that school financing on the basis of local property taxes was unconstitutional.

Regardless of the mixed outcomes of court challenges, many state legislatures have enacted school finance equity reforms during the last 15 years. Some states (California, Hawaii, New Mexico, Washington, and West Virginia, for example) have **full-funding programs** in which the state sets the same per-pupil expenditure level for all schools and districts.

Other states have adopted new funding formulas to broaden their revenue base. Level funding augmented by sales taxes, cigarette taxes, state lottery revenues, property taxes on second homes, and school-choice plans are among the solutions tried. One of the most dramatic changes in educational funding occurred in Michigan in 1993 with the passage of Proposal A, a plan that greatly reduced school funding from local property taxes and increased funding from the state's sales tax.

Because each state has been free to determine the number of districts within its boundaries, a common approach to achieving equal funding is **redistricting**, redrawing school district boundaries to reduce the range of variation in the ability of school districts to finance education. Redistricting not only equalizes funding; it can also reduce the cost of maintaining and operating schools if smaller districts are combined. The per-pupil cost of instruction, supplies, and equipment is usually lower in large districts. In addition, greater resources often allow larger districts to offer a broader curriculum and higher salaries to attract more qualified teachers.

Vertical Equity

Other states have developed various mechanisms to provide **vertical equity**, that is, allocating funds according to legitimate educational needs. Thus, additional support is given to programs that serve students from low-income backgrounds; those with limited English proficiency, or special gifts and talents; and those who need special education or vocational programs. Vertical equity is based on the assumption that "some 'unequal' students should have access to 'unequal' levels of resources" (Baker, Green, & Richards, 2008, p. 98).

Additional state-appropriated funds to cover the costs of educating students with special needs are known as **categorical aid**. Funding adjustments are also made to compensate for differences in costs within a state—higher expenses due to rural isolation or the higher cost of living in urban areas, for example. Some states even conduct periodic regional cost of living analyses, which are then used to determine adjustments in per-pupil funding.

School Choice

One of the most bitter struggles for control of schools in the United States is centered around **school choice**, the practice of allowing parents to choose the schools their children attend. The issue is especially heated for choice programs that would allow parents to choose a private school, with the public paying all or part of the tuition. According to the 2013 Phi Delta Kappa/Gallup poll of the public's attitudes toward the public schools, 70 percent opposed, and 29 percent favored, such school choice programs if the government paid the tuition (Bushaw & Lopez, 2013).

Debate continues about whether school choice programs will, in fact, promote equity and excellence. Advocates of school choice believe that giving parents more options will force public schools to adjust to free-market pressures—low-performing schools would have to improve or shut down. They also contend that parents whose children must now attend inferior, and sometimes dangerous, inner-city schools would be able to send their children elsewhere. In addition, some supporters see choice as a way to reduce the influence of top-heavy school bureaucracies and teachers' unions.

On the other hand, opponents believe that school choice would have disastrous consequences for public schools and lead to students being sorted by race, income, and religion. School choice, they argue, would subsidize the wealthy by siphoning money away from the public schools and further widen the gap between rich and poor districts.

Other critics contend that school choice could lead to the creation of segregated schools and schools that would be more committed to competing for education dollars and the most able, manageable students. A study of the impact of competition on three urban school systems concluded that "competition did not force [the districts] to substantially alter system, governance, management, or operations." And in the words of an observer at two schools, "teachers have thirty kids in their classroom just like they did last year, just like they did ten years ago. They still teach the same way. [School choice hasn't] affected what they do" (Hess, 2002, p. 198).

PROFESSIONAL REFLECTION
Learn how school choice stems from court cases, such as *Brown vs. Board of Education*.

Voucher Systems

One approach to providing educational equity that has generated considerable controversy is the **voucher system** of distributing educational funds. According to voucher plans, parents would be given government-funded vouchers to purchase educational services at the schools of their choice.

Voucher systems were first suggested more than 50 years ago by Milton Friedman, a well-known conservative economist and Nobel laureate. Friedman believes that schools would be much better if they were operated by private businesses rather than the government. "If we had a system of free choice we would also have a system of competition, innovation, which would change the character of education. . . . Reform has to come through competition from the outside, and the only way you can get competition is by making it possible for parents to have the ability to choose" (Friedman, 2003).

The most controversial voucher proposals would allow parents to choose from among public as well as private (secular, parochial, for-profit, and charter) schools; others would limit

The U.S. Supreme Court has made several rulings regarding school choice and voucher systems.

parents' choice to public schools. Voucher programs require that parents and guardians reflect on the kind of educational experiences they want for their children.

Debates about vouchers regularly make the national news. In 1999, **FLORIDA** became the first state to offer state-paid tuition to children in failing public schools to attend a public, private, or religious school of choice; however, a Florida judge ruled in 2006 that the program violated the Florida Constitution because it gave tax money to religious schools (*Bush v. Holmes*, 2006). However, in 2002, the Supreme Court ruled that a school voucher program in Cleveland did not infringe on the constitutional separation of church and state (*Zelman v. Simmons-Harris*, 2002). The Court majority said that the parents had a sufficient range of choices among secular and religious schools, and that the voucher plan did not violate the 1st Amendment prohibition against the establishment of religion.

EVALUATION OF VOUCHER PROGRAMS

Approximately a dozen different voucher programs exist in various states. Each program has different rules and regulations controlling its size and scope and the terms of participation. Because "distinguishing those voucher programs that are designed to be large, generous, and inclusive from those that are small, stingy, and restrictive sometimes requires wading through technical legal and regulatory documents" (Enlow, 2004, pp. 1–2), the Milton and Rose D. Friedman Foundation released *Grading Vouchers: Ranking America's School Choice Programs* in 2004.

The report evaluates and ranks the nation's school voucher programs on three criteria: how many students are eligible to receive a voucher (Student Eligibility), how much money the voucher is worth (Purchasing Power), and how many and what type of private schools parents can choose (School Eligibility). For each category, the program is assigned a letter grade, and the final ranking is based on the average of the three. The criteria reflect Friedman's vision of a voucher system of education in which "all students, regardless of income or any other criteria, are able to use 100 percent of the state and local funds to attend public and private schools that are largely free from government interference" (Enlow, 2004, p. 2).

According to the report, the best voucher program is Florida's McKay Scholarship, with a 3.6 GPA, or A–, whereas the lowest-scoring voucher program is the Iowa Personal Tax Credit, with a 1.76 GPA, or C–. Milwaukee's voucher program, the nation's oldest program for low-income families, receives a grade of C, and Colorado's program, one of the newest, gets a B–. (In 2003, a Denver district court judge struck down Colorado's voucher legislation.)

Another study evaluated the District of Columbia School Choice Incentive Act of 2003, the first federally funded, private school voucher program in the United States. This study evaluated the long-term effects of the program, renamed the DC Opportunity Scholarship Program (OSP), on families who were given the option to move from a public school to a participating private school of their choice. The OSP provided low-income residents, particularly those whose children attended "schools in need of improvement" or "corrective action" under the Elementary and Secondary Education Act, with "expanded opportunities to attend higher performing schools in the District of Columbia." The OSP scholarship, worth up to $7,500, could be used to cover the costs of tuition, school fees, and transportation to a participating private school.

The study compared the outcomes of 2,300 eligible applicants randomly assigned to receive a voucher (treatment group) or not receive a voucher (control group) of an OSP scholarship through a series of lotteries. Test scores, high school graduation rates, and perceptions of school safety and satisfaction were collected annually during a 4- to 5-year period. Some students offered scholarships never used them, whereas others used their scholarships to attend a participating private school at some point during the 4- to 5-year period. Study results revealed the following:

- ***There [was] no conclusive evidence that the OSP affected student achievement.*** On average, after at least 4 years students who were offered (or used) scholarships had reading and math test scores that were statistically similar to those who were not offered scholarships. The same pattern of results holds for students who applied from schools in need of improvement (SINI), the group Congress designated as the highest priority for the OSP.

- ***The OSP significantly improved students' chances of graduating from high school.*** Although students may not have raised their test scores in reading and math as a result of the OSP, they graduated at higher rates. The offer of an OSP scholarship raised students' probability of completing high school by 12 percentage points overall. The graduation rate based on parent-provided information was 82 percent for the treatment group compared to 70 percent for the control group. The offer of a scholarship improved the graduation prospects by 13 percentage points for the high-priority group of students from schools designated SINI in 2003–2005 (79 percent graduation rate for the treatment group versus 66 percent for the control group).

- ***The OSP raised parents', but not students', ratings of school safety and satisfaction.*** Parents were more satisfied and felt school was safer if their child was offered or used an OSP scholarship. The OSP had no effect on students' reports on school conditions (Wolf et al., 2010, pp. v–vi).

In addition to the federal study of OSP, the *Washington Post* found a lack of quality controls for schools involved in the program. For example, hundreds of students used their vouchers to attend nonaccredited schools or schools in "unconventional" settings—a family-run K–12 school operating out of a storefront, a Nation of Islam school based in a converted home, and a school built around the philosophy of a Bulgarian psychotherapist. Furthermore,

> the government has no say over curriculum, quality or management. And parents trying to select a school have little independent information, relying mostly on marketing from the schools . . . . While public schools must report test scores and take action when they don't meet goals, private schools participating in the D.C. voucher program are insulated from such interference . . . . The schools must administer a single standardized test, but can choose the type. Those scores are not made public, and schools can stay in the voucher program no matter how their students fare. (Layton & Brown, November 17, 2012)

It is clear that the debate over school choice will continue for the foreseeable future. Gradually, support for school choice appears to be increasing—currently, almost half of the states allow some form of "interdistrict" transfer, which allows students to attend public schools outside their home district.

Education–Business Coalitions

To develop additional sources of funding for equity and excellence, many local school districts have established coalitions with the private sector. Businesses may contribute funds or materials needed by a school; sponsor sports teams; award scholarships; provide cash grants for pilot projects and teacher development; provide mentors, volunteers, or expertise; and even construct school buildings. Among the types of education–business coalitions are Grantmakers for Education (GFE), the nation's largest network of education funders; the National Alliance of State Science and Mathematics Coalitions (NASSMC); the Business Roundtable, a group of CEOs of leading U.S. companies; and partnerships with chambers of commerce.

Private support for K–12 education, including the corporate sector, totals about $3.6 billion annually (Hills & Hirschhorn, May 2007). Reducing the achievement gap for low-income or minority students and teacher professional development were the top two funding priorities in 2012, according to a GFE survey (Grantmakers for Education, 2012).

One example of an education-business partnership is the GE Foundation's Developing Futures in Education program. Since 2005, the program has provided $200 million to improve student achievement in seven U.S. school districts: Louisville, **KENTUCKY**; Stamford, **CONNECTICUT**; Cincinnati, **OHIO**; Erie, **PENNSYLVANIA**; Atlanta, **GEORGIA**; New York, **NEW YORK**; and Milwaukee, **WISCONSIN**. The Foundation "recognizes the urgent need to improve student achievement and college and career readiness in the K–12 public education system" (GE Foundation, March 10, 2014).

With assistance from the Developing Futures in Education program, the targeted districts accomplished the following:

- Jefferson County Public Schools, **KENTUCKY**, achieved a 14-point gain on students' mathematics scores, compared with an overall state gain of 6 points.
- Cincinnati Public Schools, **OHIO**, was 13th out of 609 school districts in student achievement.
- Stamford Public Schools, **CONNECTICUT**, cut the achievement gap in mathematics almost in half.

The GE Foundation also provided a 4-year, $18 million grant to help states and school districts implement the Common Core State Standards (CCSS). The grant was used to develop exemplary sample lessons aligned to the CCSS and to provide CCSS professional development Immersion Institutes for more than 1,500 teachers and principals.

The largest amount of private support for education in the United States comes from the Bill and Melinda Gates Foundation. The Foundation has spent more than $1 billion on more than 1,500 partnerships with our nation's schools. Chicago has opened 100 new schools with the help of Gates Foundation money, and New York City has opened 200. A priority for the Foundation is the reform of high schools in urban areas and helping schools develop more academically rigorous curricula. The Foundation awarded the Chicago Public Schools $21 million to develop new curricula and to make classes more rigorous (Hills & Hirschhorn, 2007).

As mentioned above, some businesses contribute funds to build new schools. A weak economy since the 2008 recession has made the public less likely less likely to support the construction of new schools; as a result, school districts often seek support from the business community.

The need to improve school buildings goes beyond a desire for more attractive buildings. Inadequate, badly maintained, or poorly designed facilities can hinder students' learning and reduce teachers' effectiveness.

Typically, the burden of paying for school construction and renovation has fallen on local districts and their constituents. But with the needs so large and widespread, it is evident that local communities cannot carry the weight by themselves—the help of the business community is often needed.

At least five factors have contributed to the current need to improve the condition of America's school buildings: (1) gradual deterioration as buildings age, (2) increasing enrollments, (3) mounting evidence that poor facilities diminish student learning, (4) increased use of technology in schools, and (5) the continuing quest to equalize the distributions of resources for schools. If local districts are to respond effectively to these factors, it is clear that they will definitely need more assistance from the business community. In addition, school buildings constructed during the 1950s to cope with the "baby boom" generation are reaching a critical age. Many of those buildings were built quickly and cheaply, and their flaws are becoming more evident as they become older. In addition, years of deferred maintenance have worsened the substandard conditions of many of these buildings.

If schools in the United States are to succeed in meeting the challenges of the future, they will need to be funded at a level that provides quality educational experiences to students from a diverse array of backgrounds. Although innovative approaches to school funding have been developed, much remains to be done before both excellence and equity characterize all schools in the United States.

HOW IS THE PRIVATIZATION MOVEMENT AFFECTING EQUITY AND EXCELLENCE IN EDUCATION?

One of the most dramatic reforms in U.S. education during the last decade has been the development of charter schools and for-profit schools, both of which were developed to provide an alternative to the perceived inadequacies of the public schools. On many different levels—governance, staffing, curricula, funding, and accountability—the **privatization movement** is a radical departure from schools as most people have known them.

Since 1995, the number of for-profit private companies operating public schools increased from 5 to 97, and the number of schools operating has increased from 6 to 840. Enrollment at these schools has grown from approximately 1,000 students in 1995–1996 to 462,926 in 2011–2012 (Miron & Gulosino, 2013).

Charter Schools

In 1991, **MINNESOTA** passed the nation's first charter school legislation calling for up to eight teacher-created and teacher-operated, outcome-based schools that would be free of most state and local rules and regulations. When the St. Paul City Academy opened its doors in September 1992, it became the nation's first charter school. Since then, the charter school movement has grown to more than 6,000 schools operating nationwide and serving over 2.2 million students. By early 2013, 42 states and the District of Columbia had legislation authorizing charter schools (Center for Educational Reform, 2014).

Charter schools are independent, innovative, outcome-based public schools. The *Survey of America's Charter Schools 2014* provides the following portrait of charter schools in America:

> Against the odds, and far too often in hostile policy environments, charters survive and succeed grounded in the principles of choice, accountability, and autonomy. They innovate and adjust to deliver results by introducing new curriculum or creating blended learning environments to meet student needs. Even when they are part of a larger network, no two charter schools are alike, providing diverse educational options from which parents and students may choose. (Center for Educational Reform, 2014, p. 2)

To open a charter school, an original charter (or agreement) is signed by the school's founders and a sponsor (usually the local school board). The **charter** specifies the learning outcomes that students will master before they continue their studies. Charter schools, which usually operate in the manner of autonomous school districts (a feature that distinguishes them from the alternative schools that many school districts operate), are public schools and must teach all students. If admission requests for a charter school exceed the number of available openings, students are selected by drawing.

Charter schools contribute to the improvement of public education in the following ways:

- Increasing access to quality education for all students
- Providing opportunities for parents and students to choose among public schools in the local community
- Developing more accurate and rigorous measures of accountability for public education
- Encouraging new approaches to teaching
- Creating opportunities for teachers to assume leadership roles in educational reform
- Increasing the involvement of parents and community in public education
- Serving as a catalyst for the broader reform of public education

Because charter schools are designed to promote the development of new teaching strategies that can be used at other public schools, they can prove to be an effective tool for promoting educational reform and the professionalization of teaching in the future. Charter schools also give teachers unprecedented leadership opportunities and the ability to respond quickly to students' needs.

RESEARCH ON CHARTER SCHOOLS

In a report titled *Do Charter Schools Measure Up? The Charter School Experiment After 10 Years,* the American Federation of Teachers (AFT) suggested that, by mid-2002, charter schools had not lived up to the claims of their advocates. According to the AFT report, students who attended charter schools were more isolated from students of different racial and ethnic groups, and their test scores were no higher than students at traditional public schools, In addition, the report revealed that charter school teachers had less experience than their public school counterparts, and they were paid less (American Federation of Teachers, 2002).

Another study, the *National Charter School Study 2013* conducted by Stanford University's Center for Research on Education Outcomes, analyzed charter school effectiveness in 27 of the 43 states (including the District of Columbia) that allow charter schools. The researchers compared academic growth during a school year for students at charter schools and at traditional public schools. The study reported that "The analysis of the pooled 27 states shows that charter schools now advance the learning gains of their students' more than traditional public schools in reading" (Center for Research on Education Outcomes, 2013, p. 3).

A critique of the Stanford study by the National Education Policy Center at the University of Colorado-Boulder, however, pointed out that "the [Stanford] study overall shows that less than one hundredth of one percent of the variation in test performance is explainable by charter school enrollment. . . . . in practical terms these effects are so small as to be regarded, without hyperbole, as trivial. The bottom line appears to be that, once again, it has been found that, in aggregate, charter schools are basically indistinguishable from traditional public schools in terms of their impact on academic test performance" (Maul & McClelland, July 2013, p. 4).

Regardless of the mixed results on the effectiveness of charter schools, few charter schools have been closed because of failure to meet academic outcomes. Instead, charter school closings have been the result of low enrolments, problems with facilities, financial problems, or mismanagement.

In the final analysis, it is important to remember that there are "good" and "not so good" charter schools, just as there are traditional public schools that meet those descriptions. Regardless of their shortcomings, charter schools do hold out the promise of developing new approaches to teaching and school governance that can benefit the entire system of public education in the U.S.

For-Profit Schools

One of the hottest educational issues today is the practice of turning the operation of public schools over to private, for-profit companies. Advocates of privatization believe privately operated schools are more efficient, and they reduce costs and maximize "production"—that is, student achievement. For-profit schools also create a healthy competitive environment for public education—schools will have to improve, or they will be forced to close. Opponents, however, are concerned that profit, rather than increasing student achievement, is the real driving force behind **for-profit schools**. Critics of for-profit schools are also concerned that school districts may not be vigilant enough in monitoring the performance of private education companies and that limited resources for schools are used for another "layer" of administration, service fees, and profits.

For-profit companies operated 840 schools in 35 states during 2011–2012. With 79 percent of its charter schools operated by for-profit companies, **MICHIGAN** leads the nation in for-profit involvement in charter schools. The states with the greatest number of schools managed by for-profit companies are **MICHIGAN** (204), **FLORIDA** (177), **OHIO** (110), and **ARIZONA** (108). The largest for-profit company, Imagine Schools, manages 89 schools. The next largest companies are Academica (76 schools), National Heritage Academies (68 schools), K^{12} Inc. (57 schools), and Edison Learning (53 schools). Among the for-profit companies, K^{12} Inc. has the largest total enrollment (87,091 students; Miron & Gulosino, November 2013, pp. ii–iii).

K^{12} Inc.

One of the largest for-profit managers of schools, K^{12} Inc., states that its mission is to focus on "each child's potential," and the company is committed to "putting students first." Through its online private school, the company offers individualized learning programs to both public and private schools worldwide. The company also provides courses directly to students based on their needs and interests and to those involved in homeschooling.

Although K^{12}'s CEO states that the company "operates schools with high integrity and a focus on strong academic performance for all students," the company has been the target of multiple class-action suits related to academic performance and educational quality in K^{12}-managed public schools. In 2013, the company's insurance carriers paid $6.75 million to settle a class-action suit based on the following:

- Concealment of K^{12}'s academic performance and annual growth measures
- Excessive and burdensome student-to-teacher ratios
- Improper grading and attendance policies at K^{12}-managed schools
- Hiring of unqualified teachers who were not properly certified
- Failure of special education programs to meet government standards
- Misleading high parent satisfaction scores

Another class-action lawsuit was filed during February 2014 in Virginia on behalf of those who purchased stock in K^{12}. The lawsuit alleged that the company misrepresented or failed to disclose various "operational failures in the enrollment process" (Reuters, 2014).

The inability of for-profit companies like K^{12} to operate schools that truly provide quality education to all students is aptly explained by Larry Cuban, a Stanford University education professor:

> CEOs and investors learned the hard way that what worked in companies to make silicon chips, crank out case after case of soda, and create brand-new cereals flopped when managers tried to turn low-performing students around and get higher test scores . . . .And then there is K^{12}, Inc., a for-profit company, that pulled in over $800 million in 2013 through selling online courses and curriculum, software, and blended programs to private and public schools . . . . Recently, investigations have shown how K^{12} Inc. squeezed money out of each of their operations to give investors a high rate of return on their shares.
>
> Sure, there is money to be made in the education market. After all, for decades big and small companies selling textbooks, classroom furniture, transportation, low- and high-tech equipment from blackboards (oops! green and whiteboards) to smartboards have profited from providing basic products and services to this stable market. These profit-driven companies, however, do not take over schools or districts. They provide services and products for already existing agencies running schools, not the tough business of turning failing ones around. That is a sinkhole that many companies eager to turn a profit have slipped into in the past and are primed to do so now. (Cuban, 2013)

TEACHER-OWNED SCHOOLS?

An innovative approach to for-profit schools has been suggested by Richard K. Vedder (2003) in his book *Can Teachers Own Their Own Schools? New Strategies for Educational Excellence*. Vedder believes that for-profit public schools would benefit from competition and develop cost-effective ways to achieve educational quality. In addition, such schools would attract the additional funding and expertise needed to revolutionize school systems.

Vedder's approach is patterned after Margaret Thatcher's privatization of government council housing in England, privatization reforms in Latin America, and the employee stock ownership plan (ESOP) movement in the United States. He suggests that teachers, administrators, and other educational stakeholders become the owners of schools, thus acquiring an attractive financial stake in the process. Such privatization reforms could pave the way for new, cost-effective means of improving education for all students. Vedder believes that schools in which teachers, administrators, and parents have a significant financial stake would foster vibrant school communities with increased parental involvement and the innovation and efficiency essential to produce educational excellence.

One example of a teacher-owned school is Avalon, a public charter school in St. Paul, **MINNESOTA**, run by a 15-teacher cooperative. The school's 200 7th- to 12th-grade students take traditional classes and work on individual projects they design with their teachers. The school has no principal; instead, patterning their practice after doctors and lawyers, teachers decide everything, from salaries to the curriculum. As Carrie Bakken, a teacher at the school, says, "The job is more appealing when you own your school" (Hawkins, 2010).

Another example of a teacher-owned school is the GW Community School, a college-prep high school serving 9th- to 12th-grade students in Springfield, **VIRGINIA**. The mission of the school is to develop each student to their full potential and to provide them with a rigorous college-prep curriculum that emphasizes not just the acquisition of subject matter, but how to apply that knowledge to solve authentic, real-world problems (GW Community School, 2011). Teachers at the school have flexibility over the curriculum and teaching methods. As a result, classes like "Conspiracy Theories," "Political Geography," and "Sea Adventures" are offered in addition to traditional courses.

SUMMARY

Why Do You Need to Understand Educational Politics?

- Understanding educational politics is an important form of professional knowledge.
- Parents; students; teachers; administrators; taxpayers; federal, state, and local authorities; ethnic and racial groups; educational theorists and researchers; the corporate sector; and special-interest groups exert political influence on education.
- *Politics* refers to how people use power, influence, and authority within an organization to persuade others to act in desired ways.
- Educators use within-school politics to influence instructional and curricular practices within a school.
- Five dimensions of educational politics influence teachers: (1) political pressure from federal, state, and local levels; (2) conflicting ideas about what to teach

and how to teach it, (3) competition for educational resources; (4) changing legal rights and responsibilities of teachers; and (5) the push for higher standards, testing, and accountability.

How Does the Local Community Influence Schools?

- Local school districts, which vary greatly in size, locale, organizational structure, demographics, and wealth, are responsible for the management and operation of schools.
- Local school boards, whose members are usually elected, set educational policies for a district; however, many people believe that boards should be reformed to be better informed and more responsive.
- The superintendent, the chief administrator of a local district, has a complex array of responsibilities

and must work cooperatively with the school board and others in an environment that is often politically turbulent.

- Through groups like the PTA or PTO, some parents are involved in local school activities and reform efforts; others are involved with private schools; and some actively promote alternative approaches to education such as school choice, voucher systems, and home schooling.

What Powers and Influence Do States Have in Governing Schools?

- The state legislature, state courts, and the governor significantly influence education by setting policies related to the management and operation of schools within a state; many states have even passed legislation allowing them to take over academically failing school districts or individual schools.
- The state board of education, the highest educational agency in a state, regulates education and advises the governor and others on important educational policies.
- The state department of education implements policies related to teacher certification, allocation of state and federal funds, enforcement of state and federal guidelines, school accreditation, and research and evaluation projects to improve education.
- The chief state school officer oversees education within a state and, in collaboration with the governor, legislature, state board of education, and the public, provides leadership to improve education.

How Do Regional Education Agencies Assist Schools?

- The regional educational service agency (RESA), an intermediate unit of educational administration in about half of the states, provides assistance to two or more school districts for staff development, curriculum development, instructional media, and program evaluation.

How Does the Federal Government Influence Education?

- The federal government influences education at the state level through funding general and categorical programs, establishing and enforcing standards and regulations, conducting and disseminating educational research, providing technical assistance to improve education, and encouraging equity and excellence for the nation's schools.
- The national legislature, federal and state supreme courts, and the president significantly influence education by exerting moral suasion for the improvement of schools, providing categorical aid for federal programs, ensuring that school systems follow legal statutes, and funding educational research.
- The U.S. Department of Education supports and disseminates educational research, administers federal grants in education, and assists the president in developing and promoting a national agenda for education.
- At times, the roles of the federal, state, and local governments in education are in conflict.

What Role Do Teacher Leaders Play in School Governance?

- Teachers have many opportunities to provide leadership for school reform, including leadership in areas such as teaching as a profession, equity, school organization, assessment of student learning, and curriculum and instruction.

How Are Schools Financed in the United States?

- The Great Recession that began in 2008 resulted in severe shortfalls in local, state, and federal budgets, and these shortfalls are continuing to have a great impact on school funding.
- Schools are supported with revenues from the local, state, and federal levels, with most funding now coming from the state level. Local funding is provided through property taxes, which in many instances results in inequitable funding for schools located in areas with an insufficient tax base.
- One challenge to financing schools has been the development of an equitable means of taxation for the support of education.

What Are Some Trends in Funding for Equity and Excellence?

- Inequities among school districts often reflect differences in the value of property that can be taxed for the support of schools.
- Many state legislatures have enacted tax reforms, including full-funding programs, that set the same per-pupil expenditures for all schools and districts. Some states have achieved greater equity through redistricting—redrawing district boundaries to reduce funding inequities.
- Some states achieve vertical equity by providing additional funding, or categorical aid, to educate students with special needs. Also, many local districts and schools receive additional funding through partnerships with the private sector and/or community groups.
- School choice and voucher programs are two controversial approaches to providing parents the freedom to select the schools their children attend.

How Will the Privatization Movement Affect Equity and Excellence in Education?

- Charter schools and for-profit schools, both part of the privatization movement, were developed in response to perceived inadequacies of the public schools.
- Charter schools are independent, innovative, outcome-based public schools started by a group of teachers,

parents, or others who obtain a charter from a local school district, a state, or the federal government.

- Research on charter schools is mixed—some studies show that charter school students outperform students at other schools, whereas other studies show the opposite.

- K^{12}, Inc. is an example of for-profit schools operated by private corporations.
- For-profit schools owned by teachers, administrators, and other stakeholders have been suggested as one way to improve the quality of schools.

PROFESSIONAL REFLECTIONS AND ACTIVITIES

Teacher's Journal

1. As this chapter points out, many individuals and groups believe that they should play an important role in school governance. Rank order (from *greatest influence* to *least influence*) the extent to which you think each of the following individuals or groups *should* control schools: students, teachers, administrators, parents, the school board, the local school district, the state government, and the federal government. Are there certain areas of schooling that should be controlled by these individuals and groups? Compare your rankings with those of your classmates. What differences do you note?

2. Imagine that you are going to open a charter school. How would this school differ from the schools in your community? What would you say to parents to convince them to send their children to your school?

Teacher's Research

1. Use your favorite search engine to visit the websites for several charter schools. What do these schools have in common? How are they different?

2. Visit the U.S. Department of Education's charter school website and click on the State Policies for Charter Schools link. How do the states' charter school policies differ? How are they similar?

Observations and Interviews

1. Visit a private (secular, parochial, for-profit, or charter) school. Find out how teachers and other staff members are hired and how the school is organized and governed. How does the management and operation of this school differ from that of public schools?

2. Using Figure 6.2 on page 183 as a guide, interview a teacher in a local school about his or her perceptions of the political influences on teachers. Ask the teacher to select one influence and describe how it currently affects the school where the teacher works.

3. Interview a teacher and ask him or her to rank order (from *greatest influence* to *least influence*) the extent to which each of the following individuals or groups *should* control schools: students, teachers, administrators, parents, the school board, the local school district, the state government, and the federal government. How do the teacher's beliefs compare with your own?

Professional Portfolio

Prepare a profile of a school district. The district may be in your hometown, your college or university community, or a community in which you would like to teach. Information on the district may be obtained on the Internet or from your university library, public library, school district office, state board of education, or professional teacher associations.

Keeping in mind that school district statistics are more readily available in some cases than in others, your profile might include the following types of information:

- Organizational chart showing (if possible) personnel currently assigned to each position
- Tables showing numbers of school buildings, students, teachers, administrators, support personnel, and so forth
- Graduation/dropout rate
- Scores on standardized achievement tests
- Total annual budget
- Expenditures per pupil
- Entitlement programs

- Demographic characteristics of population living in the area served by the district—age, race or ethnicity, socioeconomic status, unemployment rate, and so forth
- Volunteer groups serving schools in the district

- Pupil-to-teacher ratio
- Percent of ethnic minority students, students with disabilities, students eligible for free or reduced-fee lunch, and so forth
- Percentage of students going on to college

CHAPTER QUIZ

Take this quiz to check your understanding of the content covered in this chapter.

CHAPTER SEVEN

Ethical and Legal Issues in U.S. Education

learning outcomes

After reading this chapter, you will be able to do the following:

1. Explain why teachers need to know about education and the law.
2. Explain why teachers need a professional code of ethics.
3. Itemize and explain the legal rights of teachers.
4. Compare the rights that apply to student teachers with those that apply to teachers.
5. Explain the legal responsibilities of teachers.
6. Explain the legal rights of students and parents.
7. Discuss current issues in the legal rights of school districts.

Our country has a long history of protecting human rights through the enactment of specific laws. From the early colonists who sought religious freedom to African Americans involved in the civil rights movement, Americans have sought protection under the law. During the last several decades, increased attention has been devoted to various legal aspects of education. In fact, "the path from schoolhouse to courthouse is . . . well traveled, " and the average number of education cases decided in state and federal courts has increased from about 1,500 in the 1940s to more than 6,500 during the last two decades (Dunn & West, 2009, p. 4).

WHY DO YOU NEED TO KNOW ABOUT EDUCATION AND THE LAW?

At this point in your teacher education program, understanding how the law influences schools and teachers may not seem important. However, federal and state legislation and court decisions will affect your life as a teacher. What are your legal responsibilities when you take students on a field trip? Are you responsible if a student is injured during your class? Can a parent prevent you from using curriculum materials that the parent finds offensive? What guidelines must you follow when photocopying instructional materials from books and magazines? How can you copyright-protect materials you and your students publish on the Internet? How can social networking and technologies like smartphones that empower students also place teachers and schools at risk? These are just a few legal issues you might encounter as a teacher. Without knowledge of the legal dimensions of such issues, you will be ill-equipped to protect your rights and the rights of your students. This chapter examines ethical and legal issues that affect the rights and responsibilities of teachers, administrators, students, and parents.

WHY DO YOU NEED A PROFESSIONAL CODE OF ETHICS?

Your actions as a teacher will be determined not only by what is legally required of you but also by what you know you *ought* to do. You must do what is *legally right*, and you must *do the right thing*. In many cases, doing the right thing

Learn how Public Law 94-142 changed education for special education students.

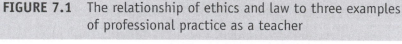

FIGURE 7.1 The relationship of ethics and law to three examples of professional practice as a teacher

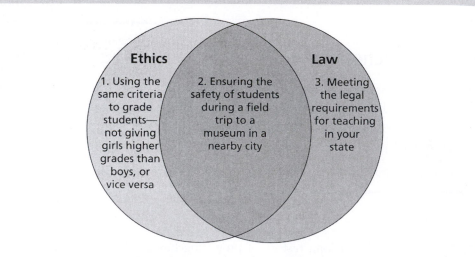

and doing what is required by law are the same. As Figure 7.1 shows, you would have an ethical and legal responsibility to ensure the safety of students during a field trip to a museum in a nearby city. The figure also shows that doing the right thing may not be required by law. For example, you should use the same criteria to grade students— giving girls higher grades than boys, or vice versa, would be unethical, but it would not be illegal. Last, meeting the legal requirements to become a teacher in your state is a legal matter, not an ethical matter.

A specific set of values will guide you as a teacher. A deep and lasting commitment to professional practice should characterize your role as a teacher. You will need to adopt a high standard of professional ethics and model behaviors that are in accord with that code of ethics. "Every teacher is charged with the responsibility of setting a good example. Not only must teachers be of good moral character, but also their general reputation must attest to this fact" (Alexander & Alexander, 2012, p. 776).

At present, the teaching profession does not have a uniform **code of ethics** similar to the Hippocratic oath, which all doctors are legally required to take when they begin practice. However, the largest professional organization for teachers, the National Education Association (NEA), has a code of ethics for members that includes the following statement: "The educator accepts the responsibility to adhere to the highest ethical standards" (NEA, 2014).

Ethical Teaching Attitudes and Practices

Teaching is an ethical enterprise; that is, a teacher has an obligation to act ethically, to follow what he or she knows to be the most appropriate professional action to take. The best interests of students, not the teacher, provide the rule of thumb for determining what is ethical and what is not. Behaving ethically is more than a matter of following the rules or not breaking the law—it means acting in a way that promotes the learning and growth of students and helps them realize their potential. The Teaching on Your Feet feature for this chapter illustrates how one teacher modified his behavior to promote the learning and growth of a "problem" student.

Unethical acts break the trust and respect on which good teacher– student relationships are based. Examples of unethical conduct would be to use grades as a form of punishment, express rage in the classroom, or intentionally trick students on tests. You can no doubt think of other examples from your own experience as a student.

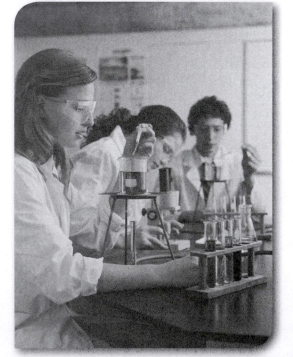

What legal responsibilities did a teacher consider when designing this laboratory experiment for students?

TEACHING ON YOUR FEET
Respect in the Classroom Is a Two-Way Street

MARK TWAIN once said, "I could live two months on one good compliment." That statement also applies to today's students. When confronted with challenging situations in the classroom, ask yourself, "Do my students feel that I respect them?" Answering that question honestly might make your day-to-day life in the classroom much more productive, as Julius Dichosa illustrates in the following excerpt.

When I was a beginning teacher, I asked several veteran teachers at my school for advice before my first day of teaching. To my surprise, they all said the same thing: "Don't smile until Christmas!" That advice was not very reassuring, since it does not fit my personality. Although they didn't mean it literally, they felt strongly about being strict and not becoming "friends" with students. After my first few weeks of teaching, I understood exactly what they meant, even if I did not totally agree with their philosophy.

I started off the first week by making sure that my students understood the rules and expectations for my class. Typical for many junior high classes, I was met with rolling eyes and witty remarks from a select few in each class. So, I put on my strictest face and made sure that those students knew that I meant business. After that, there was only one who continued to fight me on it. I'll call him Johnny.

During the next couple of months, Johnny and I disagreed on several occasions. Johnny demanded attention; he had a comment for everything that occurred in class. He would not take "no" for an answer. Each time we had a disagreement, I sent him to the guidance office, called his parents, and hoped for the best. But the next day, I would be met with even more resistance and negativity. After repeating this process several times, I decided to change my strategy. Why was Johnny giving me such a hard time? What was I doing wrong? I thought being strict and firm was the way to start off the school year, but, to be honest, it consumed all of my energy in and out of class. It was time to find a better way to reach Johnny.

After speaking to the administration and some of Johnny's other teachers, I realized that I was not alone. With one exception, they all had problems with him. To my surprise, the exception was a beginning teacher like myself. I had to know her secret. When I asked her how she "handled" Johnny, she simply said, "Some students deserve

a break." She explained that there are some students who respond to consequences and others who don't. Johnny was one who did not. He needed a "break" to be successful.

The next day, I called Johnny out of class to speak to him one-on-one. I reassured him that he wasn't in trouble—all I wanted to do was talk to him. I asked him what it was about me that he didn't like, and he responded, "You treat me like all the other teachers do." When I asked him how he wanted to be treated, he said, "I don't know . . . with respect." I proceeded to tell him that in order to get respect, you have to give it. Then he said something that surprised me. "You need to take some of your own advice." In that moment, my two-month career as a schoolteacher flashed before my eyes. I was speechless. After an awkward silence, I sent him back to class. I thought long and hard about how I was coming across to my students and came to the conclusion that, while being strict and firm (without cracking a smile) worked for the majority of my students, I was at times being disrespectful to a select few—Johnny, in particular.

Following class the next day, I thanked Johnny for our conversation. He seemed surprised by my reaction. I joked with him, telling him that he could make big money as an advisor to teachers. I apologized for the way I had been treating him in front of the class. I told him that students in the class looked up to him and saw him as a leader. I assured him that he could use his influence with students in a positive way and persuade them to act appropriately. I could tell that those words meant a lot to him. From that day forward, Johnny and I had a mutually respectful relationship. And, most important, I had an influential student who supported my approach to classroom management.

ANALYZE & REFLECT

Click here to analyze and reflect on this scenario you have just read.

JULIUS DICHOSA
Eighth-Grade Physical Science, Department Chair,
Las Palmas Middle School
Covina, **CALIFORNIA**

Ethical Dilemmas in the Classroom and School

As a teacher, you will probably encounter **ethical dilemmas** in the classroom and in the school. You will have to take action in situations in which all the facts are not known or for which no single course of action can be called right or wrong. At these times, it can be quite difficult to decide what an ethical response might be. Dealing satisfactorily with ethical dilemmas in teaching often requires the ability to see beyond short-range consequences to consider long-range consequences.

An important part of responding to an ethical dilemma is identifying possible consequences of one's actions. Consider, for example, the following three questions based on actual case studies. On the basis of the information given, how would you respond to each situation? What might be the consequences of your actions?

1. Should the sponsor of the high school literary magazine refuse to print a well-written story by a budding writer if the piece appears to satirize a teacher and a student?

2. Is a reading teacher justified in trying to increase achievement for an entire class by separating two disruptive students and placing one in a reading group beneath his reading level?

3. Should a chemistry teacher punish a student (on the basis of circumstantial, inconclusive evidence) for a laboratory explosion if the example of decisive, swift punishment will likely prevent the recurrence of a similar event and thereby ensure the safety of all students?

There are no "right" answers to these questions. To the extent possible, you want to make the "best" decision in each case. A noted scholar of professional ethics, Kenneth A. Strike, suggests the following characteristics of a "good," ethical decision:

1. The decision is supported by evidence. This evidence supports the claim that acting on this decision is more likely to achieve desired ends at an appropriate cost than other courses of action that might be taken.
2. The ends aimed at by the decision are the ends that ought to be aimed at.
3. The decision can be implemented morally.
4. The decision has been legitimately achieved. (Strike, 2007, p. 113)

WHAT ARE YOUR LEGAL RIGHTS AS A TEACHER?

With each freedom that we have comes a corresponding responsibility to others and to the community in which we live. As long as there is more than one individual on this planet, there is a need for laws to clarify individual rights and responsibilities. This necessary balance between rights and responsibilities is perhaps more critical to teaching than to any other profession. Teachers have the same rights as other citizens; however, teachers must "perform their professional duties within the boundaries of the U.S. Constitution, statutory law, case law, and school district policies" (Essex, 2012, p. xix). The primary legal rights of teachers are illustrated in Figure 7.2.

Although schools do have limited power over teachers, teachers' rights to **due process** cannot be violated. Like all citizens, teachers are protected from being treated arbitrarily by those in authority. A principal who disagrees with a teacher's methods cannot suddenly fire that teacher. A school board cannot ask a teacher to resign merely by claiming that the teacher's political activities outside school are "disruptive" to the

FIGURE 7.2 Teachers' legal rights

educational process. A teacher cannot be dismissed for "poor" performance without ample documentation that the performance was, in fact, poor and without sufficient time to meet clearly stated performance evaluation criteria.

Certification

> Suppose, for example, that Peggy Hernandez is a junior high school English teacher and lives in a state with a law specifying that a teacher must show proof of five years of successful teaching experience for a teaching certificate to be renewed. Last year was Peggy's fifth year of teaching, and her principal gave her an unsatisfactory performance rating. Peggy's principal told her that her teaching certificate cannot be renewed. Is the principal correct?

Peggy's principal is mistaken about the grounds for nonrenewal of a teaching certificate. According to the state's law, unsuccessful performance, or a failure to complete the school year, is grounds for nonrenewal of a certificate—not performance that is judged to be unsatisfactory. Because state laws vary and unsuccessful performance is defined differently in different states, however, Peggy's principal might have been correct if she taught in another state.

No teacher who meets all of a state's requirements for initial certification can arbitrarily be denied a certificate. However, receiving a certificate does not guarantee the right to keep it (NEA, 2014). For a certificate to be revoked, the reason must be job-related and demonstrably impair the teacher's ability to perform satisfactorily. In this regard, the case of a California teacher whose certificate was revoked because someone admitted to having a homosexual relationship with the teacher is often cited. The court determined that the teacher's homosexual conduct was not an impairment to the teacher's performance and ordered the certificate restored (*Morrison v. State Board of Education*, 1969).

When courts have upheld the refusal to hire and the right to terminate lesbian, gay, bisexual, or transgender (LGBT) teachers, these decisions have been influenced by factors such as sexual involvement with students or public acts of indecency (NEA, 2014). Twenty-one states and the District of Columbia prohibit discrimination on the basis of sexual orientation in regard to employment, and 17 states and D.C. also prohibit discrimination based on gender identity (Human Rights Campaign, 2014). Therefore, it is "difficult, if not impossible, for local school systems to deny employment or dismiss [teachers] on the basis of their sexual orientation" (LaMorte, 2008, p. 247).

Teachers' Rights to Nondiscrimination

> George, who pled guilty to possession of marijuana and cocaine in a criminal trial, was not reinstated in his teaching position after his criminal record was expunged. George claims that he is being discriminated against because of his past. Is he right?

States may impose certain limitations on initial certification as long as those limitations are not discriminatory with regard to race, religion, ethnic origin, sex, or age. Nearly all the states, for example, require that applicants for a teaching certificate pass a test that covers basic skills, professional knowledge, or academic subject areas. Qualifications for initial certification may also legally include certain personal qualities. George's case, for example, is based on a Louisiana case involving a man who was not reinstated in his teaching position, even though his criminal record had been expunged. The court maintained that he had committed the act, and that expunging the record did not erase that fact, nor did it erase the "moral turpitude" of the teacher's conduct (*Dubuclet v. Home Insurance Company*, 1995).

The right to **nondiscrimination** in regard to employment is protected by Title VII of the Civil Rights Act of 1964, which states:

> It shall be an unlawful employment practice for an employer (1) to fail or refuse to hire or to discharge any individual, or otherwise to discriminate against any individual with respect to his compensation, terms, conditions,

PROFESSIONAL REFLECTION
Watch a teacher discuss her legal rights when being subpoenaed.

TEACHERS' VOICES
Walk in My Shoes

**Margaret Williams
University City
High School**

University City, Missouri

This feature is adapted from Margaret Williams's Council of Chief State School Officers Teacher of the Year video retrieved January 29, 2011, from http://www .pearsonfoundation.org/ccsso-toy/2009/ vid-Missouri.html; and a Missouri Department of Elementary and Secondary Education article, "University City School District Teacher Is Missouri Teacher of the Year for 2008–09," retrieved January 29, 2011, from http://dese.mo.gov/news/2008/toy.htm.

or privileges of employment, because of such individual's race, color, religion, sex, or national origin; or (2) to limit, segregate, or classify his employees or applicants for employment in any way which would deprive or tend to deprive any individual of employment opportunities or otherwise adversely affect his status as an employee, because of such individual's race, color, religion, sex, or national origin.

However, there is currently no federal law that protects lesbian, gay, bisexual, and transgender (LGBT) individuals from employment discrimination. The Employment Non-Discrimination Act (ENDA), introduced to Congress in 2013, would prohibit workplace discrimination based on sexual orientation or gender identity. ENDA is modeled after Title VII of the Civil Rights Act and the Americans with Disabilities Act (Human Rights Campaign, 2014).

Teaching Contracts

A **teaching contract** represents an agreement between the teacher and a board of education. For a contract to be valid, it must contain these five basic elements:

1. **Offer and acceptance**—The school board has made a formal offer, and the employee has accepted the contract terms.
2. **Competent parties**—The school board is not exceeding the authority granted to it by the state, and the teacher meets the criteria for employment.
3. **Consideration**—Remuneration is promised to the teacher.
4. **Legal subject matter**—The contract terms are neither illegal nor against public policy.
5. **Proper form**—The contract adheres to state contract laws.

Before signing a teaching contract, read it carefully and be certain that it is signed by the appropriate member(s) of the board of education or board of trustees. Ask for clarification of any sections you don't understand. Any additional nonteaching duties should be spelled out in writing rather than left to an oral agreement. Because all board of education policies and regulations will be part of your contract, you should also read any available teacher handbook or school policy handbook.

The importance of carefully reading a contract and asking for clarification is illustrated in the following case:

> Victor Ming had just begun his first year as an English teacher at a high school in a city of about 300,000. Victor became quite upset when he learned that he had been assigned by his principal to sponsor the poetry club. The club was to meet once a week after school. Victor refused to sponsor the club, saying that the contract he had signed referred only to his teaching duties during regular school hours. Could Victor be compelled to sponsor the club?

Certain assignments, although not specified in a contract, may be required of teachers in addition to their regular teaching load, as long as there is a reasonable relationship between the teacher's classroom duties and the additional assignment. Such assignments can also include supervision of school events on weekends. Although Victor's contract did not make specific reference to club sponsorship, such a duty would be a reasonable addition to his regular teaching assignment.

When school authorities have assigned teachers to additional duties not reasonably related to their teaching, the courts have tended to rule in favor of teachers who file suit. For example, a school's directive to a tenured teacher of American history to assume the additional role of basketball coach was not upheld by a court of appeals (*Unified School District No. 241 v. Swanson,* 1986).

Due Process in Tenure and Dismissal

Tenure is a policy that provides the individual teacher with job security by (1) preventing his or her dismissal on insufficient grounds and (2) providing him or her with due process in the event of dismissal. Tenure is granted to teachers by the local school district after a period of satisfactory teaching, usually two to five years. In most cases, tenure may not be transferred from one school district to another.

The following case highlights the importance of tenure to a teacher's professional career:

> A teacher was dismissed from his teaching position by the school board after it learned that the teacher was a homosexual. The teacher filed suit in court, claiming that his firing was arbitrary and violated the provisions of tenure that he had been granted. The school board, on the other hand, maintained that his conduct was inappropriate for a teacher. Was the school board justified in dismissing the teacher?

The events in this case were actually heard by a court, which ruled that the teacher was unfairly dismissed (*Burton v. Cascade School District Union High School No. 5*, 1975). The court said that the board violated the teacher's rights as a tenured employee by failing to show "good and just cause" for dismissal. The teacher was awarded the balance due under his contract and an additional one-half year's salary. In a similar case, however, a court upheld the dismissal of a teacher whose sexual orientation was the target of parents' complaints and students' comments. The court ruled that the teacher could no longer effectively carry out his teaching duties (*Gaylord v. Tacoma School District No. 10*, 1977).

The practice of providing teachers with tenure is not without controversy. Some critics point out that tenure policies make it too difficult to dismiss incompetent teachers and that performance standards are high in many other fields that do not provide employees with job security. Generally, however, the courts have held the position that tenure insulates teachers from "special-interest groups and political factions, thereby enabling them to perform their professional duties without undue interference. When this occurs, the educational system is improved and students derive the benefits of quality education" (Essex, 2012, p. 250).

Just about every state today has a tenure law that specifies that a teacher may be dismissed with good cause. What counts as a good cause varies from state to state, however. The courts have ruled on a variety of reasons for **dismissal**: (1) insubordination, (2) incompetence or inefficiency, (3) neglect of duty, (4) conduct unbecoming a teacher, (5) subversive activities, (6) retrenchment or decreased need for services, (7) physical and/or mental health, (8) age, (9) causing or encouraging disruption, (10) engaging in illegal activities, (11) using offensive language, (12) personal appearance, (13) sex-related activities, (14) political activities, and (15) use of drugs or intoxicants.

For a tenured teacher to be dismissed, a systematic series of steps must be followed so that the teacher receives due process and his or her constitutionally guaranteed rights are not violated. Due process involves a careful, step-by-step examination of the charges brought against a teacher. Most states have outlined procedures that adhere to the following nine steps:

1. The teacher must be notified of the list of charges.
2. Adequate time must be provided for the teacher to prepare a rebuttal to the charges.
3. The teacher must be given the names of witnesses and access to evidence.
4. The hearing must be conducted before an impartial tribunal.
5. The teacher has the right to representation by legal counsel.
6. The teacher (or legal counsel) can introduce evidence and cross-examine adverse witnesses.
7. The school board's decision must be based on the evidence and findings of the hearing.
8. A transcript or record must be maintained of the hearing.
9. The teacher has the right to appeal an adverse decision.

These steps notwithstanding, it should be noted that due process is "a dynamic concept . . . [and] depends largely on a combination of the specific facts in a situation, the law governing the situation, the particular time in history in which judgment is being rendered, and the predilections of the individual judge(s) rendering the decision" (LaMorte, 2012, p. 5). The following case illustrates these points:

> Near the start of his fifth year of teaching at an elementary school in a small city, and two years after earning tenure, Mr. Mitchell went through a sudden and painful divorce. A few months later, a woman whom he had met around the time of his divorce moved into the house he was renting.
>
> For the remainder of the school year he and the woman lived together. During this time, he received no indication that his lifestyle was professionally unacceptable, and his teaching performance remained satisfactory.
>
> At the end of the year, however, Mr. Mitchell was notified that he was being dismissed because of immoral conduct; that is, he was living with a woman he was not married to. The school board called for a hearing and Mr. Mitchell presented his side of the case. The board, nevertheless, decided to follow through with its decision to dismiss him.
>
> Was the school board justified in dismissing Mr. Mitchell?

Although at one time teachers could readily be dismissed for living, unmarried, with a member of the opposite sex, "in today's environment, dismissal of adulterous teachers, an unmarried pregnant teacher, or an unmarried teacher living with a person of the opposite sex is rarely brought before the courts" (LaMorte, 2012, pp. 189–190). Because the board had not shown that Mr. Mitchell's alleged immoral conduct had a negative effect on his teaching, his dismissal would probably not hold up in court unless the community as a whole was upset by his behavior. Moreover, Mr. Mitchell could charge that his right to privacy as guaranteed by the 9th Amendment to the Constitution had been violated. Overall, it appears that the decision to dismiss Mr. Mitchell was arbitrary and based on the collective bias of the board. Nevertheless, teachers should be aware that courts frequently hold that teachers are role models, and the local community determines "acceptable" behavior both in school and out of school.

Teachers also have the right to organize and to join teacher organizations without fear of dismissal. In addition, most states have passed **collective bargaining** laws that require school boards to negotiate contracts with teacher organizations. Usually, the teacher organization with the most members in a district is given the right to represent teachers in the collective bargaining process.

An important part of most collective bargaining agreements is the right of a teacher to file a **grievance**, a formal complaint against his or her employer. A teacher may not be dismissed for filing a grievance, and he or she is entitled to have the grievance heard by a neutral third party. Often, the teachers' union or professional association that negotiated the collective bargaining agreement will provide free legal counsel for a teacher who has filed a grievance.

One right that teachers are not granted by collective bargaining agreements is the right to strike. Like other public employees, teachers do not have the legal right to strike in most states. Teachers who do strike run the risk of dismissal (*Hortonville Joint School District No. 1 v. Hortonville Education Association*, 1976); however, when teacher strikes occur, a school board cannot possibly replace all the striking teachers.

Academic Freedom

> A teacher of at-risk students at an alternative high school used a classroom management/motivational technique called Learnball. The teacher divided the class into teams, allowed students to elect team leaders and determine class rules and grading exercises, and developed a system of rewards that included listening to the radio and shooting baskets with a foam ball in the classroom. The school board ordered the teacher not to use the Learnball approach. Did the teacher have the right to continue using this teaching method?

This case is based on actual events involving a teacher in Pittsburgh, **PENNSYLVANIA**. The teacher brought suit against the board to prevent it from imposing a policy that banned Learnball in the classroom. The teacher cited the principle of **academic freedom** and claimed that teachers have a right to use teaching methods and materials to which school officials might object. A U.S. District Court, however, upheld the school board policy against Learnball (*Murray v. Pittsburgh Board of Public Education,* 1996).

Although the courts have held that teachers have the right to academic freedom, it is not absolute and must be balanced against the interests of society. In fact, education law expert Michael LaMorte (2012, p. 176) suggests that the concept of academic freedom "is no longer as strong a defense as it once was for teachers." For this defense to prevail, "it must be shown that the teacher did not defy legitimate state and local curriculum directives; followed accepted professional norms for that grade level and subject matter; discussed matters which were of public concern; and acted professionally and in good faith when there was no precedent or policy" (p. 176).

FAMOUS CASES

A landmark case involving academic freedom focused on John Scopes, a biology teacher who challenged a Tennessee law in 1925 that made it illegal to teach in a public school "any theory which denies the story of the Divine Creation of man as taught in the Bible, and to teach instead that man is descended from a lower order of animals." Scopes maintained that Darwin's theory about human origins had scientific merit and that the state's requirement that he teach the biblical account of creation violated his academic freedom.

Scopes's trial, which came to be known as the monkey trial, attracted national attention. Prosecuting Scopes was the "silver-tongued" William Jennings Bryan, a famous lawyer, politician, and presidential candidate. The defending attorney was Clarence Darrow.

Scopes believed strongly in academic freedom and his students' right to know about scientific theories. He expressed his views in his memoirs, *Center of the Storm*:

> Especially repulsive are laws restricting the constitutional freedom of teachers. The mere presence of such a law is a club held over the heads of the timid. Legislation that tampers with academic freedom is not protecting society, as its authors piously proclaim. By limiting freedom they are helping to make robot factories out of schools; ultimately, this produces nonthinking robots rather than the individualistic citizens we desperately need—now more than ever before. (Scopes, 1966, p. 277)

The monkey trial ended after 11 days of heated, eloquent testimony. Scopes was found guilty of violating the Butler Act and was fined $100. The decision was later reversed by the Tennessee Supreme Court on a technicality.

Since the Scopes trial, controversy has continued to surround the teaching of evolution. In many states during the 1980s, for example, religious fundamentalists won rulings that required science teachers to give equal time to both creationism and evolution in the classroom. The Supreme Court, however, in *Edwards v. Aguillard* (1987) ruled that such "balanced treatment" laws were unconstitutional. In the words of the court: "Because the primary purpose of the [Louisiana] Creationism Act is to advance a particular religious belief, the Act endorses religion in violation of the First Amendment."

In 1999, controversy over evolution again emerged when the Kansas State Board of Education removed the teaching of evolution and discussion of the origin of the universe from state science standards. A newly elected Kansas Board of Education voted to restore evolution to state science standards in 2001, however. Similarly, evolution became a topic of public debate in Ohio during 2006, when the Ohio State Board of Education voted to eliminate from state science curriculum standards a statement that encouraged students to "critically analyze" evolution.

Another case suggesting that a teacher's right to academic freedom is narrow and limited is *Krizek v. Cicero-Stickney Township High School District No. 201* (1989). In this instance, a district court ruled against a teacher whose contract was not renewed because she showed her students an R-rated film (*About Last Night*) as an example of a modern-day parallel to Thornton Wilder's play *Our Town*. Although the teacher told her students that they would be excused from viewing the film if they or their parents objected, she did not communicate directly with their parents. The teacher's attempt to consider the objections of students and parents notwithstanding, the court concluded that the length of the film indicates that its showing was more than an inadvertent mistake or a mere slip of the tongue, but rather was a planned event, and thus indicated that the teacher's approach to teaching was problematic.

Although concerned more with the right of a school to establish a curriculum than with the academic freedom of teachers per se, other cases have focused on the teacher's use of instructional materials. In *Mozert v. Hawkins County Board of Education* (1987, 1988), for example, a group of Tennessee parents objected to "secular humanist" materials used by their children's teachers. In *Smith v. Board of School Commissioners of Mobile County* (1987), 624 parents and teachers initiated a court suit alleging that 44 history, social studies, and home economics texts used in the Mobile County, Alabama, public schools encouraged immorality, undermined parental authority, and were imbued with the "humanist" faith. In both cases, the courts supported the right of schools to establish a curriculum even in the face of parental disapproval. In *Smith v. Board of School Commissioners of Mobile County* (1987), the Eleventh Circuit Court stated that "[i]ndeed, given the diversity of religious views in this country, if the standard were merely inconsistency with the beliefs of a particular religion there would be very little that could be taught in the public schools."

STATES' RIGHTS AND ACADEMIC FREEDOM

The previously described cases notwithstanding, the courts have not set guidelines for situations when the teacher's freedom conflicts with the state's right to require teachers to follow certain curriculum guidelines. The same federal court, for example, heard a similar case regarding a high school teacher who wrote a vulgar word for sexual intercourse on the blackboard during a discussion of socially taboo words. The court sidestepped the issue of academic freedom and ruled instead that the regulations authorizing teacher discipline were unconstitutionally vague and, therefore, the teacher could not be dismissed. The court did observe, however, that a public school teacher's right to traditional academic freedom is "qualified," at best, and the "teacher's right must yield to compelling public interests of greater constitutional significance."

In reviewing its decision, the court also said, "Nothing herein suggests that school authorities are not free after they have learned that the teacher is using a teaching method of which they disapprove, and which is not appropriate to the proper teaching of the subject, to suspend him [or her] until he [or she] agrees to cease using the method" (*Mailloux v. Kiley*, 1971).

Although some teachers have been successful in citing academic freedom as the basis for teaching controversial subjects, others have not. Teachers have been dismissed for ignoring directives regarding the teaching of controversial topics related to sex, polygamy, race, and religion. Although the courts have not been able to clarify just where academic freedom begins and ends, they have made it clear that the state does have a legitimate interest in what is taught to impressionable children.

Do Student Teachers Have the Same Rights as Teachers?

Do student teachers have the same legal status as certified teachers? Read the following case:

Meg Grant looked forward to the eight weeks she would spend as a student teacher in Mrs. Walker's high school English classes. Meg knew that

Mrs. Walker was one of the best supervising teachers she might have been paired with, and she was anxious to do her best.

In Mrs. Walker's senior class, Meg planned to teach *Brave New World*. Mrs. Walker pointed out to Meg that this book was controversial and some parents might object. She asked Meg to think about selecting an additional title that students could read if their parents objected to *Brave New World*. Meg felt that Mrs. Walker was bowing to pressure from conservative parents, so she decided to go ahead and teach the book.

Two weeks later Meg was called down to the principal's office where she was confronted by an angry father who said, "You have no right to be teaching my daughter this communist trash; you're just a student teacher."

What should Meg do? Does she have the same rights as a fully certified teacher?

In some states, a student teacher such as Meg might have the same rights and responsibilities as a fully certified teacher; in others, her legal status might be that of an unlicensed visitor. The most prudent action for Meg to take would be to apologize to the father and assure him that if any controversial books are assigned in the future, alternative titles would be provided. In addition, Meg should learn how important it is for a student teacher to take the advice of his or her supervising teacher.

It has been observed that a student teacher "is a special hybrid, being partially a student in higher education but not with the typical full load of campus classes and partially a teacher in K–12 education but not with the compensation and benefits of a full-fledged employee" (Zirkel & Karanxha, 2009, p. xi). Fewer than half of the states have statutes that apply specifically to student teachers (Zirkel & Karanxha, 2009). In addition, no state has a statutory provision regulating the dismissal of a student teacher, the assignment of a student teacher, or the denial of the right to student-teach (Morris & Curtis, 1983). Nevertheless, student teachers should be aware that a potential for liability exists with them just as it does with certified teachers.

One area of debate regarding student teachers is whether they can act as substitutes for their cooperating teachers or even other teachers in a school building. Unfortunately, many school districts have no policy regarding this practice. Depending on statutes in a particular state, however, a student teacher may substitute under the following conditions:

- A substitute teacher is not immediately available.
- The student teacher has been in that student-teaching assignment for a specified minimum number of school days.
- The supervising teacher, the principal of the school, and the university supervisor agree that the student teacher is capable of successfully handling the teaching responsibilities.
- A certified classroom teacher in an adjacent room or a member of the same teaching team as the student teacher is aware of the absence and agrees to assist the student teacher if needed.
- The principal of the school or the principal's representative is readily available in the building.
- The student teacher is not paid for any substitute service. (This matter is negotiable in some jurisdictions.) (Dunklee & Shoop, 2006, pp. 114–115).

Given the ambiguous status of student teachers, it is important that you begin your student-teaching assignment with knowledge of the legal aspects of teaching and a clear idea of your rights and responsibilities. During your student teaching experience, you should follow the six recommendations in Figure 7.3.

FIGURE 7.3 Legal advice for your student teaching experience

1. If the school has a faculty handbook, become familiar with its contents, particularly the roles and responsibilities that apply to teachers. If you have questions about the handbook, ask your cooperating teacher.
2. Become familiar with district guidelines that might apply to the curriculum you will teach. For example, does the district require (or prohibit) the use of certain books and/or teaching methods?
3. Understand the potential risks associated with the learning activities you plan to use during your student teaching experience. Discuss any concerns with your cooperating teacher.
4. Review with your cooperating teacher the school's rules for safety and the procedures to follow in the event of an emergency.
5. Remember that students' records are confidential. School records should be used to improve your teaching and/or to increase students' learning.
6. If you have problems with certain students or with a particular class, document your concerns and seek advice from your cooperating teacher.

WHAT ARE YOUR LEGAL RESPONSIBILITIES AS A TEACHER?

Teachers are responsible, of course, for meeting the terms of their teaching contracts. As noted previously, teachers are responsible for duties not covered in the contract if they are reasonably related to teaching. Among these duties may be club sponsorship; lunchroom, study hall, or playground duty; academic counseling of students; and record keeping.

Teachers are also legally responsible for the safety and well-being of students assigned to them. Although it is not expected that a teacher be able to control completely the behavior of young, energetic students, a teacher can be held liable for any injury to a student if it is shown that the teacher's negligence contributed to the injury.

Avoiding Tort Liability

An eighth-grade science teacher in Louisiana left her class for a few moments to go to the school office to pick up some forms. While she was gone, her students continued to do some laboratory work that involved the use of alcohol-burning devices. Unfortunately, one girl was injured when she tried to relight a defective burner.

Could the teacher be held liable for the girl's injuries?

These events actually occurred (*Station v. Travelers Insurance Co.*, 1974). The court that heard the case determined that the teacher failed to provide adequate supervision while the students were exposed to dangerous conditions. Considerable care is required, the court observed, when students handle inherently dangerous objects, and the need for this care is magnified when students are exposed to dangers they don't appreciate.

At times, teachers may have concerns about their liability for damages as a result of their actions. The branch of law concerned with compensating an individual who suffers losses resulting from another's negligence is known as tort law. "Tort law deals with a variety of matters including negligent or intentional behavior causing harm, defamation, and injuries resulting from defects in buildings or land" (Imber et al., 2014, p. 4).

According to **tort liability** law, an individual who is negligent and at fault in the exercise of his or her legal duty may be required to pay monetary damages to an

TABLE 7.1 Selected court decisions in which school personnel were found negligent for failure to meet a "standard of care"

1. A woodworking instructor allowed a student to operate a table saw without the use of a safeguard, which resulted in serious damage to his proximal interphalangeal joint. *Borbin v. State,* 506 So, 2d 888 (La. App. 1987).

2. A student dislocated his shoulder during an intramural football game, when the school provided no protective equipment and improper supervision of the game. *Locilento v. John A. Coleman Catholic High School,* 525 N.Y.S.2d 198 (A.D.3d Dept. 1987).

3. An 11-year-old student suffered serious head injuries from a blow in the head during a kick game and was without medical attention for more than an hour. The one-hour delay caused a hematoma to grow from the size of a walnut to that of an orange. *Barth v. Board of Education,* 490 N.E.2d 77 (Ill. App. 1st Dist. 1986).

4. An eight-year-old girl was seriously burned when her costume caught fire from a lighted candle on her teacher's desk. *Smith v. Archbishop of St. Louis,* 632 S.W.2d 516 (Mo. App. 1982).

5. A 12-year-old boy was killed when he fell through a skylight at school while retrieving a ball. *Stabl v. Cocolico School District,* 534 A.2d 1141 (Pa. Cmwlth. 1987).

6. A boy was seriously injured while playing on school grounds when he fell into a hole filled with glass, trash, and other debris, due to the absence of school officials to warn him of the dangerous condition. *Dean v. Board of Education,* 523 A.2d 1059 (Md. App. 1987).

7. A female student was en route to class when she pushed her hand through a glass panel in a smoke-colored door, causing severe and permanent damage. *Bielaska v. Town of Waterford,* 491 A.2d 1071 (Conn. 1985).

8. A high school student was seriously injured when he was tackled and thrown to the ground during a touch football game in gym class that was inadequately supervised and the players began to use excessive force. *Hyman v. Green,* 403 N.W.2d 597 (Mich. App. 1987).

Adapted from Nathan L. Essex. *School Law and the Public Schools: A Practical Guide for Educational Leaders,* 5th edition. Boston: Allyn & Bacon, 2012, pp. 175, 188. Copyright © by Allyn & Bacon. Reprinted by permission.

injured party. Generally, the standard of behavior applied by the courts is "the care that a reasonable and prudent person would take in the circumstances" (Imber et al., 2014, p. 287). However, teachers are held to a higher standard than ordinary citizens, and certain teachers (e.g., physical education, chemistry, and shop teachers) are held to an even higher standard because of the increased risk of injury involved in the classes they teach. Table 7.1 presents several examples of cases in which students were injured and educators were found to have breached their duty of care.

NEGLIGENCE

In contrast to the decision reached by the Louisiana court mentioned earlier, the courts have made it clear that there are many accidents that teachers cannot reasonably foresee that do result in student injuries. For example, a teacher on playground duty was found not to be negligent when a student threw a rock that struck another student in the eye. After the teacher walked past a group of boys, one boy threw a small rock that hit a larger rock on the ground and then bounced up to hit the other boy in the eye. The court ruled that "[w]here the time between an act of a student and injury to a fellow student is so short that the teacher had no opportunity to prevent injury, it cannot be said that negligence of the teacher is a proximate cause of the injury" (*Fagen v. Summers,* 1972). In another case, the court ruled that a New York teacher could not have anticipated that the paper bag she asked a student to pick up contained a broken bottle that cut the student (*West v. Board of Education of City of New York,* 1959). In two almost identical cases, the courts ruled that a teacher of a class with a good behavior record could not reasonably be expected to anticipate that a student would be injured by a pencil thrown by a classmate while the teacher was momentarily out of the room attending to her usual duties (*Ohman v. Board of Education,* 1950; *Simonetti v. School District of Philadelphia,* 1982).

PROFESSIONAL REFLECTION
Watch educators discuss the legal responsibilities of teachers to meet the needs of special education students.

When a court considers a case involving tort liability, evidence is examined to determine whether the responsible party (the school district, the administrator, or the teacher) acted negligently. For a school official to be considered liable, the following must be shown to be present: "(1) a legal duty, (2) a breach of duty, (3) a causal connection often referred to as 'proximate cause' between the conduct and the resultant injury, and (4) actual loss or damage" (LaMorte, 2012, p. 327).

As a teacher, you should be alert to conditions that might lead to accidental injury of one or more students. You will have a duty to your pupils, and you could be held liable for injuries that students incur as a result of your **negligence**. However, your liability extends only to injuries your students might suffer if you fail to provide the degree of care for pupils that a reasonable person would. A review of court cases involving the tort liability of teachers suggests that most cases involve at least one of the following:

- Inadequate supervision
- Inadequate instruction
- Lack of or improper medical treatment of pupils
- Improper disclosure of defamatory information concerning pupils—for example, release of school records that contain negative statements about a student

Teachers' concern about their potential liability for failing to prevent injury to students has been lessened by the availability of liability insurance. Many professional teacher organizations offer liability coverage as part of their membership benefits. Teachers may also purchase individual liability insurance policies. In addition, school districts in approximately half of the states have immunity from liability for torts committed by district employees (LaMorte, 2012, p. 328).

EDUCATIONAL MALPRACTICE

Since the mid-1970s, several plaintiffs have charged in their **educational malpractice** suits that schools should be responsible for a pupil whose failure to achieve is significant. In the first of such cases, the parents of Peter W. Doe charged that the San Francisco Unified School District was negligent because it allowed him to graduate from high school with a fifth-grade reading level and this handicap would not enable him to function in adult society. In particular, they charged that the "defendant school district, its agents and employees, negligently and carelessly failed to provide plaintiff with adequate instruction, guidance, counseling and/or supervision in basic academic skills such as reading and writing, although said school district had the authority, responsibility, and ability [to do so]." They sought $500,000 for the negligent work of the teachers who taught Peter.

In evaluating the claim of Peter and his parents, the court pointed out that the alleged injury was not within the realm of tort law and that many factors beyond a school's responsibility or control can account for lack of achievement. The court did not hold the school responsible for Peter's lack of achievement and made it clear that to do so would be to set a precedent with potentially drastic consequences: "To hold [schools] to an actionable duty of care, in the discharge of their academic functions, would expose them to the tort claims—real or imagined—of disaffected students and parents in countless numbers. . . . The ultimate consequences, in terms of public time and money, would burden them—and society—beyond calculation" (*Peter Doe v. San Francisco Unified School District,* 1976).

Reporting Child Abuse

Teachers are required by law to report suspected child abuse. Local, state, and federal child welfare agencies encourage teachers to be observant of children's appearance and behavior that might indicate symptoms of physical, emotional, or sexual abuse. Table 7.2 presents a list of physical and behavioral indicators of potential child abuse. Many communities, through their police departments or other public and private agencies, provide programs adapted for children to educate them about child abuse and to show them how to obtain help.

 TABLE
 7.2

Physical and behavioral indicators of child abuse and neglect

Signs of physical abuse

Physical Indicators

- Unexplained bruises and welts on the face, throat, upper arms, buttocks, thighs, or lower back in unusual patterns or shapes that suggest the use of an instrument (belt buckle, electrical cord) on an infant in various stages of healing and that regularly appear after an absence, the weekend, or a vacation.
- Unexplained burns or cigarette burns, especially found on the palms, the soles of feet, abdomen, buttocks; immersion burns producing "stocking" or "glove" demarcations on hands and feet; doughnut-shaped burns on buttocks or genital area.
- Rope burns.
- Infected burns indicating delay in treatment; burns in the shape of common household utensils or appliances.

Behavioral Indicators

- Behavioral extremes (withdrawal, aggression, regression, depression).
- Inappropriate or excessive fear of parent or caretaker.
- Antisocial behavior such as substance abuse, truancy, running away, fear of going home.
- Unbelievable or inconsistent explanation for injuries.
- Lies unusually still while surveying surroundings (for infants).
- Unusual shyness; wariness of physical contact.

Signs of sexual abuse

Physical Indicators

- Torn, stained, or bloody underclothes
- Frequent, unexplained sore throats; yeast or urinary infections
- Somatic complaints, including pain and irritation of the genitals
- Sexually transmitted diseases
- Bruises or bleeding from external genitalia, vagina, or anal region
- Pregnancy

Behavioral Indicators

- The victim's disclosure of sexual abuse
- Regressive behaviors (thumb sucking, bed-wetting, fear of the dark)
- Promiscuity or seductive behaviors
- Disturbed sleep patterns (recurring nightmares)
- Unusual and age-inappropriate interest in sexual matters
- Avoidance of undressing or wearing extra layers of clothes
- Sudden decline in school performance; truancy
- Difficulty in walking or sitting

Signs of emotional abuse

Physical Indicators

- Eating disorders, including obesity or anorexia
- Speech disorders (stuttering, stammering)
- Developmental delays in the acquisition of speech or motor skills
- Weight or height substantially below norm
- Flat or bald spots on head (infants)
- Nervous disorders (rashes, hives, facial tics, stomachaches)

Behavioral Indicators

- Habit disorders (biting, rocking, head banging)
- Cruel behavior; seeming to get pleasure from hurting children, adults, or animals; seeming to get pleasure from being mistreated
- Age-inappropriate behaviors (bed-wetting, wetting, soiling)
- Behavioral extremes: overly compliant–demanding; withdrawn–aggressive; listless–excitable

(continued)

TABLE 7.2   Physical and behavioral indicators of child abuse and neglect (continued)

Signs of neglect

Physical Indicators
- Poor hygiene, including lice, scabies, severe or untreated diaper rash, bedsores, body odor
- Squinting
- Unsuitable clothing; missing key articles of clothing (underwear, socks, shoes); overdressed or underdressed for climate conditions
- Untreated injury or illness
- Lack of immunizations
- Indicators of prolonged exposure to elements (excessive sunburn, insect bites, colds)
- Height and weight significantly below age level

Behavioral Indicators
- Unusual school attendance
- Chronic absenteeism
- Chronic hunger, tiredness, or lethargy
- Begging or collecting leftovers
- Assuming adult responsibilities
- Reporting no caretaker at home

Adapted from Childabuse.com. (2011). Anchorage, AK: Arctic Originals, Inc. Retrieved from http://www.childabuse.com/help.htm.

The Fourth Amendment guarantees protection against unlawful search and seizure, and on occasion, parents and guardians have alleged a Fourth Amendment violation, claiming that school personnel should not have questioned or examined a student to determine if child abuse had occurred. In a **PENNSYLVANIA** case, the court concluded that the Fourth Amendment had not been violated as a result of school personnel questioning a student about suspected abuse. According to the court, Pennsylvania's Child Protective Services Law required teachers and administrators to determine if there was "reason to believe" that a student had been abused (*Picarella v. Terrizzi,* 1995).

Schools usually have a process for dealing with suspected abuse cases that involves the school principal, a nurse, and the reporting teacher. Because a child's welfare may be further endangered when abuse is reported, caution and sensitivity are required.

Observing Copyright Laws

The continuing development of information technology has resulted in a new set of responsibilities for teachers regarding **copyright laws** pertaining to the use of photocopies, videotapes, and computer software. Congress revised the Copyright Act in 1976 by adding the doctrine of fair use. Although the fair-use doctrine cannot be precisely defined, it is generally interpreted as it was in *Marcus v. Rowley* (1983)—that is, one may "use the copyrighted material in a reasonable manner without [the copyright holder's] consent" as long as that use does not reduce the demand for the work or the author's income.

To "move the nation's copyright law into the digital age," the **Digital Millennium Copyright Act (DMCA)** amended the Copyright Act in 1998. The DMCA makes it illegal to circumvent copy-blocking measures (encryption and encoding, for example) that control access to copyrighted works. However, according to the statute, educational institutions may circumvent access control measures "solely for the purpose of making a good faith determination as to whether they wish to obtain authorized access to the work."

With the vast amount of material (in text, audio, video, and graphic formats) available over the Internet, teachers must consider copyright laws and restrictions that apply to this material. Unfortunately, the Copyright Act does not provide guidelines for the use of intellectual property found on the Internet. In any case, teachers should understand that content they view on the Internet is published material, and the doctrine of fair use applies to the use of such materials.

PHOTOCOPIES

To clarify the fair-use doctrine as it pertained to teachers photocopying instructional materials from books and magazines, Congress endorsed a set of guidelines developed by educators, authors, and publishers. These guidelines allow teachers to make single copies of copyrighted material for teaching or research, but they are more restrictive regarding the use of multiple copies. The use of multiple copies of a work must meet the tests of brevity, spontaneity, and cumulative effect.

- Brevity means that short works can be copied. Poems or excerpts cannot be longer than 250 words, and copies of longer works cannot exceed 1,000 words or 10 percent of the work (whichever is less). Only one chart or drawing can be reproduced from a book or an article.
- The criterion of spontaneity means that the teacher doing the copying would not have time to request permission from the copyright holder.
- The criterion of cumulative effect limits the use of copies to one course and limits the material copied from the same author, book, or magazine during the semester. Also, no more than nine instances of multiple copying per class are allowed during a semester.

VIDEOTAPES

Guidelines for the use of videotapes made by teachers of television broadcasts were issued by Congress in 1981. Videotaped material may be used in the classroom only once by the teacher within the first 10 days of taping. Additional use is limited to reinforcing instruction or evaluation of student learning, and the tape must be erased within 45 days.

COMPUTER SOFTWARE

With the explosion of computer-based technology in schools, teachers face a new ethical and legal issue—adhering to copyright laws as they relate to computer software. Making an illegal copy of software on a computer hard drive—in effect, stealing another person's intellectual property—is quite easy. "It is very common for otherwise ethical and moral people to ask for and/or offer illegal copies of software to one another" (Schwartz & Beichner, 1999, p. 193). It is important therefore that, as a teacher, you be an exemplar of ethical behavior regarding copyrighted computer software. Just as you would not allow students to plagiarize written material or submit work that was not their own, you should follow the same standard of behavior regarding the use of computer software.

Software publishers have become concerned about the abuse of their copyrighted material. Limited school budgets and the high cost of software have led to the unauthorized reproduction of software. To address the problem, the Copyright Act was amended in 1980 to apply the fair-use doctrine to software. Accordingly, as a teacher, you may now make one backup copy of a program. If you were to make multiple copies of software, the fair-use doctrine would be violated because the software is readily accessible for purchase and making multiple copies would substantially reduce the market for the software. Software publishers have several different options for licensing their software to schools, and you should be aware of the type of license that has been purchased with each software program you use.

The increased practice of networking computer programs—that is, storing a copy of a computer program on a network file server and serving the program to a computer on the network—is also of concern to software publishers. The practice has not yet been tested in the courts. As more public schools develop computer networks, however, the issue of networked software will most likely be debated in the courts.

Currently, the Copyright Act is being revised to reflect how the doctrine of fair use should be applied to digital data. Two questions currently not answered by copyright law as it pertains to the educational use of computer software are the legality of (1) installing a single program on several computers in a laboratory and (2) modifying the program for use in a computer network. The Copyright Act specifies four factors for determining whether use of copyrighted material constitutes **fair use** or an infringement: (1) the purpose and character of the use, including whether such use is of a commercial nature or is for nonprofit educational purposes; (2) the nature of the copyrighted work; (3) the amount and substantiality of the portion used in relation to the copyrighted work as a whole; and (4) the effect of the use on the potential market for or value of the copyrighted work.

E-MAIL AND THE INTERNET

With the huge increase in the transmission of documents via e-mail, copyright laws have been extended to cyberspace. Material published online may include a statement by the author(s) that the material is copyright-protected and may not be duplicated without permission. In other cases, the material may include a statement such as the following: "Permission is granted to distribute this material freely through electronic or by other means, provided it remains completely intact and unaltered, the source is acknowledged, and no fee is charged for it." If the material is published without restrictions on the Internet, one may assume that the author waives copyright privileges; however, proper credit and a citation should accompany the material if it is reproduced. The Technology in Action feature in this chapter explains how **virtual labs** can help students understand academic areas such as biology, astronomy, chemistry, and physics. If students use material from such sites in written papers and reports, they should be sure to cite the source of their information.

The following are guidelines for determining how much of a certain medium is considered fair to use without obtaining permission from the copyright holder:

- **Motion media**—Up to 10 percent or three minutes, whichever is less.
- **Text**—10 percent or 1,000 words, whichever is less.
- **Poems**—An entire poem up to 250 words may be used, but no more than three poems by one poet or five poems by different poets from any anthology. For longer poems, 250 words may be used.
- **Music, lyrics, and music video**—Up to 10 percent but no more than 30 seconds. Any alterations shall not change the basic melody or the character of the work.
- **Illustrations and photography**—No more than five images by an artist or a photographer.
- **Numerical data sets**—Up to 10 percent or 2,500 cell entries, whichever is less. (Green, Brown, & Robinson, 2008, p. 120)

PUBLISHING ON THE INTERNET

Thousands of teachers and their students around the globe are publishing material on their home pages on the Internet. Teacher- and student-produced materials can be copyright-protected by including a statement that the materials may not be duplicated without permission. In addition, teachers should be careful not to include information that would enable someone to identify children in a class. Children's last names should never be published, nor should photos of children be published with any identifying information.

Teachers and Online Social Networking

The rapid growth of online social networking sites like Facebook, Google+, Whatsapp, Twitter, Instagram, Reddit, Tumblr, and Windows Live, each of which has more

TECHNOLOGY in ACTION
Virtual Labs in a Ninth-Grade Biology Classroom

At this time each year, Mrs. Rajid's students start to squirm. She teaches introductory ninth-grade science, and the class will be dissecting frogs during the coming weeks. Many of her students will bring notes from their parents excusing them from the lesson. Mrs. Rajid has evidence of a direct correlation between those students who do not participate in the frog-dissecting activity and their gradual poor performance in high school science classes. She needs something to help her students understand the concepts of the lesson, rather than fixate on how "gross" it is to cut open a frog.

So, Mrs. Rajid goes on a frog-dissection webquest and finds several options; one is quite user-friendly, accessible on the web, and free. She decides to use the virtual lab (a software program that replicates the activities in a physical lab) in her next lesson, before the permission slips are sent home. The next day, she takes her students into the computer lab, has them open a web browser, and instructs them to navigate to the frog-dissection website. She then asks them to dissect their virtual frogs. A few students make comments like "Yuck" and "Gross," but the students perform quite well. They each have a frog preserved in formaldehyde; they dissect it and are able to identify the appropriate organs and structure.

Next week, when it is time to send home the permission slips for dissecting the real frog, she finds that a much higher percentage of her students are planning to participate. She also finds that her students are much better prepared to perform the real activity. They know what to do, how to do it, and what the goals of the activity are. Mrs. Rajid thinks that some day this virtual lab might indeed replace the need for the actual experience—at much less cost and with no formaldehyde smell.

VIRTUAL LABS: Virtual labs replicate activities that take place in a physical lab and deliver basic desired learning outcomes without the need for equipment, supplies, and dangerous materials. Although the effectiveness of virtual labs is debated among practitioners, there is no doubt that their growing popularity, combined with the technology enhancements of the industry, is a promising development for teachers. These labs usually take the form of interactive animation in which students make decisions, select tools, and perform actions, while the animation program responds appropriately. Some virtual labs use video, graphics, and audio to supplement the learning materials.

VISIT: http://www.sciencecentral.com/. This site is regularly updated with new tools and user ratings.

POSSIBLE USES: Teachers have successfully used virtual labs to help students understand biology, physics, astronomy, and chemistry. For example, virtual labs can allow students to practice appropriate stream restoration techniques, explore a human cadaver and perform an autopsy, and mix complex combinations of elements to see how those elements interact with one another.

TRY IT OUT: Open a web browser and search for the Directory of Science website. Click on the Biology link. Then enter "virtual frog" in the internal search engine. Several options will come up; pick the one that looks most appealing.

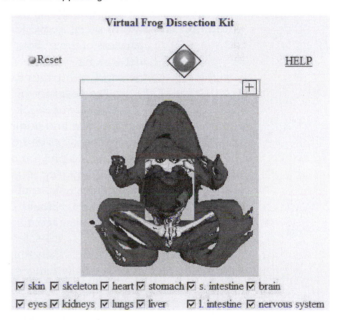

Virtual Frog Dissection Kit

Reset   HELP

☑ skin ☑ skeleton ☑ heart ☑ stomach ☑ s. intestine ☑ brain
☑ eyes ☑ kidneys ☑ lungs ☑ liver   ☑ l. intestine ☑ nervous system

Source: Copyright © 1994–2011 by Berkeley Lab. Used by permission of the Lawrence Berkeley National Lab.

---

than 100 million users, has introduced new legal and ethical concerns for teachers. Educators who use such virtual communities should realize that their postings can be seen by the public and school officials. Increasingly, the media are reporting cases of teachers being fired or disciplined because of "inappropriate" profiles on Facebook or tweets on Twitter— teachers posting personal opinions about students or uploading inappropriate pictures of themselves, for example—or inappropriate communication with students.

In Pennsylvania, a teacher was suspended after students saw photos of her on Facebook posing with a stripper. A Florida teacher was suspended after posting a note saying he "hated" his students and his school. A Washington, D.C., special education teacher faced scrutiny after school officials found this phrase about a student on her personal page: "You're a retard, but I love you." A math and science department supervisor was fired after she called her students "germ bags" on Facebook and described parents as "snobby" and "arrogant" (Sullivan, , 2010).

In some cases, teachers have encountered problems with Facebook postings made by others. Another Pennsylvania teacher was suspended for 30 days in 2010 after a friend posted a picture of her on Facebook with a stripper at a bachelorette party attended by a group of teachers. The teacher asked that the photo be removed within days, but not before it was brought to the attention of school officials. With the help of the American Civil Liberties Union (ACLU), the teacher sued her school district and won back pay (Sullivan, 2010).

Three New York City (NYC) high school teachers were fired in 2010 for having inappropriate interactions with students on Facebook—one of which culminated in a sexual relationship. One of the fired teachers, a male, "friended" several female students and wrote inappropriate comments under their Facebook photos. A female paraprofessional at an NYC high school was fired for posting a photo of her kissing an 18-year-old male former student. A male substitute teacher was barred from working in NYC schools after investigators learned that he had sent inappropriate messages to female students. Another male high school teacher, found to be giving extra credit to students who "friended" him, was not disciplined. Although New York City schools do not have a policy about teacher–student social networking, a spokeswoman said "we continually look at ways that our policies may need to evolve to keep pace with technology" (Chiaramonte & Gonen, 2010).

Some school districts in Wisconsin, New Hampshire, Ohio, and Florida have advised teachers not to "friend" students on social networking sites. For example, the Lee County School District in **FLORIDA** issued the following guidelines for teacher use of social networking sites: "It is inappropriate for employees to communicate, regardless of the reason, with current students enrolled in the district on any public social networking website. This includes becoming 'friends' or allowing students access to personal web pages for communication reasons."

The governor of **LOUISIANA** signed a law making it illegal for teachers to contact students on Facebook (Murphy, 2010). According to the governor, "It's wonderful that our teachers and administrators can now directly email our kids and work on assignments quickly over the Internet, but we cannot allow these same devices to be used as an avenue to prey on our children, out of sight of parental supervision. This new law is an important step to help protect our children from abusive and plainly inappropriate communications from educators" (Sullivan, 2010).

Schools should consider developing policies for employees' use of social networking sites, according to the Director of the Center for Safe and Responsible Internet Use: ". . . it's safer for teachers and students to be interacting on the educational plane—not a friendship plane. Socializing on Facebook can cross over into areas that are potentially dangerous" (Chiaramonte & Gonen, 2010). Similarly, an attorney for the National School Boards Association says, "If it were me, and I were a teacher, I'd say just don't do it. Don't engage in social networking with students at all. The name says it all. It's about *social* networking. Social. Those are not the kinds of relationships that teachers are supposed to have with students. . . . A wise district says to teachers that they should never engage in peer-like activity with students—ever. Every interaction between students and teacher should be professional" (Sullivan, 2010).

A 79-year-old **NEW HAMPSHIRE** teacher terminated because she had about 250 "friends" on Facebook has a different opinion, however. Upon refusing to follow school policy and "unfriend" students, the teacher said, "There's a paranoia about the Internet, and I think that we're not realizing how valuable Facebook can be [if] used properly" (Rosenfield, 2014).

WHAT ARE THE LEGAL RIGHTS OF STUDENTS AND PARENTS?

As a prospective teacher, you have an obligation to become familiar with the rights of students. Since the 1960s, students have confronted teachers and school districts more often with what they perceive to be illegal restrictions on their behavior. The following sections present brief summaries of selected major court decisions that clarify students' rights related to freedom of expression, suspension and expulsion, search and seizure, privacy, and nondiscrimination.

Freedom of Expression

The case of *Tinker v. Des Moines Independent Community School District* (1969) is perhaps the most frequently cited case concerning students' **freedom of expression**. The Supreme Court ruled in *Tinker* that three students, ages 13, 15, and 16, had been denied their First Amendment freedom of expression when they were suspended from school for wearing black armbands to protest the Vietnam War. The Court ruled that neither teachers nor students "shed their rights to freedom of speech or expression at the schoolhouse gate." In addition, the Court found no evidence that the exercise of such a right interfered with the school's operation.

CENSORSHIP

One area of student expression that has generated frequent controversy is that of student publications. Prior to 1988, the courts generally made it clear that student literature enjoyed constitutional protection and that it could be regulated only if it posed a substantial threat of school disruption, if it was libelous, or if it was judged vulgar or obscene after publication. However, school officials could use "prior **censorship**" and require students to submit literature before publication if such controls were necessary to maintain order in the school.

Within these guidelines, students frequently defended successfully their right to freedom of expression. For example, the right of high school students to place in the school newspaper an advertisement against the war in Vietnam was upheld (*Zucker v. Panitz*, 1969). Students' right to distribute information on birth control and on laws regarding marijuana was also upheld in *Shanley v. Northeast Independent School District* (1972). And other cases upheld the right of students to publish literature that was critical of teachers, administrators, and other school personnel (*Scoville v. Board of Education of Joliet Township High School District 204,* 1970, 1971; *Sullivan v. Houston Independent School District*, 1969).

In January 1988, however, the Supreme Court, in a 5–3 ruling in *Hazelwood School District v. Kuhlmeier*, departed from the earlier *Tinker* decision and gave public school officials considerable authority to censor school-sponsored student publications. The case involved a Missouri high school principal's censorship of articles in the school newspaper, the *Spectrum*, on teenage pregnancy and the impact of divorce on students. The principal believed the articles were inappropriate because they might identify pregnant students and because references to sexual activity and birth control were inappropriate for younger students. Several students on the newspaper staff distributed copies of the articles on their own and later sued the school district, claiming that their First Amendment rights had been violated.

Writing for the majority in *Hazelwood School District v. Kuhlmeier*, Justice Byron White (who had voted with the majority in *Tinker*) said school officials could bar "speech that is ungrammatical, poorly written, inadequately researched, biased or prejudiced, vulgar or profane, or unsuitable for immature audiences." White also pointed out that *Tinker* focused on a student's right of "personal expression," and the Missouri case dealt with school-sponsored publications that were part of the curriculum and bore the "imprimatur of the school." According to White, "Educators do not offend the First Amendment by exercising editorial control over the style and content of student speech in school-sponsored expressive activities so long as their actions are reasonably related to legitimate pedagogical concerns."

A case involving an attempt to regulate an underground student newspaper entitled *Bad Astra*, however, had a different outcome. Five high school students in Renton, Washington, produced a four-page newspaper at their expense, off school property, and without the knowledge of school authorities. *Bad Astra* contained articles that criticized school policies, a mock poll evaluating teachers, and several poetry selections. The students distributed 350 copies of the paper at a senior class barbecue held on school grounds.

After the paper was distributed, the principal placed letters of reprimand in the five students' files, and the district established a new policy whereby student-written, non-school-sponsored materials with an intended distribution of more than 10 were subject to pre-distribution review. The students filed suit in federal district court, claiming a violation of their First Amendment rights. The court ruled, however, that the new policy was "substantially constitutional." Maintaining that the policy was unconstitutional, the students filed an appeal in 1988 in the Ninth Circuit Court and won. The court ruled that *Bad Astra* was not "within the purview of the school's exercise of reasonable editorial control" (*Burch v. Barker,* 1987, 1988).

STUDENT EXPRESSION ON SOCIAL NETWORKING SITES

Whereas teachers are increasingly being advised not to communicate with students via social networking sites, students have few constraints to their online expression. The law is still evolving regarding what students may and may not say online about their teachers and school administrators. School districts generally have no right to control student expression off campus, unless their speech could lead to a serious disruption on campus—a riot, for example. In addition, the law is unclear about students using school computers or mobile devices while on campus to access Facebook pages that are critical of teachers and administrators (Willard, 2010).

In Florida, a student was suspended and faced other punishments for creating a Facebook fan page devoted to calling her English teacher "The worst teacher I've ever met," and inviting others to join. With help from the ACLU, the student sued and, in 2010, a U.S. District Court in Florida sided with her, forcing the school district to clear her record.

Two Pennsylvania cases similar to the Florida case resulted in different conclusions by two circuit courts. In one case, involving a middle school student who created a MySpace page insinuating that his principal was a pedophile, the court found in favor of the school, citing potential disruption. In the second case, another middle school student created a profile indicating that his principal used marijuana, and encouraged other students to do the same. Despite the fact that some of the sites were accessed on school grounds, the court found in favor of the student, saying no serious disruption of school activities occurred (Sullivan, 2010).

DRESS CODES

Few issues related to the rights of students have generated as many court cases as have dress codes and hairstyles. The demand on the courts to hear such cases prompted Supreme Court Justice Hugo L. Black to observe that he did not believe "the federal Constitution imposed on the United States Courts the burden of supervising the length of hair that public school students should wear" (*Karr v. Schmidt,* 1972). In line with Justice Black's observation, the Supreme Court has repeatedly refused to review the decisions reached by the lower courts.

In general, the courts have suggested that schools may have dress codes as long as such codes are clear and reasonable, and students are notified. However, when the legality of such codes has been challenged, the rulings have largely indicated that schools may not control what students wear unless it is immodest or is disruptive of the educational process.

Students in private schools, however, do not have First Amendment protections provided by *Tinker v. Des Moines Independent Community School District* because private schools are not state affiliated. As a result, students at private schools can be required to wear uniforms, and "[d]isagreements over 'student rights' . . . are generally resolved by applying contract law to the agreement governing the student's attendance" (LaMorte, 2008, p. 117).

At one time, educators' concerns about student appearance may have been limited to hairstyles and immodest dress; however, today's educators, as Michael LaMorte (2012, p. 141) points out, may be concerned about "T-shirts depicting violence, drugs (e.g., marijuana [leaves]), racial epithets, or characters such as Bart Simpson; ripped, baggy, or saggy pants or jeans; sneakers with lights; colored bandanas; baseball or other hats; words shaved into scalps, brightly colored hair, distinctive haircuts or hairstyles, or ponytails for males; exposed underwear; Malcolm X symbols; Walkmans, cellular phones, or beepers; backpacks; tattoos, unusual-colored lipsticks, pierced noses, or earrings; and decorative dental caps."

Because gangs, hate groups, and violence in and around public schools have become more prevalent during the last decade, rulings that favor schools are becoming more common when the courts "balance the First Amendment rights of students to express themselves against the legitimate right of school authorities to maintain a safe and disruption-free environment" (LaMorte, 2012, p. 141). This balance is clearly illustrated in *Jeglin v. San Jacinto Unified School District* (1993). In this instance, a school's dress code prohibiting the wearing of clothing with writing, pictures, or insignia of professional or college athletic teams was challenged on the grounds that it violated students' freedom of expression. The court acknowledged that the code violated the rights of elementary and middle school students, but not those of high school students. Gangs, known to be present at the high school, had intimidated students and faculty in connection with the sports-oriented clothing. The court ruled that the curtailment of students' rights did not "demand a certainty that disruption will occur, but only the existence of facts which might reasonably lead school officials to forecast substantial disruption."

After the 1999 Columbine High School shootings in Littleton, Colorado, which left 14 students and a teacher dead—including the two gunmen, who were members of a clique called the Trench Coat Mafia—many school districts made their rules for student dress more restrictive. Ten days after the shootings, a federal judge who upheld a school's decision to suspend a student for wearing a T-shirt that said "Vegan" (a vegetarian who doesn't eat animal products), said "gang attire has become particularly troubling since two students wore trench coats in the Colorado shooting." And in Jonesboro, Arkansas, where four students and a teacher were shot and killed the previous year, a group of boys and girls identifying themselves as the Blazer Mafia were suspended for 10 days (Portner, 1999).

To reduce disruption and violence in schools, some school districts now require younger students to wear uniforms. In 1994, the 90,000-student Long Beach, California, school system became the first in the nation to require K–8 students to wear uniforms. Currently, the Birmingham, Alabama; Chicago; Dayton, Ohio; Oakland, California; and San Antonio public schools require elementary-age students to wear uniforms. At the beginning of the 2002–2003 school year, Memphis took steps to become the nation's first large urban district to require all students to wear uniforms when school commissioners voted 8–1 to implement a school uniform policy for the district's 175 schools (Richard, 2002).

Between 2000 and 2010, the percentage of public schools requiring that students wear uniforms increased from 12 to 19 percent; with 10 percent of high schools requiring uniforms; 19 percent of middle schools, and 22 percent of primary schools (Robers, Kemp, & Truman, 2013). School uniform policies usually "apply to students in grades K–8 and may be either voluntary or mandatory with opt-out provisions for exemptions based on philosophical or religious objections or medical reasons" (LaMorte, 2012, p. 143). Courts have upheld mandatory school uniform policies. For example, a court ruled against a parent who challenged New York City's school uniform policy for pre-K through eighth-grade students. The parent claimed that the opt-out provision would make his daughter stick out, while the New York City Board of Education stated that the policy would "promote a more effective learning climate; foster school unity and pride; improve student performance; foster self-esteem; eliminate label competition; simplify dressing and minimize costs to parents; teach children appropriate dress and decorum in the 'workplace'; and help to improve student conduct and discipline" (*Lipsman v. New York City Board of Education*, 1999).

Due Process in Suspension and Expulsion

In February and March 1971, a total of nine students received 10-day suspensions from the Columbus, Ohio, public school system during a period of citywide unrest. One student, in the presence of his principal, physically attacked a police officer who was trying to remove a disruptive student from a high school auditorium. Four others were suspended for similar conduct. Another student was suspended for his involvement in a lunchroom disturbance that resulted in damage to school property. All nine students were suspended in accordance with Ohio law. Some of the students and their parents were offered the opportunity to attend conferences prior to the start of the suspensions, but none of the nine was given a hearing. Asserting that their constitutional rights had been denied, all nine students brought suit against the school system.

In a sharply divided 5–4 decision, the Supreme Court ruled that the students had a legal right to an education, and that this "property right" could be removed only through the application of procedural due process. The Court maintained that suspension is a "serious event" in the life of a suspended child and may not be imposed by the school in an arbitrary manner (*Goss v. Lopez*, 1975).

As a result of cases such as *Goss v. Lopez*, every state has outlined procedures for school officials to follow in the suspension and expulsion of students. In cases of short-term suspension (defined by the courts as exclusion from school for 10 days or less), the due process steps are somewhat flexible and determined by the nature of the infraction and the length of the suspension. As Figure 7.4 shows, however, long-term suspension (more than 10 days) and expulsion require a more extensive due process procedure. The disciplinary transfer of a disruptive student to an alternative school, designed to meet his or her needs, is not considered an expulsion (Alexander & Alexander, 2012; LaMorte, 2012).

In response to an increase of unruly students who disrupt the learning of others, a few districts and states have granted teachers the authority to suspend students for up to 10 days. Teachers in Cincinnati, Ohio, and Dade County, Florida, for example, have negotiated contracts that give them authority to remove disruptive students from their classrooms; however, district administrators decide how the students will be disciplined. In 1995, Indiana became the first state to grant teachers the power to suspend students, and the following year, New York's governor proposed legislation to allow teachers to remove students from their classrooms for up to 10 days for "committing an act of violence against a student, teacher, or school district employee; possessing or threatening to use a gun, knife, or other dangerous weapon; damaging or destroying school district property; damaging the personal property of teachers or other employees; or defying an order from a teacher or administrator to stop disruptive behavior" (Lindsay, 1996, p. 24).

Reasonable Search and Seizure

> You have reason to believe that a student has drugs, and possibly a dangerous weapon, in his locker. Do you, as a teacher, have the right to search the student's locker and seize any illegal or dangerous items?

According to the Fourth Amendment, citizens are protected from search and seizure conducted without a search warrant. With the escalation of drug use in schools and school-related violence, however, cases involving the legality of **search and seizure** in schools have increased. These cases suggest guidelines that you can follow if confronted with a situation such as that described here.

The case of *New Jersey v. T.L.O.* (1985) involved a 14-year-old student (T.L.O.) whom a teacher found smoking a cigarette in a restroom. The teacher took the student to the principal's office, whereupon the principal asked to see the contents of her purse. On opening the purse, the principal found a pack of cigarettes and what appeared to be drug paraphernalia and a list titled "People who owe me money." T.L.O. was arrested and later found guilty of delinquency charges.

After being sentenced to one year's probation, T.L.O. appealed, claiming that the evidence found in her purse was obtained in violation of the Fourth Amendment and that her confession to selling marijuana was tainted by an illegal search. The U.S. Supreme Court found that the search had been reasonable. The Court also developed a

FIGURE 7.4 Due process in suspension and expulsion

Suspension

1. Adequate notice must be provided to students and parents regarding the existence of rules governing student behavior. These should be clearly communicated to all affected by their implementation.
2. A record should be compiled that includes the following information:
   a. The infraction allegedly committed.
   b. The time of the alleged infraction.
   c. The place the alleged infraction occurred.
   d. Those person(s) who witnessed the alleged act.
   e. Previous efforts made to remedy the alleged misbehavior.
3. Students facing suspension should, at minimum, be provided some type of notice followed by a brief informal hearing.
4. Students should be provided either oral or written notice of charges against them, the evidence school authorities have to support the charges, and an opportunity to refute the charges.
5. Because permanent removal is not intended, no delay is necessary between the time notice is given and the time of the actual hearing. In most instances, school officials may informally discuss alleged misconduct with students immediately after it is reported.
6. During the hearing, the school official should listen to all sides of the issue. There should be adequate time provided for students to present their side of the issue without interruption.
7. Parents or guardians should be informed of the hearing and provided written notification of the action that results from the hearing. At a minimum, the written notice should include:
   a. The charge(s) brought against the student.
   b. A description of the evidence used to support the charge(s).
   c. The number of days suspended.
   d. A determination of whether suspension is an in-school or out-of-school suspension.
   e. A list of other conditions that must be net before the student returns to school (e.g., a conference with parent or guardian).
   f. A statement that informs parents or guardians that the suspension can be appealed to the district's pupil personnel director or a designee.
8. Parents or guardians should be informed by phone of the suspension, followed by written notification, which should be promptly mailed, preferably by registered mail on the day of the hearing.

Expulsion

1. Students, parents, or legal guardians should be informed based on school or district policy of specific infractions that may result in expulsion. They should also be informed of their Fourteenth Amendment rights regarding substantive and procedural due process.
2. In cases of serious misconduct for which serious disciplinary measures may be imposed, the student is entitled to written notice of the charges and has the right to a fair hearing. Written notice must be furnished to the students and parent or guardian well in advance of the actual hearing.
3. At a minimum, the following procedural steps should be considered:
   a. Written notice of charges.
   b. Right to a fair hearing.
   c. Right to inspect evidence.
   d. Right to present evidence on student's behalf.
   e. Right to legal counsel.
   f. Right to call witnesses.
   g. Right to cross-examination and to confrontation.
   h. Right against self-incrimination.
   i. Right to appeal.

Adapted from Nathan L. Essex. (2012). *School Law and the Public Schools: A Practical Guide for Educational Leaders.* Boston: Pearson, pp. 87, 90.

What are students' rights with regard to their persons, personal property, and records in school and on school grounds?
How are school districts' rights of search and seizure decided?
In what ways have students' rights to privacy been upheld?

two-pronged test of "reasonableness" for searches: (1) a school official must have a reasonable suspicion that a student has violated a law or school policy, and (2) the search must be conducted using methods that are reasonable in scope.

Another case focused on the use of trained dogs to conduct searches of 2,780 junior and senior high school students in Highland, Indiana. During a 2½- to 3-hour period, six teams with trained German shepherds sniffed the students. The dogs alerted their handlers a total of 50 times. Seventeen of the searches initiated by the dogs turned up beer, drug paraphernalia, or marijuana. Another 11 students, including 13-year-old Diane Doe, singled out by the dogs were strip-searched in the nurse's office. It turned out that Diane had played with her dog, who was in heat, that morning and that the police dog had responded to the smell of the other dog on Diane's clothing.

Diane's parents later filed suit, charging that their daughter was searched illegally. The court ruled that the use of dogs did not constitute an unreasonable search, nor did holding students in their homerooms constitute a mass detention in violation of the Fourth Amendment. The court did hold, however, that the strip searches of the students were unreasonable. The court pointed out that the school personnel did not have any evidence to suggest that Diane possessed contraband because she had emptied her pockets as requested prior to the strip search. Diane was awarded $7,500 in damages (*Doe v. Renfrow,* 1980, 1981).

Court cases involving search and seizure in school settings have maintained that school lockers are the property of the schools, not students, and may be searched by school authorities if reasonable cause exists. In addition, students may be sniffed by police dogs if school authorities have a reasonable suspicion that illegal or dangerous items may be found. Last, educators on occasion use intrusive searches, or "strip searches," when looking for drugs or weapons. Courts determine the reasonableness of such searches by considering "the student's age, the student's record and disciplinary history, the seriousness and the prevalence of the problem, and the exigency requiring an immediate warrantless search" (LaMorte, 2012, p. 137).

In general, the courts have tried to balance the school's need to obtain information and the student's right to privacy. To protect themselves from legal challenges related to searches, educators should follow guidelines that have been suggested by school law experts:

- Inform students and parents at the start of the school year of the procedures for conducting locker and personal searches.
- Base any search on "reasonable suspicion."
- Conduct any search with another staff member present.
- Avoid strip searches or mass searches of groups of students.
- Require that police obtain a search warrant before conducting a search in the school.

Some schools use drug testing as a requirement for either attendance or interscholastic participation, including sports competition, or as a means of discipline. A 1988 court case upheld a urinalysis drug test for randomly selected student athletes because those whose tests were positive were suspended only from participating in sports for a period of time and no disciplinary or academic penalties were imposed (*Schaill v. Tippecanoe School Corp.,* 1988). Similarly, the U.S. Supreme Court reversed a lower court's ruling and stated that a school district's desire to reduce drug use justified the degree of intrusion required by random tests of student athletes' urine (*Acton v. Vernonia School District,* 1995). A few school districts have attempted to implement mandatory drug testing of teachers. So far the courts have upheld the decision rendered in *Patchogue-Medford Congress of Teachers v. Board of Education of Patchogue-Medford Union Free School District* (1987) that drug testing of teachers violates the Fourth Amendment's prohibition of unreasonable searches.

Privacy

Prior to 1974, students and parents were not allowed to examine school records. On November 19, 1974, Congress passed the Family Educational Rights and Privacy Act (FERPA), which gave parents of students under 18 and students 18 and older the right to examine their school records. Every public or private educational institution must adhere to the law, known as the **Buckley Amendment**, or lose federal money.

Under the Buckley Amendment, schools must do the following:

1. Inform parents and students of their rights.
2. Provide information to parents and students about the type of educational records available and how to obtain access to them.
3. Allow parents or students to review records; request changes; request a hearing if changes are not allowed; and, if necessary, add their own explanation about the records.
4. Not give out personally identifiable information without prior written, informed consent of a parent or students.
5. Allow parents and students to see the school's record of disclosures.

The Buckley Amendment actually sets forth the minimum requirements that schools must adhere to, and many states and school districts have gone beyond these minimum guidelines in granting students access to their records. Most high schools, for example, now grant students under age 18 access to their educational records, and all students in **VIRGINIA**, elementary through secondary, are guaranteed access to their records.

EXCEPTIONS

Several exceptions are allowed by the Buckley Amendment. The teacher's gradebook, psychiatric or treatment records, notes or records written by the teacher for his or her exclusive use or to be shared with a substitute teacher, or the private notes of school law enforcement units, for example, are not normally subject to examination.

The provisions of FERPA came to the nation's attention in 2000 when Kristja Falvo challenged the practice of having students grade one another's papers (peer grading) on the grounds that it was embarrassing to her three children and resulted in grading errors. A district court disagreed and ruled in favor of the school district, maintaining that peer grading is a common school practice. However, the Tenth Circuit Court of Appeals reversed that decision and ruled that the practice of peer grading violated students' privacy because grades are entered into teachers' gradebooks and thus fit the definition of "educational records" (*Falvo v. Owasso Independent School District,* 2000). Eventually, however, the case reached the Supreme Court, which ruled 9–0 that the privacy law was not intended to protect grades on day-to-day classroom assignments and that students could grade one another's work (*Owasso Independent School District v. Falvo,* 2002).

CAMERAS IN CLASSROOMS

Another privacy-related issue emerged in 2003 when schools in Biloxi, Mississippi, became the first in the nation to use cameras to monitor activities in classrooms. Previously, some schools used cameras to monitor hallways, cafeterias, auditoriums, and parking lots.

Some observers worry that cameras in classrooms will interfere with learning activities and could be misused. Others contend that teachers' and students' privacy is violated by the use of cameras. Nevertheless, regarding the presence of 500 cameras in classrooms at the start of the school year, a Biloxi School District official pointed out: "Students, parents and teachers don't mind them at all" (Lewis, 2003).

Students' Rights to Nondiscrimination

Schools are legally bound to avoid discriminating against students on the basis of race, sex, religion, disability, sexual orientation, marital status, or infection with a disease such as HIV/AIDS that poses no threat to students. The Teachers' Voices: Being an Agent of Change feature for this chapter profiles a teacher who has developed classroom activities to promote social justice and to increase students' understanding of diversity, prejudice, and discrimination. One trend that has confronted schools with the need to develop more policies that are fair and free of discrimination has been the epidemic in teenage pregnancies.

In regard to students who are married, pregnant, or parents, the courts have been quite clear: Students in these categories may not be treated differently. A 1966 case in Texas involving a 16-year-old mother established that schools may provide separate classes or alternative schools on a voluntary basis for married and/or pregnant students. However, the district may not require such students to attend separate schools, nor may they be required to attend adult or evening schools (*Alvin Independent School District v. Cooper,* 1966).

The courts have made an about-face in their positions on whether students who are married, pregnant, or parents can participate in extracurricular activities. Prior to 1972, participation in these activities was considered a privilege rather than a right, and restrictions on those who could participate were upheld. In 1972, however, cases in Tennessee, Ohio, Montana, and Texas established the right of married students (and, in one case, a divorced student) to participate (*Holt v. Sheldon,* 1972; *Davis v. Meek,* 1972; *Moran v. School District No. 7,* 1972; and *Romans v. Crenshaw,* 1972). Since then, restrictions applicable to extracurricular activities have been universally struck down.

During the 1980s, many school districts became embroiled in controversy over the issue of how to provide for the schooling of young people with HIV/AIDS and whether school employees with HIV/AIDS should be allowed to continue working. In rulings on HIV/AIDS-related cases since then, the courts have sided with the overwhelming medical evidence that students with AIDS pose no "significant risk" of spreading the disease. "To date, courts have revealed a high degree of sensitivity to students with HIV or AIDS and to their being included in the public school mainstream" (LaMorte, 2012, p. 277). In 1987, for example, a judge prevented a Florida school district from requiring that three hemophiliac brothers who were exposed to HIV/AIDS through transfusions be restricted to homebound instruction (*Ray v. School District of DeSoto County,* 1987).

To stem the spread of HIV/AIDS, school systems in many large cities—New York, Los Angeles, San Francisco, and Seattle, to name a few—have initiated programs to distribute condoms to high school students. New York's condom-distribution program, which initially did not require parental consent, was challenged in 1993 (*Alfonso v. Fernandez*). The court ruled that the program was a "health issue" and that the district could not dispense condoms without prior parental approval. The court maintained that the program violated parents' due process rights under the Fourteenth Amendment to raise their children as they see fit; however, the program did not violate parents' or students' freedom of religion. Three years later, however, the U.S. Supreme Court declined to review a Massachusetts high court ruling that upheld a school board's decision to place condom machines in high school restrooms and allow junior- and senior-level students to request condoms from the school nurse (*Curtis v. School Committee of Falmouth,* 1995, 1996).

WHAT ARE SOME ISSUES IN THE LEGAL RIGHTS OF SCHOOL DISTRICTS?

Clearly, the law touches just about every aspect of education in the United States today. The media remind us daily that ours is an age of litigation; no longer are school districts as protected as they once were from legal problems. Corporal punishment, sexual harassment, religious expression, and homeschooling are among the issues in the legal rights of school districts.

Watch educators discuss the legal rights of school districts regarding special education.

TEACHERS' VOICES ➡ BEING AN AGENT OF CHANGE

SUSIE RENNER

TEACHING FOR SOCIAL JUSTICE

I am an eighth-grade language arts teacher in Durham, New Hampshire. My students have grown up in an environment where there is very little exposure to ethnic, racial, or LGBT (lesbian, gay, bisexual, and transgender) communities. They are ripe for learning, and are in a unique position to "be" the change.

To foster a better understanding of diversity, prejudice, and discrimination, I created a social justice unit based on readings in varied genres of literature. We begin with an overview and discussions based on segments of various videos such as *If You Cried, You Died, The Long Walk Home,* and *Come See the Paradise.* Each student chooses a topic that focuses on one particular group of people who have suffered prejudice and discrimination. Last year, student choices included American Indians, African Americans, American Muslims, Japanese-Americans during World War II, LGBT issues, Latinos, and European Jews during the Holocaust.

Once students choose a topic, they are required to read nonfiction overviews, primary sources such as diaries and letters, a book (historical fiction, a biography, or an autobiography) as well as poetry written by survivors of prejudice. As they read independently in class, students share excerpts that powerfully reflect what it feels like to experience prejudice and discrimination. They also copy these excerpts into their notes, in preparation for their writing piece.

When students finish their readings, they write a three- to five- page story based on the literature. These stories must be told from the first-person perspective, and must reflect what it is like to experience prejudice. Stories can be in the form of a narrative, journal, letters or poetry. Students weave excerpts

from the literature into their writing, and cite their sources. They then share their writing with one another, to teach or learn about other topics. Some years, younger students at our middle school are invited into our classroom, so that my eighth graders can share their knowledge with them.

As a culminating activity, I partner with the Office of Multicultural Affairs at the University of New Hampshire, and invite a panel of college students to spend the day in my classroom. The students are of varied ethnicities, sexual orientations, and races. The panel presents its own stories, invites questions, and fosters powerful discussions. At the end of this study, I ask my students to write reflections of the entire unit for their portfolios. Their thoughts and feelings show the enormous impact that this study can have on young peoples' perspectives. In fact, former students who come back to visit years later comment on the impact that this study had on their approach to tolerance and intolerance.

PERSONAL REFLECTION

1. What personal experiences have helped you develop a better understanding of diversity, prejudice, and discrimination?

2. Regarding the grade level and subject area for which you are preparing to teach, what classroom activities can you use to teach for social justice?

3. What action(s) should a teacher take if he or she observes in the school an instance of discrimination or prejudice toward others on the basis of race, gender, religion, disability, or sexual orientation?

Susie Renner teaches at Oyster River Middle School in Durham, **NEW HAMPSHIRE.** This feature is based on her article that appeared in *Teaching Tolerance,* Fall 2010, p. 15.

Corporal Punishment

The practice of **corporal punishment** has had a long and controversial history in education in the United States. Currently, policies regarding the use of corporal punishment vary widely from state to state, and even from district to district.

Critics believe that corporal punishment "is neither a necessary nor an effective response to misbehavior" (Slavin, 2015, p. 287), and some believe that the practice is "archaic, cruel, and inhuman and an unjustifiable act on the part of the state" (LaMorte, 2012, p. 124). In spite of such arguments against its effectiveness, corporal punishment continues to be widespread. Nevertheless, almost half of the states and many school districts currently ban corporal punishment, and many others restrict its use (Alexander & Alexander, 2012; LaMorte, 2012).

The most influential Supreme Court case involving corporal punishment is *Ingraham v. Wright,* decided in 1977. In Dade County, Florida, in October 1970, junior high school students James Ingraham and Roosevelt Andrews were paddled with a wooden paddle. Both students received injuries as a result of the paddlings, with Ingraham's being the more severe. Ingraham, who was being punished for being slow to respond to a teacher's directions, refused to assume the "paddling position" and had to be held over a desk by two assistant principals while the principal administered 20 "licks." As a result, Ingraham "suffered a hematoma requiring medical attention and keeping him out of school for several days."

The Court had two significant questions to rule on in *Ingraham*: Does the Eighth Amendment's prohibition of cruel and unusual punishment apply to corporal punishment in the schools? Second, if it does not, should the due process clause of the Fourteenth Amendment provide any protection to students before punishment is administered? In regard to the first question, the Court, in a sharply divided 5–4 decision, ruled that the Eighth Amendment was not applicable to students being disciplined in school, only to persons convicted of crimes. On the question of due process, the Court said, "We conclude that the Due Process clause does not require notice and a hearing prior to the imposition of corporal punishment in the public schools, as that practice is authorized and limited by the common law." The Court also commented on the severity of the paddlings in *Ingraham* and said that, in such cases, school personnel "may be held liable in damages to the child and, if malice is shown, they may be subject to criminal penalties."

Although the Supreme Court has upheld the constitutionality of corporal punishment, many districts around the country have instituted policies banning its use. Where corporal punishment is used, school personnel are careful to see that it meets minimum criteria that have emerged from other court cases involving corporal punishment:

- Specific warning is given about what behavior may result in corporal punishment.
- Evidence exists that other measures attempted failed to bring about the desired change in behavior.
- Administration of corporal punishment takes place in the presence of a second school official.
- On request, a written statement is provided to parents explaining the reasons for the punishment and the names of all witnesses. (Dunklee & Shoop, 2006, p. 154)

Sexual Harassment

Although few victims report it, 80 percent of students in a national survey reported that they had been sexually harassed, and one in three said they experienced it "often" (American Association of University Women, 2002, p. III-2). Another survey found that 64 percent of lesbian, gay, bisexual, or transgender (LGBT) students fear for their safety while at school, and about two-thirds were sexually harassed (Kosciw & Diaz, 2006). Currently, nine states have anti-bullying policies that specifically mention sexual orientation (Robinson, February/March 2008, p. 58).

In addition to harassment by the opposite sex, same-sex harassment, usually against **lesbian, gay, bisexual, and transgender (LGBT) students**, is a problem at some schools. Since the mid-1990s, several school districts have faced lawsuits filed by gay and lesbian students who claimed that school officials failed to protect them from verbal and physical antigay harassment.

In *Flores v. Morgan Hill Unified School District* (2003), several students claimed their school did not respond adequately to a seven-year period of anti-homosexual harassment they endured. In its ruling that teachers and administrators failed to enforce the school district's anti-harassment and anti-discrimination policies, the Court stated, "The record contains sufficient evidence for a jury to conclude that the defendants intentionally discriminated against the plaintiffs in violation of the Equal Protection Clause." The school district eventually agreed to pay $1.1 million to six of the students.

On the other hand, the courts have been reluctant to hold school districts liable unless the harassment was foreseeable and preventable, and they deliberately failed to intervene. School districts were not found liable for damages in the following cases: Student aides videotaped the girls' locker room and bathrooms over a two-year period

(*Harry A. v. Duncan,* 2005); a student received a punch intended for another student (*Mohammed ex rel. Mohammed v. School District of Philadelphia,* 2005); a student was verbally harassed due to ancestry and race (*Yap v. Oceanside Union Free School District,* 2004).

Regarding **sexual harassment** of students by educators, the courts have generally ruled that school districts may be held liable if the district knew or should have known of the harassment. In one case, *Franklin v. Gwinnett County Public Schools* (1992), the Supreme Court found a school district liable because district administrators knew that a teacher had repeatedly sexually abused a student and took no steps to stop the harassment. The Court ruled that the student could collect damages for sexual harassment under Title IX of the Education Act of 1972. In *Gebser v. Lago Vista Independent School District* (1998), however, the Supreme Court ruled that a school district was not liable for damages resulting from teacher-to-student harassment, unless a school official with "authority to institute corrective measures on the district's behalf has actual notice of, and is deliberately indifferent to, the teacher's misconduct."

Increased reports of sexual harassment of students by educators and the Supreme Court ruling in *Franklin v. Gwinett County Public Schools* are causing some teachers to be apprehensive about working closely with students and, particularly, touching them. In a few instances, teachers have even reported that they fear being falsely accused of sexual harassment by angry, disgruntled students. To address the problem, many school districts have suggested guidelines that teachers can follow to show concern for students, offer them encouragement, and congratulate them for their successes. Frequently, these guidelines also advise teachers to avoid behaviors such as touching or hugging that a student may experience as sexual harassment.

Cyberbullying and the Law

Cyberbullies, unlike traditional face-to-face bullies, make use of social networking sites, cell phones, instant messaging, camera phones, e-mail, and various sites on the Internet. They can bully their victims any time, from anywhere; and their user name, screen name, or stolen identity allows them to remain anonymous.

They bully their victims via text messages, postings on social networking sites like Facebook (or the more vitriolic Snubster, EnemyBook, Juicy Campus, and HateBook), and discussions in online chat rooms. They forward e-mail messages to huge groups of friends and post embarrassing, sometimes altered, photographs and video clips of their victims to the Internet. In some instances, students hack into other students' e-mail accounts or social networking sites and create havoc by sending hateful messages or posting inflammatory content that appears to have been authored by their victims (Bissonette, 2009). Figure 7.5 presents several forms of cyberbullying and examples.

By early 2012, 46 states had anti-bullying laws; 36 of these specifically prohibited cyberbullying, and "13 grant schools the authority to address off-campus behavior that creates a hostile school environment" (*Deskbook Encyclopedia of American School Law,* 2013, p. 1). An example of anti-bullying legislation is the Anti-Bullying Bill of Rights Act in **NEW JERSEY**, which requires each school to appoint an anti-bullying specialist and anti-bullying coordinator, as well as form a school safety team.

In a "Dear Colleague" letter sent to the nation's schools, the U.S. Department of Education stressed the need for schools to address bullying:

> Bullying of any student by another student, for any reason, cannot be tolerated in our schools. Bullying is no longer dismissed as an ordinary part of growing up, and every effort should be made to structure environments and provide supports to students and staff so that bullying does not occur. Teachers and adults should respond quickly and consistently to bullying

FIGURE 7.5   Forms of cyberbullying and examples

Flaming. Online fights using electronic messages with angry and vulgar language. *Joe and Alec's online exchange got angrier and angrier. Insults were flying. Joe warned Alec to watch his back in school the next day.*

Harassment. Repeatedly sending nasty, mean, and insulting messages. *Sara reported to the principal that Kayla was bullying another student. When Sara got home, she had 35 angry messages on her social networking profile. Some from complete strangers.*

Denigration. "Dissing" someone online. Sending or posting gossip or rumors about a person to damage his or her reputation or friendships. *Some students created a "We Hate Joe" group where they posted jokes, cartoons, gossip, and rumors, all dissing Joe.*

Impersonation. Pretending to be someone else and sending or posting material to get that person in trouble or danger or to damage that person's reputation or friendships. *Laura watched closely as Emma logged on to her account and discovered her password. Later, Laura logged on to Emma's account and sent a hurtful message to Emma's boyfriend, Adam.*

Outing. Sharing someone's secrets or embarrassing information or images online. *Greg, an obese high school student, was changing in the locker room after gym class. Matt took a picture of him with his cell phone camera. Within seconds, the picture was flying around the phones at school.*

Trickery. Talking someone into revealing secrets or embarrassing information, then sharing it online. *John sent a message to Jessica pretending to be interested in her. Over a few days, Jessica responded, ultimately sharing intimate personal information and a very provocative image. John then sent this image to many other people.*

Exclusion. Intentionally and cruelly excluding someone from an online group. *Millie tries hard to fit in with a group of girls at school. She recently got on the "outs" with a leader in this group. All of the girls have now deleted their friendship links to her social networking profile.*

Cyberstalking. Repeated, intense harassment and denigration that includes threats or creates significant fear. *When Annie broke up with Sam, he sent her many angry, threatening, pleading messages. He spread nasty rumors about her to her friends and posted a sexually suggestive picture she had given him in a sex-oriented discussion group, along with her e-mail address and cell phone number.*

Sexting. Sending nude sexy images and messages electronically. *Jessica was with a couple of friends. They all took nude sexy images of each other. Jessica sent some to her boy friend. Then they broke up. He was angry and sent her images to other students.*

Adapted from Willard, N. (2011). *Educator's Guide to Cyberbullying, Cyberthreat and Sexting.* Center for Safe and Responsible Use of the Internet. Retrieved February 9, 2011, from http://www.csriu.org/documents/documents/educatorsguide.pdf

behavior and send a message that bullying is not acceptable. Intervening immediately to stop bullying on the spot can help ensure a safer school environment . . . .

Addressing and reporting bullying is critical. Students who are targets of bullying behavior are more likely to experience lower academic achievement and aspirations, higher truancy rates, feelings of alienation from school, poor relationships with peers, loneliness, or depression. Bystanders, or those who only see or hear about bullying, also may be negatively affected as bullying tends to have harmful effects on overall school climate. Bullying can foster fear and disrespect and negatively affect the school experience, norms, and relationships of all students, families, and school personnel. (U.S. Department of Education, Office of Special Education and Rehabilitative Services, 2013)

Existing case law on free speech and sexual harassment does not readily apply to cyberbullying, and the limited court rulings to date have been inconsistent. As two school law experts note, "In the face of modern technology, school officials have daunting difficulties in protecting the students and the decorum of the schools. As with school officials, the judges who sit in [cyberbullying] cases find themselves largely applying 'horse and buggy laws' to modern technology" (Alexander & Alexander, 2012, p. 443).

Increasingly, though, students who are cyberbullied and their parents are filing lawsuits that name schools as defendants (Bissonette, 2009). Schools are "in a legal quandary. If they punish a student for something they did off school grounds, they could get hit with a freedom of speech claim. If they do nothing, they could get hit with failure to act litigation" (Baldas, 2007).

One case of cyberbullying was *J.C. v. Beverly Hills Unified School District* (2009). In this case, J.C. created a video of several other students disparaging C.C. and posted this video on YouTube. C.C. and her mother brought the video to the attention of the school, and J.C. was suspended.

In response to the suspension, J.C. filed suit. Eventually, the district court decided to apply the *Tinker* standard and upheld J.C.'s freedom of expression. The court decided that substantial disruption of school activities did not occur, nor was it foreseeable. The results of J.C. indicate that when districts sanction students for cyberbullying, they must be prepared to present reasonable evidence of interference with the education of the bullied student.

Religious Expression

Conflicts over the proper role of religion in schools are among the most heated in the continuing debate about the character and purposes of education in the United States. Numerous school districts have found themselves embroiled in legal issues related to school prayer, Bible reading, textbooks, creationism, intelligent design, singing of Christmas carols, distribution of religious literature, New Age beliefs, secular humanism, religious holidays, use of school buildings for religious meetings, and the role of religion in moral education, to name a few. On the one hand, conservative religious groups wish to restore prayer and Christian religious practices in the public schools; on the other hand, secular liberals see religion as irrelevant to school curricula and maintain that public schools should not promote religion. In addition, somewhere between these two positions are those who believe that although schools should not be involved in the *teaching of* religion, they should *teach about* religion.

EVOLUTION VERSUS CREATIONISM AND INTELLIGENT DESIGN

Issues related to religious expression in the schools have been most heated in regard to the teaching of evolution in science classes. School law experts Kern Alexander and M. David Alexander (2012, p. 381) explain how efforts to diminish the teaching of evolution and advance the teaching of creationism in schools have changed over the years:

> The efforts of Christian Fundamentalists to insert the biblical Book of Genesis' explanation into the teaching of science in the public school classrooms evolved in stages from direct state prohibitions to teaching Darwinian evolution, to teaching creation as a science, to balanced treatment of both creationism and evolution, and finally to the latest intelligent design movement (IDM).

LEGAL RULINGS

Scores of court cases have addressed school activities related to the First Amendment principle of separation of church and state. As two education law experts put it: "By far the most common constitutional objection raised against a school program is that it fails to respect the wall of separation between church and state" (Imber & van Geel, 2010, p. 16). In one of these landmark cases (*Engel v. Vitale*, 1962), the U.S. Supreme Court ruled that recitation of a prayer said in the presence of a teacher at the beginning of each school day was unconstitutional and violated the First Amendment, which states: "Congress shall make no law respecting an establishment of religion, or prohibiting the free exercise thereof." Justice Hugo Black, who delivered the opinion of the Court, stated, "[I]t is no part of the business of government to compose official prayers for any group of the American people to recite as a part of a religious program carried on by government."

The following year, the U.S. Supreme Court ruled that Bible reading and reciting the Lord's Prayer in school were unconstitutional (*School District of Abington Township v. Schempp,* 1963). In response to the district's claim that unless these religious activities were permitted, a "religion of secularism" would be established, the Court stated, "[W]e agree of course that the State may not establish a 'religion of secularism' in the sense of affirmatively opposing or showing hostility to religion, thus 'preferring those who believe in no religion over those who do believe.' We do not agree, however, that this decision in any sense has that effect."

To determine whether a state has violated the separation of church and state principle, the courts refer to the decision rendered in *Lemon v. Kurtzman* (1971). In this instance, the U.S. Supreme Court struck down an attempt by the Rhode Island legislature to provide a 15 percent salary supplement to teachers of secular subjects in nonpublic schools and Pennsylvania legislation to provide financial supplements to nonpublic schools through reimbursement for teachers' salaries, texts, and instructional materials in certain secular subjects. According to the three-part test enunciated in *Lemon v. Kurtzman,* governmental practices "must (1) have a secular legislative purpose; (2) have a principal or primary effect that neither advances nor inhibits religion; and (3) not foster an excessive entanglement with religion" (LaMorte, 2012, p. 33). Although criticized vigorously by several Supreme Court justices since 1971, the so-called **Lemon test** has not been overruled. Table 7.3 presents additional selected U.S. Supreme Court cases related to religion and schools.

Since the mid-1990s, lower courts have heard several cases addressing the question of whether parents' right to direct their children's upbringing meant they could demand curricula and learning activities that were compatible with their religious beliefs. Without exception, the courts have rejected parent-rights cases against the schools. Those rights, according to a U.S. Court of Appeals ruling in support of a schoolwide assembly on HIV/AIDS, "do not encompass a broad-based right to restrict the flow of information in the public schools" (*Brown v. Hot, Sexy and Safer Productions, Inc.,* 1996). In a similar case, parents objected to a Massachusetts school district's policy of distributing condoms to junior and senior high school students who requested them. The state's Supreme Judicial Court rejected the parent-rights argument and their argument that the program infringed on their First Amendment right to free exercise of religion: "Parents have no right to tailor public school programs to meet their individual religious or moral preferences" (*Curtis v. School Committee of Falmouth,* 1995).

Efforts to replace teaching of creationism in science classrooms with intelligent design (ID) theory have been similarly rejected by the courts. In a case that received nationwide attention, *Kitzmiller v. Dover Area School District* (2005), a federal court struck down an attempt by the Dover, Pennsylvania, School Board to insert the teaching of intelligent design in the classroom. The court concluded that ID is not science:

> We find that ID fails on three different levels, any one of which is sufficient to preclude a determination that ID is science. They are (1) ID violates centuries-old ground rules of science by invoking and permitting supernatural causation; (2) the argument of irreducible complexity, central to ID, employs the same flawed and illogical contrived dualism that doomed creation science in the 1980s; and (3) ID's negative attacks on evolution have been refuted by the scientific community.

TABLE 7.3 Selected U.S. Supreme Court cases related to religion and schools (listed in chronological order)

Epperson v. Arkansas (1968): Court overturned the state's anti-evolution statute on the grounds that a state may not deny students access to scientific information because of religious convictions.

Wisconsin v. Yoder (1972): Court decision exempted Amish children from mandatory school attendance beyond the eighth grade if the Amish provided a structured vocational training program for their children.

Mueller v. Allen (1983): Court upheld Minnesota's tax deductions for expenses incurred while sending children to secular elementary or secondary schools.

Wallace v. Jaffree (1985): Court invalidated Alabama's school-sponsored moment of silence in Mobile, Alabama.

Edwards v. Aguillard (1987): Court overturned Louisiana's requirement that equal time be devoted to evolution and creationism.

Stone v. Graham (1990): Court ruled that a Kentucky law mandating the posting of the Ten Commandments in public school classrooms was designed to advance a particular faith, thus violating the First Amendment's establishment of religion clause.

Board of Education of Westside Community Schools v. Mergens (1990): Court upheld the legality of the Equal Access Act (1984), which allowed student religious groups to meet in public secondary schools during noninstructional time.

Zobrest v. Catalina Foothills School District (1993): Court ruled that parochial school sign-language interpreters paid with public funds did not violate the First Amendment.

Agostini v. Felton (1997): Decision overturned the *Aguilar v. Felton* (1985) ruling that prohibited public school employees from providing remedial instruction in sectarian institutions. The *Agostini* ruling focused on Title I of the Elementary and Secondary Education Act of 1965, which required that comparable services be offered to parochial school pupils.

Mitchell v. Helms (2000): Court allowed the use of government funds to provide instructional materials to religious schools.

Santa Fe Independent School District v. Jane Doe (2000): Court ruled that a Texas school district's policy of allowing voluntary student-initiated and student-led invocations before football games violated the establishment clause of the First Amendment.

Good News Club v. Milford Central School (2001): Court ruled that a public school could not deny a Christian group from meeting in the school after hours; if a district allows community groups to use the school, it cannot deny use to religious groups.

GUIDELINES FOR RELIGIOUS ACTIVITIES IN SCHOOLS

In 2003, the U.S. Department of Education issued federal guidelines requiring school districts to allow students and teachers to engage in religious activities, including prayer, at school. Districts that violate the rules—or fail to promise in writing that they will comply with the guidelines—risk the loss of federal education funds. The following points are included in the guidelines:

- Students may "read their Bibles or other scriptures, say grace before meals, and pray or study religious materials with fellow students during recess, the lunch hour or other non-instructional time."
- Teachers should not discriminate against students who "express their beliefs about religion in homework, artwork, and other written and oral assignments."
- In certain circumstances, schools may have to grant parental requests to "excus[e] students from class" for religious reasons.
- Teachers and other school employees, "when acting in their official capacities as representatives of the state," cannot encourage or participate in prayer activities with students. Before school or during lunch, however, school employees are free to meet with other employees for prayer or Bible study (*NEA Today*, 2003, p. 13).

Today's students come from families with diverse religious backgrounds. What challenges do schools face in educating students from diverse religious backgrounds? How can teachers be sure they do not discriminate against students from religious backgrounds that differ from their own?

Homeschooling

One spin-off of the public's heightened awareness of the problems that schools face has been the decision by some parents to educate their children in the home. Although most homeschoolers view homeschooling as an opportunity to provide their children with a curriculum based on religious values, many homeschoolers are motivated not by religious doctrine but by concern about issues such as school violence, poor academic quality, or peer pressure. According to the National Center for Education Statistics, approximately 1,770,000 students are homeschooled in the United States (about 3.4 percent of the school-age population). Sixty-eight percent of homeschooled students are White, 15 percent are Hispanic, 8 percent are Black, and 4 percent are Asian or Pacific Islander (Noel, Stark & Redford, 2013).

Homeschooling is legal in all the states and the District of Columbia; however, how it is regulated, and whether resources are allocated, vary greatly. In most states, homeschoolers must demonstrate that their instruction is "equivalent" to that offered in the public schools, a standard set in *New Jersey v. Massa* (1967). Additional requirements may include participation in standardized testing, a minimum number of hours of instruction, submission of attendance records and lesson plans, adherence to a minimum curriculum, and minimum academic credentials for parents or guardians (LaMorte, 2012).

Legal support for homeschooling has been mixed. In 1998, a Massachusetts court ruled that home visits by a local superintendent were not a valid requirement for approval by school officials of a homeschooling program (*Brunelle v. Lynn Public Schools*, 1998). In 1993 and 1994, legislation to require homeschool teachers to be state certified was defeated in South Dakota and Kansas, and similar laws were overturned in Iowa and North Dakota. However, a federal district court upheld a West Virginia statute making children ineligible for homeschooling if their standardized test scores fell below the 40th percentile (*Null v. Board of Education*, 1993). In Iowa, mandatory homeschooling reports to the state were upheld in *State v. Rivera* (1993); homeschoolers in that state must submit course outlines and weekly lesson plans, and provide the amount of time spent on areas of the curriculum. A Maryland law requiring the state's monitoring of homeschooling was upheld despite a parent's claim that the state's curriculum promoted atheism, paganism, and evolution (*Battles v. Anne Arundel County Board of Education*, 1996). And courts have not been sympathetic to homeschoolers who would like to have their children participate in extracurricular activities or other after-school activities (for example, *Swanson v. Guthrie Independent School District No. 1*, 1998).

As the preceding cases related to homeschooling show, school law is not static—instead, it is continually evolving and changing. The legal issues examined in this chapter make it clear that the law touches just about every aspect of the teacher's professional life. Ours is an age of litigation, and the teacher is no longer quite as free as in the past to determine what happens behind the closed classroom door.

Although the review of school law in this chapter has answered some of the more common questions teacher education students have about their rights and responsibilities as a teacher, it may have made you aware of other questions for which you need answers. Because school law is constantly changing and laws pertaining to education vary from state to state, you may wish to consult current publications on school law in your state.

SUMMARY

Why Do You Need to Know About Education and the Law?

- Federal and state legislation and court decisions affect the daily lives of teachers, and teachers must have knowledge of school law to protect their rights and the rights of students.

Why Do You Need a Professional Code of Ethics?

- A professional code of ethics guides teachers' actions, helps them see beyond the short-range consequences of their actions to the long-range consequences, and helps them respond appropriately to ethical dilemmas in the classroom.
- Ethical decisions (1) are supported by evidence, (2) aim at ends that ought to be aimed at, (3) can be implemented morally, and (4) are legitimately achieved.

What Are Your Legal Rights as a Teacher?

- The right to due process protects teachers from arbitrary treatment by school districts and education officials regarding certification, nondiscrimination, contracts, tenure, dismissal, and academic freedom.
- The constitutional rights of teachers must be balanced against a school's need to promote its educational goals.

Do Student Teachers Have the Same Rights as Teachers?

- Student teachers should be aware that a potential for liability exists for them just as it does with certified teachers, and they should clarify their rights and responsibilities prior to beginning student teaching.

What Are Your Legal Responsibilities as a Teacher?

- Teachers are responsible for meeting the terms of their teaching contracts, including providing for their students' safety and well-being.
- Three legal responsibilities that concern teachers are avoiding tort liability, recognizing the physical and behavioral indicators of child abuse and then reporting suspected instances of such abuse, and observing copyright laws for instructional materials used in the classroom.
- Teachers' use of online social networking sites like Facebook, MySpace, and Twitter has introduced new legal and ethical concerns for teachers. Increasingly, school districts are advising teachers not to "friend" students on social networking sites and reminding them that their postings can be seen by the public and school officials.

What Are the Legal Rights of Students and Parents?

- Generally, students' freedom of expression can be limited if it is disruptive of the educational process or incongruent with the school's mission.
- The courts have indicated that students have few constraints to their online expression. School districts generally have no right to control student expression off campus and on social networking sites, unless their speech could lead to a serious disruption on campus.
- Students can be neither suspended nor expelled without due process.
- Courts have developed a two-pronged test for search and seizure actions involving students: (1) School officials must have "reasonable" suspicion that a student has violated a law or school policy, and (2) the search must be done using methods that are reasonable and appropriate given the nature of the infraction.
- Under the Buckley Amendment, students have the right to examine their school records, and schools may not give third parties information about students without the students' prior written consent.
- Schools may not discriminate against students on the basis of race, sex, religion, disability, marital status, or infection with a noncommunicable disease such as HIV/AIDS.

What Are Some Issues in the Legal Rights of School Districts?

- Some states and school districts allow the use of corporal punishment if it meets criteria that have emerged from other court cases involving corporal punishment.
- School officials can be held responsible if they fail to act on reports of sexual harassment of students by their peers or by professional staff. School officials also can be held responsible if they fail to take steps to protect gay and lesbian students from antigay harassment.
- To bully others, cyberbullies use social networking sites, cell phones, instant messaging, camera phones, e-mail, and various sites on the Internet. Existing case law on free speech and sexual harassment does not readily apply to cyberbullying; however, there is a trend for students who are cyberbullied to file lawsuits that name schools as defendants.
- The First Amendment principle of separation of church and state has been applied to numerous court cases involving religious expression in the public schools. In 2003, the U.S. Department of Education issued guidelines outlining religious activities that are allowed at school.
- Homeschooling is legal in all states, although most require homeschoolers to demonstrate that their instruction is equivalent to that in public schools.

PROFESSIONAL REFLECTIONS AND ACTIVITIES

Teacher's Journal

1. Read the National Education Association's Code of Ethics for Teachers, which is available on the Internet. Regarding Principle I, a teacher's commitment to students, describe a situation you have observed or experienced in which you think a teacher may have violated this principle. Regarding Principle II, a teacher's commitment to the profession, describe a situation in which a teacher might have violated that principle. What are your goals for ethical conduct as a teacher?

2. How can you accommodate students in your classroom who may come from backgrounds with worldviews that differ from Christianity—for example, Islam, Judaism, Buddhism, or a naturalistic worldview that is free of supernatural and mystical elements?

3. What limits do you believe should be placed on *what* teachers teach? On *how* they teach? Which of the legal cases on academic freedom discussed in this chapter support your views?

Teacher's Research

1. Go to the American Bar Association's website, where you can access its journal, a database of court decisions, and analyses of many of those decisions. Read the complete court decision for one or more legal cases mentioned in this chapter. After reading the case, do you agree with the court's decision? Why or why not?

2. Go to the websites for the National Education Association and the American Federation of Teachers. What legal information related to the legal issues discussed in this chapter do these sites provide for teachers?

Observations and Interviews

1. Interview an experienced teacher about the legal rights of teachers. Ask this teacher for examples of situations for which it was important that he or she (or another teacher) was familiar with the legal rights of teachers.

2. Interview another experienced teacher about the legal responsibilities of teachers. Ask this teacher for examples of situations in which it was important that he or she (or another teacher) was familiar with the legal responsibilities of teachers.

3. During an observation of a teacher's day, identify an ethical dilemma that the teacher confronts. Describe the dilemma and the teacher's response in a journal entry.

Professional Portfolio

Survey a group of students, teachers, and/or parents regarding a legal issue in education.

Among the legal issues and questions you might address are the following:

- Should tenure for teachers be abolished? Does tenure improve the quality of the education that students receive?
- Under what circumstances should restrictions be placed on what teachers teach and how they teach?
- Should parents be allowed to provide homeschooling for their children?
- Are parents justified in filing educational malpractice suits if their children fail to achieve in school?
- Under what circumstances should restrictions be placed on students' freedom of expression?
- Should schools have the right to implement dress codes? Guidelines for students' hairstyles? School uniforms?
- Should corporal punishment be banned? If not, under what circumstances should it be used?
- How should schools combat the problem of sexual harassment?
- To combat drug abuse, should schools implement mandatory drug testing of students? Of teachers?

- Should students have access to their educational records? Should their parents or guardians?
- As part of an HIV/AIDS prevention program, should condoms be distributed to high school students? Should parental approval be required for participation?

The report summarizing the results of your survey should include demographic information such as the following for your sample of respondents: gender, age, whether they have children in school, level of education, and so on. When you analyze the results, look for differences related to these variables.

CHAPTER QUIZ

Take this quiz to check your understanding of the content covered in this chapter.

PART THREE
THE ART OF TEACHING

DEAR MENTOR This summer I am about to start my college career at Ohio State University. I hope to stay in the Columbus area to teach after I graduate with my bachelor's degree in middle childhood education. Throughout my high school career, I had a few teaching experiences. As a result of these experiences, I have a few questions that you may help me answer and thus increase my success as a teacher.

- How do teachers develop effective classroom management techniques and learn to respond effectively to students' misbehavior when it occurs?
- What should be considered when developing a lesson plan?
- How do teachers develop a community of learners?
- How do teachers set an efficient pace for learning when the classroom is a mix of advanced students and those who are behind in their learning?
- How will I keep up with newly emerging technologies that teachers are expected to master?

I realize that you may not be able to answer all my questions; however, anything you have learned from your teaching experiences will be greatly appreciated. I look forward to your response.

THANK YOU, RICHARD PATTERSON

DEAR RICHARD

You ask many good questions. I agree; reflecting on these questions now will increase your success as a teacher.

Developing effective classroom management techniques and responding effectively really begins when your students walk through your door the first day. You need to immediately lay the foundation for mutual respect. Engaging your students in helping to develop classroom expectations and consequences, and making sure they understand these, establishes the groundwork for classroom management.

Getting to know your students—where they come from and their values and beliefs—will be invaluable in gaining their respect and developing a community of learners. Once they know they can trust you to be fair and a good listener, you will find that there are more positive behaviors than negative. Through building trust, you are building a community of learners.

I also recommend that you engage parent volunteers. This provides an opportunity to let parents be involved in their children's education, and it provides you with extra help for one-on-one or small-group intervention.

Establishing clear expectations and then making sure students are aware of the learning targets will create an atmosphere of ownership and achievement. When I develop my lesson plans, I collaborate with my colleagues on the year-long plan. Big units are developed from our state standards and essential learning skills, from which weekly learning targets are established. Using quality pre-assessments before new skills are introduced gives me the information needed to provide enrichments and interventions for students who need additional help. Having enrichment and intervention techniques built into my lessons plans each week provides me with the tools I need to address each student at his or her appropriate learning level.

Your last question concerning keeping up with new technology is a tough one. Your district should have technology experts available for in-service training. If not, there are many online training resources available, and collaborative efforts to integrate technology within your building and district should be at the top of your list.

In closing, becoming a teacher will be one of the most rewarding experiences you could ever have. I wish you well as you pursue this honorable profession!

SINCERELY, **LAURIE GRAVES**

NBCT (National Board Certified Teacher) Middle Childhood Generalist

2011 WYOMING Teacher of the Year

CHAPTER EIGHT
Today's Students

learning outcomes

After reading this chapter, you will be able to do the following:

1. Explain how diversity is reflected in the culture of the United States.

2. Explain what equal educational opportunity means.

3. Explain what is meant by bilingual education.

4. Discuss the key elements of multicultural education.

5. Explain how gender is a dimension of multicultural education.

Today's teachers must be sensitive to the needs of students from different cultural backgrounds. As a teacher, you will need to communicate effectively with students from diverse populations and cultural backgrounds. You will have students from families that differ from the idealized traditional family. Some of your students may be from biracial families, adoptive families, stepfamilies, gay families, or immigrant families. According to the U.S. Census Bureau, married couples made up less than 50 percent of U.S. households in 2014, down from 71 percent in 1970. During the same period, nontraditional households increased from 29 percent in 1970 to over 50 percent (U.S. Census Bureau, April 23, 2014).

It would be impossible to develop a different curriculum for each group of students in your multicultural classroom—that would place undue emphasis on differences among students. Instead, you can develop a curriculum that affirms all students' cultures and increases their awareness and appreciation of the rich diversity in U.S. culture.

This chapter looks at cultural diversity in the United States and the challenges of equalizing educational opportunity for all students. A goal for your professional development as a teacher, then, is to see cultural diversity as an asset to be preserved and valued, not a liability. The United States has always derived strength from the diversity of its people, and all students should receive a high-quality education so that they may make their unique contributions to society.

HOW IS DIVERSITY REFLECTED IN THE CULTURE OF THE UNITED STATES?

The percentage of ethnic minorities in the United States has been growing steadily since the end of World War II. Approximately 40.8 million foreign-born people, or 13 percent of the total U.S. population of 314 million, lived in the United States during 2014. More than half (53 percent) were born in Latin America and more than one-fourth (29 percent) in Asia. Most (56 percent) lived in just four states: California, New York, Texas, and Florida. Less than half (45 percent) were naturalized citizens (U.S. Census Bureau, 2014). Each year, more than 1 million immigrants obtain legal permanent resident status in the United States (U.S. Department of Homeland Security, 2013).

Figure 8.1 shows that more than 17 million U.S. children under age 18 had at least one foreign-born parent during 2012. The figure also shows that, nationally, more than half of immigrant children have parents from Latin American countries—Mexico, Central America and Spanish-speaking Caribbean, and South America.

The Center for Children of Immigrants (2013) describes the challenge of providing equal educational opportunity to the growing U.S. immigrant population, particularly undocumented children:

> It is critical that the specific needs of children and youth are considered in the ongoing immigration debate and that particular attention is paid to their educational opportunities. Of the approximately 5.5 million children of immigrants in the U.S., around 1 million are undocumented. Many of these children entered the country at a young age, have been educated in American schools, and have grown up speaking English and embracing American culture.
>
> While undocumented children in grades K–12 are legally allowed to attend school, they often face challenges that their peers do not. Additionally, undocumented status becomes a significant barrier after youth leave high school. Undocumented youth who graduate from high school face significant barriers to everything typically associated with youth of that age, including driving, working, and receiving financial aid for higher education. With an estimated 65,000 undocumented students graduating from American high schools every year, this is an important issue not only for these youth, but for the entire country. (p. 1)

Learn how an educator embraces cultural and linguistic diversity.

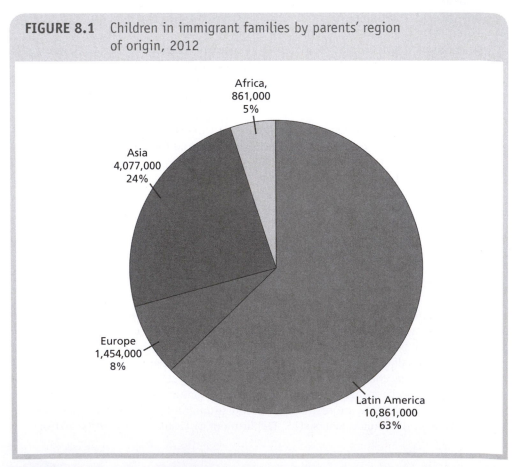

FIGURE 8.1   Children in immigrant families by parents' region of origin, 2012

Note: The share of children under age 18 either foreign-born or who have at least one foreign-born parent with at least one parent from Latin America, Europe, Asia, or Africa.

Adapted from the U.S. Census Bureau, 2012 American Community Survey. Retrieved May 7, 2014, from http://www.census.gov/acs/www/.

Minorities, which made up 37 percent of the U.S. population in 2012, are projected to comprise 57 percent of the population in 2060. During that period, the total minority population would more than double, from 116.2 million to 241.3 million. The Hispanic population would increase from 53.3 million in 2012 to 128.8 million in 2060; similarly, the Asian population would more than double, from 15.9 million in 2012 to 34.4 million in 2060 (U.S. Census Bureau, December 12, 2012).

Increasing **diversity** in the United States is reflected, of course, in the nation's schools. Nearly 48 percent of public school students were considered part of a minority group during 2011, an increase of 16 percentage points from 1988 (Keaton, 2012a). Before the middle of this century, more than half of the nation's students will be minority-group members (U.S. Census Bureau, 2012). In the nation's 25 largest cities, students of color represent half or more of the student population (National Center for Education Statistics, July 2012).

Changes in the racial and ethnic composition of student enrollments are expanding the array of languages and cultures found in the nation's public schools. Differences in student backgrounds offer opportunities to enhance the learning environment; however, these differences also raise challenges for schools. For example, there is an increased demand for bilingual programs and teachers in many parts of the country. All but a few school districts face a critical shortage of minority teachers. And there is a need to develop curricula and strategies that address the needs and backgrounds of all students—regardless of their social class; gender; sexual orientation; or ethnic, racial, or cultural identity.

The Meaning of Culture

One mission of schools is to maintain the culture of the United States. But what is the U.S. culture? Is there a single culture to which everyone in the country belongs? Before answering that question, we must define the term *culture*. Simply put, **culture** is the way of life common to a group of people. It consists of the values, attitudes, and beliefs that influence their traditions and behavior. It is also a way of interacting with and looking at the world. At one time, it was believed that the United States was like a melting pot in which ethnic cultures would melt into one; however, ethnic and cultural differences have remained very much a part of life in the United States. A salad-bowl analogy captures more accurately the **cultural pluralism** of U.S. society. That is, the distinguishing characteristics of cultures are to be preserved rather than blended into a single culture. Or, as one columnist observed regarding the continuing increase in people of mixed-race identity in the United States: "America's melting pot isn't going to create a bland, homogenous porridge so much as a deeply flavored, spicy stew" (Stuckey, 2008).

DIMENSIONS OF CULTURE

Within the United States, cultural groups differ according to other distinguishing factors, such as religion, politics, economics, and geographic region. The regional culture of New England, for example, is quite different from that of the Southeast. Similarly, Californians are culturally different from Iowans.

However, everyone in the United States does share some common dimensions of culture. James Banks (2014), an authority on multicultural education, has termed this shared culture the "national macroculture." In addition to being members of the national macroculture, people in the United States are members of ethnic groups. An **ethnic group** is made up of individuals within a larger culture who

Today's classrooms are becoming increasingly diverse. What knowledge and skills will help you meet the learning needs of students from racial/ethnic, cultural, and linguistic backgrounds that are different from yours?

share a self-defined racial or cultural identity and a set of beliefs, attitudes, and values. Members of an ethnic group distinguish themselves from others in the society by physical and social attributes. You should be aware also that the composition of ethnic groups can change over time, and that there is often as much variability within groups as between them. Clearly, the United States is a "culturally complex society . . . the most racially and ethnically diverse democracy in the world" (Wells, 2014, pp. 19–20).

CULTURAL IDENTITY

In addition to membership in the national macroculture, each individual participates in an array of subcultures, each with its customs and beliefs. Collectively, these subcultures determine an individual's **cultural identity**, an overall sense of who one is. Other possible elements that might shape a person's cultural identity include age, racial identity, exceptionalities, language, gender, sexual orientation, income level, and beliefs and values. The importance of these elements differs among people. For some, their cultural identity is most strongly determined by their occupations; for others, it is determined by their ethnicity; and for others, by their religious beliefs.

Remember that your future students will have their own complex cultural identities, which are no less valid for being different. For some of them, these identities may make them feel disconnected from the attitudes, expectations, and values conveyed by the school. You will be challenged as a teacher to understand the subtle differences in cultural identities among your students. You will need to create a learning environment that enables all students to feel connected to their school experiences.

Some of your students may have cultural backgrounds that are individualistic, whereas the backgrounds of others may be collectivistic. **Individualistic cultures** tend to emphasize the individual and his or her success and achievement. **Collectivistic cultures**, on the other hand, tend to emphasize group membership and a sense of "we," rather than "I" (Greenfield, 1994; Hofstede, 2001; Rothstein-Fisch & Trumbull, 2008; Triandis, 1989). "While self-realization is the ideal with many individualistic cultures, in the collectivist model, individuals must fit into the group, and group realization is the ideal" (Waltman & Bush-Bacelis, 1995, pp. 66–67). Figure 8.2 presents a comparison of individualistic and collectivistic cultures that can be helpful in understanding how students from different cultural backgrounds view life in classrooms. Remember, though, that everyone has values and points of view that are both individualistic and collectivistic. The two types of cultures represent "general tendencies that may emerge when the members of . . . [a] culture are considered as a whole" (Markus & Kitayama, 1991, p. 225).

FIGURE 8.2 Individualistic and collectivistic cultures: A comparison

Individualistic Cultures (United States, Canada, Western Europe, Australia)	Collectivistic Cultures (Many Asian, African, and South American Cultures)
Individual uniqueness, self-determination.	Loyalty to group and family.
Independence, self-reliance, and individual achievement.	Interdependence, cooperation, and group success.
Self-expression.	Adherence to group norms.
Individual choice.	Group consensus.
Equality of relationships.	Hierarchical relationships.
Task orientation.	Group orientation.
Individual well-being.	Group well-being.
Self-esteem.	Modesty.

LANGUAGE AND CULTURE

Culture is embedded in language, a fact that has resulted in conflict among different groups in our society. Some groups support the preservation of ethnic cultures, yet they believe that members of non-English-speaking groups must learn English if they are to function in U.S. society. Those who wish to preserve linguistic diversity are also in conflict with those who wish to establish English as a national language.

Much of the debate has focused on **bilingual education**—using two languages as the medium of instruction. Bilingual education is designed to help students maintain their ethnic identity and become proficient in both English and the language of the home, to encourage assimilation into the mainstream culture and integrate the home language and culture with a new one. Some people are strongly opposed to any form of bilingual education, and others support it as a short-term way to teach English to students.

Clearly, language diversity is an important dimension of U.S. cultural diversity. Many students come from homes where English is not spoken. About 4.7 million **limited English proficient (LEP)** students attended public schools in 2010–2011, or about 10 percent of the total enrollment (Aud et al., 2013). LEP students have limited ability to understand, read, or speak English, and they have a first language other than English. Ten percent or more of public school students were LEP in the following states during 2011: **OREGON**, **HAWAII**, **ALASKA**, **COLORADO**, **TEXAS**, **NEW MEXICO**, **NEVADA**, and **CALIFORNIA**. Among the states, California enrolled the greatest percentage of LEP students—29 percent (Aud et al., 2013).

LEP students in the United States speak more than 150 languages, with about 73 percent claiming Spanish as their native language. Next in frequency of use is Chinese, spoken by approximately 3.8 percent; Vietnamese, spoken by 2.7 percent; and French/Haitian Creole, spoken by 2.1 percent (Batalova & McHugh, 2010). Although states in the West report particularly high numbers of LEP students, Figure 8.3 indicates that the continued increase in the number of LEP students is being felt throughout the United States.

Students' language patterns became a topic of national debate in late 1996 when the Oakland, **CALIFORNIA**, school district passed a resolution on Ebonics (a blend of the words *ebony* and *phonics*), also known as African American Vernacular English (AAVE). The resolution, which recognized Ebonics as the primary language of many of the district's 28,000 African American students, called for them to be taught in their

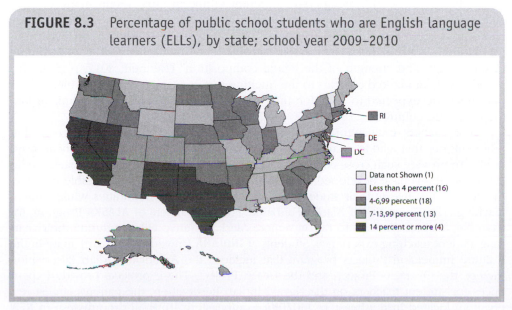

FIGURE 8.3 Percentage of public school students who are English language learners (ELLs), by state; school year 2009–2010

Legend:
- Data not Shown (1)
- Less than 4 percent (16)
- 4–6,99 percent (18)
- 7–13,99 percent (13)
- 14 percent or more (4)

Source: Aud, S., Hussar, W., Johnson, F., Kena, G., Roth, E., Manning, E., Wang, X., and Zhang, J. (2012). *The Condition of Education 2012* (NCES 2012-045). U.S. Department of Education, National Center for Education Statistics. Washington, DC, p. 31.

primary language and suggested that some students might be eligible for state and federal bilingual education or ESL money.

Critics of the resolution pointed out that Black English is a nonstandard form of English or a dialect of English—not a foreign language. Other critics were concerned that students and teachers would be taught Ebonics. In the midst of intense national debate, the district revised the resolution so that it no longer called for students to be taught in their primary language (or dialect of English). Instead, the district would implement new programs to move students from the language patterns they bring to school toward proficiency in Standard English.

Teachers should remember that "African Americans as a group include the entire spectrum of speakers from fluent native speakers of AAVE to eloquent speakers of standard English. It would therefore be a mistake to equate an African American racial heritage with Ebonics or any specific linguistic behavior" (Baugh, 2012, p. 53). In *Through Ebony Eyes: What Teachers Need to Know But Are Afraid to Ask About African American Students*, Gail Thompson (2004, p. 148) suggests that teaching African American students to speak Standard English requires

> . . . a respect for the home language that students bring to school . . . [then] these teachers can help students understand why they need to learn to speak Standard English, and to realize that the ability and willingness to use Standard English when necessary can empower them. Moreover, they can convince students they do not have to give up their home language to become empowered.

Other dialects of English and their use in the classroom have been debated from time to time—for example, Chicano English, Cajun English, or Hawaiian Creole English (more popularly known as pidgin English).

THE CONCEPT OF MULTICULTURALISM

Multiculturalism stresses the importance of seeing the world from different cultural frames of reference, and recognizing and valuing the rich array of cultures within a nation and within the global community. **Multiculturalism** affirms the need to create schools where differences related to race, ethnicity, gender, sexual orientation, disability, and social class are acknowledged and all students are viewed as valuable resources for enriching the teaching–learning process. Furthermore, a central purpose of multiculturalism is to prepare students to live in a culturally pluralistic world. In such a world, members of different ethnic groups "retain many of their cultural traditions, such as language, religion, and food preferences, so long as they conform to society as a whole. The symphony orchestra is an appropriate metaphor for cultural pluralism. Each section retains some of its uniqueness while contributing to the beauty and strength of the whole composition" (Bennett, 2011, p. 56). This worldview is in marked contrast to the "melting pot" view, according to which ethnic minorities are expected to abandon their traditions and "blend in" or assimilate into the dominant culture.

For teachers, multiculturalism also means actively seeking out experiences within other cultures that lead to increased understanding of and appreciation for those ways of life. To provide such cross-cultural experiences for their students, some teacher education programs have developed cultural immersion experiences that enable prospective teachers to live in their students' neighborhoods and communities while student teaching. The University of Alaska–Fairbanks Future Teachers of **ALASKA** Program, for example, enables students to live in remote Alaskan Native villages during their yearlong student teaching experience. Students at **INDIANA** University can participate in the Cultural Immersion Projects program that includes the American Indian Reservation Project, the Overseas Project, and the Urban Project. These projects provide experiences for student teachers on the Navajo Indian Reservation, the nation's largest reservation, located in northeastern **ARIZONA**, southeastern **UTAH**, and northwestern **NEW MEXICO**; in 13 different countries; and in inner-city Chicago. Through student teaching on a reservation, in another country, or on the Rio Grande border, students have a life-altering cultural immersion experience, as the following comments by Reservation Project participants illustrate:

- As my experience in K winds down, I can't believe that 17 weeks have gone by. I have never been affected so much by one experience in my life. I have done new things and seen new things which will be lasting impressions upon me forever. Some people will never have these experiences in their lifetime. I am proud to have taken part in such a program.
- It is ending and I am getting very sad. I've come to feel so attached to the people and their ideas—even to just the feeling of being here. I hate to see it end. I've learned just as much about myself as I have about Navajo life and culture. This place is "home" to me in many ways.
- With a little spirit, humor, spunk, ambition, and natural curiosity you can really grow and bloom out here. It is all what you make it. So, go for it!
- My cultural experiences on the Navajo Reservation are ever-present in my life. When I share my experiences with others, I feel as though I am giving a gift. Not only do I reflect on my own experiences, but I use such opportunities to educate others about Navajo culture. I recently received a letter from a student who is beginning Fort Lewis College this fall. My heart melted and I can't help but think I had some small influence in her educational success. The project has affected my life in ways I am only beginning to comprehend. I am certain it will continue to impact my life in profound ways. (Indiana University, 2014)

Ethnicity and Race

Understanding the distinction between ethnicity and race will enable you to provide students with educational experiences that reflect ethnic and racial diversity in meaningful ways. **Ethnicity** refers to a "shared sense of peoplehood, culture, identity, and shared language and dialects" (Banks, 2009, p. 16). On the other hand, **race** is a subjective concept that is used to distinguish among human beings on the basis of biological traits. Although anthropologists have yet to provide a definitive definition for the concept of race, "from evidence on how people make choices about their children's schools to the research on cultural biases in standardized curriculum and assessments, there is no doubt that race matters in U.S. public education" (Wells, 2014, p. 7).

Until recently, anthropologists tended to "reject the concept of race as a scientifically valid biological category and . . . argue[d] instead that 'race' is a socially constructed category" (Mukhopadhyay & Henze, 2003, p. 670). However, "the concept of race and how we view it culturally has changed" (Roberts, 2010). Today, anthropologists take a more nuanced view of race. As noted anthropologist John H. Relethford (2009) points out,

> race is culturally constructed, as all labels are, but it is also based on an underlying reality of biological variation. Rather than argue about whether race is a cultural construct (an idea that many unfortunately take as being equivalent to a denial of variation) or that race is 'real,' it might be more useful to consider race as a culturally constructed label that crudely and imprecisely describes real variation. (p. 20)

Similarly, another noted anthropologist, John Hartigan (2013), points out that "race is a *biosocial fact*. This assertion purposefully stands in contrast to the position that race is a social construction" (p. 4; italics in original).

As a result of the diversity among humans and the mixing of genes that has taken place over time, no single set of racial categories is universally accepted. Because many genetic factors are invisible to the naked eye (DNA, for example), noted anthropologist Ashley Montagu has suggested that there could be as few as three "races" (Negroid, Caucasoid, and Mongoloid) or as many as 300, depending on the kind and number of genetic features chosen for measurement. In his classic book, *Man's Most Dangerous Myth: The Fallacy of Race*, Montagu (1974) pointed out:

> It is impossible to make the sort of racial classification which some anthropologists and others have attempted. The fact is that all human beings are so . . . mixed with regard to origin that between different groups of individuals . . . "overlapping" of physical traits is the rule. (p. 7)

Similarly, Richard Dawkins, world-renowned scientist and former professor for the Public Understanding of Science at Oxford University, points out that "Relatively recently, maybe less than 100,000 years ago, roving bands of Homo sapiens looking pretty much like us left Africa and diversified into all the races that we see around the world today: Inuit, native Americans, native Australians, Chinese, and so on" (Dawkins, 2009, p. 186).

MIXED-RACE IDENTITY

To reflect the realities of racial identities in the United States, the questionnaire for the 2010 U.S. Census was changed so that people could select from among 15 racial categories for their racial identity, including a place to write in races not listed on the form. In addition, the "Spanish/Hispanic/Latino" category allowed respondents to choose among the following: Mexican, Mexican American, and Chicano; Puerto Rican; Cuban; and "other" Hispanic/Latino/Spanish. Similarly, respondents who self-identified as "Asian or Pacific Islander" had the following choices: Asian Indian, Chinese, Filipino, Japanese, Korean, Vietnamese, "other" Asian, Native Hawaiian, Guamanian or Chamorro, Samoan, and "other" Pacific Islander.

According to the 2010 U.S. Census, about 8 percent of marriages are mixed race. On the 2000 U.S. Census, about 7.3 million Americans, or 3 percent of the population, identified themselves as being two or more races. Forty-one percent of the mixed-race population was under age 18 (Navarro, 2008). It is estimated that the number of multiracial Americans is increasing at 10 times the rate of the White population (Stuckey, 2008). For people of mixed race, decisions about how to identify themselves are influenced by how and where they were raised, how others perceive them, what they look like, and the cultural identity with which they most strongly identify.

People with a mixed-race identity received more attention when Barack Obama, who has a White mother from Kansas and a Black father from Kenya, was elected president in 2008. As an educator who identifies herself as African American, American Indian, and White said, "I think Barack Obama [brought] these deeply American stories to the forefront. Maybe we'll get a little bit further in the dialogue on race" (Navarro, 2008).

It is also clear that racial and ethnic identities in the United States are becoming more complex. We now know that "racial and ethnic identities derive their meanings from social and historical circumstances, that they can vary over time, and that they can sometimes even be slipped on and off like a change of clothing" (Coughlin, 1993, p. 7). For example, a third-generation descendent of a Japanese immigrant may choose to refer to himself or herself as a Japanese American, an American, or an Asian American. Furthermore, it is evident that "specific racial categories acquire and lose meaning over time" (Coughlin, 1993, p. 7), and the use of ethnic and racial labels and expressions of group membership is largely self-selected and arbitrary.

There are many ethnic groups in U.S. society, and everyone belongs to at least one. However, as James Banks (2009) points out:

> An individual is ethnic to the extent that he or she shares the values, behavioral patterns, cultural traits, and identification with a specific ethnic group. Many individuals have multiple ethnic attachments; others consider themselves "American" rather than ethnic. An individual's identity with his or her ethnic group varies significantly with the period of life, economic and social status, and situations or settings. (p. 16)

The Concept of Minorities

To understand the important concept of **minorities**, it may help to remember that even though the term *minority* technically refers to any group numbering less than half of the total population, in certain parts of the country "minorities" are actually the majority. More important than the numbers themselves, however, is an appreciation of how many groups of people have continuously struggled to obtain full educational, economic, political, and social opportunities in society. Along with minority racial and ethnic groups, others who have traditionally lacked power in U.S. public life are immigrants; the poor; children and the elderly; non-English speakers; members of minority religions; people who have no religion; women; and people who are gay, lesbian, bisexual, or transgender. Groups who have been most frequently discriminated against in terms of the quality of education they have received include African Americans, Spanish-speaking Americans, Native Americans, Asian Americans, exceptional learners, people with disabilities, and females. There is mounting evidence that many students from these groups continue to receive a substandard education that does not meet their needs or empower them to participate fully and equally in life in the United States.

Minority Groups and Academic Achievement

Minority-group students are disproportionately represented among students who have failed to master minimum competencies in reading, writing, and mathematics. It has been estimated that ethnic minority students are two to four times more likely than others to drop out of high school. According to a 2013 U.S. Department of Education report, Asian/Pacific Islander students had the highest high school graduation rate, 93.5 percent, followed by 83.0 percent for White students, 71.4 percent for Hispanic students, 69.1 percent for American Indian/Alaska Native students, and 66.1 percent for Black students (Stillwell & Sable, 2013). In addition, racial- and language-minority students are often overrepresented in special education programs and more likely to be suspended or expelled from school.

From 1999 to 2008, the largest relative increase in those taking advanced-placement (AP) exams was among Black students, and Hispanic student participation in AP exams more than tripled over the same time period (Aud, Fox, & KewalRamani, 2010). In addition, the number of minority students who complete high school and continue their education in college continues to increase. Despite these gains, progress is uneven, and an **achievement gap** exists between White students and Hispanic, Black, and American Indian/Alaska Native students on many measures of educational achievement. For example, on the 2012 National Assessment of Educational Progress in reading and mathematics, White students scored 21 or more points higher on average than Black and Hispanic students (National Center for Education Statistics, 2013).

When we consider the lower achievement levels of minority students, it is important to note the much higher incidence of poverty among minority families and the research showing that socioeconomic status—not race, language, or culture—contributes most strongly to students' achievement in school (Coleman et al., 1966; Jencks et al., 1972; Jencks & Phillips 1998; National Center for Education Statistics, 1980). It is understandably difficult for poor children to learn well if they endure the stress of living in crime-ridden neighborhoods, dwelling in dilapidated homes, or going to school hungry.

In addition, it is important to remember that test scores are but a narrow measure of educational quality. A recent report from the National Education Policy Center suggests that paying attention only to comparisons of test scores among different racial and ethnic groups may lead to the mistaken notion that "only those schools that are predominantly White, or Asian, or both are considered 'good'" (Wells, 2014, p. 13). Moreover, placing undue emphasis on test scores reduces the likelihood that *all students* receive an education that prepares them for a culturally complex, diverse society:

> the current approach to accountability not only leads to more negative perceptions of racially diverse schools, but also limits educators' ability to tap into the educational benefits of the cultural diversity within those schools to

help all students thrive intellectually. The more narrow the measures used to judge schools, teachers, and students, the less likely the educational system as a whole can envision racial, ethnic, and cultural diversity as an asset in preparing all children for the 21st Century. (Wells, 2014, p. 12)

Stereotyping and Racism

Although teachers should expand their knowledge of and appreciation for the diverse cultural backgrounds of their students, they should also guard against forming stereotypes or overgeneralizations about those cultures. **Stereotyping** is the process of attributing behavioral characteristics to all members of a group. In some cases, stereotypes are formed on the basis of limited experiences with and information about the group being stereotyped, and the validity of these stereotypes is not questioned.

Within any cultural group that shares a broad cultural heritage, however, considerable diversity exists. For example, two Puerto Rican children who live in the same community and attend the same school may appear alike to their teachers when, in reality, they are very different. One may come from a home where Spanish is spoken and Puerto Rican holidays are observed; the other child may know only a few words of Spanish and observe only the holidays of the majority culture.

In addition to being alert for stereotypes they and others may hold, teachers should learn to recognize **individual racism**, the prejudicial belief that one's ethnic or racial group is superior to others. An obvious feature of racism in the United States "is that many whites see themselves as better than persons and groups of color, and as a result exercise their power to prevent people of color from securing the prestige, power, and privilege held by them" (Gollnick & Chinn, 2009, p. 63). Teachers should also be able to recognize **institutional racism**, which occurs when institutions "behave in ways that are overtly racist (i.e., specifically excluding people-of-color from services) or inherently racist (i.e., adopting policies that while not specifically directed at excluding people-of-color, nevertheless result in their exclusion)" (Randall, 2001).

In light of the arbitrariness of the concept of race, James A. Banks (2009) points out, "In most societies, *the social significance of race is much more important than the presumed physical differences among groups*" (p. 71, italics in original). Unfortunately, many people attach great importance to the concept of race. If you believe "that human groups can be validly grouped on the basis of their biological traits and that these identifiable groups inherit certain mental, personality, and cultural characteristics that determine their behavior" (Banks, 2009, p. 72) then you hold racist beliefs. When people use such beliefs as a rationale for oppressing other groups, they are practicing racism.

As a teacher, you will not be able to eliminate stereotypic thinking or racism in society. However, you have an obligation to all your students to see that your curriculum and instruction are free of any forms of stereotyping or racism. You need to assess your own cultural attitudes and values and determine whether you have stereotypes about other cultural groups.

Class and Socioeconomic Status

"One of the most critical issues that educators routinely face is that of social class and poverty" (Gollnick & Chinn, 2009, p. 339). In 2013, the federal poverty level was $22,350 a year for a family of four. As Figure 8.4 shows, the poverty rate for children under age 18 that year was 19.9 percent, higher than the rates for people aged 18 to 64 and those aged 65 and older. Additionally, in 2013, children represented 23.5 percent of the U.S. population (about 14.7 million); however, they accounted for 32.3 percent of people in poverty (DeNavas-Walt and Proctor, 2014).

The percentage of children in poverty also varies by race/ethnicity. For example, Figure 8.5 shows that among different racial groups, Asian households had the highest median income in 2013 ($67,065). The median income for non-Hispanic White households was $58,270; for Hispanic household, $40,963; and for Black households, $34,598. Figure 8.5 also shows that the real median household income for each of the race and Hispanic-origin groups has not yet recovered to its pre-2001-recession median household income peak.

FIGURE 8.4   Poverty Rates by Age: 1959 to 2013

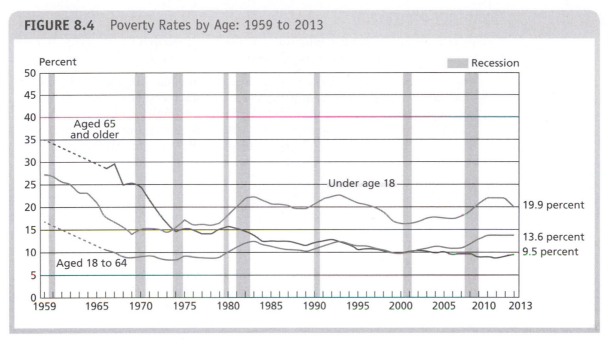

Note: The data points are placed at the midpoints of the respective years. Data for people aged 18 to 64 and 65 and older are not avaliable from 1960 to 1965. For information on recessions, see Appendix A. For information on confidentiality protection, sampling error, nonsampling error, and definitions, see <ftp://ftp2.census.gov/programs-surveys/cps/techdocs/cpsmar14.pdf>.

Source: DeNavas-Walt, Carmen and Bernadette D. Proctor, U.S. Census Bureau, Current Population Reports, P60-249, *Income and Poverty in the United States: 2013*, U.S. Government Printing Office, Washington, DC, 2014, p. 14.

FIGURE 8.5   Real Median Household Income by Race and Hispanic Origin: 1967 to 2013

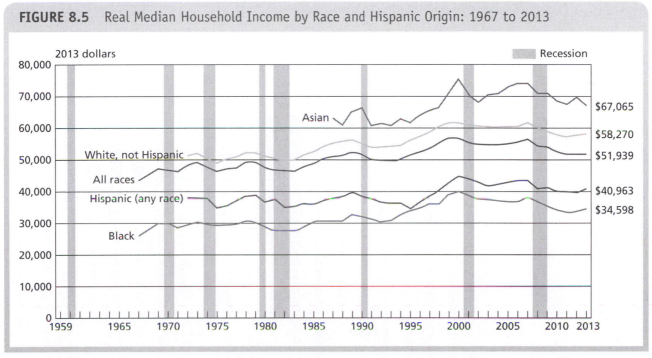

Note: Median household income data are not avaliable prior to 1967. For more information on recessions, see Appendix A. For information on confidentiality protection, sampling error, nonsampling error, and definitions, see <ftp: //ftp2.census.gov/programs-surveys/cps/techdocs/cpsmar14.pdf>.
Source: DeNavas-Walt, Carmen and Bernadette D. Proctor, U.S. Census Bureau, Current Population Reports, P60-249, *Income and Poverty in the United States: 2013*, U.S. Government Printing Office, Washington, DC, 2014, p. 5.

Teachers in inner-city schools or schools in poor rural communities may find that nearly all their students are from families who live in poverty. For children, poverty can contribute to depression, lower levels of sociability and/or initiative, problematic peer relations, and disruptive classroom behavior (Eamon, July 2001). Poverty can impede children's ability to learn and contribute to social, emotional, and behavioral problems.

Religious Pluralism

Today's schools are religiously pluralistic. As the Pew Research Center's *U.S. Religious Landscape Survey* noted, the U.S. population

> can be usefully grouped into more than a dozen major religious traditions that, in turn, can be divided into hundreds of distinct religious groups. Overall, nearly eight-in-ten (78.4%) adults report belonging to various forms of Christianity, about 5% belong to other faiths and almost one-in-six (16.1%) are not affiliated with any particular religion. (Pew Forum on Religion & Public Life, 2008, p. 10)

The *Landscape Survey* found that the United States "is on the verge of becoming a minority Protestant country" (p. 5). Religious affiliations in the United States are not only diverse, they are fluid. For example, about 28 percent of American adults have left the faith in which they were raised in favor of another religion, or no religion at all. Moreover, a 2012 Pew Research Center survey found that

> The number of Americans who do not identify with any religion continues to grow at a rapid pace. One-fifth of the U.S. public—and a third of adults under 30—are religiously unaffiliated today, the highest percentages ever in Pew Research Center polling. In the last five years alone, the unaffiliated have increased from just over 15% to just under 20% of all U.S. adults. Their ranks now include more than 13 million self-described atheists and agnostics (nearly 6% of the U.S. public), as well as nearly 33 million people who say they have no particular religious affiliation (14%). (Pew Forum on Religion & Public Life, 2012, p. 9)

Figure 8.6 illustrates the religious diversity, by race, in the United States.

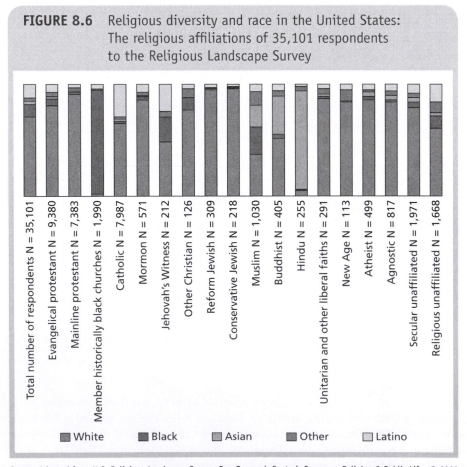

FIGURE 8.6 Religious diversity and race in the United States: The religious affiliations of 35,101 respondents to the Religious Landscape Survey

White   Black   Asian   Other   Latino

Source: Adapted from U.S. Religious Landscape Survey, Pew Research Center's Forum on Religion & Public Life, @ 2008 Pew Research Center, http://religion.pewforum.org

Different religious groups in America can have different expectations of the schools. Depending on the religious makeup of a local community, areas such as the following can emerge as points of conflict between the community and the school: sex education, teaching of evolution and/or intelligent design, and liberal points of view in textbooks. In a religiously pluralistic society such as the United States, "educators would do well to inform themselves of the religious groups in their community and in their school. In doing so, they greatly enhance their ability to function in the classroom, mindful and respectful of the religious rights of all students" (Gollnick & Chinn, 2009, p. 281).

WHAT DOES EQUAL EDUCATIONAL OPPORTUNITY MEAN?

Providing educational opportunity to all students means that teachers and schools promote the full development of students as individuals, without regard for race, ethnicity, gender, sexual orientation, socioeconomic status, religion, abilities, or disabilities. More specifically, educators fulfill this important mission by continually evaluating the appropriateness of the curricular and instructional experiences they provide to each student. The Teachers' Voices: Being an Agent of Change feature in this chapter, by Marcus Goodyear, describes how he learned that the primary goal of a teacher should be to promote the full development of students—that a teacher should "always err on the side of the student."

The following sections review the progress that has been made to provide students from diverse groups with equal educational opportunity and present strategies for teaching in diverse classrooms. Strategies for each group draw from research that suggests that particular learning styles may be associated with specific ethnic groups in U.S. society (Bennett, 2011; Hale-Benson, 1986; Shade, 1982). These strategies should not lead you to assume, however, that all students from a certain group learn in a particular way. As Christine I. Bennett (2011), an expert on multicultural education, points out:

> The notion that certain learning styles are associated with different ethnic groups is both promising and dangerous. Promise lies in the realization that low academic achievement among some ethnic minorities may sometimes be attributed to conflicts between styles of teaching and learning, not low intelligence. This leads to the possibility that teachers will alter their own instructional styles to be more responsive to the learning needs of students. Danger lies in the possibility that new ethnic stereotypes will develop while old ones are reinforced, as in "Blacks learn aurally," "Asians excel in math," "Mexican American males can't learn from female peer tutors," and "Navajos won't ask a question or participate in a discussion." (pp. 67–68)

Anglo-European Americans are omitted from the review, not because students from this very diverse group have always had equal educational opportunities but because this group represents the historically dominant culture. To a great extent, it has determined the curricular and instructional practices found in schools.

Like the groups discussed in the following sections, "Anglo-European American" is not a single, monolithic culture. Americans whose ethnic heritage is English, Polish, German, Italian, Irish, Slovakian, Russian, or Swedish, for example, often differ greatly in religious and political traditions, beliefs, and values. Their individual ethnic identity may or may not be strengthened by recent immigrants from their country of origin. European ethnics have nevertheless assimilated into the mainstream U.S. society more completely than others.

Education and African Americans

Of the more than 314 million persons living in the United States, nearly 45 million are African Americans (U.S. Census Bureau, 2012c). According to U.S. Census Bureau projections, the African American population is expected to increase to 77.8 million (18.7 percent of the total) in 2060. The incidence of social problems such as unemployment, crime, drug abuse, poverty, inadequate housing, and dropping out of school is

TEACHERS' VOICES ➡ BEING AN AGENT OF CHANGE

MARCUS GOODYEAR

DOLLARS AND POINTS

Teacher Marcus Goodyear faced a dilemma after giving a student a grade of 50 for her final research paper because half of it was plagiarized. The research paper grade gave the student a six-weeks' grade of 69 (one point short of a passing grade of 70). The failing grade made the girl ineligible to compete in athletics. However, the teacher reflects on whether he made the "right" decision after meeting with the girl's upset parents and learning that the father has serious health problems.

After almost a week, I asked my principal for advice. What would he do? I asked my department head. Miraculously neither of them had ever become cynical, and so I trusted them. "Give her the point," they said. "It isn't worth it to hold the line. They'll drag you to the school board. They'll make you look like the villain. They'll examine every minor grade under a microscope. Just give her the point and let her have a seventy."

On the grade change form I checked "teacher error." The student became eligible. She went on to the state competition that year. "What will you say to the people you beat?" I wanted to ask her. "What will you say to the students who had enough honor not to plagiarize their research papers?" But I swallowed my pride. I swallowed some of my moral self-righteousness. I even swallowed my anger at parents who will bully their way through teachers and administrators and anyone else standing between them and their entitlements. Because I hadn't known about her dad's health problems. If the girl had just told me that she thought her father might die, I would have given her extra time on the paper. I would have allowed more makeup work. I would have helped her. I should have helped her.

Part of me still felt like I was compromising academics for athletics. Part of me wanted to punish the student for the actions of her parents. But I learned an important lesson: Always err on the side of the student.

Because I do make mistakes, of course. I made a big mistake with that plagiarized paper—I assumed the worst of my student. I should have given the girl a chance to confess and rewrite the paper. Now I know to reward students for what they do well, rather than punish students for what they do poorly. Some students will need to face consequences for their mistakes, but that can never become my focus as a teacher. It would destroy me. It would make me shrivel up into bitterness and indignation that the students, the teachers, the whole educational system was just going to hell. Everyone makes mistakes in the classroom, even me. That is what the classroom is for. And those mistakes will only make me worthless and vindictive if I remain proud and absolute. Like some one-room schoolhouse tyrant. Or like the cynics down the hall.

During that conference [with the girl's parents] I also realized that no amount of points brings value to a student's education. Passing my class, passing the state achievement test, even passing the Advanced Placement test were all based on an economic view of the world. These things reduce human actions and feelings to a few numbers—either test scores or the price of a college class. These things work as external rewards, but the biggest rewards are always internal. In addition to points, I can give my students respect and trust and confidence and faith. They need to become adults; they need me to treat them like adults.

Why would I treat them any other way?

Above all I finally realized that I teach for the students. Not their parents. Not my peers. Not even for myself or the paycheck at the end of every month. I teach for my students to rise above their mistakes.

And the mistakes of their teachers.

Some of them will. I know it.

PERSONAL REFLECTION

1. Based on his account of the plagiarism incident, what are Goodyear's views about the following elements of educational philosophy: Beliefs about teaching and learning? Beliefs about students? Beliefs about knowledge? Beliefs about what is worth knowing?
2. Why does Goodyear decide to change his student's grade? Do you agree or disagree with his decision? Why?
3. What ethical dilemmas might you encounter when you begin to teach? How will you resolve those ethical dilemmas?

Marcus Goodyear formerly taught at O'Connor High School in San Antonio, TEXAS. The preceding is excerpted from his chapter that appears in Molly Hoekstra (ed.), *Am I Teaching Yet? Stories from the Teacher-Training Trenches*, Portsmouth, NH: Heinemann, 2002, pp. 70–75.

proportionally greater for African Americans than for Whites. The struggle of African Americans to improve their quality of life after the end of slavery has been hampered for generations by persistent racism, discrimination, poverty, crime, unemployment, and underemployment.

The civil rights movement of the 1960s and 1970s made it clear that African Americans had been denied full access to many aspects of U.S. life, including the right to a good education. A 1976 report by the United States Commission on Civil Rights, for example, revealed that a southern school district in the 1930s spent nearly 18 times as much for the education of White pupils as it did for the education of African Americans.

THE DESEGREGATION ERA

Perhaps the most blatant form of discrimination against African Americans has been school segregation and unequal educational opportunity. Prior to the 1950s, an attempt was made to justify segregation with the idea of separate but equal schools. It was not until the National Association for the Advancement of Colored People (NAACP) brought suit on behalf of a Kansas family (*Brown v. Board of Education of Topeka, Kansas*) in 1954 that the concept of separate but equal schools was decidedly struck down.

The parents of Linda Brown felt that the education their fourth grader was receiving in the segregated Topeka schools was inferior. When their request that she be transferred to a White school was turned down, they filed suit. In a landmark decision, the U.S. Supreme Court ruled that segregated schools are "inherently unequal" and violate the equal protection clause of the Fourteenth Amendment. U.S. citizens, the justices asserted, have a right to receive an equal opportunity for education.

As a result of opportunities created during the civil rights movement, a substantial number of African Americans are now members of the middle class. Affirmative action programs have enabled many African Americans to attain high-ranking positions in the business, medical, legal, and educational professions. For example, there were 44,900 African American physicians and surgeons, 80,000 postsecondary teachers, 48,300 lawyers, and 52,400 chief executives in the United States during 2007 (U.S. Census Bureau, 2007). And, in 2014, Census Bureau data included the following:

- Of African Americans 25 and older, 1.6 million held advanced degrees (i.e., master's, doctorate, medical, or law); in 1996, 683,000 African Americans had this level of education.
- In the fall of 2012, 3.7 million African Americans attended college, a 28 percent increase over the 2.9 million who attended college in 2007. (U.S. Census Bureau, January 16, 2014)

RESEGREGATION OF SCHOOLS IN THE UNITED STATES

As the United States continues to become more ethnically and racially diverse, there is evidence that schools have been resegregating since 1990, according to *Resegregation in American Schools*, a Harvard University report (Orfield & Yun, 1999). The report included the following findings:

- Latinos attend the most severely segregated schools.
- Since the late 1980s, schools in the South have been resegregating.
- As African Americans and Latinos move to the suburbs, they are attending segregated schools, especially in urban areas.
- States with a high proportion of African American students made progress toward desegregation in the 1970s; however, all showed increases in school segregation between 1980 and 1996.
- Segregated schools, with the exception of those for White students, tend to have a high concentration of poverty, which has a negative influence on student achievement.

One reason for the trend back to resegregation has been Supreme Court rulings that removed judicial supervision of school districts' efforts to desegregate—for example, *Board of Education of Oklahoma City Public Schools v. Dowell* (1991), *Freeman v. Pitts* (1992), and *Brown v. Unified School District No. 501* (1999). In addition, the Supreme Court ruled in *Missouri v. Jenkins* (1995) that Kansas City schools did not have to maintain desegregation through a magnet school approach until actual benefits for African American students were shown. Such rulings by the Supreme Court prompted the filing of many lawsuits to end desegregation in several large school districts.

THE LEARNING NEEDS OF AFRICAN AMERICAN STUDENTS

Research on factors related to students' success in school suggests that schools are monoethnic and do not take into account the diverse needs of ethnic minority-group students (Banks, 2009; Bennett, 2015). In the case of African American students, the failure of the school curriculum to address their learning needs may contribute to high dropout rates and below-average achievement. For example, research indicates that teaching strategies that emphasize cooperation—not competition—often result in higher achievement among African American (and Mexican American) students (Aronson & Gonzalez, 1988; Bennett, 2014). In addition, it has been suggested that because many African Americans have grown up in an oral tradition, they may learn better through oral/aural activities—for example, reading aloud and listening to audiotapes (Bennett, 2015). However, one should not assume that all African Americans learn better aurally.

The following case illustrates how Steven, a 12-year-old African American student who was having difficulty learning math and developing his reading skills, benefited from teachers who were sensitive to his learning needs. After Steven's school failed to make adequate yearly progress (AYP) as required by No Child Left Behind, teachers began to receive in-service training to meet the instructional needs of students from culturally diverse backgrounds. The school principal also started after-school tutoring programs.

> Steven participated in the after-school tutoring program, where he received direct instruction in reading and mathematics. Teachers learned that he had an interest in astronomy, and textbooks and supplemental materials on astronomy were presented to him at his readability levels. Math across the curriculum was implemented, and he saw a direct benefit from instruction in math. As a result, Steven was able to see the utility of math in several different contexts. For example, teachers participating in the after-school tutoring program created math problems around the astronomy subject matter. After several months of direct instruction . . . Steven's reading comprehension and word recall improved. (Obiakor, 2007, p. 36)

AFROCENTRIC SCHOOLS

To address the educational inequities that African American and other minority-group students may experience as a result of segregation, many communities have tried to create more ethnically and racially diverse classrooms through the controversial practice of busing students to attend schools in other neighborhoods. Also, some African Americans have recently begun to call for **Afrocentric schools**—schools that focus on African American history and cultures for African American pupils. Proponents believe that the educational needs of African American students can be met more effectively in schools that offer Afrocentric curricula and build on the strengths of the African American community.

Private Afrocentric schools, or Black academies, have sprung up across the country in recent years, many supported by the growing number of African Americans who practice Islam. Curricula in these schools emphasize the people and cultures of Africa and the history and achievements of African Americans. Teaching methods are often designed for culture-based learning styles, such as choral response, learning through movement, and sociability. One Afrocentric school is the Betty Shabbaz International Charter School (Shabazz School) in Chicago, **ILLINOIS**. Shabazz School is comprised of three Chicago campuses: Betty Shabbaz Academy (grades K–8), Barbara A. Sizemore Academy (grades K–8), and the DuSable Leadership Academy (grades 9–12), located at the former DuSable High School where the author taught for 8 years. Students at the school, the majority of whom are from families in poverty, have higher scores on state tests and higher college acceptance rates than students at other schools in the district (Ahmed-Ullah, 2013).The Shabbaz School curriculum instills pride and a community-like spirit in students as they learn how African culture has influenced countries around the world. Teaching methods and displays throughout the school emphasize African history, values, languages, arts, traditions, and ceremonies (Betty Shabbaz International Charter School, May 14, 2014).

Another Afrocentric school, the Young Geniuses Academy in Seattle, **WASHINGTON**, is collaborating with the Africatown Center for Education and Innovation to deliver programs that that develop children's talents in science, technology, engineering, and mathematics (STEM). Students at the Academy experience a culturally relevant curriculum that introduces students to the contributions African people have made in STEM fields and the arts (Africatown Center for Education and Innovation, spring 2014).

Education and Latino and Hispanic Americans

Hispanic Americans, the fastest growing minority group in the United States, account for about 17 percent of the nation's population, and it has been estimated that an additional 5 million illegal aliens who speak Spanish may be in the country. By 2060, the His-

What effects has the growing Hispanic population in the U.S. had on schools both throughout the country as well as in some states in particular? Why might some Hispanic Americans prefer assimilation over bilingual education for their children?

panic population is expected to more than double, from 53.3 million in 2012 to 128.8 million in 2060. Consequently, by the end of the period, nearly one in three U.S. residents would be Hispanic, up from about one in six today (U.S. Census Bureau, December 12, 2012).

Included in the category of Hispanic Americans are people who call themselves Latinos and Chicanos and who report their ancestry as Mexican, Puerto Rican, Cuban, Central American, or South American. Five states have populations that are more than 10 percent Hispanic: **CALIFORNIA**, **TEXAS**, **NEW MEXICO**, **ARIZONA**, and **COLORADO**. Many states have passed English-only laws and made efforts to restrict Hispanic immigrants' access to education. Prior to 1983, six states had English-language laws; however, efforts by political action groups such as U.S. English, founded by the late Senator S. I. Hayakawa of California in 1983, were instrumental in getting English-only laws passed in 31 states by 2014 (U.S. English, 2014). U.S. English has also lobbied periodically the U.S. Congress to pass legislation to make English the official language of the United States. Most recently, the English Language Unity Act of 2014 was introduced to the House of Representatives.

SOCIOECONOMIC FACTORS

Although some Spanish-speaking immigrants come to the United States hoping to escape a life of poverty in their home country, many others come because they have relatives in the United States or they wish to take advantage of business opportunities in this country. For those Spanish-speaking immigrants who lack job skills and have little education, however, adjusting to the complexities and demands of life in the United States may be difficult.

Socioeconomic factors affect the education of some Hispanics, such as the children of migrant farm workers. Among the estimated 1 million or so migrant farm workers in this country, more than 70 percent are Spanish-speaking. The dropout rate among all migrant workers is 90 percent, and 50 percent leave school before finishing the ninth grade (Bennett, 2014). Migrant children are handicapped by the language barrier, deprivation resulting from poverty, and irregular school attendance. Some states have educational intervention programs in place for reaching this group.

THE LEARNING NEEDS OF SPANISH-SPEAKING STUDENTS

What can easily happen to Spanish-speaking learners if they are taught by teachers who are not sensitive to their learning needs is illustrated in Christine I. Bennett's (2011) portrait of Jesús, an LEP student:

> Jesús Martinez was a bright, fine-looking six-year-old when he migrated with his family from Puerto Rico to New York City. At a time when he was ready to learn to read and write his mother tongue, Jesús was instead suddenly thrust into an English-only classroom where the only tool he possessed for oral communication (the Spanish language) was completely useless to him. Jesús and his teacher could not communicate with each other because each spoke a different language, and neither spoke the language of the other. Jesús felt stupid, or retarded; his teacher perceived him to be culturally disadvantaged and beyond her help. However, she and the school officials agreed to allow him to "sit there" because the law required that he be in school. (p. 7)

Bennett (2003) also captures well the dilemma that many Spanish-speaking LEP students find themselves in: "Students with limited English proficiency are often caught up in conflicts between personal language needs—for example, the need to consolidate cognitive skills in the native language—and a sociopolitical climate that views standard English as most desirable and prestigious" (p. 271).

The degree to which students from Spanish-speaking backgrounds are motivated to learn English varies from group to group. Mexican American students who live in the Southwest may retain the Spanish language to maintain ties with family and friends in Mexico. Recently arrived Cubans, on the other hand, may have a stronger motivation to learn the language of their new country. In regard to what they wish to learn, children take their cues from the adults around them. If their parents or guardians, friends, and relatives have learned English and are bilingual, then they will be similarly motivated. Many Hispanic Americans who value assimilation over their traditional culture favor English-only education.

However, the limited English proficiencies of many children raised in native Spanish-speaking families contribute significantly to the difficulties they have in school. To address the needs of these students, federally funded bilingual-bicultural programs encourage teachers to view bicultural knowledge as a bridge to the school's curriculum. Bilingual education is examined in detail later in this chapter.

Education and Asian Americans and Pacific Islanders

Asian Americans and Pacific Islanders represent about 5.6 percent, or 17.3 million, of the total population of the United States (U.S. Census Bureau, 2012 c). The U.S. Census Bureau estimates that the Asian and Pacific Islander population in the United States will increase to 40.6 million (9.67 percent of the total) in 2060 (U.S. Census Bureau, December 12, 2012). This group, comprising at least 34 ethnic groups speaking more than 300 languages and dialects (Asian Americans/Pacific Islanders in Philanthropy, 1997), is tremendously diverse and includes people from South Asia, primarily Bangladesh, India, and Pakistan; Southeast Asia, including Indochina (Laos, Thailand, Indonesia, Malaysia, and Vietnam) and the Philippines; East Asia, including China, Hong Kong, Japan, Korea, and Taiwan; and the Pacific Islands, including Hawaii, Guam, and Samoa. About 51 percent of the total Asian American and Pacific Islander population lives in the western United States (U.S. Census Bureau, 2010).

HISTORICAL, CULTURAL, AND SOCIOECONOMIC FACTORS

The six largest Asian American groups in 2012 were Chinese Americans (3.8 million), Filipinos (3.4 million), Asian Indians (3.2 million), Vietnamese (1.7 million), Koreans (1.7 million), and Japanese (1.3 million) (U.S. Census Bureau, 2012c). Although these groups differ significantly, each "came to the United States seeking the American dream, satisfied important labor needs, and became victims of an anti-Asian movement designed to prevent their further immigration to the United States. [They] also experienced tremendous economic, educational, and social mobility and success in U.S. society" (Banks, 2009, p. 398).

The California gold rush of 1849 brought the first immigrants from Asia, Chinese men who worked in mines, on railroads, and on farms, and who planned to return to their families and homeland. Early Chinese immigrants encountered widespread discrimination in their new country, with anti-Chinese riots occurring in San Francisco, Los Angeles, and Denver between 1869 and 1880. In 1882, Congress passed the Immigration Act, which ended Chinese immigration until 1902. The Chinese were oriented toward maintaining their traditional language and religion and established tight-knit urban communities, or Chinatowns. Recently, many upwardly mobile, professional Chinese Americans have been assimilated into suburban communities, while newly arrived, working-class immigrants from China and Hong Kong are settling in redeveloped Chinatowns.

Japanese immigrants began to arrive in Hawaii and the U.S. mainland in the late 1800s; most worked in agriculture, fisheries, the railroads, or industry and assimilated rapidly despite racial discrimination. The San Francisco Board of Education, for example, began to segregate all Japanese students in 1906, and the Immigration Act of 1924 ended Japanese immigration until 1952. During World War II, the United States was at war with Japan. In response to war hysteria over the "yellow peril," the U.S. government interned 110,000 Japanese Americans, most of them American-born, in 10 detention camps from 1942 to 1946. Since World War II, Japan has developed into one of the world's leading economic and technological powers—an accomplishment that has contributed, no doubt, to a recent decline in Japanese immigration to the United States.

Filipinos began to immigrate to Hawaii and the mainland as field laborers during the 1920s. They, too, encountered racism; in 1934, Congress passed the Tydings-McDuffie Act, which limited Filipino immigration to the United States to 50 persons annually. The following year, President Franklin Roosevelt signed the Repatriation Act, which provided free transportation to Filipinos willing to return to the Philippines. Whereas most early Filipino immigrants had little education and low income, recent immigrants have tended to be professional, technical workers who hope to obtain employment in the United States more suitable for their education and training than they could in the Philippines (Banks, 2009).

TEACHERS' CONCERNS ABOUT ASIAN AMERICAN STUDENTS

Asian Americans are frequently stereotyped as hard-working, conscientious, and respectful of authority, what many people view as a so-called model minority (Fong, 2007). In fact, 50 percent of Asian Americans 25 years and over have a bachelor's degree or more, compared to 28 percent for all Americans 25 and older (U.S. Census Bureau, December 2013). The unreliability of such stereotypes notwithstanding, Asian American parents do tend to require their children to respect authority and value education. However, "for many Asian American students, this image is a destructive myth," according to a report titled *An Invisible Crisis: The Educational Needs of Asian Pacific American Youth*. "As their schools fail them, these children become increasingly likely to graduate with rudimentary language skills, to drop out of school, to join gangs, or to find themselves in the low-paying occupations and on the margins of American life" (Asian Americans/Pacific Islanders in Philanthropy, 1997). Families often pressure children to be successful academically through sacrifice and hard work. At the same time, there has been an increase in the number of Asian American youth who are in conflict with their parents' way of life. Leaders in Asian American communities have expressed concern about increases in dropout rates, school violence, and declining achievement. Some Indochinese Americans, for example, face deep cultural conflict in schools. Values and practices that are accepted in U.S. culture, such as dating and glorification of the individual, are sources of conflict between many Indochinese students and their parents (Fong, 2007).

Teachers need to be sensitive to cultural conflicts that may contribute to problems in school adjustment and achievement for Asian American students and realize that

> [s]tereotypes about Asian "whiz kids" and jealousy over the relatively high percentages of Asian Americans in the nation's colleges and universities may blind some non-Asian parents, fellow students, and teachers to the deep cultural conflict many Southeast Asian Americans face in our schools. (Bennett, 2011, p. 195)

To help Asian American students adjust to the U.S. culture, Qiu Liang offers teachers the following advice based on his school experiences as a Chinese immigrant:

> They [teachers] should be more patient [with an immigrant child] because it is very difficult for a person to be in a new country and learn a new language. Have patience. If the teacher feels there is no hope in an immigrant child, then the child will think, "Well, if the teacher who's helping me thinks that I can't go anywhere, then I might as well give up myself." (Igoa, 1995, pp. 99–100)

Similarly, Dung Yoong offers these recommendations based on her educational experiences as a Vietnamese immigrant:

> Try to get them to talk to you. Not just everyday conversation, but what they feel inside. Try to get them to get that out, because it's hard for kids. They don't trust—I had a hard time trusting and I was really insecure because of that.
>
> [P]utting an immigrant child who doesn't speak English into a classroom, a regular classroom with American students, is not very good. It scares [them] because it is so different. [Teachers] should start [them] slowly and have special classes where the child could adapt and learn a little bit about American society and customs. (Igoa, 1995, p. 103)

Education and Native Americans and Alaskan Natives

Native Americans and Alaskan Natives peopled the Western Hemisphere more than 12,000 years ago. They represent about 2 percent of the total U.S. population, or about 5.2 million people (U.S. Census Bureau, 2012c). The Native American and Alaska Native population is expected to increase to 11.2 million, or 2.7 percent of the population, by 2060 (U.S. Census Bureau, December 2012).

This group consists of 566 federally recognized and 365 state-recognized tribes, each with its own language, religious beliefs, and way of life. The six largest federally recognized tribes are the Navajo Nation, with over 308,000 members enrolled in the tribe; the Cherokee Nation, 285,000; the Sioux Nation, 131,000; the Chippewa Nation, 115,000; the Choctaw Nation, 89,000; and the Apache Nation, 65,000 (U.S. Census Bureau, 2010).

More than one-half million Native Americans live on 275 reservations located primarily in the West. In rank order, the five states with the largest proportion of Native Americans and Alaskan Natives are **ALASKA** (19.6 percent), **OKLAHOMA** (13.4 percent), **NEW MEXICO** (10.4 percent), **SOUTH DAKOTA** (10.0 percent), and **MONTANA** (8.1 percent) (U.S. Census Bureau, 2012). Although most Native Americans live in cities, many are establishing connections with reservation Indians as a means of strengthening their cultural identities.

Native Americans are an example of the increasing ambiguity of racial and ethnic identities in the United States. For example, controversy exists over who is Native American. "Some full-blooded native people do not regard a person with one-quarter native heritage as qualifying, while others accept $^1/_{128}$" (Bennett, 2011, p. 141). Whereas most Native Americans consider a person with one-quarter or more tribal heritage to be a member, the U.S. Census Bureau considers anyone who claims native identity to be a member. An expert on Native Americans and Alaskan Natives, Arlene Hirschfelder

(1986), points out that 52 legal definitions of Native Americans have been identified. Native Americans were declared U.S. citizens in 1924, and Native American nations have been recognized as independent, self-governing territories since the 1930s.

HISTORICAL, CULTURAL, AND SOCIOECONOMIC FACTORS

Perhaps more than any other minority group, Native Americans have endured systematic long-term attempts to eradicate their languages and cultures. Disease, genocide, confinement on reservations, and decades of forced assimilation have devastated Native American cultures. A member of the Muscogee (Creek) Nation explains the impact of these forces on the education of Native Americans:

> For centuries, American Indian, Alaska Native, and Native Hawaiian families and communities have exercised their sovereign rights to educate their children according to their own values, goals, and circumstances. Sovereign self-education *by* Native communities has for much of the past 5 centuries been at odds with, forcibly suppressed by, or actively criminalized by colonial systems of schooling that provided an education for American Indians dedicated to 'erasing and replacing' assimilationist policies and practices. (Lomawaima, 2013, p. 104)

It was not until 2000 that the U.S. government officially apologized for the Bureau of Indian Affairs' "legacy of racism and inhumanity that included massacres, forced relocation of tribes and attempts to wipe out Indian languages and cultures" (Kelly, 2000, p. 1).

In 1492, Native American people used 2 billion acres of land; currently, they own about 94 million acres of land, or about 5 percent of U.S. territory (Bennett, 2015). Today, the rates of unemployment, poverty, and lack of educational attainment among Native Americans are among the nation's highest. Since the 1970s, however, there has been a resurgence of interest in preserving or restoring traditional languages, skills, and land claims.

There are hundreds of Native American languages, which anthropologists have attempted to categorize into six major language families (Banks, 2014). Older tribal members fluent in the original tribal language and younger members often speak a form of so-called reservation English. The challenge of educating Native Americans from diverse language backgrounds is further complicated by the difference in size of various Native American populations. These range from the more than 308,000 people enrolled in the federally recognized Cherokee Nation to the 650 or so Havasupai of **ARIZONA**. As a result of the extreme diversity among Native Americans, it has even been suggested that "There is no such thing as an 'Indian' heritage, culture, or value system. [N]avajo, Cherokee, Sioux, and Aleut children are as different from each other in geographic and cultural backgrounds as they are from children growing up in New York City or Los Angeles" (Gipp, 1979, p. 19).

Education for Native American children living on reservations is currently administered by the federal government's Bureau of Indian Affairs (BIA). The **Indian Education Act of 1972 and 1974 Amendments** supplement the BIA's educational programs and provide direct educational assistance to tribes.

What factors contribute to below-average achievement levels of Native American children? How do forces toward assimilation and cultural preservation coexist in the Native American experience?

The act seeks to improve Native American education by providing funds to school districts to meet the special needs of Native American youth, to Indian tribes and state and local education agencies to improve education for youth and adults, to colleges and universities for the purpose of training teachers for Indian schools, and to Native American students to attend college.

RESEARCH ON NATIVE AMERICAN WAYS OF KNOWING

Considerable debate has occurred over the best approaches for educating Native Americans. For example, Banks (2006) points out that "since the 1920s, educational policy for Native Americans has vacillated between strong assimilationism to self-determination and cultural pluralism" (p. 42). The number of Native American students who leave school before completion remains high, leading two observers to comment that "school systems have shown little evidence of changing to meet the human and academic needs of the Indigenous student clientele . . . The process of inflicting an educational system conceived and implemented completely by outside forces appears to be a foundational cause of alienation by Native students toward school" (Freed & Samson, 2004, p. 42).

In general, the culture-based learning styles of many Native Americans and Alaskan Natives differ from that of other students. The traditional upbringing of Native American children generally encourages them to develop a view of the world that is holistic, intimate, and shared. "They approach tasks visually, seem to prefer to learn by careful observation which precedes performance, and seem to learn in their natural settings experientially" (Swisher & Deyhle, 1987, p. 350). Bennett (2003) suggests the following guideline to ensure that the school experiences of Native American students are in harmony with their cultural backgrounds: "An effective learning environment for Native Americans is one that does not single out the individual but provides frequent opportunities for the teacher to interact privately with individual children and with small groups, as well as opportunities for quiet, persistent exploration" (p. 212).

Increasingly, Native Americans are designing multicultural programs to preserve their traditional cultures and ways of knowing. Although these programs are sometimes characterized as emphasizing separatism over assimilation, for many Native Americans they are a matter of survival. For example, the Native American Community Academy in Albuquerque, **NEW MEXICO**, was created to preserve the languages and cultures of 37 different tribes. The school offers classes in the Navajo and Lakota languages and a high school class in Dine (Navaho) Government (Native American Community Academy, 2014).

Cultural preservation is also the primary concern at Alaskan Native schools in remote parts of western **ALASKA** and Cherokee schools in the Marietta Independent School District of Stillwell, **OKLAHOMA**. In Alaska, elders come into the classroom to teach children how to skin a seal, an education that few Alaskan Native children receive today at home. In an effort to keep the Cherokee language alive, students at the Lost City School near Tulsa, Oklahoma, learn Cherokee, one of the many endangered Native American tongues. In Oklahoma, fewer than 8,000 of the 100,000 Cherokees can speak the language fluently, and most of those are over age 45 (Burns, 2003).

WHAT IS MEANT BY BILINGUAL EDUCATION?

Bilingual education programs are designed to meet the learning needs of students whose first language is not English by providing instruction in two languages. Regardless of the instructional approach used, one outcome for all bilingual programs is for students to become proficient in English. Students are also encouraged to become **bicultural**, that is, able to function effectively in two or more linguistic and cultural groups.

In 1968, Congress passed the Bilingual Education Act, which required that language-minority students be taught in both their native language and English. In response to the act, school districts implemented an array of bilingual programs that varied greatly in quality and effectiveness. As a result, many parents filed lawsuits, claiming that bilingual programs were not meeting their children's needs.

In 1974, the Supreme Court heard a class action suit (*Lau v. Nichols*) filed by 1,800 Chinese students in San Francisco who charged that they were failing to learn because they could not understand English. The students were enrolled in all-English classes and received no special assistance in learning English. In a unanimous ruling, the Court asserted that federally funded schools must "rectify the language deficiency" of students who "are certain to find their classroom experiences wholly incomprehensible." That same year, Congress adopted the Equal Educational Opportunity Act (EEOA), which stated in part that a school district must "take appropriate action to overcome language barriers that impede equal participation by its students in its instructional programs."

Although most bilingual programs serve Latino and Hispanic American students, there is an increasing need for bilingual teachers who are proficient in a variety of second languages. In fact, many school districts are offering salary bonuses for bilingual teachers.

Bilingual programs are tremendously varied. In fact, "any discussion about bilingual education should begin with the understanding that bilingual education is neither a single program nor a consistent 'methodology' for teaching language minority students" (Ovando, Combs, & Collier, 2006, p. 8). Generally, however, four types of bilingual education programs are currently available to provide special assistance to the 4.7 million language-minority students in the United States (see Figure 8.7).

PROFESSIONAL REFLECTION
Watch as teachers work effectively with bilingual students.

Research and Debate on Bilingual Programs

Research on the effectiveness of bilingual programs is mixed (Gollnick & Chinn, 2009). Some who have examined the research conclude that bilingual programs have little effect on achievement (American Institutes of Research, 2003; Hakuta, 2001a, 2001b). Others have found that well-designed bilingual programs do increase students' achievement and are superior to monolingual programs (Crawford, 2004, 2007; Krashen & McField, 2005; Nieto, 2002).

Considerable debate surrounds bilingual programs in the United States. Those in favor of bilingual education make the following points:

- Students are better able to learn English if they are taught to read and write in their native language.
- Bilingual programs allow students to learn content in their native language rather than delaying that learning until they master English.
- Further developing competencies in students' native languages provides important cognitive foundations for learning English and academic content.

FIGURE 8.7   Four types of bilingual education programs

Immersion programs: Students learn English and other subjects in classrooms where only English is spoken. Aides who speak the first language of students are sometimes available, or students may also listen to equivalent audiotape lessons in their first language.

Transition programs: Students receive reading lessons in their first language and lessons in English as a second language (ESL). Once they sufficiently master English, students are placed in classrooms where English is spoken and their first language is discontinued.

Pullout programs: On a regular basis, students are separated from English-speaking students so that they may receive lessons in English or reading lessons in their first language. These are sometimes called sheltered English programs.

Maintenance programs: To maintain the student's native language and culture, instruction in English and instruction in the native language are provided from kindergarten through twelfth grade. Students become literate.

- Second-language learning is a positive value and should be as valid for a Spanish-speaker learning English as for an English-speaker learning Spanish.
- Bilingual programs support students' cultural identity, social context, and self-esteem.

On the other hand, those opposed to bilingual programs make the following points:

- Public schools should not be expected to provide instruction in all the first languages spoken by their students, nor can schools afford to pay a teacher who might teach only a few students.
- The cost of bilingual education is high. Bilingual programs divert staff and resources away from English-speaking students.
- If students spend more time exposed to English, they will learn English more quickly.
- Bilingual programs emphasize differences among and barriers between groups; they encourage separateness rather than assimilation and unity.
- Bilingual education is a threat to English as the nation's first language.

Advice for Monolingual Teachers

Although the future of bilingual education in the United States is uncertain, teachers must continue to meet the needs of language-minority students. These needs are best met by teachers who speak their native language as well as English (Snipes, Soga, & Uro, 2007). This is often not possible, however, and monolingual teachers will find increasing numbers of LEP students in their classrooms. The following classroom strategies are useful for both monolingual and bilingual teachers:

- Be aware of each student's language abilities.
- Make sure appropriate cultural experiences are reflected in the material.
- Document the success of selected materials.
- Experiment with the materials until you find the most appropriate for your particular student.
- Make a smooth transition into the new material.
- Be sure to become knowledgeable about the cultures and heritages of your students to ensure appropriateness and compatibility of the material. (Ariza, 2006, pp. 110–111)

Additional tips for adapting material for LEP students are:

- Develop your own supplemental materials.
- Tape-record directions for the material so students can replay them for clarity.
- Provide alternatives to responding verbally to questions (e.g., use prearranged signals—give students a card to hold up, a flag, or any indicator they can use instead of speaking).
- Rewrite sections of the text to condense the reading for those with lower proficiency levels.
- Outline the material for the students before they read.
- Teach students the meaning of using bold headings, italicized words, subheadings, and transition words (*first, last, however, although,* etc.).
- Reduce the number of pages or items to be completed by the student.
- Break tasks into smaller subtasks.
- Substitute a similar, less complex task.
- Develop study guides for all students. (Ariza, 2006, p. 110)

Additionally, you should be aware that "although second language learners often present challenges within the classroom, they may also bring a number of advantages" (Adesope, Lavin, Thompson, & Ungerleider, 2010, p. 231). In an analysis of 63 research studies (including more than 6,000 participants) of the cognitive outcomes associated with bilingualism, Olusola Adesope and his colleagues (2010) found that people who are bilingual tend to have several cognitive "advantages" over monolingual people. Among these advantages are:

- greater metacognitive awareness (knowledge about one's own cognitive processes and ability to self-regulate learning strategies)
- greater cognitive flexibility and creativity
- enhanced skills for divergent thinking and abstract and symbolic reasoning
- enhanced problem-solving skills
- greater efficiency of working memory
- enhanced ability to control attention while engaged in linguistic and nonverbal tasks

WHAT IS MULTICULTURAL EDUCATION?

Multicultural education is committed to the goal of providing all students—regardless of socioeconomic status; gender; sexual orientation; or ethnic, racial, or cultural backgrounds—with equal opportunities to learn in school. Multicultural education is also based on the fact that students do not learn in a vacuum—their culture predisposes them to learn in certain ways. And finally, multicultural education recognizes that current school practices have provided—and continue to provide—some students with greater opportunities for learning than students who belong to other groups. The suggestions presented in the preceding section are examples of multicultural education in practice. The Teachers' Voices: Walk in My Shoes feature in this chapter profiles Kevin Grover, a second-grade teacher known throughout his school and community for his kindness, intelligence, and creativity in helping all students learn and become involved citizens in a multicultural, global world.

PROFESSIONAL REFLECTION
Watch how teachers plan
a "Holidays Around
the World" lesson.

As multiculturalism has become more pervasive in U.S. schools, controversy over the need for multicultural education and its purposes has emerged. "Multicultural education is sometimes criticized as focusing on differences rather than similarities among groups. On the other side, it is criticized for not adequately addressing issues of power and oppression that keep a number of groups from participating equitably in society" (Gollnick & Chinn, 2009, p. 8). Although multicultural education is being challenged by some, public dialogue and debate about how schools can address diversity more effectively is healthy—an indicator that our society is making real progress toward creating a culture that incorporates the values of diverse groups.

Dimensions of Multicultural Education

According to James A. Banks, "Multicultural education is a way of viewing reality and a way of thinking, and not just content about various ethnic, racial, and cultural groups" (Banks, 2006, p. 8). More specifically, Banks suggests that multicultural education be conceptualized as consisting of five dimensions: (1) content integration, (2) the knowledge construction process, (3) prejudice reduction, (4) an equity pedagogy, and (5) an empowering school culture and social structure (see Figure 8.8). As you progress through your teacher education program and eventually begin to prepare curriculum materials and instructional strategies for your multicultural classroom, remember that integrating content from a variety of cultural groups is just one dimension of multicultural education.

Multicultural education promotes students' positive self-identity and pride in their heritage, acceptance of people from diverse backgrounds, and critical self-assessment. In addition, multicultural education can prompt students, perhaps with guidance from their teachers, to promote social justice and to take action against prejudice and discrimination within their school. For example, students might reduce the marginalization of minority-group students in their school by inviting them to participate in extracurricular and after-school activities.

FIGURE 8.8 The dimensions of multicultural education

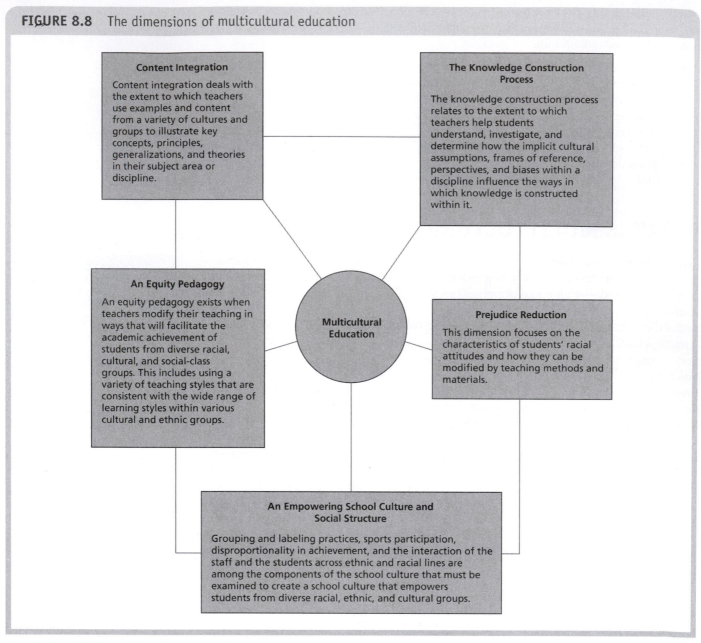

Content Integration

Content integration deals with the extent to which teachers use examples and content from a variety of cultures and groups to illustrate key concepts, principles, generalizations, and theories in their subject area or discipline.

The Knowledge Construction Process

The knowledge construction process relates to the extent to which teachers help students understand, investigate, and determine how the implicit cultural assumptions, frames of reference, perspectives, and biases within a discipline influence the ways in which knowledge is constructed within it.

An Equity Pedagogy

An equity pedagogy exists when teachers modify their teaching in ways that will facilitate the academic achievement of students from diverse racial, cultural, and social-class groups. This includes using a variety of teaching styles that are consistent with the wide range of learning styles within various cultural and ethnic groups.

Multicultural Education

Prejudice Reduction

This dimension focuses on the characteristics of students' racial attitudes and how they can be modified by teaching methods and materials.

An Empowering School Culture and Social Structure

Grouping and labeling practices, sports participation, disproportionality in achievement, and the interaction of the staff and the students across ethnic and racial lines are among the components of the school culture that must be examined to create a school culture that empowers students from diverse racial, ethnic, and cultural groups.

Source: Reprinted with the permission of James A. Banks, from James A. Banks, *An Introduction to Multicultural Education* (Fourth Edition). Upper Saddle River, NJ: Allyn & Bacon.

Multicultural Curricula

TEACHERS' VOICES
Walk in My Shoes
Kevin Grover
D. W. Lunt School
Falmouth, MAINE

As a teacher, you will teach students who historically have not received full educational opportunity—students from the many racial and ethnic minority groups in the United States; students from low-income families or communities; students with exceptional abilities or disabilities; students who are lesbian, gay, bisexual, or transgender (LGBT); and students who are male or female. You will face the challenge of reaching out to all students and teaching them that they are persons of worth who can learn. The following case about 12-year-old Yvette illustrates that challenge.

Yvette is 12 years old and lives with her older brother and younger sister in an apartment in the city. Yvette and her brother were born in Puerto Rico, and her sister was born in the United States. Yvette's mother and father brought the family to the mainland two years ago.

Three months ago, Yvette transferred into your class. It appears that the transition is difficult for her. Her work would improve if she got more involved, you think. However, she seems afraid to risk making mistakes, especially in reading and language arts.

Yvette seems to trust you, so you've decided to talk to her after school today. She usually waits in your classroom until her brother Juan arrives to walk her home.

You begin by asking, "How is school going?"

As she speaks, timidly at first and then more openly and naturally, you realize that Yvette is still struggling to adjust to the challenges of living on the mainland. She misses her grandmother, who lived with the family in Puerto Rico. She also says she does not speak English well enough. She is worried that the other children will tease her if she speaks out in class. You also learn that Yvette has missed school frequently because of bad headaches and stomach problems. When you ask Yvette if her parents are coming to the next PTA meeting, Yvette tells you they probably will not come because they do not speak English.

How can you get Yvette more involved in classroom activities? What strategies could you use to help her to increase her reading, speaking, and writing skills? How might you make Yvette's parents feel welcome and comfortable at the school?

As a teacher, you will develop a curriculum that increases students' awareness and appreciation of the rich diversity in U.S. culture. A **multicultural curriculum** addresses the needs and backgrounds of all students regardless of their cultural identity. As Banks (2009) suggests, the multicultural curriculum "enable[s] students to derive valid generalizations and theories about the characteristics of ethnic groups and to learn how they are alike and different, in both their past and present experiences. . . . [It] focus[es] on a range of groups that differ in their racial characteristics, cultural experiences, languages, histories, values, and current problems" (p. 16). Teachers who provide multicultural education hold the following beliefs:

- Cultural differences have strength and value.
- Schools should be models for the expression of human rights and respect for cultural and group differences.
- Social justice and equality for all people should be of paramount importance in the design and delivery of curricula.
- Attitudes and values necessary for the continuation of a democratic society can be promoted in schools.
- Schooling can provide the knowledge, skills, and dispositions (i.e., values, attitudes, and commitments) to help students from diverse groups learn.
- Educators working with families and communities can create an environment that is supportive of multiculturalism. (Gollnick & Chinn, 2009, p. 4)

In developing a multicultural curriculum, you should be sensitive to how your instructional materials and strategies can be made more inclusive so that they reflect cultural perspectives, or "voices," that previously have been silent or marginalized in discussions about what should be taught in schools and how it should be taught. Effective teachers attend to these previously unheard voices not as an act of tokenism, but with a genuine desire to make the curriculum more inclusive. The Teaching on Your Feet feature in this chapter describes how Romaine Washington was able to relate curriculum content to her students' cultural backgrounds.

Multicultural Instructional Materials and Strategies

To create classrooms that are truly multicultural, teachers must select instructional materials that are sensitive, accurately portray the contributions of ethnic groups, and reflect diverse points of view. Teachers must also recognize that "[s]ome of the books and other materials on ethnic groups published each year are insensitive, inaccurate, and written from mainstream and insensitive perspectives and points of view" (Banks, 2009, p. 108). Some guidelines for selecting multicultural instructional materials follow:

- Books and other materials should accurately portray the perspectives, attitudes, and feelings of ethnic groups.
- Fictional works should have strong ethnic characters.
- Books should describe settings and experiences with which all students can identify and yet should accurately reflect ethnic cultures and lifestyles.
- The protagonists in books with ethnic themes should have ethnic characteristics but should face conflicts and problems that are universal.
- The illustrations in books should be accurate, ethnically sensitive, and technically well done.
- Ethnic materials should not contain racist concepts, clichés, phrases, or words.
- Factual materials should be historically accurate.
- Multiethnic resources and basal textbooks should discuss major events and documents related to ethnic history. (Banks, 2009, pp. 109–110)

Yvonne Wilson, a first-grade teacher in Talmoon, **MINNESOTA**, and an Ojibwe Indian, points out that a teacher's willingness to learn about other cultures is very important to students and their parents:

> People in the community know if you are trying to understand their culture. Students also see it. Becoming involved—going to a powwow or participating in other cultural events—shows people that here is a teacher who is trying to learn about our culture.

TEACHING ON YOUR FEET
¡Sí Se Puede! (It Can Be Done!)

What do you do when multiculturalism gets shaved down to biculturalism and students ask why more groups are not represented in the literature? From Puritanism to the Slave Narrative, from Transcendentalism to the Harlem Renaissance, Modernists, Beat Poets, Post-Modernists, and the Black Arts Movement, students are presented with myriad voices and views of American life. Mario asked one day, "Why is everything black and white?" Melissa followed his question with, "Where are Mexicans in these stories? Weren't they around? Why don't we read about them?"

The questions Mario and Melissa raised were on my mind as I prepared to teach the poignant, readily accessible novel Of Mice and Men. From previous experience, I knew that students would love Lennie and hate Curly. We would identify the themes of loneliness and alienation. We would explore the concept of the American dream, as told by George. We would have a mock trial, and the jury would decide whether euthanasia is pardonable under certain circumstances. Yet when it is all said and done, we would still be left with the Mexican migrant worker waiting at the roadside for his story to be told.

This year my English class would be half Latino, with quite a few English language learners. I longed to engage them on another level. I recalled the legacy of Cesar Chavez, which would provide the cultural, historical, and literary connection I needed. Although he was not an activist at the time in which Of Mice and Men takes place, he was a child during that time period. He had a difficult time in school because he

was the child of migrant workers who had moved more than 35 times. In addition, he spoke only Spanish. Children at his school would be hit on the knuckles when they did not speak English. I inform my students that, despite those challenges, Chavez became a great orator and activist for migrant workers.

We speculate about the difference his presence might have made if he had been an activist during the time period of the novel. We read some of his quotes and relate them to the novel's characters and conflicts. Finally, we deconstruct a collage picture of Cesar Chavez in which his face, clothes, and the background are made up of migrant workers in the fields and holding peaceful demonstrations. All of the images in the collage symbolize important aspects of Chavez's life. I ask students to write about what they see and what they think it symbolizes. Detail by detail, they embrace the lesson. Phillip asks, "Can I have the picture we are writing about? I really like it." I respond using the slogan of the UFW (United Food Workers), "¡Sí se puede!"

ANALYZE & REFLECT

Click here to analyze and reflect on this scenario you have just read.

ROMAINE WASHINGTON
English Teacher
Los Osos High School
Alta Loma, CALIFORNIA

FIGURE 8.9   Essential knowledge and skills for successful teaching in a diverse society

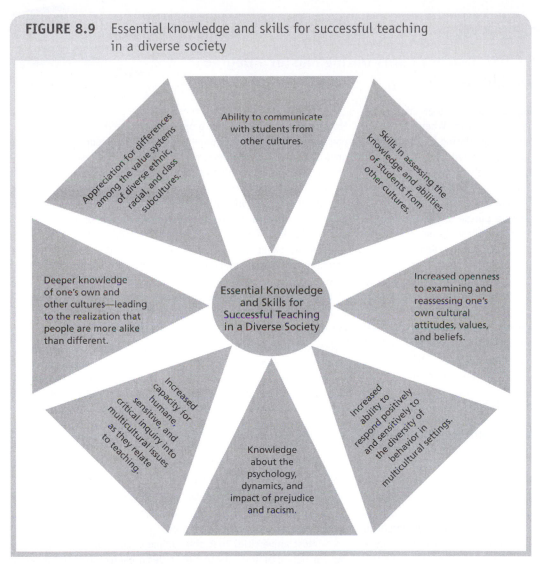

Adapted from Forrest W. Parkay and Henry T. Fillmer, "Improving Teachers' Attitudes Toward Minority-Group Students: An Experimental Approach to Multicultural Inservice," *New Horizons Journal of Education*, November 1984, pp. 178–179.

Participating wholeheartedly in cross-cultural experiences will help you to grow in the eight areas outlined in Figure 8.9 as essential for successful teaching in a diverse society. By developing knowledge and skills in these eight areas, you will be well prepared to meet the educational needs of all your students. The Technology in Action feature in this chapter profiles a teacher who earned an online master's degree with an emphasis on multicultural education.

HOW IS GENDER A DIMENSION OF MULTICULTURAL EDUCATION?

Although it may be evident that gender affects students' learning in many ways, it may not be evident that gender is an important dimension of multicultural education. However, "culturally democratic classrooms also consider gender differences" (Oakes & Lipton, 2007, p. 277). For example, the following comments by a first-year high school science teacher stress the importance of gender differences in the classroom.

> I have high expectations for all of my students, not just the boys. If I chal-
> lenge a boy to figure out the answer to a scientifically engaging problem for
> himself, and then go and give the answer to a girl, I send an unconscious

TECHNOLOGY in ACTION
High-School English Teacher Earns Online Master's Degree in Multicultural Education

Mr. Andrews teaches English at a high school in a large city on the East Coast. He has taught there for just over 5 years. When he first began teaching at the school, he had difficulty relating to his students whose cultural and linguistic backgrounds differed from his own. At the end of his first year, he even thought about not returning the following year. However, each year improved, and now he enjoys his students and looks forward to school each day.

He decided recently that he would pursue a master's degree. The problem is that he would need to take night and summer courses. With his extracurricular responsibilities and his family and community commitments, neither of these options is appealing.

Last year, a colleague of Mr. Andrews took an online course in classroom assessment. She had some very positive things to say about the experience.

After a bit of research into online courses and degrees, Mr. Andrews was surprised to find so many options available to him. Through online learning, he now had the option of "attending" a university anywhere in the world, including nationally and internationally recognized institutions.

He found a university that seemed perfect. It had a master's degree program, with an emphasis on multicultural education, designed to prepare and support teachers to be highly effective in diverse school environments. The program specifically addresses two reasons for the high level of attrition among urban teachers: preparation and mentoring support. Courses in the program include Education in a Diverse Society, Culturally Responsive Pedagogy, Second Language Teaching and Learning, and Teaching for Equity and Social Justice.

What intrigued him most was that the program was described as highly interactive. In other words, this was not a work-at-your-own-pace, all-by-yourself program. According to the program description, the academic rigor was identical to the on-campus experience.

Although unsure of these claims, Mr. Andrews enrolled in the program. He started with just one course the first semester—to measure the accuracy of the program description and to determine the level of effort needed for success. At first, it was rough going. This style of learning was quite new to him. The most difficult aspect of online learning was carving out time for the coursework. Mr. Andrews realized that he would need to create an individual calendar, based on the demands of the course that would allow him to dedicate time for specific assignments.

As he moved through the semester, Mr. Andrews found that the description of the program was very accurate. The courses were highly interactive. He connected with classmates in a discussion board area of the university's online learning management system, worked in small groups, developed projects, and made presentations. He was already looking forward to the next semester.

ONLINE DEGREE: Online degrees are one of the fastest growing educational options in the United States. As with on-campus programs, the student experience depends on the university, the subject matter, and the instructor. Most online degree programs are delivered through a learning management system. In these systems, students interact, submit assignments, make presentations, and follow a guided course experience.

POSSIBLE USES: Teachers have used online courses and degrees to update their résumés, obtain advanced degrees, and improve their teaching without relocating, traveling long distances, or giving up employment.

TRY IT OUT: Numerous online degree options are available to you. On the Internet, you can search for online degrees by level of education, subject matter, or specific institution.

Most universities that offer online degrees provide opportunities for potential students to take a demo course. Visit a university that is of interest to you and look for a demo course link.

---

message that I do not think my female student can figure it out by herself. I encourage the girls' active participation when it is easy for them to be drowned out by the louder and more aggressive boys. I encourage girls to ask questions and help them use scientific methodology to find answers. I challenge them to think about why there are more men who do science than women. (Oakes & Lipton, 2007, p. 278)

Gender Differences

Cultural differences between males and females are partially shaped by society's traditional expectations of them. Through **sex role stereotyping**, families, the media, the schools, and other powerful social forces condition boys and girls to act in certain ways regardless of abilities or interests. One dimension of the **sex role socialization** process conveys to students certain expectations about the way boys and girls are "supposed" to act. Girls are supposed to play with dolls, boys to play with trucks. Girls are supposed to be passive; boys are supposed to be active. Girls are supposed to express their feelings and emotions when in pain; boys are supposed to repress their feelings and deny pain.

Students may be socialized into particular gender-specific roles as a result of the curriculum materials they use at school. By portraying males in more dominant, assertive ways and portraying females in ways that suggest that they are passive and helpless, textbooks can subtly reinforce expectations about the way girls and boys "should" behave. Within the last few decades, however, publishers of curriculum materials have become more vigilant about avoiding these stereotypes.

Gender and Education

It was not until Title IX of the Education Amendments Act was passed in 1972 that women were guaranteed equality of educational opportunity in educational programs receiving federal assistance. Title IX has had the greatest impact on athletic programs in schools. The law requires that both sexes have equal opportunities to participate in and benefit from the availability of coaches, sports equipment, resources, and facilities. For contact sports such as football, wrestling, and boxing, sports that were not open to women, separate teams are allowed.

The right of females to equal educational opportunity was further enhanced with the passage of the **Women's Educational Equity Act (WEEA)** of 1974. This act provides the following opportunities:

- Expanded math, science, and technology programs for females
- Programs to reduce sex role stereotyping in curriculum materials
- Programs to increase the number of female educational administrators
- Special programs to extend educational and career opportunities to minority, disabled, and rural women
- Programs to help school personnel increase educational opportunities and career aspirations for females
- Encouragement for more females to participate in athletics

Despite reforms stemming from WEEA, several reports in the early 1990s criticized schools for subtly discriminating against girls in tests, textbooks, and teaching methods. Research on teacher interactions in the classroom seemed to point to widespread unintentional gender bias against girls. Two of these studies, *Shortchanging Girls, Shortchanging America* (1991) and *How Schools Shortchange Girls* (1992), both commissioned by the American Association of University Women (AAUW), claimed that girls were not encouraged in math and science and that teachers favored boys' intellectual growth over that of girls.

In the mid-1990s, however, some gender equity studies had more mixed findings. In their analysis of data on achievement and engagement of 9,000 eighth-grade boys and girls, University of Michigan researchers Valerie Lee, Xianglei Chen, and Becky A. Smerdon (1996) concluded that "the pattern of gender differences is inconsistent. In some cases, females are favored; in others males are favored." Similarly, University of Chicago researchers Larry Hedges and Amy Nowell found in their study of 32 years of mental tests given to boys and girls that, while boys do better than girls in science and mathematics, they were "at a rather profound disadvantage" in writing and scored below girls in reading comprehension (Hedges, 1996, p. 3).

Additional research and closer analyses of earlier reports on gender bias in education were beginning to suggest that boys, not girls, were most short-changed by the schools (Gurian & Stevens, 2007; Sommers, 1996, 2000). Numerous articles, as well as a PBS series that began with a program titled "The War on Boys," challenged the conclusions of the earlier AAUW report, *How Schools Shortchange Girls*. Other commentary discounted gender bias in the schools as a fabrication of radical feminism; among the first to put forth this view was Christina Hoff Sommers's (1994) controversial book, *Who Stole Feminism? How Women Have Betrayed Women*; Judith Kleinfeld (1998) followed with *The Myth That Schools Shortchange Girls: Social Science in the Service of Deception*, as did Cathy Young (1999) with *Ceasefire! Why Women and Men Must Join Forces to Achieve True Equality*.

What impact has the Women's Education Equity Act (WEEA) of 1974 had on the education of females? Why and in what ways does gender bias, for both girls and boys, persist in many U.S. classrooms and schools?

What some people had come to call the "gender wars" took another turn when the AAUW released *Where the Girls Are: The Facts About Gender Equity in Education* in 2008. The report, which examined trends in standardized test scores by gender, race, ethnicity, and family income during the past 35 years, found that family income, not gender, is most closely associated with academic success. The analysis of scores on tests such as the SAT and ACT college entrance exams led the AAUW to conclude:

> The overarching message of this report is one of good news. Overall and within racial/ethnic groups and family income levels, girls and boys are improving by most measures of educational achievement, and most achievement gaps are narrowing. The past few decades have seen remarkable gains for girls and boys in education, and no evidence indicates a crisis for boys in particular. If a crisis exists, it is a crisis for African American and Hispanic students and students from lower-income families—both girls and boys. (American Association of University Women, May 2008, p. 68)

Figure 8.10 shows, by gender and race/ethnicity, the proportion of fourth- and eighth-grade students who reached *proficient* on the 2013 National Assessment of Educational Progress (NAEP) in mathematics and reading. More than 376,000 fourth graders and 341,000 eighth graders in public and private schools completed the NAEP assessment. Compared to 1992, students made progress in mathematics and reading. However, female students have scored consistently and significantly higher in reading than male students. On the other hand, male students have scored higher in mathematics than female students, although the difference between the two groups is small. Compared to 1992, the score gaps in mathematics and reading between White and Black students and White and Hispanic students narrowed somewhat on the 2011 and 2013 NAEP assessments.

Lesbian, Gay, Bisexual, and Transgender (LGBT) Students

In addition to gender bias, some students experience discrimination on the basis of their sexual orientation. To help all students realize their full potential, teachers should acknowledge the special needs of gay, lesbian, and bisexual students because "there is an invisible gay and lesbian minority in every school, and the needs of these students [a]re often unknown and unmet" (Besner & Spungin, 1995, p. xi). One study of 120 gay and lesbian students ages 14 to 21 found that only one-fourth said that they were able to discuss their sexual orientation with school counselors, and less than one in five said they could identify someone who had been supportive of them (Tellijohann & Price, 1993). Moreover, a similar study of lesbian and gay youth reported that 80 percent of participants believed their teachers had negative attitudes about homosexuality (Sears, 1992).

Based on estimates that as much as 10 percent of society may be homosexual, a high school with an enrollment of 1,500 might have as many as 150 gay, lesbian, and bisexual students (Besner & Spungin, 1995; Stover, 1992). The National Education Association, the American Federation of Teachers and several professional organizations have passed resolutions urging members and school districts to acknowledge the special needs of these students.

The nation's first dropout prevention program targeting gay, lesbian, and bisexual students was implemented in the Los Angeles school system. Known as Project 10, the program focuses on education, suicide prevention, dropout prevention, creating a safe environment for homosexual students, and HIV/AIDS education (Uribe & Harbeck, 1991). In 1993, **MASSACHUSETTS** became the first state to adopt an educational policy prohibiting discrimination against gay and lesbian students and teachers. At one Massachusetts high school, gay and straight students created the Gay-Straight Alliance (GSA), a school-sanctioned student organization that gives students a safe place to discuss sexual orientation issues (Bennett, 1997).

FIGURE 8.10 Percentage of students at or above *Proficient* in fourth- and eighth-grade mathematics and reading, by groups: 1990, 2011, and 2013

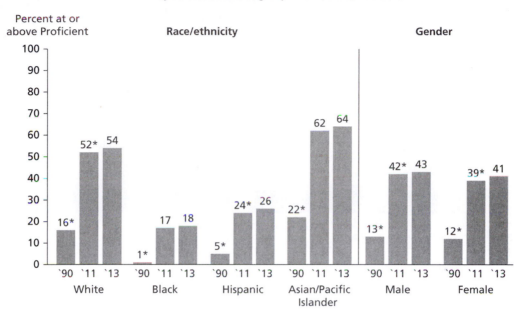

Percentage of students at or above *Proficient* in fourth-grade NAEP mathematics, by selected student groups: 1990, 2011, and 2013

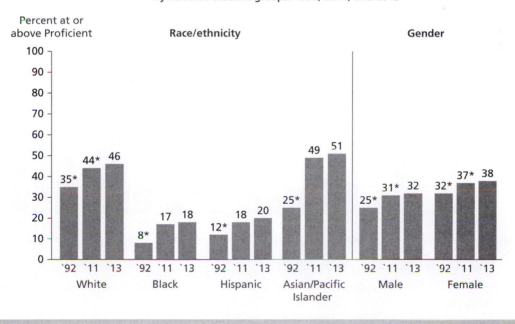

Percentage of students at or above *Proficient* in fourth-grade NAEP reading, by selected student groups: 1992, 2011, and 2013

(continued)

FIGURE 8.10 (continued)

Percentage of students at or above *Proficient* in eighth-grade NAEP mathematics, by selected student groups: 1990, 2011, and 2013

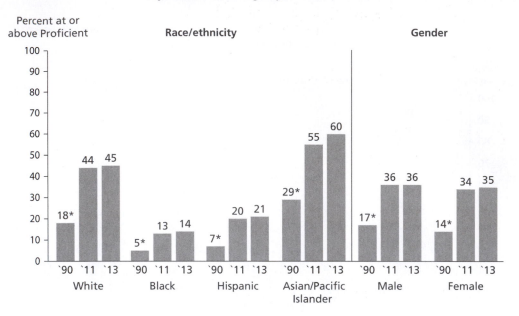

Percentage of students at or above *Proficient* in eighth-grade NAEP reading, by selected student groups: 1992, 2011, and 2013

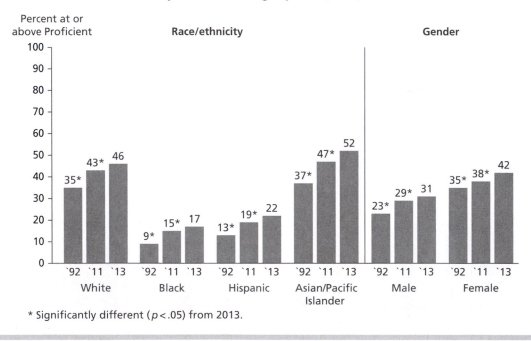

* Significantly different (*p* < .05) from 2013.

*Significantly different (*p* < .05) from 2013.

Note: Black includes African American, Hispanic includes Latino, and Pacific Islander includes Native Hawaiian. Race categories exclude Hispanic origin. Detail may not sum to totals because of rounding.

Source: The Nation's Report Card: 2013 Mathematics and Reading—What proportions of student groups are reaching *Proficient?* U.S. Department of Education, Institute of Education Sciences, National Center for Education Statistics, National Assessment of Educational Progress (NAEP), various years, 1990–2013 Mathematics and Reading Assessments. Retrieved May 12, 2014, from http://nationsreportcard.gov/reading_math_2013/#/student-groups.

In 2003, about 100 students enrolled in the Harvey Milk School, the nation's first public high school for gay, lesbian, bisexual, and transgender students. Housed in an office building in New York City, the school is named after California's first elected gay official—a member of the board of supervisors in San Francisco—who was assassinated after less than a year in office. New York City also cosponsors after-school programs, such as art and music, and counseling and support services for as many as 2,000 gay and lesbian students (Ferguson, 2003).

Homosexual students can experience school-related problems and safety risks. The hostility that gay, lesbian, and bisexual youth can encounter may cause them to feel confused, isolated, and self-destructive. This reality came to the nation's attention during fall 2010 when several homosexual students committed suicide as a result of school-based bullying they experienced. Teachers and other school personnel can provide much-needed support. Informed, sensitive, and caring teachers can play an important role in helping all students develop to their full potential. Such teachers realize the importance of recognizing diverse perspectives, and they create inclusive classroom environments that encourage students to respect differences among themselves and others and to see the contributions that persons from all groups have made to society.

Gender-Fair Classrooms and Curricula

Although research and debate about the bias boys and girls encounter in school will no doubt continue, it is clear that teachers must encourage girls and boys to develop to the full extent of their capabilities and provide them an education that is free from **gender bias**—subtle favoritism or discrimination on the basis of gender. Following is a list of basic guidelines for creating a **gender-fair classroom**.

- Become aware of differences in interactions with girls and boys.
- Promote boys' achievement in reading and writing and girls' achievement in mathematics and science.
- Reduce young children's self-imposed sexism.
- Teach about sexism and sex role stereotyping.
- Foster an atmosphere of collaboration between girls and boys.

SUMMARY

How Is Diversity Reflected in the Culture of the United States?

- The percentage of ethnic minorities in the United States has been growing steadily since World War II. Minorities, which made up 37 percent of the U.S. population in 2012, are projected to comprise 57 percent of the population in 2060, an increase from 116.2 million to 241.3 million. Currently, the majority of students in several states and many urban districts are from groups traditionally thought of as minority.
- Culture is defined as the way of life common to a group of people, including beliefs, attitudes, habits, values, and practices.
- Ethnicity refers to a commonly shared racial or cultural identity and a set of beliefs, values, and attitudes. The concept of race is used to distinguish among people on the basis of biological traits and characteristics. A minority group is a group of people who

share certain characteristics and are fewer in number than the majority of a population.

- The increase of people who identify themselves as mixed race is one indication that racial and ethnic identities in the United States are becoming more complex.
- The lower achievement levels of certain minority-group students compared to those of their Anglo-European American and Asian American counterparts reflect the strong connection between socioeconomic status and achievement.
- Stereotyping is the process of attributing certain behavioral characteristics to all members of a group, often on the basis of limited experiences with and information about the group being stereotyped. Individual racism is the prejudicial belief that one's own ethnic or racial group is superior to others, and institutional racism refers to laws, customs, and practices that lead to racial inequalities.

What Does Equal Educational Opportunity Mean?

- Equal educational opportunity means that teachers promote the full development of students without regard for race, ethnicity, gender, sexual orientation, socioeconomic status, abilities, or disabilities.
- Teachers can meet the needs of minority students by becoming familiar with their cultural and linguistic backgrounds and learning styles.
- In spite of increasing diversity in the United States, there has been a trend since 1990 for schools to resegregate.

What Is Meant by Bilingual Education?

- Bilingual education programs provide instruction in a student's first language and English. The goal of bilingual programs is for students to function effectively in two or more linguistic/cultural groups. Four approaches to bilingual education are immersion, maintenance, pullout, and transition programs.

What Is Multicultural Education?

- Five dimensions of multicultural education have been suggested: content integration, the knowledge construction process, prejudice reduction, an equity pedagogy, and an empowering school culture and social structure.
- Effective multicultural materials and instructional strategies include the contributions of ethnic groups and reflect diverse points of view, or "voices," that previously may have been silenced or marginalized in society.

How Is Gender a Dimension of Multicultural Education?

- The behavior of boys and girls in our society is influenced by sexism, sex role socialization, and sex role stereotyping.
- The latest research indicates that family income, not gender, is most closely associated with academic achievement.
- Teachers can provide an education free of gender bias by creating gender-fair classrooms and curricula and providing students with safe, supportive learning environments.

PROFESSIONAL REFLECTIONS AND ACTIVITIES

Teacher's Journal

1. Reflecting on your experiences in schools and the five dimensions of multicultural education (see Figure 8.8, page 293), describe the steps your teachers took to create an empowering school culture and social climate.
2. During your school years, did you ever experience discrimination as a member of a "different" group? Write about one outstanding incident that you feel affected your performance as a student.

Teacher's Research

1. Gather data from the National Center for Education Statistics regarding trends in achievement levels, educational attainment, and dropout rates for one of the following groups of which you are not a member: African Americans, Latino and Hispanic Americans, Asian Americans and Pacific Islanders, and Native Americans and Alaskan Natives. To what extent are achievement levels and educational attainment increasing? To what extent are dropout rates decreasing?
2. Go to the website for the National Assessment of Educational Progress (NAEP) and download the NAEP report *NAEP 2012 Trends in Academic Progress: Reading 1971–2012, Mathematics 1973–2012*. The report presents achievement data by gender, race, and ethnicity. What are some implications these data have for teachers?

Observations and Interviews

1. If possible, visit a school that has an enrollment of students whose cultural or socioeconomic backgrounds differ from your own. What feelings and questions about these students emerge as a result of your observations? How might your feelings affect your teaching and teaching effectiveness? How can you research answers to your questions?
2. Interview a teacher at the school identified in the previous activity. What special satisfactions does he or she experience from teaching at the school? What significant problems relating to diversity does he or she encounter, and how are they dealt with?

Professional Portfolio

Prepare an annotated directory of local resources for teaching students about diversity, implementing multicultural curricula, and promoting harmony or equity among diverse groups. For each entry, include an annotation—that is, a brief description of the resource materials and their availability. Resources for your personalized directory should be available through local sources such as your university library, public library, community agencies, and so on. Among the types of resources you might include are the following:

- Films, videos, audiocassettes, books, and journal articles
- Simulation games designed to improve participants' attitudes toward diversity

- Motivational guest speakers from the community
- Ethnic museums and cultural centers
- Community groups and agencies dedicated to promoting understanding among diverse groups
- Training and workshops in the area of diversity

CHAPTER QUIZ

Take this quiz to check your understanding of the content covered in this chapter.

CHAPTER NINE

Addressing Learners' Individual Needs

learning outcomes

After reading this chapter, you will be able to do the following:

1. Explain how students' needs change as they develop.
2. Explain why students vary in intelligence.
3. Discuss how students vary in ability and disability.
4. Explain special education and inclusion.
5. Explain how you can teach all learners in your inclusive classroom.

READERS' VOICES

Why should teachers address students' individual needs?

Effective teachers understand that students are not the same—they have different needs, different learning styles, and different experiences. They learn best from teachers who know how to adjust their teaching methods and materials for different types of students.

—SHAWNDRA, Teacher Education program, first year

As the preceding reader's comment suggests, when you become a teacher you must understand and appreciate students' unique learning and developmental needs. You must be willing to learn about students' abilities and disabilities and to explore the special issues and concerns of students at three broad developmental levels—childhood, early adolescence, and late adolescence. Learning about your students as individuals is essential, as Sheryl Fontaine, a chemistry teacher at Reed High School in Sparks, **NEVADA** points out:

> I appreciate it when people treat *me* as an individual. Because our classes are so big, students do get treated like a number a lot of the time. So a little bit of individual attention goes a long way for them. I don't do it with every kid every day, but I do try to do it often enough that they remember that I know that they're there. (College Board and Phi Delta Kappa, 2009, p. 15)

Understanding how students' interests, questions, and problems will change throughout their school years will help you serve them in the present. This chapter examines how students' needs change as they develop and how their needs reflect various intelligences, abilities, and disabilities.

HOW DO STUDENTS' NEEDS CHANGE AS THEY DEVELOP?

Development refers to the predictable changes that all human beings undergo as they progress through the life span—from conception to death. It is important to remember that students develop at different rates. Within a given classroom, for example, some students will be larger and physically more mature than others, some will be socially more sophisticated, and some will be able to think at a higher level of abstraction.

As humans progress through different **stages of development**, they mature and learn to perform the tasks that are a necessary part of daily living. There are several different types of human development. For example, as children develop physically, their bodies undergo numerous changes. As they develop cognitively, their mental capabilities expand so that they can use language and other symbol systems to solve problems. As they develop socially, they learn to interact more effectively with other people—as individuals and in groups. And as they develop morally, their actions come to reflect a greater appreciation of principles such as equity, justice, fairness, and altruism.

Because no two students progress through the stages of cognitive, social, and moral development in quite the same way, teachers need perspectives on these three types of development that are flexible, dynamic, and, above all, useful. By becoming familiar with models of cognitive, social, and moral development, teachers at all levels, from preschool through college, can better serve their students. Three such models are Piaget's theory of **cognitive development**, Erikson's stages of **psychosocial development**, and Kohlberg's stages of **moral reasoning**.

Piaget's Model of Cognitive Development

Jean Piaget (1896–1980), the noted Swiss biologist and philosopher, made extensive observational studies of children. He concluded that children reason differently from adults and even have different perceptions of the world. Piaget surmised that children learn through actively interacting with their environments, much as scientists do, and proposed that a child's thinking progresses through a sequence of four cognitive stages (see Figure 9.1 on page 307). According to Piaget's theory of cognitive development, the rate of progress through the four stages varies from individual to individual.

During the school years, students move through the **preoperational stage**, the **concrete operations stage**, and the **formal operations stage**; however, because of individual interaction with the total environment, each student's perceptions and learning will be unique. According to Piaget:

> The principal goal of education is to create [learners] who are capable of doing new things, not simply repeating what other generations have done—[learners] who are creative, inventive, and discoverers. [We] need pupils who are active, who learn early to find out by themselves, partly by their own spontaneous activity and partly through material we set up for them; who learn early to tell what is verifiable and what is simply the first idea to come to them. (quoted in Ripple & Rockcastle, 1964, p. 5)

Figure 9.2, based on Piaget's work and more recent research, presents strategies for teaching children as their thinking abilities develop during the preoperational stage, the concrete operations stage, and the formal operations stage.

Erikson's Model of Psychosocial Development

Erik Erikson's (1902–1994) model of psychosocial development delineates eight stages, from infancy to old age (see Table 9.1). For each stage, a **psychosocial crisis** is central in the individual's emotional and social growth. Erikson expresses these crises in polar terms; for instance, in the first stage, that of infancy, the psychosocial crisis is trust versus mistrust. Erikson explains that the major psychosocial task for the infant is to develop a sense of trust in the world but not to give up totally a sense of distrust. In the tension between the poles of trust and mistrust, a greater pull toward the more positive pole is considered healthy and is accompanied by a virtue. In this case, if trust prevails, the virtue is hope.

Shortly before his death in 1994 at the age of 91, Erikson postulated a ninth stage in the human life cycle, *gerotranscendence,* during which some people mentally transcend the reality of their deteriorating bodies and faculties. In the final chapter of an extended version of Erikson's *The Life Cycle Completed*, first published in 1982, his wife and lifelong colleague, Joan M. Erikson (1901–1997), described the challenge of the ninth stage:

> Despair, which haunts the eighth stage, is a close companion in the ninth, because it is almost impossible to know what emergencies and losses of physical ability are imminent. As independence and control are challenged, self-esteem and confidence weaken. Hope and trust, which once provided firm support, are no longer the sturdy props of former days. To face down despair with faith and appropriate humility is perhaps the wisest course. (Erikson, 1997, pp. 105–106)

FIGURE 9.1 Piaget's stages of cognitive growth

1. **Sensorimotor Intelligence (birth to 2 years):** Behavior is primarily sensory and motor. The child does not yet "think" conceptually; however, "cognitive" development can be observed.

2. **Preoperational Thought (2–7 years):** Development of language and rapid conceptual development are evident. Children begin to use symbols to think of objects and people outside of their immediate environment. Fantasy and imaginative play are natural modes of thinking.

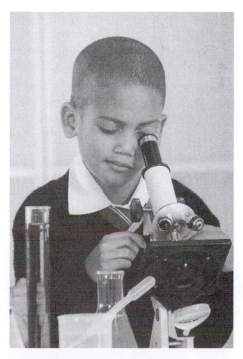

3. **Concrete Operations (7–11 years):** Children develop ability to use logical thought to solve concrete problems. Basic concepts of objects, number, time, space, and causality are explored and mastered. Through use of concrete objects to manipulate, children are able to draw conclusions.

4. **Formal Operations (11–15 years):** Cognitive abilities reach their highest level of development. Children can make predictions, think about hypothetical situations, think about thinking, and appreciate the structure of language as well as use it to communicate. Sarcasm, puns, argumentation, and slang are aspects of adolescents speech that reflect their ability to think abstractly about language.

FIGURE 9.2   Suggested strategies for teaching children at Piaget's stages of cognitive growth

Preoperational Stage

1. Use concrete objects and visual aids—pictures, drawings, photos, etc.
2. Provide opportunities to classify and group objects—by color, shape, size, use, etc.
3. Provide short instructions and explanations of ideas and concepts.
4. Use words and actions to instruct and explain.
5. Build skills by providing hands-on practice.
6. Teach simple skills first, then build on these to teach more complex skills.
7. Provide activities that give students a wide variety of learning experiences.

Concrete Operations Stage

1. Use concrete objects and visual aids to teach more complex material.
2. Provide explanations and readings that are short, clear, and well organized.
3. Explain more complex ideas and concepts by comparing them to familiar examples.
4. Provide opportunities to classify and group increasingly complex objects and concepts.
5. Present problems that require logical, analytical, scientific, and creative thinking.

Formal Operations Stage

1. Study topics in increasing depth.
2. Go beyond "facts" and teach increasingly complex concepts, ideas, and theories.
3. Provide increasingly sophisticated explanations for what students observe and experience.
4. Ask students to explain the meaning of proverbs—for example: "The pen is mightier than the sword." "There is no free lunch." "Necessity is the mother of invention."
5. Discuss social, political, moral, and ethical issues that relate to subject matter.
6. Have students design experiments to test hypotheses related to subject matter.

When we examine the issues and concerns of students in childhood and early and late adolescence later in this chapter, we will return to Erikson's model of psychosocial development. For further information on this significant and useful theory of development, you may wish to read Erikson's first book, *Childhood and Society* (1963).

Kohlberg's Model of Moral Development

According to Lawrence Kohlberg (1927–1987), the reasoning process people use to decide what is right and wrong evolves through three levels of development. Within each level, Kohlberg has identified two stages. Figure 9.3 shows that at Level I, the preconventional level, the individual decides what is right on the basis of personal needs and rules developed by others. At Level II, the conventional level, moral decisions reflect a desire for the approval of others and a willingness to conform to the expectations of family, community, and country. At Level III, the postconventional level, the individual has developed values and principles that are based on rational, personal choices that can be separated from conventional values.

Kohlberg (2014) suggests that "over 50 percent of late adolescents and adults are capable of full formal reasoning [i.e., they can use their intelligence to reason abstractly, form hypotheses, and test these hypotheses against reality], but only 10 percent of these adults display principled (Stages 5 and 6) moral reasoning" (p. 184). In addition, Kohlberg found that maturity of moral judgment is not highly related to IQ or verbal intelligence.

Kohlberg's model has been criticized because it focuses on moral reasoning rather than actual behavior, and it tends to look at moral development from a male perspective. Carol Gilligan, for example, suggests that male moral reasoning tends to address the rights of the individual, whereas female moral reasoning addresses the individual's responsibility to other people. In her book *In a Different Voice: Psychological Theory and Women's Development* (1993), Gilligan refers to women's principal moral voice as the "ethics of care," which emphasizes care of others over the

TABLE 9.1   Erikson's eight stages of psychosocial development

Stage	Approximate Age	Psychosocial "Crisis"	Description	"Basic Strength" (Positive Result if Crisis Is Adequately Resolved)
1. Infancy	Birth to 18 months	Trust versus basic mistrust	Infant needs to be nurtured and loved; if not, he or she becomes insecure and mistrustful.	Drive and hope
2. Early childhood	18 months to 3 years	Autonomy versus shame	Child focuses on developing physical skills—toilet training, walking, talking, feeding self; inadequate resolution of crisis leads to feelings of shame and doubt.	Self-control, courage, and will
3. Play age	3 to 6 years	Initiative versus guilt	Child learns to develop skills through play and cooperation; inadequate resolution of crisis leads to sense of guilt and fearfulness.	Purpose and direction
4. School age	6 to 12 years	Industry versus inferiority	Child acquires new skills, knowledge; develops sense of achievement; inadequate resolution of crisis leaves child feeling inadequate and inferior.	Competence and method
5. Adolescence	12 to 20 years	Identity versus role confusion, identity diffusion	Adolescent focuses on clarifying identity, developing social relationships with peers and others, and grappling with moral issues; inadequate resolution of crisis leads to self-doubt and self-consciousness.	Fidelity and devotion
6. Young adulthood	20 to 35 years	Intimacy versus isolation	Young adult seeks companionship and love through relationships with friends and becoming intimate with a "significant other"; inadequate resolution of crisis leads to feelings of isolation and distance from others.	Love and affiliation
7. Middle adulthood	35 to 65	Generativity versus self-absorption or stagnation	Adult focuses on family relationships, parenting, and creative and meaningful work; inadequate resolution of crisis leads to feelings of stagnation and alienation.	Care and production
8. Late adulthood	65 to death	Integrity versus despair	Adult focuses on meaning and purpose in one's life, lifetime accomplishments and contributions, acceptance of oneself and fulfillment; inadequate resolution of crisis leads to feelings of failure, disdain for world, and fear of death.	Wisdom and acceptance

more male-oriented "ethics of justice." Thus, when confronted with a moral dilemma, females tend to suggest solutions based more on altruism and self-sacrifice than on rights and rules (Gilligan, 1993).

The question remains: Can moral reasoning be taught? Can you help students develop so that they live according to principles of equity, justice, caring, and empathy? Kohlberg suggests the following three conditions that can help children internalize moral principles:

1. Exposure to the next higher stage of reasoning
2. Exposure to situations posing problems and contradictions for the child's current moral structure, leading to dissatisfaction with his [her] current level
3. An atmosphere of interchange and dialogue combining the first two conditions, in which conflicting moral views are compared in an open manner. (Kohlberg, 2014, p. 189)

FIGURE 9.3   Kohlberg's theory of moral reasoning

I. Preconventional Level of Moral Reasoning

Child is responsive to cultural rules and labels of good and bad, right or wrong, but interprets these in terms of consequences of action (punishment, reward, exchanges of favors).

Stage 1:   *Punishment-and-obedience orientation*
Physical consequences of action determine its goodness or badness.
Avoidance of punishment and deference to power are valued.

Stage 2:   *The instrumental-relativist orientation*
Right action consists of that which satisfies one's own needs and occasionally the needs of others.
Reciprocity is a matter of "you scratch my back and I'll scratch yours."

II. Conventional Level of Moral Reasoning

Maintaining the expectations of the individual's family, group, or nation is perceived as valuable, regardless of consequences.

Stage 3:   *The interpersonal concordance or "good boy–nice girl" orientation*
Good behavior is that which pleases or helps others and is approved by them.

Stage 4:   *The "law and order" orientation*
Orientation toward fixed rules and the maintenance of the social order. Right behavior consists of doing one's duty and showing respect for authority.

III. Postconventional, Autonomous, or Principled Level of Moral Reasoning

Effort to define moral principles that have validity and application apart from the authority of groups.

Stage 5:   *The social-contract, legalistic orientation*
Right action defined in terms of rights and standards that have been agreed on by the whole society.
This is the "official" morality of the U.S. government and Constitution.

Stage 6:   *The universal-ethical-principle orientation*
Right is defined by conscience in accord with self-chosen ethical principles appealing to logic and universality.

Adapted from Kohlberg, L. (2014). "The cognitive developmental approach to moral education." In F. W. Parkay, E. J. Anctil, & G. Hass (Eds.), *Curriculum leadership: Readings for developing quality educational programs* (10th ed., p. 182). The original version appeared in *Journal of Philosophy, 70*(18), 1973, 631–632.

One approach to teaching values and moral reasoning is known as **character education**, a movement that "promotes the teaching of core values that can be taught directly through course curricula, especially in literature, social studies, and social science classes" (Power et al., 2008, p. xxxvi). There is no single way for teachers to develop students' character; however, in comments made shortly after the shooting deaths of 14 students and a teacher at Columbine High School in Colorado, well-known sociologist and organizer of several White House conferences on character education Amitai Etzioni (1999) said, "What schools should help youngsters develop—if schools are going to help lower the likelihood of more Columbines—are two crucial behavior characteristics: the capacity to channel impulses into prosocial outlets, and empathy with others." Figure 9.4 illustrates a 12-point strategy teachers can use to create moral classroom communities.

Many schools, such as the Hyde Schools in Bath, **MAINE**, and Woodstock, **CONNECTICUT**, emphasize specific moral values in their curricula. The character-based educational program at the Hyde Schools focuses on five words: *Courage, Integrity, Leadership, Curiosity,* and *Concern* (Hyde Schools, 2014). Kennedy Middle School in Eugene, **OREGON**, implemented the P.R.I.D.E. program, based on the following words: *Positive Attitude, Respect, Integrity, Discipline,* and *Excellence.* To demonstrate their commitment to these character traits, students must follow behavioral guidelines

FIGURE 9.4 A 12-point comprehensive approach to character education

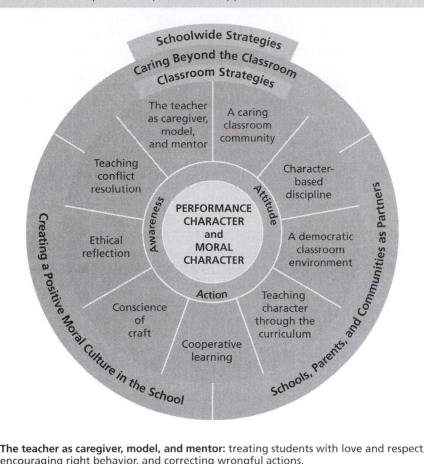

1. **The teacher as caregiver, model, and mentor:** treating students with love and respect, encouraging right behavior, and correcting wrongful actions.

2. **A caring classroom community:** teaching students to respect and care about each other.

3. **Character-based discipline:** using rules and consequences to develop moral reasoning, self-control, and a generalized respect for others.

4. **A democratic classroom environment:** using the class meeting to engage students in shared decision making and in taking responsibility for making the classroom the best it can be.

5. **Teaching character through the curriculum:** using the ethically rich content of academic subjects as vehicles for values teaching.

6. **Cooperative learning:** fostering students' ability to work with and appreciate others.

7. **Conscience of craft:** developing students' sense of academic responsibility and the habit of doing their work well.

8. **Ethical reflection:** developing the cognitive side of character through reading, research, writing, and discussion.

9. **Teaching conflict resolution:** teaching students how to solve conflicts fairly, without intimidation or violence.

10. **Caring beyond the classroom:** using role models to inspire altruistic behavior and providing opportunities for school and community service.

11. **Creating a positive moral culture in the school:** developing a caring school community that promotes the core virtues.

12. **School, parents, and communities as partners:** helping parents and the whole community join the schools in a cooperative effort to build good character.

Source: Thomas Lickona. (2014). Center for the 4th and 5th Rs. Cortland, NY: SUNY School of Education. Retrieved from http://www2.cortland.edu/centers/character/12-pt-comprehensive-approach.dot

appropriate for each word. For example, students demonstrate a Positive Attitude by participating in class discussions, following directions, encouraging others to do their best, and communicating in a positive manner. They demonstrate Excellence by learning as much as they can, taking pride in their schoolwork, always doing their best, and completing assignments and turning them in on time (Kennedy Middle School, 2014).

Maslow's Model of a Hierarchy of Needs

Students' developmental levels also vary according to how well their biological and psychological needs have been satisfied. Psychologist Abraham Maslow (1908–1970) formulated a model of a **hierarchy of needs** (see Figure 9.5) suggesting that people are first motivated by basic needs for survival and safety. When these basic needs have been met sufficiently, people naturally seek to satisfy higher needs, the highest of which is self-actualization—the desire to use one's talents, abilities, and potentialities to the fullest. Students whose needs for safety have been fairly well satisfied will discover strong needs for friendship, affection, and love, for example. If efforts to satisfy the various needs are thwarted, the result can be maladjustment and interruption or delay in the individual's full and healthy development.

Students differ markedly in terms of where they are on Maslow's hierarchy of needs. Many families lack the resources to provide adequately for children's basic needs. Children from families that are concerned with day-to-day survival may not receive the support that could help them succeed in school. They come to school tired and hungry and may have trouble paying attention in class. Others may be well fed and clothed but feel unsafe, alienated, or unloved; they may seek to protect themselves by withdrawing emotionally from activities around them.

FIGURE 9.5   Maslow's hierarchy of needs

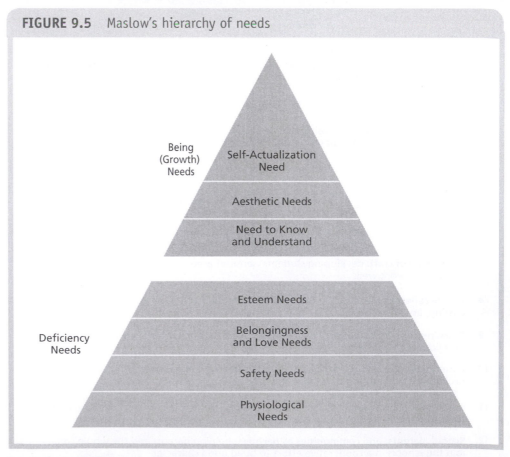

Note: The four lower-level needs are called *deficiency needs* because the motivation to satisfy them decreases when they are met. On the other hand, when *being (growth) needs* are met, motivation to fulfill them increases.

Source: Based on Abraham H. Maslow, *Toward a Psychology of Being*. 3rd Edition. New York: John Wiley & Sons, 1959; and *Motivation and Personality*, 3rd Edition. Boston: Addison-Wesley, 1987.

Developmental Stresses and Tasks of Childhood

During Erikson's school-age stage, children strive for a sense of industry and struggle against feelings of inferiority. If successful, they gain the virtue of competence, believing in their abilities to do things. If children find evidence that they are inferior to others, if they experience failure when they try new tasks, and if they struggle without ever gaining a sense of mastery, then they feel incompetent.

Children gain the sense of industry needed at this age by playing seriously, mastering new skills, producing products, and being workers. When they first go to school, they are oriented toward accomplishing new things. (Some kindergartners expect to learn to read on their first day of school and are disappointed when they don't!) For young schoolchildren, the idea of work is attractive; it means that they are doing something grown-up.

What developmental tasks do middle school students need to accomplish as part of their psychosocial development? How can their teachers help with those developmental tasks?

Is childhood a time of carefree play or a period of stress? Certainly the answer depends on the life circumstances and personality of the individual child. In a study of stressful events in the lives of more than 1,700 children in the second through the ninth grades in six countries, Karou Yamamoto and his associates found that the most stressful events "threaten[ed] one's sense of security and occasion[ed] personal denigration and embarrassment" (Yamamoto et al., 1996, p. 139). Other studies have shown that serious stress is experienced by latchkey children, for example, who are left on their own or in each other's care for part or all of the day.

Developmental Stresses and Tasks of Adolescence

Many psychologists believe that adolescence contains two distinct stages: an early period covering the ages of 10 to 12 through the ages of 14 to 16, and a late period from approximately 15 to 16 through 19. Although continuity exists in each individual's life, the psychosocial issues of adolescence—coping with change and seeking identity—vary in form and importance as individuals progress through the transition from childhood to adulthood.

In Erik Erikson's eight-stage model of human development, identity versus role diffusion is the psychosocial crisis for the adolescent years. Although the quest for identity is a key psychosocial issue for both early and late adolescence, many believe that Erikson's identity-versus-role-diffusion stage fits best for early adolescence. During this time, young adolescents, using their new thinking abilities, begin integrating a clearer sense of personal identity. Erikson's role diffusion refers to the variety of roles that adolescents have available to them.

According to Erikson's theory, when adolescents identify themselves with a peer group, with a school, or with a cause, their sense of fidelity—the virtue of this stage—is clear and strong. At this stage, adolescents are loyal and committed, sometimes to people or ideas that may dismay or alarm their parents, sometimes to high ideals and dreams.

In late adolescence, the quest for identity shifts from relying on others to self-reliance. Young people continue to work on strengthening their sense of identity in late adolescence, but as they do so, they draw less on the reactions of their peers and more on their own regard for what matters. Although late adolescents possess an array of interests, talents, and goals in life, they share a desire to achieve independence. More like adults than children, late adolescents are anxious to use newly acquired strengths, skills, and knowledge to achieve their own purposes, whether through marriage, parenthood, full-time employment, education beyond high school, a career, or military service.

The vulnerability of today's adolescents is evident in the results of a survey based on 40 "developmental assets" youth need to become healthy, mature adults. For optimal development, youth should have the following "external" and "internal" assets: *external assets*—support, empowerment, boundaries and expectations, and constructive use of time; *internal assets*—commitment to learning, positive values, social competencies, and positive identity. The survey of almost 150,000 6th- to 12th-grade youth in 202 communities revealed that

> the average young person experiences only 18.6 of the 40 assets. In general, older youth have lower average levels of assets than younger youth. And boys experience fewer assets than girls. While there is no "magic number" of assets young people should have . . . data indicate that 31 is a worthy, though challenging, benchmark for experiencing their positive effects most strongly. Yet . . . only 8 percent of youth have 31 or more assets. More than half have 20 or fewer assets. (Search Institute, 2010)

Moreover, "a solid majority of American adults—two thirds—spontaneously describe adolescents in starkly negative terms: *wild, rude, irresponsible.* Half give those descriptions even to younger children" (Scales, 2001, p. 64). The list of alarming concerns in adolescence includes academic failure and retention, accidents, assaultive behavior, criminal activity, cultism, depression, discipline problems, dropping out, drug abuse, eating disorders, homicides, incest, prostitution, running away, school absenteeism, suicide, teenage pregnancy, vandalism, and the contraction of sexually transmitted infections.

As a teacher, what can you do to help children and adolescents develop to their full potential? To help prevent the problems that place them at risk, an energetic, creative, and multifaceted approach is necessary. Figure 9.6 presents several strategies for helping students develop competence, positive self-concepts, and high esteem and for intervening to prevent or address problems that place them at risk.

FIGURE 9.6   What teachers can do to help children and adolescents develop

1. **Provide opportunities and encouragement for students to develop competence.**
   - Provide a learning environment in which students can risk making mistakes.
   - Assign work that students can perform successfully and still be challenged.
   - Have realistic but high expectations for students.
   - Express belief in students' ability to succeed.
   - Encourage industry by letting students work on goals or projects of their choosing.
   - Provide opportunities for students to take special responsibility.
   - Assign older students to work with younger ones.
   - Reward industry and competence.

2. **Promote the development of positive self-concept and high self-esteem.**
   - Give praise more than criticism.
   - Take students and their work seriously.
   - Respect students' dignity.
   - Plan individual and group activities that boost morale.
   - Provide opportunities for students to interact and work cooperatively.
   - Teach and model acceptance of human diversity and individuality.
   - Develop systems for the recognition and reward of individual and group achievement.
   - Support students' efforts to achieve and appropriately express independence.

3. **Intervene to prevent or address problems that place students at risk.**
   - Provide a safe and structured learning environment where students feel secure.
   - Practice effective leadership and classroom management.
   - Provide opportunities to discuss preferences, values, morals, goals, and consequences.
   - Teach and model critical thinking, decision making, and problem solving.
   - Teach and model prosocial attitudes and behaviors and conflict resolution strategies.
   - Provide information on subjects of special concern to students and parents.
   - Cultivate family involvement.
   - Collaborate, consult, network, and refer on behalf of students.

HOW DO STUDENTS VARY IN INTELLIGENCE?

In addition to developmental differences, students differ in terms of their intellectual capacity. Unfortunately, test scores, and sometimes intelligence quotient (IQ) scores, are treated as accurate measurements of students' intellectual ability because of their convenience and long-time use. What is intelligence, and how has it been redefined to account for the many ways in which it is expressed?

Although many definitions of **intelligence** have been proposed, the term has yet to be completely defined. One view is that intelligence is the ability to learn. As David Wechsler (1958), the developer of the most widely used intelligence scales for children and adults, said: "Intelligence, operationally defined, is the aggregate or global capacity to act purposefully, to think rationally, and to deal effectively with the environment" (p. 7). Other perspectives on intelligence include the following:

- It is *adaptive*. It involves modifying and adjusting one's behavior to accomplish new tasks successfully.
- It is related to *learning ability*. Intelligent people learn information more quickly and easily than less intelligent people.
- It involves the *use of prior knowledge* to analyze and understand new situations effectively.
- It involves the complex interaction and coordination of *many different thinking and reasoning processes*.
- It is *culture-specific*. What is "intelligent" behavior in one culture is not necessarily intelligent behavior in another culture. (Ormrod, 2006, p. 153)

Intelligence Testing

The intelligence tests that we now use can be traced to the 1905 Metrical Scale of Intelligence designed by French psychologists Alfred Binet and Theodore Simon, who were part of a Paris-based commission that wanted a way to identify children who would need special help with their learning. Binet revised the scale in 1908, which was adapted for American children in 1916 by Lewis Terman, a psychologist at Stanford University. Terman's test was further adapted, especially by the U.S. Army, which transformed it into a paper-and-pencil test that could be administered to large groups. The use of such intelligence tests has continued throughout the years. Approximately 67 percent of the population have an IQ between 85 and 115—the range of normal intelligence.

Individual intelligence tests are presently valued by psychologists and those in the field of special education because they can be helpful in diagnosing a student's strengths and weaknesses. However, group intelligence tests given for the purpose of classifying students into like-score groups have received an increasing amount of criticism.

Group IQ tests have been criticized because test items and tasks are culturally biased, drawn mostly from White middle-class experience. Thus, the tests are more assessments of how informed students are about features in a specific class or culture than of how intelligent they are in general. This complaint became a formal, legal challenge when, on the basis of their IQ test scores, a group of African American children were put into special classes for mentally retarded children. Their parents brought the complaint to the courts in 1971 and persisted with it all the way to the federal appellate court, where a decision was eventually made in their favor in 1984. In that well-known case, *Larry P. v. Riles* (1984), the court decided that IQ tests were discriminatory and culturally biased. However, in another case, *PASE v. Hannon* (1980), an Illinois district court ruled that when IQ tests were used in conjunction with other forms of assessment, such as teacher observation, they were not discriminatory for placement purposes. Although the criticism continues, psychometricians are attempting to design culture-free intelligence tests.

PROFESSIONAL REFLECTION

Watch how teachers meet the needs of their diverse learners by addressing Gardner's multiple intelligences.

Multiple Intelligences

Many theorists believe that intelligence is a basic ability that enables one to perform mental operations in the following areas: logical reasoning, spatial reasoning, number ability, and verbal meaning. However, other theorists believe "that conventional notions of intelligence are incomplete and hence inadequate. [One's] ability to achieve success depends on capitalizing on one's strengths and correcting or compensating for one's weaknesses through a balance of analytical, creative, and practical abilities" (Sternberg, 2002, pp. 447–448). For example, Howard Gardner believes that human beings possess seven to ten separate forms of intelligence, each of which functions like a computer— "one . . . computes linguistic information, another spatial information, another musical information, another information about other people, and so on" (Gardner, 2013).

Drawing on the theories of others and research findings on savants, prodigies, and other exceptional individuals, Gardner originally suggested in *Frames of Mind* (1983) that human beings possessed seven human intelligences: logical-mathematical, linguistic, musical, spatial, bodily-kinesthetic, interpersonal, and intrapersonal. In the mid-1990s, he identified an eighth intelligence, that of the naturalist. In *The Disciplined Mind* (Gardner, 1999, p. 72), he suggests that "it is possible that human beings also exhibit a ninth, existential intelligence—the proclivity to pose (and ponder) questions about life, death, and ultimate realities" and a tenth, spiritual intelligence. According to Gardner, every person possesses at least the eight intelligences (see Figure 9.7), yet each person has his or her particular blend of the intelligences.

Gardner's theory of **multiple intelligences** is valuable for teachers. As Robert Slavin suggests, "You should avoid thinking about children as smart or not smart, because there are many ways to be smart" (2015, p. 92).

Some students are talented in terms of their interpersonal relations and exhibit natural leadership abilities. Others seem to have a high degree of what some researchers have termed **emotional intelligence**—awareness of and ability to manage their feelings (Salovey & Feldman-Barrett, 2002; Salovey, Mayer, & Caruso, 2002; Salovey & Sluyter, 1997). Differences in musical, athletic, and mechanical abilities can be recognized by even the minimally informed observer. Because these intelligences are not tested or highlighted, they may go unnoticed and possibly wasted. Thirty years after the publication of *Frames of Mind,* Gardner made the following suggestions for teachers:

1. Teachers should individualize their teaching by learning as much as possible about each student and then teaching them in ways that help them learn best. Gardner acknowledged that smaller class sizes make it easier for teachers to individualize.
2. Teachers should teach important content in more ways than one—for example, use role plays, stories, and projects. By using different methods, teachers can be effective with students who learn differently. Moreover, the ability to present content in different ways shows students what it means to understand content deeply. According to Gardner, a teacher's understanding of content is limited if he or she can teach it in only one way. (Gardner, 2013)

Learning Styles

Students vary greatly in regard to **learning styles**, the approaches to learning that work best for them. These differences have also been called *learning style preferences* or *cognitive styles*. The National Task Force on Learning Style and Brain Behavior suggests that there is a "consistent pattern of behavior and performance by which an individual approaches educational experiences. It is the composite of characteristic cognitive, affective, and physiological behaviors that serve as relatively stable indicators of how a learner perceives, interacts with, and responds to the learning environment" (cited in Bennett, 1990, p. 94).

Students' learning styles are determined by a combination of hereditary and environmental influences. Some more quickly learn things they hear; others learn faster when they see material in writing. Some need a lot of structure; others learn best when they can be independent and follow their desires. Some learn best in formal settings;

FIGURE 9.7   The eight intelligences

Logical-mathematical intelligences enables individuals to use and appreciate abstract relations. Scientists, mathematicians, and philosophers all rely on this intelligence. So do the students who "live" baseball statistics or who carefully analyze the components of problems—either personal or school-related—before systematically testing solutions.

Linguistic intelligence allows individuals to communicate and make sense of the world through language. Poets exemplify this intelligence in its mature form. Students who enjoy playing with rhymes, who pun, who always have a story to tell, who quickly acquire other languages—including sign language—all exhibit linguistic intelligence.

Musical intelligence allows people to create, communicate, and understand meanings made out of sound. While composers and instrumentalists clearly exhibit this intelligence, so do the students who seem particularly attracted by the birds singing outside the classroom window or who constantly tap out intricate rhythms on the desk with their pencils.

Spatial intelligence makes it possible for people to perceive visual or spatial information, to transform this information, and to re-create visual images from memory. Well-developed spatial capacities are needed for the work of architects, sculptors, and engineers. The students who turn first to the graphs, charts, and pictures in their textbooks, who like to "web" their ideas before writing a paper, and who fill the blank space around their notes with intricate patterns are also using their spatial intelligence.

Bodily-kinesthetic intelligence allows individuals to use all or part of the body to create products or solve problems. Athletes, surgeons, dancers, choreographers, and craftspeople all use bodily-kinesthetic intelligence. The capacity is also evident in students who relish gym class and school dances, who prefer to carry out class projects by making models rather than writing reports, and who toss crumpled paper with frequency and accuracy into wastebaskets across the room.

Interpersonal intelligence enables individuals to recognize and make distinctions about others' feelings and intentions. Teachers, parents, politicians, psychologists, and salespeople rely on interpersonal intelligence. Students exhibit this intelligence when they thrive on small-group work, when they notice and react to the moods of their friends and classmates, and when they tactfully convince the teacher of their need for extra time to complete the homework assignment.

Intrapersonal intelligence helps individuals to distinguish among their own feelings, to build accurate mental models of themselves, and to draw on these models to make decisions about their lives. Although it is difficult to assess who has this capacity and to what degree, evidence can be sought in students' uses of their other intelligences—how well they seem to be capitalizing on their strengths, how cognizant they are of their weaknesses, and how thoughtful they are about the decisions and choices they make.

Naturalist intelligence allows people to distinguish among, classify, and use features of the environment. Farmers, gardeners, botanists, geologists, florists, and archaeologists all exhibit this intelligence, as do students who can name and describe the features of every make of car around them.

others learn best in informal, relaxed environments. Some need almost total silence to concentrate; others learn well in noisy, active environments. Some are intuitive learners; some prefer to learn by following logical, sequential steps.

FOCUS ON DIVERSITY: LEARNING STYLES AND CULTURE

There is no one "correct" view of learning styles to guide teachers in their daily decision making. Culture-based differences in learning styles are subtle, variable, and difficult to describe (Zhang & Sternberg, 2001), and learning styles change as the individual matures. Moreover, critics maintain that there is little evidence to support the validity of dozens of conceptual models for learning styles and accompanying assessment instruments (e.g., Pashler, McDaniel, Rohrer, & Bjork, 2008). Nevertheless, you should be aware of the concept of learning styles and realize that any given classroom activity may be more effective for some students than for others. Knowledge of your own and your students' learning styles will help you to individualize instruction and motivate

As a teacher, you will quickly learn that no one instructional approach matches the learning styles and needs of every student. How can you gather information about your students' preferred approaches to learning?

your students. As a teacher, you should keep track of information related to students' learning styles, academic progress, and individual learning needs.

LEARNING WITH STYLE

An example of how one school modified its educational programs is Libertyville High School in Libertyville, **ILLINOIS**. All Libertyville freshmen take a 5-week course called Learning with Style during the second half of their lunch period. At the beginning of the course, students complete the Learning Preference Inventory (Hanson & Silver, 2000) to help the students and their teachers understand their personal learning styles.

During the course, students learn about different approaches to learning, and they begin to reflect on their own learning behaviors. With the help of teachers, guidance counselors, and parents, each student develops a set of skills and learning strategies that matches his or her interests.

Students also learn about the strengths and weaknesses of each style. Students develop "personal growth plans" and explore careers that fit their learning styles. Students map out their high school careers, meeting regularly with their guidance counselors to discuss and revise their goals in light of new learning and experiences.

All teachers at the high school are trained in learning styles. They work closely with the teacher of the Learning with Style course and the guidance counselors. Parents are also encouraged to attend an adult version of the learning style course at night. Parents then help their children and the school make the best decisions about the child's education and future career.

During the adult learning style course, the teacher reviews student profiles and explains to parents how their children learn, what they need to be successful, and what areas may need special attention. Parents learn about how a student's learning style can influence decisions about college, vocation, and becoming a lifelong learner. The teacher of the learning style course sums up how knowledge of students' learning styles can help teachers establish authentic learning communities in their classrooms: "It keeps the learning environment fresh by helping us to remember that every student has unique interests, talents, and needs and that as an educational institution, we really can treat all our students to the personalized learning program they need and deserve" (Strong, Silver, & Perini, 2001, pp. 92–93).

PROFESSIONAL REFLECTION
Watch as a group of educators discusses a student's abilities and disabilities.

HOW DO STUDENTS VARY IN ABILITY AND DISABILITY?

Students also differ according to their special needs and talents. Some enter the world with exceptional abilities or disabilities, others encounter life experiences that change their capabilities significantly, and still others struggle with conditions that medical scientists have yet to understand. To the fullest extent possible, all children and youth with exceptionalities are given a public education in the United States. The Teachers' Voices: Walk in My Shoes feature in this chapter profiles Anthony Mullen, a former New York City homicide detective, who is committed to teaching students with special needs.

Students with Special Needs

"General education teachers today have more students with disabilities in their classrooms than ever. In fact, only a small proportion of students with disabilities currently receives more than 60% of their education outside the general education classroom" (Mastropieri & Scruggs, 2010, p. 6). To realize their potential, **students with disabilities** are provided with special education and related services. Among the **exceptional learners** teachers may encounter in the classroom are students who have physical, mental, or emotional disabilities and students who are gifted or talented.

Students with special needs are often referred to synonymously as *handicapped* or *disabled*. However, it is important for teachers to understand the following:

> Many individuals with disabilities believe that the terms *disability* and *handicap* have very different meanings and interpretations. They are convinced that it is because of their *disabilities* (e.g., conditions and impairments) that society *handicaps* them (e.g., presents challenges and barriers). . . . Thus the ways in which people are treated by society and by other individuals are what present the real barriers that influence people's outcomes. Difficult situations occur not because of a condition or disability but, rather, because people with disabilities are denied full participation in society as a consequence of their minority status. (Smith, 2007, pp. 9–10)

For example, Stephen W. Hawking, a gifted physicist, has amyotrophic lateral sclerosis (also known as Lou Gehrig's disease), which requires him to use a wheelchair for mobility and a speech synthesizer to communicate. If Hawking had to enter a building accessible only by stairs, or if a computer virus infected his speech synthesizer program, his disability would then become a handicap. As Hawking pointed out in his widely read book *A Brief History of Time: From the Big Bang to Black Holes* (1988), "I was fortunate that I chose theoretical physics, because it is all in the mind. So my disability has not been a serious handicap."

In addition, as a teacher you should know that current language use emphasizes the concept of "people first." In other words, a disabling condition should not be used as an adjective to describe a person. Thus, you should say "a child with a visual impairment," not a "blind child" or even a "visually impaired child."

You should also realize that the definitions for disabilities are generalized, open to change, and significantly influenced by the current cultural perception of normality. For example, the American Association on Mental Retardation (AAMR) has changed its definition of mental retardation several times since 1950 to reflect shifting views of people with cognitive disabilities. In 2010, President Obama signed "Rosa's Law," which replaced the term *mental retardation* with *intellectual disability* in federal education, health, and labor laws. The parents of Rosa Marcellino, a 9-year-old with Down syndrome, worked for 2 years to remove the words *mentally retarded* from the health and education code in **MARYLAND**. Upon signing the law, President Obama quoted Rosa's brother, Nick: "What you call people is how you treat them. If we change the words, maybe it will be the start of a new attitude towards people with disabilities" (White House Press Release, October 8, 2010).

Cautions about labeling should also apply to gifted and talented students. Unfortunately, people commonly have a negative view of gifted and talented youngsters. Like many ethnic groups, gifted students are "different" and thus have been the target of many myths and stereotypes. However, a landmark study of 1,528 gifted males and females begun by Lewis Terman (Terman, Baldwin, & Bronson, 1925; Terman & Oden, 1947, 1959) in 1926 and continued until 2010 has "exploded the myth that high-IQ individuals [are] brainy but physically and socially inept. In fact, Terman found that children with outstanding IQs were larger, stronger, and better coordinated than other children and became better adjusted and more emotionally stable adults" (Slavin, 2015, p. 315).

FOCUS ON DIVERSITY: STUDENTS WITH SPECIAL NEEDS

Figure 9.8 shows that more than 6.4 million students, or about 13 percent of those enrolled in public schools, participated in federally supported education programs

TEACHERS' VOICES
Walk in My Shoes

Anthony Mullen
2009 National Teacher
of the Year
Greenwich High School
Greenwich, Connecticut

Gifted and talented students benefit from enriched learning experiences and individualized plans that give them the opportunity to grow at an accelerated rate. What are some forms of enrichment you will offer your students?

for students with special needs during 2011. Various tests and other forms of assessment are used to identify persons in different categories of disability. The following brief definitional characteristics are based on the Individuals with Disabilities Education Act (IDEA) and definitions used by professional organizations dedicated to meeting the needs of persons in each category.

1. **Specific learning disabilities (LD)**—learning is significantly hindered by difficulty in listening, speaking, reading, writing, reasoning, or computing
2. **Speech or language impairments**—significant difficulty in communicating with others as a result of speech or language disorders
3. **Intellectual disability**—significant limitations in cognitive ability
4. **Serious emotional disturbance (SED)**—social and/or emotional maladjustment that significantly reduces the ability to learn
5. **Hearing impairments**—permanent or fluctuating mild to profound hearing loss in one or both ears
6. **Orthopedic impairments**—physically disabling conditions that affect locomotion or motor functions
7. **Other health impairments**—limited strength, vitality, or alertness caused by chronic or acute health problems
8. **Visual impairments**—vision loss that significantly inhibits learning
9. **Multiple disabilities**—two or more interrelated disabilities
10. **Deaf-blindness**—vision and hearing disability that severely limits communication
11. **Autism and other**—significantly impaired communication, learning, and reciprocal social interactions

Figure 9.8 shows that about 37 percent of the 6.4 million children and youth receiving special education services had a specific learning disability. Since the term **learning disability (LD)** was first introduced in the early 1960s, there has been no universally accepted definition. According to the National Joint Committee on Learning Disabilities (2008), a learning disability is a neurological disorder. People with a learning disability are no less intelligent than others; however, they have difficulty with cognitive processes such as reading, writing, spelling, and remembering information. Teachers should teach students with learning disabilities in ways that reduce the effects of the disability.

Some students have trouble remembering verbal instructions or recognizing words in print (*dyslexia*), whereas others have trouble working with numbers (*dyscalculia*). A learning disability can't be cured or fixed; it is a lifelong issue. With the right support and intervention, however, children with learning disabilities can succeed in school and go on to successful, often distinguished careers later in life. Parents can help children with learning disabilities achieve such success by encouraging their strengths, knowing their weaknesses, understanding the educational system, working with professionals, and learning about strategies for dealing with specific difficulties. The Teaching on Your Feet feature in this chapter profiles Tonia Grimes, who learned how to meet the needs of a "hard-to-reach" student with a learning disability.

FIGURE 9.8   Children 3 to 21 years old served under Individuals with Disabilities Education Act, Part B, by type of disability: 2010–11

Type of disability	Number served (in thousands)	Number served as a percent of total enrollment[2]
All disabilities	**6,419**	**13.0**
Autism	417	0.8
Deaf-blindness	1	#
Developmental delay	381	0.8
Emotional disturbance	389	0.8
Hearing impairments	78	0.2
Intellectual disability	447	0.9
Multiple disabilities	130	0.3
Orthopedic impairments	63	0.1
Other health impairments[1]	714	1.4
Preschool disabled	†	†
Specific learning disabilities	2,357	4.8
Speech or language impairments	1,390	2.8
Traumatic brain injury	26	0.1
Visual impairments	28	0.1

(a) Number served and percentage of total school enrollment, by primary type of disability

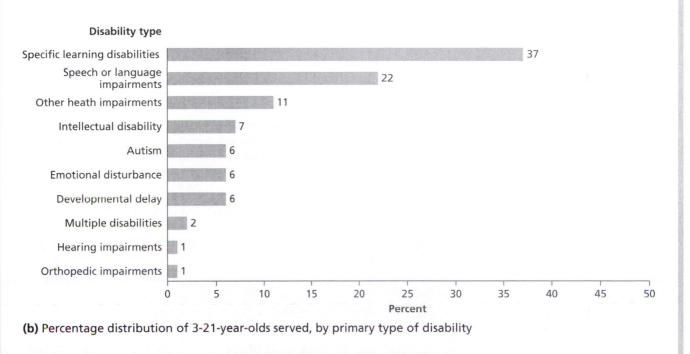

(b) Percentage distribution of 3-21-year-olds served, by primary type of disability

a. † Not applicable.
    # Rounds to zero.
    [1] Other health impairments include having limited strength, vitality, or alertness due to chronic or acute health problems such as a heart condition, tuberculosis, rheumatic fever, nephritis, asthma, sickle cell anemia, hemophilia, epilepsy, lead poisoning, leukemia, or diabetes.
    [2] Based on the total enrollment in public schools, prekindergarten through 12th grade.

b. *Note:* Deaf-blindness, traumatic brain injury, and visual impairments are not shown because they each account for less than 1 percent of children served under IDEA. Due to categories not shown, detail does not sum to total.

Adapted from Snyder, T. D., and Dillow, S. A. (2013). *Digest of Education Statistics 2012* (NCES 2014-015). National Center for Education Statistics, Institute of Education Sciences, U.S. Department of Education. Washington, DC, p. 89, and Aud, S., Wilkinson-Flicker, S., Kristapovich, P., Rathbun, A., Wang, X., and Zhang, J. (2013). *The Condition of Education 2013* (NCES 2013-037). U.S. Department of Education, National Center for Education Statistics. Washington, DC, p. 58.

TECHNOLOGY in ACTION
Word-Prediction Software in the Classroom

"I don't like to write." "I don't know how to spell." Miss Hernandez often hears comments like these from her eighth-grade students with disabilities. She understands that some students with learning disabilities may not be able to retain ideas in their memories long enough to express them in writing, whereas others may have difficulty with spelling. Students with motor disabilities may be challenged when forming letters with a pen or pencil or making repetitive keystrokes on a word processor.

Recently, Miss Hernandez visited Mr. Wu's classroom to observe how one of his students with a motor disability that affects her ability to write is using word-prediction software to reduce the number of keystrokes needed to type words. As Miss Hernandez watched, the student would type the first letter of a word, and then a numbered list of words beginning with that letter would appear on the computer screen. If the desired word was on the list, the student would enter the number and the word would be typed automatically. Miss Hernandez watched as the student wrote the word *tonight* to complete the sentence "I will watch TV tonight." First, she entered a "t" and the list of common "t" words shown in screen #1 appeared. Because the word *tonight* was not on this list, she typed an "o" and screen #2 appeared. Because *tonight* was on this list, she typed a number "3" and the word was entered automatically. Thus, the seven keystrokes needed to write *tonight* were reduced to three.

WORD-PREDICTION SOFTWARE: Word-prediction software can be installed on most word-processing programs. The software is even included on some versions of Microsoft Word. Word-prediction software helps students by guessing the words that they are typing into the word processor and saving keystrokes. Students can save more than 40 percent of the keystrokes they would normally enter into a traditional word processor.

Most good word-prediction software programs also work phonetically. For example, if a student puts a "k" for the first letter of the word *campus*, the software would overlook the error. Some word-prediction software programs can also correct for dyslexic spelling errors, where some characters may be transposed. The following list describes additional features of various word-prediction software programs.

- **Synthesized speech output**—To provide additional support for students while they write, some word-prediction programs also have synthesized speech output. For students with limited reading abilities, this feature helps them monitor the structure and meaning of their work.

- **Prediction methods**—Some programs predict on the basis of spelling only, while others consider the words that have come before in the sentence; for example, only nouns are listed after the word *a* or *an*.

- **List updating**—After "learning" a student's vocabulary, the word prediction program tailors the word prediction lists to the student's usage. Some programs update automatically, whereas others allow the user to decide when to update.

- **Prediction window customizing**—Some programs have prediction lists that appear with a set number of words in a fixed-size window in a specific location on the screen. Others allow users to customize the size, the screen location, and the amount of words in the window.

- **Keyboard sensitivity adjustment**—Keyboard sensitivity can be adjusted to prevent repetition if keys are not quickly released.

POSSIBLE USES: In addition to helping students with learning disabilities or motor disabilities, word-prediction software is helpful for general education students who are challenged by the writing process. With word-prediction software, students are better able to complete written assignments and thus experience greater success in the classroom. As an administrator at a district that makes word-prediction software available to *all* students at the district's 122 schools points out, "We're operating on the premise that adaptive technology is necessary for students with learning disabilities and good for all students. Good teaching dictates that we hit all of the learning modalities that kids need. Just because a student is doing well or moderately well doesn't mean that they couldn't benefit from adaptive technology. There are children other than our kids with learning disabilities who are stronger verbally than they are in a written context" (Kinross, 2009).

TRY IT OUT: Some word-prediction software sites on the Internet allow you to download a free demonstration version of the software. Also, some sites have links to videos that show how to install and use the software.

Imagine that you are concerned about two of your new students—Mary and Bill. Mary has an adequate vocabulary and doesn't hesitate to express herself, but her achievement in reading and mathematics doesn't add up to what you believe she can do. Often, when you give the class instructions, Mary seems to get confused about what to do. In working with her one on one, you've noticed that she often reverses letters and numbers the way much younger children do—she sees a *b* for a *d* or a *6* for a *9*. Mary may have a learning disability, causing problems in taking in, organizing, remembering, and expressing information. Like Mary, students with learning disabilities often show a significant difference between their estimated intelligence and their actual achievement in the classroom.

Bill presents you with a different set of challenges. He is obviously bright, but he frequently seems to be out of sync with classroom activities. He gets frustrated when he has to wait for his turn. He sometimes blurts out answers before you've even asked a question. He can't seem to stop wiggling his toes and tapping his pencil, and he often comes to school without his backpack and homework. Bill may have **attention deficit hyperactivity disorder (ADHD)**, one of the most commonly diagnosed disabilities among children. It is estimated that between 3 and 5 percent of children have ADHD in the United States. In a classroom of 25 to 30 students, at least one will probably have ADHD. Students with an **attention deficit disorder (ADD)** have difficulty focusing their attention long enough to learn well. Children with ADD/ADHD do not qualify for special education unless they also have another disability in a federally defined category.

Treatment for students with ADD/ADHD includes behavior modification and medication. Since the early 1980s, Ritalin has become the most commonly prescribed drug for ADD/ADHD, and more than 1 million American children are currently estimated to take Ritalin to increase their impulse control and attention span.

Teachers can help in the early identification of students with learning disabilities so they can receive the instructional adaptations or special education services they need by being alert for students who exhibit several of the following academic and behavioral characteristics:

- Significant discrepancy between potential and achievement
- Inability to problem-solve
- Substantial delay in academic achievement
- Lack of engagement with learning tasks
- Poor language and/or cognitive development
- Lack of basic reading and decoding skills
- Lack of attention during lectures or class discussion
- Excessive movement, hyperactivity
- Impulsivity
- Poor motor coordination and spatial relation skills
- Poor motivation

FOCUS ON DIVERSITY: STUDENTS WHO ARE GIFTED AND TALENTED

Gifted and talented students, those who have demonstrated a high level of attainment in intellectual ability, academic achievement, creativity, or visual and performing arts, are evenly distributed across all ethnic and cultural groups and socioeconomic classes. Although you might think it is easy to meet the needs of gifted and talented students, you will find that this is not always the case. "Students with special gifts or talents often challenge the system of school, and they can be verbally caustic. Their superior abilities and unusual or advanced interests demand teachers who are highly intelligent, creative, and motivated" (Hallahan & Kauffman, 2000, p. 497). The ability of such students to challenge the system is reflected in a U.S. Department of Education study that found that gifted and talented elementary schoolchildren have mastered 35 percent to 50 percent of the grade curriculum in five basic subject areas before starting the school year.

Variations in criteria used to identify gifted and talented students are especially evident in the reported incidence of giftedness from state to state; for example, Massachusetts and Rhode Island identify only 0.7 and 1.4 percent, respectively, of their students as gifted and talented, whereas Maryland and Kentucky identify 16.1 and 14.6 percent, respectively (Snyder & Dillow, 2010). Depending on the criteria used, estimates of the number of gifted and talented students range from 3 to 5 percent of the total population. Among the characteristics of the gifted are the following:

- **Precocity**—verbal precocity
- **Perceptual sensitivity**—good at detecting critically relevant, salient cues; notices what others fail to notice

TEACHING ON YOUR FEET
Connecting with a Hard-to-Reach Student

I navigated through my first year [as a fifth-grade teacher] fairly successfully, while working to form relationships with my students in an effort to keep one step ahead of them, which was no easy feat! There was one child in particular, Alexander, who I just couldn't seem to connect with. He was a student with special needs who had learning disabilities in both math and reading. He rarely bathed, his clothes were filthy, and the other children were sometimes very cruel to him. He was a difficult child to get to open up, but I was dogged in my efforts.

You can imagine my delight when finally, in late spring, Alexander raised his hand during math class. Not only did it go up, but it was accompanied by "Ooh, ooh, ooh," as he waved it frantically. Thrilled that Alexander was eager to participate in our discussion for the first time ever, I immediately called on him.

Well, you can imagine my surprise when he suddenly lunged into a story about his grandma, whom he was excited to tell us, had a hole in her head. You see, we were studying fractions that day, and I had just explained that a fraction is "a part of a whole." Alexander obviously didn't realize the difference between W-hole and H-ole. "Homophones," I told myself, "had better be tomorrow's English lesson!"

Acknowledging Alexander that day was exactly what he needed from me. We had suddenly bonded. Alexander felt such a connection to me after that, that he even went one step further.

I arrived at the school the following morning and was genuinely surprised to find Alexander and his grandma waiting for me. Grandma began by saying, "Alexander said he told you that I have a hole in my head." I smiled nervously and said, "Don't worry. You know kids! They have great imaginations!" Grandma replied, "You didn't believe him, did you?" "No, of course not," I stammered. Well, just that quick, Grandma proudly popped out her glass eye, revealing that she truly did have a hole in her head!

I will never forget that day, and the lessons that I learned from being Alexander's teacher. He taught me:

1. *Students with learning disabilities can connect to a word or phrase, even if it is a homophone, and then just need to vocalize their thoughts.*
2. *I can connect with the hard-to-reach students if I allow them to speak when they are ready to.*
3. *The child who sits by himself, who is shunned by his peers, and who appears to be "on another planet" most days, may just be waiting for the right moment to share something with you. He is testing you to see if you really do care about him.*
4. *We need to look beyond the "package" that our students and their families come wrapped in, so that we can see inside them, and find out what motivates them.*
5. *If a child ever again tells me about a family member with a hole in his or her head . . . BELIEVE HIM!*

ANALYZE & REFLECT

Click here to analyze and reflect on this scenario you have just read.

TONIA L. GRIMES
Warren Primary Center
South Bend, INDIANA

Grimes was Indiana's 2009 Teacher of the Year. The preceding is excerpted from her online article at http://www. beliefnet.com/Inspiration/Chicken-Soup-For-The-Soul/2010/03/Connecting.aspx.

- **Persistent concentration**—ability to attend to a task intensively, without being distracted by noise in the environment
- **Superior memory**—may be restricted to domain(s) of excellence
- **Efficient coordination**—ability to coordinate two or more tasks
- **Curtailed learning and reasoning**—ability to "intuit" solutions without following step-by-step procedures; solves problems by making "intuitive leaps"
- **Flexible thinking**—knowing when to call upon inner resources and deciding which resources to apply for the best result
- **Metacognitive awareness**—awareness of one's own thinking; keeping track of one's understanding of a problem
- **Speedy processing**—ability to process information quickly
- **Philosophical thinking**—concern with "larger questions" that focus on, for example, the future of humankind or the cosmos. (Hoh, 2008, pp. 57–83)

Effective teachers of the **gifted and talented** have many of the same characteristics as their students. "Characteristics that reoccur across the studies of exemplary teachers of the gifted include: intellectualism, subject matter expertise, a personal rapport with high-ability learners, and enjoyment in teaching them" (Robinson, 2008, p. 676). Four innovative approaches for meeting the educational needs of gifted students are acceleration, self-directed or independent study, Individual Education Programs (IEPs), and alternative or magnet schools.

ACCELERATION

The effectiveness of accelerated programs for intellectually precocious students is "striking" (Gross, 2008, p. 248). For example, in a review of hundreds of research findings in education, Kulik (2004) was "not able to find any educational treatment that consistently yielded higher effect size (i.e., positive results) than [acceleration]" (p. 20). The following acceleration options have proven to be the most beneficial at different grade levels:

- **Elementary school**—early entrance, grade skipping, nongraded classes, and curriculum compacting (modifying the curriculum to present it at a faster pace)
- **Junior high school**—grade skipping, grade telescoping (shortening the amount of time to complete a grade level), concurrent enrollment in a high school or college, subject acceleration, and curriculum compacting
- **Senior high school**—concurrent enrollment, subject acceleration, advanced-placement (AP) classes, mentorships, credit by examination, and early admission to college

One example of **acceleration** is a suburban Chicago, **ILLINOIS**, alternative school where high-potential at-risk students work at their own pace in high-tech classrooms. They engage in integrative accelerative learning, which offers advanced curricula and encourages individual creativity, positive reinforcement, and relaxation. At the National Research Center on Gifted and Talented Education, teachers in experimental classrooms practice thematic curriculum compacting, which encourages brighter students to forge ahead in the regular curriculum while all students work to their strengths, and less able students still get the time and attention they need. Also, many colleges and universities now participate in accelerated programs whereby gifted youth who have outgrown the high school curriculum may enroll in college courses.

SELF-DIRECTED OR INDEPENDENT STUDY

For some time, self-directed or independent study has been recognized as an appropriate way for teachers to maintain the interest of gifted students in their classes. Gifted students usually have the academic backgrounds and motivation to do well without constant supervision and the threat or reward of grades.

INDIVIDUAL EDUCATION PROGRAMS (IEPs)

Since the passage of PL 94-142 and the mandating of IEPs for special education students, IEPs have been promoted as an appropriate means for educating gifted students. Most IEPs for gifted students involve various enrichment experiences; self-directed study; and special, concentrated instruction given to individuals or small groups in pullout programs. For example, QuestBridge, part of the Quest Scholars Program, links gifted and talented students with the nation's best colleges and universities. QuestBridge links exceptional students with colleges and universities, scholarship providers, employers, and organizations seeking gifted and talented students who have excelled despite obstacles (QuestBridge, 2014).

ALTERNATIVE OR MAGNET SCHOOLS

Several large-city school systems have developed magnet schools organized around specific disciplines, such as science, mathematics, fine arts, basic skills, and so on. The excellent programs at these schools are designed to attract superior students from all parts of the district. Many of these schools offer outstanding programs for gifted and talented youth.

WHAT ARE SPECIAL EDUCATION AND INCLUSION?

Prior to the 20th century, children with special needs were usually segregated from regular classrooms and taught by teachers in state-run and private schools. Today, an array of programs and services in general and special education classrooms is aimed at developing

Observe this discussion of the benefits of inclusion of students with special needs.

the potential of exceptional students. Two critical concepts to promote the growth, talents, and productivity of exceptional students are special education and inclusion.

Special education refers to "services and supports that teachers provide to meet the needs of students who are identified with disabilities" (McLeskey, Rosenberg, & Westling, 2010, p. 9). Teachers who are trained in special education become familiar with special materials, techniques, equipment, and facilities for students with special needs. For example, children with visual impairment may require reading materials in large print or Braille; students with hearing impairment may require hearing aids and/or instruction in sign language; those with physical disabilities may need special equipment; those with emotional disturbances may need smaller and more highly structured classes; children with special gifts or talents may require access to working professionals. "[R]elated services may include parent counseling and training, physical therapy, occupational therapy, school health services, or special transportation" (Mastropieri & Scruggs, 2010, p. 19).

Special Education Laws

Until 1975, the needs of students with disabilities were primarily met through self-contained special education classes within regular schools. That year, however, Congress passed the **Education for All Handicapped Children Act (Public Law 94-142)**. This act guaranteed to all children with special needs a free and appropriate public education. The law, which applied to every teacher and every school in the country, outlined extensive procedures to ensure that exceptional students between the ages of 3 and 18 were granted due process in regard to identification, placement, and educational services received. As a result of PL 94-142, the participation of students with special needs in all classrooms and school programs became routine.

In 1990, PL 94-142 was replaced by the **Individuals with Disabilities Education Act (IDEA)**. IDEA included the major provisions of PL 94-142 and extended the availability of a free, appropriate education to youth with special needs between the ages of 3 and 21. IDEA, which is one of the most important and far-reaching pieces of educational legislation ever passed in this country, has several provisions with which all teachers should be familiar. In 1997, the **Amendments to the Individuals with Disabilities Education Act (IDEA 97)** were passed. IDEA 97, and its reauthorization in 2004, went beyond IDEA's focus on public school *access* for students with special needs to emphasize educational *outcomes*, modified eligibility requirements, IEP guidelines, public and private placements, student discipline guidelines, and procedural safeguards.

IDEA requires that all children with special needs be educated in the **least restrictive environment**. In other words, a student must be "mainstreamed" into a general education classroom whenever such integration is feasible and appropriate and the child would receive educational benefit from such placement. Figure 9.9 shows the educational service options for students with disabilities, from the least restrictive to the most restrictive. Among schools with high-incidence disabilities (those with a child count over 100,000), students with speech or language impairments and specific learning disabilities are served in the regular classroom for most of the school day. Students with emotional disturbance, mental retardation, and multiple disabilities typically receive services outside the regular classroom for more than 60 percent of the school day (President's Commission on Excellence in Special Education, 2002).

RESPONSE TO INTERVENTION (RTI)

Prior to IDEA 2004, the criterion of "unexpected underachievement" was used to identify students with learning disabilities. Unexpected underachievement was based on a "severe discrepancy" between a student's expected achievement level and actual achievement level. However, this approach was criticized because, often, a student needed to have a history of significant academic failure before a severe discrepancy was found to exist. According to some critics, this amounted to a "wait-to-fail" approach for identifying students with learning disabilities (Fletcher, Denton, & Francis, 2005).

After passage of IDEA 2004, however, states were required to use a systematic approach to provide *early intervention* for students having academic difficulty but not

FIGURE 9.9   Educational service options for students with disabilities

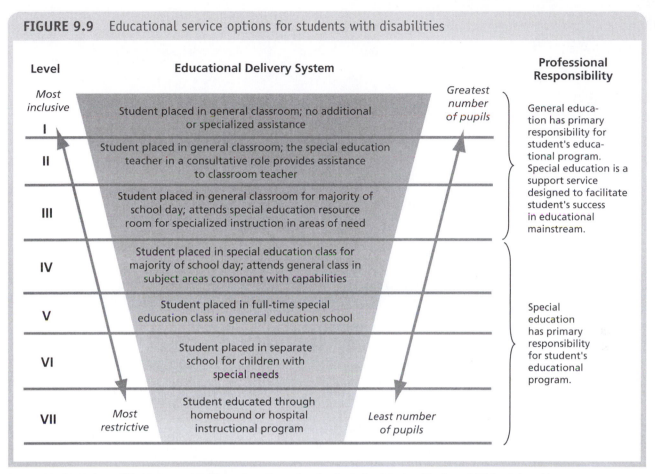

Source: Michael L. Hardman, Clifford J. Drew, and M. Winston Egan, *Human Exceptionality: Society, School, and Family,* 11th Edition. Independence, KY: Cengage Learning, 2014, p. 34.

yet identified as needing special education services. A new approach was mandated because previous methods of identifying students with learning disabilities were often not reliable or valid (Fletcher, Lyon, Fuchs, & Barnes, 2007). According to IDEA 2004, to be identified as eligible for special education services, a student's academic difficulty must be the result of a learning disability rather than a lack of good teaching.

To meet the requirements of IDEA 2004, many states adopted the **response to intervention (RTI) model**. According to RTI, general education teachers work with special education teachers on schoolwide screenings and academic progress monitoring to ensure that students are "responsive" to instruction they receive in the classroom. The RTI approach ensures that students who do not make adequate academic progress and who are at risk for reading and other learning disabilities receive increasingly intensive instructional services that include "scientific, research-based interventions." The RTI model is designed to determine, as early as possible, if a student's low achievement is due to instructional or behavioral factors or whether the student has a possible learning disability. The goal is to provide the student with appropriate instruction and educational assistance *before* he or she experiences years of low achievement.

Figure 9.10 illustrates a three-tier RTI model that many school districts follow to identify students with reading and/or learning problems. As the figure shows, a student who continues to struggle academically, even after receiving three "tiers" of increasingly intensive, individualized instruction, is then referred to a special education team that determines if the student has a learning disability.

INDIVIDUAL EDUCATION PROGRAM

Every child with a disability must have a written **Individual Education Program (IEP)** that meets the child's needs and specifies educational goals, methods for

FIGURE 9.10   Response to intervention (RTI): A three-tiered model for identifying students with learning disabilities

Special Education Services

Student does not respond as expected to previous three tiers of high-quality instruction. Student is then referred to intervention team to determine if student has a learning disability and should receive special education services.

Tier 3, Tertiary Intervention
Teachers monitor academic progress and determine that student continues to struggle academically. More intensive, individualized instruction is then provided, with weekly monitoring of academic progress.

Tier 2, Secondary Intervention
Screening measures determine that student continues to struggle academically, in spite of highly effective instructional strategies. Student receives Tier 2 intervention—e.g., more systematic, structured teaching; small-group instruction; and/or peer tutoring.

Tier 1, Primary Intervention
Student in general education class receives high-quality instruction in core areas such as reading and mathematics.

achieving those goals, and the number and quality of special educational services to be provided. The IEP must be reviewed annually by five parties: (1) a parent or guardian, (2) the child, (3) a teacher, (4) a professional who has recently evaluated the child, and (5) others, usually the principal or a special education resource person from the school district. Figure 9.11 presents an example of an IEP.

RELATED SERVICES

IDEA 97 ensures that students with special needs receive any related services that will help them benefit from special education services. Related services may include "physical therapy, occupational therapy, audiological services, counseling, rehabilitation counseling, social work services, parent counseling, psychological services, school health services, medical services, early identification, transportation, recreation services, or other services identified by the case conference committee" (Mastropieri & Scruggs, 2010, p. 37).

CONFIDENTIALITY OF RECORDS

IDEA also ensures that records on a child are kept confidential. Parental permission is required before any official may look at a child's records. Parents can amend a child's records if they feel information in it is misleading, inaccurate, or violates the child's rights.

FIGURE 9.11 A sample individualized education program (IEP) for Diane: An elementary-age student with disabilities

Student's Primary Classification: Serious Emotional Disturbance
Secondary Classification: None

Student Name <u>Diane</u>
Date of Birth <u>5-3-98</u>

Primary Language

HOME <u>English</u> Student <u>English</u>
Date of IEP Meeting <u>April 27, 2011</u>
Entry Date to Program <u>April 27, 2011</u>
Projected Duration of Services <u>One school year</u>
Required <u>Specify amount of time in educational and/or related services per day or week</u>
General Education Class <u>4 to 5 hours/day</u>
Resource Room <u>1 to 2 hours/day</u>

Special Ed Consultation in General Ed Classroom

<u>Co-teaching and consultation with general education teacher in the areas of academic and adaptive skills as indicated in annual goals</u>

Self-Contained <u>None</u>

Related Services <u>Group counseling sessions twice weekly with guidance counselor. Counseling to focus on adaptive skill development as described in annual goals and short-term objectives</u>

P.E. Program <u>45 minutes daily in general ed PE class with support from adapted PE teacher as necessary</u>

Assessment

Intellectual <u>WISC_R</u>
Educational <u>Key Math Woodcock Reading</u>
Behavioral/Adaptive <u>Burks</u>
Speech/Language _____
Other _____
Vision <u>Within normal limits</u>
Hearing <u>Within normal limits</u>

Classroom Observation Done

Dates <u>1/15-2/25/2011</u>
Personnel Conducting Observation <u>School Psychologist, Special Education Teacher, General Education Teacher</u>

Present Level of Performance Strengths

1. <u>Polite to teachers and peers</u>
2. <u>Helpful and cooperative in the classroom</u>
3. <u>Good grooming skills</u>
4. <u>Good in sports activities</u>

Access to General Education Curriculum

<u>Diane will participate in all content areas within the general education curriculum. Special education supports and services will be provided in the areas of math, reading, and social skills development.</u>

Effect of Disability on Access to General Education Curriculum

<u>Emotional disabilities make it difficult for Diane to achieve at expected grade-level performance in general education curriculum in the areas of reading and math.</u>

<u>It is expected that this will further impact her access to the general education curriculum in other content areas (such as history, biology, English) as she enters junior high school.</u>

Participation in Statewide or District Assessments

<u>Diane will participate in all state and district-wide assessments of achievement. No adaptations or modifications required for participation.</u>

Justification for Removal from General Education Classroom

<u>Diane's objectives require that she be placed in a general education classroom with support from a special education teacher for the majority of the school day. Based on adaptive behavior assessment and observations, Diane will receive instruction in a resource room for approximately 1 to 2 hours per day in the areas of social skills development.</u>

Reports to Parents on Progress toward Annual Goals

<u>Parents will be informed of Diane's progress through weekly reports of progress on short-term goals, monthly phone calls from general ed teachers, special education teachers, and school psychologist, as well as regularly scheduled report cards at the end of each term.</u>

Areas Needing Specialized Instruction and Support

1. Adaptive Skills
   - <u>Limited interaction skills with peers and adults</u>
   - <u>Excessive facial tics and grimaces</u>
   - <u>Difficulty staying on task in content subjects, especially reading and math</u>
   - <u>Difficulty expressing feelings, needs, and interests</u>
2. Academic Skills
   - <u>Significantly below grade level in math—3.9</u>
   - <u>Significantly below grade level in reading—4.3</u>

Annual Review   Date _____
Comments/Recommendations
_____
_____
_____
_____
_____

Team Signatures   IEP Review Date _____
LEA Rep. _____
Parent _____
Sp Ed Teacher _____
Gen Ed Teacher _____
School Psych _____
Student (as appropriate) _____
Related Services Personnel (as appropriate) _____
Objective Criteria and Evaluation Procedures _____

Source: Michael L. Hardman, Clifford J. Drew, and M. Winston Egan, *Human Exceptionality: Society, School, and Family*, 11th Edition. Independence, KY: Cengage Learning, 2014, pp. 39–40.

DUE PROCESS

IDEA gives parents the right to disagree with an IEP or an evaluation of their child's abilities. If a disagreement arises, it is settled through an impartial due process hearing presided over by an officer appointed by the state. At the hearing, parents may be represented by a lawyer, give evidence, and cross-examine, and are entitled to receive a transcript of the hearing and a written decision on the case. If either the parents or the school district disagrees with the outcome, the case may then be taken to the civil courts.

Meeting the Inclusion Challenge

To help you satisfy the provisions of IDEA, you will probably have opportunities as a teacher to participate in in-service programs designed to acquaint classroom teachers with the unique needs of students with special needs. In addition, your teacher education program may require a course on teaching students with special educational needs.

The guidelines for IDEA suggest that schools must make a significant effort to include, or mainstream, all children in the classroom. However, it is not clear how far schools must go to meet this inclusion requirement. For example, should children with severe disabilities be included in general education classrooms if they are unable to do the academic work? Recent court cases have ruled that students with severe disabilities must be included if there is a potential benefit for the child, if the class would stimulate the child's language development, or if other students could act as appropriate role models for the child. In one case, the court ordered a school district to place a child with an IQ of 44 in a regular second-grade classroom and rejected as exaggerated the district's claim that the placement would be prohibitively expensive (*Board of Education, Sacramento City Unified School District v. Holland,* 1992). In another case, the court rejected a school district's argument that inclusion of a child with a severe disability would be so disruptive as to significantly impair the learning of the other children (*Oberti v. Board of Education of the Borough of Clementon School District,* 1992).

To meet the inclusion challenge, you must have knowledge of various disabilities and the teaching methods and materials appropriate for each. Because teachers with negative attitudes toward students with special needs can convey these feelings to all students in a class and thereby reduce the effectiveness of inclusion (Lewis & Doorlag, 2006), as a teacher you must have positive attitudes toward students receiving special education. An accepting, supportive climate can significantly enhance the self-confidence of students with special needs.

In addition, you should be prepared to participate in the education of exceptional learners. You should be willing to do the following:

1. Make maximum effort to accommodate individual students' needs
2. Evaluate academic abilities and disabilities
3. Refer [students] for evaluation [as appropriate]
4. Participate in eligibility conferences [for special education]
5. Participate in writing individualized education programs
6. Communicate with parents or guardians
7. Participate in due process hearings and negotiations
8. Collaborate with other professionals in identifying and making maximum use of exceptional students' abilities (Hallahan & Kauffman, 2006, pp. 19–20, 22)

The Debate over Inclusion

Whereas "mainstreaming" refers to the application of the least restrictive environment clause of PL 94-142, **inclusion** goes beyond mainstreaming to integrate all students with disabilities into general education classes and school life with the active support of special educators and other specialists and service providers, as well as **assistive technology** and adaptive software. Advocates of inclusion have a philosophy similar to Joe Clifford, principal of West Hernando Middle School in Brooksville, **FLORIDA**:

> Our philosophy is that when a kid comes into West Hernando Middle School, our teachers and other staff engage in collaborative decision making to decide how to support the kid and help him fit in. We don't have programs for students with certain labels. We look at the individual student, and figure out what will work so the student will fit in. They're everyone's kids and part of our community. We're all responsible for making sure they're successful. This is inclusion for us. (McLeskey et al., 2010, pp. 4, 9)

Full inclusion goes even further and maintains that "the general education classroom is the most appropriate full-time placement for all students with disabilities—not only those with mild learning and behavior problems, but also those with more severe disabilities" (Lewis & Doorlag, 2006, p. 4). According to the full-inclusion approach, if a child needs support services, these are brought *to the child*; the child does not have to participate in a pullout program to receive support services. Advocates of full inclusion maintain that pullout programs stigmatize participating students because they are separated from their general education classmates, and pullout programs discourage collaboration between general and special education teachers. Those who oppose full inclusion maintain that classroom teachers, who may be burdened with large class sizes and be assigned to schools with inadequate support services, often lack the training and instructional materials to meet the needs of all exceptional students.

In addition, some parents of children with disabilities believe that full inclusion could mean the elimination of special education as we know it, along with the range of services currently guaranteed by federal special education laws. Full inclusion, they reason, would make them depend on individual states, not the federal government, to meet their children's needs. Some parents believe that special education classes provide their children with important benefits.

How do students in general education classrooms feel about their classmates with disabilities? Fifth-grade classmates of Jessica, a student who is nonverbal, nonambulatory, and unable to feed, dress, or care for herself, made these comments (presented in their original form):

- I feel that Jessica has changed my life. How I feel and see handicapped people has really changed. . . . I used to think about handicapped people being really weak and if I would touch her I would hurt her but now I think differently.
- I really like Jessica in my class. Before I met her I never really cared about handycapt people. Jessie is really nice and I like her a lot. Jessica is almost like a sister to me. I like to spend my recess playing with her. I thought a handycapt kid would never be part of my life, but now one and alot more are.
- I think it is great that Jessica is in our room. Jessica is very fun. She laughs and smiles a lot. Sometimes she crys but that is OK. I have learned that Handicapped people are just like the others. I used to say "ooh" look at the person but now I don't I have a big fear for handicapped because they are interesting they can do things that other people can't do. I think Jessica has changed because she is with lots of other kids. (Lewis & Doorlag, 2006, p. 12)

Lin Chang, an eighth-grade teacher, addresses the concerns that general education teachers may have about the availability of resources to help them be successful in inclusive classrooms:

> At first I was worried that it would all be my responsibility. But after meeting with the special education teacher, I realized that we would work together

and I would have additional resources if I needed them. (Vaughn, Bos, & Schumm, 1997, p. 18)

In addition, the following comments by Octavio Gonzalez, a ninth-grade English teacher who has three students with disabilities in two of his five sections of English, express the satisfaction that teachers can experience in inclusive classrooms:

> At first I was nervous about having students with disabilities in my class. One of the students has a learning disability, one student has serious motor problems and is in a wheelchair, and the third student has vision problems. Now I have to say the adaptations I make to meet their special learning needs actually help all of the students in my class. I think that I am a better teacher because I think about accommodations now. (Vaughn et al., 1997, p. 18)

The attitudes of the two teachers just quoted are confirmed in research on teachers' attitudes toward inclusion. Two studies, for example, found that teachers who had experience with inclusion and opportunities for professional development had more positive attitudes toward inclusion and more confidence in their ability to fulfill students' IEPs (Avramidis, Bayliss, & Burden, 2000; Van Reusen, Shoho, & Barker, 2000). The Teachers' Voices: Being an Agent of change feature in this chapter profiles Michelle Shearer, 2011 National Teacher of the Year. Shearer successfully includes students with a variety of special needs in her high school AP chemistry classes. Moreover, she has encouraged many of her students to continue their education beyond high school. For example, a former student at the Maryland School for the Deaf says Shearer's belief in him was the primary reason he was able to earn his bachelor's degree in mathematics (Hicks, 2011).

FOCUS ON DIVERSITY: EQUAL OPPORTUNITY FOR EXCEPTIONAL LEARNERS

Like many groups in our society, exceptional learners have not often received the kind of education that most effectively meets their needs. More than 6.4 million learners in public schools, approximately 13 percent of the school-age population, are classified as exceptional (Snyder & Dillow, 2013). Exceptional learners require special education because they differ significantly from most children. They may have intellectual disabilities, learning disabilities, emotional or behavioral disorders, physical disabilities, disorders of communication, autism, traumatic brain injury, impaired hearing, impaired sight, or special gifts or talents.

Just as there are no easy answers for how teachers should meet the needs of students from diverse cultural backgrounds, there is no single strategy for teachers to follow to ensure that all exceptional students receive an appropriate education. The key, however, lies in not losing sight of the fact that "the most important characteristics of exceptional children are their abilities, not their disabilities" (Hallahan & Kauffman, 2006, p. 7).

To build on students' strengths, classroom teachers must work cooperatively and collaboratively with special education teachers, and students in special education programs must not become isolated from their peers. In addition, teachers must understand how some people can be perceived as "different" and presumed to be "handicapped" because of their appearance or physical condition. Evidence suggests, for example, that people who are short, obese, or unattractive are often victims of discrimination, as are people with conditions such as AIDS, cancer, multiple sclerosis, or epilepsy. It is significant that many individuals with clinically diagnosable and classifiable impairments or disabilities do not perceive themselves as handicapped. The term itself means "permanently unable to be treated equally."

TEACHERS' VOICES ➡ BEING AN AGENT OF CHANGE

MICHELLE SHEARER

"CREATING AN INCLUSIVE ENVIRONMENT . . . HAS ALWAYS BEEN MY MISSION."

Since I began teaching AP chemistry over a decade ago, I have successfully accommodated exceptional students with low vision, dyslexia, dysgraphia, attention deficit disorder, and Asperger's syndrome into my AP chemistry classroom. In 2003, after building rapport and a relationship with both profoundly deaf and hard-of-hearing students at the Maryland School for the Deaf (MSD), I taught AP chemistry, offered for the first time in the school's 135-year history. I conducted the class exclusively in American Sign Language and will always remember the unique experience of discussing complex concepts such as kinetics, electrochemistry, and chemical equilibria with students communicating solely with our hands. When I suggested that these students also study AP calculus, they looked at me with inquisitive expressions and signed, "WHY?" I signed back: "BECAUSE YOU CAN." For the next 2 years, I taught during my planning period so that these enthusiastic, academically motivated students would have the opportunity to study AP calculus and probability and statistics, which otherwise would not have been offered. I proudly share inspirational stories of MSD students who have proven that deaf and hard-of-hearing individuals can succeed in rigorous classes, pass AP exams, earn college degrees, and build successful careers as professionals in our society.

Creating an inclusive environment in which all students are able to experience the world of chemistry has always been my mission as a teacher. One of my greatest rewards is the tremendous growth of our current AP chemistry program and the diversity of the students it attracts. There were 11 students enrolled in AP chemistry when I returned to Urbana High in 2006; there are 92 students enrolled this year. This eight-fold increase is a testament to the high level of commitment and interest on behalf of our students and evidence of their confidence in my ability to provide a meaningful, relevant, rigorous, and yes "fun," chemistry program accessible to a broad range of students.

I am most proud of the fact that every student I have ever taught in AP chemistry, regardless of age, gender, race, hearing status, or learning challenge, has finished the journey with pride and completed the exam to the best of his or her ability. Many continue to keep me informed of their scientific accomplishments as professionals in the fields of health, engineering, and scientific research. Even the self-proclaimed "non-scientists" who finish my course reflect on the experience with a profound sense of pride in their personal achievements. One such student recently e-mailed, "Who knew that I could enjoy chemistry so much? Thank you for helping me to not dread taking science in college!" It is especially rewarding to collaborate with former students, now professional educators in STEM areas, who implement some of the teaching strategies I utilized when they were students in my classroom. I have connected with so many students whom I consider members of my ever-expanding "extended family," and I never tire hearing of the personal and professional accomplishments they have achieved beyond my classroom!

PERSONAL REFLECTION

1. Recall a teacher who helped you overcome self-doubt and believe that you could learn complex, difficult subject matter. How did the teacher do that?
2. Write a short note to the teacher referenced above, thanking him or her for helping you see yourself as a capable learner.

Michelle Shearer teaches chemistry at Urbana High School in Ijamsville, **MARYLAND**. She was the 2011 National Teacher of the Year.

The preceding is excerpted from Michelle Shearer's application for the National Teacher of the Year award at http://www.ccsso.org/Documents/2011/news/2011_NTOY_Press.pdf.

Officially labeling students has become a necessity with the passage of laws that provide education and related services for exceptional students. The classification labels help determine which students qualify for the special services, educational programs, and individualized instruction provided by the laws, and they bring to educators' attention many exceptional children and youth whose educational needs could otherwise be overlooked, neglected, or inadequately served. Detrimental aspects include the fact that classification systems are imperfect and have arbitrary cutoff points that sometimes lead to injustices. Also, labels tend to evoke negative expectations, which can cause teachers to avoid and underteach these students, and their peers to isolate or reject them, thereby stigmatizing individuals, sometimes permanently. The most serious detriment, however, is that students so labeled are taught to feel inadequate, inferior, and limited in terms of their options for growth.

HOW CAN YOU TEACH ALL LEARNERS IN YOUR INCLUSIVE CLASSROOM?

Teachers have a responsibility to address all students' developmental, individual, and exceptional learning needs. Although addressing the range of student differences in the inclusive classroom is challenging, it can also be very rewarding. Consider the comments of three teachers who reflect on their experiences teaching diverse learners:

> This is a note I wrote on the bottom of her [final] report card: "Sara is a sweet, bright child. As much as she could be a challenge, she made me a better teacher by keeping me on my toes. I will truly, truly miss her!" (teacher of a student with Turner syndrome)
>
> It was a gratifying year. I had no idea at the beginning that we would see the progress that we did. . . . Irina came back for a visit today. She ran right up to me and gave me a hug. A year ago, such an obvious display of emotion would have been unthinkable! (teacher of a student with an attachment disorder resulting from a lack of human contact during the years she spent in a Romanian orphanage)
>
> On complex and difficult days, it sometimes feels like it would be a lot easier not to have children with special needs in my classroom. . . . But, you know, I really mourned having to give Daniel up at the end of the school year. There was a special connection I made with that child, and I wanted to be sure that his next teacher felt the same way. (teacher of a student with Down syndrome) (Kostelnik, Onaga, Rohde, & Whiren, 2002, pp. 55, 92–93, 149)

Attention to three key areas will enable you to create a truly inclusive classroom: collaborative consultation with other professionals, partnerships with parents, and assistive technology for special learners.

Collaborative Consultation with Other Professionals

One approach to meeting the needs of all students is known as **collaborative consultation**, an approach in which a classroom teacher meets with one or more other professionals (a special educator, school psychologist, or resource teacher, for example) to focus on the learning needs of one or more students. Collaborative consultation often involves shared decision making and co-teaching relationships (Mastropieri & Scruggs, 2010), and participants assume equal responsibility for meeting students' needs. When working with a consultant, your role will include "preparing for meetings, using data to describe your concern about the student [or students], being open to the consultant's suggestions, implementing the agreed-upon strategies systematically, and documenting the effectiveness of the ideas you try" (Friend & Bursuck, 2015, p. 87).

To meet the educational goals of a student's IEP, regular education teachers are part of an IEP team that includes special educators, other support personnel, and parents. The following special education professionals are among those who consult with and/or collaborate with regular education teachers:

Consulting teacher—a special educator who provides technical assistance such as arranging the physical setting, helping to plan for instruction, or developing approaches for assessing students' learning

Resource-room teacher—a special educator who provides instruction in a resource room for students with disabilities

School psychologist—consults with the general education teacher and arranges for the administration of appropriate psychological, educational, and behavioral assessment instruments; may observe a student's behavior in the classroom

Speech and language specialist—assesses students' communication abilities and works with general education teachers to develop educational programs for students with speech and/or language disorders

Physical therapist—provides physical therapy for students with physical disabilities

Occupational therapist—instructs students with disabilities to prepare them for everyday living and work-related activities

Partnerships with Parents

In addition to working with education professionals to meet the learning needs of all students, effective teachers develop good working relationships with parents. As the following comment by the mother of a daughter with Rett syndrome makes clear, parents of children with special needs expect their teachers to be committed to meeting the learning needs of their children: "My child will never be considered a poster child. She does not give professionals the satisfaction of making great progress, nor is she terribly social. But I need the same type of investment by professionals as any other parents of children without disabilities. The most important thing any

The IEP for this student with multiple disabilities provides for assistive technology, which enables her to create and respond to language.

educator can do for me is to love my Mary" (Howard, Williams, Port, & Lepper, 2001, p. 123). Parents of exceptional children can be a source of valuable information about the characteristics, abilities, and needs of their children. Also, they can be helpful in securing necessary services for their children, and they can assist you by reviewing skills at home and praising their children for their learning.

Assistive Technology for Special Learners

The ability of teachers to create inclusive classrooms has increased dramatically as a result of many technological advances that make it easier for exceptional students to learn and communicate. However, no more than 35 percent of students with diagnosed disabilities are receiving assistive technology as part of their federally mandated IEP (Bran, Gray, & Silver-Pacuila, June 10, 2008).

The array of assistive technologies for students with disabilities is extensive. For example, personal digital assistants (PDAs), BlackBerrys, and iPhones enable students to access the Internet, send and receive e-mail, and keep track of school assignments. Other examples include computer-based word-processing and math tutorials that greatly assist students with learning disabilities in acquiring literacy and computational skills. Students with hearing impairments can communicate with other students by using telecommunications equipment, and students with physical disabilities can operate computers through voice commands or with a single switch or key.

Assistive technology also allows persons with disabilities to express themselves in new ways. For example, a young autistic woman posts video on YouTube about her condition. Using a device that enables her to communicate, she explains the thoughts and feelings behind her movements and gestures. Additional recent developments in assistive technology include the following:

- Talking word processor
- Speech synthesizer
- Touch-sensitive computer screens
- Computer screen image enlarger
- Teletypewriter (TTY) (connects to telephone and types a spoken message to another TTY)
- Customized computer keyboards
- Ultrasonic head controls for computers
- Voice-recognition computers
- Television closed captioning
- Kurzweil reading machine (scans print and reads it aloud)

Assistive technology also includes devices to enhance the mobility and everyday activities of people with special needs (wheelchairs, lifts, adaptive driving controls, scooters, laser canes, feeders). Many technology-related special education resources and curriculum materials are available on the Internet. One of these sites, the TechMatrix, is maintained by the National Center for Technology Innovation (NCTI), funded by the U.S. Department of Education, Office of Special Education Programs. TechMatrix is an online database to help educators and families find educational and assistive technology resources and help for students with special needs. Users can even follow TechMatrix on Twitter. The dazzling revolution in microelectronics will continue to yield new devices to enhance the learning of all students.

SUMMARY

How Do Students' Needs Change as They Develop?

- *Development* refers to predictable changes throughout the human life span.
- People move through different stages of cognitive, psychosocial, and moral development throughout their lives.
- Piaget maintains that children pass through four stages of cognitive development as they mature. Effective teachers are aware of the characteristics of school-age children's thinking during three of these stages: the preoperational stage, the concrete operations stage, and the formal operations stage.
- According to Erikson's model of psychosocial development, people pass through eight stages of emotional and social development throughout their lives. Each stage is characterized by a "crisis" with a positive and negative pole. Healthy development depends on a satisfactory, positive resolution of each crisis.
- Kohlberg believes that moral development, the reasoning people use to decide between right and wrong, evolves through three levels. Evidence suggests that males and females base their moral reasoning on different factors.
- Character education emphasizes teaching values and moral reasoning.
- Maslow suggests that human growth and development depend on how well the individual's biological and psychological needs have been met.

How Do Students Vary in Intelligence?

- Conflicting definitions of intelligence range from "what IQ tests measure" to "goal-directed adaptive behavior." Some theorists believe intelligence is a single, basic ability, although recent research suggests that there are many forms of intelligence.
- According to Gardner's theory of multiple intelligences, there are at least eight (perhaps 10) human intelligences.
- Although there is conflict about the concept of learning styles, effective teachers are aware of differences among students regarding their preferences for learning activities.

How Do Students Vary in Ability and Disability?

- Some students are called "exceptional" because they have abilities or disabilities that distinguish them from other students. Students with physical, cognitive, or emotional disabilities and students who are gifted and talented have unique learning needs.
- Learning disabilities are the most common disability among students, with attention deficit hyperactivity disorder (ADHD) and attention deficit disorder (ADD) the most common learning disabilities.

What Are Special Education and Inclusion?

- Special education includes a variety of educational services to meet the needs of exceptional students. Key provisions of the Individuals with Disabilities Education Act (IDEA) include least restrictive environment, Individual Education Program (IEP), confidentiality of records, and due process.
- Response to intervention (RTI) is a systematic approach to identifying students with learning disabilities.
- Mainstreaming is the process of integrating students with disabilities into regular classrooms.
- Inclusion integrates all students with disabilities into regular classrooms, with the support of special education services as necessary. Full inclusion is the integration of students with disabilities in general education classrooms at all times regardless of the severity of the disability.

How Can You Teach All Learners in Your Inclusive Classroom?

- Through collaborative consultation, an arrangement whereby the regular classroom teacher collaborates with other education professionals, teachers can meet the needs of exceptional students. Collaborative consultation is based on mutuality and reciprocity, and all participants assume responsibility for meeting students' needs.
- An array of assistive technologies and resources is available to help exceptional students learn and communicate in inclusive classrooms.

PROFESSIONAL REFLECTIONS AND ACTIVITIES

Teacher's Journal

1. Relate Erikson's stages of psychosocial development to your own experiences as a child and as an adolescent. How did sources of stress, psychosocial crises, and your resolutions of them affect your learning in school?

2. Do you know your IQ or recall participating in an IQ test? How do you regard yourself in terms of intelligence and how did you come by your beliefs about your intelligence? Do you think these beliefs influenced your motivation, choices, and achievement as a student? Do you think they influenced your school or class placements? Do you think they influenced the way your teachers and peers responded to you? What criteria would you now use to evaluate the fairness of IQ testing and the appropriate use of IQ scores?

3. Describe your preferred learning environment. Where, when, and how do you learn best? Think about how you acquire new information—are you analytical and abstract or more concrete, relying on common sense? Do you prefer to learn alone, in a small group, or in a large group? When given an assignment, do you prefer structure and details or open-ended, unstructured assignments?

Teacher's Research

1. Visit the TechMatrix website and compile a list of assistive technology resources to meet the needs of students with the disabilities listed in Figure 9.8 on page 321.

2. Select two of the major educational journals that focus on the subject area and grade level for which you are preparing to teach. Collect articles that present tips and resources for adapting teaching for students with special needs. In addition, you may wish to look at journals that focus on special education—for example, *Teaching Exceptional Children, Learning Disabilities Research and Practice, Exceptional Children, Remedial and Special Education, Focus on Exceptional Children,* and *Journal of Special Education.*

Observations and Interviews

1. Observe in a classroom that has exceptional students. What steps does the teacher take to meet the needs of these students? Interview the teacher to determine what he or she sees as the challenges and rewards of teaching exceptional students. What does the teacher think are the advantages and disadvantages of inclusion?

2. Visit a local school that provides services for exceptional students. What teams serve students with special needs, and who serves on those teams? How often do they meet, and how do they work with general education teachers? If possible, observe a team meeting. Who are members of the team? To what extent do they have similar recommendations for students' individual education plans? To what extent do they have different recommendations?

Professional Portfolio

For the grade level and content area you are preparing to teach, identify learning activities that address each of the eight multiple intelligences identified by Gardner. For example, you might plan activities such as the following. For one activity in each category, list the preparations you would need to make and/or the materials you would need to gather, and add this information to your portfolio.

Logical-Mathematical

- Design an experiment on . . .
- Describe the rules for a new board game called . . .

Linguistic

- Write a short story about . . .
- Write a biographical sketch of . . .

Musical

- Write song lyrics for . . .
- Locate music that sounds like . . .

Spatial

- Draw, paint, or sculpt a . . .
- Create an advertisement for . . .

Bodily-Kinesthetic

- Role-play a person who is . . .
- Do a dance that shows . . .

Intrapersonal

- Assess your ability to . . .
- Describe how you feel about . . .

Interpersonal

- Show one or more of your classmates how to . . .
- In a small group, construct a . . .

Naturalist

- Identify the trees found in . . .
- Classify the rocks found in . . .

CHAPTER QUIZ

Take this quiz to check your understanding of the content covered in this chapter.

CHAPTER TEN
Creating a Community of Learners

learning outcomes

After reading this chapter, you will be able to do the following:

1. Identify and describe the factors that determine the culture of a classroom.
2. Explain how teachers create a positive learning environment.
3. Identify and explain the keys to successful classroom management.
4. Describe the teaching methods that effective teachers use.
5. Explain how teachers help to build learning communities.
6. Explain how teachers participate in teacher collaboration.

What determines the culture of a classroom?

Classroom culture is determined by the ability of a teacher to develop a good, positive environment—an environment that meets each student's needs and takes into account each student's diverse cultural background.

—ALICIA, Teacher Education student, first year

As the Reader's Voices comment points out, a teacher's primary responsibility is to create a positive learning environment—a cohesive community of learners. Successful teachers know that they must make careful decisions about curriculum goals and objectives, instructional strategies, and classroom management techniques. They understand that, to create a community of learners, they must know not only *what* to teach, but *how* to teach it.

For teacher education students like you, making the transition between the study of teaching and actual teaching can be a challenge. You will make that transition smoothly, however, if you understand that to create a cohesive community of learners, you will need to "(1) earn the respect and affection of students; (2) be consistent and, therefore, credible and dependable; (3) assume responsibility for seeing that [your] students learn; and (4) value and enjoy learning and expect students to do so, too" (Good & Brophy, 2008, p. 77).

WHAT DETERMINES THE CULTURE OF THE CLASSROOM?

A community of learners has a strong positive culture. One definition of culture is the way of life common to a group of people. In much the same way, each classroom develops its own culture. Classroom culture is determined by the manner in which teachers and students participate in common activities.

As a teacher, the activities you and your students engage in will be influenced by several factors. You will make countless decisions that will shape the physical and social milieus of your classroom. From seating arrangements, to classroom rules and procedures, to the content and relevance of the curriculum, to the quality of your interactions with students from diverse cultural and linguistic backgrounds, you will have a strong influence on the culture that emerges in your classroom. You will have many methodological choices to make—when to shift from one activity to another, when to use discussion rather than lecture, how to respond to misbehavior, or whether to make one requirement rather than another.

Classroom Climate

One dimension of classroom culture is **classroom climate**—the atmosphere or quality of life in a classroom. The climate of your classroom will be determined

FIGURE 10.1   Factors for improving student achievement (% major impact)

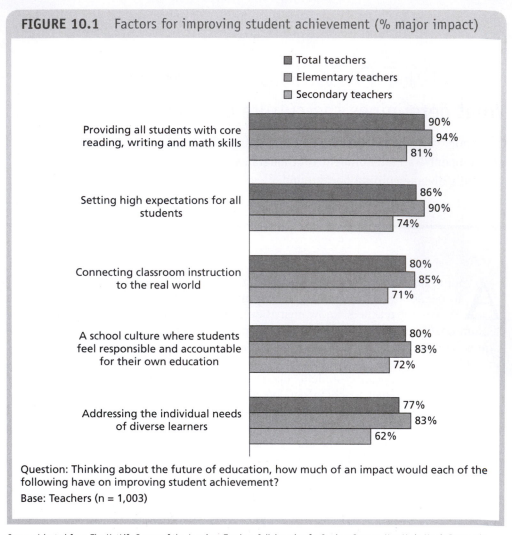

Question: Thinking about the future of education, how much of an impact would each of the following have on improving student achievement?

Base: Teachers (n = 1,003)

Source: Adapted from *The MetLife Survey of the American Teacher: Collaborating for Student Success.* New York: Harris Interactive, April 2010, p. 29.

by how you interact with your students and "by the manner and degree to which you connect with your students, show warmth and support, encourage cooperation, and allow for independent judgment and choice" (Borich, 2014, p. 79).

From the students' perspective, your classroom climate should convince them that you care about them and believe they can learn, are sensitive to their differing needs and abilities, are familiar with their cultural backgrounds, know the subject matter, and can maintain effective discipline. Teachers themselves have a similar view of what is important in the classroom, as shown in Figure 10.1. The figure shows five classroom factors and the percentage of teachers who believe each factor has a "major impact" on student achievement. From the teacher's perspective, the classroom climate should emphasize reading, writing, and math skills; convey high expectations to all students; enable students to see connections between what they are learning and the real world; encourage them to be responsible and accountable for their learning; and show that the teacher is sensitive to their differing needs and abilities.

The climate of your classroom will be complex and multidimensional; its character will be determined by a wide array of variables, many of which will be beyond your control. However, many classroom variables will be within your control. You can take specific steps to create a classroom climate with the following eight characteristics:

1. A productive, task-oriented focus
2. Group cohesiveness
3. Open, warm relationships between teacher and students

4. Cooperative, respectful interactions among students
5. Low levels of tension, anxiety, and conflict
6. Humor
7. High expectations
8. Frequent opportunities for student input regarding classroom activities

The degree to which these dimensions of classroom climate are present within your classroom will be influenced by your style of communicating and treating students. As the following case illustrates, creating a classroom climate characterized by these eight dimensions is not easy. The moment-to-moment decisions teachers make about how to respond to classroom events can enhance or reduce group cohesiveness and students' motivation to learn.

> Dari feels uncomfortable as she makes the seemingly endless trip from her desk to the drinking fountain at the back of the room. If she had a choice, she wouldn't make the trip at all. She is well aware that her classmates resent her being allowed to get a drink whenever she wants to, whereas they have to wait until recess or lunch. They know that the medicine she takes every morning makes her thirsty, but they still tease her about being "Teacher's Pet."
>
> "Why can't the others get drinks when they want to?" she wonders. "It wouldn't be any big deal. Besides, Ms. Patterson is *always* drinking her coffee. She carries that stupid coffee mug around so much that it looks as if it's attached to her body."
>
> "Hey, Ms. Patterson, can I get a drink?" Craig calls out. "It's a really hot day, and I'm thirsty."
>
> "Of course not, Craig. You know my rule about that." Ms. Patterson is obviously annoyed at his question.
>
> Craig persists. "It's not fair. *You* can drink your coffee whenever you want to."
>
> "I never said life is fair," Ms. Patterson replies. "I'm the teacher, so I have certain privileges. I need to have something to drink because I do most of the talking and my mouth gets dry. Besides, my job is to make sure that you children learn, and I can't do that if you're running to the drinking fountain all the time. It won't kill you to wait until recess to get a drink."
>
> "But we could use a water bottle," Huong suggests.
>
> "No, that won't work. A couple of years ago, I let my students bring water bottles to school, and they used them to squirt one another all the time. When are you people going to learn that *no* means *no*?"
>
> "But you let Dari go to the fountain whenever she wants to," Shelby points out.
>
> "Dari has medical problems," Ms. Patterson responds. "Anyway, I know that she'll only get a drink if she really, really needs one. Right, Dari?"
>
> Dari nods self-consciously and then tries to make herself smaller by scrunching low in her seat.
>
> "Yeah, she's special, all right," Guy scoffs. "She's Teacher's Pet." (Ormrod & McGuire, 2007, p. 111)

How would you describe this classroom climate using the eight dimensions listed earlier? Should Ms. Patterson allow her students to get a drink during class? Is it fair that she drinks coffee in front of her students? Could Ms. Patterson help Dari feel more socially connected to her classmates?

Although how you regard and treat students influences your classroom climate, the instructional decisions you make also influence it. Your decisions can result in three types of relationships among members of the class: cooperative or positive interdependence, competitive or negative interdependence, and individualistic or no interdependence (Johnson & Johnson, 1999). A group project to measure classroom furniture would promote *cooperative interdependence*. A race to be the first student to measure the furniture would call for *competitive interdependence*. And having a student measure the furniture independently would be an example of *no interdependence*. Obviously, you should use strategies that foster all three forms of interactions, depending on your instructional goals. In most cases, though, your primary emphasis will be on furthering cooperative interdependence.

Classroom Dynamics

Interactions between teachers and students are at the very core of teaching. As a teacher, the quality of your interactions with students reveals how you feel about them. In addition, high-quality "teacher-child relationships play an important role in children's socio-emotional and behavioral development." Such relationships act as "protective factors" and "help prevent behavior problems" (O'Connor, Dearing, & Collins, 2011, pp. 120, 125).

If you empathize with students, genuinely respect them, and expect them to learn, you are more likely to develop a classroom climate free of management problems. In classrooms with positive group dynamics, teachers and students work toward a common goal—learning. In classrooms with negative interactions, the energy of teachers and students may be channeled into conflict rather than into learning.

There is no precise formula to guarantee success in the classroom; however, a classroom climate characterized by the following four qualities results in greater student motivation to learn and more positive teacher–student and student–student interactions:

1. Learning activities are well organized, progress smoothly, and are free from distractions or interruptions.
2. The teacher is caring, patient, and supportive, and never ridicules or criticizes students for their efforts to learn.
3. The curriculum is challenging but not so difficult that students become frustrated and decide not to learn.
4. Learning activities are authentic and, to the degree possible, relevant to students' interests and experiences.

COMMUNICATION SKILLS

Successful teachers possess effective communication skills. They express themselves verbally and nonverbally (and in writing) in a manner that is clear, concise, and interesting. They "are able to communicate clearly and directly to their students without wandering, speaking above students' levels of comprehension, or using speech patterns that impair their presentation's clarity" (Borich, 2014, p. 8). In addition, they are good listeners. Their students feel that not only are they heard, they are understood.

Effective teachers relish the interactive, spontaneous dimensions of classroom discourse. They respond appropriately to events that could sabotage the plans of less effective teachers—a student's misbehavior, announcements on the PA system, interruptions by other teachers or parents, arguments between students, or the mood of the class at a given time.

INTERACTIONS AMONG STUDENTS

In addition to engaging in positive, success-oriented interactions with their students, effective teachers foster positive, cooperative interactions among students. In culturally diverse classroom settings, students easily and regularly interact with peers from different cultural and linguistic backgrounds. As a result, students feel supported by their peers and free to devote their attention to learning. The climate of such a classroom is "mature" and "self-renewing" (Schmuck & Schmuck, 2001). Typically, the classroom climate has evolved through four stages of group development (see Figure 10.2).

During stage 1, students are on their best behavior. Teachers can use this honeymoon period to their advantage. They can discuss classroom rules and procedures, outline learning goals, and clarify expectations. During stage 2, teachers can encourage student participation and communication, while discouraging the formation of cliques.

FIGURE 10.2   Characteristics of groups at four stages of development

STAGE 1	STAGE 2	STAGE 3	STAGE 4
Teacher acceptance Peer acceptance Sense of membership Sense of trust	Subgroups or cliques Conflict patterns Communication patterns Influence patterns	Conflict resolution Group identity Group cohesiveness Common goals Common procedures High productivity	Effective lasting learning Group commitment Group self-renewal Flexible group norms Individual expression

Groups that have reached stage 2 then move into stage 3, which may last for the remainder of the school year. In stage 3, the group sets clear goals, shares tasks, and agrees on deadlines. A fully evolved group reaches stage 4. In this stage, group members accept responsibility for the quality of life in the group, and they continuously strive to improve it.

Teachers who facilitate group processes in their classrooms recognize that students as well as teachers exert leadership in the classroom. Accomplished teachers identify student leaders and are able to influence these students to use their leadership abilities to help the entire group reach its goals.

HOW CAN YOU CREATE A POSITIVE LEARNING ENVIRONMENT?

A positive classroom climate and positive classroom dynamics are essential for a good learning environment. Developing and then maintaining such an environment is a complex challenge. No single set of strategies will ensure success in all situations. However, educational researchers have identified teacher behaviors that tend to be associated with high levels of student learning. Effective teachers know how to use these behaviors and *for what purposes* they are best suited. The following sections address three important dimensions of positive learning environments: the caring classroom, the physical classroom environment, and classroom organization, including procedures for grouping students for instruction and managing time.

PROFESSIONAL REFLECTION
Watch as a teacher shares what she does to create a positive and productive learning environment.

The Caring Classroom

At this point in your preparation to become a teacher, you may doubt your ability to create a positive classroom climate and to orchestrate the complex dynamics of the classroom so that you and your students become a cohesive, productive, and mutually supportive group. In your quest to develop these abilities, remember that an authentic spirit of caring is at the heart of an effective learning environment. "*[C]aring pedagogy* [italics added] can . . . create or restore self-confidence needed for participating in the positive learning opportunities in the classroom. It can also help form the moral foundation of responsible citizenship, productive community membership and leadership, and lifelong engagement in learning" (Paul & Colucci, 2000, p. 45). This chapter's Teaching on Your Feet feature profiles a teacher who cared enough about a troubled, angry student to figure out a way for the student to make his own unique contribution to a positive learning environment.

FOCUS ON DIVERSITY: CARING AND MULTICULTURAL CLASSROOMS

How can you establish a **caring classroom** in today's culturally diverse schools? First, you can demonstrate caring through your efforts to help all students learn to their fullest potential. You can learn as much as you can about your students' abilities, their

TEACHING ON YOUR FEET
I See a Story in Every Learner

I see the world in stories. I relish in the transformative power of language that can divide and unite us. When I look in a classroom, I see a story in every learner, unique and yearning to be read. Creating a community for learning means creating more than a classroom; it means constantly intertwining our stories in a way that reveals our potential . . . .

Several years ago I taught New Start English where the 28 students who had failed Freshman English came to me, disengaged and disgruntled, each with a story that seemed to explain why. To stay positive, I ate lunch in my room so I could respond to a daily journal I had started with each student. Then, just before they would arrive, I would remind myself what I liked about each.

One particularly troubled student, Tyler, [was] troubled and angry, intelligent and formidable; lost and scared. [He] wielded an uncanny power over his peers. They knew he was smart, both in mind and experience. He was their hero, the tough and seemingly confident person they all wanted to be. In many ways, understanding Tyler meant understanding the class.

I discovered through these daily journals that Tyler loved to draw and for several weeks I invited him to bring in some of his artwork until he finally did.

One day, he came into the room, angrier than usual, but calmed by his art. At the end of class he took his sketch, complex in emotion and execution, and tacked it to the bulletin board. Later, my AP class came in and aptly noticed the new addition. They immediately recognized in it the literary archetypes we'd been studying. I quickly grabbed a pile of sticky notes, asked the students to write down their thoughts and post the notes on the illustration.

The next morning before school I had the office call Tyler into my classroom where I had a note ready for him: "The greatest measure of an artist's worth is the impact he can make on others. Look what you've done," I nodded towards his illustration.

That afternoon he put another [illustration] up and received more sticky notes. Soon after, I discovered how many artists I had in class, all wanting feedback on their work. It became routine—my at-risk learners posted their artwork, my AP learners responded to it.

This didn't magically transform my 5th hour class, but those kids, Tyler especially, came and said hello nearly every day for the next two years as they struggled time and again, just to graduate.

ANALYZE & REFLECT

Click here to analyze and reflect on this scenario you have just read.

SARAH BROWN WESSLING
English Teacher, Johnston Community School District
Johnston, IOWA

Wessling was the 2010 National Teacher of the Year.

The preceding is adapted and excerpted from Sarah Brown Wessling's application for the 2010 National Teacher of the Year award at http://www.ccsso.org/Documents/NTOY/Applications/2010NTOYAPP.pdf.

This dynamic kindergarten class exhibits many of the characteristics of a caring classroom climate. Relations are open and trusting; everyone is accepted and actively engaged; a sense of order prevails even in an activity format that calls for self-expression.

cultural and linguistic backgrounds, and what motivates them to do their best. You should actually become a *student of your students*—as a 10th-grade student states: An effective teacher "[gets] to know all students well" (Harris Interactive, 2001). In addition, as the teacher profiled in the Teachers' Voices: Being an Agent of Change feature in this chapter explains, you can make your classroom a welcoming place for all students—a place where "students from 'different sides of the tracks' [intermingle] on their own accord."

You should also realize that how you speak and listen to students determines the extent to which they believe you care about them. A synthesis of research on classroom environments that enhance students' learning found that "students learn more when their classes are satisfying, challenging, and friendly and they have a voice in decision

TABLE 10.1   Fifteen dimensions of classroom environment

Dimension	Learning		Percent Positive Influence on Description
Satisfaction	100%	(17)	Students enjoy classroom work and find it satisfying.
Challenge	87	(16)	Students find the work difficult and challenging.
Cohesiveness	86	(17)	Students know one another well and are helpful and friendly toward one another.
Physical environment	85	(15)	Adequate books, equipment, space, and lighting are available.
Democracy	85	(14)	Students share equally in making decisions that affect the entire class.
Goal direction	73	(15)	Learning goals are clear.
Competition	67	(9)	Competition among students is minimized.
Formality	65	(17)	Class is informal, with few formal rules to guide behavior.
Speed	54	(14)	Students have sufficient time to finish their work.
Diversity	31	(14)	Students' interests differ and are provided for.
Apathy	14	(15)	Students don't care about what the class does.
Favoritism	10	(13)	All students do not enjoy the same privileges; the teacher has favorites.
Cliquishness	8	(13)	Certain students work only with close friends and refuse to interact with others.
Disorganization	6	(17)	Activities are disorganized and confusing, rather than well organized and efficient.
Friction	0	(17)	Tension and quarreling among students characterize the classroom.

Note: Percent indicates the percentage of research studies that reported a positive influence on learning for that dimension; number in parentheses indicates number of research studies that investigated that dimension.

Source: Adapted from Herbert J. Walberg and Rebecca C. Greenberg, "Using the Learning Environment Inventory," *Educational Leadership,* May 1997, p. 47.

making. [When] classes are unfriendly, cliquish, and fragmented, they leave students feeling rejected and therefore impede learning" (Walberg & Greenberg, 1997, p. 46). Table 10.1 is based on this study; it presents 15 dimensions of classroom life and how each influences students' learning at the junior and senior high school levels.

Although students learn best in caring classrooms, students must also learn to care for others. Toward this end, Stanford University professor Nel Noddings (2002) recommends reorganizing the school curriculum around "themes of care" and suggests that "all students should be engaged in a general education that guides them in caring for self, intimate others, global others, plants, animals, the environment, objects and instruments, and ideas" (p. 99). In addition, Noddings (2007) points out that "relations of care and trust should improve (or at least not hurt) achievement, [and] they also might contribute to greater safety, stronger social ties, better citizenship, and greater satisfaction for both teachers and students" (p. 83).

The Physical Environment of the Classroom

When you become a teacher, the physical environment of your school will probably be similar to that of schools you attended. With the help of your students, however, it is possible to improve your surroundings. Fresh air; plants; clean, painted walls; displays of students' work; a comfortable reading or resource area; and a few prints or posters help to create a positive learning environment. Seating arrangements and the placement of other classroom furniture also do much to shape the classroom environment. Although seating by rows may be very appropriate for whole-group instruction or examinations, other arrangements may be more beneficial for other activities. For

FIGURE 10.3   Learning centers in an elementary classroom

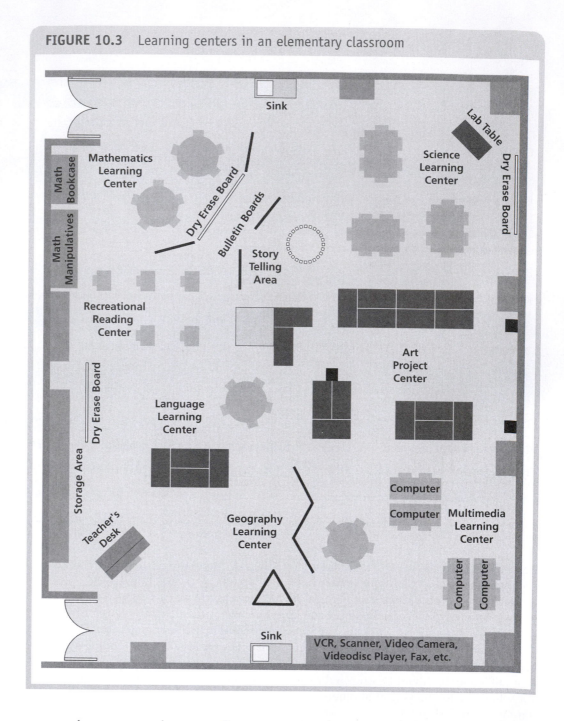

example, you can enhance small-group activities by moving desks into small clusters in different parts of the room. Figure 10.3 shows the arrangement of a classroom at an exemplary elementary school. The room is designed to encourage students to learn through discovery at learning centers located around the room.

However you design your classroom, be certain that seating arrangements do not reduce the opportunity of some students to learn. For example, students in some classrooms receive more attention if they are seated in the so-called *action zone*, the middle front-row seats and seats on the middle aisle. Teachers often stand near this area and unknowingly give students seated there more opportunities to speak.

Classroom Organization

A critical factor in creating a positive learning environment is **classroom organization**—how teachers and students are grouped for instruction, how

TEACHERS' VOICES ➡ BEING AN AGENT OF CHANGE

R. ANDRE STEMM-CALDERON

ENCOURAGING GLOBAL CITIZENSHIP IN THE CLASSROOM

Schools should stop the extreme focus on testing and conceive of a broader view of education that takes into account the whole, creative child who is a citizen of the world. I do not oppose standardized testing. In an ideal world, students would simply pause for a few days at the end of the year to take tests and then return to their creative, motivating curriculum.

However, the testing culture has invaded all aspects of our school. Typically, these tests do not assess the right-brain aptitudes of our students; therefore, we stop developing it, leaving our students at a huge disadvantage when it comes to global understanding. However, many American families embrace the concept of global citizenship and desire such an education for their children.

Currently, I am teaching in a program that embraces a global perspective. This program joins two cultures, two languages, and, in some ways, two classes of people. The two-way dual language program brings Spanish-speaking, Mexican Americans from predominately lower-income communities together with English-speaking Anglo students from predominately middle-class backgrounds. In my 10 years of teaching, I have never witnessed the things I see in my classroom. I see students from "different sides of the tracks" intermingling on their own accord. I see friendships between a middle-class Anglo girl and a very poor Mexican American girl blossom. These girls do not understand how rare this is in American education. They have never visited the highly segregated schools that exist across America that separate by class and race. Our program has normalized this type of interaction. It is true that at the beginning of the year

they will sit together, segregated in their "tribes" (White with White, Hispanic with Hispanic, etc.). However, by March we have students interacting in all sorts of configurations. Unfortunately, two-way dual language programs are still rare in the United States, although some reports suggest a growing trend. Programs that represent other cultures, languages, and even social classes expand the opportunities for our students and prepare them to function and thrive in a diverse and complex world.

As an immigrant to the United States, I understand the importance of global citizenry. I was raised in a bicultural, bilingual home all around California and Texas, where learning about cultures was encouraged. I also had the privilege of traveling during and after college. These opportunities have increased my curiosity about other places in the world. These experiences have broadened my thinking, challenged my values, and opened my mind to other ideas and philosophies. I am challenged to think about world problems from a human level instead of solely an American point of view. In the end, my global citizenry makes me a better teacher, equipped with the perspective and compassion to work alongside my fellow world citizens.

PERSONAL REFLECTION

1. With reference to the grade level and subject area for which you are preparing to teach, how can you foster global citizenship? How can you develop a welcoming tone for all students and their families?

2. What challenges can a teacher face when trying to foster global citizenship and develop a welcoming tone in his or her classroom? How can a teacher overcome these challenges?

R. Andre Stemm-Calderon is a teacher at Mission View Elementary School in Wenatchee, **WASHINGTON**. Andre taught in **TEXAS** for 8 years and was 2003–2004 Teacher of the Year at Jenard Gross Elementary School in Houston.

---

learning tasks are structured, and how other resources are used. The following sections focus on these aspects of classroom organization.

GROUPING STUDENTS BY ABILITY

Two common approaches for grouping students on the basis of shared characteristics are between-class ability grouping, often called tracking, and within-class ability grouping. Students who attend schools where **between-class ability grouping** is practiced are assigned to classes on the basis of ability or achievement (usually determined by scores on standardized tests). Another form of between-class ability grouping, especially at the high school level, is based on students' goals after graduation. Many high schools, for example, have a college preparatory track, a vocational track, and a business education track.

For the most part, between-class ability grouping does not contribute to greater achievement (Good & Brophy, 2008). Supporters nevertheless claim that teachers are better able to meet the needs of students in homogeneous groupings. Among the alternatives to between-class ability grouping are heterogeneous (or mixed-ability) grouping, regrouping by subject area, the Joplin Plan (regrouping students for reading instruction by ability across grade levels), and cooperative learning.

Within-class ability grouping is often used for instruction in reading and mathematics within a class, where a teacher instructs students in homogeneous, small groups. Within-class grouping is used widely in elementary classrooms. You may recall learning to read in a small group with a name such as the Eagles, the Redbirds, or the Mustangs. Like tracking, within-class ability grouping can heighten preexisting differences in achievement between groups of students, especially if teachers give high-achieving groups more attention. Also, once students are grouped, they tend not to be regrouped, even when differences in achievement are reduced.

At best, evidence to support student groupings is mixed. Whether students are grouped on the basis of ability, curricular interests, or disabling condition, there is a danger that some group labels can evoke negative expectations, causing teachers to under-teach certain students, and their peers to isolate or reject them. The most serious consequence, of course, is that students so labeled are taught to feel inadequate, inferior, and limited in their options for growth.

GROUPING STUDENTS FOR COOPERATIVE LEARNING

Cooperative learning is an approach to teaching in which students work in small groups, or teams, sharing the work and helping one another complete assignments. Student-Team-Learning, for example, is a cooperative approach teachers use to increase the basic skills achievement of at-risk students. In cooperative learning arrangements, students are motivated to learn in small groups through rewards that are made available to the group as a whole and to individual members of the group. **Cooperative learning** includes the following key elements:

- Small groups (four to six students) work together on learning activities.
- Assignments require that students help one another while working on a group project.
- In competitive arrangements, groups may compete against one another.
- Group members contribute to group goals according to their talents, interests, and abilities.

Cooperative learning also enables students to learn a variety of roles and responsibilities, as the Technology in Action feature in this chapter describes how a fifth-grade social studies teacher combined cooperative learning and podcasting as a way for her students to study the history of the local community.

FOCUS ON DIVERSITY: COOPERATIVE LEARNING AND CROSS-CULTURAL INTERACTION

In addition, cooperative learning is an instructional method that can strengthen students' interpersonal skills. When students from different racial, ethnic, and cultural backgrounds and students with special needs all contribute to a common group goal, friendships increase and group members tend to view one another as more equal in status and worth. The contribution that cooperative learning can make to the culture of the classroom is supported by research that indicates that "students of color and White students have a greater tendency to make cross-racial friendships choices [if] they have participated in interracial learning teams. [Also], the academic achievement of students of color . . . is increased . . . while the academic achievement of White students remains about the same in both cooperative and competitive learning situations" (Banks 2014, p. 122).

DELIVERING INSTRUCTION

The delivery of instruction is a key element in creating positive learning environments. What the teacher and the students do has a powerful influence on learning and on the quality of classroom life. A common activity format in elementary schools consists of students doing seatwork on their own or listening to their teachers and participating in

FIGURE 10.4   An authentic learning activity

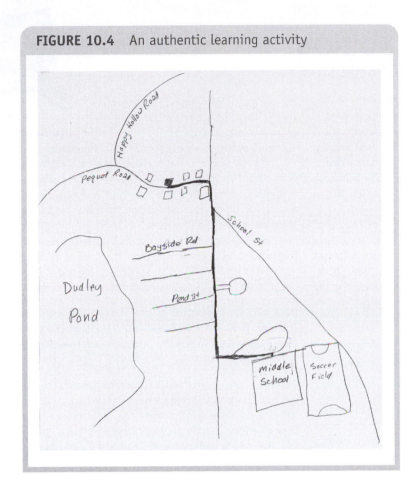

whole-class recitations. In addition, students participate in reading groups, games, and discussions; take tests; check work; view films; give reports; gather information from the Internet; help clean up the classroom; and go on field trips.

As a teacher, you must answer the question, What activity will enable me to accomplish my instructional goals? You should also realize that learning activities should meet students' goals; that is, the activities must be meaningful and authentic for students. **Authentic learning tasks** enable students to see the connections between classroom learning and the world beyond the classroom—both now and in the future. For example, Figure 10.4 is an example of an authentic assignment to create a map of the route to school.

To understand how authentic learning tasks can motivate students to learn, reflect on your own school experiences. Do you recall memorizing facts only because they would appear on a test? Did you ever wonder why a teacher asked you to complete a learning task? Did you ever feel that a teacher asked you to do busywork? What kinds of learning tasks motivated you the most? How often were you involved in authentic learning activities such as the following?

- Giving oral reports based on research you conducted
- Writing an editorial for the school or local newspaper
- Representing the pro or con side in a debate
- Conducting an experiment and then writing the results
- Creating a model to illustrate a process like photosynthesis, a solar eclipse, or combustion in a gasoline engine
- Completing an art project and then participating in an art exhibit for the community
- Tutoring younger children in reading, mathematics, or science

TECHNOLOGY in ACTION
Podcasting in Fifth-Grade Social Studies

Mrs. Warren teaches fifth-grade social studies at Miliken Elementary School. She is a firm believer in connecting her students to their community. Each year, she has her students research historical and current events from their community and write up the stories they uncover. In the past, she posted these written stories on the school's website, printed them in a newspaper format, or compiled them in a hard-copy book. This year, she decides to try something different: Mrs. Warren wants to podcast her students' stories.

To start, she divided her students into groups of four. Each group was formed around a series of basic skill sets. Each group had a student who was comfortable with podcasting technologies, a student who had strong writing skills, a student who was comfortable speaking into a microphone, and a student who had research skills. The groups were asked to identify an aspect of their community that they wanted to explore. They were also asked to identify one historical event and one current event to report on.

Once Mrs. Warren approved the topics, the students started researching those topics. They developed research notes, a storyboard, and a script for narration. When they had these components, they started creating their audio files. Mrs. Warren allowed the students to either record directly on the computer or use a mobile recording device. Selection of a device depended on the needs of the group. Some groups performed in teams, with one student reading, then another. Some of the groups chose to act out historical events. Members of the group would take on the roles of historical figures from the community, like an old-time radio broadcast. Other groups delivered their podcast as a news report. Some students interviewed members of the community, some acted as news anchors, and others as roving reporters. Mrs. Warren was very impressed with the creativity and accuracy of the reports and the excitement that the activity generated among the students.

What made the activity a true success was Mrs. Warren's approach to publicizing the podcasts. After the first podcast was created, Mrs. Warren made an announcement over the school's public address (PA) system. She alerted the whole school to the availability of the podcasts and where they could get information on accessing the podcasts. Most important, she informed them of a competition. She offered free merchandise at the school store if students answered questions about the stories in the podcasts.

At any moment, walking down the hallway, in the lunchroom, or in class, Mrs. Warren would ask questions. For each correct answer, a student was entered into a drawing. Friday morning of each week, Mrs. Warren would draw a name from the pool of entries and announce the winners over the PA system.

By the second week, students in the school were downloading the podcast to their MP3 players, the computers at school, and—according to parents she spoke with—computers at home. Without a doubt, students were really learning about their community.

PODCASTING: Podcasting is the delivery of audio files over the Internet. What makes podcasting unique is syndication. Syndication allows subscribers to receive, through a web feed, frequently updated web content.

POSSIBLE USES: Teachers have used podcasts to deliver lecture material to students, to improve their teaching by accessing relevant professional development materials, to improve student reading comprehension, to improve learning through student-generated material, and to update parents on the daily events that transpire in their classrooms.

TRY IT OUT: To create a podcast, you need access to a computer, a microphone, and a web server. The first step is to create an audio file. You can use any audio recording software to create the file—programs such as Audacity work well. Once the audio file is created, you need to convert it to an MP3 format. Once your audio file is converted to MP3, you need to upload that file, along with a Really Simple Syndication (RSS) file, to a web server. If you are familiar with basic HTML, then creating an RSS file is quite simple. If you are not familiar with basic HTML, a quick tutorial will get you ready in a short time. Once the MP3 and RSS file are uploaded to your web server, the file is ready for prime time and is accessible to your registered audience.

- Developing a website to document an in-class project
- Creating an infomercial using video-editing software and then getting reactions to the infomercial from other classes in your school
- Developing a science webquest and then posting the webquest for evaluation

A comprehensive nationwide study of successfully restructured schools reported that "authentic pedagogy" helps students to (1) "construct knowledge" through the use of higher-order thinking, (2) acquire "deep knowledge" (relatively complex understandings of subject matter), (3) engage in "substantive conversations" with teachers and peers, and (4) make connections between substantive knowledge and the world beyond the classroom (Newmann et al., 1996; Newmann & Wehlage, 1995). In addition, the study found that highly authentic pedagogy classes boost achievement for students at all grade levels.

HOW TIME IS USED

How teachers use time affects student learning. **Allocated time** is the time teachers allocate for instruction in various areas of the curriculum. Teachers vary widely in their instructional use of time. For example, "some students [may receive] as much as four times more instructional time in a given subject than other students in the same grade" (Good & Brophy, 2003, p. 29).

Researchers have shown that **time on-task**—the amount of time students are actively engaged in learning activities—is directly related to learning. As anyone who has ever daydreamed while appearing to pay attention can confirm, time on-task is difficult to measure. In response to this difficulty, researchers have introduced the concept of **academic learning time**—the amount of time a student spends working on academic tasks with a high level of success (80 percent or higher). Not surprisingly, learning time, like allocated time, varies greatly from classroom to classroom. For example, a study of how elementary teachers actually use the more than 1,000 hours most states mandate for instruction revealed that students were truly engaged in meaningful, appropriate tasks for only about 300 hours. The other 700 hours were devoted to activities such as the following: recess, lunch, transitions, clerical and administrative tasks, "off-task" behaviors by students (Weinstein & Migano, 2010).

An additional concept that is proving useful in understanding teachers' use of time in the classroom is known as **opportunity to learn (OTL)**. OTL is based on the premise that teachers should use time to provide all students with challenging content through appropriate instruction. Many states are developing OTL standards for how teachers should use time in the classroom.

Claudia Meek, a third-grade teacher in California, points out in her *Phi Delta Kappan* article that state- and district-mandated testing and the time needed to prepare students for testing reduce the amount of instructional time available to teachers. During a 1-year period, approximately 32 hours of her class time were devoted to testing. That same year, 262 hours were devoted to fundraising, disaster preparedness, socialization, holidays, assemblies, regular interruptions, and miscellaneous time losses. Taken together, more than one-third of Meek's classroom time was devoted to these activities. Her observations are based on a large-scale research study conducted by the National Center for Education Statistics and an analysis of data collected from her own classroom (Meek, 2003). To increase the time available for active learning, many high schools have implemented block scheduling arrangements. **Block scheduling** uses longer blocks of time each class period, with fewer periods each day. Longer blocks of time allow more in-depth coverage of subject matter and lead to deeper understanding and higher-level applications. Block scheduling also gives teachers more time to pre-sent complex concepts and students more time to practice applying those concepts to authentic problems.

WHAT ARE THE KEYS TO SUCCESSFUL CLASSROOM MANAGEMENT?

For most new teachers, classroom management is a primary concern. How can you prevent discipline problems from arising and keep students productively engaged in learning activities? Effective **classroom management** cannot be reduced to a cookbook recipe. However, you can take definite steps to create an effective learning environment in your classroom.

Consider the following scenarios of two middle-level classrooms—the same group of students with two different teachers. In which classroom is misbehavior more likely to emerge?

Classroom 1 is a beehive of activity as students continue to study global warming in their science class. Students are working in small groups at four multimedia centers, each with a desktop computer. Each group is developing questions they will post on the class blog for scientists participating on the Andrill Research Immersion for Science Educators (ARISE) team stationed in Antarctica. "What do you eat in Antarctica?" "How cold is it right now?" "Have you seen any polar bears, seals, penguins, or other wildlife?" The teacher circulates from group to group—listening, asking clarifying questions, and encouraging each group's effort. Some students suggest questions; others clarify the group's thinking—clearly, the students are deeply engaged in the activity.

Classroom 1 is filled with instructional materials. Student work—clay models of igloos, polar bears, and penguins, for example—is on the shelves that line the walls. On the classroom walls are maps of Antarctica drawn by students, color photos of Antarctica printed out on the printer at each learning center, and color printouts of PowerPoint presentations on Antarctica.

Science class is over, and students are now in classroom 2, studying language arts. Students are seated in rows, staring at their literature books while student after student reads two paragraphs from the book. The teacher sits on the desk at the front of the room and occasionally asks a question or makes a comment about the material just read. Several commercially printed posters are on the classroom walls—"Elements of a Novel or Short Story," "Punctuation Rules," and "What Good Readers Do." On one side of the room, beneath the windows, paperback and hardcover books are neatly lined up on the shelves of two bookcases. The room is quiet except for the sound of the student reading, the teacher's occasional comment or question, and the loud ticking of the clock above the classroom door.

These two scenarios illustrate the fact that good classroom management focuses on "establishing a productive learning environment, rather than control of misbehavior" (Good & Brophy, 2008, p. 77). Sound classroom management techniques are based on the guidelines for creating an effective learning environment presented previously in this chapter—in other words, (1) creating a caring classroom, (2) organizing the physical classroom environment, (3) grouping students for instruction, (4) providing authentic learning tasks, and (5) structuring the use of time to maximize students' learning. Positive leadership and preventive planning thus are central to effective classroom management.

In addition, you should remember that classroom management refers to how teachers structure their learning environments to prevent, or minimize, behavior problems. *Discipline* refers to the methods teachers use *after* students misbehave. *Classroom management* is prevention-oriented, while discipline is control-oriented. The goal of classroom management is to structure the classroom environment to *maximize student attention* and *minimize disruptive behavior*. The following strategies will help you create a well-managed classroom environment:

PROFESSIONAL REFLECTION

Watch how a teacher implements successful classroom management and discusses her keys to its success.

- Arrange classroom furniture (desks, tables, and chairs) so that you can easily monitor students' behavior for signs of inattention, boredom, and misbehavior from any point in the room.
- Arrange classroom furniture so that students can move from place to place without disturbing their classmates.
- Keep very interesting instructional materials (for example, a replica of a human skeleton, a model of the solar system, or a large collection of insects) out of sight until you need to use them.
- Separate friends who tend to misbehave and get off-task when they are seated near one another, or separate students who dislike one another and are more likely to misbehave if they are seated close to one another.
- Assign chronically misbehaving students to seats close to your desk.

The Democratic Classroom

Teachers who allow students to participate in making decisions about the physical classroom environment, classroom rules and procedures, modifications to the curriculum, and options for learning activities also have fewer discipline problems. Students in **democratic classrooms** have more power and more responsibility than students in conventional classrooms. If students are to live in a democracy, they must learn to manage freedom responsibly; teachers model democracy by giving their students some choices and some control over classroom activities.

William Glasser, well-known psychiatrist and author of *Quality School* (1998a), *The Quality School Teacher* (1998b), *Choice Theory* (1998c), and (with Karen Dotson) *Choice Theory in the Classroom* (1998), recommends that teachers develop "quality" classrooms based on democratic principles. According to Glasser, many teachers struggle with classroom management because their actions are guided by stimulus-response theory. They try to coerce students through rewards or punishment, or what many teachers term logical consequences. Instead, Glasser believes that teachers should establish "quality" environments in the classroom by following choice theory. Choice theory recognizes that human beings make choices that enable them to create "quality worlds" that satisfy four needs: the need to belong, the need for power, the need for freedom, and the need for fun.

From a **choice theory** perspective, misbehavior in the classroom arises when students' learning experiences do not enable them to create quality worlds for themselves. Therefore, teachers "must give up bossing and turn to 'leading'" (Glasser, 1997, p. 600). We follow leaders, Glasser says, because we believe they are concerned about our welfare. To persuade students to do quality schoolwork, teachers must establish warm, noncoercive relationships with students; teach students meaningful skills rather than ask them to memorize information; enable them to experience satisfaction and excitement by working in small teams; and move from teacher evaluation to student self-evaluation.

Creating a democratic classroom community is not easy; however, the benefits can be significant. Teachers who create a democratic classroom environment often report that their classrooms were teacher-centered at the beginning of the school year; however, as the year progressed, they were able to transition to a communal environment. In such an environment, students understood that the guiding question for the class was "*What are we going to do?*" rather than "*What does the teacher want us to do?*"

Preventive Planning

What other strategies can you use to prevent discipline problems from occurring? The key to prevention is excellent planning and an understanding of life in classrooms. In addition, if you master the essential teaching skills, you will have fewer discipline problems because students will recognize that you are prepared, are well organized, and have a sense of purpose. You will be confident of your ability to teach all students, and your task-oriented manner will tend to discourage misbehavior.

In a seminal study of how teachers prevent discipline problems, Jacob Kounin looked at two sets of teachers: (1) those who managed their classrooms smoothly and productively, with few disruptions, and (2) those who seemed to be plagued with discipline problems and chaotic working conditions. He found that the teachers who managed their classrooms successfully had certain teaching behaviors in common: They (1) displayed the proverbial eyes in the back of the head, a quality of alertness Kounin referred to as *with-it-ness*; (2) used individual students and incidences as models to communicate to the rest of the class their expectations for student conduct—Kounin's *ripple effect*; (3) supervised several situations at once effectively; and (4) were adept at handling transitions smoothly (Kounin, 1970).

In addition to the principles of effective classroom management that Kounin found, two key elements of preventive planning are (1) establishing rules and procedures and (2) organizing and planning for instruction.

ESTABLISHING RULES AND PROCEDURES

Successful classroom managers have carefully planned rules and procedures, which they teach early in the year using clear explanations, examples, and

From this photo, what can you tell about this teacher's proficiency in planning and preparation, structuring the classroom environment, and instruction?

practice (Emmer & Evertson, 2013; Evertson & Emmer, 2013; Good & Brophy, 2008). Your classroom rules should be clear, concise, reasonable, and few in number. For example, four general rules for elementary-age students might include: (1) respect and be polite to all people, (2) be prompt and be prepared, (3) listen quietly while others are speaking; and (4) obey all school rules (Evertson & Emmer, 2013, pp. 33–34). Rules for the middle and secondary levels might stipulate the following: (1) bring all needed materials to class, (2) be in your seat and ready to work when the bell rings, (3) respect and be polite to all people, (4) listen and stay seated when someone is talking, (5) respect other people's property, (6) listen and stay seated while someone else is speaking, and (7) obey all school rules (Emmer & Evertson, 2013, p. 31).

It is important to enforce classroom rules consistently and fairly. "Consistency is a key reason some rules are effective while others are not. Rules that are not enforced or not applied consistently over time result in a loss of respect for the person who has created the rules and is responsible for enforcing them" (Borich, 2014, p. 85).

Procedures—the routines your students follow as they participate in learning activities—are also essential for smooth classroom functioning and minimizing opportunities for misbehavior. How will homework be collected? How will supplies be distributed? How will housekeeping chores be completed? How will attendance be taken? How do students obtain permission to leave the classroom? Part of developing classroom rules and procedures is to decide what to do when students do not follow them. Students must be made aware of the consequences for failing to follow rules or procedures. For example, consequences for rule infractions can range from an expression of teacher disapproval to penalties such as loss of privileges, detention after school, disciplinary conference with a parent or guardian, or temporary separation from the group.

ORGANIZING AND PLANNING FOR INSTRUCTION

Organizing instructional time, materials, and activities so that classes run smoothly enables you to keep your students engaged in learning, thereby reducing the need for discipline. Time spent planning authentic learning activities that are appropriate for students' needs, interests, and abilities enables you to enjoy the professional satisfaction that comes from having a well-managed classroom.

The following examples illustrate how one eighth-grade teacher began the school year by carefully organizing and planning for instruction. The teacher across the hall, however, was not as well organized; as a consequence, she is more likely to experience misbehavior in her classroom as the year progresses.

> Donnell Alexander is waiting at the door for her eighth graders with prepared handouts as students come in the room. She distributes them and says, "Take your seats quickly, please. You'll find your name on the desk. The bell is going to ring in less than a minute and everyone needs to be at his or her desk and quiet when it does. Please read the handout while you're waiting." She is standing at the front of the room, surveying the class as the bell rings. When it stops, she begins, "Good morning, everyone."
>
> Vicki Williams, who also teaches eighth graders across the hall from Donnell, is organizing her handouts as the students come in the room. Some take their seats while others mill around, talking in small groups. As the bell rings, she looks up and says over the hum of the students. "Everyone take your seats, please. We'll begin in a couple minutes," and she turns back to finish organizing her materials. (Kauchak & Eggen, 2012, p. 82)

Effective Responses to Student Behavior

When students do misbehave, effective teachers draw from a repertoire of problem-solving strategies. These strategies are based on their experience and common sense, their knowledge of students and the teaching–learning process, and their knowledge of human psychology.

There are many structured approaches to classroom management; some are based on psychological theories of human motivation and behavior, while others reflect various philosophical views regarding the purposes of education. None of these approaches, however, is appropriate for all situations, for all teachers, or for all students. The usefulness of a given method depends, in part, on the teacher's individual personality and leadership style and the ability to analyze the complex dynamics of classroom life. In addition, what works should not be the only criterion for evaluating structured or packaged approaches to discipline; what they teach students about their self-worth, ability to meet challenges, and prospects for future success is also important.

SEVERITY OF MISBEHAVIOR

Your response to student misbehavior will depend, in part, on whether an infraction is mild, moderate, or severe, and whether it is occurring for the first time or is part of a pattern of chronic misbehaviors. For example, a student who throws a wad of paper at another student might receive a warning for the first infraction. Another student who repeatedly throws objects at other students might receive an after-school detention. Definitions of the severity of misbehavior vary from school to school and from state to state. Figure 10.5 shows the percentage of public schools, categorized by locale, that reported different types of discipline problems.

ZERO TOLERANCE

In response to concerns about violence, drugs, and weapons, some schools have implemented zero tolerance policies. The purpose of **zero tolerance policies** is to communicate to students the types of misbehavior that will result in automatic suspension and/or expulsion. Zero tolerance policies are based on the assumption that awareness of automatic, severe consequences for certain types of misbehavior will deter students from those misbehaviors. Evidence indicates, however, that such policies have little effect on students who are inclined to engage in serious misbehavior, and they do not help to create conditions that deter such misbehavior (Losinski, Katsiyannis, Ryan, & Baughan, 2014; National Association of School Psychologists, 2008). In light of such evidence, the National Association of School Psychologists (2008) has concluded, "Systemic school-wide violence prevention programs, social skills curricula and positive behavioral supports lead to improved learning for all students and safer school communities" (p. 3).

CONSTRUCTIVE ASSERTIVENESS

The effectiveness of your responses to students' misbehavior depends, in part, on your ability to use constructive assertiveness (Emmer & Evertson, 2013; Evertson & Emmer, 2013). Constructive assertiveness "lies on a continuum of social response between aggressive, overbearing pushiness and timid, ineffectual submissiveness. Assertiveness skills allow you to communicate to students that you are serious about teaching and about maintaining a classroom in which everyone's rights are respected. Assertiveness does not limit or hamper teachers' and students' caring for one another" (Evertson & Emmer, 2013, p. 166). Communication based on constructive assertiveness is not hostile, sarcastic, defensive, or vindictive; it is clear, firm, and concise. **Constructive assertiveness** includes three basic elements:

- A direct, clear statement of the problem
- Body language that is unambiguous (e.g., direct eye contact with students, erect posture, and facial expressions that are congruent with the content and tone of corrective statements)
- Firm, unwavering insistence on correct behavior

Lee Canter developed an approach to discipline based on teacher assertiveness. The approach calls on teachers to establish firm, clear guidelines for student behavior and to follow through with consequences for misbehavior. Canter (1989, p. 58) comments on how he arrived at the ideas behind assertive discipline: "I found that, above all, the master teachers were assertive; that is, they taught students how to behave.

FIGURE 10.5   Percentage of public schools reporting selected discipline problems that occurred at school, by locale: School year 2009–10

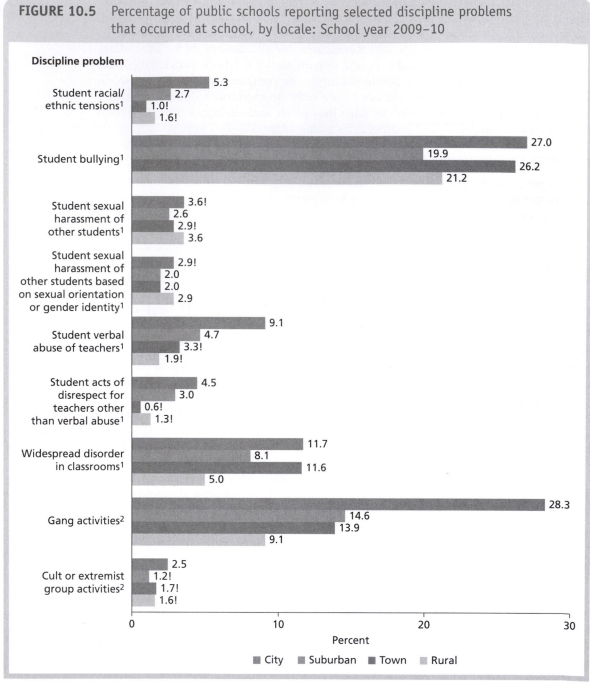

Discipline problem

Student racial/ethnic tensions[1]: City 5.3; Suburban 2.7; Town 1.0!; Rural 1.6!

Student bullying[1]: City 27.0; Suburban 19.9; Town 26.2; Rural 21.2

Student sexual harassment of other students[1]: City 3.6!; Suburban 2.6; Town 2.9!; Rural 3.6

Student sexual harassment of other students based on sexual orientation or gender identity[1]: City 2.9!; Suburban 2.0; Town 2.0; Rural 2.9

Student verbal abuse of teachers[1]: City 9.1; Suburban 4.7; Town 3.3!; Rural 1.9!

Student acts of disrespect for teachers other than verbal abuse[1]: City 4.5; Suburban 3.0; Town 0.6!; Rural 1.3!

Widespread disorder in classrooms[1]: City 11.7; Suburban 8.1; Town 11.6; Rural 5.0

Gang activities[2]: City 28.3; Suburban 14.6; Town 13.9; Rural 9.1

Cult or extremist group activities[2]: City 2.5; Suburban 1.2!; Town 1.7!; Rural 1.6!

Percent (0, 10, 20, 30)

■ City   ■ Suburban   ■ Town   ■ Rural

! Interpret data with caution. The coefficient of variation (CV) for this estimate is between 30 and 50 percent.
[1] Includes schools that reported the activity happens either at least once a week or daily.
[2] Includes schools that reported the activity happens at all at their school during the school year.

Note: Responses were provided by the principal or the person most knowledgeable about crime and safety issues at the school. "At school" was defined for respondents to include activities that happen in school buildings, on school grounds, on school buses, and at places that hold school-sponsored events or activities. Respondents were instructed to respond only for those times that were during normal school hours or when school activities or events were in session.

Source: Robers, S., Kemp, J., and Truman, J. (2013). *Indicators of School Crime and Safety: 2012* (NCES 2013-036/NCJ 241446). National Center for Education Statistics, U.S. Department of Education, and Bureau of Justice Statistics, Office of Justice Programs, U.S. Department of Justice. Washington, DC, p. 33.

They established clear rules for the classroom, they communicated those rules to the students, and they taught students how to follow them." **Assertive discipline** requires teachers to do the following:

1. Make clear that they will not tolerate anyone preventing them from teaching, stopping learning, or doing anything else that is not in the best interest of the class, the individual, or the teacher.

FIGURE 10.6   Assertive discipline policy

JEFFERSON AREA SR. HIGH SCHOOL ASSERTIVE DISCIPLINE PLAN
2013-2014
Room A104-Mrs. Janet Grout

CLASS RULES
1. Be in your assigned seat when the bell rings
2. Bring needed materials to class
3. Listen quietly when Mrs. Grout is talking
4. Show respect to others and the lab equipment

Negative Consequences if you choose to break a rule:
1st time: Verbal warning
2nd time: A stronger warning (This may also include a reassigned seat, isolation, or other suitable measure.)
3rd time: Lunch time quiet table
4th time: Call home and/or 45 minute after-school detention
5th time: Office referral

> ✓ If for any reason you can not serve your detention, you must notify me at least 24 hours in advance. Otherwise, you will receive an additional detention.

Severe Clause: A student may be sent directly to the office for repeated offenses or extreme offenses (fighting, abusive language, damaging property, insubordination, etc.)

Positive Rewards:
1. **Occasionally,** the class may have 5 minutes of free time at the end of class.
2. Various reward activities throughout the year for classes showing exemplary classroom manners.
3. The joy of learning in a positive environment each day of the school year!

Sign and return the bottom portion to Mrs. Grout. Keep the top portion in your class folder.

_____

Students: I have read the rules, consequences, and rewards and I understand them. I agree to abide by this plan while in Room A104

_____   _____
(Student Name Printed)   **(Date)**

Parents: My son/daughter has discussed this plan with me. I understand it and will support it.

_____   _____
(Parent Signature)   **(Date)**

Source: Jefferson Area High School, Jefferson, OH. Retrieved June 6, 2014, from http://www.jefferson.k12.oh.us/webpages/jgrout/files/2013%20assertivedisciplineplan.pdf.

2. Instruct students clearly and in specific terms about what behaviors are desired and what behaviors are not tolerated.
3. Plan positive and negative consequences for predetermined acceptable or unacceptable behaviors.
4. Plan positive reinforcement for compliance. Reinforcement includes verbal acknowledgment, notes, free time for talking, and, of course, tokens that can be exchanged for appropriate rewards.
5. Plan a sequence of steps to punish noncompliance. These range from writing a youngster's name on the board to sending the student to the principal's office. (MacNaughton & Johns, 1991, p. 53).

Figure 10.6 presents the assertive discipline policy used by a junior and senior high school computer teacher in Jefferson, **OHIO**.

Research on the effectiveness of assertive discipline is mixed. Some research studies suggest that rewarding students for good behavior may reduce their intrinsic motivation to learn and/or to conform to the teacher's expectations (Oakes & Lipton, 2007). In such cases, students come to expect "rewards" for behaving properly. This has led some teachers to discontinue using assertive discipline.

TEACHER PROBLEM SOLVING

If your efforts to get a student to stop misbehaving are unsuccessful, a problem-solving conference with the student is warranted. A problem-solving conference may give you additional understanding of the situation, thus paving the way for a solution. A conference also helps you and the student understand one another's perspectives better and begin to build a more positive relationship.

The goal of a problem-solving conference is for the student to accept responsibility for his or her behavior and make a commitment to change it. Although there is no right way to conduct a problem-solving conference, Glasser's choice theory lends itself to a conferencing procedure that is flexible and appropriate for most situations. Students will usually make good choices (that is, behave in an acceptable manner) if they experience success and know that teachers care about them. The following steps are designed to help misbehaving students see that the choices they make may not lead to the results they want:

1. Have the misbehaving student evaluate and take responsibility for his or her behavior. Often, a good first step is for the teacher to ask, "What are you doing?" and then, "Is it helping you?"
2. Have the student make a plan for a more acceptable way of behaving. If necessary, the student and the teacher brainstorm solutions. Agreement is reached on how the student will behave in the future and the consequences for failure to follow through.
3. Require the student to make a commitment to follow the plan.
4. Don't accept excuses for failure to follow the plan.
5. Don't use punishment or react to a misbehaving student in a punitive manner. Instead, point out to the student that there are logical consequences for failure to follow the plan.
6. Don't give up on the student. If necessary, remind the student of his or her commitment to desirable behavior. Periodically ask, "How are things going?"

DEVELOPING YOUR OWN APPROACH TO CLASSROOM MANAGEMENT

No approach to classroom management is effective with all students at all times. How you respond to misbehavior in your classroom depends on your personality, value system, and beliefs about children and ranges along a continuum from the minimum power of giving students nonverbal cues to the maximum power of physical intervention.

To summarize, most teachers tend to rely on one of the following three general approaches to maintaining discipline in the classroom

1. The *humanist approach* involves the use of minimum power and requires that the teacher develop caring relationships with students and actively listen to their concern. This approach is based on the assumption that misbehavior often reflects a student's inner turmoil or lack of confidence. The teacher uses a problem-solving approach to help the student change his or her behavior and to become more self-disciplined. Glasser's choice theory is an example of the humanist approach (Glasser, 1998 a, 1998b, 1998c).
2. The *behaviorist approach* draws from research on human behavior and emphasizes behavior modification techniques and reinforcement of desired behavior in the classroom. Constructive assertiveness is an example of this approach (Canter, 1989, 2009).
3. The *classroom management approach* emphasizes preventive planning, establishing reasonable rules and procedures, and organizing and planning for instruction.

The classroom management approach focuses on preventing discipline problems from occurring.

In your journey toward becoming a professional teacher, you will draw from these three approaches and develop a repertoire of strategies for classroom management. When you encounter a discipline problem in the classroom, you can analyze the situation and respond with an effective strategy. The ability to do so will give you confidence, as the following beginning teacher told the author:

> I went into the classroom with some confidence and left with lots of confidence. I felt good about what was going on. I established a comfortable rapport with the kids and was more relaxed. Each week I grew more confident. When you first go in, you are not sure how you'll do. When you know you are doing okay, your confidence improves.

This chapter's Teachers' Voices: Walk in My Shoes presents the advice one teacher gives to a student teacher who is uncertain about how to deal with management-related challenges that can arise in an elementary classroom.

WHAT TEACHING METHODS DO EFFECTIVE TEACHERS USE?

Beliefs about teaching and learning, students, knowledge, and what is worth knowing influence the instructional methods a teacher uses. In addition, variables such as the teacher's style, learners' characteristics, the culture of the school and surrounding community, and the resources available all influence the methods a teacher uses. All of these components contribute to the model of teaching you use in the classroom. A model of teaching provides you with rules of thumb to follow to create a particular kind of learning environment. As the authors of *Models of Teaching* point out, "models of teaching are really models of *learning*. As we help students acquire information, ideas, skills, values, ways of thinking, and means of expressing themselves, we are also teaching them how to learn" (Joyce, Weil, & Calhoun, 2015, p. 7). Table 10.2 presents brief descriptions of four widely used models of teaching.

Effective teachers use a repertoire of teaching models and assessment strategies, depending on their situations and the goals and objectives they wish to attain. Your teaching strategies in the classroom will most likely be eclectic—that is, a combination of several models and assessment techniques. Also, as you gain classroom experience and acquire new skills and understanding, your personal model of teaching will evolve, enabling you to respond appropriately to a wider range of teaching situations.

Methods Based on Learning New Behaviors

Many teachers use instructional methods that have emerged from our greater understanding of how people acquire or change their behaviors. **Direct instruction**, for example, is a systematic instructional method that focuses on the transmission of knowledge and skills from the teacher (and the curriculum) to the student. Direct instruction is organized on the basis of observable learning behaviors and the actual products of learning. Generally, direct instruction is most appropriate for step-by-step knowledge acquisition and basic skill development, but it is not appropriate for teaching less structured, higher-order skills such as writing, the analysis of social issues, and problem solving.

Extensive research was conducted in the 1970s and 1980s on the effectiveness of direct instruction (Gagné, 1974, 1977; Good & Grouws, 1979; Rosenshine, 1988; Rosenshine & Stevens, 1986). The following eight steps represent a synthesis of research on direct instruction and may be used with students ranging in age from elementary to senior high school:

1. Orient students to the lesson by telling them what they will learn.
2. Review previously learned skills and concepts related to the new material.

TEACHERS' VOICES
Walk in My Shoes
Gaetan Pappalardo

Gaetan Pappalardo is a third-grade teacher and blogger. The preceding is excerpted from his blog titled "Classroom Management Strategies for Elementary Teachers" that appeared on January 28, 2011, at the George Lucas Educational Foundation's *Edutopia* site. Retrieved from http://www.edutopia.org/blog/classroom-management-strategies-elementary-teacher.

TABLE 10.2 Four instructional models

	Goals and Rationale	Methods
Cooperative learning	Students can be motivated to learn by working cooperatively in small groups if rewards are made available to the group as a whole and to individual members of the group.	• Small groups (four to six students) work together on learning activities. • Assignments require that students help one another while working on a group project. • In competitive arrangements, groups may compete against one another. • Group members contribute to group goals according to their talents, interests, and abilities.
Theory into practice	Teachers make decisions in three primary areas: content to be taught, how students will learn, and the behaviors the teacher will use in the classroom. The effectiveness of teaching is related to the quality of decisions the teacher makes in these areas.	The teacher follows seven steps in the classroom: 1. Orients students to material to be learned 2. Tells students what they will learn and why it is important 3. Presents new material that consists of knowledge, skills, or processes students are to learn 4. Models what students are expected to do 5. Checks for student understanding 6. Gives students opportunity for practice under the teacher's guidance 7. Makes assignments that give students opportunity to practice what they have learned on their own
Behavior modification	Teachers can shape student learning by using various forms of enforcement. Human behavior is learned, and behaviors that are positively reinforced (rewarded) tend to increase and those that are not reinforced tend to decrease.	• Teacher begins by presenting stimulus in the form of new material. • The behavior of students is observed by the teacher. • Appropriate behaviors are reinforced by the teacher as quickly as possible.
Nondirective teaching	Learning can be facilitated if teachers focus on personal development of students and create opportunities for students to increase their self-understanding and self-concepts. The key to effective teaching is the teacher's ability to understand students and to involve them in a teaching–learning partnership.	• Teacher acts as a facilitator of learning. • Teacher creates learning environments that support personal growth and development. • Teacher acts in the role of a counselor who helps students to understand themselves, clarify their goals, and accept responsibility for their behavior.

3. Present new material, using examples and demonstrations.
4. Assess students' understanding by asking questions; correct misunderstandings.
5. Allow students to practice new skills or apply new information.
6. Provide feedback and corrections as students practice.
7. Include newly learned material in homework.
8. Review material periodically.

A direct instruction method called **mastery learning** is based on two assumptions about learning: (1) almost all students can learn material if they are given enough time and taught appropriately, and (2) students learn best when they participate in a structured, systematic program of learning that enables them to progress in small, sequenced steps (Bloom, 1981; Carroll, 1963). The following five steps present the mastery learning cycle:

1. Set objectives and standards for mastery.
2. Teach content directly to students.

3. Provide corrective feedback to students on their learning.
4. Provide additional time and help in correcting errors.
5. Follow a cycle of teaching, testing, reteaching, and retesting.

In mastery learning, students take diagnostic tests and then are guided to complete corrective exercises or activities to improve their learning. These may take the form of programmed instruction, workbooks, computer drill and practice, or educational games. After the corrective lessons, students are given another test and are more likely to achieve mastery.

Methods Based on Child Development

These students are building on prior knowledge and using inquiry to acquire new knowledge. What kinds of learning activities require students to use their cognitive abilities this way?

As you know from reflecting on your own development as a human being, children move through stages of cognitive, psychosocial, and moral development. Effective instruction includes methods that are developmentally appropriate, meet students' diverse learning needs, and recognize the importance of learning that occurs in social contexts. For example, one way that students reach higher levels of development is to observe and then imitate their parents, teachers, and peers, who act as models. "Modeling provides students with specific demonstrations of working with the content. . . . The teacher explicitly demonstrates how the students can be successful in the lesson" (Dell'Olio & Donk, 2007, p. 79).

Effective teachers also use **modeling** by thinking out loud and following three basic steps of mental modeling: (1) demonstrating to students the thinking involved in a task, (2) making students aware of the thinking involved, and (3) focusing students on applying the thinking. In this way, teachers can help students become aware of their learning processes and enhance their ability to learn. "For example, as a teacher demonstrates cutting out a construction paper square to serve as a math manipulative during the next lesson, she might 'think out loud' in class, saying, 'I am cutting this square very carefully because we will be using it today to create fractional shapes. I need the sides of my square to be very neat. My smaller, fraction pieces should be accurate in size'" (Dell'Olio & Donk, 2007, p. 80).

Since the mid-1980s, several educational researchers have examined how learners construct understanding of new material. "Constructivist views of learning, therefore, focus on how learners make sense of new information—how they construct meaning based on what they already know" (Parkay, Anctil, & Hass, 2014, p. 229). Teachers with this constructivist view of learning focus on students' thinking about the material being learned and, through carefully orchestrated cues, prompts, and questions, help students arrive at a deeper understanding of the material. The common elements of **constructivist teaching** include the following:

- The teacher elicits students' prior knowledge of the material and uses this as the starting point for instruction.
- The teacher not only presents material to students but also responds to students' efforts to learn the material. While teaching, the teacher must learn about students' learning.
- Students not only absorb information but also actively use that information to construct meaning.

- The teacher creates a social milieu within the classroom, a community of learners, that allows students to reflect and talk with one another as they construct meaning and solve problems.

Constructivist teachers provide students with support, or scaffolding, as they learn new material. By observing the child and listening carefully to what he or she says, the teacher provides **scaffolding** in the form of clues, encouragement, suggestions, or other assistance to guide the student's learning efforts. The teacher varies the amount of support given on the basis of the student's understanding—if the student understands little, the teacher gives more support; conversely, the teacher gives progressively less support as the student's understanding becomes more evident. Overall, the teacher provides just enough scaffolding to enable the student to "discover" the material on his or her own.

The concept of scaffolding is based on the work of L. S. Vygotsky, a well-known Soviet psychologist. Vygotsky (1978, 1986) coined the term *zone of proximal development* to refer to the point at which students need assistance to continue learning. The effective teacher is sensitive to the student's zone of proximal development and ensures that instruction neither exceeds the student's current level of understanding nor underestimates the student's ability.

Methods Based on the Thinking Process

Some teaching methods are derived from the mental processes involved in learning, thinking, remembering, problem solving, and creativity. **Information processing**, for example, is a branch of cognitive science concerned with how people use their long- and short-term memory to access information and solve problems. The computer is often used as an analogy for information-processing views of learning:

> Like the computer, the human mind takes in information, performs operations on it to change its form and content, stores the information, retrieves it when needed, and generates responses to it . . . According to this model, stimuli from the environment (input) flow into the sensory registers, one for each sensing modality (see, hearing, tasting, etc.). From there, some information is encoded and moves to short-term memory. Short-term memory holds information very briefly, combines it with information from long-term memory, and with enough effort, moves some information into long-term memory storage. Short-term memory is also responsible for generating responses or output (Woolfolk, 2013, p. 284).

Although several systematic approaches to instruction are based on information processing—teaching students how to memorize, think inductively or deductively, acquire concepts, or use the scientific method, for example—they all focus on how people acquire and use information. Psychologists have identified three types of memory stores used in information processing:

1. **Sensory memory**—information stored briefly until it can be processed by the information-processing system; sensory memory retains information for about 1 second for vision and 2 to 4 seconds for hearing (Leahey & Harris, 2001; Pashler & Carrier, 1996).
2. **Working memory**—holds information while a person processes it; working memory is the conscious part of our information-processing system.
3. **Long-term memory**—a permanent store of information; working memory is limited to about seven items of information for a few seconds; however, long-term memory is vast and may remain for a lifetime (Schunk, 2012).

Table 10.3 presents general teaching guidelines based on these three types of memory stores.

In **inquiry learning** and **discovery learning**, students are given opportunities to inquire into subjects so that they discover knowledge for themselves. When

TABLE 10.3 Applying an understanding of memory stores in your classroom

Sensory Memory

1. To keep students from losing a sensory memory trace, give them a chance to attend to one stimulus before presenting a second one.
   - **Elementary:** A second-grade teacher asks one question at a time and gets an answer before asking a second question.
   - **Middle school:** A pre-algebra teacher displays two problems on the overhead and waits until students have copied them before she starts talking.
   - **High school:** In a geography lesson, a teacher places a map on the overhead and says, "I'll give you a minute to examine the geography of the countries on this map in the front of the room. Then we'll go on."

Working Memory

2. To avoid overloading students' working memories, conduct lessons with questioning.
   - **Elementary:** A first-grade teacher gives students directions for seatwork by presenting them slowly and one at a time. He asks different students to repeat the directions before he has them begin.
   - **Middle school:** A teacher in a woodworking class begins by saying, "The hardness and density of wood from the same kind of tree vary, depending on the amount of rainfall the tree has received and how fast it grows." Then, she waits a moment, holds up two pieces of wood, and says, "Look at these wood pieces. What do you notice about the rings on them?"
   - **High school:** An Algebra II teacher walks students through the solution to problems by having a different student describe each succeeding step to the solution.

3. Provide frequent practice to develop automaticity and present information in both verbal and visual forms.
   - **Elementary:** A first-grade teacher has his students practice their writing by composing two sentences each day about an event of the previous evening.
   - **Middle school:** To capitalize on the dual-processing capability of working memory, an eighth-grade history teacher prepares a flowchart of the events that led up to the Revolutionary War. As she questions the students about the topic, she refers to the flowchart for each important point and encourages students to use the chart to organize their note taking.
   - **High school:** As a physics teacher discusses the relationship between force and acceleration, he demonstrates by pulling a cart along the desktop with a constant force so the students can see that the cart accelerates.

Long-Term Memory

4. To develop schemas, encourage students to explore relationships between ideas, and between new ideas and prior understanding.
   - **Elementary:** During story time, a second-grade teacher asks students to explain how the events in a story contribute to the conclusion.
   - **Middle school:** In developing the rules for solving equations by substitution, an algebra teacher asks, "How does this process compare to what we did when we solved equations by addition? What do we do differently? Why?"
   - **High school:** To help his students understand cause-and-effect relationships in their study of ancient Greece, a world history teacher asks questions such as: "Why was shipping so important in ancient Greece?" "Why was Troy's location so important, and how does its location relate to the location of today's big cities?" and "Why did Greek city-states exist (instead of larger nation-states)?"

Source: From Paul D. Eggen & Donald P. Kauchak. *Educational Psychology: Windows on Classrooms,* 8th edition. Published by Merrill, an imprint of Pearson Education. Copyright 2010 by Pearson Education. Reprinted by permission. All rights reserved.

teachers ask students to go beyond information in a text to make inferences, draw conclusions, or form generalizations, and when teachers do not answer students' questions, preferring instead to have students develop their own answers, they are using methods based on inquiry and discovery learning. These methods are best suited for teaching concepts, relationships, and theoretical abstractions, and for having students formulate and test hypotheses. The following example shows how inquiry and discovery learning in a first-grade classroom fostered a high level of student involvement and thinking.

> The children are gathered around a table on which a candle and jar have been placed. The teacher, Jackie Wiseman, lights the candle and, after it has burned brightly for a minute or two, covers it carefully with the jar. The candle grows dim, flickers, and goes out. Then she produces another

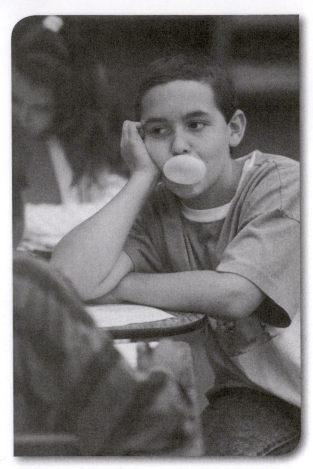

Many factors influence the attitude of students display in class. How might a "hidden curriculum" result in negative attitudes among students? How can the concept of a hidden curriculum be used to promote positive behavior?

candle and a larger jar, and the exercise is repeated. The candle goes out, but more slowly. Jackie produces two more candles and jars of different sizes, and the children light the candles, place the jars over them, and the flames slowly go out. "Now we're going to develop some ideas about what has just happened," she says. "I want you to ask me questions about those candles and jars and what you just observed." (Joyce et al., 2015, p. 24)

Methods Based on Peer-Mediated Instruction

Student peer groups can be a deterrent to academic performance (Sternberg, Dornbusch, & Brown, 1996), but they can also motivate students to excel. Because school learning occurs in a social setting, **peer-mediated instruction** provides teachers with options for increasing students' learning. Cooperative learning, described earlier in this chapter, is an example of peer-mediated instruction.

Another example is **group investigation**, in which the teacher's role is to create an environment that allows students to determine what they will study and how. Students are presented with a situation to which they "react and discover basic conflicts among their attitudes, ideas, and modes of perception. On the basis of this information, they identify the problem to be investigated, analyze the roles required to solve it, organize themselves to take these roles, act, report, and evaluate these results" (Thelen, 1960, p. 82).

The teacher's role in group investigation is multifaceted; he or she is an organizer, guide, resource person, counselor, and evaluator. The method is very effective in increasing student achievement (Sharan & Sharan, 1989/1990, pp. 17–21), positive attitudes toward learning, and the cohesiveness of the classroom group. The model also allows students to inquire into problems that interest them and enables each student to make a meaningful, authentic contribution to the group's effort based on his or her experiences, interests, knowledge, and skills.

Other common forms of peer-mediated instruction include peer tutoring and cross-age tutoring. In **peer-tutoring** arrangements, students are tutored by other pupils in the same class or the same grade. **Cross-age tutoring** involves, for example, sixth-grade students tutoring second-grade students in reading. With proper orientation and training, cross-age tutoring can greatly benefit both "teacher" and learner (Henriques, 1997; Schneider & Barone, 1997; Utay & Utay, 1997; Zukowski, 1997). Pilot programs pairing students at risk of dropping out of school with younger children and with students with special needs have proved especially successful.

HOW DO TEACHERS HELP TO BUILD LEARNING COMMUNITIES?

In addition to the community of learners they develop in the classroom, effective teachers recognize the importance of being part of the learning community beyond the classroom. Success in your first year of teaching will be determined not only by the relationships you develop with students, but also the relationships you develop with their families, your colleagues, school administrators, and other members of your school community. Ideally, all of these groups will work together to create a learning community—a school environment "where teachers and principals can continually expand their capacity to create the results they desire, where emergent patterns of thinking are nurtured, where collective aspiration is liberated, and where people are constantly learning how to learn" (Hoy & Hoy, 2013, p. 19).

Relationships with Students

Without a doubt, your relationships with students will be the most important (and complex) you will have as a teacher. The quality of your relationships with students will depend in large measure on your knowledge of students and commitment to improving your interactions with them.

Your relationships with students will have many dimensions. Your primary responsibility as a professional teacher will be to see that each student learns as much as possible. You will need to establish relationships with *all* students based on mutual respect, caring, and concern. Without attention to this personal realm, your effectiveness as a teacher will be limited, as will your ability to have a positive influence on students' attitudes and behaviors.

Relationships with Colleagues and Staff

Each working day, you will interact with other teachers and staff members, and they can provide much needed support and guidance. If you have a problem, they can suggest solutions. Often, you will learn that they, too, have experienced the same problem. From the beginning of your first teaching assignment, let your colleagues know that you are willing to learn all you can about your new job and to be a team player. In most schools, it is common practice to give first-time teachers less desirable assignments (classes that have a greater number of lower-ability students, for example), reserving the more desirable assignments (honors or advanced-placement classes, for example) for more experienced teachers. By demonstrating your willingness to take on these assignments with good humor and to give them your best effort, you will do much to establish yourself as a valuable colleague.

It is important that you get along with your colleagues and contribute to a spirit of professional cooperation or collegiality in the school. Some you will enjoy being around; others you may wish to avoid. Some will express obvious enthusiasm for teaching; others may be bitter and pessimistic about their work. Be pleasant and friendly with both types. Accept their advice with a smile, and then act on what you believe is worthwhile.

Relationships with Administrators

Pay particular attention to the relationships you develop with administrators, department heads, and supervisors. Although your contacts with them will not be as frequent as those with other teachers, they can do much to ensure your initial success. The following comments illustrate the information new teachers often desire from their school principals:

- "I would like affirmation from my principal that I am doing things OK. If not, I would like to know about it so I can address and correct the situation."
- "I would like to meet monthly with my principal to discuss things like 'hidden agendas,' culture and traditions of the school, expectations, regular events, and what to expect, as well as an opportunity to bitch and gripe a bit."
- "The principal should express the expectations that he has for students in the school. I needed to know about the parameters of the grading system. I needed to know expectations for lesson plans." (Brock & Grady, 2001, pp. 18–19)

Principals are well aware of the difficulties you might encounter as a first-year teacher, and they are there to help you succeed. Because the demands on their time are intense, however, you should not hesitate to be proactive about meeting with them to discuss issues of concern.

The principal of your new school will most likely be the one to introduce you to other teachers, members of the administrative team, and staff. He or she should inform you if there are assistant principals or department heads who can help you enforce school rules, keep accurate records, and obtain supplies, for example. The principal may also assign an experienced teacher to serve as a mentor during your first year.

Relationships with Parents or Guardians

Developing positive connections with your students' parents or guardians can contribute significantly to students' learning and to your success as a teacher. In reality, teachers and parents or guardians are partners—both concerned with the learning and growth of the children in their care. As President Barack Obama told students during his 2010 Back to School speech at Julia R. Masterman Middle-High School in Philadelphia, **PENNSYLVANIA**:

> America has an obligation to you to make sure you're getting the best education possible. And making sure you get that kind of education is going to take all of us working hand-in-hand. . . . It will take an outstanding principal and outstanding teachers like the ones here at Masterman; teachers who go above and beyond for their students. And it will take parents who are committed to your education. (White House Press Release, September 13, 2010)

It is important that you become acquainted with parents or guardians at school functions, at meetings of the parent-teacher association (PTA) or parent-teacher organization (PTO), at various community events, and in other social situations. To develop good communication with parents or guardians, you will need to be sensitive to their needs, such as their work schedules and the language spoken at home.

Additionally, you should be aware of the information parents or guardians expect teachers to provide regarding their children's learning at school. For example, a survey of more than 1,000 parents revealed that the following percentages of parents believe it is "absolutely essential" or "very important" that their children's teachers do the following: notify them if a child is having academic or social problems (absolutely essential, 63 percent; very important, 31 percent); respond to parental requests for information (absolutely essential, 50 percent; very important, 42 percent); provide information about homework policies and school procedures (absolutely essential, 42 percent; very important, 44 percent); inform parents of concerns if child's well-being is affecting child's

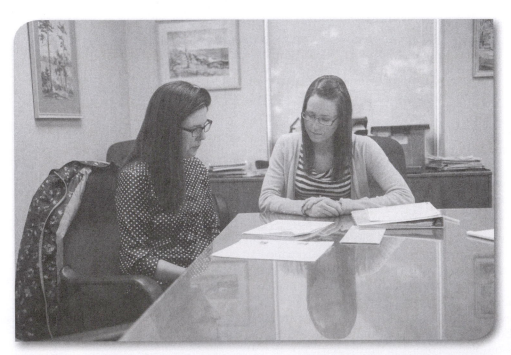

Parents and guardians expect teachers to provide them with important information about their child's performance at school, particularly concerns about factors that might affect a child's success.

success (absolutely essential, 51 percent; very important, 36 percent); provide ideas about how parents can help their child succeed (absolutely essential, 36 percent; very important, 48 percent); and be willing to meet with parents at times and locations convenient for them (absolutely essential, 28 percent; very important, 46 percent) (Harris Interactive, March 2012).

HOW DO TEACHERS PARTICIPATE IN TEACHER COLLABORATION?

The relationships that build a learning community involve **collaboration**—working together, sharing decision making, and solving problems. As a member of a dynamic, changing profession, your efforts to collaborate will result in an increased understanding of the teaching–learning process and improved learning for all students. By working with others on school governance, curriculum development, school partnerships, and educational reform, you will play an important role in creating a professional learning environment at your school and increasing **collegiality**. Teachers are reporting increased time for collaboration with other teachers and professional development opportunities, according to a recent survey of 1,000 public K-12 teachers in the U.S. For example, in 2011, 24 percent of teachers reported increased time to collaborate with other teachers during the past 12 months; in 2012, 33 percent of teachers reported increased time. Similarly, in 2011, 26 percent of teachers reported an increase in professional development opportunities during the past 12 months; in 2013, 35 percent of teachers reported increased opportunities (Harris Interactive, February 2013).

The heart of collaboration is meaningful, authentic relationships among professionals. Of course, such relationships do not occur naturally; they require commitment and hard work. Collaboration has several characteristics: it is voluntary and based on mutual goals; it requires parity among participants; and it depends on shared responsibility for participation and decision making. In addition, individuals who collaborate share resources and accountability for outcomes; they value collaboration; and they trust one another (Friend & Cook, 2013). Schools that support the essential elements of collaboration are collegial schools "characterized by purposeful adult interactions about improving schoolwide teaching and learning" (Glickman, Gordon, & Ross-Gordon, 2014, p. 6). The following sections examine four expressions of teacher collaboration: peer coaching, professional development, team teaching, and co-teaching.

Listen to an educator explain how she participates in teacher collaboration and co-teaching.

Peer Coaching

Experienced teachers traditionally help novice teachers, but more formal peer-coaching programs extend the benefits of collaboration to more teachers. **Peer coaching** is an arrangement whereby teachers grow professionally by observing one another's teaching and

Opportunities for teachers to collaborate help to create a professional learning environment and lead to improved learning for all students.

providing constructive feedback. The practice encourages teachers to learn together in an emotionally safe environment. According to the authors of *Models of Teaching*, peer coaching is an effective way to create communities of professional educators, and all teachers should be members of coaching teams:

> If we had our way, all school faculties would be divided into coaching teams—that is, teams who regularly observe one another's teaching and learn from watching one another and the students. In short, we recommend the development of a "coaching environment" in which all personnel see themselves as coaches. (Joyce et al., 2015, p. 440)

Through teacher-to-teacher support and collaboration, peer-coaching programs improve teacher morale and teaching effectiveness.

Professional Development

Today, teachers often contribute to the design of professional development programs that encourage collaboration, risk-taking, and experimentation. Some programs, for example, give teachers the opportunity to meet with other teachers at similar grade levels or in similar content areas for the purpose of sharing ideas, strategies, and solutions to problems. A day or part of a day may be devoted to this kind of workshop or idea exchange. Teachers are frequently given released time from regular duties to visit other schools and observe exemplary programs in action.

One example of a collaborative professional development program is being implemented at Hartville Elementary School in Hartville, **MISSOURI**, population 613. The program, called eMINTS (Enhancing Missouri's Instructional Networked Teaching Strategies), trains teachers to use technology to enhance inquiry-based learning in their classrooms. The program consists of up to 200 hours of learning time over a 2-year period and includes coaching and follow-up training sessions. To date, more than 250,000 students have been taught by eMINTS-trained teachers, and these students consistently outperform their peers on state standardized tests.

Hartville Elementary, located in a community hard hit by the nationwide economic slump, had few technology resources and professional development opportunities before eMINT began. As a result of the eMINT professional development program, however, the school's principal made the following comment: "By helping our teachers with training they can apply directly in their classrooms, we not only improved our test results, we changed the entire culture of our school. And our focus has grown from improvement to excellence" (Markus, 2012).

Team Teaching

In team-teaching arrangements, teachers share the responsibility for two or more classes, dividing the subject areas between them, with one preparing lessons in mathematics, science, and health, for instance, while the other plans instruction in reading and language arts. The division of responsibility may also be made in terms of the performance levels of the children, so one teacher may teach the lowest- and highest-ability reading groups and the middle math group, for example, while the other teaches the middle-ability reading groups and the lowest and highest mathematics group.

The practice of **team teaching** is often limited by student enrollments and budget constraints. As integrated curricula and the need for special knowledge and skills increase, however, the use of collegial support teams will become more common. A **collegial support team (CST)** provides teachers with a safe zone for professional growth. The members of a team make wide-ranging decisions about the instruction of students assigned to the team, such as when to use large-group instruction or small-group instruction; how teaching tasks will be divided; and how time, materials, and other resources will be allocated.

Co-Teaching

In co-teaching arrangements, two or more teachers, such as a classroom teacher and a special education teacher or other specialist, teach together in the same classroom. **Co-teaching** builds on the strengths of two teachers and provides increased learning opportunities for all students (Friend & Bursuck, 2015). Typically, co-teaching arrangements occur during a set period of time each day or on certain days of the week. Among the several possible co-teaching variations, Friend (2014, pp. 120–122) has identified the following:

- **One teach, one observe**—one teacher teaches the lesson; the other observes.
- **One teach, one assist**—one teacher leads the lesson; the other assists.
- **Station teaching**—the lesson is divided into two parts; one teacher teaches one part to half of the students while the other teaches the other part to the rest. The groups then switch and the teachers repeat their part of the lesson. If students can work independently, a third group may be formed, or a volunteer may teach at a third station.
- **Parallel teaching**—a class is divided in half, and each teacher instructs half the class individually.
- **Alternative teaching**—a class is divided into one large group and one small group. For example, one teacher may provide remediation or enrichment to the small group, while the other teacher instructs the large group.
- **Teaming**—teachers fluidly share teaching responsibilities.

SUMMARY

What Determines the Culture of the Classroom?

- From seating arrangements to classroom rules and procedures, to the content and relevance of the curriculum, to the quality of interactions with students from diverse cultural and linguistic backgrounds, teachers make many decisions that influence the culture of the classroom.
- Classroom climate refers to the atmosphere or quality of life in a classroom. An important element of a positive learning environment is a caring classroom climate.

How Can You Create a Positive Learning Environment?

- Teachers show care for students by providing support, structure, and appropriate expectations.
- The physical environment of a classroom—seating arrangements and the placement of other classroom furniture, for example—can make a positive contribution to students' learning.
- Classroom organization—how students are grouped for instruction and how time is used—is an important element of the effective learning environment.

What Are the Keys to Successful Classroom Management?

- Teachers who prevent problems before they occur foster effective, harmonious interpersonal interactions; understand how their leadership style influences students; and facilitate the development of the classroom group so that it becomes more cohesive and supportive.
- When management problems occur, effective teachers base their responses on three elements of constructive assertiveness: a clear statement of the problem or concern; unambiguous body language; and a firm, unwavering insistence on appropriate behavior.
- Most teachers tend to rely on one of three general approaches to maintaining discipline in the classroom: the humanist approach, the behaviorist approach, or the classroom management approach.

What Teaching Methods Do Effective Teachers Use?

- Direct instruction and mastery learning are based on the view that learning is the acquisition of new behaviors.

- Modeling, constructivism, and scaffolding are based primarily on an understanding of how students construct meaning as they learn new material.
- Psychologists have identified three types of memory stores used in information processing: sensory memory, working memory, and long-term memory.
- Peer-mediated instruction, which views learning as taking place in social situations, includes cooperative learning, group investigation, and peer- and cross-age tutoring.

How Do Teachers Help to Build Learning Communities?

- Effective teachers recognize the importance of being part of the learning community beyond the classroom.

- The learning community includes students, their families, colleagues, and members of the community.
- Teachers and parents generally agree on the importance of what teachers can do for parents.

How Do Teachers Participate in Teacher Collaboration?

- Teachers collaborate through participation in school governance, curriculum development, school–community partnerships, and educational reform.
- Four approaches to teacher collaboration are peer coaching, professional development, team teaching, and co-teaching.

PROFESSIONAL REFLECTIONS AND ACTIVITIES

Teacher's Journal

1. Recall the teachers and classmates you had during your school career. Select one class and analyze its group processes in terms of the stages of group development discussed in this chapter. At what stage of development was the group near the end of the school year? What conditions facilitated or impeded the development of this group?

2. Describe the "ideal" physical classroom environment for you. How would the seating arrangement facilitate the attainment of your instructional goals and objectives? How would you involve students in arranging the classroom?

3. Describe your leadership style as it relates to classroom management. In which aspects of leadership and classroom management do you feel most and least confident? What might you do, or what skills might you acquire, to strengthen your effectiveness in areas where you feel you lack confidence? Develop your ideas into a statement of professional goals.

Teacher's Research

1. Visit the home pages for a few of the following educational research publications on the Internet.

   - *American Educational Research Journal*
   - *Cognition and Instruction*
   - *Contemporary Educational Psychology*
   - *Educational Psychologist*
   - *Educational Psychology Review*

- *Educational Researcher*
- *Journal of Educational Psychology*
- *Journal of Teaching and Teacher Education*
- *Review of Educational Research*
- *Review of Research in Education*
- *Social Psychology of Education*

Select an article of interest related to increasing student learning. Summarize the article and present a brief oral report to your class. Based on the research findings presented in the article, what are the implications for teaching?

2. Visit several school district websites to examine their discipline policies. What similarities and differences do you note among the policies? To what extent do the policies address the following topics: democratic classrooms, choice theory, constructive assertiveness, assertive discipline, caring classrooms, zero tolerance, bullying, sexual harassment, and gangs?

Observations and Interviews

1. Observe several teachers at the level for which you are preparing to teach and try to identify the teaching methods they are using as part of their instructional repertoires.

Professional Portfolio

Prepare a poster depicting a classroom arrangement appropriate for the subject area and grade level for which you are preparing to teach. The poster should indicate the seating arrangement, location of other classroom furniture, and educational technology areas. In addition, make a list of classroom rules that will be posted in the room. You may wish to organize the rules according to the following categories.

- Rules related to academic work
- Rules related to classroom conduct

- Rules that must be communicated on your first teaching day
- Rules that can be communicated later

CHAPTER QUIZ

Take this quiz to check your understanding of the content covered in this chapter.

CHAPTER ELEVEN
School Curricula and Standards

learning outcomes

After reading this chapter, you will be able to do the following:

1. Explain what students learn from the different types of curricula they experience at school.
2. Explain how the school curriculum is developed.
3. Describe influences on the curriculum development process.
4. Explain the role of standards in today's classrooms.
5. Describe the key features of standards-based education.
6. Explain how the Common Core State Standards Initiative is influencing U.S. education.
7. Explain the controversies that surround the push to raise standards.

READERS' VOICES

What do students learn from the curriculum?

The curriculum teaches students how to survive in today's competitive world. Students learn not only knowledge of content, but also people skills in order to live in today's society.

—DREW, Teacher Education program, first year

WHAT DO STUDENTS LEARN FROM THE CURRICULUM?

Think back to your experiences as a student at the elementary, middle, junior, and high schools you attended. What did you learn? The curriculum you experienced certainly included reading, computation, penmanship, spelling, geography, and history. In addition to these topics, though, did you learn something about cooperation, competition, stress, football, videogames, social networking, smartphones, popularity, and the opposite sex? Or did you perhaps learn to love chemistry and to hate English grammar?

The countless things you learned in school make up the curriculum that you experienced. Curriculum theorists and researchers have suggested several different definitions for **curriculum**, with no single definition that is universally accepted. Here are some definitions in current use:

1. A course of study, derived from the Latin *currere,* meaning "to run a course"
2. Course content, the information or knowledge that students are to learn
3. Planned learning experiences
4. Intended learning outcomes, the results of instruction as distinguished from the means (activities, materials, etc.) of instruction
5. All the experiences that students have while at school

None of these five is in any sense the "right" definition. The way we define the word *curriculum* depends on our purposes and the situation we find ourselves in. If, for example, we are advising a high school student on the courses he or she needs to prepare for college, our operational definition of curriculum would most likely be "a course of study." However, if we were interviewing sixth-grade students for their views on the K–6 elementary school they had just graduated from, we would probably want to view curriculum as "all the experiences that students have while at school." Let us posit an additional definition of curriculum: *Curriculum refers to the experiences, both planned and unplanned, that enhance (and sometimes impede) the education and growth of students.*

Kinds of Curricula

Elliot Eisner, a noted educational researcher, has said that "schools teach much more—and much less—than they intend to teach. Although much of what is taught is explicit and public, a great deal is not" (Eisner, 2002, p. 87). For this reason, we need to look at the four curricula that all students experience: the explicit curriculum, the

FIGURE 11.1 Four kinds of curricula students experience

hidden curriculum, the null curriculum, and the extracurricular/cocurricular program. Figure 11.1 illustrates that the ultimate goal of these experiences is the learning and growth of students. The more we understand these curricula and how they influence students, the better we will be able to develop educational programs that do, in fact, promote learning and growth.

EXPLICIT CURRICULUM

The explicit, or overt, curriculum refers to what a school intends to teach students. This curriculum is made up of several components: (1) the goals, aims, and learning objectives the school has for all students; (2) the actual courses that make up each student's course of study; and (3) the specific knowledge, skills, and attitudes that teachers want students to acquire. If we asked a principal to describe the educational program at his or her school, our question would be in reference to the explicit curriculum. Similarly, if we asked a teacher to describe what he or she wished to accomplish with a particular class, we would be given a description of the explicit curriculum.

In short, the **explicit curriculum** represents the publicly announced expectations the school has for its students. These expectations range from learning how to read, write, and compute to learning to appreciate music, art, and cultures other than one's own. In most instances, the explicit curriculum takes the form of written plans or guides for the education of students. Examples of such written documents are course descriptions, curriculum guides that set forth the goals and learning objectives for a school or district, texts and other commercially prepared learning materials, and teachers' lesson plans. Through the instructional program of a school, then, these curricular materials are brought to life.

HIDDEN CURRICULUM

The **hidden curriculum** (also called the *implicit curriculum*) refers to the behaviors, attitudes, and knowledge the culture of the school unintentionally teaches students (Parkay, Anctil, & Hass, 2014). What students learn via the hidden curriculum can be positive or negative, depending on their day-to-day experiences at school. For example, from teachers who are knowledgeable, well organized, and personable, students are likely to develop positive habits and abilities—cooperating with others, taking responsibility, planning ahead, and forgoing immediate gratification to obtain long-range goals. On the other hand, from teachers who are ill prepared, apathetic, or aloof, students are likely to acquire habits and attitudes that are negative and that discourage personal growth and development—for example, a dislike for learning, the ability to deceive or defy adult authority figures, or a tendency to procrastinate.

In the following excerpts from letters written about their teachers, four students describe the hidden curricula they experienced in school. In examples 1 and 2, the hidden curricula "taught" students to be more confident in their ability to learn. In examples 3 and 4, the hidden curricula undermined the students' confidence and desire to learn.

Example 1

I was in your grade 10 English class. I sure felt safe to take a risk in your class. I actually tried hard, knowing I might fail, but felt safe enough to do so. (Paul, Christensen, & Falk, 2000, p. 23)

Example 2

I was in your grade 9 class and you praised me for my creative writing. Until that time, I had never thought of myself as a very creative person but your faith in me spurred me on to choose English as my major at the university. (Paul et al., 2000, p. 23)

Example 3

The teacher just put [material] on the board and if you don't know how, the teacher get angry. I try to get help but when I come after school, they gotta go somewhere and can't help you . . . like when I ask somebody to help me, just because some other kid won't need help, then they think others won't either; some kids are smarter. (Wilson & Corbett, 2001, p. 38)

Example 4

I was in your 11th-grade biology class. I loved science and biology until I took your class. You gave me a great disdain for the subject. Your teaching methods bored the class to tears. We read each chapter out loud at the beginning of the week and spent the rest of the week working quietly on the questions at the end of the chapter along with the endless dittos you passed out. We never discussed anything and you never taught us anything. We were graded on how well we could come up with the answers you thought were right and heaven forbid if we did not head our paper using the "correct" format. I think the only thing I learned in your class was conformity. (Colucci, 2000, p. 38)

As a result of the hidden curriculum of schools, students learn more than their teachers imagine. As a teacher, you will not be aware of all that students are learning through the hidden curriculum of your classroom. However, you can increase the likelihood that what it teaches will be positive. By allowing students to help determine the content of the explicit curriculum, by providing them with challenges appropriate for their stage of development, and by encouraging them to put forth their best effort and to persevere when learning new material, teachers can ensure that the outcomes of the hidden curriculum will be largely positive. This chapter's Walk in My Shoes feature highlights an eighth-grade language arts teacher who learned through his own elementary-level hidden curriculum that he loved learning. The hidden curriculum he experienced enabled him to grow beyond consistently being "in trouble" to being an eager learner. Years later, as a teacher, he received national visibility for his program to teach students math, science, and programming skills to design their own videogames—in 2011, he was named **KANSAS** Teacher of the Year.

TEACHERS' VOICES
Walk in My Shoes
"I learned that
I love learning"
Curtis Chandler
Wamego Middle School
Wichita, Kansas

NULL CURRICULUM

Discussing a curriculum that cannot be observed directly is like talking about dark matter or black holes, unseen phenomena in the universe whose existence must be inferred because their incredible denseness and gravitational fields do not allow light to escape. In much the same way, we can consider the curriculum that we do not find in the schools; it may be as important as what we do find. Elliot Eisner (2002) has labeled the intellectual processes and content that schools do not teach "the **null curriculum**—the options students are not afforded, the perspectives they may never know about, much less be able to use, the concepts and skills that are not a part of their intellectual repertoire" (pp. 106–107).

The kind of thinking that schools foster among students is largely based on manipulations of words and numbers—skills that neuroscience informs us are performed by the left hemisphere of the brain. Right-hemispheric thinking that is imaginative, subjective, and poetic is stressed only incidentally. School curricula in non-Western cultures frequently show a great integration of right- and left-hemispheric thinking. Japanese schools, for example, require considerably more art, music, and literature than most U.S. schools. In addition, all Japanese students must study handicrafts and calligraphy. It is possible that many of the well-documented successes of Japanese business and industry may be traced back to curricula that go beyond verbal and numerical thinking to include the development of aesthetic capabilities. Unlike some of their U.S. counterparts, the Japanese would be reluctant to consider eliminating art, music, or physical education (which includes dance) from the curriculum.

Perhaps you have wondered why schools teach what they do. Why is so much of the K–12 curriculum devoted to language arts, mathematics, science, and history or social studies? Why are students seldom taught anthropology, sociology, psychology, law, economics, filmmaking, or architecture? Eisner (2002) points out that "certain subject matters have been traditionally taught in schools not because of a careful analysis of the range of other alternatives that could be offered but rather because they have traditionally been taught. We teach what we teach largely out of habit, and in the process neglect areas of study that could prove to be exceedingly useful to students" (p. 103).

EXTRACURRICULAR/COCURRICULAR PROGRAMS

The curriculum includes school-sponsored activities—music, drama, special-interest clubs, sports, student government, and honor societies, to name a few—that students may pursue in addition to their studies in academic subject areas. When such activities are perceived as additions to the academic curriculum, they are termed *extracurricular*. When these activities are seen as having important educational goals—and not merely as extras added to the academic curriculum—they are termed *cocurricular*. To reflect the fact that these two labels are commonly used for the same activities, I use the term *extracurricular/ cocurricular activities*. Although **extracurricular/cocurricular programs** are most extensive at the secondary level, many schools at the elementary, middle, and junior high levels also provide their students with a broad assortment of extracurricular/cocurricular activities. For those students who choose to participate, such activities provide an opportunity to use social and academic skills in many different contexts.

The larger a school is, the less likely it is that a student will take part in extracurricular/cocurricular activities. At the same time, those who do participate tend to have higher self-concepts than those who do not (Coladarci & Cobb, 1996). The actual effects that extracurricular/cocurricular activities have on students' development, however, are not entirely clear.

Students who participate in extracurricular/cocurricular activities tend to receive higher grades than nonparticipants and are more frequently identified as gifted (Gerber, 1996; Jordan & Nettles, 1999; Modi, Konstantopoulos, & Hedges, 1998). However, it is not known whether participation influences achievement, or whether achievement influences participation. Nevertheless, participation has a positive influence on the decision to remain in school (Mahoney & Cairns, 1997), educational aspirations (Modi et al., 1998), and the occupation one aspires to and eventually attains (Brown, Kohrs, & Lanzarro, 1991; Holland & Andre, 1987). Furthermore, students themselves tend to identify extracurricular/cocurricular activities as a high point in their school careers.

It is also clear that students who might benefit the most from participating in extracurricular/cocurricular activities—those below the norm in academic achievement and students at risk—tend not to participate. In addition, students from low socioeconomic backgrounds participate less often (Aud et al., 2013).

Curriculum Content and Student Success

The content of the curricula in U.S. schools has changed frequently since our colonial period. These modifications came about as the goals of the schools were debated, additional needs of society became evident, and student populations became more diverse. Over time, schools have had to focus on a wide variety of goals set by society. Since our nation's founding, the following are among the goals society has set, to varying degrees, for schools:

- Prepare students to carry out religious and family responsibilities
- Provide employers with a source of literate workers
- Desegregate society
- Reduce crime, poverty, and injustice
- Help the U.S. maintain its competitive edge in the world economy
- Provide the scientists, mathematicians, and engineers needed to keep our country strong
- Educate students for intelligent participation in a democracy

What might be one of the pressures felt by U.S. teachers and students as a result of the increased emphasis on international comparisons of student achievement?

The nation's schools teach what the larger society believes young people should learn to be successful. For example, Figure 11.2 shows how teachers, parents, students, and Fortune 1000 executives view the importance of skills and knowledge for college and career readiness. The data presented in the figure show that many teachers, parents, students, and Fortune 1000 executives think that global awareness is important to be ready for college and a career, but most do not consider it to be as important as problem-solving and critical thinking skills, the ability to write well, and the ability to work independently and in teams. Nevertheless, the following comments by survey respondents typify the concern many people have about the importance of global understanding in the school curriculum:

> "We need an education system that will prepare students to meet the challenges of participating in a global community—the challenge is for educators to value these language and cultural perspectives."
>
> "Teachers will have to broaden their own knowledge and be more aware of global issues students will face."
>
> "Globalization [means a] need for high-level technical solutions on par with international peers." (Harris Interactive, Inc., 2011, p. 15)

Although the primary aim of school curricula is to promote student success in the future, success is not easy to achieve in our increasingly complex, interdependent world. To realize their full potential, students must navigate an environment shaped by forces such as continually evolving technology, economic volatility, and climate change. This requires more than content knowledge and intellectual accomplishments. For example, we know that high-achieving individuals usually possess certain attitudes, dispositions, social skills, intrapersonal resources, and interpersonal competencies that contribute to their success. Moreover, these qualities are, to a great extent, teachable, and they should be made part of the school curriculum. As the director of the U.S. Department of Education's Institute of Educational Sciences said: "The test score accountability movement has pushed aside many of the so-called 'non-cognitive' or 'soft'; skills, and they belong back on the front burner" (Easton, 2012, p. 19). Figure 11.3 illustrates three noncognitive areas that are receiving more attention in school curricula: grit, tenacity, and perseverance; academic mindset; and mindfulness/meditation skills.

GRIT, TENACITY, AND PERSEVERANCE

A moment's reflection likely provides evidence of how success in your own life has resulted from grit, tenacity, and perseverance. Throughout your life, these personal

FIGURE 11.2   Importance of skills and knowledge for college and career readiness

Base	Teachers n = 1000	Parents n = 580	Students n = 2002	Fortune 1000 Executives n = 301
Problem solving skills				
Absolutely essential/Very important (NET)	98%	93%	92%	99%
Absolutely essential	64%	60%	55%	73%
Critical thinking skills				
Absolutely essential/Very important (NET)	97%	91%	93%	99%
Absolutely essential	64%	61%	56%	71%
Ability to write clearly and persuasively				
Absolutely essential/Very important (NET)	96%	90%	88%	97%
Absolutely essential	53%	57%	50%	59%
Ability to work independently				
Absolutely essential/Very important (NET)	95%	93%	92%	90%
Absolutely essential	55%	59%	55%	40%
Ability to work in teams				
Absolutely essential/Very important (NET)	86%	85%	83%	94%
Absolutely essential	42%	42%	41%	59%
Knowledge of other nations and cultures and international issues				
Absolutely essential/Very important (NET)	63%	63%	49%	65%
Absolutely essential	19%	24%	15%	18%
Knowledge and ability in higher-level science such as chemistry and physics				
Absolutely essential/Very important (NET)	50%	71%	64%	31%
Absolutely essential	11%	29%	24%	4%
Knowledge and ability in higher-level mathematics, such as trigonometry or calculus				
Absolutely essential/Very important (NET)	46%	69%	66%	40%
Absolutely essential	11%	31%	27%	8%

Question: How important do you think of the following is for a student to be ready for college and a career?

Base: Teachers (n = 1000), Parents (n = 580), Students (n = 2002), Fortune 1000 Executives (n = 301)

Source: The MetLife Survey of the American Teacher—Preparing Students for College and Careers Part I: Clearing the Path, p. 13. New York: Harris Interactive, Inc., 2011.

qualities have enabled you to work toward long- and short-term goals. Today, they are helping you to follow through on your decision to become a teacher. Tomorrow, they will help you become a successful beginning teacher.

In *Promoting Grit, Tenacity, and Perseverance: Critical Factors for Success in the 21st Century*, the U.S. Department of Education's Office of Educational Technology stated that ". . . conventional educational approaches have tended to focus on intellectual aspects of success, such as content knowledge. However, this is not sufficient. If students are to achieve their full potential, they must have opportunities to engage and develop a much richer set of skills. Indeed, a growing body of research suggests that noncognitive factors can have just as strong an influence on

FIGURE 11.3   Three non-cognitive factors that contribute to academic achievement

academic performance and professional attainment as intellectual factors" (Shecht-man et al., 2013, p. 75).

Individuals who possess a high level of grit, tenacity, and perseverance tend to characterize themselves with the following phrases: "I am diligent," "Setbacks don't discourage me," and "I have overcome setbacks to conquer an important challenge." Grit, tenacity, and perseverance enable students to work hard to meet challenges and to maintain commitment and interest over time, in spite of occasional failure, hardships, and plateaus in progress toward goals. They have a distinct "advantage" over students who lack grit, tenacity, and perseverance. Whereas disappointment, boredom, and set-backs lead some students to "cut their losses" and quit, students with grit, tenacity, and perseverance "stay the course" until they succeed. The following describes how these students view themselves as learners:

> What do academically tenacious students look like? First, they believe that they belong in school academically and socially. Second, they are engaged in learning, view effort positively, and can forgo immediate pleasures for the sake of school work. Third, difficulty, be it intellectual or social, does not derail them. They see a setback as an opportunity for learning or a problem

TEACHING ON YOUR FEET
Confronting "Tough" Questions

I must confess that I was not particularly surprised to see eyes roll as several of my students chimed in and interrupted my heartfelt paean to Shakespeare as they ruefully exclaimed, "*Hamlet* is way too complicated and confusing!" I suppose they felt that their plaintive cries were necessary at the time to try to curb my rampant enthusiasm before things really got out of hand in my 12th-grade British Literature class.

Struggling to overcome the temptation to launch into a passionate defense of Shakespeare's literary honor, I realized this was probably the best opportunity in recent times to turn that nascent cynicism on its head. So I quickly brought out copies of Tom Stoppard's *Rosencrantz & Guildenstern Are Dead*—a contemporary, comedic play based on the perspectives of two minor characters from *Hamlet*—and asked my detractors to read with me. I directed them to the scene where they play Questions and Answers, where words ricochet back and forth in rapid succession as if they were on a tennis court. Rosencrantz and Guildenstern desperately want to extract some answers from Hamlet as they attempt to delve into the cause of his apparent madness, but all they really have are unanswered questions, which ironically become self-reflective as they ponder their own existence and purpose, or lack thereof. I kept pushing the pace of the reading with crisp and emphatic enunciation, and smiles and even wide grins slowly began to break out over their faces as they got caught up in the escalating torrent.

When the exchange finally ended, I deliberately made solid eye contact with my students, and affirmed with complete sincerity that the tough questions that challenge and address the very nature of what we truly are as human beings will always be of great value. We should never be satisfied with oversimplified, pedantic answers when reading a great work of literature such as *Hamlet*, which deserves the highest respect because, to this very day, it still evokes questions with remarkable power to provoke contemplation of the profound, ironic, and even the absurd.

Almost in unison, my students nodded their heads in agreement. In their eyes, I saw genuine appreciation for the important lesson they had learned that day—not so much about the particular merits of *Hamlet* per se, but rather that we can and should ascribe value to things that are hard and challenging, because embedded within are the questions that have been and will continue to be meaningful and great.

ANALYZE & REFLECT

Click here to analyze and reflect on this scenario you have just read.

ELMER LEE
Teacher; Mountain Peak Charter School; Vista, **CALIFORNIA**

to be solved rather than as a humiliation, a condemnation of their ability or worth, a symbol of future failures, or a confirmation that they do not belong. This is true at the level of a given task and at the level of their studies in general. Tenacious students know how to remain engaged over the long haul and how to deploy new strategies for moving forward effectively. (Dweck, Walton, & Cohen, 2011, pp. 5–6).

It is important to remember that grit, tenacity, and perseverance are not related to IQ. In fact, research indicates that grit, tenacity, and perseverance predict success over and above other attributes like intelligence, self-control, and grade point average (Duckworth & Allred, 2012; Duckworth, Kirby, Tsukayama, Berstein, & Ericsson, 2010; Duckworth, Peterson, Matthews, & Kelly, 2007). This chapter's Teaching on Your Feet feature illustrates how one teacher's students learned that "we can and should ascribe value to things that are hard and challenging."

ACADEMIC MINDSET

Students who have grit, tenacity, and perseverance also have what might be called an "academic mindset." As Figure 11.3 illustrates, students with an **academic mindset** have positive views of themselves as learners, and they understand that effort is required to develop ability and competence related to their schoolwork. The degree to which a student possesses an academic mindset, of course, depends upon having positive relationships while at school—positive relationships with teachers, classmates, and other school staff.

In addition, students with an academic mindset employ learning strategies to help themselves learn. They know how to plan, set priorities, define tasks, monitor their progress, and deal with obstacles as they learn new, challenging material. Put differently, they have self-discipline—"knowing how to manage your emotions and thoughts, and knowing how to plan your behavior so you can reach your goals" (Duckworth, 2009, p. 536).

MINDFULNESS/MEDITIATION SKILLS

As humans, each of us experiences a more or less continuous flow of thoughts and feelings. Our minds flit from one thought to another, occasionally making it difficult to concentrate on an important task at hand. This flow of thoughts and feelings can even make us anxious and stressed, thus reducing our ability to perform. One way to become more of *an observer of*, rather than *a reactor to*, our thoughts and feelings as they come and go is to learn mindfulness/meditation skills. According to the Association of Mindfulness in Education, the following practices can enhance students' attention and well-being:

- Becoming aware of the breath
- Feeling the various physical sensations of an emotion
- Noticing thoughts as they pass through the mind
- Paying attention to all the sounds in the room
- Noticing what happens in the body when there is stress
- Watching the thoughts that arise when there is boredom
- Feeling the stomach rise and fall with each breath (Association of Mindfulness in Education, 2014)

Those who have mastered complex, demanding skills and can perform at an elite level—athletes, musicians, brain surgeons, and trapeze artists, for example—provide us with everyday examples of how becoming more aware of how our minds work and developing mindfulness/meditation skills can enhance performance. Prior to performing, these individuals focus their attention, laser-like, on the forthcoming event; "tune out" surrounding external distractions; and greatly reduce their mind's tendency to flit from thought to thought. William James, the great psychologist and founder of experimental psychology, commented on the benefit of such mental concentration and the role that education ought to play in developing this skill: "The faculty of voluntarily bringing back a wandering attention, over and over again, is the very root of judgment, character, and will . . . An education which should improve this faculty would be the education par excellence" (James, 1890).

Like elite performers, students can benefit from developing mindfulness/meditation skills. Whether dealing with the stress of a forthcoming exam; responding to a bully on the playground; coping with the trauma of violence in their neighbourhoods; preparing for a musical or sports event; improving communication with peers, teachers, and parents/guardians; or reducing anxiety about their future, mindfulness/meditation skills can enhance students' ability to respond to the challenges that life brings.

Currently, fewer than 100 U.S. schools include mindfulness/meditation skills as part of the curriculum, a fact that led the former Superintendent of the San Francisco Unified School District to comment, "Isn't it ironic that we teach students about everything except about themselves?" (David Lynch Foundation, 2014).

In 2007, Vistacion Valley Middle School (VVMS) in the San Francisco Bay area became the first public school nationwide to include mindfulness/meditation skills in the curriculum. The neighborhood around VVMS is frequently punctuated with gunfire—nine shootings occurred during December 2013, for example. Most students know someone who's been shot or did the shooting, and the school employs a full-time grief counselor to help students deal with frequent murders (Kirp, January 12, 2014).

In response to such chronic stress, VVMS students were often out of control, fighting in the hallways, scrawling graffiti on the walls, or cursing their teachers. Absenteeism and suspensions were among the city's highest. Stressed-out teachers routinely called in sick; and, not surprisingly, students' academic achievement was low. As the principal of VVMS explains in the following, the school tried various approaches to improve the school's climate, but conditions remained the same:

> In the first eight years of my tenure as principal we introduced many new initiatives, engaging community organizations offering afterschool tutoring,

sports, music, peer support and counseling services in an attempt to improve the school conditions. There was improvement, but at the end of 2006 there was still a lot of stress and violence. Even though we established clear behavior goals for all students and common standards for all teachers to uphold, high tension and turmoil remained, impairing the learning experience. Fighting was prevalent in our school throughout the day, so much so that we were known as the "fight school" in the district. Fear, sadness and tension dominated the school climate. (Dierke, 2012, pp. 14–15)

In his search for options to address the stress that was impacting students' ability to learn, the principal came across Quiet Time, a stress-reduction program developed by a Washington, D.C., school principal in the early 1990s. When they learned about the program, 95 percent of the school's teachers adopted a "what-do-we-have-to-lose" attitude and voted in favor of adopting the program.

Quiet Time (QT) at VVMS occurs during two 15-minute periods, one in the morning and one in the afternoon. After teachers take attendance in the morning, a tingling bell marks the beginning of QT. Most students close their eyes and meditate, whereas others read silently. For 15 minutes, the entire school is silent. Students and all school staff experience 15 minutes of quiet, peacefulness, and safety. QT allows students to quiet their minds, relax, and restore their readiness to learn.

As part of QT, the vast majority of students and teachers accepted the invitation to receive training in Transcendental Meditation, an easy-learn, nonreligious approach to meditation. With few exceptions, parents and guardians signed approvals so their children could learn how to meditate. Hundreds of research studies support the effectiveness of Transcendental Meditation, and its educational outcomes include increases in the following:

- Brain functioning
- Verbal and analytical thinking
- Holistic thinking and ability to synthesize
- Ability to resist distractions and social pressure
- Transfer of information in the brain
- Academic performance and learning
- Creativity, memory, problem solving, perception,
- Self-confidence and self-actualization (David Lynch Foundation, 2014)

Transcendental Meditation also reduces the following:

- Hostility, anxiety, and depression
- Anger, absenteeism, misbehavior, and suspensions (David Lynch Foundation, 2014))

SRI International (formerly Stanford Research Institute) is partnering with VVMS and other schools to research further QT outcomes. SRI has conducted numerous large-scale educational research projects, and its sources of funding include the U.S. Department of Education and the National Science Foundation.

During the first year of QT at VVMS, the number of suspensions fell by 45 percent; within 4 years, the suspension rate was among the lowest in the city. Daily attendance rates increased to 98 percent, well above the city-wide average. Grade point averages improved significantly, and about 20 percent of graduates are now admitted to Lowell High School, San Francisco's elite high school; before QT, few VVMS students were admitted to this school. Last, in the annual California Healthy Kids Survey, VVMS students recorded the highest happiness levels in San Francisco. Reports are similarly positive in the three other schools that have adopted Quiet Time. Currently, 15 other schools in the San Francisco Bay area are on a waiting list to implement QT (Dierke, 2012, p. 16).

Upon his retirement, the principal who launched QT at VVMS observed, "[QT] is by far the most impactful, transformational program that I have seen in my 40 years of education. By reducing the individual and collective stress levels and fostering a positive school climate, it creates a foundation for all of our other school initiatives to be more successful. Students are engaged and learning more" (Dierke, 2012, p. 16).

CURRICULA TO ENHANCE NONCOGNITIVE STRENGTHS

To prepare students for successful lives in the future, the school curriculum must not only provide them with knowledge and skills, it should help them increase their grit, tenacity, and perseverance; academic mindset; and mindfulness/meditation skills. Although the preceding noncognitive strengths may be "teachable" to some extent, students' strengths in these areas will increase if their overall curricular experiences are rigorous, supportive, and growth-promoting. Specifically, the curriculum is characterized by the following:

- Goals are challenging and optimally meaningful to students.
- Goals require that students plan, set priorities, define tasks, monitor their progress, and overcome obstacles.
- Teachers convey the expectation that all students, with effort, can achieve these goals.
- The classroom culture emphasizes the importance of an "academic mindset," effortful control, and developing strategies and tactics to reach goals.
- Students are encouraged to develop grit, perseverance, and tenacity.
- Failure should be seen as part of learning,
- Students are given constructive feedback and encouraged to improve their work.

In what ways can mindfulness/meditation enhance a student's learning?

HOW IS THE SCHOOL CURRICULUM DEVELOPED?

The title of Franklin Bobbitt's classic work *How to Make a Curriculum* (1924) might suggest that developing a curriculum is a straightforward process. According to Bobbitt, a curriculum should be developed "scientifically" by analyzing the daily activities of adult life and then creating behavioral objectives for those activities.

Bobbitt's approach suggests that one need only apply curriculum theory and research to the processes of curriculum development. However, curriculum theory and research do not set forth, in cookbook fashion, exactly how one should develop a curriculum. Instead, it may be helpful to think of curriculum theory and research as providing "rules of thumb" for curriculum development.

Clearly, there is no single right way to develop a curriculum. As John Dewey (1929) pointed out in *The Sources of a Science of Education,* "No conclusion of scientific research can be converted into an immediate rule of educational art. For there is no educational practice whatever which is not highly complex; that is to say, which does not contain many other conditions and factors than are included in the scientific finding." The significance of any one research study for curriculum development, then, can be determined only as the results of that study are balanced with an understanding of the "conditions and factors" that influence the curriculum.

Although there is no easy-to-follow set of procedures for developing curriculum, Ralph Tyler (1902–1994), a University of Chicago professor instrumental in shaping the Elementary and Secondary Education Act of 1965, has provided four fundamental questions that must be answered in developing any curriculum or plan

PROFESSIONAL REFLECTION
Listen as a group of educators discusses curriculum and related issues in their school.

of instruction. These four questions, known as the **Tyler rationale**, are as follows (Tyler, 1949, p. 1):

1. What educational purposes should the school seek to attain?
2. What educational experiences can be provided that are likely to attain these purposes?
3. How can these educational experiences be effectively organized?
4. How can we determine whether these purposes are being attained?

When first introduced, Tyler's model represented a modern view of curriculum design. Developing the curriculum, according to Tyler, required a mechanical, rational approach that could be followed systematically in any context, with any group of students. Today, however, some educators believe the Tyler rationale underestimates the complexities of curriculum development because it advocates a straightforward, step-by-step process that is difficult to follow in the real classroom, and it does not make allowances for diverse points of view regarding what should be taught. Nevertheless, Tyler's classic work has been used by a great number of school systems to bring some degree of order and focus to the curriculum development process.

The Focus of Curriculum Planning

In discussing curriculum development, it is helpful to clarify the focus of curriculum planning. Figure 11.4 illustrates two dimensions of this planning process: the focus

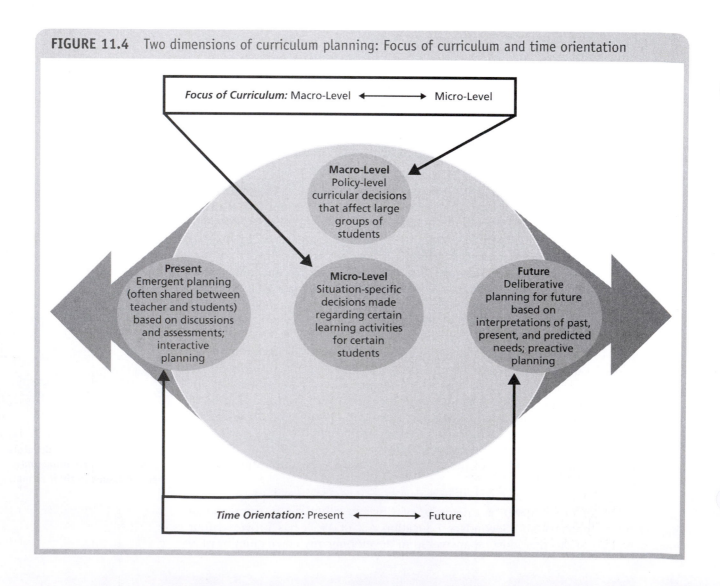

FIGURE 11.4   Two dimensions of curriculum planning: Focus of curriculum and time orientation

Focus of Curriculum: Macro-Level ⟷ Micro-Level

Macro-Level
Policy-level curricular decisions that affect large groups of students

Present
Emergent planning (often shared between teacher and students) based on discussions and assessments; interactive planning

Micro-Level
Situation-specific decisions made regarding certain learning activities for certain students

Future
Deliberative planning for future based on interpretations of past, present, and predicted needs; preactive planning

Time Orientation: Present ⟷ Future

of curriculum and the time orientation. The focus of curriculum planning may be at the macro- or the micro-level. At the macro-level, decisions about the content of the curriculum apply to large groups of students. Curriculum guidelines developed by state departments of education are examples of macro-level curricular decisions. At the micro-level, curriculum decisions are made that apply to groups of students in a particular school or classroom. To some extent, you will be a micro-level curriculum developer—that is, you will make numerous decisions about the curricular experiences you provide students in your classroom.

Another dimension of curriculum planning is the time orientation—does the planning focus on the present or the future? In addition to state-level curriculum guidelines, the semester-long or monthly plans or unit plans that teachers make are examples of future-oriented curriculum planning. Present-oriented curriculum planning usually occurs at the classroom level and is influenced by the unique needs of specific groups of students. The daily or weekly curriculum decisions and lesson plans that teachers make are examples of present-oriented curriculum planning.

Student-Centered Versus Subject-Centered Curricula

A key concern in curriculum development is whether greater emphasis should be given to the requirements of the subject area or to the needs of the students. It is helpful to imagine where a school curriculum might be placed on the following continuum:

Although no curriculum is entirely subject- or student-centered, curricula vary considerably in the degree to which they emphasize one or the other. The **subject-centered curriculum** places primary emphasis on the logical order of the discipline students are to study. The teacher of such a curriculum is a subject-matter expert and is primarily concerned with helping students understand the facts, laws, and principles of the discipline. Subject-centered curricula are more typical of high school education.

Some teachers develop curricula that reflect greater concern for students and their needs. Although teachers of the **student-centered curriculum** also teach content, they emphasize the growth and development of students. This emphasis is generally more typical of elementary school curricula. A major challenge of keeping students engaged in learning a curriculum is maintaining their interest, especially when the curriculum is primarily subject-centered. As a teacher, you should try to make subject-centered curricula relevant to students' lives and timely. You might accomplish this by using examples from current events, students' personal experiences, and real-world scenarios or case studies.

The Integrated Curriculum

To provide students with more meaningful learning experiences, you may decide to use an integrated approach to developing the school curriculum. Used most frequently with elementary-age students, the **integrated curriculum** draws from several different subject areas and focuses on a theme or concept rather than on a single subject. Early childhood education expert Suzanne Krogh (2000) suggests that an integrated approach based on thematic webs is a more natural way for children to learn:

> [Children] do not naturally learn through isolating specific subjects. These have been determined by adult definition. Children's natural learning is more likely to take place across a theme of interest: building a fort, exploring a sandbox, interacting with the first snow of winter. Teachers can create a good deal of their curriculum by building webs made up of these themes of interest. Done with knowledge and care, a web can be created that incorporates most, or even all, of the required and desired curriculum. (p. 340)

According to a national survey of elementary teachers' views on the integrated curriculum, 89 percent believed that integration was the "most effective" way to present the curriculum. As one teacher who was surveyed said, "I'm not interested in presenting isolated facts which children seem to memorize and forget. I want to help students put each lesson in perspective" (Boyer, 1995, p. 83). In *The Basic School: A Community for Learning*, Ernest Boyer (1928–1995), a U.S. commissioner of education and president of the Carnegie Foundation for the Advancement of Teaching, suggested that the elementary school curriculum should be integrated according to eight themes or "core commonalities": The Life Cycle, The Use of Symbols, Membership in Groups, A Sense of Time and Space, Response to the Aesthetic, Connections to Nature, Producing and Consuming, and Living with Purpose (Boyer, 1995).

WHAT INFLUENCES THE CURRICULUM DEVELOPMENT PROCESS?

Various agencies and people outside the school are involved in the curriculum development process. Textbook publishers, for example, influence what is taught because many teachers use textbooks as curriculum guides. The federal government contributes to curriculum development by setting national education goals, and state departments of education develop both broad aims for school curricula and specific minimum competencies for students to master.

Within a given school, the curriculum planning team and the classroom teacher plan the curriculum that students actually experience. As a teacher you will draw from a reservoir of curriculum plans prepared by others, thus playing a vital role in the curriculum planning process. Whenever you make decisions about what material to include in your teaching, how to sequence content, and how much time to spend teaching certain material, you are planning the curriculum.

From the earliest colonial schools to schools of the 21st century, curricula have been broadly influenced by a variety of religious, political, and utilitarian agendas. Figure 11.5 illustrates the influence of community pressures, court decisions, students' life situations, testing results, national reports, teachers' professional organizations, research results, and other factors. The inner circle of the figure represents factors that have a more direct influence on curriculum development (such as students' needs and interests, and school policies). The outer circle represents factors that are more removed from the school setting or have less obvious effects on the curriculum. Individual schools respond to all these influences differently, which further affects their curricula. Let us examine some of these influences in greater detail.

SOCIAL ISSUES AND CHANGING VALUES

Values that affect curriculum planning include prevailing educational theories and teachers' educational philosophies. In addition, curriculum planners respond to social issues and changing values in the wider society. As a result, current social concerns find their way into textbooks, teaching aids, and lesson plans. Often curriculum changes are made in the hope that changing what students learn will help solve social problems or achieve local, statewide, or national goals.

Because the United States is so culturally diverse, proposed curriculum changes also reflect divergent interests and values. This divergence then leads to controversies over curriculum content and conflicting calls for reform. For example, the courts have become involved in legal issues surrounding the demands of some groups that Christian teachings and observances be included in the public school curricula or that materials regarded as objectionable on religious grounds be censored or banned. Additionally, curriculum controversies have erupted in the nearly 30 states that have passed English-only laws (Zuckerman, 2010). Other curriculum controversies have arisen over calls for the elimination of all activities or symbols that have their origins in organized religion, including even secularized or commercialized ones such as Halloween and

FIGURE 11.5   Influences on the school curriculum

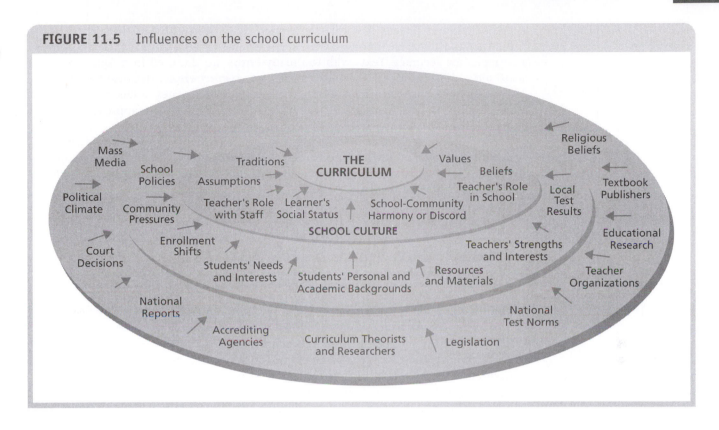

the Easter bunny. Curriculum changes to promote greater social integration or equity among racial or ethnic groups may draw complaints of irrelevancy or reverse discrimination. Traditionalists may object to curriculum changes that reflect feminist views.

As you can imagine, consensus on many curriculum reform issues is never achieved. Because of their public accountability, however, schools must consider how to respond to those issues. One survey revealed that during a 1-year period, half the school districts in Florida received complaints about curriculum content. Included were complaints claiming that the schools were undermining family values, overemphasizing globalism, underemphasizing patriotism, permitting profanity and obscenity, and teaching taboo subjects such as Satanism and sex (Sheuerer & Parkay, 1992, pp. 112–118). In the end, the creative and evaluative tasks of choosing and developing curriculum materials are a source of both empowerment and frustration for teachers. Budget constraints, social and legal issues, and state and local curriculum mandates often determine curriculum choices.

TEXTBOOK PUBLISHING

Textbooks greatly influence the curriculum. Without a doubt, most teachers base classroom lessons and homework on textbooks. In addition, textbook publishers influence school curricula by providing teaching objectives, learning activities, tests, audiovisual aids, and other supplements to assist their customers.

Like curriculum planners, textbook authors and publishers are influenced by trends in education and by social issues. In response to criticism, for example, publishers now tend to avoid bias in terms of gender, religion, sexual orientation, class, race, and culture. However, because the goal of business is profit, publishers are most responsive to market trends and customer preferences. They are often reluctant to risk losing sales by including subjects that are controversial or that may be offensive to their bigger customers. They may also modify textbooks to appeal to decision makers in populous states that make statewide adoptions of textbooks, such as California and Texas. As an editor at a major publishing house reveals: "When it comes to setting the agenda for textbook publishing, only the 22 states that have a formal adoption process count. The other 28 are irrelevant—even though they include populous giants like New York, Pennsylvania, and Ohio—because they allow all publishers to come in and market programs directly to local school districts" (Ansary, 2010, p. 301). In addition, California and Texas are among several states that systematically review state-approved textbooks for accuracy. Texts with too many errors are dropped from state-approved lists, and publishers are levied fines for failing to correct errors. Because highly populated states influence publishers more than less populated states, it has been observed that as California and Texas go regarding the development of state-approved textbook adoption lists, so goes the rest of the nation.

Educators have criticized textbooks for inoffensiveness to the point of blandness, for artificially lowered reading levels (called "dumbing down"), and for pedagogically questionable gimmicks to hold students' attention. Although the publishing industry continually responds to such criticisms, you would be wise to follow systematic guidelines in evaluating and selecting textbooks and other curriculum materials.

WHAT ROLE WILL STANDARDS PLAY IN YOUR CLASSROOM?

As the media remind us almost daily, the public is concerned about low test scores, U.S. students' performance on international comparisons of achievement, and our nation's standing in a competitive global economy. Calls from parents, citizen groups, and politicians to hold teachers accountable for student learning have led to a push for school curricula based on higher standards. To meet these demands for higher standards, schools have undertaken numerous curriculum reforms over the years and used more sophisticated methods for measuring the educational outcomes of these reforms.

Curriculum standards are key elements in the move to hold educators more accountable for student learning. Parents and guardians want to know that schools are educating their children well, and the community wants to know that its investment in school buildings, teachers' salaries, and curricular resources is returning educational dividends. Clearly, curriculum standards will be a fact of life during your career as a teacher.

As adults, we are familiar with standards. To obtain a driver's license, we must demonstrate the knowledge and skills needed to drive a car. At work, we must meet our employer's standards. In this regard, a *standard* refers to a level of knowledge or skill that is generally acknowledged as necessary to perform a specific task or to occupy a particular role in society. In education, for example, standards represent the criteria students must meet to receive a grade of A, to be promoted to the next grade, or to graduate from elementary or high school.

In education, standards can take different forms. The type of standards most important to the individual often depends on whether one is a school administrator, teacher, or student. Administrators, for example, are very concerned about standards related to *students' performance on standardized tests of achievement*. In such instances, the administrator (and his or her school board) might focus on a standard such as the following: "During the next five years, the percentage of students scoring above the norm will increase by at least two percent each year."

Teachers, of course, are also concerned about standards related to students' performance on standardized tests. In addition, teachers understand that another important standard is their expectations for *student performance and behavior at the classroom level*. Teachers demonstrate their commitment to high standards by giving students intellectually demanding reading and writing assignments; providing extensive, thoughtful feedback on students' work; and presenting intellectually stimulating lessons.

The following example illustrates how a science teacher conveys high standards to students. Rather than merely transmit information about how scientists conduct experiments, the teacher uses an intellectually challenging activity to foster students' critical thinking and problem-solving skills. Students experience, firsthand, what it means to think like a scientist.

Scott Sowell, a middle school science teacher, wants to provide his students with experience in problem solving and designing and conducting

Listen to a principal's view on the role of standards in today's classrooms.

experiments. Because simple pendulums are concrete and easy to assemble, he decides to have his students try to determine what will influence the frequency of a simple pendulum. . . .

Scott begins by demonstrating a simple pendulum with paper clips attached to a piece of string. He attaches the string to a ring stand and hooks a paper clip in a loop at the end of it. He then pulls the paper clip aside and watches as the pendulum swings back and forth like the pendulum in a grandfather clock. He explains that frequency means the number of swings in a certain time period such as 15 seconds, and asks students what factors they think will influence the frequency. After some discussion, they suggest length, weight, and angle of release as possibilities. (In reality, only the length of the pendulum determines its frequency.)

"Okay, your job as a group is to design your own experiment," Scott continues. "Think of a way to test how each affects the frequency. Use the equipment at your desk to design and carry out the experiment." (Eggen & Kauchak, 2012, pp. 224, 229)

Students often have yet another perspective on standards; for them, the school curriculum should meet the *standard of being personally relevant, interesting, and meaningful*. The school curriculum should help them meet the developmental challenges of moving from childhood to adulthood. It should help them realize the goals they have set for themselves.

According to the MetLife Survey of the American Teacher, most teachers and principals believe their school has high academic standards. Figure 11.6, for example, shows that 83 percent of teachers and 86 percent of principals at the elementary level, and 67 percent of teachers and 74 percent of principals at the secondary level, "strongly agree" that their schools have high standards. However, only 50 percent of secondary school students polled in the MetLife Survey believe that their teachers "very much encourage them to do their best," whereas 72 percent of elementary students believe their teachers encourage them to do their best (Harris Interactive, 2010, p. 32).

Administrators, teachers, students, and parents frequently have different perspectives on standards. During the last decade, however, **standards** in education (on occasion called *content standards, goals, expectations, learning results,* or *learning outcomes*) have come to be seen primarily as statements that reflect what students should know and be able to do within a particular discipline or at a particular grade level.

FIGURE 11.6   Agreement that most teachers hold high standards for all students (% strongly agree) by school level

■ Elementary school   □ Secondary school

Teachers: 83%, 67%
Principals: 86%, 74%

Question: How much do you agree or disagree with the following statement: Most teachers in my school hold high standards for all of the students?
Base: Teachers (n = 1,003); Principals (n = 500)

Source: The MetLife Survey of the American Teacher: Collaborating for Student Success. New York: Harris Interactive, April 2010, p. 30.

HOW IS STANDARDS-BASED EDUCATION SHAPING SCHOOL CURRICULA?

Current efforts at educational reform in the United States emphasize **standards-based education (SBE)**—that is, basing curricula, teaching, and assessment of student learning on rigorous, world-class standards. SBE is based on the belief that all students are capable of meeting high standards. In the past, expectations for students from poor families and students who are members of minority groups were sometimes lower than for other students. Today, SBE is seen as a way of ensuring that excellence and equity become part of our nation's public school system. For example, in his 2011 State of the Union Address, Barack Obama pointed out how the federal Race to the Top program has raised academic standards throughout the nation: "When a child walks into a classroom, it should be a place of high expectations and high performance. . . . Race to the Top is the most meaningful reform of our public schools in a generation. . . . it has led over 40 states to raise their standards for teaching and learning" (White House Press Release, January 25, 2011).

To meet the demand for higher standards, each state has adopted state standards for what students should know and be able to do. For example, here are standards in geometry from three states:

Colorado: Students use geometric concepts, properties, and relationships in problem-solving situations and communicate the reasoning used in solving these problems.

North Dakota: Students understand and apply geometric concepts and spatial relationships to represent and solve problems in mathematical and nonmathematical situations.

Wyoming: Students apply geometric concepts, properties, and relationships in problem-solving situations. Students communicate the reasoning used in solving these problems.

As these examples show, state standards are broad statements of learning outcomes against which student achievement can be measured.

Content and Performance Standards

Standards documents prepared by state education agencies, local school districts, and professional associations typically refer to two types of standards—content standards and performance standards. **Content standards**, as the term implies, refer to the content—or knowledge and skills—students should acquire in various academic disciplines. A common phrase in standards documents is that content standards represent "what students should know and be able to do."

Content standards are often subdivided into benchmarks (frequently called *indicators*). **Benchmarks** are content standards that are presented as specific statements of what students should understand and be able to do *at specific grade levels or developmental stages*. Here are three statements from the **IOWA** Core Content Benchmarks:

Reading, grades 3–5: Students can draw conclusions, make inferences, and deduce meaning.

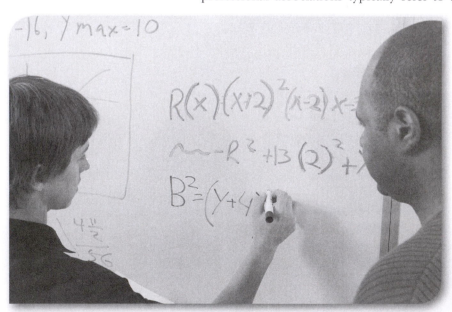

What type of assessment might this teacher be using?

Mathematics, grades 6–9: Students can understand and apply concepts and procedures of algebra.

Science, grades 9–12: Students can understand and apply the processes and skills of scientific inquiry.

In addition, many standards documents refer to performance standards. A **performance standard** specifies "how good is good enough." Performance standards are used to assess the degree to which students have attained standards in an academic area. Performance standards require teacher judgment about the quality of performance or level of proficiency required. Unlike content standards, performance standards reflect levels of proficiency. For example, Iowa performance standards specify the following levels: High Performance Level (Distinguished, Accomplished), Intermediate Performance Level (Skilled, Moderate), and Low Performance Level (Marginal, Weak). Here are samples of Iowa performance standards for reading, mathematics, and science:

Grade 3 Literacy Standards

- **Distinguished:** Understands factual information and new words in context. Can make inferences and interpret either non-literal language or information in new contexts. Can determine a selection's main ideas and analyze its style and structure.
- **Moderate:** Usually understands factual information and new words in context. Often is able to make inferences and interpret either non-literal language or information in new contexts. Sometimes can determine a selection's main ideas and analyze its style and structure.
- **Weak:** Seldom understands factual information or new words in context. Rarely is able to make inferences and interpret either non-literal language or information in new contexts. Seldom can determine a selection's main ideas and analyze aspects of its style and structure.

Grade 8 Mathematics

- **Distinguished:** Understands math concepts and is able to solve word problems. Usually can use estimation methods. Is able to interpret data from graphs and tables.
- **Moderate:** Usually can understand math concepts and sometimes is able to solve word problems. Sometimes can use estimation methods and interpret data from graphs and tables.
- **Weak:** Seldom can understand math concepts or solve word problems. Rarely can use estimation methods or interpret data from graphs and tables.

Grade 11 Science

- **Distinguished:** Makes inferences or predictions from data, judges the relevance and adequacy of information, and recognizes the rationale for and limitations of scientific procedures.
- **Moderate:** Sometimes makes inferences or predictions from data, judges the relevance and adequacy of information, and usually recognizes the rationale for and limitations of scientific procedures.
- **Weak:** Seldom makes inferences or predictions from data, sometimes judges the relevance and adequacy of information, and rarely recognizes the rationale for and limitations of scientific procedures.

Standards Developed by Professional Associations

In addition to national, state, and local efforts to raise standards, professional associations are playing a key role in SBE by developing standards in the subject-matter disciplines. In many cases, professional associations have developed specific, grade-level **performance expectations**—established levels of achievement, quality of performance, or level of proficiency—for recommended standards as well as classroom activities related to standards.

Standards developed by professional associations are used in the following ways:

- State departments of education, school districts, and schools can use the standards as a guide for developing curricula and assessments of student learning.
- Teachers can use standards to (1) develop goals and objectives for units and courses, (2) evaluate their teaching, and (3) develop ideas for instructional activities and classroom assessments.
- Parents and community members can use standards to assess the quality of education in their local schools and to monitor the achievement levels of their children.

Figure 11.7 presents several professional associations that have recommended curriculum standards in various academic disciplines. You can obtain complete sets of standards from the websites these associations maintain.

Aligning Curricula and Textbooks with Standards and Curriculum Frameworks

An important part of SBE in the United States is aligning curricula and textbooks with national and state standards and curriculum frameworks. **Curriculum alignment** may take two forms. Horizontal alignment occurs when teachers within a specific grade level coordinate instruction across disciplines and examine their school's curriculum to ensure that course content and instruction dovetail across and/or within subject areas. Vertical alignment occurs when subjects are connected across grade levels so that students experience increasingly complex instructional programs as they move through the grades.

A **curriculum framework** is a document, usually published by a state education agency, that provides guidelines, recommended instructional and assessment strategies, suggested resources, and models for teachers to use as they develop curricula

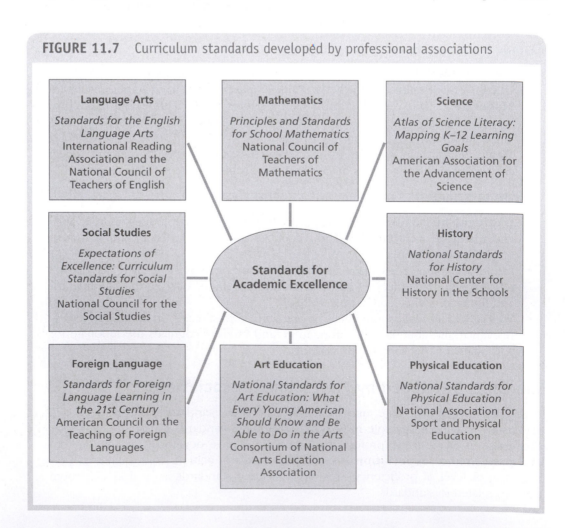

FIGURE 11.7 Curriculum standards developed by professional associations

Language Arts

Standards for the English Language Arts
International Reading Association and the National Council of Teachers of English

Mathematics

Principles and Standards for School Mathematics
National Council of Teachers of Mathematics

Science

Atlas of Science Literacy: Mapping K–12 Learning Goals
American Association for the Advancement of Science

Social Studies

Expectations of Excellence: Curriculum Standards for Social Studies
National Council for the Social Studies

History

National Standards for History
National Center for History in the Schools

Foreign Language

Standards for Foreign Language Learning in the 21st Century
American Council on the Teaching of Foreign Languages

Art Education

National Standards for Art Education: What Every Young American Should Know and Be Able to Do in the Arts
Consortium of National Arts Education Association

Physical Education

National Standards for Physical Education
National Association for Sport and Physical Education

Standards for Academic Excellence

that are aligned with national and state standards. Curriculum frameworks are usually written by teams of teachers and state agency personnel, and they serve as a bridge between national and state standards and local curriculum and instructional strategies. In **ALASKA**, for example, curriculum frameworks in CD-ROM format and Frameworks Resource Kits in specific subjects are given to teachers by the Department of Education & Early Development. The CD-ROM provides state-of-the-art information in different formats, including videoclips of educators explaining standards-based curricula. Figure 11.8, taken from the Alaska frameworks, presents English/language arts process skills for writing.

FIGURE 11.8   English/language arts process skills

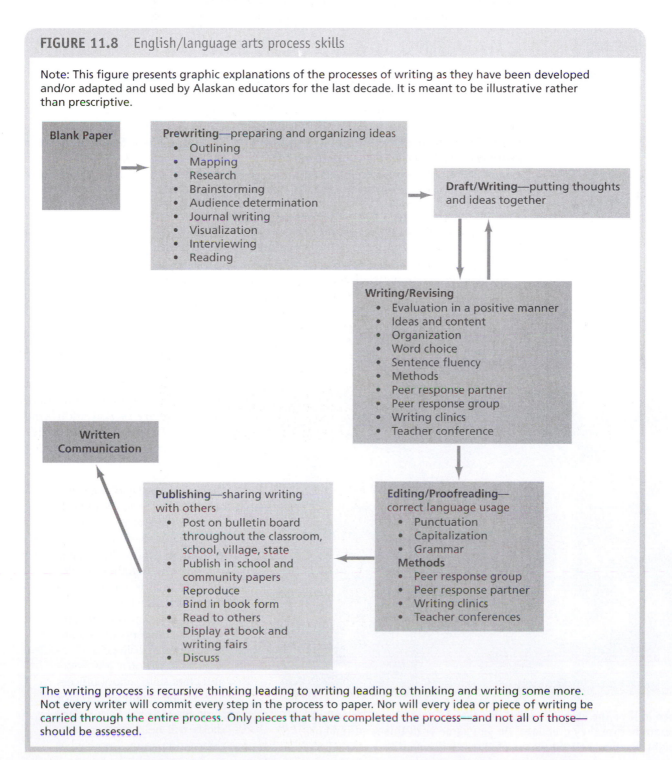

Note: This figure presents graphic explanations of the processes of writing as they have been developed and/or adapted and used by Alaskan educators for the last decade. It is meant to be illustrative rather than prescriptive.

Blank Paper

Prewriting—preparing and organizing ideas
- Outlining
- Mapping
- Research
- Brainstorming
- Audience determination
- Journal writing
- Visualization
- Interviewing
- Reading

Draft/Writing—putting thoughts and ideas together

Writing/Revising
- Evaluation in a positive manner
- Ideas and content
- Organization
- Word choice
- Sentence fluency
- Methods
- Peer response partner
- Peer response group
- Writing clinics
- Teacher conference

Written Communication

Publishing—sharing writing with others
- Post on bulletin board throughout the classroom, school, village, state
- Publish in school and community papers
- Reproduce
- Bind in book form
- Read to others
- Display at book and writing fairs
- Discuss

Editing/Proofreading—correct language usage
- Punctuation
- Capitalization
- Grammar

Methods
- Peer response group
- Peer response partner
- Writing clinics
- Teacher conferences

The writing process is recursive thinking leading to writing leading to thinking and writing some more. Not every writer will commit every step in the process to paper. Nor will every idea or piece of writing be carried through the entire process. Only pieces that have completed the process—and not all of those—should be assessed.

Source: Used with permission of the Alaska Department of Education & Early Development Curriculum Frameworks Project. Retrieved April 16, 2011 from http://www.eed.state.ak.us/tls/frameworks/langarts/30contnt.htm

Like teachers, textbook authors and publishers are influenced significantly by the development of academic standards throughout the nation. Many publishers are revising their textbooks so they are in alignment with state standards and curriculum frameworks, particularly in populous states that make statewide adoptions of textbooks, such as **CALIFORNIA** and **TEXAS**. In states such as these, school districts can purchase only those textbooks that are on state textbook adoption lists.

HOW IS THE COMMON CORE STATE STANDARDS INITIATIVE CHANGING U.S. EDUCATION?

The Common Core State Standards Initiative (CCSSI)

To bring uniformity to the "patchwork quilt" of 50 sets of state standards, the Council of Chief State School Officers (CCSSO) and the National Governors Association Center for Best Practices (NGA Center) organized the **Common Core State Standards Initiative (CCSSI)**. In March 2010, CCSSI released a draft set of K–12 standards in English/language arts and mathematics for public comment. According to the CCSSI, Common Core Standards

- are aligned with college and work expectations;
- are clear, understandable, and consistent;
- include rigorous content and application of knowledge through higher-order skills;
- build upon strengths of and lessons learned from current state standards;
- are informed by other top-performing countries, so that all students are prepared to succeed in a global economy and society; and
- are evidence- and research-based.

With the exception of Texas and Alaska, 48 states, two territories, and the District of Columbia participated in developing the standards.

Although the federal government had no role in developing the standards, U.S. Secretary of Education Arne Duncan pointed out that the standards would play a key role in strengthening U.S. education:

> The release today of the Common Core State Standards is an important step toward the improvement of quality education nationwide. States have come together to develop standards that are internationally benchmarked and include the knowledge and skills that students must learn to succeed in college and career. The nation's governors and chief state school officers are to be commended for their leadership. These standards will help teachers, students and parents know what

More than half of the states require students to pass an exit or end-of-course exam before they graduate. Do you agree with this requirement? What might be some consequences of this requirement?

is needed for students to succeed in college and careers, and will enable states, school districts and teachers to more effectively collaborate to accelerate learning and close achievement gaps nationwide.

As the nation seeks to maintain our international competitiveness, ensure all students regardless of background have access to a high quality education, and prepare all students for college, work, and citizenship, these standards are an important foundation for our collective work. (U.S. Department of Education, June 2, 2010)

Watch as a principal discusses key features of standards-based education that are communicated to parents.

The overall goal of the Common Core's English and Language Arts and Literacy in History/Social Studies, Science, and Technical Subjects Standards is to ensure that high school graduates are college and/or career ready in literacy. The standards address five essential elements of literacy: Reading, Writing, Speaking and Listening, Language, and Media and Technology.

In response to the criticism that U.S. mathematics is "a mile wide and an inch deep," the goal of the mathematics standards is to achieve greater "focus and coherence" in the curriculum. The mathematics standards focus on two broad areas: Mathematical Practice and Mathematical Content. Mathematical Practice emphasizes eight types of practice that are to be taught, as appropriate, from kindergarten through 12th grade:

1. Make sense of problems and persevere in solving them.
2. Reason abstractly and quantitatively.
3. Construct visible arguments and critique the reasoning of others.
4. Model with mathematics.
5. Use appropriate tools strategically.
6. Attend to precision.
7. Look for and make us of structure.
8. Look for and express regularity in repeated reasoning.

Mathematical Content focuses on several mathematical *domains* that are emphasized from kindergarten through eighth grade and at the high school level. For example, at the kindergarten level, the domain Counting and Cardinality is emphasized; and these four domains are emphasized, as appropriate, from kindergarten through fifth grade: Operations and Algebraic Thinking, Number and Operations in Base 10, Measurement and Data, and Geometry. At the high school level, the Standards do not specify the content to be studied at each grade level; instead, six conceptual *categories* are covered: Number and Quantity, Algebra, Functions, Modeling, Geometry, and Statistics and Probability.

Early Reactions to the Common Core

Many observers responded positively to the release of the Common Core Standards. Some suggested that the standards were long overdue:

After more than 20 years of messy thinking, mistakes, and misguided direction, policy makers have finally given teachers and students a solid set of standards in mathematics and literacy. The Common Core of Standards only begins the process of moving academic performance in these subjects to the levels we need, but it's such a relief to have them. Now, the Race to the Top funding and the federal investments in state assessment systems have targets that make sense. (Philips & Wong, 2010, p. 37).

U.S. Secretary of Education Arne Duncan pointed out that the standards would enable students to move from state to state without having to adjust to a different set of expectations, and teachers located in different states could share lesson plans:

. . . literally for the first time in American history, a child in Mississippi will face the same expectations as a child in Massachusetts. Today a fourth grade teacher in New Mexico can develop a lesson plan at night and, the very next day, a fourth grade teacher in New York can use it and share it with others if she wants to. Today, the child of a Marine officer, who is transferred from Camp Pendleton in California to Camp Lejeune in North Carolina, will be able to make that academic transition without a hitch, instead of having to start over in a widely different place academically. (U.S. Department of Education, June 25, 2013)

However, a vigorous debate over the Standards soon emerged, and "manifestos" setting forth very different views were released within a year. First, the Albert Shanker Institute (2011), named for the late, long-time leader of the American Federation of Teachers, released *A Call for Common Content*, in which more than 100 leading educators and policymakers asserted that

> We therefore applaud the goals of the recently released Common Core State Standards, already adopted in most states, which articulate a much clearer vision of what students should learn and be able to do as they progress through school. For our nation, this represents a major advance toward declaring that "equal educational opportunity" is a top priority—not empty rhetoric. . . . [O]ur nation must finally answer questions it has avoided for generations: What is it, precisely, that we expect all educated citizens to have learned? What explicit knowledge, skills, and understanding of content will help define the day-to-day work of teaching and learning?

A "counter-manifesto" titled "Closing the Door on Innovation: Why One National Curriculum is Bad for America" and signed by a "broad coalition of over 100 educational and other leaders"—took the opposite position and made the following points:

1. There is no constitutional or statutory basis for national standards, national assessments, or national curricula.
2. There is no consistent evidence that a national curriculum leads to high academic achievement.
3. The national standards on which the administration is planning to base a national curriculum are inadequate.
4. There is no body of evidence for a "best" design for curriculum sequences in any subject.
5. There is no evidence to justify a single high school curriculum for all students. (Evers, Greene, Forster, Stotsky, & Wurman, May 2, 2011)

Upon release of the Common Core Standards, CCSSI made it clear that the standards are "voluntary"—they *were not* a federal initiative. And, three years after the standards were released, the U.S. Secretary of Education pointed out, emphatically, that the standards *were not* a federal initiative: "I believe the Common Core State Standards may prove to be the single greatest thing to happen to public education in America since *Brown versus Board of Education*—and the federal government had nothing to do with creating them. The federal government didn't write them, didn't approve them, and doesn't mandate them. And we never will. Anyone who says otherwise is either misinformed or willfully misleading" (U.S. Department of Education, June 25, 2013).

However, the Obama administration stated that federal funding to the states would be contingent upon the states adopting the "voluntary" standards. For example, the administration's reauthorization of the Elementary and Secondary Education Act would tie $14.5 billion in Title 1 money for low-income districts to the adoption of Common Core Standards. In addition, federal Race to the Top grant awards would be directed to "early adopters" of the Common Core Standards.

TECHNOLOGY in ACTION
Using Text-to-Speech in a Third-Grade Reading Class

Mrs. Kelly teaches English as a second language (ESL) at Wilson Elementary. Although she understands the importance of one-on-one instruction, she has found that the varied English proficiency of her students makes it difficult to work with individual students for any extended period of time. She prefers to work with students individually, helping them pronounce words, reading along with them, and helping when they encounter words they do not understand. The problem with this approach is the time it requires—there are only so many hours in a day.

Mrs. Kelly knows it is important for her ESL students to hear the words they are reading. Often, she stands at the front of her classroom and reads to students as they follow along in their books. The problem with this approach is that each student has a different level of English proficiency. If students speak up when they have difficulty (which is rare due to the large class size), she finds that the more proficient speakers are impatient as she helps a student who is having difficulty.

To solve this problem, Mrs. Kelly decides to introduce a text-to-speech (TTS) program in her class. (TTS uses a synthesized computer voice to read text on a computer screen or in an electronic file.) Students now sit at the computer and read along with the TTS program as it highlights the text that is being spoken. With this program, students can select an appealing voice: male or female, older or younger, softer or more authoritative.

Mrs. Kelly finds that the text-to-speech program provides the individual instruction that her students need. It has improved their reading ability, vocabulary retention, and pronunciation. For example, when she listens to her students read, she identifies words that are difficult for a particular student to pronounce, and she writes a list of these words for each student. The student then plugs those words into the TTS program and listens to the correct pronunciation of the words. Each student can listen to a word as many times as needed. Her students see the TTS program as a second teacher and now identify difficult pronunciations before they read for Mrs. Kelly.

TEXT-TO-SPEECH: Text-to-speech programs convert electronic text to digital audio. The TTS program reads the text and then speaks the words for the listener. There are two approaches for converting text to speech. The first is user-directed, the other author-directed. The user-directed application requires that the user of TTS identify the text to be converted. This can be done by highlighting the identified text or uploading an electronic file of the text to the TTS program. The author-directed application requires the author of the website, videogame, or text file to identify the text to be spoken. Several text-to-speech programs are available today. The most popular programs use a realistic human voice.

POSSIBLE USES: Teachers have used text-to-speech programs to proofread student writing, listen to term papers on their iPods during their commutes to and from work, help students with reading or vision difficulties, create e-books for their students, and improve ESL instruction.

TRY IT OUT: Three of the most popular text-to-speech products are NeoSpeech, TextAloud, and NaturalReader. All of these products have demonstrations on their websites. For example, the NaturalReader website allows users to click on an application demonstration that presents TTS in e-mail, PDF, Word, and a W=web browser. Although there are several variation of TTS, a visit to most TTS websites will provide a good introduction to text-to-speech technology. There are also text-to-speech options in the Ease of Use settings for Windows and System Preferences on Mac that are included with the operating systems.

WHAT CONTROVERSIES SURROUND THE EFFORT TO RAISE STANDARDS?

The Common Core State Standards Initiative intensified an already widespread, often heated national debate about the role of standards in educational reform. By mid 2013, several states had introduced and passed legislation to delay or withdraw from using the Common Core Standards. **INDIANA**, for example, signed a bill into law that "paused" the implementation of the standards until more studies and evaluations could be completed.

The U.S. Secretary of Education pointed out that the standards had become "a topic for dueling newspaper editorials. Why? That's because a new set of standards—rigorous, high-quality learning standards, developed and led by a group of governors and state education chiefs—are under attack as a federal takeover of the schools" (U.S. Department of Education, June 25, 2013).

Without a doubt, responses to the Common Core have been mixed, and many questions about raising standards remain unanswered. What are minimum acceptable standards? Who should set those standards? How should students' attainment of those standards be assessed? What should schools do about students who fail to meet those standards? Can standards be raised without increasing dropout rates? Are both excellence and equal opportunity possible if standards are raised? Last, will expanded testing programs based on higher standards discriminate against minority-group students who traditionally score lower on such tests?

Arguments in Support of Raising Standards

"We are moving in this country from a local to a national view of education and we need better arrangements to guide the way." So observed Ernest Boyer (1928–1995) when he was president of the Carnegie Foundation for the Advancement of Teaching. As Boyer's comment implies, the United States, like other nations of the world, needs national goals and standards to motivate its people to excel. Without them, people may become complacent and satisfied with mediocrity. Also, like other countries in our increasingly interdependent world, the United States needs to compare the achievement of its students with those of other countries. Just as a runner will run faster when paced by another, the U.S. educational system can become more effective as a result of comparisons with educational systems in other countries.

Those who advocate raising standards and assessing students' attainment of those standards put forth several additional arguments in favor of standards-based education:

- Standards enable the states, and the nation, to define clearly what is to be taught and the level of performance that demonstrates mastery of those standards.
- Standards that are set and measured annually promote educational growth and achievement for all students, and the results can be reported easily to parents and other stakeholders.
- Standards provide a way to track the educational achievement of minority-group students and thus promote equal educational opportunity and narrowing the "achievement gap" between White and minority-group students.
- State-level standards provide a way of comparing educational programs among the 50 states and the District of Columbia.

In addition to the arguments just outlined, it is clear that the United States—as a society rich in ethnicities, religions, nationalities, and language groups—also needs common, rigorous standards for unity. With increasing immigration to the country, which brings diverse groups of people to its urban and suburban neighborhoods and rural areas, schools need to provide a common core of knowledge about the democratic heritage of our country and a common curriculum based on high academic standards.

As a mobile society, the United States needs common educational standards so that children from one area will not fall behind when they move to another. Children from a farming community in Minnesota should be able to move to the heart of Dallas without finding themselves behind or ahead of their peers in school. Children from a school in Seattle should be able to transfer to a school in Cincinnati and recognize the curricula studied there.

Concerns About Raising Standards

Opponents of the effort to develop world-class standards as the centerpiece of educational reform point out that the failure of many schools to achieve adequate yearly progress as mandated by No Child Left Behind is evidence that a new approach to educational reform is needed. Instead, they contend, we should become more aware of the lack of uniformity in schools around the country and the needs of the children they serve. As Jonathon Kozol's books *Savage Inequalities* (1991) and *The Shame of the Nation* (2005) vividly illustrate, equal education in the United States is an illusion. To compare the performance of a student in a poor Chicago housing project with that of a student in the city's wealthy suburbs is to confront the "savage inequalities" found throughout our educational system.

In addition, test score gains attributed to the standards movement have been shown not to reflect real gains in the knowledge and skills the tests were designed to measure. A phenomenon known as *score inflation* results in students' scores on high-stakes tests rising faster than their scores on other standardized tests given at the same time and measuring the same subjects. Students don't actually know as much as we think they do based only on the high-stakes test scores. Actually, the standards movement may result in test scores that are less accurate than they were prior to the addition of high-stakes assessments (Stecher & Hamilton, 2002).

Also, sanctions imposed on low-performing schools will not ensure that students in those schools are not left behind. The record of success when sanctions such as staff reassignment and school takeover have been imposed is mixed. Students in low-performing schools may not be helped by sanctions, and there is some risk that they will be harmed (Stecher & Hamilton, 2002). Thus, higher standards would further bias educational opportunities in favor of students from advantaged backgrounds, intensify the class-based structure of U.S. society, and increase differences between well-funded and poorly funded schools.

Opponents of efforts to develop world-class standards in U.S. schools have raised numerous additional concerns. The following are among their arguments:

- Raising standards might lead to a national curriculum and an expanded role of the federal government in education.
- The push to raise standards is fueled by conservative interest groups that want to undo educational gains made by traditionally underrepresented groups.
- A focus on higher standards diverts attention from more meaningful educational reform.
- Increased emphasis on tested subjects often results in a decrease in emphasis on subjects not tested.
- World-class standards are often vague and not linked to valid assessments and scoring rubrics.
- Standards frequently describe learning activities, not the knowledge and skills students are expected to learn—for example, "Students will experience various forms of literature."
- The scope and sequence of what students should learn with reference to standards and benchmarks has been unclear; in other words, to what degree and in what order should students learn material?
- Grade-level benchmarks have been created that are unrealistic and developmentally inappropriate for some students; often students are hurried through their learning without sufficient time and instruction to acquire underlying concepts and skills.
- SBE and high-stakes tests based on those standards lead to the practice of teaching to the test, giving priority to academic content covered by the tests and deemphasizing areas of the curriculum not covered. For example, a study of Kentucky's assessment system (Jones & Whitford, 1997) found that test-related sanctions and rewards influenced teachers to "focus on whatever is thought to raise test scores rather than on instruction aimed at addressing individual student needs" (p. 277).

As a teacher, you and your colleagues will no doubt participate in an ongoing dialogue about academic standards at your school. Thus, the role that standards will play in your professional life will be significant. The following eight questions may help you decide the nature of SBE in your school:

1. Where will we get our standards?
2. Who will set the standards?
3. What types of standards should we include?
4. In what format will the standards be written?
5. At what levels will benchmarks be written?
6. How should benchmarks and standards be assessed?
7. How will student progress be reported?
8. How will we hold students accountable? (Marzano, 1997)

TEACHERS' VOICES ➡ BEING AN AGENT OF CHANGE

CAROLYN FOOTE

A "TECHNO-LIBRARIAN" SHARES NEW IDEAS ACROSS THE GLOBE

Providing our students opportunities to be prepared for the future is crucial. Across the nation, thousands of dedicated educators and librarians are leading the charge to help students investigate, create, collaborate and communicate effectively, and to reach beyond the walls of their own schools.

Connected librarians across the nation . . . play a uniquely significant role in assisting teachers as they become comfortable with new technologies, and who link teachers and students with the tools and resources that help them become "connected" learners. While librarians have always been resource mavens and curriculum specialists, our roles have broadened to include the technology tools and strategies that prepare our students for an always connected future. That can mean connecting our ASL (American Sign Language) students via Skype so they can teach a Canadian student sign language, hosting a robotics makerspace in the library, building a list of web resources for our Vietnam memorial project, or discovering new devices that will aid student research.

When tablets entered the commercial marketplace, for example, I was eager to pilot them in the library in order to determine their efficacy for our teachers and students. As an early adopter, I began with just six tablets to gather information on their usefulness for student learning both within the library and the classroom. Three years later, with the dedication of a tribe of people, we are now a one-to-one tablet district k–12 and are entering our third year hosting an annual conference for tablet users across the country.

As a librarian (in concert with technology staff), I supported the initiative in many ways: redesigning the library to include a tech "help desk," building lists of appropriate apps, developing projects with students and teachers, and documenting our initiative on a campus blog. I have networked with librarians around the country as they grapple with similar issues from e-books to library redesign; even when we redesigned our own library six years ago, many of the future-friendly features that make our library a vibrant hub were inspired by other colleagues online.

As a librarian, I play a vital leadership role with my unique expertise about research and literacy. But I and other librarians cannot develop our skills in a vacuum. Wired librarians across the globe have banded together to build resources for one another, like the Teacher Librarian Virtual café. This program, led by volunteers, hosts monthly online programming and supports weekly Twitter chats. I also engage with Texas librarians during the weekly Texas Library Twitter chat and network during national events like the Connected Educator month with U.S. Education Secretary Arne Duncan, and the free K12online Conference, which gave me the first thrilling taste of connecting with educators globally.

These ongoing connections have imbued my own practice with the most empowering professional learning I have ever been a part of; I can wake up chatting with educators in Australia, connect with colleagues on campus during the day, and go to bed having chatted with colleagues on the West Coast. Rather than work alone, librarians have grown wide networks of colleagues that both support and challenge us, and we, and our schools, are better for it.

We care fiercely about educating our students and about moving our schools forward. And these connections make our work much richer.

PERSONAL REFLECTION

1. Foote calls herself a "techno-librarian." With reference to the grade level and subject area for which you are preparing to teach, describe the curriculum your students would experience if you were a "techno-teacher." For example, as a "techno-elementary teacher," what would you want students to learn? As a "techno-science teacher"? As a "techno-English teacher"? As a "techno-music teacher"?
2. Foote's blog post describes how she "reached beyond the walls" of her school. As a teacher, explain how you will develop a curriculum that "reaches beyond the walls" of your school.

Carolyn Foote is a "techno-librarian" at Westlake High School in Austin, **TEXAS**. She wrote a chapter about her school's iPad program for the book *New Landscapes in Mobile Learning* (Routledge, May 2013).

The preceding is excerpted from her November 26, 2013, blog post upon being selected by the White House as a Connected Educator Champion of Change. Retrieved from "A "Techno-Librarian" Shares New Ideas Across the Globe" by Carolyn B. Foote, http://futura.edublogs.org/2014/07/25/librarians-sharing-new-ideas-across-globe/. Used with permission of Dinah McGuire.

SUMMARY

What Do Students Learn from the Curriculum?

- A general definition of curriculum refers to the experiences, both planned and unplanned, that either enhance or impede the education and growth of students.
- Students experience four types of curricula: what teachers intend to teach (the explicit curriculum), the hidden curriculum, the null curriculum, and extracurricular/cocurricular programs.
- Curriculum content reflects the beliefs of society and what the larger society believes young people should learn.
- Curricula are based on the needs and interests of students and also reflect a variety of professional, commercial, local, state, national, and international pressures.
- Three noncognitive factors are receiving more attention in school curricula: grit, tenacity, and perseverance; academic mindset; and mindfulness/meditation.
- Students' strengths in noncognitive areas will increase if their overall curricular experiences are rigorous, supportive, and growth-promoting.

How Is the School Curriculum Developed?

- Many school systems develop curricula by addressing the four questions in the Tyler rationale: (1) What educational purposes should the school seek to attain? (2) What educational experiences can be provided that are likely to attain these purposes? (3) How can these educational experiences be organized effectively? (4) How can we determine whether these purposes are being attained?
- Curriculum planning focuses on a continuum between the macro-level and the micro-level, and on a continuum between the present and the future.
- Curricula vary in the degree to which they are student-centered or subject-centered.
- The integrated curriculum draws from several different subject areas and focuses on a theme or concept rather than on a single subject.

What Influences the Curriculum Development Process?

- Community pressures, court decisions, students' life situations, testing results, national reports, teachers' professional organizations, textbook publishing, and educational research are among the factors that influence the school curriculum.

What Role Will Standards Play in Your Classroom?

- Standards at the state and national levels are part of the movement to hold educators and schools more accountable for student learning.
- School administrators, teachers, and students have different perspectives on standards. Administrators are primarily concerned with students' performance on standardized tests of achievement; teachers are primarily concerned with student performance and behavior at the classroom level; and students are primarily concerned with the learning being personally relevant, interesting, and meaningful.

How Is Standards-Based Education Shaping School Curricula?

- Developing rigorous academic standards, assessing students' mastery of those standards, and holding students and teachers accountable for meeting those standards are key elements of standards-based education.
- Professional associations have developed standards that reflect the knowledge, skills, and attitudes students should develop in the subject-matter disciplines.
- A good school curriculum is aligned both horizontally and vertically.
- Curriculum frameworks provide guidelines, recommended instructional and assessment strategies, suggested resources, and models for teachers to use as they develop curricula that are aligned with national and state standards.

How Is the Common Core State Standards Initiative Changing U.S. Education?

- The Council of Chief State School Officers (CCSSO) and the National Governors Association Center for Best Practices (NGA Center) organized the Common Core State Standards Initiative (CCSSI), a set of K–12 standards in English/language arts and mathematics.
- Since the release of the Common Core Standards in 2010, a vigorous debate over the standards has emerged.

What Controversies Surround the Effort to Raise Standards?

- By mid-2013, several states had introduced and passed legislation to delay or withdraw from using the Common Core Standards.
- Some critics of the Common Core have mistakenly maintained that the Common Core Standards are a federal "takeover" of education in the United States.
- Proponents of higher standards argue that standards increase student achievement. Opponents argue that higher standards may result in decreased emphasis on subjects not tested.
- As part of the No Child Left Behind Act, schools are to provide evidence each year that students are making adequate yearly progress (AYP). Schools that fail to make AYP will be identified as "in need of improvement."

- State-mandated tests often have high-stakes consequences for students, such as determining eligibility to participate in extracurricular activities or to graduate.
- For teachers, administrators, and schools, test results can be linked to merit rewards, increased funding, or sanctions.
- An unintended consequence of high-stakes tests is that they overemphasize differences in achievement (often termed the "achievement gap") between White students and minority-group students and students from low-income families; the tests can also unfairly highlight achievement differences between students who attend "resource-rich" schools and those who attend "resource-poor" schools.
- High-stakes tests increase the likelihood that minority-group students and students from low-income families will drop out.

PROFESSIONAL REFLECTIONS AND ACTIVITIES

Teacher's Journal

1. Reflect on the 12,000 or so hours that you have spent as a student in K–12 classrooms. How would you characterize the academic standards you were expected to meet? How were these expectations conveyed to you?
2. Many people believe that high-stakes tests address only a narrow portion of the school curriculum. If a school district decided to "take a break" from high-stakes testing for five years, what data would parents, teachers, and others use to judge whether a school and its students were "successful"?
3. List in order of importance the five factors that you believe have the greatest impact on the curriculum. Then list the five factors that you believe ideally should have the greatest influence. What differences do you notice between your actual and ideal lists? What might be done to reduce the differences between the two lists?
4. Reflect on the 12,000 or so hours that you have spent as a student in K–12 classrooms. What did the nonexplicit curricula in the classes teach you about yourself?
5. What are the biggest barriers to student engagement with the curriculum? As a teacher, how might you address these barriers and foster learning for all students?

Teacher's Research

1. Find the professional curriculum standards for your subject area online and compare them to the curriculum standards for that subject area in a state where you plan to teach (most state department of education websites include state-mandated standards). For example, you might download the National Council of Teachers of Mathematics (NCTM) standards and then compare them with the mathematics curriculum in the state where you plan to teach. How are the two sets of standards similar? How are they different? Is one set of standards clearer than the other?
2. Find an online blog by a teacher that discusses his or her experiences related to the Common Core State Standards. Post a thoughtful response to the teacher's blog.

Observations and Interviews

1. Spend a half day at a school at the level you plan to teach, recording your impressions about the degree to which teachers hold students accountable for meeting high academic standards. How do teachers convey their standards or expectations for student learning?
2. As a collaborative project, conduct an informal survey of what people think about retaining elementary, middle, and secondary students at their current grade level as a solution to the dilemma of

what to do with students who do not meet standards for promotion. Do you note any differences at the three levels of schooling?

Professional Portfolio

Prepare a catalog of interactive multimedia resources and materials in a curricular area of interest. For each entry, include an annotation that briefly describes the resource materials, how teachers might use them, and where they may be obtained. As with the selection of any curriculum materials, try to find evidence of effectiveness, such as results of field tests, published reviews of educational software, awards, or testimonials from educators.

CHAPTER QUIZ

Take this quiz to check your understanding of the content covered in this chapter.

CHAPTER TWELVE

Assessing Student Learning

learning outcomes

After reading this chapter, you will be able to do the following:

1. Explain the role of assessment in teaching.
2. Explain how standardized assessments are used in education.
3. Explain how "high-stakes" tests are part of the current push for accountability in education.
4. Describe several approaches to assessing students' learning.
5. Describe several emerging trends in classroom assessment.
6. Explain how teachers develop high-quality classroom assessments.

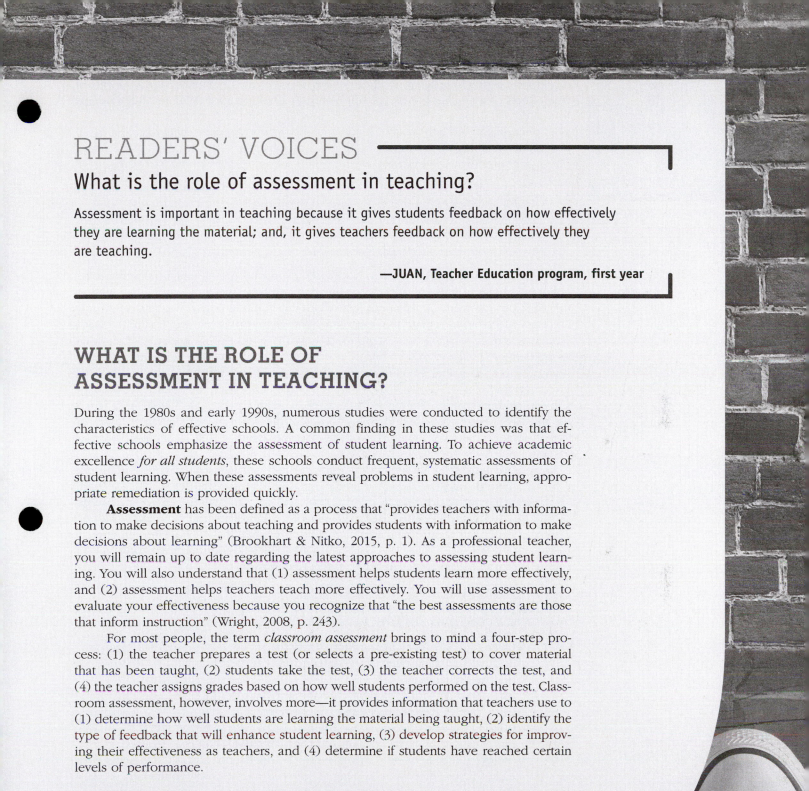

READERS' VOICES

What is the role of assessment in teaching?

Assessment is important in teaching because it gives students feedback on how effectively they are learning the material; and, it gives teachers feedback on how effectively they are teaching.

—**JUAN, Teacher Education program, first year**

WHAT IS THE ROLE OF ASSESSMENT IN TEACHING?

During the 1980s and early 1990s, numerous studies were conducted to identify the characteristics of effective schools. A common finding in these studies was that effective schools emphasize the assessment of student learning. To achieve academic excellence *for all students*, these schools conduct frequent, systematic assessments of student learning. When these assessments reveal problems in student learning, appropriate remediation is provided quickly.

Assessment has been defined as a process that "provides teachers with information to make decisions about teaching and provides students with information to make decisions about learning" (Brookhart & Nitko, 2015, p. 1). As a professional teacher, you will remain up to date regarding the latest approaches to assessing student learning. You will also understand that (1) assessment helps students learn more effectively, and (2) assessment helps teachers teach more effectively. You will use assessment to evaluate your effectiveness because you recognize that "the best assessments are those that inform instruction" (Wright, 2008, p. 243).

For most people, the term *classroom assessment* brings to mind a four-step process: (1) the teacher prepares a test (or selects a pre-existing test) to cover material that has been taught, (2) students take the test, (3) the teacher corrects the test, and (4) the teacher assigns grades based on how well students performed on the test. Classroom assessment, however, involves more—it provides information that teachers use to (1) determine how well students are learning the material being taught, (2) identify the type of feedback that will enhance student learning, (3) develop strategies for improving their effectiveness as teachers, and (4) determine if students have reached certain levels of performance.

Challenges of Assessing Students' Learning

Assessing students' learning is not as straightforward as one might imagine. First, it is difficult to assess with 100 percent accuracy everything that students actually learn as a result of being taught. The ultimate purpose of teaching is to lead the student to a greater understanding of the things and ideas of this world. However, a moment's reflection on our own experiences reminds us that it is difficult, perhaps impossible,

Watch as these educators explain how they incorporate assessment into their classrooms.

to determine precisely what another person does or does not understand. Moreover, "the effects of a teacher's work are still maturing a half-century or more after students' formal education is completed" (Joyce, Weil, & Calhoun, 2015, p. xix).

Second, although the outcomes of teaching may be specified with exacting detail, one of the realities of teaching is that some of what students learn may be beyond direct measurement. For example, a junior high school teacher points out that

> There is no clear end result. . . . That frustrates me. I want so badly for my joy [of teaching] to be neatly tied up so that I can look at it admiringly. . . . I want so badly to see my successes—I don't know, give me certificates or badges or jelly beans. Then I can stack them up, count them, and rate myself as a teacher. (Henry, Huntley, McKamey, Harper, 1995, pp. 68–69)

In spite of continued emphasis on statewide testing programs that hold schools accountable for students' performance, the conventional wisdom among teachers is that they are often uncertain about just what their students learn. We have enormous amounts of assessment data, but very little knowledge of what lies behind a child's written response, or little understanding of how the child experiences the curriculum. As one educational researcher concludes: "The inaccessibility of data is similar both in science and in learning. We cannot directly 'see' subatomic particles, nor can we 'see' the inner-workings of the mind and emotions of the child. Both are inferential: both are subject to human interpretation" (Costa, 1984, p. 202). On the one hand, then, teachers must recognize their limited ability to determine what students actually learn; on the other, they must continuously work to become aware of the latest approaches to assessing students' learning.

A third challenge of assessing students' learning was suggested by Albert Einstein, a former member of the American Federation of Teachers, when he pointed out that: "Not everything that counts can be counted, and not everything we count, counts" (quoted in Weingarten, spring 2014, p. 1). Similarly, the recipient of the 2011 National Teacher of the Year Award, high school chemistry teacher Michelle Shearer, reminds us that many important learning outcomes cannot be reduced to numerical scores. As she said in her application for the Teacher of the Year Award:

> What should be the basis of teacher accountability? Consider the following examples from my teaching, formatted as the multiple-choice question, *"Which of the following is the best evidence of effective teaching?"*
>
> A. Over the past three years, Mrs. Shearer's AP chemistry students have achieved passage rates of 91%, 91%, and 88% percent (with 100% student participation).
> B. Mrs. Shearer's former student, a 2000 graduate, recently earned his Ph.D. from Yale University in biophysical chemistry and is currently exploring options for teaching science at the high school and college levels.
> C. Mrs. Shearer's 2005 class of deaf and hard-of-hearing students, identified as "below grade," frequently arrived at class before the bell and asked to begin early because they were so eager to see what awaited them in the lab.
> D. Five of Mrs. Shearer's seniors asked to return *after* graduation to participate in the post-AP exam lab activities.
> E. A minority student hesitant to take AP Chemistry considered her final "B" average one of her greatest personal achievements, one that gave her the confidence to attend college to pursue a scientific major.
> F. All of the above.
>
> (*Correct answer:* F!)
>
> Numerical data [are] concrete, objective, and easily communicated, yet teacher accountability for student success cannot be tied solely to test scores. I am accountable not only for my students' AP scores, but also for fostering habits of mind such as creativity, innovation, problem-solving, and skills essential to success in college and careers. I am accountable for

ensuring students' self-confidence, independence, resilience, perseverance, and traits essential to success in *life*. . . . Teaching is too complex and awesome a task for any simple measure of accountability . . . (Shearer, 2011)

HOW ARE STANDARDIZED ASSESSMENTS USED IN EDUCATION?

Standardized assessments (or standardized tests) are pencil-and-paper tests that are taken by large groups of students and scored in a uniform manner. The test items, conditions under which students take the test, how the tests are scored, and how the scores are interpreted are standardized for all who take the test. This standardization enables educators to compare scores for different groups of students in different schools around the country. Standardized assessments are administered at the district, state, and national levels.

The first standardized test in the United States was administered by Horace Mann (1796–1859) in the mid-1800s. Mann, who eventually came to be known as the "father of the common school," wanted to classify students by ability and gather evidence for the effectiveness of the state school system. He hoped to use the results of the state test to further his educational reform efforts. Prior to the use of this standardized test, teachers conducted their own assessments at the individual classroom level.

Current examples of standardized tests are the Iowa Test of Basic Skills, California Achievement Test, Metropolitan Achievement Tests, the Stanford Achievement Test, the Scholastic Assessment Test (SAT), and the ACT Assessment (ACT). In addition, the federal government funds the National Assessment of Educational Progress (NAEP). Periodically, the NAEP is used to sample student achievement around the country. On a biannual basis, the performance of national samples of 9-, 13-, and 17-year-olds is assessed. Educational policymakers then use the results—reported by geographic region, gender, and ethnic background—to guide their decision making. First administered in 1969, the NAEP has assessed student learning in all areas of the curriculum.

INTERNATIONAL ASSESSMENTS

In 1991, the first **International Assessment of Educational Progress (IAEP)** was conducted, and the achievement of U.S. students was compared to that of students in more than 30 nations. The results indicated that the achievement levels of U.S. students were often below those of students from other countries. The United States also participates in several other international assessments—for example, the **Trends in International Mathematics and Science Study (TIMSS)** and the **Progress in International Reading Literacy Study (PIRLS)**, both conducted by the International Association for the Evaluation of Educational Achievement (IEA).

In 2012, U.S. students participated in the **Program for International Student Assessment (PISA)**, an assessment of 15-year-olds' performance in reading, mathematics, and science. PISA is conducted every 3 years by the 34 member countries of the Organization for Economic Cooperation and Development (OECD). PISA 2012 results included assessments from OECD members and 31 "partner" countries and economies.

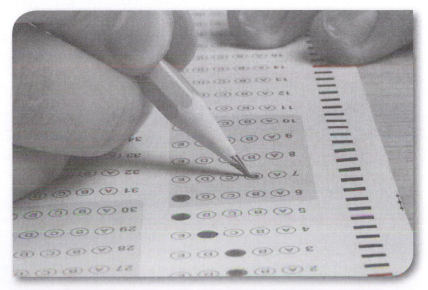

How can teachers best prepare students to take important standardized assessment tests?

PISA 2012 results (see Figure 12.1) show the mean scores of students in mathematics, reading, and science. The figure shows that U.S. students' scores were below the OECD mean in mathematics (481 compared to 494) and science (497 compared to 501). U.S. students' scores were slightly above the OECD mean in reading (498 compared to 496). The figure also shows that, in mathematics, the U.S. share (percentage) of "low achievers" was higher than the OECD average, whereas the share of "high achievers" was lower than the OECD average. Last, the figure shows that the scores of the top three countries/economies (Shanghai—China, Singapore, and Hong Kong—China) were significantly higher compared to those received during their earliest participation in PISA.

Since the publication of *A Nation at Risk* in 1983, there has been an unbroken trend for the media and some observers of U.S. education to decry the perceived poor performance of U.S. students on international comparisons of achievement. A closer examination of international comparisons, however, reveals the seldom-reported fact that the United States' position in country-by-country rankings is based on *aggregate* achievement scores—in other words, achievement scores of all students are used to make the comparisons. Not taken into account is the United States' commitment to educating all students—not just the academically able or those from home environments that encourage education. For example, *50 Myths and Lies That Threaten America's Public Schools: The Real Crisis in Education* points out that

> the modest U.S. national average [on international tests] is reasonably attributed to a child poverty rate . . . that exceeds 20%—considerably higher than comparable countries. . . . In the United States, if we looked only at the students who attend schools where child poverty rates are under 10%, we would rank as the number one country in the world, outscoring countries like Finland, Japan, and Korea. (Berliner & Glass, 2014, p. 15)

50 Myths and Lies includes the following additional points, suggesting that international comparisons of achievement should be made very cautiously, if at all:

- Comparing achievement across countries is very different from comparing Olympic rankings.
- Trends in International Mathematics and Science Study (TIMMS) tests use the metric system, not the imperial system used in the United States.
- Translation issues make it unlikely that achievement tests written in different languages have the same level of cognitive difficulty.
- Contrary to popular belief, the United States has never led the world on international achievement tests; the relative ranking of U.S. students has changed little since international assessments began.
- International test scores do not reflect the quality of a nation's educational system; nor do they predict future national prosperity.
- During the 1970s, the United States was one of four nations that decided their students would not be allowed to use calculators on the TIMMS tests.

NORM-REFERENCED ASSESSMENTS

Some standardized assessments are norm-referenced—that is, students' scores are compared with scores of other students who are similar. The comparison group of students, called the *norm group*, is usually from the same age group and grade level. An individual student's score is then compared to the average, or mean, score for the total group. Norm-referenced tests are used to determine where a student is compared to the typical performance of other students at the same age and grade level. Thus, **norm-referenced assessments** enable teachers to rank students in terms of their achievement.

To understand the meaning of scores on a norm-referenced assessment, imagine that a student received a total of 75 points on a 100-point norm-referenced assessment. If the mean, or average, score for the comparison group of students was also 75, the student would be at the 50th percentile. That is, 50 percent of the students in the comparison

Countries/economies with a mean performance/share of top performers above the OECD average
Countries/economies with a share of low achievers below the OECD average

Countries/economies with a mean performance/share of low achievers/share of top performers not statistically significantly different from the OECD average

Countries/economies with a mean performance/share of top performers below the OECD average
Countries/economies with a share of low achievers above the OECD average

	Mathematics				Reading		Science	
	Mean score in PISA 2012	Share of low achievers in mathematics (Below Level 2)	Share of top performers in mathematics (Level 5 or 6)	Annualized change in score points	Mean score in PISA 2012	Annualized change in score points	Mean score in PISA 2012	Annualized change in score points
OECD average	494	23.0	12.6	−0.3	496	0.3	501	0.5
Shanghai–China	613	3.8	55.4	4.2	570	4.6	580	1.8
Singapore	573	8.3	40.0	3.8	542	5.4	551	3.3
Hong Kong–China	561	8.5	33.7	1.3	545	2.3	555	2.1
Chinese Taipei	560	12.8	37.2	1.7	523	4.5	523	−1.5
Korea	554	9.1	30.9	1.1	536	0.9	538	2.6
Macao–China	538	10.8	24.3	1.0	509	0.8	521	1.6
Japan	536	11.1	23.7	0.4	538	1.5	547	2.6
Liechtenstein	535	14.1	24.8	0.3	516	1.3	525	0.4
Switzerland	531	12.4	21.4	0.6	509	1.0	515	0.6
Netherlands	523	14.8	19.3	−1.6	511	−0.1	522	−0.5
Estonia	521	10.5	14.6	0.9	516	2.4	541	1.5
Finland	519	12.3	15.3	−2.8	524	−1.7	545	−3.0
Canada	518	13.8	16.4	−1.4	523	−0.9	525	−1.5
Poland	518	14.4	16.7	2.6	518	2.8	526	4.6
Belgium	515	19.0	19.5	−1.6	509	0.1	505	−0.9
Germany	514	17.7	17.5	1.4	508	1.8	524	1.4
Viet Nam	511	14.2	13.3	m	508	m	528	m
Austria	506	18.7	14.3	0.0	490	−0.2	506	−0.8
Australia	504	19.7	14.8	−2.2	512	−1.4	521	−0.9
Ireland	501	16.9	10.7	−0.6	523	−0.9	522	2.3
Slovenia	501	20.1	13.7	−0.6	481	−2.2	514	−0.8
Denmark	500	16.8	10.0	−1.8	496	0.1	498	0.4
New Zealand	500	22.6	15.0	−2.5	512	−1.1	516	−2.5
Czech Republic	499	21.0	12.9	−2.5	493	−0.5	508	−1.0
France	495	22.4	12.9	−1.5	505	0.0	499	0.6
United Kingdom	494	21.8	11.8	−0.3	499	0.7	514	−0.1
Iceland	493	21.5	11.2	−2.2	483	−1.3	478	−2.0
Latvia	491	19.9	8.0	0.5	489	1.9	502	2.0
Luxembourg	490	24.3	11.2	−0.3	488	0.7	491	0.9
Norway	489	22.3	9.4	−0.3	504	0.1	495	1.3
Portugal	487	24.9	10.6	2.8	488	1.6	489	2.5
Italy	485	24.7	9.9	2.7	490	0.5	494	3.0
Spain	484	23.6	8.0	0.1	488	−0.3	496	1.3
Russian Federation	482	24.0	7.8	1.1	475	1.1	486	1.0
Slovak Republic	482	27.5	11.0	−1.4	463	−0.1	471	−2.7

(continued)

FIGURE 12.1 2012 program for international student assessment (PISA): Snapshot of performance in mathematics, reading and science (*continued*)

	Mathematics				Reading		Science	
	Mean score in PISA 2012	Share of low achievers in mathematics (Below Level 2)	Share of top performers in mathematics (Level 5 or 6)	Annualized change in score points	Mean score in PISA 2012	Annualized change in score points	Mean score in PISA 2012	Annualized change in score points
United States	481	25.8	8.8	0.3	498	−0.3	497	1.4
Lithuania	479	26.0	8.1	−1.4	477	1.1	496	1.3
Sweden	478	27.1	8.0	−3.3	483	−2.8	485	−3.1
Hungary	477	28.1	9.3	−1.3	488	1.0	494	−1.6
Croatia	471	29.9	7.0	0.6	485	1.2	491	−0.3
Israel	466	33.5	9.4	4.2	486	3.7	470	2.8
Greece	453	35.7	3.9	1.1	477	0.5	467	−1.1
Serbia	449	38.9	4.6	2.2	446	7.6	445	1.5
Turkey	448	42.0	5.9	3.2	475	4.1	463	6.4
Romania	445	40.8	3.2	4.9	438	1.1	439	3.4
Cyprus[1,2]	440	42.0	3.7	m	449	m	438	m
Bulgaria	439	43.8	4.1	4.2	436	0.4	446	2.0
United Arab Emirates	434	46.3	3.5	m	442	m	448	m
Kazakhstan	432	45.2	0.9	9.0	393	0.8	425	8.1
Thailand	427	49.7	2.6	1.0	441	1.1	444	3.9
Chile	423	51.5	1.6	1.9	441	3.1	445	1.1
Malaysia	421	51.8	1.3	8.1	398	−7.8	420	−1.4
Mexico	413	54.7	0.6	3.1	424	1.1	415	0.9
Montenegro	410	56.6	1.0	1.7	422	5.0	410	−0.3
Uruguay	409	55.8	1.4	−1.4	411	−1.8	416	−2.1
Costa Rica	407	59.9	0.6	−1.2	441	−1.0	429	−0.6
Albania	394	60.7	0.8	5.6	394	4.1	397	2.2
Brazil	391	67.1	0.8	4.1	410	1.2	405	2.3
Argentina	388	66.5	0.3	1.2	396	−1.6	406	2.4
Tunisia	388	67.7	0.8	3.1	404	3.8	398	2.2
Jordan	386	68.6	0.6	0.2	399	−0.3	409	−2.1
Colombia	376	73.8	0.3	1.1	403	3.0	399	1.8
Qatar	376	69.6	2.0	9.2	388	12.0	384	5.4
Indonesia	375	75.7	0.3	0.7	396	2.3	382	−1.9
Peru	368	74.6	0.6	1.0	384	5.2	373	1.3

[1] Footnote by Turkey: The information in this document with reference to "Cyprus" relates to the southern part of the Island. There is no single authority representing both Turkish and Greek Cypriot people on the Island. Turkey recognizes the Turkish Republic of Northern Cyprus (TRNC). Until a lasting and equitable solution is found within the context of the United Nations, Turkey shall preserve its position concerning the "Cyprus issue."

[2] Footnote by all the European Union Member States of the OECD and the European Union: The Republic of Cyprus is recognized by all members of the United Nations with the exception of Turkey. The information in this document relates to the area under the effective control of the Government of the Republic of Cyprus.

The annualized change is the average annual change in PISA score points from a country's/economy's earliest participation in PISA to PISA 2012. It is calculated taking into account all of a country's/economy's participation in PISA.

Countries and economies are ranked in descending order of the mean mathematics score in PISA 2012.

Note: Countries/economies in which the annualized change in performance is statistically significant are marked in bold.

Source: OECD (2014), PISA 2012 Results in Focus: What 15-Year-Olds Know And What They Can Do With What They Know, http://www.oecd.org/pisa/keyfindings/pisa-2012-results-overview.pdf.

group scored higher, and 50 percent scored lower. However, if the mean score for the comparison group was 90, the student would be in the 30th percentile. That is, 70 percent of the students in the comparison group scored higher, and 30 percent scored lower.

The preceding example can also be used to illustrate how scores on norm-referenced tests should be interpreted carefully. Norm-referenced test scores can be misused. If the student scored in the 30th percentile, it would be a mistake to assume that the score is evidence that the student is doing poorly. The student might not have done well on the material covered by the norm-referenced assessment; however, the student might be doing quite well in other areas not included in the test. Four examples of norm-referenced interpretations of students' performance follow:

1. Alfredo won the 1-mile race.
2. On the test of basic skills, Jiling's scores were near the average.
3. On the chemistry test given district-wide, our school had the best scores.
4. On the test of physical fitness, Susan was in the 90th percentile.

CRITERION-REFERENCED ASSESSMENTS

Other standardized assessments are criterion-referenced—that is, students' learning is compared with clearly defined criteria or standards rather than the performance of other students. **Criterion-referenced assessments** do not indicate what is average or typical for students from the same age group and grade level. Criterion-referenced assessments indicate what students know and can do within a specific subject area. Students' scores are not compared with the scores of other groups of students.

A teacher might use a criterion-referenced assessment to assess a student's ability to calculate the square root of a number, to write a well-organized paragraph, or to type 60 words per minute on a computer keyboard. In other words, the assessment is made with reference to an instructional objective, rather than the performance of other students on the assessment. Similarly, the student's score is interpreted without reference to how other students performed. Following are four examples of criterion-referenced interpretations of students' performance:

1. In the chemistry lab, Mary can light a Bunsen burner correctly.
2. Juan can identify each element on a periodic table.
3. Yiming can calculate the sine, cosine, and tangent of angles.
4. Using a map of the world, Lashandra can identify the countries that were involved in World War II.

WHAT ARE "HIGH-STAKES" TESTS AND ACCOUNTABILITY?

Today's schools and teachers are held accountable for students' mastery of state-mandated educational standards. As part of this push for **accountability**, some states—Florida and South Carolina, for example—rank schools on how well their students learn. In **FLORIDA**, schools are graded from A through F. A school's grade determines if the school receives supplemental funding, if a change in principals is necessary, if students can transfer out, or if the school can be closed. In 2010, school superintendents across Florida asked the state Department of Education to hold off on issuing school grades, as they had concerns about the validity of that year's Florida Comprehensive Assessment Test (FCAT) scores. As the chief executive officer (CEO) of the Florida Association of District School Superintendents stated: "Simply put, we all need to have confidence in an assessment system that has so many consequences, and at this point, we do not" (McGrory, August 5, 2010).

SOUTH CAROLINA'S School Report Cards rate schools as either *Excellent, Good, Average, Below Average,* or *At-Risk.* An "Average" rating means a district or school meets the standard that "all students graduate with the knowledge and skills necessary to compete successfully in the global economy, participate in a democratic society, and contribute positively as members of families and communities." Report Cards also contain Growth Ratings that compare student test scores from one year to the next.

Every state has mandated a standardized test to assess students' mastery of academic standards, and most districts are assisting schools in bringing standards-based reform into classrooms. As a result of standards-based reforms at the state level, *how* and *what* teachers teach is changing, and in many cases student achievement is increasing. This chapter's Teachers' Voices: Walk in My Shoes profiles a **WASHINGTON** State teacher who, each year, prepares her students to take the state's standardized test.

High-Stakes Testing

Testing students to assess their learning is not new. However, state-mandated tests often have high-stakes consequences for students, teachers, and administrators. For example, performance on **high-stakes tests** may determine whether a student can participate in extracurricular activities or graduate, or whether teachers and administrators are given merit pay increases.

Approximately seven out of ten public school students in the U.S. are affected by high school exit exams. Figure 12.2 shows that twenty-four states required members of the Class of 2014 to pass comprehensive exit exams or end-of-course exams to receive a high school diploma. Figure 12.2 also shows that nine states used high school tests as a portion of students' final course grades, and six states planned, as of 2012, to eliminate their exit exam policy in the future. In many states that have exit exams, students who do not pass the exam can take an alternative route to obtain a standard diploma. For example, students in the following states can take an alternative route to obtain a diploma:

Massachusetts—Students with an Individual Education Program (IEP) can submit a portfolio of work that displays knowledge and skills at grade-level expectations for a 10th grader.

Alaska and Oklahoma—Students with disabilities can submit a portfolio of their work.

Maryland and Nevada—Students who have repeatedly failed the state exit exam may use the portfolio option.

Oregon—Students can submit a "collection of evidence" instead of state assessments to fulfill the Essential Skills component of the state graduation requirements.

CONSEQUENCES OF HIGH-STAKES TESTS

At the conclusion of the 2009–2010 school year, 25 states withheld high school diplomas based on exit exams. Exit exams result in approximately 35,000–70,000 more dropouts each year (Urbina, 2010). For 12th graders who must pass a high school exit exam and have no alternate pathway to a high school diploma, the dropout rate increases by about 23 percent. For African American 12th graders, this rate increases to more than 50 percent for boys and 65 percent for girls (Hemelt & Marcotte, 2013, p. 346).

In **CALIFORNIA**, 17 percent of students in 2011 failed the required English language arts exit exam on the first attempt, and 16 percent failed the mathematics exam (Center on Education Policy, September 2012). In **FLORIDA**, hundreds of seniors from the class of 2009 who failed the Florida Comprehensive Assessment Test (FCAT), a requirement for graduation, transferred their high school credits to North Atlantic Regional High School in Lewiston, **MAINE**, where there is no FCAT exit exam. The Florida students thus received a standard high school diploma from the accredited, state-authorized high school in Maine (PRWeb, 2009). And, in **MASSACHUSETTS**, diplomas were withheld from 2,500 seniors in 2011 who failed to pass the Massachusetts Comprehensive Assessment System (MCAS) exam in science (Vaznis, July 26, 2011).

In some cases, the large numbers of students who failed the exams prompted states to modify their requirements. **ALABAMA**, **ARIZONA**, and **WASHINGTON** delayed the start of the exit exam requirement in 2008 and lowered standards after seeing that many students, including a disproportionate number of minorities, would fail the tests (Urbina, 2010).

FIGURE 12.2   Past, Present, and Future: State High School Exit Exams

THEN (Class of 2012)	NOW (Class of 2014)	FUTURE
25 states have an exit exam requirement	**24 states** have an exit exam requirement	**As many as 21 states** could have an exit exam requirement
Alabama, Alaska, *Arkansas*, Arizona, California, Florida, Georgia, Idaho, Indiana, Louisiana, Maryland, Massachusetts, Minnesota, Mississippi, Nevada, New Jersey, New Mexico, New York, Ohio, Oklahoma, Oregon, South Carolina, Texas, Virginia, Washington	*Alabama, Alaska, Arizona,* California, Florida, Georgia, Idaho, Indiana, Louisiana, Maryland, Massachusetts, *Minnesota,* Mississippi, Nevada, New Jersey, New Mexico, New York, Ohio, Oklahoma, Oregon, *South Carolina,* Texas, Virginia, Washington	California, **Connecticut**, Florida, Idaho, Indiana, Louisiana, Maryland, Massachusetts, Mississippi, Nevada, New Jersey, New Mexico, New York, Ohio, Oklahoma, Oregon, **Pennsylvania, Rhode Island**, Texas, Virginia, Washington
14 states plan to maintain an exit exam requirement after adopting Common Core	**9 states** use high school tests as a portion of students' final course grades	**At least 11 states** plan to use high school tests as a portion of students' final course grades
Arizona, Arkansas, California, Florida, Idaho, Louisiana, Massachusetts, Mississippi, Nevada, New Mexico, New York, Oklahoma, Oregon	Florida, Kentucky, Louisiana, Missouri, North Carolina, Pennsylvania, South Carolina, Tennessee, *Texas*	**Alabama, Arizona**, Florida, **Georgia**, Kentucky, Louisiana, Missouri, North Carolina, Pennsylvania, South Carolina, Tennessee
2 states plan to eliminate an exit exam requirement		**7 states** will have eliminated an exit exam requirement
Alabama, Georgia		Alabama, Alaska, Arizona, Arkansas, Georgia, Minnesota, South Carolina
6 states undecided on a future exit exam requirement after adopting Common Core		
Indiana, Maryland, New Jersey, Ohio, South Carolina, Washington		

Notes: Italicized states are those that plan to eliminate their policy in the future, while states in bold are those that plan to adopt the policy for the first time in the future. Georgia is eliminating all of its exit exams, with the exception of its comprehensive writing test.

Source: 2011–12 data are from the Center on Education Policy's 2012 state survey "State High School Exit Exams: A Policy in Transition." Questions about states' exit exam plans related to Common Core did not include states that had not adopted the standards (e.g., Texas). Newer data are from a New America analysis, which does not include state surveys but is inclusive of all 50 states, plus Washington, D.C.

HIGH-STAKES TESTS AND EDUCATOR ACCOUNTABILITY

For teachers and administrators, test results are frequently linked to merit rewards, increased funding, or sanctions. Some states and large school districts provide additional funds for high-performing schools or bonuses for educators at those schools. For example, **CALIFORNIA** has several merit-based incentive programs for teachers, schools, and administrators, including the Governor's Performance Awards that give money to schools based on their academic performance index. Similarly, the **NEW YORK** City school system gives bonuses of up to $15,000 to principals and other administrators whose schools show significant gains on test scores. School system administrators group schools into three performance categories—low, middle, and high—taking into account students' economic circumstances. For high schools, factors such as dropout rates are also used.

On the other hand, schools and even entire districts that do poorly on tests can be taken over by the state or in some cases closed. Currently, 26 states allow full state control of low-performing schools or districts (State Policy Report Card, 2014). Several of those states allow students to leave low-performing schools, taking their proportional amount of state funding aid with them. A few of these states directly punish

TEACHERS' VOICES
Walk in My Shoes
Kathy Addleman
Eastmont High School
Wenatchee, **WASHINGTON**

low-performing schools by taking aid away from them. Whereas some states use test scores as one of several accountability indicators, many rely solely on scores.

Testing can also have significant consequences when schools are ranked according to how well they attain a state or district's performance goals. Usually, school rankings are reported in relation to schools of similar size and demographics because test results are closely linked to students' economic backgrounds, with the lowest scores often earned by schools that serve the neediest children (Fetler, 2001; Lindjord, 2000).

High-stakes testing and the push to hold teachers accountable for student learning has led many districts and schools to place great emphasis on preparing students for the tests. In fact, critics assert that the curricular emphasis in schools is shifting from academic content to test preparation. Many teachers feel compelled to teach to the test, or to emphasize item teaching rather than curriculum teaching.

FOCUS ON DIVERSITY: UNINTENTIONAL CONSEQUENCES OF HIGH-STAKES TESTS

An unintended consequence of high-stakes tests is that they place too much emphasis on differences in achievement (often termed the "achievement gap") between White students and students who are Black, Latina/Latino, Native American, English language learners (ELL), or from low-income families. High-stakes tests can also unfairly highlight achievement differences between students who attend "resource-rich" schools and those who attend "resource-poor" schools. Moreover, "tests reinforce the social status quo, and to focus on them exclusively runs the risk of freezing the existing social order, injustices, inequities, exclusivities, and the prevailing power distribution of the here and now into the future" (English, 2010, p. 107).

The Center on Education Policy's 2010 analysis of high school exit exams found that they "have a negative impact on certain student populations, such as low-performing students, students of color, or students from low-income families" (Center on Education Policy, 2010, p. 6). Similarly, one study found that Black and Hispanic students as well as students from low-income families were more likely to drop out after "barely failing" on their first attempt to pass the **NEW JERSEY** High School Proficiency Assessment (HSPA) exam (Ou, 2009).

Some researchers are critical of high-stakes tests and how they lead to a narrow emphasis on test score differences among students from different groups. Instead, they urge educators to move beyond "gap gazing" to emphasize effective teaching strategies for students of color and students from low-income families (Gutierrez, 2008; Matthews, 2008; Rodriguez, 2001). In an article titled "A 'Gap-Gazing' Fetish in Mathematics Education? Problematizing Research on the Achievement Gap," Gutierrez (2008, p. 362) calls for the following changes:

- Less research that documents the achievement gap
- Less research that identifies causes of the achievement gap
- Less research that focuses on single variables to predict student success
- More research on effective teaching and learning environments for Black, Latina/Latino, First Nations, English language learning, and working-class students, plus richer descriptions of those environments, including their origins and development
- More focus on making that research accessible to and usable by practitioners

Clearly, the debate over the effectiveness and consequences of high-stakes tests based on state-mandated standards will continue for some time. However, professional teachers understand that participating in these programs is only part of their assessment responsibility—they must develop high-quality classroom assessments for day-to-day use in the classroom. The ability to develop and implement high-quality assessments of students' learning is a fundamental part of professional accountability for today's teachers. Teachers must know whether their methods of assessing students' learning are, in fact, enhancing students' ability to learn.

FIGURE 12.3   Effective classroom assessment

Goal of Assessment	Method of Assessment	Evaluation	Use	Feedback
How will this assessment contribute to my students' ability to learn or my ability to teach them?	How will I gather this information?	What standards and criteria will I use to interpret the results of my assessments or observations?	How will I use the results?	What feedback will I give students? Parents?

Quantitative Measurement?   Qualitative Observation?

Formative Evaluation?   Summative Evaluation?

WHAT METHODS WILL YOU USE TO ASSESS STUDENT LEARNING?

Figure 12.3 illustrates the essential elements of effective classroom assessment and the questions that will guide your decision making in this important area of teaching. Assessment-related decisions require an understanding of the following: formal and informal assessments, qualitative and quantitative assessments, measurement and evaluation, and formative and summative evaluation.

Formal and Informal Assessments

Assessment of student learning can be both formal and informal. **Formal assessments** are developed prior to having students complete the assessments. Formal assessments include final exams, tests, and quizzes on subject matter studied; in-class seatwork and homework; and critiques of performances, for example, tryouts for a school play or athletic team.

Informal assessments occur during teaching, and they are made spontaneously. You might, for example, note students' facial expressions to determine their level of understanding of the material taught, listen carefully to a student's explanation of how she solved a problem in mathematics, or ask questions to monitor students' level of understanding during a lecture. Teachers frequently make informal assessments of their students at the beginning of each school day or class session.

Informal assessments are less obvious to the classroom observer. In other words, during a classroom observation, an observer may not know just when a teacher is making

What type of assessment might this teacher be using?

PROFESSIONAL REFLECTION

Watch as educators discuss what they learn from observing in classrooms.

informal assessments of student learning. Actually, professional teachers continuously assess students' responses to their teaching.

Quantitative and Qualitative Assessment

To assess student learning, you can use both quantitative and qualitative approaches. Quantitative approaches make use of measurement and evaluation techniques—such as teacher-made classroom tests comprised of multiple-choice, true/false, matching, or essay items—or performance-based assessments. **Quantitative assessments** yield numerical scores that teachers use to evaluate student learning as well as the effectiveness of their teaching.

Qualitative approaches may include formal and informal observations of students' performance on various learning tasks, the manner with which they approach those learning tasks, or students' self-reports of their interests and attitudes. For example, teachers routinely assess students' **work habits**. *Work habits* is a term suggested by the Coalition of Essential Schools for various dispositions important for effective thinking and learning, including reading with curiosity; reflecting critically on one's own work; developing independence, clarity, and incisiveness of thought; willingness to work hard; an ability to manage time effectively; persistence; accuracy and precision; and working collaboratively. **Qualitative assessments** are more subjective than quantitative assessments. However, quantitative assessments are also subjective because teachers must interpret the meaning of the scores.

Measurement and Evaluation

To assess student learning, you will use measurement and evaluation techniques. **Measurement** is the gathering of quantitative data related to the knowledge and skills students have acquired. Measurement yields scores, rankings, or ratings that teachers can use to determine the degree to which students have attained specified standards. For example, an elementary teacher might use an informal reading inventory test to identify students' strengths and weaknesses in reading.

Evaluation is a critical teaching skill. In your role as an evaluator, you will make judgments about the performance of students and about your own effectiveness as a teacher. **Evaluation** involves making judgments about or assigning a value to measurements the teacher makes of student learning.

Formative and Summative Evaluation

When teachers measure students' attainment of knowledge and skills for the purpose of making decisions about their teaching, they are engaging in **formative evaluation**. Teachers use the results of formative evaluations to make decisions about what learning activities are appropriate for students. For example, as an aid to planning for a new unit of instruction, you may assess students' understanding of a subject by having them take a short diagnostic test or quiz, complete homework or seatwork assignments, or participate in a group project.

As a teacher, you will also conduct informal formative evaluations while you are teaching. For example, you will pay close attention to what students say, you will use probing questions to gauge students' understanding of the subject, and you will note students' facial expressions and behavior. During these informal formative evaluations, you will not only assess students' understanding; you will also assess students' attitudes toward learning the subject. For example, in the following, Amy James, a high school science teacher in **KENTUCKY**, makes some candid comments about how she learned to use informal formative evaluations while teaching:

> When I began teaching, I would teach a concept over one to two weeks assuming that my students were "getting it" along the way and then would

quiz students over that concept. The quiz did very little to inform my instruction, but instead rewarded those students who "got it" and punished those who didn't. . . . Now I am probing constantly for understanding with both formal and informal styles of formative assessment. I give both verbal and written feedback, as opposed to simply grades, so that both the student and I know what they understand and where they are struggling. I have broken units of study into manageable chunks, or specific learning targets, and assess students in a progressive manner on each learning target. Remediation occurs immediately, allowing students to revisit learning targets that they struggle with. This allows for easy differentiation and grouping, focusing on what each individual student needs help with and allowing those students who have reached understanding to delve deeper into the concepts. (quoted in Chappuis, Stiggins, Chappuis, & Arter, 2012, pp. 104–105)

When teachers use measurements to determine grades at the end of a unit, semester, or year and to decide whether students are ready to proceed to the next phase of their education, they are engaging in **summative evaluation**. Summative evaluations usually provide the teacher with an overview of student learning across a broad range of knowledge and skills. Formative evaluations, on the other hand, are usually more focused and cover a narrower range of knowledge and skills. Teachers also use summative evaluations to make changes in their teaching that might be beneficial with the next group of students.

WHAT ARE EMERGING TRENDS IN CLASSROOM ASSESSMENT?

As mentioned at the beginning of this chapter, there is a trend to assess student learning with ever-increasing numbers of tests. More recently, however, new forms of assessment are being used. Innovations in assessment are partly in response to criticisms of the fairness and objectivity of standardized tests, such as the Iowa Test of Basic Skills, the Scholastic Assessment Test (SAT), and the American College Test (ACT). Educators and the public have criticized these tests not only for class and gender bias in their content but also for failing to measure accurately students' true knowledge, skills, and levels of achievement. For all these reasons, educators are increasingly going beyond traditional pencil-and-paper tests, oral questioning, and formal and informal observations. In addition, they are using an array of new assessment tools—individual and small-group projects, portfolios of work, exhibitions, videotaped demonstrations of skills, and community-based activities, to name a few.

Increasingly, teachers are using **alternative assessments**—that is, assessments that "directly measure student performance through 'real-life tasks'" (Kauchak & Eggen, 2012, p. 421). Alternative assessments require that students apply knowledge and skills to solve problems rather than merely regurgitate isolated facts. The following sections examine several forms of alternative assessments: authentic assessment, portfolio assessment, peer assessment, self-assessment, performance-based assessment, alternate assessment, and project-based learning.

AUTHENTIC ASSESSMENT

Authentic assessment (sometimes called *alternative assessment*) requires students to use higher-level thinking skills to perform, create, or solve a real-life problem, not just choose one of several designated responses, as on a multiple-choice test item. A teacher might use authentic assessment to evaluate the quality of individual and small-group projects, videotaped demonstrations of skills, or participation in community-based activities. In science, for example, students might design and conduct an experiment to solve a problem and then explain in writing how they solved the problem.

Authentic assessments require students to solve problems or to work on tasks that approximate as much as possible those they will encounter beyond the classroom. For example, **authentic assessment** might allow students to select projects on which they will be evaluated, such as writing a brochure, making a map, creating a recipe, writing and directing a play, critiquing a performance, inventing a working machine, producing a video, creating a model, writing a children's book, and so on. In addition, authentic assessment encourages students to develop their own responses to problem situations by allowing them to decide what information is relevant and how that information should be organized and used.

When teachers use authentic assessment to determine what students have learned—and the depth to which they have learned—student achievement and attitudes toward learning improve. For example, a study of 11 pairs of K–12 science and math teachers found that when teachers assess student learning in real-life problem-solving situations, learning and attitudes toward school improve (Appalachia Educational Laboratory, 1993). Similarly, a synthesis of research on successfully restructured schools (Newmann & Wehlage, 1995) revealed that teachers in those schools emphasized authentic assessment. Their assessments focused on students' ability to think; develop in-depth understanding; and apply academic learning to important, realistic problems.

Watch as educators explain how authentic assessments are used in their classrooms.

PORTFOLIO ASSESSMENT

Portfolio assessment is based on a collection of student work that "offers an ideal way to assess final mastery, effort, reflection, and growth in learning. In sum, it tells the learner's story of achievement" (Borich, 2014, p. 405). In short, a portfolio provides examples of important work undertaken by a student, and it represents that student's best work. For example, a high school physics student might include in a portfolio (1) a written report of a physics lab experiment illustrating how vector principles and Newton's laws explain the motion of objects in two dimensions, (2) photographs of that experiment in progress, (3) a certificate of merit received at a local science fair, and (4) an annotated list of Internet sites related to vector principles and Newton's laws. For students, an important part of **portfolio assessment** is clarifying the criteria used to select work to be included in the portfolio, and then organizing and presenting that work for the teacher to assess.

There are three types of portfolios:

1. A *working portfolio* represents works in progress. It serves as a depository for student accomplishments that are on the way to being selected and polished for a more permanent assessment or display portfolio.
2. A student selects his or her best works from a working portfolio for a *display* or *show portfolio*. With the aid of the teacher, the student learns to critically judge the works, focusing on those qualities that make some stand above others.
3. An *assessment portfolio* may contain all or some of the selections in a display portfolio as well as some of those that began in a working portfolio. Although the purpose of the working portfolio is to develop good products and the purpose of the display portfolio is to show off finished products, some of the contents of these collections are often used for the purpose of assessment. The teacher, therefore, is the primary audience of the assessment (Borich, 2014, p. 405).

As students prepare portfolios, four general guidelines should be followed to maximize the learning that results from their involvement in the process of portfolio development:

1. Have students individualize their portfolios—that is, portfolios should focus on the attainment of instructional goals that are important and meaningful for the students.
2. Portfolios should focus on students' accomplishments, their best work—not on their mistakes or limitations.
3. Portfolios should be collaboratively evaluated by teacher and students.
4. Use students' portfolios to discuss their progress with parents, counselors, and other teachers.

Watch how one teacher incorporates portfolios in her classroom.

Among the states that require exit exams to graduate from high school, several also require that students present a portfolio. **OHIO** has replaced the Ohio Graduation Test (OGT) with a three-part assessment system that, beginning with the 2014–2015 school year, will require high school students to complete a senior portfolio project. Similarly, **RHODE ISLAND** has a new exit exam policy that, in addition to state assessments in reading and math and completion of required coursework, requires that students complete exhibitions and portfolios.

Several states that do not require an exit exam for high school graduation do require a portfolio. For example, **CONNECTICUT** will require a one-credit "demonstration project" beginning with the graduating class of 2018. In **HAWAII**, students working toward receiving an advanced Board of Education Recognition diploma must enroll in a one-credit senior project course that includes a portfolio. And, **SOUTH DAKOTA**'s High School 2025 plan includes opportunities for high school students to complete a relevant and rigorous capstone experience by the end of their senior year, such as an entrepreneurship experience, youth internship, or pre-apprenticeship. Students who complete a senior experience will receive credit for creating a portfolio, product, research paper, and presentation related to the capstone experience.

PEER ASSESSMENT

Peer assessment occurs when students assess one another's work. Typically, peer assessment is done informally during a class session. At times, a student may be more open to accepting critical feedback from a peer than from the teacher. Also, a peer may use a manner of speaking typical of his or her age level (word choice, for example), and it may be easier for another student to understand the feedback. The Teaching on Your Feet feature in this chapter provides an example of how feedback from their peers enabled one teacher's students to understand a concept that they had not understood previously.

In the following, fourth-grade language arts team teachers Jessica Barylski, Audrey Eckert, and Robyn Eidam explain how they modeled for students the process of giving quality feedback during the **peer assessment** process:

> When concluding a writing lesson, we used to have students conduct a peer review of their work with a partner. We would provide them with checklists and tell them to use these checklists, assuming that they would know what to do. While students were giving each other feedback, we would monitor their conversations. We noticed that students simply read their writing pieces to each other and gave very few suggestions to improve their writing because they believed that was what peer review was. . . .
>
> To introduce peer review now, we list the criteria for quality peer feedback. Then we show the students a videotape of ourselves modeling weak and strong examples of peer feedback. Including this component adds a visual model to help the students engage. As students watch the clips, they are looking for the criteria that will help them identify the strong example. After thoroughly discussing each video clip, the students apply the peer feedback criteria to their own writing pieces. . . .

What are some of the advantages of using peer assessment in the classroom?

They took ownership of their peer review process, they followed the peer feedback model and criteria, and they took their time and allowed for corrections. They used constructive criticism and their conversations were more meaningful than in the past. We saw growth and improvement in our students' final writing pieces as well (quoted in Chappuis et al., 2012, pp. 29–30).

SELF-ASSESSMENT

Self-assessment occurs when students assess their own work and their thought processes while completing that work. It has been suggested that "[self-assessment] is the most underused form of classroom assessment but has the most flexibility and power as a combined assessment and learning tool" (Tileston, 2004, p. 99). When students assess their own work, they become more aware of the factors that promote or hinder their learning. Students may, for example, ask assessment questions such as the following: What have I learned as a result of this activity? What problems did I encounter during my learning? How will I overcome these problems in the future?

As a teacher, you should help your students, particularly low-achieving students, develop skills of self-assessment. As the following teacher indicates, once students develop self-assessment skills, their learning can improve dramatically:

The kids are not skilled in what I am trying to get them to do. I think the process is more effective long term. If you invest time in it, it will pay off big dividends, this process of getting the students to be more independent in the way that they learn and to take the responsibility themselves. (Black, Harrison, Lee, Marshall, & Wiliam, 2004, p. 14)

Some teachers have taught students how to assess their work using the analogy of a common traffic light. Students label their work green, yellow, or red based on whether they have good, partial, or little understanding, respectively. The teacher then has the "greens" and the "yellows" meet in small groups to help one another, while the teacher meets with the "reds" to address their learning problems.

PERFORMANCE-BASED ASSESSMENT

Put simply, **performance-based assessment** is based on observation and judgment (Stiggins & Chappuis, 2012). We observe a student perform a task or review a student-produced product, and we judge its quality. We could observe a student's science experiment and judge the quality of the thinking involved, or we could read a student's research report in history and judge the quality of argumentation and writing. Performance assessment is used to determine what students can do as well as what they know. In some cases, the teacher observes and then evaluates an actual performance or application of a skill; in others, the teacher evaluates a product created by the student.

Performance-based assessment focuses on students' ability to apply knowledge, skills, and work habits through the performance of tasks they find meaningful and engaging. Whereas traditional testing helps teachers answer the question, "Do students *know* content?" performance-based assessment helps answer the question, "How well can students *use* what they know?"

Students should find that performance tasks are interesting and relevant to the knowledge, skills, and work habits emphasized in the

This teacher is using performance-based assessment. What types of performance-based assessment might you use as a teacher?

TEACHING ON YOUR FEET
The Benefits of Peer Assessment

Despite my lesson plans, the suggestions I took from the text, and the numerous examples I gave during the day, nothing seemed to work— my sixth-grade class did not understand adjectives. I needed to find a new way to teach my students.

Then it hit me! Have them describe something they see in their bedrooms or on the way home from school each afternoon. So, I changed that night's homework assignment to observing their environment in preparation to write about it the next day. I didn't tell them that I was going to have them share their writing with a classmate.

The next day students came ready to share what they had observed. We did a 5-minute brainstorm before they wrote their descriptions. After 20 minutes of nonstop writing, I had the students switch papers with a neighbor. The neighbor was to draw exactly what the writing described.

I gave them 20 minutes to draw the picture, then hand it back to their neighbor. That's when I heard, "Man, you didn't put any grass in the park. I told you the sun was shining!" "Where's the color? My comforter is blue with white trim. You didn't show that."

Those were the responses I hoped to hear. Because students had not used adjectives, their peers' drawings did not portray what they thought they described. "Ms. Gore, are you saying that using adjectives helps the reader see what I am describing?" asked Melissa. "Now, I get it. Adjectives are colors and sizes. They make things come to life, right? Can we try it again, please?"

Aha! They finally understood adjectives. The assignment for that night was to rewrite their descriptions, which they would again share in class.

The next day, students came in eager to share their writing and then see their classmates' drawings. The results were wonderful—at last, my students understood the importance of using adjectives.

ANALYZE & REFLECT

Click here to analyze and reflect on this scenario you have just read.

LESLIE U. GORE
Literacy Coach
Horace Mann Middle School
Los Angeles, CALIFORNIA

---

curriculum. If appropriate, students can help teachers construct performance-based assessments. For example, elementary-level and high-school-level students helped their teachers construct the following two performance-based assessments, each of which required students to create graphs:

Example 1—Elementary Level

At various times during the school day, students observe and count, at 15-minute intervals, the number of cars and trucks that cross an unlit intersection near their school. Students also gather the same information for a lit intersection near the school. Using data for both intersections, students construct graphs to illustrate the results. If the data suggest the need for a light at the unlit intersection, the graphs will be sent to the local police department.

As students work on various parts of this performance task, the teacher would observe students and make judgments about the quality of their work. Do the counts of cars and trucks appear to be accurate? Do the graphs illustrate the results clearly? Is the students' decision about the need for a traffic light supported by the data they have gathered?

Example 2—High School Level

Students go online to find data on traffic accidents in their state. Based on the data they locate, students prepare graphs that show, by driver's age, various types of accidents, fatalities, speed at the time of accident, and so on. Exemplary graphs will be displayed in the driver education classroom.

As with the elementary-level example, the teacher would make judgments about the quality of the high school students' work. Naturally, these judgments would reflect the teacher's beliefs about the characteristics of exemplary student work at the high school level. Did students visit online sites that have extensive, accurate data on traffic accidents? Were students exhaustive in their online search? Do their graphs show a high degree of technical accuracy? Do the graphs "look professional"?

Many states have developed statewide performance-based curriculum goals. **WASHINGTON** State, for example, uses the Measurements of Student Progress (MSP) exam to assess students' performance in reading, mathematics, writing, and science. Teachers, parents, community members, and business representatives developed Performance-Level Descriptors (PDLs) for the knowledge and skills a student should demonstrate on the MSP. The PDLs are at three performance levels: Basic, Proficient, and Advanced.

ALTERNATE ASSESSMENTS

Alternate assessments are designed to measure the performance of students who are unable to participate in the traditional large-scale assessments used by districts and states. This approach to assessment emerged as a result of the reference to "alternate assessment" in the 1997 reauthorization of the Individuals with Disabilities Education Act (IDEA), which called for states to have alternate assessments in place by the year 2000. An alternate assessment is an alternative way of gathering data about what a student, regardless of the severity of his or her disability, knows and can do. Alternate strategies for collecting data might consist of observing the student during the school day, asking the student to perform a task and noting the level of performance, or interviewing parents or guardians about the student's activities outside school.

The primary purpose for alternate assessments in state assessment systems is to provide information about how well a school, district, or state is doing in terms of enhancing the performance of *all* students. Gathering data through alternate assessments requires rethinking traditional assessment methods.

An alternate assessment is neither a traditional large-scale assessment nor an individualized diagnostic assessment. For students with special needs, alternate assessments can be administered to students who have a unique array of educational goals and experiences and who differ greatly in their ability to respond to stimuli, solve problems, and provide responses.

Most states are in the process of developing alternate assessments for students with special needs. The National Center on Educational Outcomes at the University of Minnesota suggests six principles for developing inclusive assessment and accountability systems:

> **Principle 1**—All students with disabilities are included in the assessment system.
>
> **Principle 2**—Decisions about how students with disabilities participate in the assessment system are the result of clearly articulated participation, accommodation, and alternate assessment decision-making processes.
>
> **Principle 3**—All students with disabilities are included when student scores are publicly reported, in the same frequency and format as for all other students, whether they participate with or without accommodations, or in an alternate assessment.
>
> **Principle 4**—The assessment performance of students with disabilities has the same impact on the final accountability index as the performance of other students, regardless of how the students participate in the assessment system (i.e., with or without accommodation, or in an alternate assessment).
>
> **Principle 5**—There is improvement of both the assessment system and the accountability system over time, through the processes of formal monitoring, ongoing evaluation, and systematic training in the context of emerging research and best practice.
>
> **Principle 6**—Every policy and practice reflects the belief that all students must be included in state and district assessment and accountability systems (Guenemoen, Thompson, Thurlow, & Lehr, 2001).

The U.S. Department of Education decided in 2003 that the achievement of students with severe learning problems could be compared to the achievement of students without learning problems. The new ruling would enable more schools to demonstrate that they had made adequate yearly progress (AYP), a key requirement of the No Child Left Behind Act.

Prior to the Department of Education ruling, students who took alternate assessments could not be considered "proficient." In addition, many schools failed to make adequate yearly progress because their students with disabilities scored low on "regular" assessments or did not take the assessments. Thus, schools were "penalized" when they reported their yearly achievement scores for all students. Furthermore, schools that received federal aid for the poor but failed to make AYP could face increasing sanctions from the government.

According to the new ruling, states could develop their own criteria to identify students with "significant cognitive disabilities." The federal government required that standards for students with disabilities be tied to state academic standards, however. Identified students would be tested against standards appropriate for their intellectual development, and their scores counted as part of their schools' overall academic performance.

PROJECT-BASED LEARNING (PBL)

A growing body of research supports the use of project-based learning as a way to engage students, cut absenteeism, boost cooperative learning skills, and improve test scores. In **project-based learning (PBL)**, students work in teams to explore real-world problems and create presentations to share what they have learned. Compared with learning solely from textbooks, this approach has many benefits for students, including deeper knowledge of subject matter, increased self-direction and motivation, and improved research and problem-solving skills.

Students find PBL very engaging, as George Lucas, founder of the George Lucas Educational Foundation and director of *Star Wars*, points out: "Project learning, student teams working cooperatively, children connecting with passionate experts, and broader forms of assessment can dramatically improve student learning. New digital multimedia and telecommunications can support these practices and engage our students" (George Lucas Educational Foundation, June 2008).

PBL, which transforms teaching from teachers telling to students doing, includes five key elements:

1. Engaging learning experiences that involve students in complex, real-world projects through which they develop and apply skills and knowledge
2. Recognizing that significant learning taps students' inherent drive to learn, their capability to do important work, and their need to be taken seriously
3. Learning for which general curricular outcomes can be identified up-front, while specific outcomes of the students' learning are neither predetermined nor fully predictable
4. Learning that requires students to draw from many information sources and disciplines to solve problems
5. Experiences through which students learn to manage and allocate resources such as time and materials

These five key elements are reflected in the following examples of project-based learning:

- At Mountlake Terrace High School in Mountlake Terrace, **WASHINGTON**, teams of students in a high school geometry class design a state-of-the-art high school for the year 2050. The students create a site plan, make simple architectural drawings of rooms and a physical model, plan a budget, and write a narrative report. They present their work to real architects, who judge the projects and "award" the contract.
- At Newsome Park Elementary School in Newport News, **VIRGINIA**, second graders curious about the number of medicines a classmate takes and her frequent trips to the doctor investigate—with the classmate's permission—the causes of cystic fibrosis. They invite experts to tell them about the disease, write their research, use graphs and PowerPoint presentations to tell the story, sell pledges to a cystic fibrosis walkathon, and participate in the walkathon.

TEACHERS' VOICES ➡ BEING AN AGENT OF CHANGE

REBECCA MIELIWOCKI

Good Teachers Don't Shy Away from Assessment Data

Teachers must be held accountable for their students' success, from helping them meet personal or schoolwide learning goals to achieving on district- and state-level assessments. Good teachers don't shy away from assessment data and what it can tell them about their students' performance and their own. Data drives instruction and provides an essential reflective tool in the process of improvement, for the teacher AND the student.

When [students] leave my classroom, they are better people than when they walked through my door. They are children who know they are important and that a great future lies ahead for them if they are willing to match their talents with effort and creativity. They know that learning is exciting. They learn strong communication skills that will help them make the most of their lives. They leave able to write clearly and compellingly about what they believe. They know life will throw them many curveballs, but they have all the tools they need to handle them. They leave enthralled with reading and knowing that the great mysteries of life can be answered through close and careful study of the written word. They begin to make adventures of their own lives.

I feel driven to let my fellow teachers know, in ways large and small, how valued they are and how proud I am to see us pushing ourselves to be better each day. I collaborate with my peers frequently, sharing great ideas, best practices, and novel ways to reach students. I volunteer my time mentoring new teachers and coaching veteran teachers through challenging moments in the classroom. I spend time and energy making sure our school environment is one that celebrates teachers and heightens morale.

I would like to see every school provide opportunities for teacher collaboration, strategy sharing, modeling and observation of best practices, collective data-analysis, and problem-solving. Mentoring, formally and informally, must exist so that new teachers and veterans alike can receive support and grow in their craft. Individual goal-setting and self-directed professional development must be an ongoing process for every teacher. Every school should foster an environment of collaboration with open door policies and constructive feedback loops for all staff members.

Every day, teachers with patience and creativity are opening doors for children to reach deep within themselves to learn more, solve problems, build skills, and nurture their dreams. It happens every day in America's classrooms, and this good news deserves to be shared.

PERSONAL REFLECTION

1. What does Mieliwocki mean when she says "Data drives instruction"? With reference to the grade level and subject area for which you are preparing to teach, develop a hypothetical example of how data might influence a teacher's instruction.
2. When you become a teacher, what can you do to ensure that your "school environment is one that celebrates teachers and heightens morale"?

Rebecca Mieliwocki teaches at Luther Burbank Middle School in Burbank, CALIFORNIA. She was the 2012 National Teacher of the Year.

Source: The preceding is adapted from Rebecca Mieliwocki's application for the 2012 National Teacher of the Year award at http://www.ccsso.org/ntoy/National_Teachers/Teacher_Detail.html?id=3487.

- At the Mott Hall School in **NEW YORK** City's Harlem, a fifth-grade project on kites involves using creative-writing skills in poems and stories with kite themes. Students design their own kites on the computer and then make them by hand. They learn about electromagnetism and the principles of ratios and proportions. A casual remark by one student leads to an in-depth study of the role of kites in various cultural celebrations.

HOW CAN YOU DEVELOP HIGH-QUALITY CLASSROOM ASSESSMENTS?

You should use various criteria to grade the assignments students complete and the tests they take. Among the criteria you may consider are effort, neatness, correctness, how well students did compared with other students or with their own past performance, and how long students had been studying the topic. These criteria, of course, focus on what *students* do to demonstrate their learning. To develop high-quality classroom assessments, however, you must focus on what *you* do to ensure that assessments

TECHNOLOGY in ACTION
Autograded Quizzes and Exams in Eighth-Grade Social Studies

Mr. Winchell has been using a quiz creator for the past year to create autograded self-assessments. (Autograded quiz-making tools allow teachers to construct their own assessments.) The quiz creator allows Mr. Winchell to create Flash-driven quizzes that include audio, animation, and text. The quizzes can be true/false, short answer, clickable maps, multiple-choice, and other auto-reply formats. The tool allows him to create assessments that review classroom discussion, group projects, and current events, and it quickly and easily puts them in a format that allows students to access the assessments and receive immediate feedback on their responses—not just with right or wrong answers, but with detailed explanations of the correct answer.

At the end of each lesson, Mr. Winchell has his students submit questions that cover the day's events. They provide the questions, the correct answers, and several not-so-correct answer choices. If Mr. Winchell uses a student's question in the daily quiz, the student receives several extra-credit points for that day. Mr. Winchell then loads the questions, the correct answers, and the incorrect choices into the quiz creator. The other students then access the questions, take the quiz, and see how they performed. They can take the quiz as many times as they want for as long as they want.

Mr. Winchell found that, as effective as the autograded quiz tool is, the exercise of having students write questions works equally well in helping students retain course-specific information. By the end of the year, Mr. Winchell has an extensive series of questions and answers covering the entire term and that students can review at any time. And, best of all, he never had to grade a single question!

AUTOGRADED TOOLS: Several quiz-making tools are available to teachers. Most of these tools allow teachers to import questions and answers from other sources like Excel or Word; insert screen shots, animation, music, and sound; randomize question-and-answer sets; provide automated feedback on performance and correct responses for each question; and provide detailed reporting to teachers. Some quiz creators include a management system that allows the teacher to group students and assign quizzes to that group. Teachers often post quiz-creator links to social media or their own websites so students can take quizzes for practice.

VISIT: Several quiz-making sites provide visitors with opportunities to try the quiz-creation tool, see examples of autograded assessment instruments, and obtain technical requirements for running the tool.

POSSIBLE USES: Teachers have used autograded assessments to improve student performance, save time, provide for diverse student self-assessment opportunities, and help students take control of their learning experience.

---

fairly and accurately measure students' knowledge, skills, and levels of achievement. To assess student learning, you should be skilled in the following:

- Choosing and/or developing assessment methods appropriate for attaining instructional goals and objectives
- Administering, scoring, and interpreting the results of both externally produced and teacher-produced assessment methods
- Using assessment results when making decisions about individual students, planning teaching, developing curriculum, and school improvement
- Developing valid grading procedures based on high-quality assessment of student learning
- Communicating assessment results to students, parents, other nonteaching audiences, and other educators
- Recognizing unethical, illegal, and otherwise inappropriate assessment methods and uses of assessment information

The teacher profiled in the Technology in Action feature in this chapter figured out a way to assess his students' understanding of complex concepts. As a result of his classroom-based inquiry and reflection, he began to use a quiz creator to develop autograded self-assessments for his students.

VALIDITY AND RELIABILITY

Two important qualities of classroom assessments—whether teacher-made or commercially prepared—are validity and reliability. Because high-quality assessments are directly related to teaching effectiveness, assessments must be valid and reliable. **Validity** refers to the extent to which assessments measure what they are supposed to measure. If assessments fail to do this, they are useless. Valid assessments, however, ensure that what students are asked to do is a direct reflection of stated standards, goals, expectations, and/or targeted learning outcomes. If assessments are valid, teachers can use that information to improve their teaching, and students can use that information to improve their learning.

Surprisingly, examples of assessments that lack sufficient validity can be found among state-mandated tests of student learning. For example, a former classroom teacher and founding director of the Center for Teaching the Way Children Learn, located in **NEW YORK**, observed that:

> Numerous accountability systems use tests that have little relation to the standards they are supposed to evaluate. . . . Although the rhetoric of new and lofty standards is used when discussing what the tests measure, their actual content includes few performance items, and their formats provide scant opportunities for students to demonstrate the higher-order thinking of the new standards. (Falk, 2002, p. 614)

Reliability refers to the degree to which an assessment provides results that are consistent over time. In other words, an entire test (or individual test item) is considered to be reliable if it yields similar results at different times and under different conditions. For example, imagine that Mr. Hernandez wants to assess his students' multiplication and division skills using whole numbers by giving them a 40-point quiz (20 points for multiplication, 20 points for division). After scoring his students' quizzes, Mr. Hernandez is uncertain about whether he should begin teaching the more complex skills of multiplying and dividing using fractions. He decides to gather more information by giving another quiz 3 days later on the same multiplication and division skills. The following table presents the scores several students received on both quizzes:

Student	Multiplication			Division	
	Quiz 1	Quiz 2		Quiz 1	Quiz 2
Carlos	20	18		17	9
Kim	14	13		13	17
Shawn	11	11		12	17
Nong	16	17		16	12
Mary	20	19		15	14

The items that assessed students' multiplication skills, Mr. Hernandez notes, are quite consistent (or reliable). On quizzes 1 and 2, all five students received comparable scores, with Carlos and Mary receiving the highest scores on both quizzes, and Shawn and Kim receiving the lowest scores. On the other hand, the items that assessed students' division skills are less consistent (or reliable). On quiz 1, Carlos and Nong received the highest scores on the division items, while Kim and Shawn received the highest scores on the items for quiz 2.

At this point, Mr. Hernandez must make a judgment about the reliability of the information he has gathered. Because the results for the multiplication items are fairly consistent and those for the division items are fairly inconsistent, he decides to spend one more class session instructing students on division using whole numbers before he proceeds to teach multiplication and division using fractions.

Scoring Rubrics

Rubrics are an important element of quality classroom assessments. Sometimes called *scoring guides*, **scoring rubrics** are rating scales that consist of pre-established performance criteria. As a teacher, you can use rubrics to differentiate between levels of student performance on a rating scale, and students can even use them to guide their learning. Rubrics can be used to specify performance criteria for a variety of learning activities—writing an essay, conducting a science experiment, or delivering an informative speech, for example.

Students benefit from seeing examples of excellent work appropriate to their grade and ability levels. "Given clear requirements for success, students can approach learning from a more efficacious perspective; that is, they are better able to gauge the appropriateness of their own preparation and thus gain control over their own academic well-being. Students who feel in control of their own chances for success are more likely to care and to strive for excellence" (Stiggins & Chappuis, 2012, p. 43).

In addition to developing rubrics, you should collect models of exemplary performances and products by your students. Besides using a scoring rubric to learn about the specific elements that will be used to assess the quality of their work, students must see what quality looks (sounds, feels, smells, or tastes) like. Over time, you should collect sets of excellent work such as graphs, nonfiction writing, solutions to open-ended math problems, and designs for science experiments from students. Less-than-exemplary work may also be used in the process of teaching students how to use the rubrics.

Rubrics are typically used as scoring instruments when teachers evaluate student performances or products resulting from a performance task. There are two types of rubrics: holistic and analytic. A **holistic rubric** requires the teacher to score the overall process or product as a whole, without judging the component parts separately (Brookhart & Nitko, 2015; Stiggins & Chappuis, 2012). Figure 12.4 presents a generic framework for developing a holistic scoring rubric based on a 4-point scale.

As an illustration, a high school English teacher might use the framework presented in Figure 12.4 for holistic assessment of students' ability to write a clear, well-organized essay. A score of 5 would mean the essay reflected characteristics such as clear organization, accurate and precise use of words, adequately developed ideas, insightful analysis of the topic, and effective transitions from paragraph to paragraph. An essay with a score of 3 might have grammatical errors, problems with logic, confusing sentences, and a lack of transitions from paragraph to paragraph. And an essay with a score of 1 might be very confusing and contain only a few sentences that are clear and understandable.

Unlike the holistic scoring rubric, an **analytic rubric** requires that the teacher score separate, individual parts of the product or performance according to prespecified criteria, then add the individual scores to obtain a total score (Brookhart & Nitko, 2015; Stiggins & Chappuis, 2012). Figure 12.5 presents a generic framework for developing an analytic scoring rubric based on a 4-point scale.

Let's continue with the example that focuses on teaching essay writing at the high school level. A teacher might evaluate students' essays with reference to the following four criteria, each of which would be evaluated according to the description of performances in Figure 12.5 at the "beginning," "developing," "accomplished," and "highly accomplished" levels:

- Criterion 1: The essay is organized clearly—the introduction sets the stage for what follows and the conclusion summarizes key ideas.

FIGURE 12.4 Generic framework for a holistic scoring rubric

Score	Description
5	Performance or product reflects complete understanding of the assessment task or problem. The performance or product reflects all requirements of the task or problem.
4	Performance or product reflects considerable understanding of the assessment task or problem. The performance or product reflects all requirements of the task or problem.
3	Performance or product reflects partial understanding of the assessment task or problem. The performance or product reflects nearly all requirements of the task or problem.
2	Performance or product reflects little understanding of the assessment task or problem. Many requirements of the task or problem are missing.
1	Performance or product reflects no understanding of the assessment task or problem.
0	Task or problem not undertaken.

FIGURE 12.5 Generic framework for an analytic rubric

Criterion	Beginning	Developing	Accomplished	Highly Accomplished	Score
Criterion 1	Performance or product reflects beginning level of performance.	Performance or product reflects emerging performance at the mastery level.	Performance or product reflects performance at the mastery level.	Performance or product reflects performance at the highest level of mastery.	
Criterion 2	Performance or product reflects beginning level of performance.	Performance or product reflects emerging performance at the mastery level.	Performance or product reflects performance at the mastery level.	Performance or product reflects performance at the highest level of mastery.	
Criterion 3	Performance or product reflects beginning level of performance.	Performance or product reflects emerging performance at the mastery level.	Performance or product reflects performance at the mastery level.	Performance or product reflects performance at the highest level of mastery.	
Criterion 4	Performance or product reflects beginning level of performance.	Performance or product reflects emerging performance at the mastery level.	Performance or product reflects performance at the mastery level.	Performance or product reflects performance at the highest level of mastery.	

- Criterion 2: The essay is free of grammatical errors.
- Criterion 3: The essay has a unifying idea that is clear and easy to follow.
- Criterion 4: Effective paragraphing and transitions from one paragraph to the next provide an organizing structure and facilitate movement from one idea to the next.

To help you develop scoring rubrics for eventual use in your classroom, Figure 12.6 presents a step-by-step process for designing holistic and analytic scoring rubrics.

Multiple Measures of Student Learning

There is no single right way to assess student learning. Clearly, it will be important for you to provide your students with multiple opportunities to demonstrate what they know and are able to do. If your students know that they have different ways to demonstrate their success, they will develop more positive views of themselves as learners. They will find learning to be an enjoyable experience.

Students who previously disliked a subject because they associated assessments of learning in that area with failure can develop positive views about a subject if they know they have different ways to demonstrate their learning—in other words, multiple opportunities to be successful. As four assessment experts put it: "Used with skill, assessment can motivate the reluctant, revive the discouraged, and thereby increase, not simply measure, achievement" (Chappuis et al., 2012, p. 1).

FIGURE 12.6   Designing scoring rubrics: A step-by-step procedure

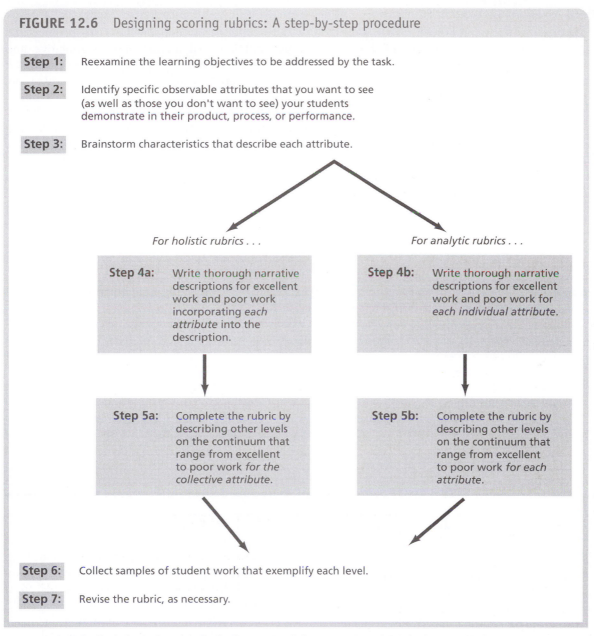

Step 1:   Reexamine the learning objectives to be addressed by the task.

Step 2:   Identify specific observable attributes that you want to see (as well as those you don't want to see) your students demonstrate in their product, process, or performance.

Step 3:   Brainstorm characteristics that describe each attribute.

For holistic rubrics . . .   *For analytic rubrics . . .*

Step 4a: Write thorough narrative descriptions for excellent work and poor work incorporating *each attribute* into the description.

Step 4b: Write thorough narrative descriptions for excellent work and poor work for *each individual attribute.*

Step 5a: Complete the rubric by describing other levels on the continuum that range from excellent to poor work *for the collective attribute.*

Step 5b: Complete the rubric by describing other levels on the continuum that range from excellent to poor work *for each attribute.*

Step 6:   Collect samples of student work that exemplify each level.

Step 7:   Revise the rubric, as necessary.

Source: Craig A. Mertler, "Designing Scoring Rubrics for the Classroom, *Practical Assessment, Research & Evaluation*, 2001, 7(25). Used with permission.

SUMMARY

What Is the Role of Assessment in Teaching?

- Effective schools frequently and systematically assess student learning.
- Classroom assessments of student learning enable teachers to make judgments about the performance of students and about their own performance as teachers.
- Assessment is a process that provides teachers with information about the effectiveness of their teaching and students with information about their learning.
- Classroom assessment provides information that teachers use to (1) determine how well students are learning the material being taught, (2) identify the type of feedback that will enhance student learning, (3) develop strategies for improving their effectiveness as teachers, and (4) determine if students have reached certain levels of performance.

How Are Standardized Assessments Used in Education?

- Standardized assessments (or standardized tests) are pencil-and-paper tests taken by large groups of students and are scored in a uniform manner.
- Norm-referenced assessments compare students' scores with scores of other students who are similar.
- Criterion-referenced assessments compare students' learning with clearly defined criteria or standards.

What Are "High-Stakes" Tests and Accountability?

- State-mandated tests often have high-stakes consequences for students, such as determining eligibility to participate in extracurricular activities or to graduate.
- For teachers, administrators, and schools, test results can be linked to merit rewards, increased funding, or sanctions.
- An unintended consequence of high-stakes tests is that they overemphasize differences in achievement (often termed the "achievement gap") between White students and minority-group students and students from low-income families; the tests can also unfairly highlight achievement differences between students who attend "resource-rich" schools and those who attend "resource-poor" schools.
- High-stakes tests increase the likelihood that minority-group students and students from low-income families will drop out.

What Methods Will You Use to Assess Student Learning?

- To assess student learning, teachers use informal and formal and informal assessments, quantitative and qualitative assessments, measurement and evaluation techniques, and formative and summative evaluation.

What Are Emerging Trends in Classroom Assessment?

- Among the various types of alternative assessments are authentic assessments, portfolio assessments, peer assessments, self-assessments, performance-based assessments, alternate assessments, and project-based learning.

How Can You Develop High-Quality Classroom Assessments?

- Validity and reliability are two qualities of high-quality classroom assessments.
- Scoring rubrics are rating scales that consist of pre-established performance criteria.
- Holistic rubrics are used to evaluate student performance or products related to a performance task.
- Analytic rubrics are used to score separate, individual parts of a performance or product.
- There is no single right way to assess student learning, and students' views of themselves as learners improve if they know that they have different ways to demonstrate their learning.

PROFESSIONAL REFLECTIONS AND ACTIVITIES

Teacher's Journal

1. As a K–12 student, what were your experiences with standardized and state-mandated tests? Did you have teachers who "taught to the test"? Did teaching to the test promote (or hinder) your own learning? Explain your answers.

2. Reflect on the many different assessments you experienced when you were a student in K–12 schools. Describe one or two assessments that you felt were accurate assessments of your knowledge and abilities and that motivated you to continue learning. Similarly, describe one or two assessments that you felt were *not* accurate assessments of your knowledge and abilities and that did *not* motivate you to continue learning. What implications do your own experiences have for your future assessment activities as a teacher?

3. In grading group projects, should a teacher give everyone in the group the same grade or assign different grades on the basis of how much each student contributed to the group's effort? Explain your answer.

4. Many people believe that high-stakes tests address only a narrow portion of the school curriculum. If a school district decided to "take a break" from high-stakes testing for five years, what data would parents, teachers, and others use to judge whether a school and its students were "successful"?

Teacher's Research

1. On the Internet, review the most recent results of one of the following international assessments: International Assessment of Educational Progress (IAEP), Trends in International Mathematics and Science Study (TIMSS), Progress in International Reading Literacy Study (PIRLS), or Program for International Student Assessment (PISA). How does the achievement of U.S. students compare with the achievement of students from other countries? Based on what you have learned in this chapter's section on international assessments, what cautions should you keep in mind when examining such comparative data?

2. Visit the George Lucas Educational Foundation online and, with reference to the subject matter and

grade level for which you are preparing to teach, find two examples of project-based learning activities that are featured at the site. How is student learning assessed in these project-based learning activities? How might you adapt or modify these assessment activities when you become a teacher?

Observations and Interviews

1. Spend a half day at a school at the level you plan to teach, recording your impressions about the various approaches teachers use to assess students' learning. Which of the assessment approaches discussed in this chapter are used by the teachers?

2. As a collaborative project, conduct an informal survey of what people think about requiring students to pass an exit exam before they graduate from high school. What conclusions can you draw from the results? Do you agree with those conclusions?

Professional Portfolio

Prepare a set of guidelines or strategies for students to follow when they take a standardized test. The strategies might include items such as the following:

- Survey the test, checking for missing pages.
- Read directions carefully.
- Notice use of double negatives.
- Note use of terms such as *always, never, best*, etc.
- Read all choices for multiple-choice test items.
- Check answers.

CHAPTER QUIZ

Take this quiz to check your understanding of the content covered in this chapter.

CHAPTER THIRTEEN

Integrating Technology into Teaching

learning outcomes

After reading this chapter, you will be able to do the following:

1. Explain how technology is transforming teaching and learning.
2. Describe the digital technologies that can be integrated into teaching.
3. Discuss the availability and use of the latest technologies in the classroom.
4. Summarize key findings from recent research on technology integration and student learning.
5. Explain several challenges related to integrating technology into teaching.

READERS' VOICES

How is technology transforming teaching and learning?

Technology is having a huge impact on how, when, and where students learn. With a smartphone or tablet in their hand, students can learn at any hour of the day, wherever they might be.

—KENDRA, Teacher Education Program, first year

Since the 2001 edition, *Becoming a Teacher* has included a separate chapter on integrating technology into teaching. In 2001, it was clear that technology was influencing schools and the profession of teaching. However, few people could have predicted just how this influence would accelerate during the next 15 years. The magnitude of technology's impact on education is evident in a sampling of session titles from the 2014 International Society for Technology in Education (ISTE) conference attended by more than 18,000 educators and technology leaders from around the world:

- How games have changed how we teach
- Lights! Camera! Student moviemakers in action!
- Coaching teachers to implement student-centered, technology-rich BYOD (Bring Your Own Device) instruction
- STEM (Science, Technology, Education, and Mathematics) app-tivities for the Common Core
- Create a world-class robotics program at your school
- Elementary microblogging: Connect your classroom with the global community
- Using mobile devices and multimedia in multicultural and multilingual projects
- Student tech leaders to support digital transformation
- Gamifying the classroom: Mastery for digital-age learners
- Apps workflow for project-based learning
- Arts and bots: Encouraging students to learn by building robots
- Augmented reality: The unimaginable visualized through kid-created tutorials (International Society for Technology in Education [ISTE] Conference Program, June 28–July 1, 2014).

Today, it is abundantly clear that technology has transformed how, when, and where students can learn. "New technologies are providing opportunities with the potential to advance education far beyond what has been possible before. . . . Across formal and informal learning settings, blended learning situations are increasingly integrating classroom-based activities with technologies such as web-based digital learning resources, intelligent tutoring systems, online courses and learning communities, feedback systems such as 'clickers,' games that engage players as they learn content, and simulations of complex real-world phenomena" (U.S. Department of Education, Office of Educational Technology, February 14, 2013, pp. 7–8).

Often referred to as the *iGeneration, Generation M²*, *digital natives, netgens, millennials, Generation Z,* or *generation tech*, today's students live in a world that is connected to and continuously transformed by technology. To them, a network password is more important than a Social Security number. With few exceptions, students are more "wired" than their teachers. Generations ago, students came to school with notebooks, pencils, and pens; today, they come to school with smartphones, iPods, iPads, and MP3 players. In addition, they "spend their days immersed in a 'media diet,' devouring entertainment, communication, [and] any form of electronic media. They are master multitaskers, social networkers, electronic communicators, and the first to rush to buy any new technology" (Rosen, 2010, p. 2). Members of Generation Z, those born after 1995, have even been called "a new species—'screenagers,' the first tribe of 'digital natives.' [They are] wired-from-the-crib and differ from 'digital immigrants,' for whom the Internet is a second language" (Kingston, 2014).

A report titled *Generation M²: Media in the Lives of 8- to 18-Year-Olds* revealed that youth spend an average of 7 hours and 38 minutes with media each day (see Figure 13.1). Because today's students are skilled at multitasking, their total media exposure is 10 hours and 45 minutes a day, an increase of almost 2½ hours of media exposure since 2004. The figure also shows that the most popular computer activities are social networking sites like Facebook, Twitter, Pinterest, Slingshot, Snapchat, Tumblr, and Instagram; playing computer games; and watching videos on sites like YouTube. Another study found that only 27 percent of youth aged 12 to 15 met the National Center for Health's (NCH) recommended limit of 2 hours or less of TV plus computer use daily outside of school (Herrick, Fakhouri, Carlson, & Fulton, 2014).

FIGURE 13.1   (a) Media use over time; (b) computer time by activity

Among all 8- to 18-year-olds, average amount of time spent with each medium in a typical day:

	2009	2004	1999
TV content	4:29	3:51	3:47
Music/audio	2:31	1:44	1:48
Computer	1:29	1:02	:27
Video games	1:13	:49	:26
Print	:38	:43	:43
Movies	:25	:25	:18
TOTAL MEDIA EXPOSURE	10:45	8:33	7:29
Multitasking proportion	29%	26%	16%
TOTAL MEDIA USE	7:38	6:21	6:19

Total media exposure is the sum of time spent with all media. **Multitasking proportion** is the proportion of media time that is spent using more than one medium concurrently. **Total media use** is the actual number of hours out of the day that are spent using media, taking multitasking into account.

(a)

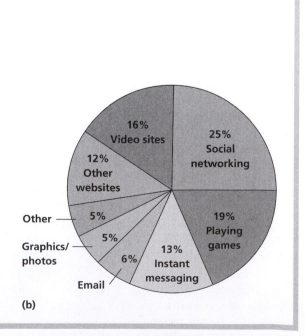

(b)

Adapted from Victoria J. Rideout, Ulla G. Foehr, and Donald F. Roberts, *Generation M²: Media in the Lives of 8- to 18-Year-Olds—A Kaiser Family Foundation Study.* January 2010, pp. 2, 21.

HOW IS TECHNOLOGY TRANSFORMING TEACHING AND LEARNING?

For today's students, *anywhere, anytime learning* is a reality. Their learning options include online instruction, various forms of e-learning, and **blended learning**—that is, a blending of traditional face-to-face instruction and online learning. Frequently, all or most of their learning materials and resources are available on the Internet, 24 hours a day, 7 days a week. In this chapter's Teachers' Voices: Being an Agent of Change, Melissa Meyers explains how students with learning disabilities benefit from her approach to blended learning.

Technology has transformed teaching and learning. Each day, students use social networking sites like Facebook and Twitter to communicate with other students around the block and around the world. Students search the web for information about whales, the Brazilian rain forest, or the planet Mars; and then they create podcasts based on what they have learned. They send text messages to students in other countries and collaborate with them on global networking projects.

Figure 13.2, based on a 2013 survey of pre-K–12 teachers, shows that most "embrace digital resources to propel learning." Approximately three-quarters of the teachers report that technology enables them to reinforce and expand on content (74 percent), to motivate students to learn (74 percent), and to respond to a variety of learning styles (73 percent). More than two-thirds of teachers want more technology in the classroom, and this number is even greater (76 percent) for teachers in low-income schools. Seven in 10 teachers (69%) surveyed said educational technology allows them to "do much more than ever before" for their students, and 65 percent of teachers reported that technology allows them to demonstrate something they cannot show in any other way.

Technology enables students to experience events or study phenomena that they could not witness firsthand. By integrating technology into various learning tasks and across subject areas, teachers can provide students with learning experiences that would have been impossible a few years ago. Careful and purposeful use of educational technology changes the roles of teachers and students and enhances students' higher-order and problem-solving skills, as a school superintendent points out after the district integrated smartphones into fifth- and seventh-grade classrooms: "The biggest change that I've seen with our staff is the role of the teacher has gone from the person who delivers the instruction to the person who facilitates learning. Students are now empowered to be leaders, to deliver instruction, to problem-solve, and to come up with their own solutions, versus waiting for the teacher" (Ash, 2010, p. 26). Read the following three teacher-authored vignettes and consider how the use of educational technology changes the roles of teachers and students.

PROFESSIONAL REFLECTION
Watch as an educator shares how technology transforms teaching and learning by meeting the individual needs of each student with different computer programs.

Vignette 1: The Tech Detectives: Students Take Ownership of Technology

Picture it: a middle school in Anytown, U.S.A., has a teacher that is struggling to figure out why her SmartBoard is acting up. Typically she would submit a "tech request" and wait an extended period of time for it to be fixed. One issue, though—she needs the device *now* for a very important math lesson. She suddenly remembers that a group of students called the "Tech Detectives" can come to the rescue and fix the problem. Within minutes, several students arrive, play around with a few wires and buttons, and the malfunction is addressed in no time.

The Tech Detectives Club was created at Black River Middle School in Chester, **NEW JERSEY**, as a way for students to take ownership of the technology they utilize during their various learning experiences. Based on feedback from various school stakeholders who have a passion for technology, it was deemed necessary to start a club that arms students with a strong technological skill set. On a regular basis, students create tutorials, assist teachers, learn about technology trends, collaboratively problem solve issues, and gain exposure to career readiness.

FIGURE 13.2   Teachers embrace digital resources to propel learning

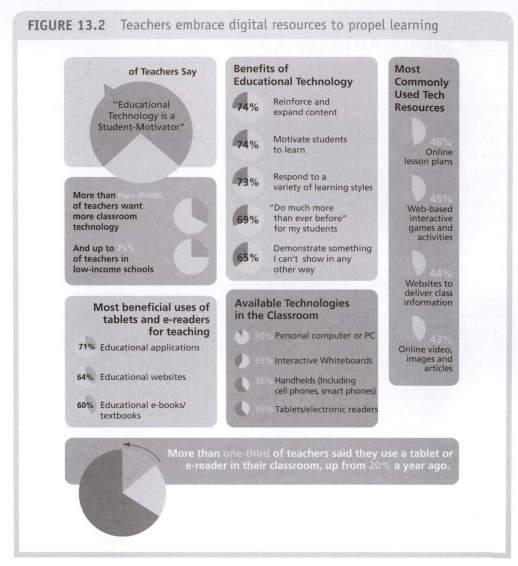

Source: PBS Learning Media. (February 4, 2013). Press Release: PBS Survey Finds Teachers Are Embracing Digital Resources to Propel Student Learning. Retrieved July 4, 2014, from http://wwwtc.pbs.org/about/media/about/cms_page_media/615/PBS%20 LearningMedia%20Digital%20Resources%20Infographic-2-4-13.pdf.

The backbone behind the success of this program is a vision that encompasses student empowerment, collaboration, and career readiness. Right at the top, though, is a strong teacher or teachers to harness the energy of a group of students ready to solve all of the school's technology issues one emergency at a time. While this club does not replace the school's support technicians, it does deflect some of the simple troubleshooting to students who can help. (Currie, 2014)

Vignette 2: SOLE Motivates Students to Teach Themselves (and Each Other)

An eighth-grade teacher uses the Self-Organized Learning Environment (SOLE) to teach geography to his students. His students organize themselves into small groups, and each group works at one of four learning centers in the classroom. Each learning center has a computer with Internet access and a few software programs that enable students to acquire geographic knowledge and skills.

As part of the SOLE environment, the teacher gave each group a list of Internet resources related to various topics in geography; then, he let each group choose what it wanted to learn. With their teacher's encouragement, students soon became excited about being able to direct their own learning and to learn from one

TEACHERS' VOICES ➡ Being an Agent of Change

MELISSA MEYERS

IS BLENDED LEARNING WORTH THE HYPE?

Yesterday afternoon in my 12th-grade World Literature class, I put my students through Hell, literally. Thanks to a fantastic interactive website called Virtual Inferno, my English class embarked upon a tour of Dante's Hell, from Dante's mysterious awakening in the Dark Wood of Error down, down through nine levels until we reached the Cocytus where Satan himself resides, encased in ice forever.

In the coming weeks, my English students will research and write about the visually stunning *Dante's Inferno* video game, listen to Franz Liszt's *A Symphony to Dante's Divine Comedy* accompanied by Gustave Dore's illustrations on YouTube, and explore Dante-era Florence through the "Firenze-Virtual History" iPad app. They will also read *Inferno* (of course!) and listen to the audio book on their iPads.

As I walked in the front door of my school this morning, one of my students told me that he had spent the long MLK [Martin Luther King] holiday weekend reading the full version of Longfellow's *Inferno* translation online. Another student brought in a graphic novel of it to share with the class. A third asked if he could write an extra-credit short story about the text from the point of view of Virgil, Dante's spiritual guide. I would like to think that my students are just a bunch of gifted, enthusiastic readers, but the truth is that all of them are LD [learning disabled] learners with severe dyslexia, disorder of written expression, and various forms of speech and language difficulties.

Reading is neither pleasurable nor natural for them. Technology isn't a fun extra at my school; it's a voice for dyslexic readers, an essential communication and social device for autistic students, a tool for the dysgraphic, and an organizational must-have for everyone. Is technology in the classroom worth the hype at *my* school? Absolutely.

Occasionally, I come upon a questioning parent who wants to know why students spend so much time using technological do-dads instead of doing good old-fashioned reading and writing. For these naysayers, I rattle off a whole list of reasons why I integrate technology: multi-modal instruction, supplements for remediation or enrichment, 21st-century skill-building, text-to-world connections, collaboration, student buy-in, not to mention marked improvement in essay writing and reading comprehension. And though we study ancient pieces of literature, we view texts through modern eyes, with technology as our lens. This begs the question of why we're not evolving at a faster rate if there are, by Apple's count, 1.5 million iPads in American classrooms and increased funding for 1:1 computer initiatives in all public schools.

The answer is ugly: teachers themselves slow down this evolution when they aren't sufficiently trained to use technology or resist the idea of change altogether. According to a 2009 survey conducted through the National Center for Education Statistics, 99 percent of public school teachers have computer access throughout the day, whereas only 29 percent of them are using computers "often" during instruction. Such a wasted opportunity!

Technology is certainly worth the hype, but it will remain only empty, extravagant claims if teachers aren't trained to use it effectively and aren't as enthusiastic—and evolved—as their students already are. It's time to play catch-up.

PERSONAL REFLECTION

1. Meyers believes that technology integration in teaching is "certainly worth the hype." To what extent do you agree with her?
2. Why do you think some teachers might resist the integration of technology into teaching?

Melissa Meyers teaches at Stanbridge Academy, a small, private K–12 special education school in San Mateo, **CALIFORNIA**.

The preceding is her contribution to a February 8, 2012, blog post made by Bob Lenz, instructor of a graduate-level technology course she took. Retrieved July 12, 2014, from http://www.edutopia.org/blog/blended-learning-example-classroom-lesson-bob-lenz.

another. For example, one group decided to follow their interests and to make a movie and a PowerPoint presentation about the water shortage in their state. According to the teacher, the SOLE approach is very effective: "Since I began to use SOLE, students find learning more fun; they are more engaged; and they are learning to collaborate."

Vignette 3: Teaching in a Technology-Rich 1:1 iPad Classroom

An English teacher at a high school that gave an iPad to each student at the start of the school year is eager to integrate several new technologies into his teaching. He agreed to be the English Department's "technology coach" and share with other teachers how to teach in a one-on-one iPad environment.

At first, he was concerned that students might use the iPads primarily for playing games or using social media. Two weeks into a unit on American literature, however, he realizes that his concern was unfounded. Students are actually using the iPads to improve their learning. For example, students make frequent use of a free, online learning management system (LMS) and social network that enables users to create and to share academic content. Students are also using a note-taking and annotation app available on the Internet. His students tell him that the LMS and the note-taking app enable them to be more organized and better able to keep track of their learning.

During a unit on *The Red Badge of Courage*, he decides to use a free online quiz creator that allows him to use a game-show format to quiz students on their reading. In addition, he uses a student response system that allows students to use "clickers" to answer questions. During the unit, he has four game-show quizzes. During each quiz, students are excited and deeply engaged.

During the quizzes, he uses a graph provided at the end of each question to assess and correct immediately students' understanding of the material. After each quiz, he downloads a spreadsheet with each student's answers and then meets individually with students to review the questions they missed.

The three preceding vignettes illustrate the "Digital Learning Farm" model as described in Alan November's book *Who Owns the Learning?* (2012). When family farms were common in the United States, November explains, children had to help out on the farm. They had jobs that were essential for the success of the farm and the family. Similarly, many older students in one-room schoolhouses across the United States functioned as the "teacher's helper" and helped younger students learn. With the decline of one-room schoolhouses, "We lost the value of children as contributors to the culture of school" (November, 2012, p. 5).

The Digital Learning Farm model once again gives students opportunities to perform tasks that are "real" and increase the learning of all students. The model "leverages inexpensive and easy-to-use technologies to challenge and support more active participation of students and to give them more ownership in the educational process as tutorial designers, scribes, researchers, global communicators and collaborators, and more. This approach restores the dignity and integrity of the child as a contributor, even as it teaches students skills that will help them compete with peers from around the world" (November, 2012, p. 12). Figure 13.3 compares the Digital Learning Farm model with the "traditional" approach to education.

Anywhere, Anytime Learning

As mentioned, anywhere, anytime learning is a reality. Increasingly, teachers are blending online and face-to-face instruction. Depending on the purposes of the lesson, the percentage of time spent online and in the face-to-face classroom varies. The following describes a blended learning experience for seventh-graders:

> A seventh-grade teacher takes her students on once-a-week field trips to a nearby river where they use handheld computers to analyze water samples. Back in the classroom, they upload their data to a program that aggregates the data and analyzes the results.
>
> Next, students log onto a class Wiki about the river's water quality, and they document their most recent field trip, invite teachers in the district to evaluate their work, read about what another seventh-grade class on the other side of the state has learned about water quality in the same river, and share their ongoing inquiry with the school's parent-teacher association.
>
> At a university in the same city, the professor who heads up a research team studying the river's water quality analyzes the students' aggregated data and concludes that the students' data show that the river is being polluted not only by a paper mill at the river's edge, but by runoff from streets and parking lots near the river. He sends a text message to the teacher and her students, thanking them: "Gathering this data would have been

FIGURE 13.3 How the digital learning farm compares to the traditional educational model

Traditional Educational Model	Digital Learning Farm Model
It features the same prescribed assignments and rubrics for all students.	Students design more of their own assignments and rubrics.
There is an audience of one (the teacher).	It has the capacity for a worldwide, authentic audience.
Reward and punishment are external (in the form of a grade).	There is opportunity for more intrinsic rewards.
Student work is not leveraged to help all students learn.	All students contribute to the learning processes of the entire class and to learners around the world.
The critical skill is to know how to be taught.	The critical skill is to learn how to learn.
The limit of learning is what the teacher already knows.	Students research content beyond the teacher's knowledge.
The curriculum is covered regardless of students' mastery.	There are more opportunities for mastery.
Students rely on their teacher for help.	Students rely on their teacher and the whole class for help.
Parents have limited access to day-to-day student creativity.	There is an increased opportunity for parents to see creative student work.
Technology reinforces the current industrial culture.	Technology is used as a transformational tool to change the culture of teaching and learning.

impossible without your help," he says. "I simply don't have the staff. But I have the evidence I need now to submit a report to the local government so we can stop this pollution from destroying our rivers."

The students are excited to be part of an effort to save the beach and rivers they love; they don't want to stop there. They set up a blog to publicize their findings. This ultimately leads to a news story, increased local awareness of the pollution problem, a response from the local government, and an eventual reduction in runoff and pollution. The students are galvanized by their success. That they learned a great deal about government, scientific study, and ecosystems is evident from their test scores. And school personnel—even across school boundaries—enjoyed collaborating on the project. (Consortium for School Networking, 2008)

The following are among the advantages that teachers and students realize from such blended learning activities:

- **Virtual field trips**—Students and their teachers can go anywhere in or out of this world.
- **Open discussion**—Online discussions allow for reflection, and archived discussions can be evaluated later.
- **Accessibility**—Students can access learning resources, assignments, and assessment activities from any place that has a computer and an Internet connection.
- **Guest lectures**—Experts from a global community can participate in classroom activities.
- **Vast resources**—Almost limitless resources include data banks, publishers' materials, online labs, and virtual worlds.
- **Accommodation of learning styles**—Online activities allow for audio, video, text, graphics, and interactive animation that appeal to a variety of learning styles.
- **Assessment and tracking**—Most online interactions can be archived and reviewed at any time by teachers.

Realizing the Full Impact of Technology on Learning

Without a doubt, the World Wide Web; Web 2.0 that enables users to interact through social networking sites, blogs, video-sharing sites, and other host-provided services; mobile learning devices (MLDs); and related telecommunications technologies can transform teaching and learning. However, one of the education questions for the future is, How committed are teachers, administrators, policymakers, parents and guardians, and the general public to enabling all students to realize the *full impact* that technology can have on their learning? As the following comments by the author of *Rewired: Understanding the iGeneration and the Way They Learn* suggest, the future of schools may depend on educators' response to this challenge:

> Although many schools have tried to integrate technology into the curriculum, I feel that they have gone about it the wrong way. These kids are so technologically advanced that simple adaptations to technology and media in the classroom and in school is *borrrrrring*. . . . One twelve-year-old told me: *"My teacher thinks she is so cool and with it because she makes these PowerPoints for each lecture with text and graphics that fly in, twist and turn, and display the same information that is in the book and that she lectures about. Maybe when I was 8 that might have been fun and interesting, but it is so yesterday."* (Rosen, 2010, p. 16)

Educators must also develop new assessment techniques to evaluate students' learning that occurs through the use of advanced telecommunications like the Internet and the World Wide Web. The number of correct responses on homework, quizzes, and examinations will no longer suffice to measure students' learning.

Online Schools and Online Learning

Westwood Cyber High School, near Detroit, **MICHIGAN**, does not have traditional classrooms, academic departments, courses, or tests. Instead, the school is patterned after a British model known as the "Not School." Westwood students do most of their work on the Internet from home, and they report to the school for 2 hours a week to meet with teachers. The rest of the time they work interactively with school personnel and the school's learning management system.

Westwood is one of a growing number of **online schools** in the nation. The curriculum at Westwood emphasizes project-based learning that incorporates multiple subject areas. Students create individualized portfolios of creative work tailored to their interests. Teachers certified by the state of Michigan grade students' portfolios with reference to state learning standards.

The Westwood School District, which had been losing enrollment, has increased enrollment by 33 percent since starting the Cyber School. The school itself has retained 90 percent of its students (U.S. Department of Education, Office of Educational Technology, November 2010, p. 69).

In addition to virtual schools, several hundred high schools in the United States offer **online learning** through the Virtual High School (VHS), a consortium of high schools run by VHS Inc., a nonprofit foundation. VHS partners with schools to provide "rigorous, student-centered online courses that help expand versus replace existing curriculum options." Members of the VHS consortium include over 15,000 enrolled students and 750 member schools in 30 U.S. states and 26 countries (Virtual High School, 2014). The VHS was one of the nation's first two online programs for high schools—the other was the e-school run by the **HAWAII** Department of Education.

As Figure 13.4 shows, 30 states plus the District of Columbia had at least one multi-district fully online school operating statewide at the end of 2013. Approximately 310,000 students were enrolled in these schools (Evergreen Education Group, 2013).

FIGURE 13.4   States with multi-district fully online schools

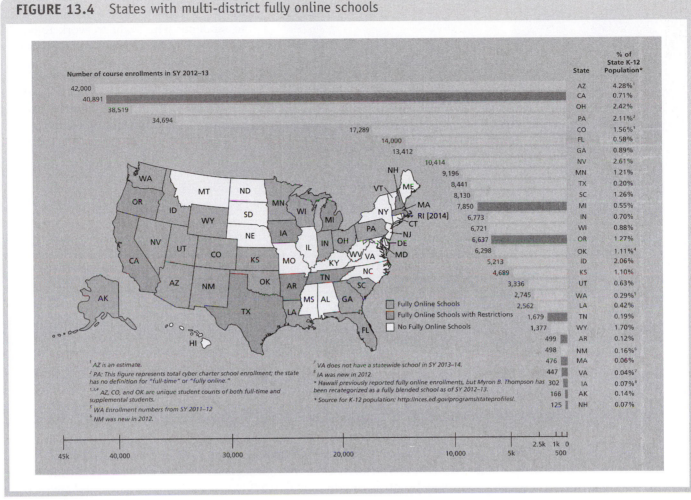

Source: Evergreen Education Group. (2013). *Keeping Pace with K–12 Online & Blended Learning: An Annual Review of Policy and Practice,* p. 23.

In addition, 39 states had online learning initiatives offered through schools within the state. Their sizes varied greatly—some schools had fewer than 2,500 course enrollments (one student taking one semester-long course), whereas the **FLORIDA** Virtual School (FLVS), the largest in the country, had more than 210,000 course enrollments. The **NORTH CAROLINA** Virtual Public School (NCVPS) was the second largest, with almost 74,000 course enrollments—a 369 percent increase from the previous year! And, the **ALABAMA** Virtual Academy, with over 31,000 course enrollments, was the third largest. Nationwide, state virtual school course enrollments were about 450,000 in 2010, an increase of nearly 40 percent over 2009 (Evergreen Education Group, 2013).

Many districts are creating full-time **blended schools** that combine online and face-to-face instruction. During the 2013–2014 school year, more than 75 percent of the nation's school districts offered at least some online learning, involving more than 5 percent of the total U.S. K–12 student population (Evergreen Education Group, 2014). The following programs illustrate a few of the online learning options available to students during the 2013–2014 school year:

- In Chicago, **ILLINOIS**, the Virtual Opportunities Inside a School Environment (VOISE) Academy, a public high school, uses a blended learning approach in which students attend the physical school, but online courses act as the primary source of course content.

Whether in special classes or extracurricular programs, students in today's schools receive a great deal of hands-on involvement with technology. How does this prepare them for postgraduate life?

- Riverside Virtual School in **CALIFORNIA** offers a blended online learning option to students who want to work remotely. They must communicate with teachers via e-mail throughout the week.
- In **NORTH CAROLINA**, Polk County Early College annually allows up to 20 students to complete high school while earning college credits, leading to early completion of an associate's degree while earning a high school diploma.
- Myron B. Thompson Academy in **HAWAII** is a blended charter school serving about 500 students statewide. Students take some courses face-to-face at the onsite location and other courses mostly online with some face-to-face requirements. The face-to-face requirements are unique to each island.
- In **RHODE ISLAND**, the Village Green Virtual Public Charter High School and Sheila C. "Skip" Nowell Leadership Academy opened in fall 2013 and are the state's first two fully blended charter schools. Students spend 15 hours in the classroom and 15 hours working online each week (Evergreen Education Group, 2014).

With the spread of virtual schools and online learning, some educators, policymakers, and researchers have expressed concern about exaggerated claims for online learning. In addition, they are worried about what is lost when students do not meet face to face with their classmates and teachers. Alan Warhaftig, a Los Angeles, **CALIFORNIA**, high school English teacher who earned certification from the National Board for Professional Teaching Standards (NBPTS), said there is an "overall weakness to that notion that online schools can replace the school environment." He doubts that online classrooms can provide the "looking-in-the-eyes" factor that teachers use to monitor students' understanding of a lesson or how they might be feeling (Trotter, 2002).

In *50 Myths and Lies That Threaten America's Public Schools: The Real Crisis in Education,* David Berliner and Gene Glass (2014) make the following points about cyberschooling:

- When the performance of the children who receive their education at cyberschools is assessed, the results are dismal. Dropout rates during the school year are staggering, often exceeding 50%. Graduation rates are abysmal, and achievement lags far behind that of their peers in brick-and-mortar schools. For the 2012–13 school year, Tennessee Virtual Academy—operated by K12 Inc.—scored lower than any of the other 1,300 elementary schools on the state standardized test. (p. 33)
- Legislators are often big proponents of cyberschooling, for which they can pay a fraction of the cost of educating a child in a traditional brick-and-mortar school. . . . The cyberschool industry operates in the grand tradition of crony capitalism, essentially buying the support of politicians through such things as campaign contributions and personal perks like junkets to foreign countries to study other education systems. (p. 34)
- Only about a quarter of online cyberschools meet "adequate yearly progress" as defined by the No Child Left Behind act, as compared

with about 50% of traditional schools. In 2011–12, state department of education ratings of virtual schools' academic performance showed that more than 70% were rated academically unacceptable. Students in cyberschools have scored substantially lower than their counterparts in traditional brick-and-mortar schools in math and reading. The on-time graduate rate for students in cyberschools is about two-thirds the rate for traditional schools. (p. 35)

In spite of evidence such as this, the public is generally supportive of virtual schools. According to the 2013 Phi Delta Kappan/Gallup Poll (Bushaw & Lopez, 2013, p. 17) public school parents approve, by 63 percent to 36 percent, of allowing high school students to earn high school credits online; and they favor allowing high school students to earn college credits by 80 percent to 19 percent.

The trend toward virtual schools and online learning no doubt will continue. Meanwhile, several questions need to be addressed to ensure that virtual students have high-quality online learning experiences:

- Although online learning may be appropriate for high school students, should online learning be made available to elementary and middle school students?
- Should online courses be aligned with state academic standards?
- Who should provide for students' technological needs while they take an online course?
- Are online teachers trained effectively to teach via the Internet?
- Should parent approval be required before a child enrolls in an online course?
- Should students receive the same credit for an online course as they would for an interactive, face-to-face class?
- How can school officials ensure the quality of online courses, especially those offered by teachers in other states or countries?

FLIPPED CLASSROOMS

One form of blended learning is known as a **flipped classroom**. In a flipped classroom, students first learn new content at home by watching online video lectures by the teacher or other online videos related to the subject matter. Then, during time in class, they apply their new knowledge by solving problems or completing "homework," with the teacher providing individual assistance. **Flipped teaching** allows teachers to use their time in class differently. Instead of acting in the well-known role of the "sage on the stage," the teacher is able to be more like the "guide on the side." Teachers can work with individual students or groups of students.

An early innovator of flipped teaching was Clintondale High School in MICHIGAN. The principal, who had been posting YouTube videos of baseball skills for his son's team, worked with a social studies teacher to offer two class with the same material and assignments—one class was flipped, the other traditional. After 20 weeks, students in the flipped class were outperforming traditional students.

Clintondale had been identified as among the state's worst 5 percent of schools. In 2010, more than half of ninth graders had failed science, and almost half had failed math. That same year, the ninth grade flipped. The English failure rate dropped from 52 percent to 19 percent; math, from 44 percent to 13 percent; science, from 41 percent to 19 percent; and social studies, from 28 percent to 9 percent. Following those results, the school decided to flip every class in 2011. After that, the now-flipped school's failure rate dropped from 30 to 10 percent. Graduation rates soared above 90 percent. College attendance went from 63 percent in 2010 to 80 percent in 2012 (Rosenberg, 2013).

Approaches to flipped classrooms and flipped teaching continue to be developed, and their impact on student achievement is being studied. Two high school chemistry teachers in Woodland Park, COLORADO, Jonathan Bergmann and Aaron

Sams, report impressive results in their book *Flip Your Classroom: Reach Every Student in Every Class Every Day*. In the following, they explain how they developed the flipped model:

> One day, Aaron had an insight that would change our world. It was one simple observation: "The time when students really need me physically present is when they get stuck and need my individual help. They don't need me there in the room with them to yak at them and give them content; they can receive content on their own."
>
> He then asked this question: "What if we prerecorded all of our lectures, students viewed the video as 'homework,' and then we used the entire class period to help students with the concepts they don't understand?". . .
>
> We implemented the flipped model for one year and we were very pleased with how our students were learning. We had evidence our model worked and was better for kids. (Bergman & Sams, 2012, pp. 4–5)

At this point, the effects of flipped classrooms on students' learning appear to be impressive; however, these results are largely anecdotal and have not been subject to rigorous research studies. Nevertheless, flipped classrooms and flipped teaching provide a model for how technology can be integrated into teaching.

WHAT DIGITAL TECHNOLOGIES CAN BE INTEGRATED INTO TEACHING?

Today's teachers can integrate a dazzling array of digital technologies into their teaching. Until the 1970s, the technology available to teachers who wished to use more than the chalkboard was limited to an overhead projector; a 16-mm movie projector; a tape recorder; and, in a few forward-looking school districts, a television set. Today, teachers are using increasingly powerful online tools to help students learn from the ever-expanding sea of information available on the Internet and to make their own creative contributions to it.

The following sections examine several of the exciting ways that teachers are integrating digital technologies into their teaching. Each section illustrates how integrating technology into teaching involves much more than providing students with access to the Internet. Instead, students must learn to use technology to solve problems, to inquire, to create, and to connect with the global community.

PROFESSIONAL REFLECTION
Listen as an educator identifies four types of technology that can be integrated into teaching.

Online Social Networking

Online social networking refers to an online community of people who share common interests. Participants in **online social networking** can interact in a variety of ways; chat, e-mail, blogging, voice chat, and discussion groups are among the ways group members communicate.

Social networks usually allow a user to create a profile of him- or herself using text, audio, graphics, video, and pictures; then other individuals or groups can access the profile. As a user's circle of "friends" grows, so does a sense of community. Most social networks have security features that permit users to choose who can view their profile or contact them. Several social networking services are available to teachers and students. The social networking services discussed in the following are but a small sample of those available on the Internet.

FACEBOOK, TWITTER, AND TUMBLR

According to the Facebook website, "Millions of people use Facebook every day to keep up with friends, upload an unlimited number of photos, share links and videos, and learn more about the people they meet. Facebook's mission is to give people the power to share and make the world more open and connected." Similarly, the Twitter website states, "Twitter is a real-time information network that connects you to the latest information about what you find interesting. Simply find the public streams you find most compelling and follow the conversations. At the heart of Twitter are small bursts of information called Tweets. Each Tweet is 140 characters in length . . . Connected to each Tweet is a rich details pane that provides additional information, deeper context and embedded media." And, according to Tumblr, "Tumblr lets you effortlessly share anything. Post text, photos, quotes, links, music, and videos from your browser, phone, desktop, email or wherever you happen to be. You can customize everything, from colors to your theme's HTML." Teachers have successfully used Facebook, Twitter, and Tumblr to facilitate small-group projects, highlight exemplary work, build a sense of community outside the classroom, and showcase student creative expressions.

As a teacher-user of Facebook, Twitter, or Tumblr, remember that you are in the public eye at all times. Occasionally, there are media reports about teachers being fired or disciplined because of "inappropriate" profiles on Facebook—for example, teachers posting personal opinions about students, uploaded pictures of teachers engaged in activities deemed inappropriate, and inappropriate communication between teachers and students. Additionally, some school districts have advised teachers not to "friend" students on social networking sites; teacher–student communication via social networking, districts maintain, is inappropriate. For example, the Lee County School District in **FLORIDA** issued the following guidelines for teacher use of social networking sites: "It is inappropriate for employees to communicate, regardless of the reason, with current students enrolled in the district on any public social networking website. This includes becoming 'friends' or allowing students access to personal web pages for communication reasons" (Murphy, 2010).

Classroom Example

Mr. Labronski collaborates with three sophomore English teachers at three other high schools and uses Twitter to teach creative writing. One of his students tweets the first line of a short story around the network of participating schools and invites contributions to the story line. Once all Twitter network participants have contributed, students in each class take the tweeted material and develop a coherent, polished short story. In addition to learning about creative writing, students learn to write clear, concise statements because of the 140-character limitation for Twitter.

YOUTUBE

Another website that today's students visit regularly is YouTube.

YouTube is an online video clearinghouse where students can watch, upload, and share online videos. Videos range from footage captured with a cell phone to high-end film productions. Users can establish profiles and share favorite videos with their friends. In addition to being a site for watching videos, YouTube is a form of online social networking because it can build a sense of community for users. Teachers are using YouTube in a variety of ways: to access international news coverage, political debates, and diverse opinions, and to enhance classroom lessons with stimulating content.

Many schools block access to YouTube because much of the material is inappropriate for educational settings and the videos vary widely in quality. In addition, it can be very time consuming for teachers to preview videos to make sure they are relevant to their educational goals. In lieu of YouTube, many teachers use **TeacherTube**, which allows them to share video materials with classrooms around the world. Another similar site, **SchoolTube**, mainly hosts videos produced by students in class with the help of their teachers.

Classroom Example

English as a second language (ESL) teacher Ms. Hernandez uses YouTube to reinforce correct pronunciation and grammar. She gives students the URLs for several YouTube channels that emphasize learning English.

BLOGS

A **blog** (short for *web log*) is an online journal constructed by an individual and reacted to by those who visit the blog. A blog usually consists of text, but it can include pictures, links to other websites, and media sources that support the author's views on various topics. Blogging can be interactive because the visitor can offer opinions about the author's statements.

Classroom Example

Mr. Sanchez uses a professional blog to recap the day's events in his seventh-grade classroom. He encourages students and their parents or guardians to join the conversation about activities in his classroom. He finds that blogging is a good way to connect with parents or guardians and to get them involved in their children's education.

WIKIS

A **wiki** is a website created, edited, and maintained by groups of people. A wiki website grows based on user creation and is validated by user reviews. Coming out of the social networking movement, wikis follow the logic that many voices are better than one and allow collaborative work by various authors. A wiki website allows anyone or designated members of a group to create, delete, and/or edit the content on the website. One high school, for example, uses wikis for five functions:

1. To support the school's professional learning community (PLC),
2. To provide transparency to the community and to one another about how the school operates,
3. To provide teachers with technology to increase the rigor of their classroom instruction,
4. To provide a platform for student to create online portfolios that document their learning, and
5. To provide evidence of student learning for school accreditation (Roe, 2010).

Classroom Example

Mrs. Rioas uses a wiki as a build-your-own-story writing assignment. She divides students into groups of five and then asks them to write a shared story on a classroom wiki space. The students have to come up with the topic, develop the story line, and create and edit the work—all in their wiki space. As students work on the wiki, Mrs. Rioas examines different iterations of the story, checks progress, provides feedback, and shares the stories with parents and colleagues.

3D VIRTUAL REALITY WORLDS

Three-dimensional (3D) virtual reality worlds are a dynamic part of online social networking; **3D virtual reality worlds** can be a powerful learning tool for active, engaged learning with visually rich, hands-on experiences; trial-and-error activities; and virtual participation in events. For example, a teacher might assume the identity of a personal avatar (an online visual image) and take students on a virtual field trip to a museum, an active volcano, a chemistry lab, a spaceship, or other planets and galaxies. Participants are free to navigate, communicate, access resources, and in some cases manipulate

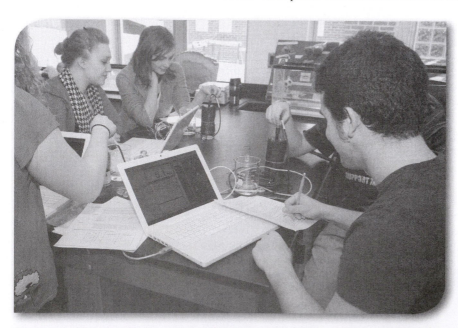

These students receive immediate feedback and reinforcement, are more engaged and motivated, and are acquiring important workplace skills by using the latest software programs. Are there any drawbacks to the use of technology in schools?

the environment as they choose. Dozens of virtual reality worlds are available on the Internet. Among educators, one of the most popular virtual worlds is **Second Life**.

Classroom Example

Ms. Wang, a history teacher, uses Second Life to help students understand past events and apply their understanding to life today. For example, when studying ancient Greece, she locates an "island" at the Second Life site that resembles ancient Athens. Then she develops roles that students can assume and a problem that confronts them—perhaps conflict with Sparta. Students then clothe their avatars according to their roles and then behave as people actually did in ancient Greek society. Ms. Wang, of course, assumes the role of Zeus and guides the action in the Second Life virtual world.

PODCASTS

A **podcast** is a digital media file delivered over the Internet. These files can be played on a computer or mobile device such as an MP3 player or cell phone. A podcast allows for a syndication feed, which delivers digital files to the user automatically once new content is loaded to the site. A podcast can be compared to online radio delivered on the web, with the recipient able to decide what he or she will hear and when.

Classroom Example

Mr. Pendergrass uses podcasting in his advanced-placement (AP) chemistry class. He clips on a small wireless microphone at the beginning of the class period. The microphone is connected to his computer, which is set up to record audio. As he presents content and responds to students' questions, these interactions are recorded in an electronic file. When the session is finished, Mr. Pendergrass opens the audio file, looks for long periods of silence, and edits those out. He then publishes the file to his podcasting site. Students can then download and listen to material he has presented over a week, month, or year.

E-PORTFOLIOS

An e-portfolio can serve many different functions; however, it is best known as an assessment tool. An **e-portfolio** allows students to place work they have completed, or resources they have gathered, in a web-based portfolio. E-portfolios allow teachers and students to track growth and understanding.

Classroom Example

Susanna is a high school senior. She began using an e-portfolio during her freshman year. Originally, she saw the e-portfolio as a place where she could store her electronic artwork. As she began to publish her work in her portfolio space, however, she expanded the content to include all of her creative academic work. Susanna credits her e-portfolio for the scholarship she received to a prestigious university. In her e-portfolio, Susanna included her senior project, a photo-log of her service-learning activities for the victims of the earthquake in Haiti. She included a story she had been working on since her freshman year. She included audio files of music she created and graphics of her artwork. Most impressive, though, are her personal reflections describing her philosophy of life and her professional goals for the future. As she says, "If you want to know who I am, what I can do, and where I can go, look at my e-portfolio."

MOBILE LEARNING

Mobile learning (sometimes termed *m-learning*) involves the use of mobile technologies to enhance students' learning experiences. Teachers are using smartphones with Internet access like the Blackberry and the iPhone, the iTouch (an iPhone without the phone), personal digital assistants (PDAs), and Pocket PCs to engage and motivate learners, at any time and anywhere. They realize the potential of mobile learning; they understand that "more and more of what [students] want and need is available in their pocket on demand" (Prensky, 2010, p. 2). For example, the Pew Research Center's Internet & American Life Project surveyed nearly 2,500 middle and high school teachers and found that 42 percent allow students to use smartphones to look up information in class, but only 11 percent allow students to text in class as part of an assignment (Pew Research Center, 2013).

Classroom Example

Mr. Atkins uses cell phones in his beginning Spanish classes at a middle school. His students call in and are recorded as they read aloud Spanish-language passages. Mr. Atkins then uploads the recordings to his iPod and listens to them after school hours. He also conducts monthly, mobile-based scavenger hunts for his students. He divides each class into teams of four students and sends them clues in Spanish.

Digital Resources for Teaching and Learning

The digital resources available on the web for teaching and learning are almost endless. Truly, the web is like a giant wholesale warehouse for consumers and producers alike. With Web 2.0 interactive sites, teachers and students are not just "consumers," they are "producers" as well. Materials in the warehouse enable them to create brand new products or to develop new ways to use existing products. So much information is available that it can be hard to decide which resources to use. Knowing where to look for quality materials is as important as the materials themselves. To make the most out of your time in this warehouse, it is helpful to know about learning objects and open-source materials.

LEARNING OBJECTS

Learning objects are digital resources that can be reused to support learning. Learning objects are small digital resources that can be:

- Used by themselves, without any additional resources
- Used repeatedly to support learning in a variety of situations
- Combined with other learning objects and organized in various ways—for example, as a unit within a traditional course or as an entire course
- Found easily by using a search engine that looks for descriptive "metadata"—e.g., the instructional topic(s) or learning objective(s) associated with the learning object (Beck, 2008)

The idea behind learning objects is simple. Large chunks of information are broken down into smaller bits of information. For example, a lesson on the Civil War might have smaller pieces consisting of a video on railroads in operation during the Civil War, an animated map of the Battle of Gettysburg, or ideas for activities related to Civil War–era clothing. These objects are then made available to teachers. Teachers may use the objects sequenced in a manner that fits their instructional objectives.

Several online resources are devoted to creating and storing learning objects. Some are discipline-specific, such as the National Science Digital Library funded by the National Science Foundation. Others are very broad, such as the STEM Education Resource Center maintained by PBS Teachers. The STEM Education Resource Center provides television and online content that teachers can use to help students expand their knowledge and skills related to science, technology, engineering, and mathematics (STEM) (PBS Teachers, 2014).

Classroom Example

Mr. Denta has been a substitute teacher at three local high schools during the past year. He is making quite a name for himself as a teacher prepared to teach any subject. Recently, the biology teacher at one of the high schools came down with the flu. The school district called Mr. Denta at 5:00 P.M. and asked him to sub for the teacher. Mr. Denta learned that the teacher was teaching about DNA.

To prepare a lesson on DNA, Mr. Denta went to the site for Multimedia Educational Resource for Learning and Online Teaching (MERLOT), as he had done several times during the last few years. At merlot.org, he entered "DNA" in the search box. He located an excellent lesson on teaching DNA to high school students. The lesson included animations illustrating the formation of DNA and drag-and-drop animated DNA assessments.

OPEN-SOURCE MATERIALS

The open-source initiative grew out of the freeware or shareware approach to disseminating software and creating communities of users during the 1990s. **Open-source materials** are developed by a community of programmers and are distributed for free on the Internet. Users of the materials can, in turn, modify the materials and redistribute them. Although open source is usually associated with software development, the open-source movement is spreading to other areas of education as well, such as the open courseware initiative. The MIT OpenCourse-Ware project is one such example. MIT has made all of its 2,150 courses available for free online. Teachers can examine syllabi, lecture notes, resources, assessments, and teaching materials.

Classroom Example

Mrs. Banari is, by all accounts, obsessed with computers. She wants her high school students to become as passionate about computers as she is. She has offered elective computer science and advanced mathematics courses for several years. Usually, a small core of high-ability students takes these courses. After visiting the MIT OpenCourseWare site, she decided to offer one of the MIT courses, Mathematics for Computer Science, as an elective. Students who signed up for the course knew about MIT's highly ranked programs and were eager to test their abilities at this advanced level.

Digital Resources for Different Subject Areas

As the previous classroom examples suggest, the Internet contains a vast amount of free, high-quality learning materials to use in your teaching. The following sections provide a brief sampling of the myriad ways these materials can be used in different subject areas.

THE FINE ARTS

The fine arts—art, music, theater, and dance—offer numerous opportunities to integrate technology into the fine arts classroom. Teachers have used technology in the fine arts classroom to provide students with opportunities to:

- View famous pieces of art in museums around the world.
- Create and share compilations of art, music, theater, and dance.
- View legendary performances by various fine artists.
- Experience diverse cultural styles of the fine arts.
- Express themselves artistically.
- Share ideas and thoughts about the fine arts with others.

Classroom Example

In smaller school districts, the opportunity to perform with other musicians can be limited. Technology, however, can be used to overcome the isolation of the artist. For example, Musigy makes it possible for people to perform live music together over the Internet. A performer at one location plugs a guitar, keyboard, microphone, or any other electronic instrument into a computer and connects with other musicians interested in jamming. Teachers have set up global jazz bands, string quartets, and rock-and-roll bands with partner schools around the world. In addition to the audio connection, Musigy includes a video connection that allows performers to view others who are performing at the same time.

LANGUAGE ARTS

Language arts—reading, writing, oral communication—offer many opportunities for teachers to integrate technology. Language arts teachers have used technology in the classroom to:

- Access great works of literature from special or rare book collections.
- Show students videos of famous speeches.
- Improve student writing by using online writing labs.
- Combat plagiarism by using online plagiarism detection programs.
- Access hard-to-find journals.
- Improve students' word recognition and pronunciation by using animation and audio.
- Increase students' reading comprehension by using audio textbooks or e-books.

The Teachers' Voices: Walk in My Shoes feature for this chapter describes how an English teacher became aware of her students' extensive out-of-class reading on the Internet and learned how to relate her classroom teaching to students' interest in developing online projects.

Classroom Example

Good Readers, a movie produced by a first-grade class at Highland Ranch Elementary School in San Diego, **CALIFORNIA** is a powerful example of technology integration in the language arts classroom. The teacher divided students into teams, each of which included a cinematographer, a director, and a spokesperson. Each student was given an opportunity to try out each role. During the week, each team wrote a script that highlighted the six strategies of "good readers." Then, students learned to speak their lines loudly and clearly while being filmed. After filming, students edited the raw footage using a video editing program. Making the film about "good readers" enabled students to "see" good reading strategies in action; as a result, they became better readers themselves (Poway Unified School District, 2008).

MATHEMATICS

Technology has been a part of mathematics for centuries—from the abacus to the supercomputer. Mathematicians have long relied on technology to help solve complex problems. Similarly, mathematics teachers have integrated technology into their teaching to:

- Help students understand numerical relationships.
- Do math calculations such as addition, subtraction, multiplication, and division; find the square root; and solve trigonometry functions and linear equations.
- Help students estimate and measure.
- Help students deal with the symbolic manipulations needed in algebra and calculus.
- Reduce student anxiety about memorizing complex formulas in geometry and trigonometry.
- Help students understand more complex mathematical concepts and ideas.
- Allow for the application of mathematical solutions to real-world problems.

Classroom Example

Ms. Stone teaches solid geometry at the local high school. With their iPods, her students have 24/7 access to the class website. The site includes links to podcasts and notes from her in-class lectures, video clips on related topics, and information about assignments and exams. Ms. Stone also gives multiple-choice quizzes on iPods, which automatically calculate scores and give students immediate feedback on their knowledge of content.

SCIENCE

Science teachers from the elementary through high school levels have made extensive use of technology in the classroom. Technology integration has enabled them to:

- Tour the solar system with students.
- Become miniaturized and travel throughout the human body.
- Visit the ocean floor.
- Experience an earthquake.

Many science teachers have their students conduct **webquests**—online inquiry research projects that consist of five parts:

1. An introduction to spark students' interest in the quest
2. A task description explaining the purpose and outcomes of the quest
3. Steps to follow during the quest and resources to be used
4. Evaluation consisting of rubrics and assessment guidelines
5. Conclusion to provide closure

In the following, a science teacher comments on the benefits of having students search for information on the Internet:

> I think [the Internet] provides more opportunities for the kids than relying primarily on a textbook. I think that the Web allows them to go out and see things that the book just can't show them. If they want they can go out and see excellent schematics of the human cell. They can go out and see excellent photographs of cells. They can spend all day looking underneath a microscope and never see a cell as nice as they can find online because they put the best ones out there. (Wallace, 2004, p. 462)

Classroom Example

Students at a rural high school use Second Life to study the human brain in biology class. Students and their teacher will have a virtual meeting with a neurosurgeon from a large urban hospital at a virtual model of the human brain located on a public island in Second Life. At a prearranged time, they meet at the brainstem. After a brief lecture by the doctor and a short question-and-answer session, the doctor leads them to the cerebrum, where she discusses the basic functions of the lobes. Students are able to manipulate the lobes and observe how the lobes react. From the cerebrum, they will visit the cerebellum for a similar experience.

SOCIAL STUDIES

Social studies teachers have used technology to explore economics, geography, political science, psychology, and sociology. For example, social studies teachers have used technology to:

- Allow students to be floor traders on the Wall Street stock market.
- Enable students to become a leader of state and understand how their political decisions affect the countries they lead.
- Cope with the poverty, hunger, and political corruption that characterize the lives of people in many developing countries.
- Examine important primary source documents from different historical periods.
- Help students experience how crime and violence affect the lives of victims.

Classroom Example

Mrs. Muralia's students have been studying the Israeli–Palestinian conflict for the past week. They have read the textbook, watched a video, listened to historical speeches online, researched articles and current events, and discussed the situation in class. However, it was not until students experienced a videogame that allowed them to role-play various characters in this historical conflict that they

TEACHERS' VOICES
Walk in My Shoes
Tracy J. Tarasuik
Park Campus School
Round Lake, ILLINOIS

The preceding is excerpted from the following article by Tracy J. Tarasuik: "Combining Traditional and Contemporary Texts: Moving My English Class to the Computer Lab," *Journal of Adolescent & Adult Literacy, 53*(7), April 2010, pp. 543–552.

understood how complex and difficult the situation is. In the videogame, students assumed roles of the Israeli prime minister, local Palestinian political leaders, Israeli settlers, Palestinians working in Gaza, or Israeli soldiers. Each student's role called for an action followed by a reaction, followed by another action, and so on. Allowing students to navigate through this complex political landscape in various roles enabled them to begin to think critically and to understand the various points of view that make up the Israeli–Palestinian situation.

HOW AVAILABLE AND FREQUENTLY USED ARE THE LATEST TECHNOLOGIES IN THE CLASSROOM?

As the preceding sections illustrate, a dazzling array of digital technologies can be used in the classroom. However, are these technologies readily available to teachers and to students? Are they part of students' day-to-day learning experiences in schools? What obstacles do teachers encounter when they incorporate technology into their teaching? To determine the availability and use of educational technology in schools, the U.S. Department of Education gathered data for a report titled *Teachers' Use of Educational Technology in U.S. Public Schools*.

Availability and Use of Technology in the Classroom

Table 13.1 shows the percentage of teachers who report the availability of various digital tools in the classroom and the percentage who report using those tools "sometimes" or "often" during their classes. Among teachers who have LCD (liquid crystal display) or DLP (digital light processing) projectors available, 72 percent use them "often" or "sometimes"; 57 percent use interactive whiteboards "often" or "sometimes"; and 49 percent use digital cameras "often or "sometimes."

Watch as educators discuss and evaluate the types of technology they use with students.

The Internet is a remarkable resource for planning lessons, delivering in-class instruction, and fostering home–school communication. It is a dynamic, unlimited resource that invites contributions by anyone, anywhere, at any time. According to a U.S. Department of Education survey, 94 percent of K–12 public school teachers report using the Internet "sometimes" or "often" for classroom preparation or in-class instruction (Thomas & Lewis, 2010). However, the survey also revealed that fewer than half of the teachers use software for administering tests; and one-third, or fewer, use simulation and visualization programs, blogs and/or wikis, and social networking sites in the classroom.

Many school districts have taken steps to encourage teachers to increase their use of technology in the classroom. These districts understand the importance of meeting the professional development needs of teachers, like the following sixth-grade teacher who stated, "As professionals, we (educators) . . . need to embrace the new technology. I am ready!" (Egbert, 2009, p. 17). An example of a school district that fosters teachers' use of software and the Internet is **WASHINGTON** State's Kent School District. At the district's Technology Integration website (see Figure 13.5), teachers can access a variety of resources to use in the classroom. At the site, Kent teachers can also sign up for professional development activities.

Another example is the IBM-funded "Reinventing Education" grant program implemented by the **WEST VIRGINIA** and **VERMONT** Departments of Education. Teachers throughout both states can access the Riverdeep Learning Village (RLV), a suite of online applications that support communication and collaboration among teachers, parents, community members, and students. The applications enable teachers to access curriculum content and to create customized lessons and activities based on individual student needs. Through the RLV, parents and guardians can stay informed about their children's academic progress and activities.

TABLE 13.1

Percent of teachers reporting the availability of various technology devices, and of those with the devices available, percent that reported using the devices sometimes or often for instruction during their classes

Characteristic	LCD or DLP projector			Videoconference unit			Interactive whiteboard			Classroom response system[1]		
	Availability		Use sometimes or often	Availability		Use sometimes or often	Availability		Use sometimes or often	Availability		Use sometimes or often
	Available as needed	In classroom every day		Available as needed	In classroom every day		Available as needed	In classroom every day		Available as needed	In classroom every day	
All public school teachers	36	48	72	21	1	13	28	23	57	22	6	35
School instructional level[2]												
Elementary	37	44	68	19	1	12	31	23	58	21	7	35
Secondary	33	56	78	23	2	15	23	23	58	24	6	34

Characteristic	Digital camera			MP3 player/iPod			Document camera[1]			Handheld device		
	Availability		Use sometimes or often	Availability		Use sometimes or often	Availability		Use sometimes or often	Availability		Use sometimes or often
	Available as needed	In classroom every day		Available as needed	In classroom every day		Available as needed	In classroom every day		Available as needed	In classroom every day	
All public school teachers	64	14	49	18	5	36	22	17	56	8	4	50
School instructional level[2]												
Elementary	67	14	53	14	4	34	23	19	60	8	5	60
Secondary	57	13	41	24	6	37	23	13	48	8	2	28

[1] Wireless systems allowing teachers to pose questions and students to respond using—clickers or hand-held response pads, with responses compiled on a computer.
[2] Data for combined schools (those with both elementary and secondary grades) are included in the totals.
[3] Devices that transmit images of 2- or 3-dimensional objects, text, or graphics to a computer monitor or LCD projector.

Source: Adapted from Gray, L., Thomas, N., and Lewis, L. (2010). Teachers' Use of Educational Technology in U.S. Public Schools: 2009 (NCES 2010-040). National Center for Education Statistics, Institute of Education Sciences, U.S. Department of Education. Washington, DC., pp. 7–8.

FIGURE 13.5   Technology integration, Kent School District

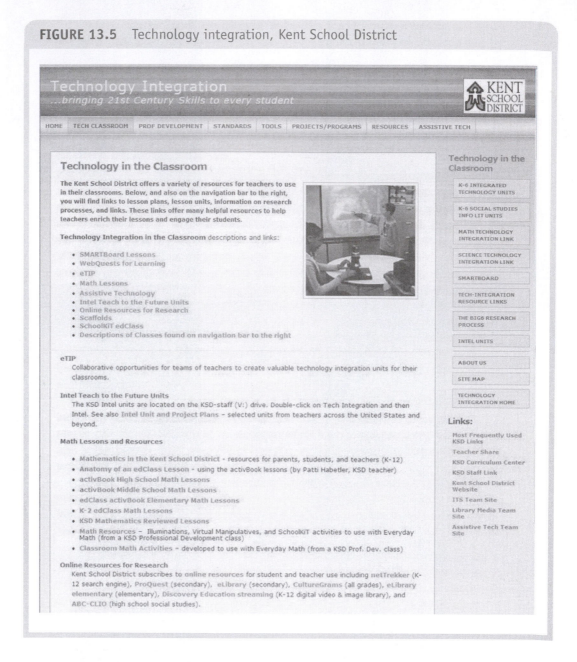

Student Use of Technology in the Classroom

Table 13.2 shows the percentage of teachers reporting how frequently their students use educational technology "rarely," "sometimes," or "often" for various purposes during their classes. The results show that the following are the most frequent uses of technology by students: learning or practicing basic skills (69 percent); conducting research (66 percent); preparing written text (61 percent); creating or using graphics or visual displays (53 percent); solving problems, analyzing data, or performing calculations (45 percent); and developing and presenting multimedia presentations (42 percent). On the other hand, the results indicate that students are less likely to use technology for the following: accessing social networking sites (7 percent); contributing to blogs or wikis (9 percent); designing and producing a product (13 percent); developing or running demonstrations, models, or simulations (17 percent); conducting experiments or performing measurements (25 percent); or creating art, music, movies, or webcasts (25 percent).

TABLE 13.2

Percent of teachers reporting how frequently their students performed various activities using educational technology during their classes, based on teachers reporting that the activity applied to their students.

Characteristic	Prepare written text		Create or use graphics or visual displays		Learn or practice basic skills		Conduct research		Correspond with others		Contribute to blogs or wikis		Use social networking websites	
	Rarely	Sometimes or often	Rarely	Sometimes or often	Rarely	Sometimes or often	Rarely	Sometimes or often	Rarely	Sometimes or often	Rarely	Sometimes or often	Rarely	Sometimes or often
All public school teachers	24	61	27	53	17	69	22	66	21	31	12	9	9	7
School instructional level[1]														
Elementary	27	57	29	49	15	76	23	64	20	26	10	7	7	6
Secondary	20	67	24	59	21	53	20	69	24	40	16	13	12	9

Characteristic	Solve problems, analyze data, or perform calculations		Conduct experiments or perform measurements		Develop and present multimedia presentations		Create art, music, movies, or webcasts		Develop or run demonstrations, models, or simulations		Design and produce a product	
	Rarely	Sometimes or often	Rarely	Sometimes or often	Rarely	Sometimes or often	Rarely	Sometimes or often	Rarely	Sometimes or often	Rarely	Sometimes or often
All public school teachers	23	45	25	25	42	25	24	25	23	17	17	13
School instructional level[1]												
Elementary	21	45	24	23	35	26	25	21	21	14	15	11
Secondary	25	46	27	30	53	24	24	32	26	25	20	17

[1] Data for combined schools (those with both elementary and secondary grades) are included in the totals.

Source: Adapted from Gray, L., Thomas, N., and Lewis, L. (2010). *Teachers' Use of Educational Technology in U.S. Public Schools: 2009* (NCES 2010-040). National Center for Education Statistics, Institute of Education Sciences, U.S. Department of Education. Washington, DC., pp. 13–14.

WHAT DOES RESEARCH SAY ABOUT TECHNOLOGY INTEGRATION AND STUDENT LEARNING?

The integration of technology into teaching and learning has grown enormously since the early 1990s. Now, teachers and other educators want to know if technology integration enhances student learning. Regarding the effects of technology on learning, research results are just now beginning to appear. However, as one observer noted, "Technology integration can be one of the most challenging topics to find quality research on. The term itself is a broad umbrella for numerous practices that may have little in common with each other. In addition, technology tools change rapidly, and outcomes can vary depending on implementation" (Vega, 2013).

Apple Classrooms of Tomorrow Project (ACOT)

One of the most informative research studies is based on the Apple Classrooms of Tomorrow (ACOT) project launched in seven K–12 classrooms in 1986. Participating students and teachers each received two computers—one for school and one for home. Eight years later, study results indicated that all ACOT students performed as well as expected without computers, and some performed better. More important, perhaps, "students in the technology-rich ACOT classrooms were more apt to work together, which made school more interesting and, consequently, improved students' attitudes about themselves and their learning. Rather than merely fulfilling what was asked of them is assignments, these students surpassed original goals, challenging themselves to explore new and creative projects, and often choosing to work during their free time" (Bitter & Legacy, 2008, p. 149). Also, 90 percent of ACOT students went on to college after graduating from high school, whereas only 15 percent of non-ACOT students did.

An additional positive finding of the ACOT study was how teachers gradually began to use the computers in new ways in the classroom. "When [ACOT] teachers were able to move past that pervasive teacher-centered view of education, students and teachers, as communities of learners, were able to benefit from the range of individual areas of expertise represented by the entire group" (Bitter & Legacy, 2008, p. 146). Teachers rearranged their classrooms to enable students to work collaboratively on projects, and they frequently made arrangements for students who wished to stay after school to work on multimedia projects.

INTEGRATING TECHNOLOGY

Teacher participants in the ACOT study were volunteers, many of whom had little experience with educational technology. As with teachers learning any new instructional strategy, the ACOT teachers frequently struggled to adjust to their new computer-filled rooms. Researchers found that the teachers progressed through five distinct stages as they integrated the technology into their teaching (Bitter & Legacy, 2008):

1. **Entry stage**—For many teachers, this was a period of painful growth and discomfort; learning to use computers presented challenges similar to those faced by beginning teachers.
2. **Adoption stage**—Becoming more proactive toward the challenge of integrating computers, teachers began to teach students how to use the computers and software.
3. **Adaptation stage**—Teachers turned from teaching the technology to using the technology as a tool to teach content.
4. **Appropriation stage**—Teachers moved from merely accommodating computers in their daily routines to personally exploring new teaching possibilities afforded by the technology.
5. **Invention stage**—Eager to move beyond teacher-centered instruction, teachers began to collaborate with peers in developing authentic, inquiry-oriented learning activities.

APPLE CLASSROOMS OF TOMORROW—TODAY (ACOT²)

To implement the findings of the ACOT study and "to help high schools get closer to creating the kind of learning environment [today's] generation of students' needs, needs, wants, and expects so they will stay in school" (Apple, Inc., 2008, p. 3), the Apple Classrooms of Tomorrow—Today (ACOT²) project was launched in 2008. The first phase of the project involved the development of six "essential design principles" for the 21st-century high school:

- Understanding of 21st-century skills and outcomes
- Relevant and applied curriculum
- Informative assessment
- A culture of innovation and creativity
- Social and emotional connections with students
- Ubiquitous access to technology

This teacher uses technology to develop authentic, inquiry-oriented learning activities for his students.

The second phase involved providing participating high schools with online resources based on the six principles. The resources emphasized Web 2.0 sites like You-Tube, MySpace, and Second Life that allow students to produce content, not just consume content.

The third phase will involve the development of "200 Days for a Lifetime of Success," a freshman-year curriculum to prepare students for success. The curriculum will reflect the fact that "students today expect to learn in an environment that mirrors their lives and their futures—one that seamlessly integrates today's digital tools, accommodates a mobile lifestyle, and encourages collaboration and teamwork in physical and virtual spaces" (Apple, Inc., 2008, p. 9).

"Wired" Students and Their Ability to Focus

Evidence is beginning to emerge that technology may have a negative effect on students' ability to focus on learning tasks. For example, the Pew Research Center's Internet & American Life Project (November 1, 2012) analyzed data from more than 2,400 teachers and concluded:

> Overwhelming majorities . . . agree with the assertions that "today's digital technologies are creating an easily distracted generation with short attention spans" (87%) and "today's students are too 'plugged in' and need more time away from their digital technologies" (86%). Two-thirds (64%) agree with the notion that "today's digital technologies do more to distract students than to help them academically." (p. 7)

An expert in the "psychology of technology," Larry Rosen (2013), makes similar points in his book *iDisorder: Understanding Our Obsession with Technology and Overcoming Its Hold on Us*. According to Rosen, "iDisorder" can change the brain's ability to process information and even lead to psychological disorders, such as stress, sleeplessness, and a compulsive need to monitor technological devices. "What we are looking at is a new disorder, one that combines elements of many psychiatric maladies and is centered on the way we all relate to technology and media: an iDisorder" (p. 4).

Rosen and his research team observed 263 middle school, high school, and university students studying during a 15-minute period in their homes. The researchers wanted to find out if students could maintain focus, and, if not, what distracted them.

Rosen and his team found that "these students were only able to stay on task for an average of three to five minutes before losing their focus. Universally, their distractions came from technology, including: (1) having more devices available in their studying environment such as iPods, laptops, and smart phones; (2) texting; and (3) accessing Facebook." Additionally, the researchers found that "The worst students were those who consumed more media each day and had a preference for switching back and forth between several tasks at the same time." Moreover, the researchers were "stunned" to find that "If the students checked Facebook just once during the 15-minute study period, they had a lower grade-point average. It didn't matter how many times they looked at Facebook; once was enough" (Rosen, November 13, 2012).

Findings from Other Research Studies

A powerful way to determine whether certain educational practices actually influence students' learning is to conduct meta-analyses, that is, to "take the findings from single studies and calculate a way to compare them with each other. The goal is to synthesize the findings statistically and determine what the studies reveal when examined all together" (Kirkpatrick & Cuban, 1998). In addition, meta-analyses address the complications and difficulties involved in determining the effects of computers on learning, particularly when much of the research in that area has been shown to be methodologically flawed. For example, research studies of technology integration "are of little use unless they elaborate the children's ages, the subject, the software used, the kinds of outcomes that were sought, and how the study was done."

One of the largest meta-analytic studies of online learning was conducted by the U.S. Department of Education (May 2009). The study, titled *Evaluation of Evidence-Based Practices in Online Learning: A Meta-Analysis and Review of Online Learning Studies,* sought to compare the effectiveness of online learning with face-to-face instruction. Surprisingly, on its first review of research published between 1996 and 2006, the Department of Education team found *no rigorously conducted studies* comparing K–12 online learning with face-to-face instruction (p. xiv). A second review of research, this time through 2008, evaluated more than 1,000 studies of online learning. However, the review identified only 5 K–12 studies and 44 studies of undergraduate and older learners that met the criteria for quality.

The analysis of these studies found that "on average, students in online learning conditions performed better than those receiving face-to-face instruction" (U.S. Department of Education, May 2009, p. xiv). However, because the results were based largely on older learners, the research report urged "caution" in applying the results to K–12 settings. In fact, the report stated that "without new random assignment or controlled quasi-experimental studies of the effects of online learning options for K–12 students, policymakers will lack scientific evidence of the effectiveness of these emerging alternatives to face-to-face instruction" (U.S. Department of Education, May 2009, p. xvii).

The results of several additional meta-analytic studies of integrating technology into education are presented in the following.

- **A Meta-Analysis of the Effects of Computer Technology on School Students Mathematics Leaning**—This meta-analytic study found generally positive impacts of technology on K–12 students' math learning. Stronger effects were found for students with special needs and elementary, rather than secondary, students. The greatest effects were found when teachers used constructivist, rather than traditional teaching methods (Li & Ma, 2010).
- **What Forty Years of Research Says About the Impact of Technology on Learning: A Second-Order Meta-Analysis and Validation Study**—This study examined 25 meta-analyses that encompassed more than 1,000 studies. Results indicate that the use of technology has a small to moderate positive effect on student learning. Greater effects were linked to using technology to support knowledge formation rather than using technology to present content. Teacher effectiveness and technology skills may have a greater effect on student learning than the type of technology used (Tamim, Bernard, Borokhovski, Abrami, & Schmid, 2011).

- **The Effectiveness of Educational Technology Applications for Enhancing Mathematics Achievement in K–12 Classrooms**—This meta-analysis focused on 74 well-designed studies that included more than 56,000 K–12 students. Results revealed that computer applications have a small but positive effect on math achievement. Math programs (for example, *Jostens, PLATO, Larson Pre-Algebra,* and *SRA Drill and Practice*) based on individual needs and offered as a supplement to traditional instruction had greater effects on math achievement (at all grade levels) if used for more than 30 minutes a week (Cheung & Slavin, 2011).

- **The Effectiveness of Educational Technology Applications for Enhancing Reading Achievement in K–12 Classrooms: A Meta-Analysis**—This meta-analysis focused on 84 well-designed studies that included more than 60,000 K–12 students. The largest effects on reading achievement were found for approaches that integrated computer and noncomputer instruction (for example, *READ 180, Voyager Passport,* and *Writing to Read*) and included extensive professional development for teachers. For example, in *READ 180* classrooms, "Each period begins with a 20-minute shared reading and skills lesson, and then students in groups of five rotate among three activities: computer-assisted instruction in reading, modeled or independent reading, and small-group instruction with the teacher" (Cheung & Slavin, 2012, p. 19). This meta-analysis also confirmed previous research and found that supplemental computer-assisted programs to augment regular classroom instruction (for example, *Destination Reading, Plato Focus, Waterford Early Reading Program, Headsprout, Academy of Reading,* and *LeapTrack*) **did not** show meaningful effects on reading achievement for K–12 students (Cheung & Slavin, 2012).

- **What Is Our Current Understanding of One-to-One Computer Projects?: A Systematic Narrative Research Review**—This research focused on research studies of 1:1 computer projects in school settings during a 5-year period. Generally, laptops were used for searching and exploration (for example, physics simulations), student expression (student presentations and written reports using PowerPoint and Word), communication (e-mail, discussion boards, and instant messaging [IM], between students and between students and teachers), and organization (for example, OneNote). Studies found that laptops tended to improve student motivation and engagement in learning. The use of laptops "slightly improved" students' writing and technology skills, and "very slightly improved" students' scores on high-stakes tests (Fleischer, 2012).

- **Our Princess Is in Another Castle: A Review of Trends in Serious Gaming for Education**—According to the researchers, digital learning games "target the acquisition of knowledge as its own end, and foster habits of mind and understanding that are generally useful within an academic context." The researchers found "promising but inconclusive" evidence that games promote learning in some K–12 settings. The strongest effects on learning were found for language-learning videogames, physical education and tactile videogames (for example, *Wii* videogames), and history videogames (for example, role-playing videogames). The review found little support for gaming in science and mathematics (Young et al., 2012).

Research studies such as the preceding indicate that technology *can have* modest, positive effects on students' learning. As more funds are made available to purchase advanced technologies and software, train teachers, and provide technical support, these effects will, no doubt, become even stronger.

Although research has yet to support the hype that surrounded the integration of technology into teaching during the early 1990s, technology will influence all aspects of education even more in the future. Thus, researchers should pose not just a single question about educational technology—Is it effective? Instead, multiple questions should be posed. Answers to questions such as the following will enable educators to understand how and under what circumstances educational technology can powerfully enhance students' learning: In what educational settings is educational technology most effective? For which students is educational technology most effective? For attaining what educational purposes is educational technology most effective? For teachers with what styles of teaching is educational technology most effective?

WHAT ARE THE CHALLENGES OF INTEGRATING TECHNOLOGY INTO TEACHING?

There continue to be challenges related to integrating technology into teaching. Failure to meet these challenges will shortchange students and prevent them from participating fully in the digital age. Three of the most significant challenges are access to technology for all students, funding for technology and technical support, and training in technology for teachers.

FOCUS ON DIVERSITY: ACCESS TO TECHNOLOGY FOR ALL STUDENTS

Internet access is a vital part of a school's capacity to benefit from the vast resources found in cyberspace. Prior to the mid-1990s, about 35 percent of public schools had access to the Internet, and the richest schools had almost 50 percent more Internet-linked classrooms per teacher—a disparity that came to be known as the "digital divide." Today, classroom Internet access is now almost universal and schools have reduced the number of students per computer; however, there is evidence of a **digital divide** if the ownership and use of technology at home are compared to family income. For example, the Pew Research Center's Internet & American Life Project found that broadband access at home, cell phone ownership, and Internet usage are significantly related to family income (see Figure 13.6). The project also found that ownership and use of technology at home are not significantly related to community type (rural, suburban, urban), education level, race, gender, or age (Pew Research Center, 2010, pp. 9–10). Last, a survey by the Pew Research Center's Internet & American Life Project found that households earning $75,000 or more are much more likely than households earning less than $30,000 to own the following technologies:

- desktop computers
- laptop computers
- iPods or other types of MP3 players
- game consoles
- e-book readers
- iPads or other types of tablet computers (Pew Research Center, 2010)

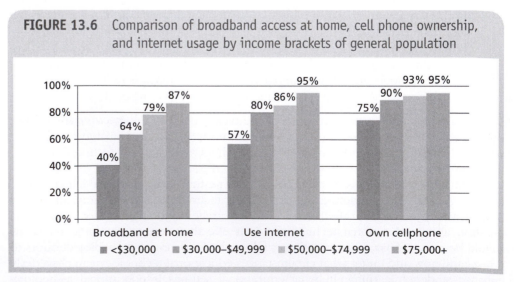

FIGURE 13.6 Comparison of broadband access at home, cell phone ownership, and internet usage by income brackets of general population

Source: Pew Research Center's Internet & American Life Project, August 9–September 13, 2010. Tracking Survey, N = 3,001 adults and the margin of error is +/− 2.5 percentage points. *Use of the Internet in Higher-Income Households,* November 24, 2010, Washington, DC: Pew Research Center, p. 2.

To reduce the digital divide, the Broadband Affordability Act was introduced to Congress in in 2011. The act would offer more affordable Internet service to low-income households. Although Congress failed to enact the act she introduced, Congresswoman Doris Matsui has continued to stress the importance of affordable broadband access:

> As part of our nation's economic security in the 21st Century, we will need to continue to strive to address a looming crisis that largely gets overlooked, and that is closing our nation's digital divide and improving digital literacy. . . . Unfortunately, it is estimated that nearly 100 million Americans have not yet adopted broadband Internet at home, many of whom simply can't afford the high-cost of broadband service . . . It is imperative that our nation close this economic digital divide. (Matsui, 2013)

Funding for Technology and Technical Support

Funding provided by No Child Left Behind (NCLB), Title II, Part D, is playing a key role in helping the states incorporate educational technology. Nearly a quarter of the states report that NCLB funds are the only source of funds for technology, and half of the states report that these funds are their "primary" source for educational technology funding (State Educational Technology Directors Association, 2005). Only 10 states have funding programs in place to regularly replace or update technology in all schools (*Education Week,* 2005, p. 50). As schools continue to incorporate technology, about 69 percent of their total technology spending is devoted to purchasing hardware, 15 percent to purchasing software, 9 percent to outside services, and 6 percent to providing staff development (*Education Week,* 2005, p. 8).

Although schools are getting more computer hardware, most cannot afford to hire sufficient support staff for technology. Only 31 percent of public schools report having full-time staff in the school whose only responsibility is technology support and/or technology integration. Forty-seven percent of secondary schools and 27 percent of elementary schools have full-time technology staff (Gray, Thomas, & Lewis, 2010, p. 10). As a result, most schools rely on central district personnel or computer-savvy teachers and/or students for support.

High-Quality, Continuous Training in Technology for Teachers

Using technology to enhance students' learning requires more than investing in the latest hardware, software, and connectivity to the Internet. E-mailing students, parents, and peers; conducting classroom demonstrations augmented with multimedia; using presentation graphics to address students' varied learning styles; and designing lessons that require students to use the Internet as a resource for inquiry should be second nature for teachers. Just as new technological skills are needed in the workplace, a high degree of technological literacy is needed in the classroom. Thus, acquiring proficiency in the ever-evolving array of technologies and developing the ability to evaluate software and websites should be an important part of professional development for new and veteran teachers. However, teachers frequently complain of a lack of training in how to use technology to reach their curriculum goals. A U.S. Department of Education survey of more than 2,000 public K–12 schools found that 36 percent disagreed with the following statement: "Teachers are sufficiently trained to integrate technology into classroom instruction." In addition, 31 percent disagreed with the following: "Teachers construct lessons in which students use a range of educational technologies" (Gray et al., 2010, p. 17). To help you evaluate computer-based instructional materials, Figure 13.7 presents criteria for evaluating software programs, and Figure 13.8 presents criteria for evaluating websites.

FIGURE 13.7 Criteria for evaluating software programs

	Poor	Fair	Excellent
User Friendliness			
How easy is it to start the program?	☐	☐	☐
Is there an overview or site map for the program?	☐	☐	☐
Can students easily control the pace of the program?	☐	☐	☐
Can students exit the program easily?	☐	☐	☐
Can students create their own paths through the program and develop their own links among elements?	☐	☐	☐
After first-time use, can students bypass introductory or orientation material?	☐	☐	☐
Does the program include useful hotlinks to Internet sites?	☐	☐	☐
Inclusiveness			
Can students with hearing or visual impairments make full use of the program?	☐	☐	☐
Can students navigate the program by making simple keystrokes with one hand?	☐	☐	☐
Does the material avoid stereotypes and reflect sensitivity to racial, cultural, and gender differences?	☐	☐	☐
Textual Material			
How accurate and thorough is the content?	☐	☐	☐
Is the content well organized and clearly presented?	☐	☐	☐
Is the textual content searchable?	☐	☐	☐
Can the content be integrated into the curriculum?	☐	☐	☐
Images			
Is the image resolution high quality?	☐	☐	☐
Is the layout attractive, user friendly, and uncluttered?	☐	☐	☐
Do the graphics and colors enhance instruction?	☐	☐	☐
How true are the colors of the images?	☐	☐	☐
Are the images large enough?	☐	☐	☐
Does the program have a zoom feature that indicates the power of magnification?	☐	☐	☐
Does the program make effective use of video and animation?	☐	☐	☐
Audio			
Are the audio clips high quality?	☐	☐	☐
Does the audio enhance instruction?	☐	☐	☐
Technical			
Is installation of the program easy and trouble-free?	☐	☐	☐
Are instructions clear and easy to follow?	☐	☐	☐
Is user-friendly online help available?	☐	☐	☐
Are technical support people easy to reach, helpful, and courteous?	☐	☐	☐
Motivational			
Does the program capture and hold students' interest?	☐	☐	☐
Are students eager to use the program again?	☐	☐	☐
Does the program give appropriate, motivational feedback?	☐	☐	☐
Does the program provide prompts or cues to promote students' learning?	☐	☐	☐

FIGURE 13.8 Criteria for evaluating websites

	Poor	Fair	Excellent
Authoritativeness			
The author(s) are respected authorities in the field.	☐	☐	☐
The author(s) are knowledgeable.	☐	☐	☐
The author(s) provide a list of credentials and/or educational background.	☐	☐	☐
The author(s) represent respected, credible institutions or organizations.	☐	☐	☐
Complete information on references (or sources) is provided.	☐	☐	☐
Information for contacting the author(s) and webmaster is provided.	☐	☐	☐
Comprehensiveness			
All facets of the subject are covered.	☐	☐	☐
Sufficient detail is provided at the site.	☐	☐	☐
Information provided is accurate.	☐	☐	☐
Political, ideological, and other biases are not evident.	☐	☐	☐
Presentation			
Graphics serve an educational, rather than decorative, purpose.	☐	☐	☐
Links are provided to related sites.	☐	☐	☐
What icons stand for is clear and unambiguous.	☐	☐	☐
The website loads quickly.	☐	☐	☐
The website is stable and seldom, if ever, nonfunctional.	☐	☐	☐
Timeliness			
The original website was produced recently.	☐	☐	☐
The website is updated and/or revised regularly.	☐	☐	☐
Links given at the website are up-to-date and reliable.	☐	☐	☐

The following comments by the father of a 12-year-old student highlight the critical need for teachers to receive high-quality, continuous training in how to integrate technology into teaching:

> I just don't get what his school must be thinking. He comes home, turns on his laptop, pulls out his homework and starts doing paper-and-pencil worksheets. He keeps peeking at Facebook or whatever is on the screen and checking his text messages. He's a good student and I may be naïve, but why can't the school figure out how to combine his paper-and-pencil homework (which bores him literally to tears some nights) with his love of everything he does on the computer? I try to help him by finding websites that present interesting ways to understand his homework but it really isn't my job, is it? The school has lots of computers in his classroom but mostly they are used for playing educational games that my son (and I), quite frankly, find boring and tedious. (Rosen, 2010, pp. 4–5)

Not surprisingly, 17 percent of schools report that students help school staff integrate technology into instruction to a "major" or "moderate extent"; and 39 percent report that students help to a "minor extent" (Gray et al., 2010, p. 13). The Teaching on Your Feet feature in this chapter describes how one teacher's students came up with a solution to the shortage of equipment for the multimedia projects to be completed by small collaborative learning groups. A nationwide example of how tech-savvy students can help teachers integrate technology is Generation YES.

THE GenYES MODEL: STUDENT-LED TECHNOLOGY INTEGRATION

The GenYES model of student-facilitated professional development for teachers began in 1996 as a program funded by the U.S. Department of Education in the Olympia School District in WASHINGTON State. **GenYES** is a teacher professional development model that empowers students to play a major role in facilitating technology integration in the school. To date, more than 2,000 schools and 75,000 teachers have collaborated with GenYES students to integrate technology to improve student learning. GenYES provides training, resources, materials, and online tools that support meaningful student involvement in all areas of technology and allow them to play a role in designing professional development activities for teachers.

The GenYES approach teaches students how technology is used in education, and then pairs teachers and students, with students helping teachers to integrate technology into their classrooms. These teacher–student teams produce technology-infused lessons for the teacher's classroom that are aligned with curriculum standards. The GenYES program consists of the following three components:

> **GenYES—Student-Supported Professional Development**—Students in grades 4–12 partner with classroom teachers to develop technology-infused lessons.
>
> **TechYES—Student Technology Literacy Certification**—Students in grades 6–9 take on the major responsibility for becoming technology literate by creating projects that meet No Child Left Behind (NCLB) requirements for eighth-grade tech literacy. Peer mentors are trained to assist students and assess projects.
>
> **GenerationTECH—Student-Led Technology Support**—Students in grades 8–12 learn troubleshooting, communication, and documentation skills as they help schools keep their technology up and running.

Evaluation studies of the GenYES model "have shown increases in student achievement and engagement, increases in teacher ability to teach with technology and understand how technology integrates into curriculum and satisfaction that the GenYES model is an effective and powerful way to engage students and increase the authentic use of technology in schools" (GenYES Corp., 2010, p. 1). In addition, the U.S. Department of Education's Expert Panel on Educational Technology concluded that, in addition to fostering learning gains for students, "there is complete and compelling demonstration that the program promotes coherent organizational change" (GenYES Corp., 2010, p. 4).

Ten years of data collected by the Northwest Regional Educational Laboratory (NWREL) show schoolwide increases in technology integration as a result of student leadership for technology integration. In addition, the program is an "effective alternative for schools wishing to integrate technology into their regular curriculum and increase their use of project-based, student-centered learning practices" (Harper, 2006, p. 3).

Surveys of teachers who have received technology integration support from GenYES students reveal that they had "overwhelmingly positive responses to collaborating with students and believed it had a real impact on the way they would use technology to teach their classes" (Harper 2006, p. 3). The following are among the results of GenYES surveys:

- Eighty-nine percent agree that as a consequence of GenYES, their students learned content better.
- Ninety-six percent report that they will continue adding technology to their lessons as a result of what they learned from their GenYES student partner.
- Eighty-two percent report that the GenYES experience will change the way they teach in the future. (Harper, 2006, p. 3)

In response to the uneven quality of professional development and technical support, several state departments of education, school districts, and individual schools are taking steps to ensure that teachers have the help they need to integrate technology

TEACHING ON YOUR FEET
Half of Teaching Is Learning

"You have a screen name?" they query in disbelief. Screen name, IM, blogging, DVD, iPod, podcasts, YouTube, MySpace, HDTV, text messaging, iMac . . . this is the jargon of the *millennials*—my seventh-grade students. Their world is filled with technology; they accept it—and expect it. They use it to communicate, connect, and create. And they use it constantly and confidently.

Yes, I tell them. I have a screen name . . . It's mrsheebz. I blog, instant message (IM), Google, make podcasts, publish online books, and text message. I visit MySpace, Facebook, and YouTube. I use Garageband, Comic Life, iPhoto, iTunes, Frontpage, iMovie, Keynote, and Noteshare. I love the world of technology. Of course, my students think I'm kidding when I tell them I grew up with a rotary phone . . . and a black-and-white TV with three stations of snow. No microwave, no World Wide Web, no cell phones . . . and certainly no computers. But my family did own a typewriter and a complete set of World Book Encyclopedias. I had all the tools necessary to give me an edge in school—then.

Fast-forward 40 years. The 12-year-olds I teach still have the encyclopedia as a wonderful window to the world. But the typewriter is long gone. Instead they possess iMac G4 laptops with the World Book just one of the many promising programs at their fingertips. It's a powerful tool that gives my kids—and me—an edge on learning.

There is no tool that has changed my teaching practice as much as the laptop. All seventh and eighth graders in the state of Maine have 24/7 access to their own wireless laptops. In 2001, the Maine Learning and Teaching Initiative (MLTI) was voted and approved; as a result, 1 percent of Maine's educational funds was spent on one-to-one computing—a laptop for every seventh grader in the state. The following year, the eighth grade was added, for a total of 35,000 laptops. This was a lofty goal aimed at evening the digital divide by providing the World Wide Web to all students in our largely rural state. This was a true democratic ideal: equal opportunity regardless of economic status. At this time, this initiative was the only program of its kind in the world. . . . Teachers spouted clichés like a potato sprouts eyes: a mixed blessing, throwing money in the wind, a two-edged sword, Christmas in July, can't teach an old dog new tricks. The program was embraced by some teachers, scorned by others. I chose to embrace. To learn. Or at least try to learn. For to teach "is to learn twice" (Joseph Joubert). And that has made all the difference in who I am as a teacher.

Using technology has transformed my curriculum and my teaching style. In particular, one-on-one computing has made the single biggest impact on my 27 years of teaching. My entire belief system has been tested and strengthened not only by the advent, but also by the intrusion of the laptop into my classroom. I'm no longer the expert, the disseminator of all-that-needs-to-be-known. I'm a learner, growing along with my students and along with my colleagues. We are a true community of explorers compelled by the MLTI motto: "If you know how to do it, teach someone else. If you don't know how, ask someone else." It's an energizing environment in which to learn: it's the environment of the connected generation.

Today's students are often more technologically savvy than their teachers. At many schools, students play an important role in integrating technology into teaching. What are the benefits of this approach to technology integration?

I teach seventh-grade language arts in a coastal town in southern Maine. The majority of my students come from professional families who have the ability to travel widely, vacation often, own lovely homes, and pay for higher education. It's a homogeneous community, with poor and minority students few and far between. Ninety-two percent of the families in my district had access to the Internet at home when the MLTI program began, so the digital divide was never a huge issue for my students. Yet access to computers at school for word processing and research had always been minimal. Prior to the laptop program, I'd been lucky to obtain an hour a week in the computer lab for my students. Laptops have given us a portable writing lab, instant access to research, and assistive technology.

My teaching philosophy is simple. I strive to create a democratic classroom—an energetic community of caring people engaged in learning. The laptop is a tool, a powerful communication device that has increased my ability to enact democratic ideals on a daily basis. Engagement, energy, and caring: these are more important to me than the content I teach.

ANALYZE & REFLECT

Click here to analyze and reflect on this scenario you have just read.

Merry Herbert teaches seventh-grade language arts at a middle school in MAINE.

The preceding is excerpted from her contribution to the National Network for Educational Renewal's Teacher Case Story Collection. The Collection is "dedicated to providing a public forum for teachers to share their stories." National Center for Educational Renewal © 2008. Retrieved and adapted from http://nnerpartnerships.org/stories/herbert.html.

fully into their teaching. About one-third of states require technology training and/ or coursework for an initial teacher license, and nine states require a technology test (*Education Week*, 2009).

Also, many teacher education programs have taken innovative steps such as the following to ensure that their graduates possess the ability to integrate technology into the classroom:

- At Washington State University, students develop an online portfolio of literacy strategies that are critiqued by teachers around the state.
- At the University of Virginia, students use the Internet to link with students at 11 other universities to analyze case studies based on commonly occurring problems in classrooms; students also write their own cases and post them on the web.
- At San Diego State University, student teachers, along with classroom teachers and school administrators, participate in a weekly Multimedia Academy taught by university staff and former student teachers.
- At the University of Northern Iowa, students learn from television-mediated observations of "live" classrooms at a pre-K–12 laboratory school and conduct question-and-answer sessions with the laboratory school teachers.
- At Indiana University, students, as well as visitors from around the world, learn about educational technology at the Center for Excellence in Education, a new state-of-the-art facility with 700 computers, an "enhanced technology suite," a building-wide video distribution system, and a two-way video distance-learning classroom.
- At Boise State University, students complete a 15-hour technology fieldwork internship in a public school classroom with a teacher who effectively integrates technology into the curriculum.

In spite of progress in integrating technology into schools, schools will need extensive support as they strive to meet the challenges outlined in this section. Teachers, professional associations, the private sector, state and federal governments, and local communities must continue to work together to enable digital technologies to enhance every student's learning. To promote such broad-based collaboration, the U.S. Department of Education and the Office of Educational Technology released the *National Education Technology Plan* near the end of 2010. The plan includes a "Model of Learning, Powered by Technology" that, "in contrast to traditional classroom instruction, which often consists of a single educator transmitting the same instruction to all learners in the same way, . . . puts students at the center and empowers them to take control of their own learning by providing flexibility on several dimensions" (see Figure 13.9). The plan also sets forth the following goals in five key areas—*learning, assessment, teaching, infrastructure,* and *productivity:*

1.0 **Learning:** Engage and Empower
All learners will have engaging and empowering learning experiences both in and out of school that prepare them to be active, creative, knowledgeable, and ethical participants in our greatly networked society.

2.0 **Assessment:** Measure What Matters
Our education system at all levels will leverage the power of technology to measure what matters and use assessment data for continuous improvement.

3.0 **Teaching:** Prepare and Connect
Professional educators will be supported individually and in teams by technology that connects them to data, content, resources, expertise, and learning experiences that enable and inspire more effective teaching for all learners.

FIGURE 13.9   A model of learning powered by technology

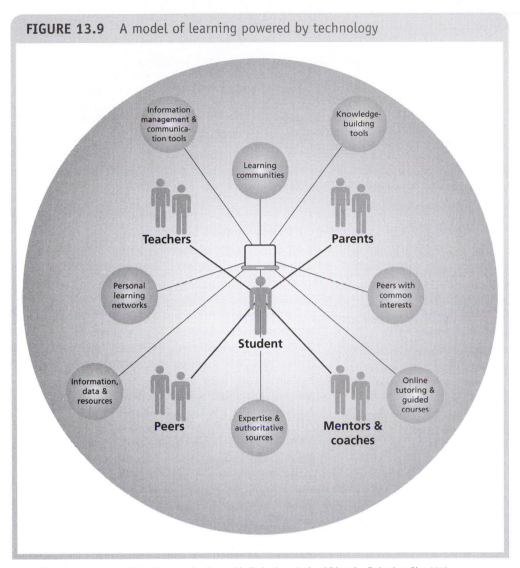

Source: Transforming American Education: Learning Powered by Technology, National Education Technology Plan 2010,
U.S. Department of Education, Office of Educational Technology, Washington, DC, p. 11.

4.0   Infrastructure: Access and Enable
All students and educators will have access to a comprehensive infrastructure for learning when and where they need it.

5.0   Productivity: Redesign and Transform
Our education system at all levels will redesign processes and structures to take advantage of the power of technology to improve learning outcomes while making more efficient use of time, money, and staff. (U.S. Department of Education, Office of Educational Technology, November 2010, pp. xvi–xx)

Clearly, yet-to-be-invented technologies will impact education during the years to come. As teachers, and others who have an interest in education, prepare for that unknown future, they are becoming more sophisticated in understanding the strengths and limitations of technology as a tool to promote learning. They know full well that, like another educational tool—the book—computers and related technologies can be a powerful, almost unlimited medium for instruction and learning, if they carefully reflect on how it will further the attainment of the goals and aspirations they have for their students.

SUMMARY

How Is Technology Transforming Teaching and Learning?

- Today's students have grown up in a technology-rich environment and, with few exceptions, they are more comfortable with technology than their teachers.
- Anywhere, anytime learning is a reality for today's students.
- Many teachers are using blended learning—face-to-face instruction blended with online learning activities.
- Most teachers support the use of digital technologies to promote students' learning and maintain that technology enables them to expand on content, motivate students, and respond to a variety of learning styles.
- The "Digital Learning Farm" model, much like farms of yesteryear, gives students ownership in their education and assign them "jobs" like tutorial designers, scribes, researchers, and global communicators and collaborators.
- E-learning and virtual schools are increasing in number.
- Although evidence suggests that virtual schools are not as effective as brick-and-mortar schools, the public is generally supportive of virtual schools.
- In a flipped classroom, students first learn new content at home by watching online videos related to the subject matter, then apply their new knowledge by solving problems or completing "homework" in class, with the teacher providing individual assistance.

What Digital Technologies Can Be Integrated into Teaching?

- Increasingly, teachers are integrating online social networking methods such as Facebook, Tumbler, Twitter, YouTube, blogs, wikis, 3D virtual reality worlds, podcasts, e-portfolios, and mobile learning devices (MLDs) into their teaching.
- Digital resources for teaching and learning in all academic areas include a vast array of learning objects on the Internet and open-source materials.

How Available and Frequently Used Are the Latest Technologies in the Classroom?

- The vast majority of classrooms—regardless of school size, community type, or level of poverty—have at least one computer with Internet connectivity and a projector.
- Most teachers report that their students are using cell phones, digital cameras and recorders, readers, and tablet computers in the classroom.
- The most common challenges teachers face when integrating technology are lack of time, pressure to teach to assessments, and lack of resources and technical support.

- As part of their learning experiences in schools, students frequently go online to conduct research, download and submit assignments, edit work, and collaborate with each other.
- Teachers of students from low-income families are more likely to report that their students do not have sufficient access to digital tools both in school and at home.

What Does Research Say About Technology Integration and Student Learning?

- To date, research studies show that technology has a limited to slight positive impact on students' achievement and attitudes.
- Teachers progress through five stages as they integrate technology into teaching: entry, adoption, adaptation, appropriation, and invention.
- Evidence is beginning to emerge that technology may have a negative effect on students' ability to focus on learning tasks.
- A U.S. Department of Education meta-analytic study, *Evaluation of Evidence-Based Practices in Online Learning*, found that students in online learning conditions tend to perform better than those receiving face-to-face instruction—however, most of the studies analyzed were of older learners; thus, the results have limited applicability to K–12 settings.
- Several meta-analytic studies have shown that technology can have modest, positive effects on students' learning.
- Overall, research has yet to support the hype that surrounded the integration of technology into teaching during the early 1990s.

What Are the Challenges of Integrating Technology into Teaching?

- Three challenges must be met so that all students can participate fully in the digital age while at school: providing (1) access to technology for all students; (2) funding for technology and technical support; and (3) high-quality, continuous training in technology for teachers.
- Although classroom Internet access is almost universal, there is evidence that a "digital divide" exists, as low-income families are less likely to own and to use advanced technologies.
- Although school district spending on technology training for teachers is often inadequate and the quality of that training uneven, state departments of education, school districts, and individual schools are developing new approaches to providing teachers with support for integrating technology.

- GenYES is a nationwide program that enables tech-savvy students to help teachers integrate technology.
- Many teacher education programs have developed innovative approaches to preparing technologically competent teachers. Many teachers, however, still believe they are ill-prepared to integrate technology into the curriculum.

- In 2010, the U.S. Department of Education and the Office of Educational Technology released the *National Education Technology Plan* that sets forth goals in five key areas: *learning, assessment, teaching, infrastructure,* and *productivity.*

PROFESSIONAL REFLECTIONS AND ACTIVITIES

Teacher's Journal

1. In your opinion, what are the most important benefits of technology for education, and what are its most important drawbacks?
2. A concern voiced by some is that the use of computers and advanced digital technologies in education will lead to a depersonalization of the teacher–student relationship. How valid is this concern?

Teacher's Research

1. With regard to the subject area and grade level for which you are preparing to teach, identify several online learning objects that you might use in your teaching. Then, in a written narrative, explain how you would use them.
2. Construct a webquest on integrating technology into teaching with reference to the grade level and subject area for which you are preparing to teach.

Observations and Interviews

1. Survey teachers at a local school district to determine the educational technologies they use. How and how often are these technologies used for instruction? What is the availability of computers, advanced digital technologies, and software for use by students?
2. Interview two or more teachers at a local elementary, middle, or high school to find out how they integrate technology into their teaching. Ask them to describe their greatest successes at integrating technology. What do they see as the greatest challenges to using technology in the classroom?

Professional Portfolio

Create an e-portfolio that includes at least three learning objects you developed using three different educational technologies. Include in your e-portfolio a statement that presents two or more principles for effectively integrating these learning objects into your teaching.

CHAPTER QUIZ

Take this quiz to check your understanding of the content covered in this chapter.

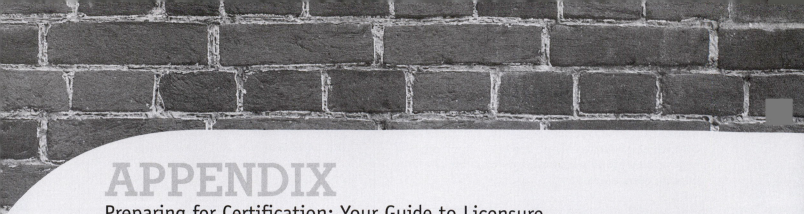

APPENDIX
Preparing for Certification: Your Guide to Licensure

Learning About the *Praxis Series*™ Statewide Testing Licensure

Many states require prospective teachers to take standardized tests for licensure. The questions and answers in this appendix will help you learn more about this important step to becoming a teacher.

WHAT KINDS OF TESTS DO STATES REQUIRE FOR CERTIFICATION?

Some tests assess students' competency in the basic skills of reading, writing, and mathematics, often prior to admission to a professional teacher education program. Many states also require standardized tests at the end of a teacher education program; these tests assess prospective teachers' competency and knowledge in their subject area and about teaching and learning.

DO ALL STATES USE THE SAME TEST FOR CERTIFICATION?

No. Some states have developed their own tests. The most commonly used test is the *Praxis Series*™, published by the Educational Testing Service (ETS). As of December 2014, 38 states and the District of Columbia required some form of the *Praxis Series*™ for certification. You can learn about each state's testing requirements by checking its department of education website or contacting the state department of education by mail or telephone. The University of Kentucky has developed a website with the web addresses for all 50 states' and the District of Columbia's certification requirements (https://2b.education.uky.edu/certification-requirements-by-state/).

WHAT IS THE *PRAXIS SERIES*™, AND WHAT IS THE DIFFERENCE BETWEEN PRAXIS I, PRAXIS II, AND PRAXIS III?

The *Praxis Series*™ is a set of three levels of standardized tests developed by the Educational Testing Service.

Praxis I assesses reading, writing, and mathematics skills. Many states require minimum passing scores on the three Praxis I subtests (also sometimes called the **Preprofessional Skills Test**, or **PPST**) prior to admission to a teacher education program. Computer-based and pencil-and-paper formats are available for the Praxis I assessment, which is given early in a student's teacher education program.

Praxis II measures prospective teachers' knowledge of the teaching and learning process and the subjects they will teach. Praxis II includes tests on Principles of Learning and Teaching (PLT) and Professional Knowledge, specific subject assessments, and multiple subject assessments. The PLT is available in three versions: K–6, 5–9, and 7–12. Many states require that prospective teachers pass both a subtest on principles of teaching and learning appropriate to the grade level to be taught and either a single-subject or multiple-subject test appropriate to the area of certification. It is important to check with an adviser, testing center, or state certification office about the appropriate Praxis II tests to take for certification.

Praxis III focuses on classroom performance assessment and is usually taken by teachers in their first year of teaching. Prospective teachers who are applying for initial certification are not required to take Praxis III.

IF MY STATE USES THE *PRAXIS SERIES*™, HOW DO I KNOW WHICH TESTS TO TAKE?

Contact your adviser or student services center if you are currently a student in a teacher education program. If you are applying for certification through an alternative certification program, contact the state department of education's certification office.

WHAT IS THE FORMAT OF THE PRINCIPLES OF LEARNING AND TEACHING (PLT) TEST?

The Principles of Learning and Teaching tests are two hours in length, and consist of 45 multiple-choice questions and six constructed-response (short-answer) questions. Each test includes three case histories followed by seven multiple-choice and two short-answer questions and 24 additional multiple-choice questions.

WHAT DOES THE PLT TEST COVER?

The PLT covers four broad content categories:

- Organizing Content Knowledge for Student Learning
- Creating an Environment for Student Learning
- Teaching for Student Learning
- Teacher Professionalism

ETS provides descriptions of topics covered in each category on its website (www.ets.org/praxis) and in its free *Test at a Glance* booklet.

WHAT COURSES IN MY TEACHER PREPARATION PROGRAM MIGHT APPLY TO THE PLT?

Almost all of your teacher preparation courses relate to the PLT in some way. This book, *Becoming a Teacher*, addresses many concepts that are assessed in the PLT tests, particularly in the areas of Creating an Environment for Student Learning and Teacher Professionalism. You have probably studied or will study concepts and knowledge related to the four content categories in courses such as educational foundations, educational psychology or human growth and development, classroom management, curriculum and methods, and evaluation and assessment. You may have had or will have field experiences and seminars that provide knowledge about these concepts.

HOW SHOULD I PREPARE FOR THE PLT?

Test-taking tips are provided in the next section.

Test-Taking Tips for the *Praxis Series*™ and State Certification Tests

TEST-TAKING TIP 1: KNOW THE TEST

- **Review the topics covered in the exam.** For the *Praxis Series*™, the ETS booklet *Test at a Glance* (available online at www.ets.org/praxis or free by mail) includes detailed descriptions of topics covered in each of the four content categories.
- **Take the sample tests.** The ETS provides sample tests for the *Praxis Series*™ on its website and in its print materials. Analyze the kinds of questions asked, the correct answers, and the knowledge necessary to answer the questions correctly.
- **Analyze the sample questions and the standards used for scoring the responses to open-ended (constructed response) questions.** Read the scoring guides carefully; the test readers will use these criteria to score your written responses. Write your own responses to the sample questions and analyze them using the test-scoring guide. If your responses do not meet all the criteria for a score of 3 on Praxis (or the highest score for your test), revise them.

TEST-TAKING TIP 2: KNOW THE CONTENT

- **Plan ahead.** You can begin preparing for Praxis and other standardized teacher certification tests early in your program. Think about how each of your courses relates to the concepts and content of the exam.
- **Review what you learned in each course in relation to the topics covered in the test.** Review course textbooks and class notes for relevant concepts and information. At the end of each course, record reminders of how the course's content and knowledge relate to concepts on the test.
- **Think across courses.** The Praxis case studies draw on knowledge from several courses. As you prepare for the exam, think about how knowledge, skills, and concepts from the courses that you took relate to each other. For example, you might have learned about aspects of working with parents in a foundations course, an educational psychology course, or a methods course. Be prepared to integrate that knowledge.
- **Review the content with others.** Meet with a study group and review the test and your course work together. Brainstorm about relevant content using the ETS descriptions or other descriptions of each test's categories and representative topics as a guideline.

TEST-TAKING TIP 3: APPLY GOOD TEST-TAKING STRATEGIES

- **Read the test directions carefully.** Even though you have previewed the test format and directions as part of learning about the test, make sure you understand the directions for this test.

For multiple-choice questions:

- **Read each question carefully.** Pay attention to key words such as *not, all, except, always,* or *never.*
- **Try to anticipate the answer to the question before looking at the possible responses.** If your answer is among the choices, it is likely to be correct. Before automatically choosing it, however, carefully read the alternative answers.
- **Answer questions you are certain of first.** Return to questions you are uncertain about later.

If you are unsure of the answer, eliminate obviously incorrect responses first.

For short open-ended response questions:

- **Read the directions carefully.** Look for key words and respond directly to exactly what is asked.
- **Repeat key words from the question to focus your response.** For example, if you are asked to list two advantages of a method, state "Two advantages are (1) . . . and (2) . . ."
- **Be explicit and concrete.** Short-answer responses should be direct and to the point.

For essay questions:

- **Read the question carefully and pay close attention to key words, especially verbs.** Make sure you understand all parts of the question. For example, if the question asks you to list advantages and disadvantages, be sure to answer both parts.
- **Before you write your response, list key points or make an outline.** The few minutes you take to organize your thoughts will pay off in a better-organized essay.
- **Use the question's words in your response.** For example, if the question asks for three advantages, list each in a sentence, "The first advantage is . . . ," "The second advantage is . . . ," and "The third

advantage is. . . ." Make it easy for the reader to score your response.

- **Stay on topic.** Answer the question fully and in detail, but do not go beyond what the question asks or add irrelevant material.

SAMPLE STATE LICENSURE TEST QUESTIONS

The following sample questions illustrate the kinds of questions in the *Praxis Series*™ Principles of Learning and Teaching tests and other state licensure tests. The case study focuses on elementary education, which is the focus of Principles of Learning and Teaching: Grades K–6 (0522). Praxis tests for Principles of Learning and Teaching: Grades 5–9 (0523) and Principles of Learning and Teaching: Grades 7–12 (0524) would include case histories appropriate to those grade levels.

The Principles of Learning and Teaching tests focus on four broad content categories:

- Organizing Content Knowledge for Student Learning
- Creating an Environment for Student Learning
- Teaching for Student Learning
- Teacher Professionalism

The sample questions that follow include one case study followed by three related multiple-choice questions, two short-answer constructed-response questions, and three additional discrete multiple-choice questions. An actual Praxis Principles of Learning and Teaching test would include three case histories, each with seven related multiple-choice questions, two constructed-response questions, and 24 additional discrete multiple-choice questions. It would draw from many courses and field experiences in your teacher education program.

These sample questions focus only on content and issues presented in *Becoming a Teacher*; they are not representative of the actual test in scope, content, or difficulty. Learn more about Praxis and try more sample questions on the Educational Testing Service website at www.ets.org/praxis/.

Following the sample questions are answers with explanations and references to Praxis topics and appropriate parts of this book.

SAMPLE CASE STUDY AND RELATED QUESTIONS

CASE HISTORY: K–6

Columbus, New Mexico, is an agricultural community near the international boundaries separating Mexico and the United States. It's a quiet town where traditional views of community and territory are being challenged. Just three miles from the border is Columbus Elementary School, a bilingual school for kindergarten through fifth-grade students.

Of the some 340 students enrolled at Columbus Elementary, approximately 97 percent are on free or reduced-price lunches. The school is unique because about 49 percent of the students live in Mexico and attend Columbus Elementary at U.S. taxpayer expense. Columbus Elementary is a fully bilingual school. In the early grades, basic skills are taught in Spanish, but by the third-grade level, students have begun to make the transition to English. Most of the teachers at Columbus Elementary School are English speakers; some have limited Spanish skills. The school also employs teaching assistants who are fluent in Spanish and can assist the teachers in these bilingual classrooms.

Dennis Armijo, the principal of Columbus Elementary School, describes the unique relationship between Columbus and its neighboring community, Palomas, Mexico. "Most of the people who live in Columbus, New Mexico, have relatives in Palomas, Mexico. At one point or another, many Columbus residents were Mexican residents and they came over and established a life here. And so they still have ties to Mexico and a lot of uncles and aunts and grandparents still live in Palomas. They have a kind of family togetherness, where they just go back and forth all the time. The kids that are coming over from Mexico, most of those are U.S. citizens who have been born in the United States. Now the parents may not be able to cross because of illegal status, but the kids are U.S. citizens; they have been born in U.S. hospitals."

Columbus Elementary School's international enrollment poses special challenges for family and parental involvement. Mr. Armijo notes that parental contact is often not as frequent as he would like it to be. The school occasionally runs into problems reaching parents because many don't have telephones and must be reached through an emergency number in Mexico that might be as far as three blocks away or through a relative on the United States side of the border. In many cases, school personnel go into Mexico and talk to the parents or write them a letter so they can cross the border legally to come to the school. Despite these barriers, however, Mr. Armijo says that cooperation from the parents is great. "They'll do anything to help out this school."

The parents who send their children across the border to Columbus Elementary are willing to face the logistical difficulties of getting their children to Columbus each day because they want their children to have the benefits of a bilingual education. Mr. Armijo notes that the only reason that many parents from across the border send their kids to Columbus is to learn English. He describes a potential conflict that sometimes arises from this expectation:

There's—I wouldn't call it a controversy, but there's some misunderstanding, mainly because parents don't understand what a bilingual program is. Some of them don't want their children to speak Spanish at all; they say they are sending the children to our school just to learn English. A true bilingual program will take kids that are monolingual speakers of any language and combine them together. At Columbus Elementary, for example, if you have a monolingual English speaker and a monolingual Spanish speaker, if they are in a true bilingual program you hope that the Spanish speaker will learn English and the English speaker will learn Spanish. And if they live here for the rest of their lives, they will be able to communicate with anybody. So when the students from Mexico come over, they need, as far as I know, they need to learn the skills or the way of life, the American way of life, the American dream, if you will, of an education. Because at some point or another, they might want to come over. Remember, these students are United States citizens, even though they live with their parents in Mexico. I'm almost sure that most of those kids are going to come over across to the United States and live here and so they need to have this education.

Perspective of Linda Lebya, Third-Grade Teacher

Linda Lebya is [in] her third year of teaching third grade at Columbus Elementary School. She lives nearby on a ranch with her husband, who is a deputy sheriff. She speaks conversational Spanish, although she is not a native Spanish speaker. About 95 percent of her third-grade students are Spanish-speaking.

Linda's classroom is small but inviting. Colorful posters and pictures on the wall reflect the students' culture, and many words and phrases are posted in Spanish and English. Desks are grouped in clusters of four so students can sit together facing one another. A list of vocabulary words, written in English and Spanish, is on the blackboard.

Linda describes her teaching approaches and some of the challenges she faces. First, she describes a typical spelling lesson:

On Monday as an introduction for spelling vocabulary we have 10 vocabulary words written in English and Spanish. The intent is for [students] to learn it in English; I also put up the Spanish words with the intent of helping them to learn what the English word means. We discuss the words in English and Spanish, then use them in sentences in each language.

Columbus Elementary is a poor school, and Linda reports that resources are limited:

Lack of books is a problem because we're supposed to be teaching in Spanish for part of the day but the only thing we have in Spanish are the readers. All the other materials are in English so that is a problem.

One resource that Ms. Lebya does have is a Spanish-speaking instructional assistant. She describes the assistant's role in her classroom:

All of the teachers here at Columbus K–3 have an instructional assistant to help out with different things. My assistant this year is really wonderful;

she helps out a great deal. She teaches the Spanish reading to the students because I'm not as fluent to teach it. I can speak it and I can understand, but to actually teach it, I wouldn't know how; my Spanish is not strong enough.

Linda describes her understanding of multicultural education:

Multicultural education here means that most of the students are from a different culture. We have a few Anglos but most of the students are Mexicans or Hispanics, and when you are teaching multicultural education, you want to make sure that the students understand that their culture is just as important as the dominant culture. For example, one of our vocabulary words was "fiesta" or "party." Some of our students were not in school that day because they were making their First Holy Communion and their families were having a big celebration. We talked about official fiestas like Cinco de Mayo and family or traditional fiestas like today and the students made English and Spanish sentences about fiestas and parties. It all helps them to value their culture while they learn about the culture of the United States.

And as far as the Spanish sentences, that's just giving them an opportunity to do something well because they already know it in Spanish. They have the vocabulary in Spanish, so they're able to do a good job in making the sentences, and that's something they can feel good about and help their self-esteem. (Kent, Larsen, & Becker, 1998)

Sample Test Questions

SAMPLE MULTIPLE-CHOICE QUESTIONS

DIRECTIONS: Each of the multiple-choice questions below is followed by four choices. Select the one that is best in each case.

1. Which approach best describes the philosophy of the bilingual program at Columbus Elementary School?
   A. Children should receive instruction in both English and their native language and culture throughout their school years, making a gradual transition to English.
   B. Students should make the transition to English through ongoing, intensive instruction in English as a second language.
   C. Students should be removed from their regular classes to receive special help in English or in reading in their native language.
   D. Students should be immersed in English, then placed in English-speaking classes.

2. Sleeter and Grant describe five approaches to multicultural education. Which approach best characterizes the

Columbus Elementary School program, based on the comments of Ms. Lebya?
A. Human relations approaches
B. Single-group studies
C. Teaching the exceptionally and culturally different
D. Education that is multicultural and social reconstructionist

3. Ms. Lebya's instructional approach to teaching vocabulary could best be described as
A. Individualized instruction
B. Cooperative learning
C. Inquiry learning
D. Direct instruction

SAMPLE SHORT-ANSWER QUESTIONS

The Principles of Learning and Teaching tests include two open-ended short-answer questions related to the case study. A well-constructed short-answer response demonstrates an understanding of the aspects of the case that are relevant to the question; responds to all parts of the question; supports explanations with relevant evidence; and demonstrates a strong knowledge of appropriate concepts, theories, or methodologies relevant to the question. Two readers who are practicing teachers will score the responses according to an ETS scoring guide. (To view the scoring guide, go to the ETS web page: www.ets.org/ praxis.)

The following sample open-ended questions draw from knowledge and concepts covered in this book only. In an actual Praxis Principles of Learning and Teaching test, respondents should use knowledge and concepts derived from all parts of their teacher education program.

4. Ms. Lebya says that she relies on her instructional assistant to teach reading in Spanish because "I'm not as fluent to teach it. I can speak it and I can understand, but to actually teach it, I wouldn't know how." List at least one positive and one negative possible consequence of this teaching arrangement.

5. Is it possible to teach well without textbooks? If so, in what situations? If not, why not?

Sample Discrete Multiple-Choice Questions

The Principles of Learning and Teaching tests include 24 discrete multiple-choice questions that cover an array of teaching and learning topics. In an actual Praxis Principles of Learning and Teaching test, respondents would draw from knowledge and concepts learned in all aspects of an undergraduate teacher preparation program. In this sample test, items are drawn from concepts discussed in *Becoming a Teacher*.

6. On the first day of school, Mr. Jones told his eighth-grade class that all students must arrive at class on time

and with all their materials. He posted the same rule on the bulletin board by the door.

On Tuesday of the second week of school, a classroom visitor observed the following: two students arrived about five minutes late for class and took their seats without any comment from Mr. Jones; one student received permission to go to his locker to get an assignment the class was reviewing; another student borrowed a pen from Mr. Jones so she could complete an in-class activity.

The student actions and teacher response suggest which of the following:
A. Mr. Jones did not establish a set of expectations at the beginning of the year.
B. Mr. Jones did not make consequences clear and apply them consistently.
C. Mr. Jones taught and retaught desired behaviors.
D. Mr. Jones demonstrated "with-it-ness" when working with the students.

7. Mr. Williams placed a pitcher of water and several containers of different sizes and shapes on a table. He asked a small group of students, "Which container holds the most water? Which holds the least? How can you figure it out?"

Mr. Williams's philosophical orientation probably is:
A. behaviorism
B. perennialism
C. constructivism
D. essentialism

8. Ms. Jackson was planning a unit of study for her eleventh-grade American history class. She wanted to determine what students already know and want to know about the topic prior to beginning the unit. Which forms of pre-assessment would be most useful?
A. a norm-referenced test
B. a teacher-made assessment
C. a criterion-referenced test
D. a summative assessment

ANSWERS

1. The best answer is A. In the Columbus School's bilingual program, children learn primarily in Spanish during their first few grades and then begin the transition to English in the third grade. They are not experiencing an intensive English instruction or pullout program, nor are they immersed in English.

Related Praxis topics: I. Organizing Content Knowledge for Student Learning/Needs and characteristics of students from diverse populations; II. Creating an Environment for Student Learning/Appropriate teacher responses to individual and cultural diversity; III. Teaching for Student Learning/Needs and characteristics of students from diverse populations
Related material in this book: Chapter 8: Today's Students

2. The best answer is C. Both Mr. Armijo and Ms. Lebya emphasize that the purpose of their bilingual program is to help the students assimilate into American culture and acquire language and skills that will help them be successful if they choose to live in the United States.

Related Praxis topics: I. Organizing Content Knowledge for Student Learning/Needs and characteristics of students from diverse populations; II. Creating an Environment for Student Learning/Appropriate teacher responses to individual and cultural diversity

Related material in this book: Chapter 8: Today's Students

3. The best answer is D. Ms. Lebya uses a teacher-directed approach, in which she asks specific questions of the students and provides praise or corrective feedback.

Related Praxis topics: I. Organizing Content Knowledge for Student Learning/Creating or selecting teaching methods, learning activities, and instructional materials or other resources that are appropriate for the students and are aligned with the goals of the lesson; III. Teaching for Student Learning/Repertoire of flexible teaching and learning strategies

Related material in this book: Chapter 10: Creating a Community of Learners; Chapter 13: Integrating Technology into Teaching

4. A strong response to this open-ended question will explicitly state at least one potential positive consequence and one potential negative consequence to the teaching arrangement. The respondent will use or paraphrase the question and answer explicitly in complete sentences.

Sample response: One potential positive consequence of having the Spanish-speaking teaching assistant teach reading in Spanish is that the students will acquire better reading skills in Spanish. If they become good readers in Spanish, they may find it easier to become good readers in English later. One potential negative consequence of having the Spanish-speaking teaching assistant teach reading in Spanish is that she may not have the knowledge or skills to teach reading. (Many teaching assistants have not had the educational preparation that licensed teachers have.) Ms. Lebya's Spanish may not be strong enough to pick up on those problems or correct them. Thus, the children may not become strong readers in Spanish.

Related Praxis topic: III. Teaching for Student Learning/Making content comprehensible to students; IV. Teacher Professionalism/Reflecting on the extent to which learning goals were met

Related material in this book: Chapter 8: Today's Students

5. A strong response to this open-ended question will explicitly take a position on the necessity of textbooks and will defend that position. The respondent will use or paraphrase the question and answer explicitly in complete sentences.

Sample response: It is entirely possible to teach well without textbooks. Although textbooks can be an invaluable resource for teachers, they are only one kind of resource that can be used for instruction. Instead of textbooks, teachers could use a collection of printed materials, such as articles or primary resources, or websites from the Internet. The teacher could also use multimedia resources, such as films, videotapes, or audiotapes. To teach well without textbooks, however, the teacher must have clear goals and spend time looking for good alternative materials.

Related Praxis topic: I. Organizing Content Knowledge for Student Learning/Creating or selecting teaching methods, learning activities, and instructional materials or other resources that are appropriate for the students and are aligned with the goals of the lesson

Related material in this book: Chapter 10: Creating a Community of Learners; Chapter 13: Integrating Technology into Teaching

6. The best answer is B. Although Mr. Jones established and posted classroom procedures at the beginning of the school year, he did not make consequences clear. When students did not follow the procedures, he did not correct the students or remind them of the established classroom expectations.

Related Praxis topic: II. Creating an Environment for Student Learning/Establishing and maintaining consistent standards of classroom behavior

Related material in this book: Chapter 10: Creating a Community of Learners

7. The best answer is C. Mr. Williams encouraged the students to construct meaning or make sense of information for themselves, one of the characteristics of constructivism.

Related Praxis topic: I. Organizing Content Knowledge for Student Learning/Major theories of human development and learning; III. Teaching for Student Learning/Stages and patterns of cognitive and cultural development

Related material in this book: Chapter 4: Philosophical Foundations of U.S. Education

8. The best answer is B. Ms. Jackson can best find out what students know and want to know by designing her own instrument.

Related Praxis topic: I. Organizing Content Knowledge for Student Learning/Structuring lessons based on the knowledge, experiences, skills, strategies, and interests of the students in relation to the curriculum.

Related material in this book: Chapter 10: Creating a Community of Learners; Chapter 11: School Curricula and Standards; Chapter 12: Assessing Student Learning

References

Educational Testing Service (ETS). (2011). *Praxis II® Overview.* Available online: http://www.ets.org/praxis/about/praxisii/

Kent, T. W., Larsen, V. A., & Becker, F. J. (1998). *Educational border culture in New Mexico.* Boston: Allyn & Bacon.

GLOSSARY

A

academic freedom: the right of teachers to teach, free from external constraint, censorship, or interference.

academic learning time: the amount of time students spend working on academic tasks with a high level of success (80 percent or higher).

academic mindset: a positive view of oneself as a learner and an understanding that effort is required to develop ability and competence related to academic work.

academies: early secondary schools with broader and more practical curricula than those found in grammar schools of the previous era.

acceleration: the process of providing academically enriched programs to meet the needs of intellectually advanced students for example, early entrance, grade skipping, rigorous curricula, credit by examination, and early entrance to college.

accountability: the practice of holding teachers responsible for adhering to high professional and moral standards and creating effective learning environments for all students.

achievement gap: the continuing gap in academic achievement between White students and Hispanic, African American, and American Indian/Alaska Native students.

adequate yearly progress (AYP): a provision of the No Child Left Behind Act of 2001 requiring that schools provide evidence each year that students are making adequate yearly progress.

aesthetics: the branch of axiology concerned with values related to beauty and art.

Afrocentric schools: schools that focus on African American history and cultures for African American pupils.

allocated time: the amount of time teachers allocate for instruction in various areas of the curriculum.

alternate assessment: an alternative way of measuring the performance of students who are unable to participate in traditional approaches to assessment.

alternative assessments: approaches that assess students ability to complete real-life tasks rather than merely regurgitate facts.

alternative school: a small, highly individualized school separate from a regular school; designed to meet the needs of students at risk.

alternative teacher certification: a provision allowing people who have completed college but not a teacher education program to become certified teachers.

Amendments to the Individuals with Disabilities Education Act (IDEA 97): amendments to IDEA that emphasize educational outcomes for students with disabilities and provide greater access through changes in eligibility requirements, IEP guidelines, public and private placements, student discipline guidelines, and procedural safeguards.

American Federation of Teachers (AFT): a national professional association for teachers, affiliated with the AFL-CIO.

analytic rubric: a rating scale, or scoring guide, for evaluating part of a students product or performance.

ASCD: a professional organization for educators interested in school improvement at all levels (formerly, the Association for Supervision and Curriculum Development [ASCD]).

assertive discipline: an approach to classroom discipline requiring that teachers establish firm, clear guidelines for student behavior and follow through with consequences for misbehavior.

assessment: the process of gathering information related to how much students have learned.

assistive technology: technological advances (usually computer-based) that help exceptional students learn and communicate.

attention deficit disorder (ADD): a learning disability characterized by difficulty in concentrating on learning.

attention deficit hyperactivity disorder (ADHD): a learning disability characterized by difficulty in remaining still so that one can concentrate on learning.

authentic assessment: an approach to assessing students' learning that requires them to solve problems or work on tasks that approximate as much as possible those they will encounter beyond the classroom.

authentic learning tasks: learning activities that enable students to see the connections between classroom learning and the world beyond the classroom.

axiology: the study of values, including the identification of criteria for determining what is valuable.

B

back-to-basics: a movement begun in the mid-1970s to establish the basic skills of reading, writing, speaking, and computation as the core of the school curriculum.

behaviorism: based on behavioristic psychology, this philosophical orientation maintains that environmental factors shape peoples behavior.

benchmarks: statements of what students should understand and be able to do at specific grade levels or developmental stages.

between-class ability grouping: the practice of grouping students at the middle and high school levels for instruction on the basis of ability or achievement, often called tracking.

bicultural: the ability to function effectively in two or more linguistic and cultural groups.

bilingual education: a curriculum for non-English-speaking and English-speaking students in which two languages are used for instruction and biculturalism is emphasized.

blended learning: a blending of online and face-to-face instruction.

blended schools: schools that provide a combination of traditional, face-to-face instruction and online learning.

block grants: a form of federal aid given directly to the states, which a state or local education agency may spend as it wishes with few limitations.

block scheduling: a high school scheduling arrangement that provides longer blocks of time each class period, with fewer periods each day.

blog: an online journal constructed by an individual and reacted to by those who visit the blog (short for web log).

A Blueprint for Reform: The Reauthorization of the Elementary and Secondary Education Act: the Obama administrations plan for revising the No Child Left Behind Act (NCLB) and reauthorizing the Elementary and Secondary Education Act; released in 2010, the Blueprint supports state and local efforts to ensure that all students graduate prepared for college and a career.

Brown v. Board of Education of Topeka: a 1954 landmark U.S. Supreme Court case rejecting the separate but equal doctrine used to prevent African Americans from attending schools with Whites.

Buckley Amendment: a 1974 law, the Family Educational Rights and Privacy Act, granting parents of students under 18 and students over 18 the right to examine their school records.

C

caring classroom: a classroom in which the teacher communicates clearly an attitude of caring about students learning and their overall well-being.

categorical aid: state-appropriated funds to cover the costs of educating students with special needs.

censorship: the act of removing from circulation printed material judged to be libelous, vulgar, or obscene.

character education: an approach to education that emphasizes the teaching of values, moral reasoning, and the development of good character.

charter: an agreement between a charter schools founders and its sponsors specifying how the school will operate and what learning outcomes students will master.

charter schools: independent schools, often founded by teachers, that are given a charter to operate by a school district,
state, or national government, with the provision that students must demonstrate mastery of predetermined outcomes.

chief state school officer: the chief administrator of a state department of education and head of the state board of education, often called the commissioner of education or superintendent of public instruction.

choice theory: an approach to classroom management, developed by psychiatrist William Glasser, based on a belief that students will usually make good choices (i.e., behave in an acceptable manner) if they experience success in the classroom and know that teachers care about them.

classroom climate: the atmosphere or quality of life in a classroom, determined by how individuals interact with one another.

classroom culture: the way of life characteristic of a classroom group; determined by the social dimensions of the group and the physical characteristics of the setting.

classroom management: day-to-day teacher control of student behavior and learning, including discipline.

classroom organization: how teachers and students in a school are grouped for instruction and how time is allocated in classrooms.

code of ethics: a set of guidelines that defines appropriate behavior for professionals.

cognitive development: the process of acquiring the intellectual ability to learn from interaction with ones environment.

cognitive science: the study of the learning process that focuses on how individuals manipulate symbols and process information.

collaboration: the practice of working together, sharing decision making, and solving problems among professionals.

collaborative consultation: an approach in which a classroom teacher meets with one or more other professionals (such as a special educator, school psychologist, or resource teacher) to focus on the learning needs of one or more students.

collective bargaining: a process followed by employers and employees in negotiating salaries, hours, and working conditions; in most states, school boards must negotiate contracts with teacher organizations.

collectivistic cultures: cultures that tend to emphasize group membership and a sense of "we" rather than "I" in contrast to individualistic cultures that emphasize the individual and his or her success and achievement.

collegiality: a spirit of cooperation and mutual helpfulness among professionals.

collegial support team (CST): a team of teachers created according to subject area, grade level, or teacher interests and expertisewho support one anothers professional growth.

Commission on the Reorganization of Secondary Education: an NEA committee that called for a high school curriculum designed to accommodate individual differences in scholastic ability and based on seven educational goals, or "cardinal principles" (1913).

Committee of Fifteen: an NEA committee that recommended an academically rigorous curriculum for elementary students (1895).

Committee of Ten: an NEA committee that recommended an academically rigorous curriculum for high school students (1893).

Common Core State Standards Initiative (CCSSI): a set of voluntary K12 curriculum standards developed and endorsed by 48 of the 50 states.

common schools: free state-supported schools that provide education for all students.

compensatory education programs: federally funded educational programs designed to meet the needs of low-ability students from low-income families.

concrete operations stage: the stage of cognitive development (7 to 11 years of age) proposed by Jean Piaget in which the individual develops the ability to use logical thought to solve concrete problems.

constructive assertiveness: an approach to classroom management that calls for the teacher to communicate to misbehaving student(s) a direct, clear statement of the problem; maintain direct eye contact with the student(s); and insist upon correct behavior.

constructivism: a psychological orientation that views learning as an active process in which learners construct understanding of the material they learn in contrast to the view that teachers transmit academic content to students in small segments.

constructivist teaching: a method of teaching based on students prior knowledge of the topic and the processes they use to construct meaning.

content standards: the content or knowledge and skills students should acquire in various academic disciplines.

cooperative learning: an approach to education in which students work in small groups, or teams, sharing the work and helping one another complete assignments.

copyright laws: laws limiting the use of photocopies, videotapes, and computer software programs.

corporal punishment: physical punishment applied to a student by a school employee as a disciplinary measure.

co-teaching: an arrangement whereby two or more teachers teach together in the same classroom.

Council for the Accreditation of Educator Preparation (CAEP): an accrediting agency formed in 2010 by the merger of the National Council for Accreditation of Teacher Education (NCATE) and the Teacher Education Accreditation Council (TEAC).

criterion-referenced assessments: assessments of achievement that compare students performance with clearly defined criteria or standards.

critical pedagogy: an educational orientation that emphasizes education as a way to promote social justice and equity for those who do not enjoy positions of power and influence in society.

cross-age tutoring: a tutoring arrangement in which older students tutor younger students; evidence indicates that cross-age tutoring has positive effects on the attitudes and achievement of tutee and tutor.

cultural identity: an overall sense of oneself, derived from the extent of one's participation in various subcultures within the national macroculture.

cultural pluralism: the preservation of cultural differences among groups of people within one society. This view is in contrast to the melting-pot theory that says that ethnic cultures should melt into one.

culture: the way of life common to a group of people; includes knowledge deemed important, shared meanings, norms, values, attitudes, ideals, and view of the world.

curriculum: the school experiences, both planned and unplanned, that enhance (and sometimes impede) the education and growth of students.

curriculum alignment: the process of ensuring that the content of curricula and textbooks reflects desired learning outcomes, or academic standards, for students.

curriculum framework: a document that provides guidelines, instructional and assessment strategies, resources, and models for teachers to use as they develop curricula aligned with academic standards.

cyber bullying: using information and/or communication technologies to harass or threaten an individual or group.

D

dame schools: colonial schools, usually held in the homes of widows or housewives, for teaching children basic reading, writing, and mathematical skills.

democratic classroom: a classroom in which the teachers leadership style encourages students to take more power and responsibility for their learning.

departmentalization: an organizational arrangement for schools in which students move from classroom to classroom for instruction in different subject areas.

desegregation: the process of eliminating schooling practices based on the separation of racial groups.

digital divide: the gap between people at different socioeconomic levels and their access to, and use of, information technologies and the Internet.

Digital Millennium Copyright Act (DMCA): an amendment to the Copyright Act of 1998, making it illegal to reproduce copyrighted material in digital format.

direct instruction: a systematic instructional method focusing on the transmission of knowledge and skills from the teacher to the students.

discovery learning: an approach to teaching that gives students opportunities to inquire into subjects so that they discover knowledge for themselves.

dismissal: the involuntary termination of a teachers employment; termination must be made for a legally defensible reason with the protection of due process.

distance learning: the use of technology such as video transmissions that enables students to receive instruction at multiple, often remote, sites.

diversity: differences among people in regard to gender, race, ethnicity, culture, and socioeconomic status.

due process: a set of specific guidelines that must be followed to protect individuals from arbitrary, capricious treatment by those in authority.

E

early childhood education: educational programs for children from birth to age 8, also termed pre-K education.

educational malpractice: liability for injury that results from the failure of a teacher, school, or school district to provide a student with adequate instruction, guidance, counseling, and/or supervision.

educational philosophy: a set of ideas and beliefs about education that guide the professional behavior of educators.

educational politics: how people use power, influence, and authority to affect instructional and curricular practices within a school or school system.

educational reform movement: a comprehensive effort made during the 1980s and into the 1990s to improve schools and the preparation of teachers.

Education Consolidation and Improvement Act (ECIA): a 1981 federal law giving the states a broad range of choices for spending federal aid on education.

Education for All Handicapped Children Act (Public Law 94-142): a 1975 federal act that guarantees a free and appropriate education to all children with handicaps (often referred to as the mainstreaming law or Public Law 94–142).

Elementary and Secondary Education Act: part of President Lyndon B. Johnson's Great Society Program, this act allocated federal funds on the basis of the number of poor children in school districts.

emergency certification: temporary, substandard certification requirements set by a state in response to a shortage of teachers.

emotional intelligence: the capacity to be aware of and to manage ones feelings.

English-language learners (ELLs): students whose first language is not English.

entitlements: federal programs to meet the educational needs of special populations.

epistemology: a branch of philosophy concerned with the nature of knowledge and what it means to know something.

e-portfolio: an online site where an individual can place products that represent accomplishments in an area of interest.

essentialism: formulated in part as a response to progressivism, this philosophical orientation holds that a core of common knowledge about the real world should be transmitted to students in a systematic, disciplined way.

ethical dilemmas: problem situations in which an ethical response is difficult to determine; that is, no single response can be called right or wrong.

ethics: a branch of philosophy concerned with principles of conduct and determining what is good and evil, right and wrong, in human behavior.

ethnic group: individuals within a larger culture who share a racial or cultural identity and a set of beliefs, values, and attitudes and who consider themselves members of a distinct group or subculture.

ethnicity: a shared feeling of common identity that derives, in part, from a common ancestry, common values, and common experiences.

evaluation: making judgments about, or assigning a value to, measurements of students learning.

exceptional learners: students whose growth and development deviate from the norm to the extent that their educational needs can be met more effectively through a modification of regular school programs.

existentialism: a philosophical orientation that emphasizes the individuals experiences and maintains that each individual must determine his or her own meaning of existence.

expanded learning time (ELT) schools: schools that add time to the school day as a way to increase student achievement, provide opportunities for enrichment, and partner with community organizations.

expenditure per pupil: the amount of money spent on each pupil in a school, school district, state, or nation; usually computed according to average daily attendance.

explicit curriculum: the behavior, attitudes, and knowledge that a school intends to teach students.

extracurricular/cocurricular programs: activities perceived as additions to the academic curriculum.

F

fair use: the right of an individual to use copyrighted material in a reasonable manner without the copyright holder's consent, provided that use meets certain criteria.

female seminaries: schools established in the early nineteenth century to train women for higher education and public service outside the home.

feminist pedagogy: a philosophical orientation that emphasizes caring, respect for individual differences, and collaboration to achieve the aims of a democratic and just society.

field experiences: opportunities for teachers-in-training to experience firsthand the world of the teacher by observing, tutoring, and instructing small groups.

flipped classroom: a classroom in which students learn new content at home by watching online video lectures by the teacher or other online videos related to the subject matter. During in-class sessions, students apply their new knowledge by solving problems or completing "homework," with the teacher providing individual assistance.

flipped teaching: an approach to teaching in which teachers prepare online video lectures that students watch at home; during in-class sessions, teachers then help students apply their new knowledge to solving problems or completing "homework."

formal operations stage: the stage of cognitive development (11 to 15 years of age) proposed by Jean Piaget in which cognitive abilities reach their highest level of development.

formal assessments: assessments of student learning developed prior to having students complete the assessment—tests, quizzes, homework, and critiques of performance, for example.

formative evaluation: an assessment, or diagnosis, of students learning for the purpose of planning instruction.

for-profit schools: schools that are operated, for profit, by private educational corporations.

Freedmens Bureau: a U.S. government agency to provide assistance to former slaves after the Civil War.

freedom of expression: freedom, granted by the First Amendment to the Constitution, to express ones beliefs.

fringe benefits: benefits (i.e., medical insurance, retirement, and tax-deferred investment opportunities) that are given to teachers in addition to base salary.

full-funding programs: state programs to ensure statewide financial equity by setting the same per-pupil expenditure level for all schools and districts.

full inclusion: the policy and process of including exceptional learners in general education classrooms.

full-service community schools: schools that provide students and their families with medical, social, and human services, in addition to their regular educational programs.

G

gender bias: subtle bias or discrimination on the basis of gender; reduces the likelihood that the target of the bias will develop to the full extent of his or her capabilities.

gender-fair classroom: education that is free of bias or discrimination on the basis of gender.

GenYES: a teacher professional development model that empowers students to play a major role in integrating technology in the school.

G.I. Bill of Rights: a 1944 federal law that provides veterans with payments for tuition and room and board at colleges and universities and special schools; formally known as the Servicemens Readjustment Act.

gifted and talented: exceptional learners who demonstrate high intelligence, high creativity, high achievement, or special talents.

grievance: a formal complaint filed by an employee against his or her employer or supervisor.

group investigation: an approach to teaching in which the teacher facilitates learning by creating an environment that allows students to determine what they will study and how.

H

Head Start: a federal program that promotes the school readiness of children ages birth to 5 years from low-income families by enhancing their cognitive, social, and emotional development.

hidden curriculum: the behaviors, attitudes, and knowledge that the school culture unintentionally teaches students.

hierarchy of needs: a set of seven needs, from the basic needs for survival and safety to the need for self-actualization, that motivate human behavior as identified by Abraham Maslow.

highly qualified teachers (HQTs): teachers who have the following qualifications as contained in No Child Left Behind legislation: bachelors degree, full state certification, and knowledge of the subject(s) they teach.

High School: A Report on Secondary Education in America: a book by Ernest Boyer calling for a strengthened academic core curriculum in high schools (1983).

high-stakes tests: achievement tests that have high-stakes consequences for students, teachers, and administrators for example, a test that determines if a student is eligible to graduate or whether educators receive merit pay increases.

holistic rubric: a rating scale, or scoring guide, for evaluating a students overall product or performance.

horn book: a copy of the alphabet covered by a thin transparent sheet made from a cows horn.

humanism: a philosophy based on the belief that individuals control their own destinies through the application of their intelligence and learning.

humanistic psychology: an orientation to human behavior that emphasizes personal freedom, choice, awareness, and personal responsibility.

hybrid teacher: a teacher who combines part-time classroom teaching with leadership roles in a school or district.

I

inclusion: the practice of integrating all students with disabilities into general education classes.

Indian Education Act of 1972 and 1974 Amendments: a federal law and subsequent amendment designed to provide direct educational assistance to Native American tribes and nations.

individualistic cultures: cultures that tend to emphasize the individual, his or her success and achievement, and a sense of "I"—in contrast to collectivistic cultures that emphasize group membership and a sense of we.

individualized education program (IEP): a plan for meeting an exceptional learners educational needs, specifying goals, objectives, services, and procedures for evaluating progress.

individual racism: the prejudicial belief that ones ethnic or racial group is superior to others.

Individuals with Disabilities Education Act (IDEA): a 1990 federal act providing a free, appropriate education to disabled youth between 3 and 21 years of age. IDEA superseded the earlier Education for All Handicapped Children Act (Public Law 94–142).

induction programs: programs of support for beginning teachers, usually during their first year of teaching.

informal assessments: spontaneous assessment of student learning that teachers make while teaching—noting students' facial expressions, asking questions to gauge students' understanding, and listening to students' explanations of how they solved problems, for example.

information processing: a branch of cognitive science concerned with how individuals use long- and short-term memory to acquire information and solve problems.

inquiry learning: an approach to teaching that gives students opportunities to explore or inquire into subjects so that they develop their own answers to problem situations.

institutional racism: institutional policies and practices, intentional or not, that result in racial inequities.

integrated curriculum: a school curriculum that draws from two or more subject areas and focuses on a theme or concept rather than on a single subject.

intelligence: the ability to learn; the cognitive capacity for thinking.

International Assessment of Educational Progress (IAEP): a program established in 1991 for comparing the achievement of students in the United States with that of students from other countries.

Interstate Teacher Assessment and Support Consortium (InTASC): a consortium of states that has developed performance-based standards for what beginning teachers should know and be able to do and professional practice standards that apply throughout the developmental stages of a teachers career.

K

Kentucky Education Reform Act (KERA): comprehensive school-reform legislation requiring all Kentucky schools to form school-based management councils with authority to set policies in eight areas.

kindergarten: a school for children before they begin formal schooling at the elementary level; based on the ideas of German educator Friedrich Frvebel, kindergarten means garden where children grow.

L

Lanham Act: a U.S. government program during World War II that provided funding for training workers in war plants, construction of schools, and child care for working parents.

latchkey children: children who, because of family circumstances, must spend part of each day unsupervised by a parent or guardian.

Latin grammar school: colonial schools established to provide male students with a precollege education; comparable to todays high schools.

learning disability (LD): a limitation in ones ability to take in, organize, remember, and express information.

learning objects: digital resources containing a small amount of information that can be reused to support learning for example, learning objects stored at the National Science Digital Library or at PBS Teachers.

learning styles: cognitive, affective, and physiological behaviors through which an individual learns most effectively; determined by a combination of hereditary and environmental influences.

least restrictive environment: an educational program that meets a disabled students special needs in a manner that is identical, insofar as possible, to that provided to students in general education classrooms.

Lemon test: a three-part test, based on Lemon v. Kurtzman, to determine whether a state has violated the separation of church and state principle.

lesbian, gay, bisexual, and transgender (LGBT) students: students whose sexual orientation may subject them to discrimination and/or harassment in school settings.

limited English proficiency (LEP): a designation for students with limited ability to understand, read, or speak English and who have a first language other than English.

local school council (LSC): a group of community members that is empowered to develop policies for the operation of local schools.

local school district: an agency at the local level that has the authority to operate schools in the district.

logic: a branch of philosophy concerned with the processes of reasoning and the identification of rules that will enable thinkers to reach valid conclusions.

M

magnet school: a school offering a curriculum that focuses on a specific area such as the performing arts, mathematics, science, international studies, or technology. Magnet schools, which often draw students from a larger attendance area than regular schools, are frequently developed to promote voluntary desegregation.

mainstreaming: the policy and process of integrating disabled or otherwise exceptional learners into regular classrooms with nonexceptional students.

Massachusetts Act of 1642: a law requiring each town to determine whether its young people could read and write.

Massachusetts Act of 1647: a law mandating the establishment and support of schools; often referred to as the Old Deluder Satan Act because education was seen as the best protection against the wiles of the devil.

mastery learning: an approach to instruction based on the assumptions that (1) nearly all students can learn material if given enough time and taught appropriately and (2) learning is enhanced if students can progress in small, sequenced steps.

McGuffey readers: an immensely popular series of reading books for students in grades 1 through 6, written in the 1830s by Reverend William Holmes McGuffey.

McKinney-Vento Act: the nations first law to provide assistance to homeless persons, including free public education for children.

measurement: the gathering of data that indicate how much students have learned.

mentor: a wise, knowledgeable individual who provides guidance and encouragement to someone.

mentoring: an intensive form of teaching in which a wise and experienced teacher (the mentor) inducts a student (the protégé) into a professional way of life.

metaphysics: a branch of philosophy concerned with the nature of reality.

microteaching: a brief, single-concept lesson taught by a teacher education student to a small group of students; usually designed to give the education student an opportunity to practice a specific teaching skill.

minorities: groups of people who share certain characteristics and are smaller in number than the majority of a population.

mobile learning: learning that involves the use of mobile technologies such as smartphones.

modeling: the process of thinking out loud that teachers use to make students aware of the reasoning involved in learning new material.

monitorial system: an instructional method whereby a teacher instructs hundreds of pupils through the use of student monitors—older students selected for their academic abilities; developed by Joseph Lancaster (1778-1838).

Montessori method: a method of teaching, developed by Maria Montessori, based on a prescribed set of materials and physical exercises to develop childrens knowledge and skills.

moral reasoning: the reasoning process people follow to decide what is right or wrong.

Morrill Land-Grant Act: an 1862 act that provided federal land that states could sell or rent to raise funds to establish colleges of agriculture and mechanical arts.

multiage classrooms: elementary classrooms with students from different grade levels.

multicultural curriculum: a school curriculum that addresses the needs and backgrounds of all students regardless of their cultural identity and includes the cultural perspectives, or voices, of people who have previously been silent or marginalized.

multicultural education: education that provides equal educational opportunities to all students regardless of socioeconomic status; gender; or ethnic, racial, or cultural backgrounds and is dedicated to reducing prejudice and celebrating the rich diversity of U.S. life.

multiculturalism: a set of beliefs based on the importance of seeing the world from different cultural frames of reference and valuing the diversity of cultures in the global community.

multiple intelligences: a perspective on intellectual ability, proposed by Howard Gardner, suggesting that there are at least eight, and maybe as many as ten, types of human intelligence.

N

National Association of State Directors of Teacher Education and Certifications (NASDTEC) Interstate Agreement: a reciprocity agreement among approximately 47 states and the District of Columbia whereby a teaching certificate obtained in one state will be honored in another; developed by the National Association of State Directors of Teacher Education and Certification (NASDTEC).

National Board for Professional Teaching Standards (NBPTS): a board established in 1987 that began issuing professional certificates in 1994–95 to teachers who possess extensive professional knowledge and the ability to perform at a high level.

National Council for Accreditation of Teacher Education (NCATE): an agency that accredits, on a voluntary basis, almost half of the nations teacher education programs.

National Defense Education Act: a 1958 federally sponsored program to promote research and innovation in science, mathematics, modern foreign languages, and guidance.

National Education Association (NEA): the oldest and largest professional association for teachers and administrators.

National Governors Association (NGA): an association of state governors that influences policies in several areas, including teacher education and school reform.

A Nation at Risk: a 1983 national report critical of U.S. education.

NEAFT Partnership: an agreement between the National Education Association and the American Federation of Teachers to work collaboratively to attain mutually desired goals for the teaching profession.

negligence: failure to exercise reasonable, prudent care in providing for the safety of others.

No Child Left Behind (NCLB) Act of 2001: a federal law that mandates statewide testing in reading and mathematics each year in grades 38 and holds schools accountable for students performance on state proficiency tests.

nondiscrimination: conditions characterized by the absence of discrimination; for example, employees receive compensation, privileges, and opportunities for advancement without regard for race, color, religion, sex, or national origin.

normal schools: schools that focus on the preparation of teachers.

norm-referenced assessments: achievement tests that compare students scores with scores of other students who are similar.

null curriculum: the intellectual processes and subject content that schools do not teach.

O

observations: field experiences wherein a teacher education student observes a specific aspect of classroom life such as the students, the teacher, the interactions between the two, the structure of the lesson, or the setting.

online learning: education that is delivered via the Internet.

online schools: schools at which students complete all or most of their coursework online.

online social networking: an online community of people who share common interests and use methods such as e-mail, chat rooms, blogging, voice chat, and discussion groups to communicate.

open source materials: software, learning materials, and other digital resources that are available for free on the Internet.

open-space schools: schools that have large instructional areas with movable walls and furniture that can be rearranged easily.

opportunity to learn (OTL): the time during which a teacher provides students with challenging content and appropriate instructional strategies to learn that content.

out-of-school time (OST) activities: growth-oriented activities for students that take place beyond the school day; often called extracurricular activities.

P

Paideia Proposal: a book by philosopher Mortimer Adler calling for a perennialist core curriculum based on the Great Books (1982).

parochial schools: schools founded on religious beliefs.

pedagogical content knowledge: the knowledge accomplished teachers possess regarding how to present subject matter to students through the use of analogies, metaphors, experiments, demonstrations, illustrations, and other instructional strategies.

peer assessment: the practice of having students assess one anothers work; usually done informally and during a class session.

peer coaching: an arrangement whereby teachers grow professionally by observing one anothers teaching and providing constructive feedback.

peer-counseling programs: an arrangement whereby students, monitored by a school counselor or teacher, counsel one another in areas such as low achievement, interpersonal problems, substance abuse, and career planning.

peer-mediated instruction: approaches to teaching, such as cooperative learning and group investigation, that use the social relationships among students to promote their learning.

peer mediation: experiential activities, such as role-playing and simulations, that encourage students to be more accepting of differences and to develop empathy, social skills, and awareness of prejudice.

peer-mentoring programs: an arrangement whereby students, monitored by a school counselor or teacher, mentor one another in areas such as low achievement, interpersonal problems, substance abuse, and career planning.

peer tutoring: an arrangement whereby students tutor other students in the same classroom or at the same grade level.

perennialism: a philosophical orientation that emphasizes the ideas contained in the Great Books and maintains that the true purpose of education is the discovery of the universal, or perennial, truths of life.

performance-based assessment: the process of determining students ability to apply knowledge, skills, and work habits to the performance of specific learning tasks; determining what students can do as well as what they know.

performance expectations: established levels of achievement, quality of performance, or level of proficiency.

performance standard: academic standards that reflect levels of proficiency for example, 1 outstanding, 2 exemplary, 3 proficient, 4 progressing, and 5 standard not met.

Phi Delta Kappa (PDK): a professional and honorary fraternity of educators with 650 chapters and 130,000 members.

philosophy: the use of logical reasoning to inquire into the basic truths about being, knowledge, and conduct.

podcast: delivery of digital-media files over the Internet and played back on portable media players such as iPods.

portfolio assessment: the process of determining how much students have learned by examining collections of work that document their learning over time.

postmodernism: a philosophical orientation that maintains there are no absolute truths; instead, there are many truths and many voices that need to be heard.

practicum: a short field-based experience during which teacher education students spend time observing and assisting in classrooms.

Praxis Series: Professional Assessments for Beginning Teachers: a battery of tests available to states for the initial certification of teachers. Consists of assessments in three areas: academic skills, knowledge of subject, and classroom performance.

pre-K education: educational programs for children from birth to age 8, also termed early childhood education.

preoperational stage: the stage of cognitive development (2 to 7 years of age) proposed by Jean Piaget in which the individual begins to use language and symbols to think of objects and people outside the immediate environment.

privatization movement: umbrella term for reform initiatives that seek to run public schools as private enterprises.

problem-solving orientation: an approach to teaching that places primary emphasis on the teachers role as a decision maker and problem solver.

profession: an occupation that requires a high level of expertise, including advanced study in a specialized field, adherence to a code of ethics, and the ability to work without close supervision.

professionalization of teaching: the steadily increasing political influence and status of teaching as a profession; increased political influence and status reflect changes such as expanding leadership opportunities for teachers, national board certification, peer review, shared decision making, and teacher-mentor programs.

Program for International Student Assessment (PISA): an international assessment of students reading, mathematics, and science literacy skills in 34 nations.

Progress in International Reading Literacy Study (PIRLS): an international assessment of students reading and literacy skills in 44 nations.

progressive movement: a movement during the 1920s and 1930s to create schools that emphasized democracy, childrens interests and needs, and closer connections between school and community.

progressivism: a philosophical orientation based on the belief that life is evolving in a positive direction, that people may be trusted to act in their own best interests, and that education should focus on the needs and interests of students.

project-based learning (PBL): an approach to learning in which students work in teams on complex, real-world projects that allow them to develop and apply skills and knowledge.

property taxes: local taxes assessed against real estate and, in some areas, against personal property in the form of cars, household furniture and appliances, and stocks and bonds.

prosocial values: values such as honesty, patriotism, fairness, and civility that promote the well-being of a society.

psychosocial crisis: a life crisis at one of eight different stages of growth and development. According to psychologist Erik Erikson, individuals must resolve each crisis to reach the next stage.

psychosocial development: the progression of an individual through various stages of psychological and social development.

Q

qualitative assessments: subjective assessments of student learning for example, formal and informal observations of students performance on learning tasks and/or the manner in which they approach those tasks.

quantitative assessments: assessments of student learning that yield numerical scores that teachers use to evaluate student learning as well as the effectiveness of their teaching.

R

race: a concept of human variation used to distinguish people on the basis of biological traits and characteristics.

Race to the Top Program: a competitive program launched by the Obama administration to provide funding to states that have developed innovative reforms to increase student achievement, close achievement gaps, improve high school graduation rates, and ensure that students are prepared for success in college and careers.

reading and writing schools: colonial schools, supported by public funds and fees paid by parents, that used a religiously oriented curriculum to teach boys reading and writing skills and, to a lesser degree, mathematics.

recertification: the practice in some states of requiring experienced teachers to undergo periodic testing to maintain their teaching certificates.

redistricting: the practice of redrawing district boundaries to equalize educational funding by reducing the range of variation in the ability of school districts to finance education.

reflection: the process of thinking carefully and deliberately about the outcomes of ones teaching.

reflective teaching log: a journal of classroom observations in which the teacher education student systematically analyzes specific episodes of teaching.

regional educational service agency (RESA): a state educational agency that provides supportive services to two or more school districts; known in some states as education service centers, intermediate school districts, multicounty education service units, boards of cooperative educational services, or educational service regions.

reliability: the degree to which an assessment provides results that are consistent over time.

response to intervention (RTI) model: to determine if a student has a learning disability, increasingly intensive instruction is provided; if the student is not responsive to the instruction, the student receives appropriate special education services.

restructuring: reorganizing how schools are controlled at the local level so that teachers, principals, parents, and community members have greater authority.

S

scaffolding: an approach to teaching based on the students current level of understanding and ability; the teacher varies the amount of help given (for example, clues, encouragement, or suggestions) to students based on their moment-to-moment understanding of the material being learned.

school-based case management: an approach to education in which professionally trained case managers work directly with teachers, the community, and families to coordinate and deliver appropriate services to at-risk students and their families.

school-based management (SBM): various approaches to school improvement in which teachers, principals, students, parents, and community members manage individual schools and share in the decision-making processes.

school board: the primary governing body of a local school district.

school choice: various proposals that would allow parents to choose the schools their children attend.

school culture: the collective way of life characteristic of a school; a set of beliefs, values, traditions, and ways of thinking and behaving that distinguish it from other schools.

school improvement research: research studies that identify the characteristics of schools that improve over time.

school traditions: those elements of a schools culture that are handed down from year to year.

SchoolTube: an online video clearinghouse that hosts videos produced by students with the help of their teachers.

school-within-a-school: an alternative school (within a regular school) designed to meet the needs of students at risk.

scientific management: the application of management principles and techniques to the operation of big business and large school districts.

scoring rubrics: rating scales that consist of preestablished criteria for evaluating student performance on learning tasks.

search and seizure: the process of searching an individual and/or his or her property if that person is suspected of an illegal act; reasonable or probable cause to suspect the individual must be present.

Second Life: a popular, Internet-based virtual reality world.

self-assessment: the process of measuring ones growth in regard to the knowledge, skills, and attitudes possessed by professional teachers.

self-contained classroom: an organizational structure for schools in which one teacher instructs a group of students (typically, 20 to 30) in a single classroom.

service learning: an approach to teaching in which students participate in community-based service activities and then reflect on the meaning of those experiences.

sex role socialization: socially expected behavior patterns conveyed to individuals on the basis of gender.

sex role stereotyping: beliefs that subtly encourage males and females to conform to certain behavioral norms regardless of abilities and interests.

sexual harassment: unwanted and unwelcome sexual behavior directed toward another person, whether of the same or opposite sex.

social justice: a philosophical orientation that emphasizes equity and equal social benefits for all individuals and groups.

social reconstructionism: a philosophical orientation based on the belief that social problems can be solved by changing, or reconstructing, society.

Socratic questioning: a method of questioning designed to lead students to see errors and inconsistencies in their thinking, based on questioning strategies used by Socrates.

special education: a teaching specialty for meeting the special educational needs of exceptional learners.

stages of development: predictable stages through which individuals pass as they progress through life.

standardized assessments: pencil-and-paper achievement tests taken by large groups of students and scored in a uniform mannersome examples are the Iowa Test of Basic Skills, California Achievement Test, and the Scholastic Aptitude Test.

standards: statements that reflect what students should know and be able to do within a particular discipline or at a particular grade level.

standards-based education (SBE): basing curricula, teaching, and assessment of student learning on rigorous academic standards.

state aid: money given by a state to its cities and towns to provide essential services, including the operation of public schools.

state board of education: the highest educational agency in a state, charged with regulating the states system of education.

state department of education: the branch of state government, headed by the chief state school officer, charged with implementing the states educational policies.

state takeover: takeover of a chronically low-achieving school or district by the state.

stereotyping: the process of attributing behavioral characteristics to all members of a group; formulated on the basis of limited experiences with and information about the group, coupled with an unwillingness to examine prejudices.

student-centered curriculum: curriculum that is organized around students needs and interests.

student diversity: differences among students in regard to gender, race, ethnicity, culture, and socioeconomic status.

students at risk: students whose living conditions and backgrounds place them at risk for dropping out of school.

students with disabilities: students who need special education services because they possess one or more of the following disabilities: learning disabilities, speech or language impairments, mental retardation, serious emotional disturbance, hearing impairments, orthopedic impairments, visual impairments, or other health impairments.

student variability: differences among students in regard to their developmental needs, interests, abilities, and disabilities.

subject-centered curriculum: a curriculum that emphasizes learning an academic discipline.

substitute teaching: instruction provided by temporary teachers who replace regular teachers absent due to illness, family responsibilities, personal reasons, or attendance at professional workshops and conferences.

summative evaluation: an assessment of student learning made for the purpose of assigning grades at the end of a unit, semester, or year and deciding whether students are ready to proceed to the next phase of their education.

superintendent: the chief administrator of a school district.

T

Teacher Education Accreditation Council (TEAC): an agency founded in 1997 that accredits teacher education programs that provide evidence of having met TEACs three Quality Principles.

teacher-leader: a teacher who assumes a key leadership role in the improvement and/or day-to-day operation of a school.

teacher preneur: a teacher-leader who influences educational policies in entrepreneurial ways.

teachers craft knowledge: the knowledge teachers develop about teaching that derives from their experiences in the classroom, particularly the actions they have taken to solve specific problems of practice.

teachers thought processes: the thoughts that guide teachers actions in classrooms. These thoughts typically consist of thoughts related to planning, theories and beliefs, and interactive thoughts and decisions.

teacher supply and demand: the number of school-age students compared to the number of available teachers; may also be projected on the basis of estimated numbers of students and teachers.

TeacherTube: an online video clearinghouse where teachers and students can watch, upload, and share videos.

Teach for America: a program that enables recent college graduates without a teaching certificate to teach in districts with critical shortages of teachers and, after taking professional development courses and after supervision by state and school authorities, earn a teaching certificate.

teaching certificate: a license to teach issued by a state or, in a few cases, a large city.

teaching contract: an agreement between a teacher and a board of education that the teacher will provide specific services in return for a certain salary, benefits, and privileges.

teaching simulations: an activity in which teacher education students participate in role-plays designed to create situations comparable to those actually encountered by teachers.

team teaching: an arrangement whereby a team of teachers teaches a group of students equal in number to what the teachers would have in their self-contained classrooms.

tenure: an employment policy in which teachers, after serving a probationary period, retain their positions indefinitely and can be dismissed only on legally defensible grounds.

3D virtual reality worlds: computer-based simulated environments that a user inhabits through use of an avatar, a users representation of himself or herself; a popular 3D virtual reality program is Second Life.

time on task: the amount of time students are actively and directly engaged in learning tasks.

Title IX: a provision of the 1972 Education Amendments Act prohibiting sex discrimination in educational programs.

tort liability: conditions that would permit the filing of legal charges against a professional for breach of duty and/or behaving in a negligent manner.

Trends in International Mathematics and Science Study (TIMSS): an international assessment of mathematics and science achievement among fourth-, eighth-, and twelfth-grade students in 41 nations.

Tyler rationale: a four-step model for curriculum development in which teachers identify purposes, select learning experiences, organize experiences, and evaluate.

V

validity: the degree to which assessments measure what they are supposed to measure.

vertical equity: an effort to provide equal educational opportunity within a state by providing different levels of funding based on economic needs within school districts.

virtual labs: computerized, online simulations of scientific laboratories that enable students to conduct scientific inquiry in a virtual environment.

voucher system: funds allocated to parents that they may use to purchase education for their children from public or private schools in the area.

W

webquests: online inquiry research projects for students that require them to gather material from the web.

wiki: a website created, edited, and maintained by a group of people with a common interest.

within-class ability grouping: the practice of creating small, homogeneous groups of students within a single classroom for the purpose of instruction, usually in reading or mathematics, at the elementary level.

Womens Educational Equity Act (WEEA): a 1974 federal law that guarantees equal educational opportunity for females.

work habits: dispositions important for effective thinking and learning for example, reading with curiosity and willingness to work hard.

Y

YouTube: an online video clearinghouse where people watch, upload, and share videos.

Z

zero tolerance policies: school policies related to discipline and safety that provide for automatic, severe consequences for certain types of misbehavior that involves drugs, violence, sexual harassment, or bullying, for example.

REFERENCES

Abrahamsson, B. (1971). *Military profession-alization and political power*. Stockholm: Allmanna Forlagret.

Acton v. Vernonia School District, 66 F.3d 217 (9th Cir.), rev'd, 515 U.S. 646, 115 S. Ct. 2386 (1995).

Addy, Engelhardt, & Skinner. (January 2013). *Basic Facts about Low-Income Children, 2011, Children Under 18 Years*. National Center for Children in Poverty, New York: Columbia University-Mailman School of Public Health.

Adesope, O. O., Lavin, T., Thompson, T., & Ungerleider, C. (2010, June). A systematic review and meta-analysis of the cognitive correlates of bilingualism. *Review of Educational Research, 80*(2), 207–245.

Adler, M. (1982). *The paideia proposal: An educational manifesto*. New York, NY: Macmillan.

Africatown Center for Education and Innovation. (2014, Spring). The Young Geniuses Academy. Retrieved from http://www.africatowncenter.org/programs/

Afterschool Alliance. (2010, September 22). Afterschool in Hawaii. Retrieved from http://www.afterschoolalliance.org/states_docs/pdfs/2010/Hawaii_Fact_Sheet.pdf

Aguilar v. Felton, 473 U.S. 402 (1985).

Agostini v. Felton, 521 U.S. 203 (1997).

Ahmed-Ullah, N. S. (2013, February 27). CPS cracks down on underperforming charters. *Chicago Tribune*. Retrieved from http://articles.chicagotribune.com/2013-02-27/news/ct-met-cps-board-meeting-0228-20130228_1_charter-schools-beth-purvis-schools-ceo-barbara-byrd-bennett

Albert Shanker Institute. (2011). A call for common content. *American Educator, 35*(1), 41–45.

Alexander, K., & Alexander, M. D. (2012). *American public school law* (8th ed.). Belmont, CA: Wadsworth, Cengage Learning.

Alfonso v. Fernandez, 606 N.Y.S.2d 259 (N.Y. App. Div. 1993).

Alvin Independent School District v. Cooper, 404 S.W.2d 76 (Tex. Civ. App. 1966).

American Association of University Women (AAUW). (1991). *Shortchanging girls, shortchanging America*. Washington, DC: Author.

American Association of University Women (AAUW). (1992). *How schools shortchange girls: The AAUW report*. Researched by Wellesley College Center for Research on Women. Washington, DC: The AAUW Educational Foundation.

American Association of University Women (AAUW). (2002). *Harassment-free hallways: How to stop sexual harassment in schools: A guide for students, parents, and teachers, Section III for schools*. Washington, DC: Author.

American Association of University Women (AAUW). (2008, May). *Where the girls are: The facts about gender equity in education*. Washington, DC: Author.

American Federation of Teachers. (2002, July). *Do charter schools measure up? The charter school experiment after 10 years*. Washington, DC: Author.

American Federation of Teachers. (2013, November 26). About AFT. Retrieved from http://www.aft.org/about/.

American Institutes of Research. (2003). *Effects of the implementation of Proposition 227 on the education of English learners, K–12, year 3 report*. Submitted to the California Department of Education, October 29, 2003.

Annie E. Casey Foundation. (2010). *The Annie E. Casey Foundation 2010 kids count data book*. Baltimore, MD: Author.

Annie E. Casey Foundation. (2013). *2013 kids count data book: State trends in child well-being*. Baltimore, MD: Author.

Ansari, Z. (2011, February). Advancing our common interests. *American Teacher, 95*(4), 14.

Ansary, T. (2010). The muddle machine: Confessions of a textbook editor. In F. W. Parkay, E. J. Anctil, & G. Hass (Eds.), *Curriculum leadership: Readings for developing quality educational programs* (9th ed., pp. 298–303). Upper Saddle River, NJ: Allyn & Bacon/Pearson.

Anyon, J. (1996). Social class and the hidden curriculum of work. In E. Hollins (Ed.), *Transforming curriculum for a culturally diverse society* (pp. 179–203). Mahwah, NJ: Lawrence Erlbaum.

Appalachia Educational Laboratory. (1993). *Alternative assessment in math and science: Moving toward a moving target*. Charleston, WV: Author.

Apple, Inc. (2008). *Apple classrooms of tomorrow—today: Learning in the 21st century*. Cupertino, CA: Author.

Ariza, E. N. W. (2006). *Not for ESOL teachers: What every classroom teacher needs to know about the linguistically, culturally, and ethnically diverse student*. Upper Saddle River, NJ: Pearson.

Armour, R. (2006). We can finally close the achievement gap. Retrieved from http://armourachievement.blogspot.com/

Armstrong, P. A. (2008). *What teachers expect in reform: Making their voices heard*. Lanham, MD: Rowman & Littlefield Education.

Aronson, E., & Gonzalez, A. (1988). Desegregation, jigsaw, and the Mexican-American experience. In P. A. Katz & D. A. Taylor (Eds.), *Eliminating racism: Profiles in controversy*. New York, NY: Plenum Press.

Artz, S. (1999). *Sex, Power, and the Violent School Girl*. New York, NY: Teachers College Press.

Ash, K. (March 18, 2010). Teachers testing mobile methods. *Education Week*. Retrieved July 3, 2014, from http://www.edweek.org/ew/articles/2010/03/18/26mobiletools.h29.html.

Ashby, A. (2010, May 19). West Virginia to use Second Life for teacher training. Engage Digital Media. Retrieved from http://www.engagedigital.com/2010/05/19/west-virginia-to-use-second-life-for-teacher-training/

Ashton-Warner, S. (1963). *Teacher*. New York, NY: Simon & Schuster.

Asian Americans/Pacific Islanders in Philanthropy. (1997). *An invisible crisis: The educational needs of Asian Pacific American youth*. New York, NY: Author.

Association of Mindfulness in Education. (2014, January 26). What is mindfulness? Retrieved from http://www.mindfuleducation.org/whatismindfulness.html

Aud, S., Fox, M., & KewalRamani, A. (2010). *Status and trends in the education of racial and ethnic groups* (NCES 2010-015). U.S. Department of Education, National Center for Education Statistics. Washington, DC: U.S. Government Printing Office.

Aud, S., Wilkinson-Flicker, S., Kristapovich, P., Rathbun, A., Wang, X., & Zhang, J. (2013). *The condition of education 2013* (NCES 2013-037). U.S. Department of Education, National Center for Education Statistics. Washington, DC: U.S. Government Printing Office.

Aud, S., Fox, M., & KewalRamani, A. (2010). *Status and trends in the education of racial and ethnic groups*. Washington, DC: U.S. Department of Education.

Austin, W., & Adcock, P. (2002). Alternative classroom observation through two-way audiovideo conferencing systems. In D. Willis et al. (Eds.), *Proceedings of Society for Information Technology & Teacher Education International Conference 2002*, pp. 2416–2417. Chesapeake, VA.

Avramidis, E., Bayliss, P., & Burden, R. (2000). A survey into mainstream teachers' attitudes towards the inclusion of children with special educational needs in the ordinary school in one local education authority. *Educational Psychology, 20*(2), 191–211.

Ayers, W. C., & Miller, J. L. (Eds.). (1998). *A light in dark times: Maxine Greene and the unfinished conversation*. New York, NY: Teachers College Press.

Bagwell, M. (2012, August 10). The intangible rewards of teaching English as a second language. Retrieved from http://rossieron-line.usc.edu/the-intangible-rewards-of-teaching-english-as-a-second-language/.

Baker, B. D., Green, P., & Richards, C. E. (2008). *Financing education systems*. Upper Saddle River, NJ: Pearson.

Baldas, T. (2007, December 10). As "cyber-bullying" grows, so do lawsuits. *National Law Journal*. Retrieved from http://www.law.com/jsp/article.jsp?id=1197281074941

Ballantine, J. H. (1997). *The sociology of education: A systematic analysis* (4th ed.). Upper Saddle River, NJ: Prentice Hall.

Banks, J. A. (2014). *An introduction to multicultural education* (5th ed.). Boston, MA: Pearson.

Banks, J. S. (2006). *Cultural diversity and education: Foundations, curriculum and teaching* (5th ed.). Boston, MA: Allyn & Bacon/Pearson.

Banks, J. S. (2009). *Teaching strategies for ethnic studies* (8th ed.). Boston, MA: Allyn & Bacon/Pearson.

Batalova, J., & McHugh, M. 2010. *Top languages spoken by English language learners nationally and by state*. Washington, DC: Migration Policy Institute.

Battles v. Anne Arundel County Board of Education, 904 F. Supp. 471 (D. Md. 1995), *aff'd*, 95 F.3d 41 (4th Cir. 1996).

Baugh, J. (2012). African American vernacular English (Ebonics). In James A. Banks (Ed.), *Encyclopedia of diversity in education* (pp. 49–54). Thousand Oaks, CA: Sage Publications, Inc.

Beck, R. J. (2008). What are learning objects? Retrieved from http://www.uwm.edu/Dept/CIE/AOP/LO_what.html

Bell, J. S., Thacker, T., & Schargel, F. P. (2014). *Schools where teachers lead*. New York, NY: Routledge.

Bennett, C. I. (1990). *Comprehensive multicultural education: Theory and practice* (2nd ed.). Boston, MA: Allyn & Bacon.

Bennett, C. I. (2003). *Comprehensive multicultural education: Theory and practice* (5th ed.). Boston, MA: Allyn & Bacon.

Bennett, C. I. (2011). *Comprehensive multicultural education: Theory and practice* (7th ed.). Upper Saddle River, NJ: Pearson.

Bennett, C. I. (2015). *Comprehensive multicultural education: Theory and practice* (8th ed.). Upper Saddle River, NJ: Pearson.

Bennett, L. (1997). Break the silence: Gay and straight students in Massachusetts team up to make a difference. *Teaching Tolerance, 6*, 24–31.

Bennett, W. (1987). *James Madison High School: A curriculum for American students*. Washington, DC: U.S. Department of Education.

Bergman, J. and Sams, A. (2012). Flip your classroom: Reach every student in every class every day. International Society for Technology in Education.

Berliner, D. C. & Glass, G. V. (2014). 50 myths and lies that threaten America's public schools: The real crisis in education. New York: Teachers College Press.

Bernstein, B. B. (1996). *Pedagogy, symbolic control and identity: Theory, research, critique (critical perspectives on literacy and education)*. New York, NY: Taylor and Francis.

Bertocci, P. A. (1960). *Education and the vision of excellence*. Boston, MA: Boston University Press.

Berry, B., et al. (2011). *Teaching 2030: What we must do for our students and our public schools—now and in the future*. New York, NY: Teachers College Press and Washington, DC: National Education Association.

Besner, H. F., & Spungin, C. I. (1995). *Gay and lesbian students: Understanding their needs*. Washington, DC: Taylor and Francis.

Betty Shabazz International Charter School. (2014, May 14). African centered education. Retrieved from http://www.bsics.net/apps/pages/index.jsp?uREC_ID=179005&type=d

Bissonette, A. M. (2009). *Cyber law: Maximizing safety and minimizing risk in classrooms*. Thousand Oaks, CA: Corwin.

Bitter, G. G., & Legacy, J.M. (2008). *Using technology in the classroom* (7th ed.). Boston: Allyn & Bacon.

Black, P., Harrison, C., Lee, C., Marshall, B., & Wiliam, D. (2004, September). Working inside the black box: Assessment for learning in the classroom. *Phi Delta Kappan*, 9–21.

Bloom, B. S. (1981). *All our children learning: A primer for parents, teachers, and other educators*. New York, NY: McGraw-Hill.

Board of Education, Sacramento City Unified School District v. Holland, 786 F. Supp. 874 (E.D. Cal. 1992).

Board of Education of Oklahoma City Public Schools v. Dowell, 498 U.S. 237, 249–250 (1991).

Board of Education of Westside Community Schools v. Mergens, 496 U.S. 226 (1990).

Bobbit, J. F. (1924). *How to make a curriculum*. New York: Houghton Mifflin. Bond, N. (Ed.). (2014). The power of teacher leaders: Their roles, influence, and impact. Routledge.

Borich, G. D. (2014). *Effective teaching methods: Research-based practice* (8th ed.). Upper Saddle River, NJ: Pearson Education.

Boser, U. (2011, November). Teacher diversity matters: A state-by-state analysis of teachers of color. Washington, DC: Center for American Progress.

Boyer, E. (1983). *High school: A report on secondary education in America*. New York, NY: Harper & Row.

Boyer, E. (1995). *The basic school: A community for learning*. Princeton, NJ: Carnegie Foundation for the Advancement of Teaching.

Bradley, A. (1998, February 4). Unions agree on blueprint for merging. *Education Week on the Web*.

Bradley, L. June 19, 2014. SOLE: Motivate students to teach themselves (and each other). Blog post. Retrieved July 13, 2014 from http://www.edutopia.org/discussion/sole-motivate-students-teach-themselves-and-each-other.

Brameld, T. (1956). *Toward a reconstructed philosophy of education*. New York, NY: Holt, Rinehart and Winston.

Bran, A., Gray, T., & Silver-Pacuila, H. (2008, June 10). Berberi's tools: Technology can level the learning field. George Lucas Educational Foundation. Retrieved from http://www.edutopica.org/assistive-technology-devices-visually-impaired

Brock, B. L., & Grady, M. L. (2001). *From first-year to first-rate: Principals guiding beginning teachers*. Thousand Oaks, CA: Corwin Press.

Brookhart, S.M. and Nitko, A.J. (2015). *Educational assessment of students*, seventh edition. Boston: Pearson.

Broudy, H. S. (1979). Arts education: Necessary or just nice? *Phi Delta Kappan, 60,* 347–350.

Broughman, S. P., Swaim, N. L., & Hryczaniuk, C. A. (2011). *Characteristics of private schools in the United States: Results from the 2009–10 Private School Universe Survey* (NCES 2011-339). National Center for Education Statistics, Institute of Education Sciences, U.S. Department of Education. Washington, DC: U.S. Government Printing Office.

Brown, F. B., Kohrs, D., & Lanzarro, C. (1991). The academic costs and consequences of extracurricular participation in high school. Paper presented at the Annual Meeting of Educational Research Association.

Brown v. Board of Education of Topeka, Kansas, 347 U.S. 483 (1954).

Brown v. Hot, Sexy and Safer Productions, Inc., 68 F.3d 525 (1st Cir. 1995), *cert. denied*, 516 U.S. 1159 (1996).

Brown v. Unified School District No. 501, 56 F. Supp. 2d 1212 (D. Kan. 1999).

Brunelle v. Lynn Public Schools, 702 N.E.2d 1182 (Mass. 1998).

Bucky, P. A. (1992). *The private Albert Einstein*. Kansas City: Andrews and McMeel.

Burch v. Barker, 651 F. Supp. 1149 (W.D. Wash. 1987).

Burch v. Barker, 861 F.2d 1149 (9th Cir. 1988).

Bureau of Justice Statistics and National Center for Education Statistics. (2009). *Indicators of schools, crime and safety, 2009.* Washington, DC: Author.

Burney, D. (2004). Craft knowledge: The road to transforming schools. *Phi Delta Kappan, 85*(7), 526–531.

Burns, J. (2003, September 20). Immersion aims to undo damage of assimilation policies. Associated Press.

Burton v. Cascade School District Union High School No. 5, 512 F.2d 850 (9th Cir. 1975).

Bush v. Holmes, 767 So. 2d 668, 675 (2006).

Bushaw, W. J., & Lopez, S. J. (2010). A time for change: The 42nd annual Phi Delta Kappa/Gallup Poll of the public's attitudes toward the public schools. *Phi Delta Kappan, 92*(1), 8–26.

Bushaw, W. J., & Lopez, S. J. (2013). Which way do we go? The 45th annual Phi Delta Kappa/Gallup Poll of the public's attitudes toward the public schools. *Phi Delta Kappan, 95*(1), 9–25.

Button, H. W., & Provenzo, E. F. (1989). *History of education and culture in America* (2nd ed.). Upper Saddle River, NJ: Prentice Hall.

Canter, L. (1989). Assertive discipline—more than names on the board and marbles in a jar. *Phi Delta Kappan, 71*(1), 57–61.

Canter, L. (2009). Assertive discipline: *Positive behavior management for today's classroom.* Bloomington, IN: Solution Tree.

Carnegie Corporation of New York. (2008). *Teachers for a new era.* Retrieved from http://www.teachersforanewera.org/index.cfm?fuseaction=home.home

Carnegie Council on Adolescent Development. (1989). *Turning points: Preparing American youth for the 21st century.* New York, NY: Author.

Carroll, J. (1963). A model of school learning. *Teachers College Record, 64.*

Carver, P. R., & Lewis, L. (2010). *Alternative schools and programs for public school students at risk of educational failure: 2007–08* (NCES 2010–026). U.S. Department of Education, National Center for Education Statistics. Washington, DC: U.S. Government Printing Office.

Center for Children of Immigrants. (2013, December). *Access to education: Challenges and opportunities for immigrant students.* Washington, DC: Author. Retrieved from http://www.firstfocus.net/sites/default/files/Education%20Access%20for%20Immigrant%20Students.pdf.

Center for Research on Education Outcomes, Stanford University. (2013). *National charter school study* 2013.

Center on Education Policy. (2010, December). *State high school tests: Exit exams and other assessments.* Washington, DC: Author.

Center on Education Policy. (December 2012). *State high school exit exams: A policy in transition.* Washington, DC: Author.

Centers for Disease Control and Prevention. (2009, Summer). *Suicide: Facts at a glance.* Atlanta, GA: Author.

Centers for Disease Control and Prevention. (2012, August 15). *Youth suicide.* Atlanta, GA: Author. Retrieved from http://www.cdc.gov/violenceprevention/pub/youth_suicide.html

Chappuis, J., Stiggins, R. J., Chappuis, S., and Arter, J. A. (2012). *Classroom assessment for student learning: Doing it right—Using it well,* 2nd edition. Boston: Pearson.

Cheung, A., & Slavin, R. E. (2012). The Effectiveness of Educational Technology Applications for Enhancing Reading Achievement in K-12 Classrooms. Baltimore, MD: Johns Hopkins University, Center for Research and Reform in Education.

Chicago Public Schools. (2013, December). Guidelines: Service learning. Retrieved from http://www.cps.edu/ServiceLearning/Pages/Guidelines.aspx.

Chiaramonte, P., & Gonen, Y. (2010, October 18). Teachers fired for flirting on Facebook with students. Retrieved from http://www.nypost.com/p/news/local/teachers_friending_spree_JVfEO8TmN7XCnWpX5s5hnO

Children's Defense Fund. (2012). *The state of America's children handbook, 2012.* Washington, DC: Author.

Coalition for Community Schools. (2013). Community schools results. Retrieved from http://www.communityschools.org/assets/1/AssetManager/Community%20School%20Results%202013.pdf.

Cohen, S. (Ed.). (1974). *Massachusetts school law of 1648. Education in the United States.* New York, NY: Random House.

Coladarci, T., & Cobb, C. D. (1996). Extracurricular participation, school size, and achievement and self-esteem among high school students: A national look. *Journal of Research in Rural Education, 12*(2), 92–103.

Coleman, J. S., Campbell, E. Q., Hobson, C. J., McPartland, J., Mood, A. L., Weinfeld, F. D., et al. (1966). *Equality of educational opportunity.* Washington, DC: U.S. Government Printing Office.

College Board and Phi Delta Kappa. (2009). *Teachers are the center of education: Profiles of eight teachers.* New York and Bloomington, IN: Authors.

Collier-Thomas, B. (1982, Summer). Guest editorial: The impact of black women in education: An historical overview. *The Journal of Negro Education 51*(3), 173–180.

Collins, A. & Halverson, R. (2009). Rethinking education in the age of technology: The digital revolution and schooling in America. New York, NY: Teachers College Press.

Colucci, K. (2000). Negative pedagogy. In J. L. Paul & K. Colucci (Eds.), *Stories out of school: Memories and reflections on care and cruelty in the classroom* (pp. 27–44). Stamford, CT: Ablex.

Comer, J. P. (2009). *What I learned in school.* San Francisco, CA: Jossey-Bass.

Commager, H. S. (1958, October). Noah Webster, 1758–1958. *Saturday Review 41,* 18.

Commager, H. S. (1962). *Noah Webster's American spelling book.* New York, NY: Teachers College Press.

Concerned Black Men. (2010, September 20). About us. Retrieved from http://www.cbm-national.org/aboutus

Consortium for School Networking. (2008). *Executive summary: Collaboration in K–12 schools: Anywhere, anytime, any way.* Washington, DC: Author. Retrieved from http://www.cosn.org/resources/emerging_technologies/collaboration.cfm

Cornman, S.Q. (2013). *Revenues and expenditures for public elementary and secondary education: School year 2010–11 (fiscal year 2011)* (NCES 2013-342). U.S. Department of Education. Washington, DC: National Center for Education Statistics.

Cossentino, J., & Whitcomb, J. A. (2007). In D. T. Hansen (Ed.), *Ethical visions of education: Philosophies in practice.* New York, NY: Teachers College Press.

Costa, A. L. (1984). A reaction to Hunter's knowing, teaching, and supervising. In P. L. Hosford (Ed.), *Using what we know about teaching.* Alexandria, VA: Association for Supervision and Curriculum Development.

Coughlin, E. K. (1993, March 24). Sociologists examine the complexities of racial and ethnic identity in America: Number and variety of immigrants since 1965 inspire growing body of research. *The Chronicle of Higher Education 39,* no. 29: 7–8.

Council for the Accreditation of Educator Preparation. (2010, October 25). *Press release.* Washington, DC: Author.

Council for the Accreditation of Educator Preparation. (2013, August 29). *CAEP accreditation standards.* Washington, DC: Author.

Council of Chief State School Officers. (2008, May 26). Chief state school officers: Method of selection. Retrieved from http://www.ccsso.org/chief_state_school_officers/method_of_selection/index.cfm

Counts, G. (1932). *Dare the school build a new social order?* New York, NY: John Day.

Crawford, J. (2004). *Education of English learners: Language diversity in the classroom* (5th ed.). Los Angeles: Bilingual Education Services.

Crawford, J. (2007). The decline of bilingual education: How to reverse a troubling trend. *International Multilingual Research Journal, 1*(1), 33–37.

Cremin, L. A. (1961). *The transformation of the school: Progressivism in American education, 1876–1957.* New York, NY: Alfred A. Knopf.

Cuban, L. (2003). *Why is it so hard to get good schools?* New York, NY: Teachers College Press.

Cuban, L. (October 2, 2013). Making money in K–12 schools is hard to do . . . for some companies. Retrieved from http://larrycuban.wordpress.com/2013/10/02/

making-money-in-k-12-schools-is-hard-to-do-for-some-companies/

Cunningham, C. (2003). *Trends and issues: Social and economic context*. Eugene, OR: University of Oregon, Clearinghouse on Educational Management.

Currie, B. (July 1, 2014). The Tech Detectives: Students take ownership of technology. *Edutopia*. Retrieved September 17, 2014, from http://www.edutopia.org/blog/tech-detectives-students-take-ownership-brad-currie.

Curtis v. School Committee of Falmouth, 652 N.E.2d 580 (Mass. 1995), *cert. denied*, 516 U.S. 1067 (1996).

Davey, M. (2013, August 26). In Chicago, campaign to provide safe passage on way to school. *New York Times*. Retrieved from http://www.nytimes.com/2013/08/27/education/in-chicago-campaign-to-provide-safe-passage-on-way-to-school.html?_r=0

David Lynch Foundation. (2014, January 26). *The quiet time program: Restoring a positive culture of academics and well-being in high-need school communities*. New York, NY: Author. Retrieved from http://www.davidlynchfoundation.org/pdf/Quiet-Time-Brochure.pdf

Davis v. Meek, 344 F. Supp. 298 (N.D. Ohio 1972).

Dawkins, R. (2009). *The greatest show on earth: The evidence for evolution*. New York, NY: Free Press.

Deal, T. E., & Peterson, K. D. (2009). *Shaping school culture: Pitfalls, paradox, & promises* (2nd ed.). San Francisco, CA: Jossey-Bass.

Dell'Olio, J. M., & Donk, T. (2007). *Models of teaching: Connecting student learning with standards*. Thousand Oaks, CA: Sage.

Deskbook encyclopedia of American school law 2013. Malvern, PA: Center for Education & Employment Law.

Dewey, J. (1904). The relation of theory to practice in education. In Third *Yearbook for the National Society for the Scientific Study of Education*, Part 1. Bloomington, IN: Public School Publishing Co.

Dewey, J. (1916). *Democracy and education: An introduction to the philosophy of education*. New York, NY: Macmillan.

Dewey, J. (1929). *The sources of a science of education*. New York: Horace Liveright.

Dewey, J. (1955). Quoted in *Organizing the teaching profession: The story of the American Federation of Teachers*. Glencoe, IL: Commission on Educational Reconstruction.

Dierke, J. S. (2010, September/October). A quiet transformation. *Leadership* (Association of California School Administrators), pp. 14—17.

Doe v. Renfrow, 631 F.2d 91, *reh'g denied*, 635 F.2d 582 (7th Cir. 1980), *cert. denied*, 451 U.S. 1022 (1981).

Dryfoos, J. G., Quinn, J., & Barkin, C. (Eds.). (2005). *Community schools in action: Lessons from a decade of practice*. Oxford: Oxford University Press.

Dubuclet v. Home Insurance Co., 660 So. 2d 67 (La. Ct. App. 1995).

Duckworth, A. L. (2009). Backtalk: Self-Discipline is empowering. *Phi Delta Kappan*, Vol. 90, No. 07, March 2009, p. 536.

Duckworth, A. L., & Allred, K. M. (2012). Temperament in the classroom. In R. L. Shiner & M. Zentner (Eds.), *Handbook of temperament* (pp. 627–644). New York, NY: Guilford Press.

Duckworth, A. L., Kirby, T., Tsukayama, E., Berstein, H., & Ericsson, K. (2010). Deliberate practice spells success: Why grittier competitors triumph at the National Spelling Bee. *Social Psychological and Personality Science, 2*, 174–181.

Duckworth, A. L., Peterson, C., Matthews, M. D. & Kelly, D. R. (2007) Grit: Perseverance and passion for long-term goals. *Journal of Personality and Social Psychology, 92*(6), 1087–1101.

Dunklee, D. R., & Shoop, R. J. (2002). *The principal's quick-reference guide to school law: Reducing liability, litigation, and other potential legal tangles* (2nd ed.). Thousand Oaks, CA: Corwin Press.

Dunn, J. M., & West, M. R. (Eds.). (2009). *From schoolhouse to courthouse: The judiciary's role in American education*. Washington, DC: The Brookings Institution.

Durkheim, E. (1956). *Education and sociology* (S. D. Fox, Trans.). Glencoe, IL: Free Press.

Dweck, C., Walton, G. M., & Cohen, G.L. (2011). Academic tenacity: Mindsets and skills that promote long-term learning. Paper presented at the Gates Foundation, Seattle, WA.

Eamon, M. K. (2001, July). The effects of poverty on children's socio/emotional development: An ecological systems analysis. *Social Work, 46*(3), 256–266.

Easton, J. Q. (2012, April 14). The power of measurement. Paper presented at the National Council on Measurement in Education, Inaugural Opening Plenary Session, Vancouver, BC.

Edelman, M. W. (2008, April 11). *Child watch column: Celebrating young people who beat the odds*. Retrieved from http://www.childrensdefense.org/site/MessageViewer?em_id=7901.0

Education Commission of the States. (2011). Exit exams. Retrieved from http://www.ecs.org/html/offsite.asp?document=http%3A%2F%2Fwww%2Eecs%2Eorg%2Fhtml%2Feducationissues%2FHighSchool%2Fhighschooldb1%5Fintro%2Easp%3Ftopic%3Dee

Education Trust. (2008, November). *Core problems: Out-of-field teaching persists in key academic courses and high-poverty schools*. Washington, DC: Author.

Education Week. (2005, May 5). Technology counts 2005: Electronic transfer: Moving technology dollars in new directions.

Education Week. (2009, March 26). Technology counts 2005: Breaking away from tradition.

Education Week. (2014, January 3). District pressure cookers test recipes for success: Buffeted by social and fiscal forces, local educators seek new takes on governance. Retrieved from http://www.edweek.org/ew/articles/2014/01/09/16execsum.h33.html?intc=EW-QC14-TOC

Educational Testing Service. (2007, December 17). *Teacher quality in a changing policy landscape: Improvements in the teacher pool*. Princeton, NJ: Author.

Educational Testing Service. (2010). *Overview of the Praxis III assessments*. Princeton, NJ: Author. Retrieved from http://www.ets.org/praxis/institutions/praxisiii/

Educators with Disabilities Caucus, Council for Exceptional Children. (2008). CEC's Educators with Disabilities Caucus (EDC). Retrieved from http://www.cec.sped.org/Content/NavigationMenu/AboutCEC/Communities/Caucuses/Educatorswith Disabilities/default.htm

Edwards v. Aguillard, 482 U.S. 578 (1987).

Egbert, J. (2009). *Supporting learning with technology: Essentials of classroom practice*. Upper Saddle River, NJ: Pearson Education.

Eggen, P., & Kauchak, D. (2012). *Strategies and models for teachers: Teaching content and thinking skills* (6th ed.). Upper Saddle River, NJ: Pearson.

Eisner, E. (2002). *The educational imagination: On the design and evaluation of school programs* (3rd ed.). New York, NY: Macmillan College.

Eisner, E. (2006, March). The satisfactions of teaching: How we teach is ultimately a reflection of why we teach. *Educational Leadership, 44*–46.

Eisner, E. W. (1998). *The kind of schools we need: Personal essays*. Portsmouth, NH: Heinemann.

Emmer, E. T., & Evertson, C. M. (2013). *Classroom management for middle and high school teachers* (9th ed.). Boston, MA: Pearson Education.

Engel v. Vitale, 370 U.S. 421 (1962).

English, F. W. (2010). *Deciding what to teach & test: Developing, aligning, and leading the curriculum* (3rd ed.). Thousand Oaks, CA: Corwin.

Enlow, R. (2004). *Grading vouchers: Ranking America's school choice programs*. Indianapolis, IN: Milton and Rose D. Friedman Foundation.

Epperson v. Arkansas, 393, U.S. 97 (1968).

Erickson, H. L. (2008). *Stirring the head, heart, and soul: Redefining curriculum, instruction, and concept-based learning*. Thousand Oaks, CA: Corwin Press.

Erikson, E. H. (1963). *Childhood and society* (2nd ed.). New York, NY: Norton.

Erikson, E. H. (1997). *The life cycle completed: Extended version with new chapters on the ninth stage of development by Joan M. Erikson*. New York, NY: W. W. Norton.

Essex, N. L. (2012). *School law and the public schools: A practical guide for educational leaders* (5th ed.). Boston, MA: Pearson.

Etzioni, A. (1969). *The semi-professions and their organization: Teachers, nurses, social workers.* New York, NY: Free Press.

Etzioni, A. (1999, June 9). The truths we must face to curb youth violence. *Education Week on the Web.*

Evans, L. (2002). Teacher attraction: Are magnet school teachers more professionalized than traditional schoolteachers in urban secondary schools? *Education and Urban Society, 34*(3), 312–333.

Evergreen Education Group. (2013). *Keeping pace with K–12 online learning: An annual review of policy and practice.* Durango, CO: Author.

Evers, B, Greene, J.P., Forster, G., Stotsky, S., & Wurman, Z. (2011, May 2). Closing the door on innovation: Why one national curriculum is bad for America. Retrieved from http://educationnext.org/closing-the-door-on-innovation/.

Evertson, C. M., & Emmer, E. T. (2013). *Classroom management for elementary teachers* (9th ed.). Upper Saddle River, NJ: Pearson Education.

Fagen v. Summers, 498 P.2d 1227 (Wyo. 1972).

Falk, B. (2002, April). Standards-based reforms: Problems and possibilities. *Phi Delta Kappan*, 612–620.

Falvo v. Owasso Independent School District, 233 F.3d 1203 (10th Cir. 2000).

Fashola, O. (1999). *Review of extended-day and after-school programs and their effectiveness.* Baltimore, MD: Johns Hopkins University, Center for Research on the Education of Students Placed at Risk.

Feistritzer, C. E., & Haar, C. K. (2008). *Alternate routes to teaching.* Upper Saddle River, NJ: Pearson Education.

Feistritzer, E. (1999). *A report on teacher preparation in the United States.* Washington, DC: National Center for Education Information.

Feistritzer, E. (2009). Teaching while learning: Alternate routes fill the gap. *EDge 5*(2), 3–15.

Ferguson, C. (2003, August 30). Gay high school draws criticism from conservatives and civil libertarians. Associated Press.

Ferlazzo, L., & Sypnieski, K. H. (2012, April 17). Seven tips for building positive relationships with English-language learners. Retrieved from http://www.edutopia.org/blog/building-positive-relationships-ELL-larry-ferlazzo-katie-hull-sypnieski.

Ferrari, T. M., Arnett, N., & Cochran, G. (2007). *Preparing teens for success: Building 21st century skills through a 4-H work-based learning program.* Columbus, OH: Ohio State University Extension. Retrieved from www.ohio4h.org/workforceprep/documents/2007JournalofYouthDevelopment_JET.pdf

Fetler, M. (2001). Student mathematics achievement test scores, dropout rates, and teacher characteristics. *Teacher Education Quarterly, 28*(1), 151–168.

Firestone, D. (2008). Alternative schools: When teachers unite to run school. *New York Times.* Retrieved from http://query.nytimes.com/gst/fullpage.html?res=990CE1DF1039F937A15756C0A963958260

Fleischer, H. (2012). What is our current understanding of one-to-one computer projects: A systematic narrative research review. *Educational Research Review, 7*, 107–122.

Fletcher, J., Denton, C., & Francis, D. (2005). Validity of alternative approaches for the identification of learning disabilities: Operationalizing unexpected underachievement. *Journal of Learning Disabilities, 38*(6), 545–552.

Fletcher, J., Lyon, R., Fuchs, L., & Barnes, M. (2007). *Learning disabilities: From identification to intervention.* New York, NY: Guilford Press.

Flores vs. Morgan Hill Unified School District, 324 F.3d 1130 (9th Cir. 2003).

Fong, T. P. (2007). *The contemporary Asian American experience: Beyond the model minority* (3rd ed.). Upper Saddle River, NJ: Prentice Hall.

Franklin, B. (1931). Proposals relating to the education of youth in Pennsylvania. In T. Woody (Ed.), *Educational views of Benjamin Franklin.* New York, NY: McGraw-Hill.

Franklin, C., Harris, M. B., & Allen-Meares, P. (Eds.). (2006). The school services sourcebook: A guide for school-based professionals. Oxford University Press.

Franklin, J. H. (1947). *From slavery to freedom: A history of Negro Americans* (3rd ed.). New York, NY: Vintage Books.

Freed, C. D., & Samson, M. (2004). Native Alaskan dropouts in Western Alaska: Systemic failure in Native Alaskan schools. *Journal of American Indian Education 43*(2), 33–45.

Freeman v. Pitts, 503 U.S. 467 (1992).

Freire, P. (1970). *Pedagogy of the oppressed.* New York, NY: Continuum.

Friedman, M. (2003, March 24). Milton Friedman interview on CNBC: Friedman on school vouchers.

Friend, M. (2014). *Special education: contemporary perspectives for school professionals* (4th ed.). Boston: Pearson.

Friend, M., & Bursuck, W. D. (2015). *Including students with special needs: A practical guide for classroom teachers* (7th ed.). Boston, MA: Pearson.

Friend, M., & Cook, L. (2013). *Interactions: Collaboration skills for school professionals* (7th ed.). Boston, MA: Pearson.

Fryer, R. G. (2011). Teacher incentives and student achievement: Evidence from New York City public schools. Retrieved from http://scholar.harvard.edu/files/fryer/files/teacher_incentives_and_student_achievement_evidence_from_new_york_city_public_schools.pdf

Gabor, A. (2013, September). The great charter tryout: Are New Orleans's schools a model for the nation—or a cautionary tale? *Newsweek.* Retrieved from http://www.theinvestigativefund.org/investigations/politicsandgovernment/1848/the_great_charter_tryout?page=3

Gagné, R. M. (1974). *Essentials of learning for instruction.* Hinsdale, IL: Dryden.

Gagné, R. M. (1977). *The conditions of learning* (3rd ed.). New York, NY: Holt, Rinehart and Winston.

Galante, M. (April 18, 2012). Why a middle school in New York is paying teachers $125,000 a year. Business Insider. Retrieved August 15, 2014, from http://www.businessinsider.com/the-equity-project-charter-school-pays-teachers-125000-a-year-2012-4.

Gale (2014). *Encyclopedia of associations: National organizations of the U.S., 53rd edition.* Farmington Hills, MI: Gale.

Gandara, P., & Fish, J. (1994, Spring). Year-round schooling as an avenue to major structural reform. *Educational Evaluation and Policy Analysis*, p. 16.

Garan, E. M. (2004). *In defense of our children: When politics, profit, and education collide.* Portsmouth, NH: Heinemann.

Garbarino, J. (1999). *Lost boys: Why our sons turn violent and how we can save them.* New York, NY: Free Press.

Garbarino, J. (2010, December 19). How a boy becomes a killer. Retrieved from http://www.cnn.com/2012/12/19/opinion/garbarino-violence-boys/.

Gardner, H. (2013, October 16). "Multiple intelligences" are not "learning styles." *Washington Post.* Retrieved from http://www.washingtonpost.com/blogs/answer-sheet/wp/2013/10/16/howard-gardner-multiple-intelligences-are-not-learning-styles/

Gardner, H. (1983). *Frames of mind.* New York, NY: Basic Books.

Gardner, H. (1999). *The disciplined mind: What all students should understand.* New York, NY: Simon & Schuster.

Garringer, M. and MacRae, P. (2008, September). *Building effective peer mentoring programs in schools: An introductory guide.* The Mentoring Resource Center, U.S. Department of Education, Office of Safe and Drug-Free Schools. Washington, DC: Author.

Gates, B. (2013, September 5). What teachers mean to me. Retrieved from http://www.thegatesnotes.com/Topics/Education/TEACH

Gaylord v. Tacoma School District No. 10, 599 P.2d 1340 (Wash. 1977).

Gebser v. Lago Vista Independent School District, 524 U.S. 274 (1998).

GE Foundation. (March 10, 2014). *Developing futures.* Retrieved August 28, 2014, from http://www.gefoundation.com/education/developing-futures/.

GenYES Corp. (2010, December 27). *Summary of GenYES research: Student-led technology professional development.* Olympia, WA: Generation YES. Retrieved from http://msd.geny.org/media/programs/genyes/genyes_research_summary.pdf

George Lucas Educational Foundation. (2008, June). *A word from George Lucas: Edutopia's role in education.* Retrieved from http://www.edutopia.org/lucas

George Lucas Educational Foundation. (2010, April). Learning the lingo.

Retrieved from http://www.edutopia.org/global-language-education-schools-online

Gerber, S. B. (1996). Extracurricular activities and academic achievement. *Journal of Research and Development in Education, 30*(1), 42–50.

Gill, B., Zimmer, R., Christman, J., & Blanc, S. (2007). *State takeover, school restructuring, private management, and student achievement in Philadelphia.* Santa Monica, CA: Rand Corporation.

Gilligan, C. (1993). *In a different voice: Psychological theory and women's development.* Cambridge, MA: Harvard University Press.

Gipp, G. (1979, August–September). Help for Dana Fast Horse and friends. *American Education,* p. 15.

Glasser, W. R. (1997, April). A new look at school failure and school success. *Phi Delta Kappan,* 596–602.

Glasser, W. R. (1998a). *Quality school* (3rd ed.). New York, NY: Harper Perennial.

Glasser, W. R. (1998b). *The quality school teacher: Specific suggestions for teachers who are trying to implement the lead-management ideas of the quality school.* New York, NY: Harper Perennial.

Glasser, W. R. (1998c). *Choice theory: A new psychology of personal freedom.* New York, NY: HarperCollins.

Glasser, W. R., & Dotson, K. L. (1998). *Choice theory in the classroom.* New York, NY: Harper Perennial.

Glickman, C., Gordon, S. P., & Ross-Gordon, J. (2014). *Supervision and instructional leadership: A developmental approach* (9th ed.). Upper Saddle River, NJ: Allyn & Bacon/Pearson.

Gmelch, W. H., & Parkay, F. W. (1995). Changing roles and occupational stress in the teaching profession. In M. J. O'Hair & S. J. Odell (Eds.), *Educating teachers for leadership and change: Teacher education yearbook III* (pp. 46–65). Thousand Oaks, CA: Corwin Press.

Goldhaber, D., & Anthony, E. (2003, May). Teacher quality and student achievement, *ERIC Clearinghouse on Urban Education, Urban Diversity Series, 115*(1).

Goldring, R., Gray, L., & Bitterman, A. (2013). *Characteristics of public and private elementary and secondary school teachers in the United States: Results from the 2011–12 Schools and Staffing Survey* (NCES 2013-314). U.S. Department of Education. Washington, DC: National Center for Education Statistics. Retrieved from http://nces.ed.gov/pubsearch

Gollnick, D. M., & Chinn, P. C. (2009). *Multicultural education in a pluralistic society* (8th ed.). Upper Saddle River, NJ: Merrill/Pearson.

Good, T. E., & Brophy, J. E. (2003). *Looking in classrooms* (9th ed.). Boston, MA: Allyn & Bacon.

Good, T. L., & Brophy, J. E. (2008). *Looking in classrooms* (10th ed.). Upper Saddle River, NJ: Pearson Education.

Good, T. E., & Grouws, D. (1979). The Missouri mathematics effectiveness project: An experimental study in fourth-grade classrooms. *Journal of Educational Psychology, 71,* 355–362.

Good News Club v. Milford Central School, 533 U.S. 98 (2001).

Goss v. Lopez, 419 U.S. 565 (1975).

Graham, P. A. (1967). *Progressive education: From Arcady to academe: A history of the Progressive Education Association, 1919–1955.* New York, NY: Teachers College Press.

Grant, G., & Murray, C. E. (2002). *Teaching in America: The slow revolution.* Cambridge, MA: Harvard University Press.

Grant, P. G., Richard, K. J., & Parkay, F. W. (1996, April). Using video cases to promote reflection among preservice teachers: A qualitative inquiry. Paper presented at the annual meeting of the American Educational Research Association, New York.

Gray, L., Thomas, N., & Lewis, L. (2010). *Teachers' use of educational technology in U.S. public schools: 2009* (NCES 2010-040). National Center for Education Statistics. Institute of Education Sciences, U.S. Department of Education. Washington, DC: National Center for Education Statistics.

Green, T. D., Brown, A., & Robinson, L. (2008). *Making the most of the Web in your classroom: A teacher's guide to blogs, podcasts, wikis, pages, and sites.* Thousand Oaks, CA: Corwin Press.

Greene, M. (1995a). *Releasing the imagination.* San Francisco, CA: Jossey-Bass.

Greene, M. (1995b). What counts as philosophy of education? In W. Kohli (Ed.), *Critical conversations in philosophy of education* (pp. 3–23). New York, NY: Routledge.

Greenfield, P. M. (1994). Independence and interdependence as developmental scripts: implications for theory, research, and practice. In P. M. Greenfield & R. R. Cocking (Eds.), *Cross-cultural roots of minority child development* (pp. 1–37). Mahwah, NJ: Lawrence Erlbaum.

Grenda, P., & Hackmann, D. G. (2014). Advantages and challenges of distributing leadership in middle-level schools. *NASSP Bulletin, 98*(1), 53–74.

Gross, M. U. M. (2008). Highly gifted children and adolescents. In J. A. Plucker & C. M. Callahan (Eds.), *Critical issues and practices in gifted education: What the research says* (pp. 241–251). Waco, TX: Prufrock Press.

Guenemoen, R. F., Thompson, S. J., Thurlow, M. L., & Lehr, C. A. (2001). *A self-study guide to implementation of inclusive assessment and accountability systems: A best practice approach.* Minneapolis, MN: University of Minnesota, National Center on Educational Outcomes.

Gurian, M., & Stevens, K. (2007). *The minds of boys: Saving our sons from falling behind in school and life.* San Francisco, CA: Jossey-Bass.

Gutierrez, R. (2008). A "gap-gazing" fetish in mathematics education? Problematizing research on the achievement gap. *Journal for Research in Mathematics Education, 39*(4), 357–364.

GW Community School. (2011). Mission statement. Retrieved from http://www.gwcommunityschool.com/

Hakuta, K. (2001a). Follow-up on Oceanside: Communications with Ron Unz. Retrieved from http://www.stanford/edu/~hakuta/SAT9/Silence%20from%20Oceanside%202.htm

Hakuta, K. (2001b). Silence from Oceanside and the future of bilingual education. Retrieved from http://faculty.ucmerced.edu/khakuta/research/SAT9/silence1.html

Hale-Benson, J. E. (1986). *Black children: Their roots, culture, and learning styles.* Baltimore: Johns Hopkins University Press.

Hallahan, D. P., & Kauffman, J. M. (2000). *Exceptional children: Introduction to special education* (8th ed.). Boston, MA: Allyn & Bacon.

Hallahan, D. P., &, Kauffman, J. M. (2006). *Exceptional learners: An introduction to special education.* Upper Saddle River, NJ: Pearson Education.

Hamilton, B. E., Martin, J. A., & Ventura, S. J. (2013). *Births: Preliminary data for 2012.* Hyattsville, MD: National Center for Health Statistics. Retrieved from http://www.cdc.gov/nchs/data/nvsr/nvsr62/nvsr62_03.pdf

Hansen, D. T. (1995). *The call to teach.* New York, NY: Teachers College Press.

Hansen, D. T. (Ed.). (2007). *Ethical visions of education: Philosophies in practice.* New York, NY: Teachers College Press.

Hanson, J. R., & Silver, H. F. (2000). *Learning preference inventory.* Woodbridge, NJ: Thoughtful Education Press.

Hardman, M. L., Drew, C. J., & Egan, M. W. (2013). *Human exceptionality: Society, school, and family* (11th ed.). Independence, KY: Cengage Learning.

Harper, D. (2006). *Vision to action: Adding student leadership to your technology plan: Meeting the needs of all stakeholders.* Olympia, WA: Generation YES Corp.

Harrington, M. (1962). *The other America: Poverty in the United States.* New York, NY: MacMillan.

Harris Interactive, Inc. (2001). *The MetLife survey of the American teacher: Key elements of quality schools.* New York, NY: Author.

Harris Interactive, Inc. (2006). *The MetLife survey of the American teacher: Expectations and experiences.* New York, NY: Author.

Harris Interactive, Inc. (2010). *The MetLife survey of the American teacher: Collaborating for student success.* New York, NY: Author.

Harris Interactive, Inc. (2011). *The MetLife survey of the American teacher—Preparing students for college and careers part 1: Clearing the path.* New York, NY: Author.

Harris, Interactive, Inc. (2013, February). *The MetLife survey of the American teacher—Challenges for school leadership.* New York, NY: Author.

Harry A. v. Duncan, 351 F.Supp 2d 1060 (Mont. 2005).

Hartigan, J. (Ed.) (2013). *Anthropology of race: Genes, biology, and culture*. Santa Fe, NM: School for Advanced Research Press.

Hartman, A. (2008). *Education and the cold war: The battle for the American school*. New York, NY: Palgrave Macmillan.

Haselton, B., & Davis, M. (2004). Resources do produce results. *Foresight: A Publication of the Kentucky Long-Term Policy Research Center, II*(1), 7–9.

Hawking, S. W. (1988). *A brief history of time: From the big bang to black holes*. New York, NY: Bantam Books.

Hawkins, B. (2010, July 1). Teacher gets to tout St. Paul's Avalon co-op school to nation's top education officials. *MinnPost.com*. Retrieved from http://www.minnpost.com/stories/2010/07/01/19375/teacher_gets_to_tout_st_pauls_avalon_co-op_school_to_nations_top_education_officials

Hazelwood School District v. Kuhlmeier, 484 U.S. 260 (1988).

Heath, S. B. (1983). *Ways with words*. Cambridge, UK: Cambridge University Press.

Hedges, L. V. (1996). Quoted in Hedges finds boys and girls both disadvantaged in school. *Education News*. University of Chicago, Department of Education.

Hemelt, S. W., & Marcotte, D. E. (2013). High school exit exams and dropout in an era of increased accountability. *Journal of Policy Analysis and Management*, Vol. 32, No. 2, 323–349.

Hendrie, C. (1999, May 5). Battle over principals in Chicago: Administration vs. local councils. *Education Week on the Web*.

Henriques, M. E. (1997, May). Increasing literacy among kindergartners through cross-age training. *Young Children*, pp. 42–47.

Henry, E., Huntley, J., McKamey, C., & Harper, L. (1995). *To be a teacher: Voices from the classroom*. Thousand Oaks, CA: Corwin Press.

Herndon, J. (1969). *The way it spozed to be*. New York, NY: Bantam Books.

Herrick, K. A., Fakhouri, T. H., Carlson, S. A., & Fulton, J. E. TV watching and computer use in U.S. youth aged 12–15, 2012. NCHS data brief, no 157. Hyattsville, MD: National Center for Health Statistics. 2014.

Hess, F., & Meeks, O. (2010). *School boards circa 2010: Governance in the accountability area*. National School Boards Association, The Thomas Fordham Institute, and The Iowa School Boards Foundation.

Hess, F. M. (2002). *Revolution at the margins: The impact of competition on urban school systems*. Washington, DC: Brookings Institution Press.

Hess, F. M. (2004, March). The political challenge of charter school regulation. *Phi Delta Kappan*, 508–512.

Hicks, B. (2011). Letter in support of Michelle Shearer's application for National Teacher of the Year. Retrieved from http://www.ccsso.org/Documents/2011/news/2011_NTOY_Press.pdf

Hiebert, J., Gallimore, R., & Stigler, J. W. (2002). A knowledge base for the teaching profession: What would it look like and how can we get one? *Educational Researcher, 31*(5), 3–15.

Hill, P. T. (2003, May 12). School reform efforts aren't reaching underserved students. *Spokesman Review*, p. A11.

Hills, G., & Hirschhorn, J. (2007, May). *Best in class: How top corporations can help transform public education*. New York, NY: Ernst & Young.

Hirschfelder, A. B. (1986). *Happily may I walk: American Indians and Alaska Natives today*. New York, NY: Scribner.

Hletko, J. D. (1995). Reflections on NBPTS. *Voices from the Middle, 2*(4), 33–36.

Hofstede, G. (2001). *Culture's consequences: Comparing values, behaviors, institutions and organizations across nations* (2nd ed.). Thousand Oaks, CA: Sage.

Hoh, P. S. (2008). Cognitive characteristics of the gifted. In J. A. Plucker & C. M. Callahan (Eds.), *Critical issues and practices in gifted education: What the research says* (pp. 57–83). Waco, TX: Prufrock Press.

Holland, A., & Andre, T. (1987, Winter). Participation in extracurricular activities in secondary schools. *Review of Educational Research*, pp. 437–466.

Holmes, M., & Weiss, B. J. (1995). *Lives of women public schoolteachers: Scenes from American educational history*. New York, NY: Garland.

Holt, J. (1964). *How children fail*. New York, NY: Delta.

Holt v. Shelton, 341 F. Supp. 821 (M.D. Tenn. 1972).

Holt-Reynolds, D. (1999). Good readers, good teachers? Subject matter expertise as a challenge in learning to teach. *Harvard Educational Review, 69*(1), 29–50.

hooks, b. (1989). *Talking back: Thinking feminist, thinking black*. Toronto: Between the Lines.

hooks, b. (1994). *Teaching to transgress: Education as the practice of freedom*. New York, NY: Routledge.

hooks, b. (2003) *Teaching community. A pedagogy of hope*. New York, NY: Routledge.

Hortonville Joint School District No. 1 v. Hortonville Education Association, 426 U.S. 482 (1976).

Howard, V. F., Williams, B. F., Port, P. D., & Lepper, C. (2001). *Very young children with special needs*. Upper Saddle River, NJ: Merrill/Pearson.

Howell, W. G., & West, M. R. (2009, May 22). More education, less support for raising teacher salaries. *Education Next*. Retrieved from http://97.74.65.51/readArticle.aspx?ARTID=34969

Hoy, A. W., & Hoy, W. K. (2013). *Instructional leadership: A research-based guide to learning in schools* (4th ed.). Boston, MA: Allyn & Bacon.

Hoyt, W. H. (1999). An evaluation of the Kentucky Education Reform Act. In *Kentucky Annual Economic Report 1999* (pp. 21–36). Lexington: University of Kentucky, Center for Business and Economic Research.

Huber, C. R. (2011). Student teaching journal entry #10. Retrieved from http://www.cathyrutanhuber.com/student-teaching-journal-entry-10.html

Human Rights Campaign. (2014, March 20). Employment non-discrimination act. Retrieved from http://www.hrc.org/laws-and-legislation/federal-legislation/employment-non-discrimination-act

Hurwitz, S. (1999, April). New York, New York: Can Rudy Crew hang tough on vouchers and pull off a turnaround in the nation's biggest school system? *The American School Board Journal*, pp. 36–40.

Hussar, W. J., & Bailey, T. M. (2013). *Projections of education statistics to 2021* (NCES 2013-008). U.S. Department of Education, National Center for Education Statistics. Washington, DC: U.S. Government Printing Office.

Hutchins, R. M., & Adler, M. J. (1963). *Gateway to the Great Books*. Chicago: Encyclopedia Britannica. Hyde Schools. (2014). About Hyde. Retrieved from http://www.hyde.edu/about-hyde-school/

IBM MentorPlace. (2010, September 21). IBM MentorPlace. Retrieved from http://www.ibm.com/ibm/ibmgives/grant/education/programs/mentorplace.shtml

Igoa, C. (1995). *The inner world of the immigrant child*. New York, NY: Lawrence Erlbaum.

Imber, M., van Geel, T., Blokhuis, J. C., & Feldman, J. (2014). *A teacher's guide to education law* (5th ed.). New York, NY: Routledge.

Indiana University. (2014). Cultural immersion projects: About the American Indian Reservation Project. Indiana University, College of Education. Retrieved from http://portal.education.indiana.edu/tep/TeacherEducationHome/CulturalImmersionProjects/AmericanIndianReservationProject/AbouttheProject.aspx.

Ingersoll, R., & Merrill, L. (2010). Who's teaching our children? *Educational Leadership 67*(8), 14–20.

Ingraham v. Wright, 430 U.S. 651 (1977).

Innes, R. G. (2010). KERA (1990-2010): What have we learned?" Lexington, KY: Bluegrass Institute.

Institute for Educational Leadership. (2002). *Community schools: Improving student learning/strengthening schools, families, and communities*. Washington, DC: Author.

Institute for Educational Leadership. (2002). *Community schools: Improving student learning/strengthening schools, families, and communities*. Washington, DC: Author. http://icec.oise.utoronto.ca/mission.htm.

International Society for Technology in Education. (2008). *National Educational Technology Standards (NETS) for teachers 2008*. Retrieved from http://www.iste.org/Content/NavigationMenu/NETS/ForTeachers/2008Standards/NETS_for_Teachers_2008.htm

International Society for Technology in Education. (2014). Conference Program, June 28-July 1, 2014. Retrieved July 3, 2014 from https://www.isteconference.org/2014/pdfs/ISTE_2014_FPEG_PDF.pdf.

Interstate Teacher Assessment and Support Consortium (InTASC). (2010, July). *Model core teaching standards: A resource for state dialogue (draft for public comment)*. Washington, DC: Author.

J. C. v. Beverly Hills Unified School District. United States District Court for the Central District of California. (CV 08-03824 SVW, 2009). Retrieved from http://lawyersusaonline.com/wp-files/pdfs/jc-v-beverly-hills-a.pdf

Jackson, P. (1965). The way teaching is. *NEA Journal*.

Jackson, P. (1990). *Life in classrooms*. New York, NY: Teachers College Press.

James, W. (1890). *Principles of psychology*. Cambridge, MA: Harvard University Press.

Jeglin v. San Jacinto Unified School District, 827 F. Supp. 1459 (C.D. Cal. 1993).

Jencks, C., et al. (1972). *Inequality: A reassessment of the effect of family and schooling in America*. New York, NY: Basic Books.

Jencks, C., & Phillips, M. (Eds.). (1998). *The black-white test score gap*. Washington, DC: Brookings Institution Press.

Job Experience and Training (JET) Program. (2010, September 8). Job Experience and Traning (JET) Program. Retrieved from http://www.national4-hheadquarters.gov/about/pod-leadership/JET09.pdf

Johanningmeier, E. V. (1980). *Americans and their schools*. Chicago: Rand McNally.

Johnson, D. W., & Johnson, R. T. (1999). *Learning together and alone: Cooperative, competitive, and individualistic learning* (5th ed.). Boston, MA: Allyn & Bacon.

Johnston, L. D., O'Malley, P. M., Bachman, J. G., & Schulenberg, J. E. (2013). *Monitoring the Future national results on drug use: 2012 Overview, Key Findings on Adolescent Drug Use*. Ann Arbor: Institute for Social Research, The University of Michigan.

Jones, K., & Whitford, K. (1997, December). Kentucky's conflicting reform principles: High-stakes accountability and student performance assessment. *Phi Delta Kappan*, 276–281.

Jordan, W. J., & Nettles, S. M. (1999). *How students invest their time out of school: Effects on school engagement, perceptions of life chances, and achievement*. Baltimore, MD: Center for Research on the Education of Students Placed at Risk.

Joyce, B., Weil, M., & Calhoun, E. (2015). *Models of teaching* (9th ed.). Upper Saddle River, NJ: Allyn & Bacon/Pearson.

K[12], Inc. (2014, March 11). What is K12? Retrieved from http://www.k12.com/what-is-k12#.Ux-vCbeA270

Kaplan, M. (2012, May 10). Blog: Collaborative team teaching: Challenges and rewards. Retrieved from http://www.edutopia.org/blog/collaborative-team-teaching-challenges-rewards-marisa-kaplan

Karr v. Schmidt, 401 U.S. 1201 (1972).

Katyal, K. R. & Evers, C. W. (2014). *Teacher leadership: New conceptions for autonomous student learning in the age of the Internet*. New York, NY: Routledge.

Kauchak, D., & Eggen, P. (2012). *Learning & teaching: Research-based methods* (6th ed.). Upper Saddle River, NJ: Pearson.

Kaye, E. A. (Ed.). (2012). *Requirements for certification of teachers, counselors, librarians, administrators for elementary and secondary schools—seventy-seventh edition, 2012-2013* Chicago: University of Chicago Press.

Keaton, P. (2012a). *Public elementary and secondary school student enrollment and staff counts from the common core of data: School year 2010–11* (NCES 2012-327). U.S. Department of Education. Washington, DC: National Center for Education Statistics. Retrieved from http://nces.ed.gov/pubsearch

Keaton, P. (2012b). *Numbers and types of public elementary and secondary schools from the common core of data: School year 2010–11* (NCES 2012-325rev). U.S. Department of Education. Washington, DC: National Center for Education Statistics. Retrieved from http://nces.ed.gov/pubsearch

Keigher, A. (2010). *Teacher attrition and mobility: Results from the 2008–09 Teacher Follow-up Survey* (NCES 2010-353). U.S. Department of Education. Washington, DC: National Center for Education Statistics. Retrieved from http://nces.ed.gov/pubsearch

Kellner, D. (2000). Multiple literacies and critical pedagogies. In P. P. Trifonas (Ed.), *Revolutionary pedagogies—cultural politics, instituting education, and the discourse of theory* (pp. 196–221). New York, NY: Routledge.

Kelly, M. (2000, September 8). Indian Affairs head makes apology. Associated Press.

Kennedy Middle School. (2014). P.R.I.D.E. information. Retrieved from http://schools.4j.lane.edu/kennedy/documents/kms_pride.pdf.

Kennedy, M. (1999). Ed schools and the problem of knowledge. In J. D. Raths & A. C. McAninch (Eds.), *Advances in teacher education: Vol. 5. What counts as knowledge in teacher education?* (pp. 29–45). Stamford, CT: Ablex.

Kimball, J. (2010). Student teaching semester: Journal entries. Retrieved from https://seguecommunity.middlebury.edu/view/html/site/jmkimbal-jessie/node/5860424

King, M. (2008, February 3). Tribes confront painful legacy of Indian boarding schools. *Seattle Times*. Retrieved from http://seattletimes.nwsource.com/html/localnews/2004161238_boardingschool03m.html

Kingston, A. (July 15, 2014). Get ready for Generation Z. Maclean's. Retrieved August 4, 2014, from http://www.macleans.ca/society/life/get-ready-for-generation-z/.

Kinross, L. (2009). School board backs adaptive software for all students. Toronto: Bloorview. Kirkpatrick, H., & Cuban, L. (1998).

Computers make kids smarter—right? *TECHNOS Quarterly*, *7*(2), 26–31.

Kirp, D. L. (January 12, 2014). Meditation transforms roughest San Francisco schools. *SFGate*. Retrieved September 3, 2014, from http://www.sfgate.com/opinion/openforum/article/Meditation-transforms-roughest-San-Francisco-5136942.php.

Kitzmiller v. Dover Area School District, 400 F. Supp. 2d 707 (2005).

Kleinfeld, J. (1998). *The myth that schools shortchange girls: Social science in the service of deception*. Washington, DC: Women's Freedom Network.

Kohl, H. R. (1968). *36 children*. New York, NY: Signet.

Kohlberg, H. (2014). The cognitive-developmental approach to moral education. In F. W. Parkay, E. J. Anctil, & G. Hass, *Curriculum leadership: Readings for developing quality educational programs*. (10th ed., pp. 181-193147–159). Boston: Pearson.

Kosciw, J. G., & Diaz, E. M. (2006). *The 2005 national school climate survey: The experiences of lesbian, gay, bisexual, and transgender youth in our nation's schools*. New York, NY: Gay, Lesbian and Straight Education Network.

Kostelnik, M. J., Onaga, E., Rohde, B., & Whiren, A. (2002). *Children with special needs: Lessons for early childhood professionals*. New York, NY: Teachers College Press.

Kounin, J. (1970). *Discipline and group management in classrooms*. New York, NY: Holt, Rinehart and Winston.

Kozol, J. (1967). *Death at an early age*. Boston, MA: Houghton Mifflin.

Kozol, J. (1991). *Savage inequalities: Children in America's schools*. New York, NY: Crown.

Kozol, J. (2005). *The shame of the nation: The restoration of apartheid schooling in America*. New York, NY: Three Rivers Press.

Krashen, S., & McField, G. (2005). What works? Reviewing the latest evidence on bilingual education. *Language Learner, 1*(2), 7–10.

Krizek v. Cicero-Stickney Township High School District No. 201, 713 F. Supp. 1131 (N.D. Ill. 1989).

Krogh, S. L. (2000). Weaving the web. In F. W. Parkay & G. Hass (Eds.), *Curriculum planning: A contemporary approach* (7th ed., pp. 338–341). Boston, MA: Allyn & Bacon.

Kulik, J. A. (2004). Meta-analytic studies of acceleration. In N. Colangelo, S. G. Assouline, & M. U. M. Gross (Eds.), *A nation deceived: How schools hold back America's brightest students* (Vol. 2, pp. 13–22). Iowa City, IA: The Connie Belin and Jacqueline N. Blank International Center for Gifted Education and Talent Development.

LaMorte, M. W. (2008). *School law: Cases and concepts* (9th ed.). Upper Saddle River, NJ: Allyn & Bacon/Pearson.

LaMorte, M. W. (2012). *School law: Cases and concepts* (10th ed.). Upper Saddle River, NJ: Pearson.

Lange, C. M., & Sletten, S. J. (2002). *Alternative education: A brief history and research synthesis*. Alexandria, VA: Project Forum at National Association of State Directors of Special Education. Retrieved from http://www.nasdse.org/forum.htm

Larry P. v. Riles, 793 F.2d 969 (9th Cir. 1984).

Laskow, S. (2010, August 26). Necessity is the mother of invention: After Katrina, the failing schools of New Orleans were turned over to privately run charters. Five years later, they're on the mend. *Newsweek*. Retrieved from http://www.newsweek.com/2010/08/26/new-orleans-s-charter-school-revolution.html

Lau v. Nichols, 414 U.S. 563 (1974).

Laurence, D. (2000). *NEA: The grab for power: A chronology of the National Education Association*. Oklahoma City, OK: Hearthstone.

Layton, L. and Brown, E. (2012, November 17). Quality controls lacking for D.C. schools accepting federal vouchers. *Washington Post*. Retrieved from http://www.washingtonpost.com/local/education/quality-controls-lacking-for-dc-schools-accepting-federal-vouchers/2012/11/17/062bf97a-1e0d-11e2-b647-bb1668e64058_story.html

Leahy, R. (2009). *Authentic educating*. Lanham, MD: University Press of America, Inc.

Leahy, T., & Harris, R. (2001). *Learning and cognition* (5th ed.). Upper Saddle River, NJ: Merrill/Pearson.

Learning in Deed. (2004). *Learning in deed: Service learning in action*. New York, NY: National Service-Learning Partnership, Academy for Educational Development. Retrieved from http://www.learningindeed.org/tools/examples.html

Lee, V. E., Chen, X., & Smerdon, B. A. (1996). *The influence of school climate on gender differences in the achievement and engagement of young adolescents*. Washington, DC: American Association of University Women.

Leinhardt, G. (1990). Capturing craft knowledge in teaching. *Educational Researcher, 19*(2), 18–25.

Lemon v. Kurtzman, 403 U.S. 602 (1971).

Leone, P., & Weinberg, L. (2010, May). *Addressing the unmet educational needs of children and youth in the juvenile justice and child welfare systems*. Washington, DC: Georgetown University, Center for Juvenile Justice Reform.

Levenson, M. R. (2014). *Pathways to teacher leadership: emerging models, changing roles*. Cambridge: Harvard Education Press.

Lewis, C. (2003, August 13). Is it time for cameras in classrooms? *Philadelphia Inquirer*. Retrieved from http://www.philly.com

Lewis, R. B., & Doorlag, D. H. (2006). *Teaching special students in general education classrooms* (7th ed.). Upper Saddle River, NJ: Merrill/Pearson Education.

Li, Q., & Ma, X. (2010). A meta-analysis of the effects of computer technology on school students' mathematics learning. *Educational Psychology Review, 22*(3), 215–243.

Lieberman, A. & Miller, L. (2014). *Teacher leadership*. San Francisco, CA: Jossey-Bass.

Lightfoot, S. L. (1978). *Worlds apart: Relationships between families and schools*. New York, NY: Basic Books.

Lindjord, D. (2000). Families at the century's turn: The troubling economic trends. *Family Review, 7*(3), 5–6.

Lindsay, D. (1996, March 13). N.Y. bills give teachers power to oust pupils. *Education Week*.

Lipsman v. New York City Board of Education, 1999 WL 498230 (N.Y.).

Littky, D. (2004). *The big picture: Education is everyone's business*. Alexandria, VA: Association for Supervision and Curriculum Development.

Little, P. M. D., & Harris, E. (2003, July). *A review of out-of-school time program quasi-experimental and experimental evaluation results*. Cambridge, MA: Harvard University, Harvard Family Research Project.

Lomawaima, K.T. (2012). Education of American Indians. In James A. Banks (ed). *Encyclopedia of diversity in education* (pp. 104–109). Thousand Oakes, CA: Sage Publications, Inc.

Lortie, D. (1975). *School teacher: A sociological study*. Chicago: University of Chicago Press.

Losinski, M., Katsiyannis, A., Ryan, J., & Baughan, C. (2014). Weapons in schools and zero-tolerance policies. *NASSP Bulletin, 98*(2), 126–141.

MacKinnon, C. (1994). Quoted in bell hooks, *Teaching to transgress: Education as the practice of freedom*. New York, NY: Routledge.

MacLeod, J. (1995). *Ain't no makin' it: Aspirations & attainment in a low-income neighborhood*. Boulder, CO: Westview Press.

MacNaughton, R. H., & Johns, F. A. (1991, September). Developing a successful schoolwide discipline program. *NASSP Bulletin*, pp. 47–57.

Mayer, R. (1973). *A history of educational thought*. Columbus, OH: Merrill.

Magnet Schools of America. (2013, May 7). Press release: Magnet schools of America announces 2013 national award winners. Retrieved from http://www.magnet.edu/files/press-releases/2013-award-winners-press-release.pdf

Mahoney, J., & Cairns, R. B. (1997). Do extracurricular activities protect against early school dropout? *Developmental Psychology, 33*(2), 241–253.

Mailloux v. Kiley, 323 F. Supp. 1387, 1393 (D. Mass.), *aff'd*, 448 F.2d 1242 (1st Cir. 1971).

Mann, H. (1868). Annual reports on education. In M. Mann (Ed.), *The life and works of Horace Mann* (Vol. 3). Boston, MA: Horace B. Fuller.

Mann, H. (1957). Twelfth annual report. In L. A. Cremin (Ed.), *The republic and the school: Horace Mann on the education of free men*. New York, NY: Teachers College Press.

Marcus v. Rowley, 695 F.2d 1171 (9th Cir. 1983).

Markus, D. (2012, July 25). Blog: High-impact professional development for rural schools. Retrieved from http://www.edutopia.org/blog/stw-tech-integration-professional-development.

Markus, H., & Kitayama, S. (1991). Conflictways: Culture and the self: Implications for cognition, emotion, and motivation. *Psychological Review, 98*, 224–253.

Marzano, R. J. (1997). *Eight questions you should ask before implementing standards-based education at the local level*. Aurora, CO: Mid-Continent Research for Education and Learning.

Maslow, A. (1954). *Motivation and personality*. New York, NY: Basic Books.

Maslow, A. (1962). *Toward a psychology of being*. New York, NY: Basic Books.

Massachusetts 2020 and National Center on Time & Learning. (2010). *Clarence Edwards Middle School: Success through transformation*. Boston, MA: Author. Retrieved from http://www.mass2020.org/files/file/Edwards%20Case%20Study%20FINAL.pdf

Massachusetts Expanded Learning Time Initiative. (2010). *More time for learning: Promising practices and lessons learned*. Boston, MA: Author. Retrieved from http://www.timeandlearning.org/Mass%202020%20Progress%20Report.pdf

Mastropieri, M. A., & Scruggs, T. E. (2010). *The inclusive classroom: Strategies for effective instruction* (4th ed.). Upper Saddle River, NJ: Merrill/Pearson.

Matsui, D. (February 7, 2013). Press Release, Congresswoman Matsui Remarks at the FCC's Federal-State Joint Conference on Advanced Services. Retrieved September 17, 2014, from http://matsui.house.gov/press-releases/congresswoman-matsui-remarks-at-the-fccs-federalstate-joint-conference-on-advanced-services/.

Matthews, L. E. (2008). Illuminating urban excellence: A movement of change within mathematics education *Journal of Urban Mathematics Education, 1*(1), 1–4.

Mayhew, K. C., & Edwards, A. C. (1936). *The Dewey School: The University Laboratory School of the University of Chicago, 1896–1903*. New York, NY: D. Appleton-Century.

McCourt, F. (2005). *Teacher man: A memoir*. New York, NY: Simon & Schuster.

McGrory, K. (2010, August 5). Superintendents ask for delay in Florida school grades. *The Miami Herald*. Retrieved from http://www.miamiherald.com/2010/08/05/1763791/superintendents-ask-for-delay.html

McLeskey, J., Rosenberg, M. S., & Westling, D. L. (2010). *Inclusion: Effective practices for all students*. Upper Saddle River, NJ: Pearson.

McNeil, M. (January 3, 2014). Districts adjust spending to post-recession reality. Education Week. Retrieved August 28, 2014, from http://www.edweek.org/ew/articles/2014/01/09/16finance.h33.html?tkn=WMMFddnd1w6cgNx6g7O4eVzjGs2ydHXbMFnt&cmp=clp-edweek&intc=EW-QC14-EWH.

Meek, C. (2003, April). Classroom crisis: It's about time. *Phi Delta Kappan*, 592–595.

Metropolitan Federation of Alternative Schools. (2010, September 21). About us. Retrieved from http://www.mfas.org/about.html

Miami-Dade County Public Schools. (2013, May 10). Press release: M-DCPS educator named 2013 national teacher-of-the-year by Magnet Schools of America. Retrieved from http://news.dadeschools.net/releases/rls13/105_magnet.html

Miller, S. R., Allensworth, E. M., & Kochanek, J. R. (2002). *Student performance: Course taking, test scores, and outcomes*. Chicago, IL: Consortium on Chicago School Research.

Miron, G., & Gulosino, C. (2013, November). *Profiles of for-profit and nonprofit education management organizations: Fourteenth edition—2011–2012*. Boulder, CO: National Education Policy Center. Retrieved from http://nepc.colorado.edu/publication/EMOprofiles-11-12

Missouri v. Jenkins, 515 U.S. 70 (1995).

Mitchell v. Helms, 530 U.S. 793 (2000).

Modi, M., Konstantopoulos, S., & Hedges, L. V. (1998). *Predictors of academic giftedness among U.S. high school students: Evidence from a nationally representative multivariate analysis*. Paper presented at the annual meeting of the American Educational Research Association, San Diego. (Eric Document Reproduction Service No. ED422 356)

Mohammed ex rel. Mohammed, v. School District of Philadelphia, 355 F. Supp. 2d 779 (Pa. 2005).

Molino, F. (1999). My students, my children. In M. K. Rand & S. Shelton-Colangelo (Eds.), *Voices of student teachers: Cases from the field* (pp. 55–56). Upper Saddle River, NJ: Merrill.

Montagu, A. (1974). *Man's most dangerous myth: The fallacy of race* (5th ed.). New York, NY: Oxford University Press.

Morris, J. E., & Curtis, K. E. (1983, March/April). Legal issues relating to field-based experiences in teacher education. *Journal of Teacher Education*, 2–6.

Morris, V. C., & Pai, Y. (1994). *Philosophy and the American school: An introduction to the philosophy of education*. Lanham, MD: University Press of America.

Morrison v. State Board of Education, 461 P.2d 375 (Cal. 1969).

Mozert v. Hawkins County Board of Education, 827 F.2d 1058 (6th Cir. 1987), *cert. denied,* 484 U.S. 1066 (1988).

Mueller v. Allen, 463 U.S. 388 (1983).

Mukhopadhyay, C., & Henze, R. C. (2003, May). How real is race? Using anthropology to make sense of human diversity. *Phi Delta Kappan, 84*(9), 669–678.

Murphy, S. (2010, August 20). Teachers asked to "unfriend" students on Facebook. *TechNewsDaily*. Retrieved from http://www.technewsdaily.com/teachers-asked-to-unfriend-students-on-facebook-1075/

Murray v. Pittsburgh Board of Public Education, 919 F. Supp. 838 (W.D. Pa. 1996).

Nash, R. (2010). *The active mentor: Practical strategies for supporting new teachers*. Thousand Oaks, CA: Corwin.

National Association for Gifted Children. (2010, March). Redefining giftedness for a new century: Shifting the paradigm. Retrieved from http://www.nagc.org/uploadedFiles/About_NAGC/Redefining%20Giftedness%20for%20a%20New%20Century.pdf

National Association for Year-Round Education. (2008). Statistical summaries of year-round education programs. Retrieved from http://www.nayre.org/

National Association of School Psychologists. (2008). *Zero tolerance and alternative strategies: A fact sheet for educators and policymakers*. Bethesda, MD: Author. Retrieved from http://www.nasponline.org/educators/zero_alternative.pdf

National Assessment of Educational Progress. (2013). 2013 *Mathematics and Reading Assessments*. Washington, DC: U.S. Department of Education, Institute of Education Sciences, National Center for Education Statistics.

National Board for Professional Teaching Standards (NBPTS). (2002). *What teachers should know and be able to do*. Arlington, VA: Author.

National Board for Professional Teaching Standards (NBPTS). (2010). The five core propositions. Retrieved from http://www.nbpts.org/the_standards/the_five_core_propositio

National Board for Professional Teaching Standards (NBPTS). (2013, January 8). Number of Board-Certified teachers tops 100,000 as new studies show significant gains in student achievement. Retrieved from http://www.nbpts.org/nbpts-2013-01-08-nbct-student-achievement

National Board for Professional Teaching Standards (NBPTS). (2013, October 18). How National Board certification helped me find my voice. Retrieved from http://www.nbpts.org/blog/kevin-zerzan/how-national-board-certification-helped-me-find-my-voice

National Catholic Education Association. (2014). *About us*. Retrieved August 16, 2014, from http://www.ncea.org/about-us/catholic-education-information.

National Center for Education Statistics. (2008, March 25). *Digest of education statistics, 2007*. Washington, DC: Author.

National Center for Education Statistics. (2012, April). *Public elementary and secondary school student enrollment and staff counts from the common core of data: School year 2010–11*. Washington, DC: Author.

National Center for Education Statistics. (2012, July). *Characteristics of the 100 largest public elementary and secondary school districts in the United States: 2009–10*. Washington, DC: Author.

National Center for Education Statistics. (2013). *The nation's report card: Trends in academic progress 2012* (NCES 2013 456). Washington, DC: Institute of Education Sciences, U.S. Department of Education.

National Coalition for the Homeless. (2013a). Geography of homelessness. Retrieved from http://nationalhomeless.org/about-homelessness/

National Coalition for the Homeless. (2013b). Youth and homelessness. Retrieved from http://nationalhomeless.org/issues/youth/

National Commission on Excellence in Education. (1983). *A nation at risk: The imperative for educational reform*. Washington, DC: U.S. Government Printing Office.

National Conference of State Legislatures. (2010, May). *Strong leaders strong schools: 2009 state laws*. Washington, DC: Author.

National Council for Accreditation of Teacher Education (NCATE). (2008, February). *Professional standards for the accreditation of teacher preparation institutions*. Washington, DC: Author.

National Education Association. (2010, December). *Status of the American public school teacher 2005–2006*. Washington, DC: Author.

National Education Association. (2014). Rankings & estimates: Rankings of the states 2013 and estimates of school statistics 2014. Washington, DC: Author.

National Education Association. (2013, November 26). *About NEA*. Retrieved from http://www.nea.org/index.html.

National Education Association. (2014). Code of ethics. Washington, DC: Author. Retrieved August 29, 2014, from http://www.nea.org/home/30442.htm.

National Joint Committee on Learning Disabilities. (2008). LD basics: What is a learning disability? Retrieved from http://www.ldonline.org/ldbasics/whatisld

National Research Council. (2008). *Assessing accomplished teaching: Advanced-level certification programs*. Washington, DC: Author.

National Research Council. (2010). *Preparing teachers: Building evidence for sound policy*. Committee on the Study of Teacher Preparation Programs in the United States. Center for Education, Division of Behavioral and Social Sciences and Education. Washington, DC: The National Academies Press.

National trade and professional associations of the United States 2013. New York, NY: Columbia Books and Information Service.

Native American Community Academy. (2014, May 15). Who we are. Retrieved from http://www.nacaschool.org/about/

Navarro, M. (2008, March 31). New dialogue on mixed race: Many of mixed parentage feel Obama's path similar to theirs. *New York Times*. Retrieved from http://www.msnbc.msn.com/id/23875822/

NBC News, Education Nation. (2013, June 10). NBC News to host 2013 Education Nation Summit from Oct. 6-8 at the New York Public Library. Retrieved from http://www.educationnation.com/files/dmfile/2013Summit.pdf

NBC News, Education Nation. (2013, October 1). NBC Universal News Group announces 2013 "Education Nation" Summit agenda focused on "what it takes" to ensure student success. Retrieved from http://www.educationnation.com/files/dmfile/2013SummitAgenda.pdf

NEA Today. (2003, May). New federal rule supports school prayer, p. 13.

NEAFT Partnership. (2002, April 23–24). *NEAFT Partnership Joint Council communique.* Washington, DC: Author.

Neill, A. S. (1960). *Summerhill: A radical approach to child rearing.* New York, NY: Hart.

Nelson, J. L., Carlson, K., & Palonsky, S. B. (2000). *Critical issues in education: A dialectic approach* (4th ed.). New York, NY: McGraw-Hill.

New Jersey v. Massa, 231 A.2d 252 (N.J. Sup. Ct. 1967).

New Jersey v. T.L.O., 469 U.S. 325 (1985).

New York City Department of Education. (2014). About us. Retrieved from http:// schools.nyc.gov/AboutUs/default.htm

Newmann, F. M., et al. (Eds.). (1996). *Authentic achievement: Restructuring schools for intellectual quality.* San Francisco, CA: Jossey-Bass.

Newmann, F. M., & Wehlage, G. G. (1995). *Successful school restructuring: A report to the public and educators by the Center on Organization and Restructuring of Schools.* Madison, WI: University of Wisconsin, Center on Organization and Restructuring of Schools.

Nieto, S. (2002). *Language, culture, and teaching: Critical perspectives for a new century.* Mahwah, NJ: Lawrence Erlbaum.

Noddings, N. (2002). *Educating moral people: A caring alternative to character education.* New York, NY: Teachers College Press.

Noel, A., Stark, P., & Redford, J. (2013). *Parent and family involvement in education, from the National Household Education Surveys Program of 2012* (NCES 2013-028). National Center for Education Statistics, Institute of Education Sciences, U.S. Department of Education. Washington, DC: U.S. Government Printing Office. Retrieved from http://nces.ed.gov/pubsearch

November, A. (2012) *Who owns the learning?: Preparing students for success in the digital age.* Bloomington, IN: Solution Tree.

Null v. Board of Education, 815 F. Supp. 937 (D. W. Va. 1993).

Nussbaum, M. (2009). Tagore, Dewey, and the imminent demise of liberal education. In Siegel, H. (Ed.). *The Oxford handbook of philosophy of education.* New York, NY: Oxford University Press.

Oakes, J., & Lipton, M. (2007). *Teaching to change the world* (3rd ed.). Boston, MA: McGraw-Hill.

Oberti v. Board of Education of the Borough of Clementon School District, 789 F. Supp. 1322 (D.N.J. 1992).

Obiakor, F. E. (2007). *Multicultural special education: Culturally responsive teaching.* Upper Saddle River, NJ: Merrill/Pearson.

O'Connor, E. E., Dearing, E., & Collins, B. A. (2011). Teacher-child relationship and behavior problem trajectories in elementary school. *American Educational Research Journal, 48*(1), 120–162.

Ohman v. Board of Education, 93 N.E.2d 927 (N.Y. 1950).

Olson, L. (2008, March 1). Supporting teachers' success. *Education Week, 18,* 20–22.

Orfield, G., & Yun, J. T. (1999). *Re-segregation in American schools.* Cambridge, MA: Harvard University, Civil Rights Project.

Ormrod, J. E. (2006). *Essentials of educational psychology.* Upper Saddle River, NJ: Merrill/Pearson Education.

Ormrod, J. E., & McGuire, D. J. (2007). *Case studies: Applying educational psychology.* Upper Saddle River, NJ: Pearson Education.

Ou, D. (2009). To leave or not to leave? A regression discontinuity analysis of the impact of failing the high school exit exam. *Economics of Education Review, 29,* 171–186.

Ovando, C. J., Combs, M. C., & Collier, V. P. (2006). *Bilingual and ESL classrooms: Teaching in multicultural contexts.* Boston, MA: McGraw-Hill.

Owasso Independent School District v. Falvo, 233 F.3d 1203 (10th Cir. 2002).

Ozmon, H. W., & Craver, S. M. (2007). *Philosophical foundations of education* (8th ed.). Upper Saddle River, NJ: Prentice Hall.

Paige, R., & Witty, E. (2010). *The black-white achievement gap: Why closing it is the greatest civil rights issue of our time.* New York, NY: Amacom Press.

Parkay, F. W. (1983). *White teacher, black school: The professional growth of a ghetto teacher.* New York, NY: Praeger.

Parkay, F. W. (1988, Summer). Reflections of a protégé. *Theory into Practice,* pp. 195–200.

Parkay, F. W., Anctil, E., & Hass, G. (2014). *Curriculum leadership: Readings for developing quality educational programs* (10th ed.). Upper Saddle River, NJ: Pearson.

Parkay, F. W., Shindler, J., & Oaks, M. M. (1997, January). Creating a climate for collaborative, emergent leadership at an urban high school: Exploring the stressors, role changes, and paradoxes of restructuring. *International Journal of Educational Reform,* 64–74.

Parker, L., & Shapiro, J. P. (1993). The context of educational administration and social class. In C. A. Capper (Ed.), *Educational administration in a pluralistic society* (pp. 36–65). Albany, NY: State University of New York Press.

PASE (Parents in Action on Special Education) v. Hannon, 506 F. Supp. 831 (E.D. Ill. 1980).

Pashler, H., & Carrier, M. (1996). Structures, processes, and the flow of information. In E. Bjork & R. Bjork (Eds.), *Memory* (pp. 3–29). San Diego, CA: Academic Press.

Pashler, H., McDaniel, M., Rohrer, D., & Bjork, R. (2008). Learning styles: Concepts and evidence. *Psychological Science in the Public Interest, 7*(3), 105–119.

Patchin, J. W., & Hinduja, S. (2010). Cyberbullying research. *Cyberbullying Research Center.* Retrieved from http://www.cyberbullying.us/research.php

Patchogue-Medford Congress of Teachers v. Board of Education of Patchogue-Medford Union Free School District, 510 N.E.2d 325 (N.Y. 1987).

Paul, J. L., Christensen, L., & Falk, G. (2000). Accessing the intimate spaces of life in the classroom through letters to former teachers: A protocol for uncovering hidden stories. In J. L. Paul & T. J. Smith (Eds.), *Stories out of school: Memories and reflections on care and cruelty in the classroom* (pp. 15–26). Stamford, CT: Ablex.

Paul, J. L., & Colucci, K. (2000). Caring pedagogy. In J. L. Paul & T. J. Smith (Eds.), *Stories out of school: Memories and reflections on care and cruelty in the classroom* (pp. 45–63). Stamford, CT: Ablex.

PBS Teachers. (2014). STEM Education Resource Center. Retrieved July 19, 2014, from http://www.pbs.org/teachers/stem/.

Peck, D. R. (2008). New teacher experiences in two rural Washington school districts: A phenomenological study. Unpublished Ed.D. dissertation, Washington State University.

People for the American Way. (2008, May 25). *Schools and censorship.* Retrieved from http://www.pfaw.org/pfaw/general/default .aspx?oid=10038#

Peter Doe v. San Francisco Unified School District, 131 Cal. Rptr. 854 (Ct. App. 1976).

Pew Forum on Religion & Public Life. (2008, February 25). *The U.S. religious landscape survey.* Washington, DC: Author.

Pew Forum on Religion & Public Life. (2012, October 9). *"Nones" on the rise: One-in-five adults have no religious affiliation.* Washington, DC: Author.

Pew Research Center. (2010). *Internet & American Life Project, August 9–September 13, 2010.* Use of the Internet in Higher-Income Households,*November 24, 2010.* Washington, DC: Author.

Pew Research Center. (November 1, 2012*). How teens do research in the digital world.* Washington, DC: Author.

Pew Research Center (February 28, 2013). *How teachers are using technology at home and in their classrooms.* Washington, DC: Author.

Philips, V., & Wong, C. (2010). Tying together the Common Core of standards, instruction, and assessments. *Phi Delta Kappan, 91*(5), 37-–41.

Picarella v. Terrizzi, 893 F. Supp. 1292 (M.D. Pa. 1995).

Pierre, C. E. (1916, October). The work of the Society for the Propagation of the Gospel in Foreign Parts among the Negroes in the Colonies. *Journal of Negro History* 1, 349–60.

Poetter, T. S. (2014). *Teacher leadership for the 21st century.* Cincinnati, OH: Van Griner Publishers.

Ponticel, J. A., & Zepeda, S. J. (1996). Making sense of teaching and learning: A case study of mentor and beginning teacher problem solving. In D.J. McIntyre & D.M. Byrd (Eds.), *Preparing tomorrow's teachers: The field experience: Teacher Education Yearbook IV.* Thousand Oaks, CA: Corwin Press.

Portner, J. (1999, May 12). Schools ratchet up the rules on student clothing, threats. *Education Week on the Web.*

Posner, G. J. (2005). *Field experience: A guide to reflective teaching* (6th ed.). Boston, MA: Pearson Education.

Poway Unified School District. (2008). Ed tech central. Retrieved from http://powayusd .sdcoe.k12.ca.us/projects/edtechcentral/ DigitalStorytelling/default.htm

Power, E. J. (1982). *Philosophy of education: Studies in philosophies, schooling, and educational policies.* Upper Saddle River, NJ: Prentice Hall.

Power, F. C., et al. (Eds.). (2008). *Moral education: A handbook* (Vol. 1). Westport, CT: Praeger.

Prensky, M. (2010). *Teaching digital natives: Partnerships for real learning.* Thousand Oaks, CA: Corwin.

President's Commission on Excellence in Special Education. (2002). *A new era: Revitalizing special education for children and their families.* Washington, DC: Author.

Provenzano, N. (2013, September 26). If you're not reflecting, you're not trying. Retrieved from http://www.thenerdyteacher .com/2013/09/if-youre-not-reflecting- youre-not-trying.html

PRWeb. (2009, September 4). FCAT steals high school diplomas: Students transfer credits to Maine, receive standard high school diploma without FCAT. Retrieved from http://www.prweb.com/releases/2009/09/ prweb2801374.htm

QuestBridge. (2014). QuestBridge: Mission & vision. Retrieved from http://www .questbridge.org/about-questbridge/ mission-a-vision.

Rand, M. K., & Shelton-Colangelo, S. (1999). *Voices of student teachers: Cases from the field.* Upper Saddle River, NJ: Merrill.

Randall, V. R. (2001). *Institutional racism.* Dayton, OH: University of Dayton School of Law.

Ravitch, D. (1983). *The troubled crusade: American education, 1945–1980.* New York, NY: Basic Books.

Ravitch, D. (1985). *The schools we deserve: Reflections on the education crises of our times.* New York, NY: Basic Books.

Ray v. School District of DeSoto County, 666 F. Supp. 1524 (M.D. Fla. 1987).

Recovery School District. (2014, March 3). About RSD: Empowerment. Retrieved from http://www.rsdla.net/apps/pages/index .jsp?uREC_ID=205342&type=d&pREC_ ID=406074

Relethford, J. H. (2009). Race and global patterns of phenotypic variation. *American Journal of Physical Anthropology, 139,* 16–22.

Reuters. (2014, February 13). Law Offices of Howard G. Smith files class action lawsuit against K12 Inc. Retrieved from http:// www.reuters.com/finance/stocks/LRN/ key-developments/article/2921866

Richard, A. (2002, May 15). Memphis school board wants uniforms for all. *Education Week on the Web.*

Rickover, H. G. (1959). *Education and free- dom.* New York, NY: E. P. Dutton.

Rideout, V., Foehr, U. G., & Roberts. (2010). *Generation M²: Media in the lives of 8- to 18-year-olds.* Menlo Park, CA: Kaiser Family Foundation.

Rippa, S. A. (1984). *Education in a free society.* New York, NY: Longman.

Rippa, S. A. (1997). *Education in a free society: An American history* (8th ed.). New York, NY: Longman.

Ripple, R. E., & Rockcastle, V. E. (Eds.). (1964). *Piaget rediscovered: A report of the confer- ence on cognitive studies and curriculum development.* Ithaca, NY: Cornell University, School of Education.

Robers, S., Kemp, J., & Truman, J. (2013). *Indicators of school crime and safety: 2012* (NCES 2013-036/NCJ 241446). National Center for Education Statistics, U.S. Depart- ment of Education, and Bureau of Justice Statistics, Office of Justice Programs, U.S. Department of Justice. Washington, DC: U.S. Government Printing Office.

Roberts, S. (2010, January 21). Census figures challenge view of race and ethnicity. *New York Times.* Retrieved from http:// www.nytimes.com/2010/01/22/us/ 22census.html

Roberts v. City of Boston, 59 Mass. (5 Cush.) 198 (1850).

Robinson, A. (2008). Teacher characteristics. In J. A. Plucker & C. M. Callahan (Eds.), *Critical issues and practices in gifted educa- tion: What the research says* (pp. 669–680). Waco, TX: Prufrock Press.

Robinson, M. W. (2008, February/March). Scared not to be straight. *Edutopia: The New World of Learning, 4*(1), 56–58.

Rodriguez, A. J. (2001). From gap gazing to promising cases: Moving toward equity in urban systemic reform. *Journal of Research in Science Teaching, 38,* 1115–1129.

Roe, M. J. (2010). Wiki technology and the return to rigor. *Leadership, 39*(3), 20–22.

Rogers, C. (1961). *On becoming a person.* Boston, MA: Houghton Mifflin.

Rogers, C. (1982). *Freedom to learn in the eighties.* Columbus, OH: Merrill.

Romans v. Crenshaw, 354 F. Supp. 868 (S.D. Tex. 1972).

Rosen, L. (2010). *Rewired: Understanding the iGeneration and the way they learn.* New York, NY: Palgrave.

Rosen, L. (November 13, 2012). Driven to distraction: How to help wired students learn to focus. *eSchool News.* Retrieved August 8, 2014, from http://www.eschool- news.com/2012/11/13/driven-to-distraction- how-to-help-wired-students-learn-to-focus/.

Rosen, L. (2013). *iDisorder: Understanding our obsession with technology and overcoming its hold on us.* Palgrave Macmillan.

Rosenberg, T. (October 9, 2013). Turning education upside down. *New York Times.* Retrieved July 5, 2014, from http://opin- ionator.blogs.nytimes.com/2013/10/09/ turning-education-upside-down/?_ php=true&_type=blogs&_r=1&.

Rosenfield, M. (2014, April 7). NH teacher fired for refusing to "unfriend" students on Facebook. Boston, *WBZ.* Retrieved from http://boston.cbslocal.com/2014/04/07/ nh-teacher-fired-for-refusing-to-unfriend- students-on-facebook/.

Rosenkranz, T. (2002). *2001 CPS test trend review: Iowa Tests of Basic Skills.* Chicago, IL: Consortium on Chicago School Research.

Rosenshine, B. (1988). Explicit teaching. In D. Ber- liner & B. Rosenshine (Eds.), *Talks to teachers* (pp. 75–92). New York, NY: Random House.

Rosenshine, B., & Stevens, R. (1986). Teaching functions. In M. C. Wittrock (Ed.), *Handbook of research on teaching* (3rd ed.) (pp. 376–391). New York, NY: Macmillan.

Rothstein-Fisch, C., & Trumbull, E. (2008). *Managing diverse classrooms: How to build on students' cultural strengths.* Alexandria, VA: Association for Supervision and Curriculum Development.

Rury, J. L. (2002). *Education and social change: Themes in the history of American schooling.* Mahwah, NJ: Lawrence Erlbaum.

Russo, A. (Ed.). (2004). *School reform in Chicago: Lessons in policy and practice.* Cambridge, MA: Harvard Education Press.

Salas, K. D., Tenorio, R., Walters, S., & Weiss, D. (Eds.). (2004). *The new teacher book.* Mil- waukee, WI: Rethinking Public Schools, Ltd.

Salovey, P., & Feldman-Barrett, L. (Eds.). (2002). *The wisdom of feelings: Psychological pro- cesses in emotional intelligence.* New York, NY: Guilford Press.

Salovey, P., Mayer, J. D., & Caruso, D. (2002). The positive psychology of emotional intelligence. In C. R. Snyder & S. J. Lopez (Eds.), *The hand- book of positive psychology* (pp. 159–171). New York, NY: Oxford University Press.

Salovey, P., & Sluyter, D. J. (Eds.). (1997). *Emotional development and emotional intelligence: Educational implications.* New York, NY: Basic Books.

Santa Fe Independent School District v. Jane Doe, 530 U.S. 290 (2000).

Sartre, J. P. (1972). Existentialism. In J. M. Rich (Ed.), *Readings in the philosophy of educa- tion.* Belmont, CA: Wadsworth.

Sawchuk, S. (2012, September 21). In strike's wake, Chicago faces budget questions. *Education Week.* Retrieved from http://www.edweek.org/ew/ articles/2012/09/21/05strike.h32.html

Scales, P. C. (2001). The public image of ado- lescents. *Society 38*(4), 64–70.

Scering, G. E. S. (1997, January–February). Theme of a critical/feminist pedagogy: Teacher education for democracy. *Journal of Teacher Education, 48*(1), 62–68.

Schaill v. Tippecanoe School Corp., 864 F.2d 1309 (7th Cir. 1988).

Schmuck, R. A., & Schmuck, P. A. (2001). *Group processes in the classroom* (8th ed.). Boston, MA: McGraw-Hill.

Schneider, R. B., & Barone, D. (1997, Spring). Cross-age tutoring. *Childhood Education,* 136–143.

School District of Abington Township v. Schempp, 374 U.S. 203 (1963).

Schubert, W. (1986). *Curriculum: Perspective, paradigm, and possibility.* New York: Macmillan.

Schunk, D. (2012). *Learning theories: An educational perspective* (6th ed.). Upper Saddle River, NJ: Pearson.

Schwartz, J. E., & Beichner, R. J. (1999). *Essentials of educational technology.* Boston, MA: Allyn & Bacon.

Scopes, J. (1966). *Center of the storm.* New York, NY: Holt, Rinehart and Winston.

Scoville v. Board of Education of Joliet Township High School District 204, 425 F.2d 10 (7th Cir.), *cert. denied,* 400 U.S. 826, (1970).

Search Institute. (2010). *How many assets do young people have?* Minneapolis, MN: Author. Retrieved from http://www.search-institute.org/research/assets/asset-levels

Sears, J. T. (1992). Educators, homosexuality and homosexual students: Are personal feelings related to professional beliefs? *Journal of Homosexuality, 22,* 29–60.

Shade, B. J. (1982). Afro-American cognitive style: A variable in school success? *Review of Educational Research, 52*(2), 219–238.

Shanley v. Northeast Independent School District, 462 F.2d 960 (5th Cir. 1972).

Sharan, Y., & Sharan, S. (1989/90, December/January). Group investigation expands cooperative learning. *Educational Leadership,* 17–21.

Shearer, M. (2011). Application for National Teacher of the Year Award. Retrieved June 24, 2014, from *http://www.ccsso.org/Documents/2011/news/2011_NTOY_Press.pdf.*

Shechtman, N., DeBarger, A. H., Dornsife, C., Rosier, S., & Yarnall, L. (2013). *Promoting grit, tenacity, and perseverance: Critical factors for success in the 21st century.* U.S. Department of Education, Office of Educational Technology.

Sheuerer, D., & Parkay, F. W. (1992). The new Christian right and the public school curriculum: A Florida report. In J. B. Smith & J. G. Coleman, Jr. (Eds.), *School library media annual: 1992* (Vol. 10) (pp. 112–118). Englewood, CO: Libraries Unlimited.

Shulman, L. (1987, August). Teaching alone, learning together: Needed agendas for the new reform. Paper presented at the Conference on Restructuring Schooling for Quality Education, San Antonio.

Simonetti v. School District of Philadelphia, 454 A.2d 1038 (Pa. Super. 1982).

Simpkins, S. (2003, Spring). Does youth participation in out-of-school time activities make a difference? *The Evaluation Exchange, IX*(1). Harvard Graduate School of Education, Harvard Family Research Project (HFRP).

Skinner, B. F. (1972). Utopia through the control of human behavior. In J. M. Rich (Ed.), *Readings in the philosophy of education.* Belmont, CA: Wadsworth.

Slavin, R. E. (2015). *Educational psychology: Theory and practice* (11th ed.). Upper Saddle River, NJ: Pearson.

Smith, D. D. (2007). *Introduction to special education: Making a difference* (6th ed.). Upper Saddle River, NJ: Pearson.

Smith, L. G., & Smith, J. K. (1994). *Lives in education: A narrative of people and ideas* (2nd ed.). New York, NY: St. Martin's Press.

Smith v. Board of School Commissioners of Mobile County, 655 F. Supp. 939 (S.D. Ala.), *rev'd,* 827 F.2d 684 (11th Cir. 1987).

Snipes, J., Soga, K., & Uro, G. (2007). *Improving teaching and learning for English language learners in urban schools.* Council of the Great City Schools, Research Brief. Washington, DC: Author.

Snyder, T. D., & Dillow, S. A. (2010). *Digest of education statistics 2009.* National Center for Education Statistics, Institute of Education Sciences, U.S. Department of Education. Washington, DC: U.S. Government Printing Office.

Snyder, T. D., & Dillow, S. A. (2013). *Digest of education statistics 2012* (NCES 2014-015). National Center for Education Statistics, Institute of Education Sciences, U.S. Department of Education. Washington, DC: U.S. Government Printing Office.

Snyder, T. D., & Dillow, S. A. (2014). *Digest of education statistics 2013.* National Center for Education Statistics, Institute of Education Sciences, U.S. Department of Education., Washington, DC: U.S. Government Printing Office.

Sofen, L. (2010, August 27). Why I teach: Catching kids before they sink. Blog post, *Teaching Tolerance.* Retrieved from http://www.tolerance.org/blog/why-i-teach-catching-kids-they-sink

Sommers, C. H. (1994). *Who stole feminism? How women have betrayed women.* New York, NY: Simon & Schuster.

Spokesman Review. (1993, June 4). Harassment claims vex teachers.

Spring, J. (2005). *The American school: 1642–2004.* Boston, MA: McGraw-Hill.

Spring, J. (2008a). *American education* (13th ed.). Boston, MA: McGraw-Hill.

Spring, J. (2008b). *The American school: From the Puritans to No Child Left Behind.* Boston, MA: McGraw-Hill.

Spring, J. (2011). *The politics of American education.* New York, NY: Routledge.

St. Michel, T. (1995). *Effective substitute teachers: Myth, mayhem, or magic?* Thousand Oaks, CA: Corwin Press.

State Educational Technology Directors Association. (2005). *National trends: Enhancing education through technology: No Child Left Behind, Title IID-year two in review.* Los Angeles, CA: Metri Group.

State Policy Report Card. (2014). Objective: Establish state and mayoral control. Retrieved June 28, 2014, from http://reportcard.studentsfirst.org/policy/spend_wisely_govern_well/promote_governance_structures_that_streamline_accountability/establish_state_and_mayoral_control/state_by_state.

State v. Rivera, 497 N.W.2d 878 (Iowa 1993).

Station v. Travelers Insurance Co., 292 So. 2d 289 (La. Ct. App. 1974).

Stecher, B., & Hamilton, L. (2002, February 20). Test-based accountability: Making it work better. *Education Week on the Web.* Retrieved from http://www.edweek.org/ew/newstory.cfm?slug=23Stecher.h21

Sternberg, L., Dornbusch, S., & Brown, B. (1996). *Beyond the classroom: Why school reform has failed and what parents need to do.* New York, NY: Simon & Schuster.

Sternberg, R. J. (2002). Beyond g: The theory of successful intelligence. In R. J. Sternberg & E. L. Grigorenko (Eds.), *The general factor of intelligence: How general is it?* (pp. 447–479). Mahwah, NJ: Lawrence Erlbaum.

Stiggins, R. and Chappuis, J. (2012). *An introduction to student-involved assessment for learning* (6th ed.). Boston: Pearson.

Stillwell, R., & Sable, J. (2013). *Public school graduates and dropouts from the common core of data: School year 2009–10: First look (provisional data)* (NCES 2013-309rev). U.S. Department of Education. Washington, DC: National Center for Education Statistics. Retrieved from http://nces.ed.gov/pubsearch

Stone v. Graham, 599 S.W.2d 157 (Ky. 1980).

Stover, D. (1992, March). The at-risk kids schools ignore. *The Executive Educator,* pp. 28–31.

Strike, K. A. (2007). *Ethical leadership in schools: Creating community in an environment of accountability.* Thousand Oaks, CA: Corwin Press.

Strike, K. A., & Soltis, J. F. (1985). *The ethics of teaching.* New York, NY: Teachers College Press.

Strong, R., Silver, H., & Perini, M. (2001). *Teaching what matters most: Standards and strategies for raising student achievement.* Alexandria, VA: Association for Supervision and Curriculum Development.

Stuckey, M. (2008, May 28). Multiracial Americans surge in numbers. Voice: Obama candidacy focuses new attention on their quest for understanding. *MSNBC Interactive.* Retrieved from http://www.msnbc.msn.com/id/24542138/

Substitute Teaching Institute. (2011). STEDI philosophy. Retrieved from http://stedi.org/subs/aboutsti/philosophy.aspx

Sullivan, B. (October 22, 2010). Blogpost, teachers, students and Facebook, a toxic mix. Retrieved from http://redtape.msnbc.com/2010/10/the-headlines-conjure-up-every-parents-nightmare-teachers-fired-for-flirting-on-facebook-with-students-the-new-york-post-r.html

Sullivan v. Houston Independent School District, 475 F.2d 1071 (5th Cir.), *cert. denied,* 414 U.S. 1032 (1969).

Swanson v. Guthrie Independent School District No. 1, 135 F.3d 694 (10th Cir. 1998).

Swisher, K., & Deyhle, D. (1987). Styles of learning and learning styles: Educational conflicts for American Indian/Alaskan Native youth. *Journal of Multilingual and Multicultural Development, 8*(4), 345–360.

TakePart. (2013, January 3). Diary of a first-year teacher: Finally, I'm out of survival mode. Retrieved from http://www.takepart.com/article/2013/01/03/diary-first-year-teacher-first-semester

Tamim, R. M., Bernard, R. M., Borokhovski, E., Abrami, P. C., & Schmid, R. F. (2011). What forty years of research says about the impact of technology on learning: A second-order meta-analysis and validation study. *Review of Educational Research, 81*(1), 4-28.

Teacher Education Accreditation Council (TEAC). (2010, May 25). 200th member joins TEAC. Retrieved from http://www.teac.org/2010/05/200th-member-joins-teac/

Teach for America. (2014). About Teach for America. Retrieved August 15, 2014, from http://www.teachforamerica.org/sites/default/files/2013-14_press_kit_updated_09_18_13.pdf.

Teacher's Diary. (2010, February 23). The rewards of teaching English language learners. Retrieved from http://www.teachersdiary.com/teachers-diary/2010/02/teaching-ells.html

Tellijohann, S. K., & Price, J. H. (1993). A qualitative examination of adolescent homosexuals' life experiences: Ramifications for secondary school personnel. *Journal of Homosexuality, 26.*

TEP (The Equity Project Charter School). (2014). *TEP: Philosophy.* New York, NY: Author. Retrieved from http://www.tepcharter.org/philosophy.php

Terman, L. M., Baldwin, B. T., & Bronson, E. (1925). Mental and physical traits of a thousand gifted children. In L. M. Terman (Ed.), *Genetic studies of genius* (Vol. 1). Stanford, CA: Stanford University Press.

Terman, L. M., & Oden, M. H. (1947). The gifted child grows up. In L. M. Terman (Ed.), *Genetic studies of genius* (Vol. 4). Stanford, CA: Stanford University Press.

Terman, L. M., & Oden, M. H. (1959). The gifted group in mid-life. In L. M. Terman (Ed.), *Genetic studies of genius* (Vol. 5). Stanford, CA: Stanford University Press.

Thelen, H. A. (1960). *Education and the human quest.* New York, NY: Harper & Row.

Thomas, N. & Lewis, L. (2010). Teachers' use of educational technology in U.S. public schools: 2009k. National Center for Education Statistics, Institute of Education Sciences, U.S. Department of Education, Washington, DC.

Thompson, G. L. (2004). *Through ebony eyes: What teachers need to know but are afraid to ask about African American students.* San Francisco, CA: Jossey Bass.

Tileston, D. W. (2004). *What every teacher should know about student assessment.* Thousand Oaks, CA: Corwin Press.

Tinker v. Des Moines Independent Community School District, 393 U.S. 503 (1969).

Tobias, A. K., & Myrick, R. D. (1999). A peer facilitator-led intervention with middle school problem-behavior students. *Professional School Counseling, 3*(1), 27–33.

Tomal, D. R., Schilling, C. A., Wilhite, R. K. (2014). *The teacher leader: Core competencies and strategies for effective leadership.* Lanham, MD: Rowman & Littlefield Publishers.

Tormala, Alyssa. A. July 7, 2014. 5 epiphanies on learning in a 1:1 iPad classroom. Blog post retrieved July 13, 2014, from http://www.edutopia.org/blog/epiphanies-learning-ipad-classroom-alyssa-tormala.

Torres, C. A. (1994). Paulo Freire as Secretary of Education in the municipality of Sao Paula. *Comparative Education Review, 38*(2), 181–214.

Triandis, H. (1989). Cross-cultural studies of individualism and collectivism. *Nebraska Symposium of Motivation, 37, 43–133.*

Trotter, A. (2002, May 9). E-learning goes to school. *Education Week on the Web.*

Tyler, R. (1949). *Basic principles of curriculum and instruction.* Chicago: University of Chicago.

Ulich, R. (1950). *History of educational thought.* New York, NY: American Book Company.

Unified School District No. 241 v. Swanson, 717 P.2d 526 (Kan. Ct. App. 1986).

Union Alternative School. (2010, September 8). General information. Retrieved from http://www.unionps.org/index.cfm?id=260

Urban, W. J., & Wagoner, J. L. (2013). *American education: A history* (5th ed.). New York, NY: Routledge.

Urban, W. J., & Wagoner, J. L. (2009). *American education: A history* (4th ed.). New York, NY: Routledge.

Urbina, I. (2010, January 11). As school exit tests prove tough, states ease standards. *New York Times.* Retrieved from http://www.nytimes.com/2010/01/12/education/12exit.html?pagewanted=1&_r=2

Uribe, V., & Harbeck, K. M. (1991). Addressing the needs of lesbian, gay and bisexual youth. *Journal of Homosexuality, 22.*

U.S. Census Bureau. (2007). *Statistical abstract of the United States* (127th ed.). Washington, DC: U.S. Government Printing Office.

U.S. Census Bureau. (2010, March 2). Asian/Pacific American Heritage Month: May 2010. Retrieved from http://www.marc.org/.../2010%2003%2002%20-%20Asian-Pacific%20American%20Heritage%20Month%20-%20May%202010.pdf

U.S. Census Bureau. (2012). *Statistical abstract of the United States* (131st ed.). Washington, DC: U.S. Government Printing Office.

U.S. Census Bureau. (2012a). *Population projections.* Washington, DC: Author.

U.S. Census Bureau. (2012b). *Statistical abstract of the United States* (131st ed.). Washington, DC: U.S. Government Printing Office.

U.S. Census Bureau. (2012c). *2012 population estimates.* Washington, DC: Author.

U.S. Census Bureau. (December 12, 2012). *Press Release: U.S. Census Bureau projections show a slower growing, older, more diverse nation a half century from now.* Washington, DC: Author. Retrieved August 30, 2014, from http://www.census.gov/newsroom/releases/archives/population/cb12-243.html.

U.S. Census Bureau. (2012, October). School enrollment—Social and economic characteristics of students: October 2012: Detailed tables: Table 1. Retrieved from http://www.census.gov/hhes/school/data/cps/index.html

U.S. Census Bureau (2013, May 3). Who's minding the kids? Child care arrangements and payments. Retrieved from http://www.census.gov/newsroom/cspan/childcare/

U.S. Census Bureau. (2013, August). *Language use in the United States: 2011—American community survey reports.* Washington, DC: Author. Retrieved from http://www.census.gov/prod/2013pubs/acs-22.pdf

U.S. Census Bureau. (2013, December). *Percent of people 25 years and over who have completed high school or college, by race, Hispanic origin and sex: Selected years 1940 to 2012.* Washington, DC: U.S. Government Printing Office. Retrieved from http://www.census.gov/hhes/socdemo/education/data/cps/historical/index.html

U.S. Census Bureau. (2014). *American community survey 2014.* Washington, DC: Author. Retrieved from https://www.census.gov/acs/www/

U.S. Census Bureau. (2014, April 23). *America's families and living arrangements: 2013.* Washington, DC: Author. Retrieved from http://www.census.gov/hhes/families/

U.S. Census Bureau. (2014, January 16). Profile America facts for features: Black (African-American) History Month: February 2014. Retrieved from https://www.census.gov/newsroom/releases/archives/facts_for_features_special_editions/cb14-ff03.html

U.S. Charter Schools. (2008, May 28). Charter schools: Frequently asked questions. Retrieved from http://www.uscharterschools.org/pub/uscs_docs/o/faq.htm1#8

U.S. Department of Education. (2001, January). Executive summary of the No Child Left Behind Act of 2001. Retrieved from http://www2.ed.gov/print/nclb/overview/intro/execsumm.html

U.S. Department of Education. (2009, January). *Title I implementation—Update on recent evaluation findings.* Washington, DC: Author.

U.S. Department of Education. (2009, May). *Evaluation of evidence-based practices in online learning: A meta-analysis and review of online learning studies.* Washington, DC: Author.

U.S. Department of Education. (2010, March). *Office of Planning, Evaluation and Policy Development, ESEA blueprint for reform.* Washington, DC: Author.

U.S. Department of Education. (2010, May). *The condition of education 2010.* Washington, DC: Author.

U.S. Department of Education. (2010, May 7). U.S. Secretary of Education celebrates Teacher Appreciation Week in a video with his favorite teacher. Retrieved from http://www.ed.gov/news/press-releases/us-secretary-education-celebrates-teacher-appreciation-week

U.S. Department of Education. (2010, June 2). Statement on National Governors

Association and State Education Chiefs Common Core Standards. Retrieved from http://www.ed.gov/news/press-releases/statement-national-governors-association-and-state-education-chiefs-common-core-

U.S. Department of Education. (2011, February 17). U.S. Secretary of Education appoints members of Equity and Excellence Commission. Retrieved from http://www.ed.gov/news/press-releases/us-secretary-education-appoints-members-equity-and-excellence-commission

U.S. Department of Education. (2011, September 30). *Education department proposes reforms to improve teacher preparation programs and better prepare educators for classroom success.* Press release. Washington, DC: Author. Retrieved from http://www.ed.gov/news/press-releases/education-department-proposes-reforms-improve-teacher-preparation-programs-and-b

U.S. Department of Education. (2011, November). *Preparing and credentialing the nation's teachers: The Secretary's Eighth Report on Teacher Quality; based on data provided for 2008, 2009 and 2010.* Office of Postsecondary Education. Washington, DC: Author. Retrieved from http://title2.ed.gov/Public/TitleIIReport11.pdf

U.S. Department of Education. (2012, February 15). Obama administration seeks to elevate teaching profession, Duncan to launch RESPECT Project: Teacher-led national conversation. Retrieved from http://www.ed.gov/news/press-releases/obama-administration-seeks-elevate-teaching-profession-duncan-launch-respect-pro

U.S. Department of Education. (2012, December 11). Education Department announces 16 winners of Race to the Top district competition. Retrieved from http://www.ed.gov/news/press-releases/education-department-announces-16-winners-race-top-district-competition

U.S. Department of Education. (February 2013). Office of Educational Technology, *Expanding evidence approaches for learning in a digital world,* Washington, D.C.

U.S. Department of Education, Office of Educational Technology. (February 14, 2013). Promoting grit, tenacity, and perseverance: Critical factors for success in the 21st century. Washington, DC: Author.

U.S. Department of Education. (April 2013). *Blueprint for Recognizing Educational Success, Professional Excellence and Collaborative Teaching (RESPECT).* Washington, DC: Author.

U.S. Department of Education. (2013, June 25). *Duncan pushes back on attacks on Common Core Standards.* Press release. Washington, DC: Author.

U.S. Department of Education. (2013, July 2). *Education Secretary's statement on Philadelphia school district.* Washington, DC: Author.

U.S. Department of Education. (2013, August 7). Eight teachers selected for 2013–2014 Teacher Ambassador Fellowships.

Retrieved from http://www.ed.gov/blog/2013/08/eight-teachers-selected-for-2013-2014-teacher-ambassador-fellowships/

U.S. Department of Education. (2013, December 3). My child's academic success: Values—Helping your child through early adolescence. Retrieved from http://www2.ed.gov/parents/academic/help/adolescence/partx5.html.

U.S. Department of Education, Office of Educational Technology. (2010, November). *Transforming American education: Learning powered by technology.* Washington, DC: Author.

U.S. Department of Education, Office of Special Education and Rehabilitative Services. (2013, August 20). "Dear colleague" letter. Retrieved from https://www2.ed.gov/policy/speced/guid/idea/memosdcltrs/bullyingdcl-8-20-13.pdf

U.S. Department of Health and Human Services, Administration for Children and Families, Administration on Children, Youth and Families, Children's Bureau. (2013). *Child maltreatment: Facts at a glance.* Washington, DC: Author. Retrieved from http://www.cdc.gov/violenceprevention/pdf/cm-data-sheet--2013.pdf

U.S. Department of Health and Human Services, Head Start, An Office of the Administration for Children and Families Early Childhood Learning and Knowledge Center (ECLKC). (2013, April 26). Policy & regulation: Final FY 2013 funding level. Retrieved from http://eclkc.ohs.acf.hhs.gov/hslc/standards/PIs/2013/resour_pri_003_042613.html

U.S. Department of Health and Human Services, Office of Adolescent Health. (2013, December 10). Negative impacts of teen childbearing. Retrieved from http://www.hhs.gov/ash/oah/adolescent-health-topics/reproductive-health/teen-pregnancy/health-impact.html

U.S. Department of Homeland Security. (2013). *Yearbook of immigration statistics: 2012.* Washington, DC: U.S. Department of Homeland Security, Office of Immigration Statistics. Retrieved from https://www.dhs.gov/sites/default/files/publications/ois_yb_2012.pdf

U.S. Department of Justice, Office of Juvenile Justice and Delinquency Prevention. (2013, September). *Highlights of the 2011 National Youth Gang Survey.* Washington, DC: Author.

U.S. Department of Labor. (2013). *Occupational outlook handbook 2013–14 edition. Teachers—preschool, kindergarten, elementary, middle, and secondary.* Washington, DC: Author.

U.S. English. (2014). *About U.S. English: History.* Retrieved from http://www.us-english.org/view/2

Utay, C., & Utay, J. (1997). Peer-assisted learning: The effects of cooperative learning and cross-age peer tutoring with word processing on writing skills of students with

learning disabilities. *Journal of Computing in Childhood Education, 8,* 1043–1055.

Valli, L., & Buese, D. (2007, September). The changing roles of teachers in an era of high-stakes accountability. *American Educational Research Journal, 44*(3), 519–558.

Van Reusen, A. K., Shoho, A. R., & Barker, K. S. (2000). High school teacher attitudes toward inclusion. *High School Journal, 84*(2), 7–20.

Vaughn, S., Bos, C. S., & Schumm, J. S. (1997). *Teaching mainstreamed, diverse, and at-risk students in the general education classroom.* Boston, MA: Allyn & Bacon.

Vaznis, J. (July 26, 2011). Science MCAS stymies seniors. *The Boston Globe.* Retrieved June 28, 2014, from http://www.boston.com/news/education/k_12/mcas/articles/2011/07/26/failure_rate_for_science_mcas_rises_fairness_questioned/.

Vedder, R. K. (2003). *Can teachers own their own schools? New strategies for educational excellence.* Chicago, IL: Paul & Co.

Vega, V. (February 5, 2013). Technology Integration Research Review. Edutopia. Retrieved August 7, 2014, from http://www.edutopia.org/technology-integration-research-learning-outcomes.

Virtual High School. (2014). Why VHS: Commitment to quality. Retrieved July 5, 2014, from http://thevhscollaborative.org/why-vhs/commitment-quality.

Vossekuil, B., Fein, R., Reddy, M., Borum, R., & Modzeleski, W. (2002, May). *The final report and findings of the Safe School Initiative: Implications for the prevention of school attacks in the United States.* Washington, DC: U.S. Department of Education, Office of Elementary and Secondary Education, Safe and Drug-Free Schools Program and U.S. Secret Service, National Threat Assessment Center.

Vygotsky, L. S. (1978). *Mind in society: The development of higher mental process.* Cambridge, MA: Harvard University Press.

Vygotsky, L. S. (1986). *Thought and language.* Cambridge, MA: MIT Press.

Walberg, H. J. (Ed.). (2007). *Handbook on restructuring and substantial school improvement.* Lincoln, IL: Center on Innovation & Improvement.

Walberg, H. J., & Greenberg, R. C. (1997, May). Using the learning environment inventory. *Educational Leadership,* pp. 45–47.

Wallace, R. M. (2004, Summer). A framework for understanding teaching with the Internet. *American Educational Research Journal, 41*(2), 447–488.

Wallace v. Jaffree, 472 U. S. 38 (1985).

Waller, W. (1932). *The sociology of teaching.* New York, NY: John Wiley.

Waltman, J. L., & Bush-Bacelis, J. L. (1995), Contrasting expectations of individualists and collectivists: Achieving effective group interaction. *Journal of Teaching in International Business, 7*(1), 61–76.

Ward, C., & Griffin, A. (2006, March 21). *Five characteristics of an effective school board:*

A multifaceted role, defined. San Rafael, CA: George Lucas Educational Foundation.

Washington, W. (2009). A summary of Austin Independent School District's optional extended year program activities, 2007–2008. Retrieved from http://www.austinisd.org/inside/docs/ope_07-78_OEYP.pdf

Watson, J. B. (1925). *Behaviorism* (2nd ed.). New York, NY: People's Institute.

Webb, L. D., Metha, A., & Jordan, K. F. (1999). *Foundations of American education* (3rd ed.). Upper Saddle River, NJ: Prentice Hall.

Wechsler, D. (1958). *The measurement and appraisal of adult intelligence* (4th ed.). Baltimore: Williams and Wilkins.

Weingarten, R. (spring 2014). Teaching and learning over testing. *American educator.* p. 1.

Wells, A. S. (2014, March). *Seeking past the "colorblind" myth of education policy: Addressing racial and ethnic inequality and supporting culturally diverse schools.* University of Colorado Boulder, CO: National Education Policy Center.

Welner, K. (2013, September 24). The bottom line on charter school studies. *Washington Post.* Retrieved from http://www.washingtonpost.com/blogs/answer-sheet/wp/2013/09/24/the-bottom-line-on-charter-school-studies/

West v. Board of Education of City of New York, 8 A.D.2d 291 (N.Y. App. 1959).

Weston, S. P., & Sexton, R. F. (2009, December). Substantial and yet not sufficient: Kentucky's effort to build proficiency for each and every child. *Education, Equity, and the Law, 2.* Teachers College, Columbia University.

White House. (January 28, 2014). President Barack Obama's State of the Union Address. Retrieved August 28, 2014, from http://www.whitehouse.gov/the-press-office/2014/01/28/president-barack-obamas-state-union-address.

White House Press Release. (2010, March 1). President Obama announces steps to reduce dropout rate and prepare students for college and careers. Retrieved from http://www.whitehouse.gov/the-press-office/president-obama-announces-steps-reduce-dropout-rate-and-prepare-students-college-an

White House Press Release. (July 29, 2010). Remarks by the President on Education Reform at the National Urban League Centennial Conference. Retrieved August 15, 2014, from http://www.whitehouse.gov/the-press-office/remarks-president-education-reform-national-urban-league-centennial-conference.

White House Press Release. (2010, September 13). Remarks of President Barack Obama—As prepared for delivery—Back to school speech. Retrieved from http://www.whitehouse.gov/the-press-office/2010/09/13/remarks-president-barack-obama-prepared-delivery-back-school-speech

White House Press Release. (2010, October 8). Remarks by the president at the signing of the 21st Century Communications and Video Accessibility Act of 2010. Retrieved from http://www.whitehouse.gov/the-press-office/2010/10/08/remarks-president-signing-21st-century-communications-and-video-accessib

White House Press Release. (2011, January 25). Remarks by the president in State of Union Address. Retrieved from http://www.whitehouse.gov/the-press-office/2011/01/25/remarks-president-state-union-address

Willard, N. (2010, August 2). *School response to cyberbullying and sexting: The legal challenges.* Eugene, OR: Center for Safe and Responsible Internet Use. Retrieved from http://www.cyberbully.org/documents/documents/cyberbullyingsextinglegal_000.pdf

William R. Beard School. (2010, September 8). School brochure. Retrieved from http://www.syracusecityschools.com/docs/school-alt-BrochureBeardSchool2006.pdf

Wills, K. (2007, September). The advantage of disadvantage: Teachers with disabilities not a handicap. *Edutopia.* Retrieved from http://www.edutopia.org/disabled-teachers

Wilson, B. L., & Corbett, H. D. (2001). *Listening to urban kids: School reform and the teachers they want.* Albany, NY: State University of New York Press.

Wirt, F. M., & Kirst, M. W. (2009). *The political dynamics of American education* (4th ed.). Berkeley, CA: McCutchan.

Wisconsin v. Yoder, 406 U.S. 205 (1972).

Wolf, P., Gutmann, B., Puma, M., Kisida, B., Rizzo, L., Eissa, N., & Carr, M. (2010, June). *Evaluation of the DC Opportunity Scholarship Program: Final report executive summary* (NCEE 2010-4019). Washington, DC: National Center for Education Evaluation and Regional Assistance, Institute of Education Sciences, U.S. Department of Education.

Woolfolk, A. E. (2013). *Educational psychology* (11th ed.). Upper Saddle River, NJ: Allyn & Bacon/Pearson.

Wright, R. J. (2008). *Educational assessment: Tests and measurements in the age of accountability.* Los Angeles, CA: Sage.

Yamamoto, K., Davis, Jr., O. L., Dylak, S., Whittaker, J., Marsh, C., & van der Westhuizen, P. C. (1996, Spring). Across six nations: Stressful events in the lives of children. *Child Psychiatry and Human Development,* pp. 139–150.

Yap v. Oceanside Union Free School District, 303 F. Supp 2d 284 (N.Y. 2004).

Yendol-Hoppey, D., & Dana, N. F. (2010). *Powerful professional development: Building expertise within the four walls of your school.* Thousand Oaks, CA: Corwin.

Young, C. (1999). *Ceasefire! Why women and men must join forces to achieve true equality.* New York, NY: The Free Press.

Young, M. F., Slota, S., Cutter, A. B., Jalette, G., Mullin, G., Lai, B., & Yukhymenko, M. (2012). Our princess is in another castle: A review of trends in serious gaming for education. *Review of Educational Research, 82*(1), 61-89.

Zelman v. Simmons-Harris, 536 U.S. 639 (2002).

Zhang, L., & Sternberg, R. J. (2001). Thinking styles across cultures: Their relationships with student learning. In R. J. Sternberg & L. Zhang (Eds.), *Perspectives on thinking, learning, and cognitive styles* (pp. 197–226). Mahwah, NJ: Lawrence Erlbaum.

Zirkel, P. A., & Karanxha, Z. (2009). *Student teaching and the law.* Lanham, MD: Rowman & Littlefield Education.

Zobrest v. Catalina Foothills School District, 509 U.S. 1 (1993).

Zubrzycki, J. (2013, September 10). Budget, security concerns as Chicago schools open. *Education Week.* Retrieved from http://www.edweek.org/ew/articles/2013/09/11/03chicago-2.h33.html?qs=chicago+schools

Zubrzycki, J. (2014, January 3). Rival strategies for running schools put Memphis in hot seat: A variety of approaches to running and improving the system challenge local control. *Education Week.* Retrieved from http://www.edweek.org/ew/articles/2014/01/09/16hotseat.h33.html

Zucker v. Panitz, 299 F. Supp. 102 (S.D.N.Y. 1969).

Zuckerman, M. A. (2010). Constitutional clash: When English-only meets voting rights. *Yale Law and Policy Review, 28*(2). Retrieved from http://yalelawandpolicy.org/28-2/constitutional-clash-when-english-only-meets-voting-rights

Zukowski, V. (1997, Fall). Teeter-totters and tandem bikes: A glimpse into the world of cross-age tutors. *Teaching and Change,* 71–91.

NAME INDEX

Page numbers in italics refer to figures, illustrations, tables, or sidebar content.

SUBJECT INDEX

Page numbers in italics refer to figures, illustrations, tables, or sidebar content.